GRINNELL

GRINNELL

AMERICA'S ENVIRONMENTAL PIONEER AND HIS RESTLESS DRIVE TO SAVE THE WEST

JOHN TALIAFERRO

LIVERIGHT PUBLISHING CORPORATION
A Division of W. W. Norton & Company
Independent Publishers Since 1923
New York   London

For information about permission to reproduce selections from this book,
write to Permissions, Liveright Publishing Corporation, a division of
W. W. Norton & Company, Inc., 500 Fifth Avenue, New York, NY 10110

For information about special discounts for bulk purchases, please contact
W. W. Norton Special Sales at specialsales@wwnorton.com or 800-233-4830

Manufacturing by LSC Communications, Harrisonburg
Book design by JAM Design
Production manager: Anna Oler

Library of Congress Cataloging-in-Publication Data

Names: Taliaferro, John, 1952– author.
Title: Grinnell : America's environmental pioneer
and his restless drive to save the West / John Taliaferro.
Description: First edition. | New York : Liveright Publishing Corporation, A Division of
W. W. Norton & Company, 2019. | Includes bibliographical references and index.
Identifiers: LCCN 2019002370 | ISBN 9781631490132 (hardcover)
Subjects: LCSH: Grinnell, George Bird, 1849–1938. | Natural history—West (U.S.) |
West (U.S.)—History—1860–1890. | West (U.S.)—History—1890–1945. | Naturalists—
United States—Biography. | Conservationists—United States—Biography.
Classification: LCC QH31.G74 T35 2019 | DDC 508.78—dc23
LC record available at https://lccn.loc.gov/2019002370

Liveright Publishing Corporation, 500 Fifth Avenue, New York, N.Y. 10110
www.wwnorton.com

W. W. Norton & Company Ltd., 15 Carlisle Street, London W1D 3BS

1 2 3 4 5 6 7 8 9 0

FOR

John Stillman

(1945–2013)

"Happy, especially, is the sportsman who is also a naturalist; for as he roves in pursuit of his game, over hills or up the beds of streams where no one but a sportsman ever thinks of going, he will be certain to see things noteworthy, which the mere naturalist would never find, simply because he could never guess that they were there to be found. I do not speak merely of the rare birds which may be shot, the curious facts as to the habits of the fish which may be observed, great as these pleasures are. I speak of the scenery, the weather, the geological formation of the country, its vegetation, and the living habits of its denizens."

—CHARLES KINGSLEY, *Glaucus* (1855)

CONTENTS

PART SEVEN   *Gray Guardian (1919–1938)*

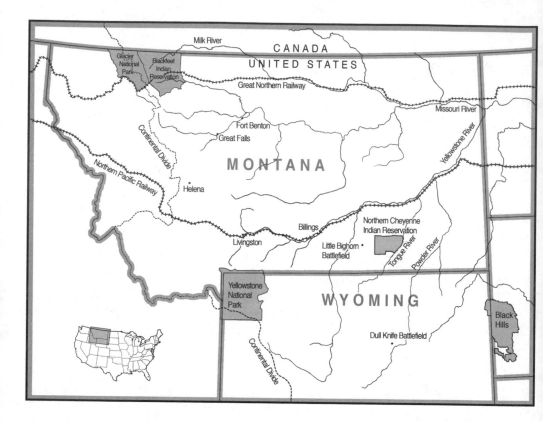

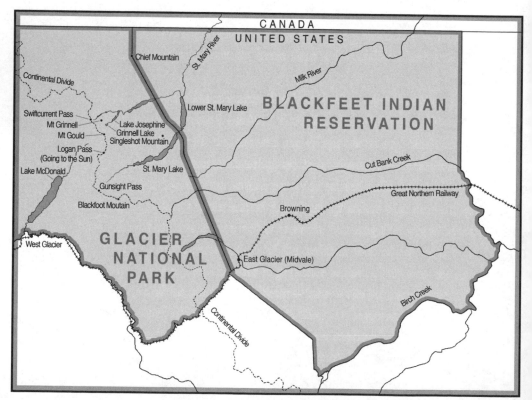

A NOTE ON NAMES

A Blackfeet is a Blackfoot, but not every Blackfoot is a Blackfeet. The Blackfoot Indians are made up of four bands: Blackfoot, Blood, Northern Piegan, and Southern Piegan. The first three of these bands reside in Canada. The Southern Piegans, also called Blackfeet, live on the Blackfeet Indian Reservation in Montana. Grinnell addressed the Southern Piegans simply as Piegans, (*pē'gans*) or as Blackfeet. Herein the author honors Grinnell's interchangeable usage of *Blackfeet* and *Piegan* and also allows Grinnell's usage of *Blackfoot* as an adjective or to describe an individual member of the Blackfeet band. Today, however, an individual member of the American Blackfeet, or Piegans, is not properly a Blackfoot, except with respect to his or her membership in the larger Blackfoot confederacy. In the course of daily life, he or she is a Blackfeet.

The term *Indian*, to describe indigenous people of North America, was in common usage in Grinnell's time, and it is nearly as common today, among both Indians and non-Indians. The author, who is white, chooses to use it in its historical context, while acknowledging that *Native American* (or in Canada, *First Nations*) is a more accurate and more respectful identifier of the people who inhabited the continent long before Europeans stepped ashore.

Transcribing Grinnell's letters and diaries, the author has taken occasional liberties with spelling, capitalization, and punctuation for the sake of consistency and clarity.

GRINNELL

EVOLUTION AND EXTINCTION

On June 16, 1926, George Bird Grinnell departed by taxi from his town-house on East Fifteenth Street and boarded the 20th Century Limited at Grand Central Station, heading westward, as he had done, almost annually, since his graduation from Yale more than fifty years earlier. He was seventy-six, his hair now a match for his gray eyes. For all his adventurousness as a younger man, Grinnell had become a creature of habit. His destinations, once wild and remote, were now quite familiar to him. After passing through Chicago, he nearly always stopped in Columbus, Nebraska, where the Loup River meets the Platte, to spend the night with venerable frontier scout Luther North. Their friendship, deep and unlikely—given their differences of class and literacy—had been forged during summers of hunting and ranching together. From Nebraska, Grinnell typically headed to the Northern Cheyenne reservation on the Tongue River of southeastern Montana; to Yellowstone National Park, whose wonders first enchanted him during an expedition with army surveyors in 1875; or to the Blackfeet reservation and the magnificent mountains of what had become, largely by Grinnell's efforts, Glacier National Park in northern Montana.

Grinnell knew this western country as well as almost anyone alive, and he had written prolifically on its native people, publishing benchmark books on the Cheyennes and Blackfeet, assessing their cultures, chronicling their histories, calling attention to their struggles, and advocating on their behalf. He had spent weeks at a time among these tribes, listening to their stories, observing the sun dance and other deep-rooted ceremonies, and making friends. As with Luther North, the bonds Grinnell made in the West, among both Indians and whites, were every bit as indelible as those that inter-stitched his cohort of Yale classmates.

For many years Grinnell had gone west alone, joining companions and guides once he crossed the prairies into Indian country and the Rocky Mountains. It went without saying that these outings were all male. But then in 1902, in his fifty-third year, Grinnell married Elizabeth Curtis Williams, a widow half his age, and she gamely accompanied him on many of the seasonal excursions that followed, scaling mountains and glaciers, camping in tepees, and contributing to Grinnell's ethnological studies by photographing everyday life on the reservation. Indeed, it was their mutual enthusiasm for Native American culture that had first drawn the pedigreed, pipe-puffing bachelor to the proud but impecunious young woman from Saratoga County.

"She is so entirely satisfied with her abilities as a trail finder," Grinnell joked after one summer's outing, "that it is a little difficult to live with her."

In June of 1926 Elizabeth joined her husband aboard the Pullman hastening from New York into the heartland of the American continent. In Grinnell's memory, this until recently had been the Great Frontier, the domain of noble, nomadic aborigines and a bounty of buffalo, pronghorn antelope, elk, bighorn sheep, mountain goats, bears, and bird life.

If there was one compelling appointment this summer, it was on Montana's Little Bighorn River, where fifty years earlier Lieutenant Colonel George Armstrong Custer and the Seventh Cavalry had attacked a large encampment of Sioux, Cheyennes, and Arapahos, only to be overrun themselves by the Indians they had so imprudently provoked.

Two hundred and sixty-three soldiers died at the Little Bighorn, but the fate of the plains tribes had already been cast. Their lifeblood, the vast buffalo herds, was draining away; railroads, settlers, and a military strategy of pursuit, destruction, punishment, and containment portended the end of the Indians' freedom and, quite possibly, their existence as a race.

Grinnell knew the drama well, along with many of its actors. In the summer of 1874 he had been the naturalist on an expedition that Custer had led into the Black Hills of Dakota Territory. A number of the soldiers and officers Grinnell had tented with during that sixty-day march had died in the legendary Last Stand. Since then Grinnell had come to know many of the Cheyennes who had fought the cavalry on the Little Bighorn. He had walked the battlefield with several of those participants, and he chronicled their retelling of that event in *The Fighting Cheyennes*, considered one of the first faithful renditions of the battle from the Indian perspective.

Two days after leaving Manhattan, Grinnell and Elizabeth detrained in Columbus and stayed the night with Luther North and his wife, Elvira. Lute North had recently turned eighty and stooped several inches shorter than Grinnell's fence-rail five-foot-ten. Yet to Grinnell, North was a figure of heroic stature and full experience. He had grown up on the Nebraska frontier among the Pawnee Indians, and after the Civil War he and his older brother, Frank, commanded a battalion of Pawnee scouts, employed with deadly effectiveness in the campaigns against their historic enemies, the Sioux and Cheyennes.

In the summer of 1870 the Pawnee scouts had been assigned by General Philip Sheridan to watch over an expedition led by Yale paleontologist Othniel C. Marsh. Grinnell had graduated that June, and he and several of his classmates supposed it might be grand sport to assist Professor Marsh in digging for dinosaurs in the wild West. Thoroughly smitten by his summer lark, Grinnell returned two years later to tag along with Lute North and the Pawnees on a traditional buffalo hunt on the Nebraska prairie. In 1874 Grinnell secured a spot for North on the Custer expedition to the Black Hills.

From Columbus the Grinnells next made their way to Sheridan, Wyoming, the nearest station to Eatons' Ranch, where they knew they would find ample peace and pleasant society for several days before the festivities at the

Little Bighorn. By the 1920s "dude" ranches had become quite fashionable, catering to a well-heeled, mostly eastern clientele; Eatons', opened in 1904, was credited as the first. Its cozy cabins nestled in the foothills of the Big Horn Mountains, formerly the hunting grounds of the Cheyennes, Sioux, and Crows. Grinnell, who chronically lamented the "passing" of the old West, had a soft spot for the Eatons' brand of hospitality.

Over the next four days they took occasional rides and walks, but Grinnell, no longer spry, was mostly content writing letters, chatting with other guests, and reading *With Lawrence in Arabia* by Lowell Thomas. Though enthralled by Lawrence's swashbuckling exploits in the deserts of the East, Grinnell, as a man of western appetites, was drawn more to the similarities between mounted Bedouin warriors and their far-off counterparts among the Plains Indians. In his diary he noted: "[Thomas] says Arabs mount horses from right side, as Indians do. Write him to learn more of this."

This was but one of the many threads that Grinnell pulled in his inquiries on wide-ranging subjects of Native American ethnology and natural history. The discipline of anthropology was in its infancy in the 1880s, when Grinnell opened his first leather-bound notebook and began interviewing Indian elders. He earned a doctorate in osteology (bones), but in practice and profession he was hardly a man of science. He learned as he went along, pursuing enthusiasms with little system. During his years as owner and editor of the sportsman's journal *Forest and Stream*, he wrote dozens of letters seeking to verify the supposed magic powers of Spanish armor worn by Indian war parties, or wondering why some female antelope shed their horns and others did not. In the end, it was his sheer energy, along with his impulse to mingle his own knowledge with that of the brightest and most vigorous minds of the day, that earned him so much authority and respect.

To know Grinnell was to appreciate that the pomp of the fiftieth anniversary of the Little Bighorn was not his cup of tea. He elected to skip the opening day of ceremonies on June 24, which began with planes flying low over the battlefield, followed by a mock cavalry charge across the Little Bighorn River—a reprise of the ill-conceived thrust by Major Marcus Reno that triggered the ensuing disaster.

Grinnell also missed the parade of soldiers and Indians in full war regalia and a tour of the battlefield guided by General Edward Godfrey, one of the few officers (then a lieutenant) to survive the massacre and the author of the most reliable account of the bloody event.

On Friday morning, June 25, Grinnell and Elizabeth were driven to the site by one of the Eaton brothers. The newspapers estimated that as many as fifty thousand were on hand for the pageantry—"a horrible crowd and what a contrast with the days of 15 or 20 years ago when people out there were very scarce," Grinnell noted somewhat grouchily. The throng of spectators was so thick that he, uncomfortable in his woolen city suit, could see little besides the tops of the Indians' headdresses and soldiers' campaign hats in the procession to the battlefield.

Grinnell was arguably one of the more distinguished figures at the anniversary. Yet he deferred preferential treatment in the programmed events and went largely unrecognized during the formal ceremony at the hilltop monument. Only later did he meet "a number of my contemporary antiques, whom I was glad to see and who seemed to be cheered by the sight of my face." One of them was Lute North, who had come out from Nebraska on his own to be with Grinnell and to catch a whiff of the bygone era. All told, only eight soldiers who had fought in the 1876 battle were on hand; once again the Indian participants outnumbered them, sixfold.

The next morning Grinnell and Elizabeth departed for the Northern Cheyenne reservation, forty or so miles to the east. The Cheyennes were the third of three North American tribes to draw Grinnell's interest. His interactions with the Pawnee scouts and the North brothers had led to his first Indian book, *Pawnee Hero Stories and Folk-Tales*. The respectful reviews it received encouraged him to turn his attention to the Blackfeet, with whom he had become acquainted during hunting and exploring trips in the mountains of the Continental Divide along the western boundary of their reservation. After publication of *Blackfoot Lodge Tales* in 1892, he would spend the next two decades learning everything he could about the Cheyennes—his urgency to transcribe old stories and document dimming lifeways tempered by the patience required for thoroughness and accuracy.

The car broke down on the rough road to the Cheyenne agency at Lame Deer, but, by and by, the Grinnells arrived at the house of trader August Stohr, where they had been welcomed on many previous visits. In the past they would stay for weeks, long enough to gather more material for the "big book." Now that *The Cheyenne Indians: Their History and Ways of Life* was complete, published in 1923, this was purely a social occasion. Grinnell spent his first day shaded up on the porch of Stohr's store, greeting old acquaintances: Hairy Hand, Squint Eye, Walks Last, and Little Sun; soon came Bobtail Horse, Big Beaver, and Red Water.

But the Grinnells could not tarry long if they expected to complete their rounds of western places. They spent the night of July 3 at the Northern Hotel in Billings, Montana, a town on the Yellowstone River that had boomed from nothing upon the completion of the Northern Pacific Railway in 1883. Fireworks and band music ruined their sleep, and Elizabeth, who had suffered sporadic, unspecified bouts of ill health throughout the marriage, felt poorly in the morning, but not to such a degree that she was unable to continue onward to Glacier National Park, which they reached on the evening of the fourth.

Arrival in Glacier and a trip next day to the Blackfeet reservation stirred a mixture of emotions in George Bird Grinnell. He had first visited the reservation in the fall of 1885 and from there had cast his eyes to the western horizon, where a thousand miles of undulating buffalo prairie is halted by a wall of primordial stone—a tectonic verge upon which one world appears to end and another abruptly begins. He had been inspired to make the trip by a series of articles in *Forest and Stream* by James Willard Schultz, who as a teenager had left behind comfortable family circumstances in upstate New York and found his way westward, to the upper Missouri River, marrying into the Blackfeet tribe. "Here as nowhere else in our whole country, has nature piled up great mountains and spread out vast prairies with a more lavish hand," Schultz wrote.

Back then Glacier National Park did not exist, and it would be another six years before rail service was completed to the Blackfeet reservation. Grinnell had ridden by stage more than two hundred miles from Helena, by way of Fort Benton, to the reservation. With Schultz as guide, he spent two days among the Blackfeet, or Piegans, as they were also known, before setting out to pursue mountain goats and bighorn sheep in the mountains above the "Walled-in Lakes" that fed the St. Mary River. The climax of their climbing came on September 15, after a steep and slippery scramble along a succession of lakes and ledges leading upward from the Swiftcurrent valley toward the Continental Divide. Exhausted, soaked to the skin, and without food, Grinnell and Schultz could not bring themselves to continue higher. Yet their investment delivered a splendid reward: "From this point we had also an excellent view of the glacier," Grinnell wrote.

Glaciers, living messengers from the Ice Age, had been identified in the United States since the 1850s; a number of those in the Sierra Nevada and Cascade Mountains had been climbed, mapped, and named by the time Grinnell caught a glimpse of the ice shelf peeking from above the final walled-in lake. Here, however, was a discovery all his own, or so he reckoned. In the climb onto the ridges above Swiftcurrent Creek, Grinnell had seen no evidence of man, ancient or recent. The Blackfoot followed certain routes over the mountains, but Grinnell was told that they rarely spent time away from the plains where buffalo roamed. Schultz could not provide names, Indian or otherwise, for the surrounding topographic features. It was possible that Grinnell was the first white man to see this particular tableau of rock and ice and running water. Certainly it was tempting to believe so.

Since his boyhood on the then-rural shore of Manhattan Island, Grinnell had wanted to be an explorer, another John James Audubon, whose estate his father had purchased in 1856. He was not so fortunate as to meet the renowned bird stalker and portraitist, but from Audubon's widow and sons he received a strong draft of the man's spirit—a mix of wanderlust and purposefulness. It was only fitting that Grinnell chose to name a society of bird lovers after the eminence whose feathery ghost still lingered on the banks of the Hudson.

The aim of exploration is discovery. Yet by the time Grinnell came of age, most of the continental United States (the territory of Alaska, purchased in 1867, was another matter) had been trod by at least one white man, from the depth of the Grand Canyon (1869) to the summit of Mount Whitney (1873). As the century neared its end, there was little, if any, frontier left to cross, much less to define; it had been smudged to irrelevance by the wheels of eastern enterprise and the footfalls of westward ambition. Hence Grinnell's exhilaration in 1885, when, after strenuous, perilous perseverance, he stumbled upon something that, as best he could tell, was absolutely *un*discovered. Virgin land after all. Perhaps the map still held blank spots not yet filled in. He vowed that he would return another year and reach the actual ice.

He kept his promise, revisiting the region again and again, taking the liberty of naming dozens of the peaks and glaciers he came upon during his concerted surveys. The glacier he "discovered" in 1885 became Grinnell Glacier—"my glacier," he allowed in a rare breach with modesty. The lake below became Grinnell Lake; the mountain on its north flank, Mount Grinnell.

The idea of creating a national park first came to Grinnell in 1891, during yet another fall hunting trip to his now-familiar stomping grounds. For years he promoted his dream—the "Crown of the Continent"—tirelessly in the pages of *Forest and Stream*. Finally in 1910 a million acres of majestic mountains, forest, lakes, and the largest concentration of glaciers in the continental United States—an alpine Valhalla straddling the Continental Divide and framed by the Canadian border, the Blackfeet reservation, and the Middle and North forks of the Flathead River—were dedicated by Congress as Glacier National Park.

In the sixteen years since the park's creation, America had beaten a path to its entrances and invaded its innermost redoubts. Grinnell and Elizabeth arrived on the evening of July 4, 1926, crossed a groomed promenade, and checked into the Glacier Park Lodge, a tourist temple on the grand scale. Blackfeet Indians, fierce and far-ranging not so long ago, now loitered about the station and the hotel, selling trinkets and entertaining dudes with desultory song and dance.

Grinnell's relationship with the Blackfeet had once been as intimate as the one he continued to enjoy with the Cheyennes. The Blackfeet agency, the center of the reservation, was twelve miles to the east at Browning, and Grinnell usually divided his trips to the region between the mountains and the Indians. His involvement went beyond the anthropological. He immersed himself not just in documenting the Blackfeet's past, but also in promoting the well-being and betterment of the tribe, as they ran a brutal gantlet of starvation, disease, corrupt agents, invasive stock raisers, and a steady onslaught of ineffective and downright bad policies drawn up by spoilsmen and would-be reformers in faraway Washington. Though Grinnell carried no official credential, the Blackfeet came to count on him as their broker with the Bureau of Indian Affairs, Congress, and the White House. He received no compensation, other than the satisfaction of helping friends through hard times toward "civilization"—a condescending term and a paternalistic role, to be sure, but Grinnell believed that, for the Blackfeet, theirs was a clear-cut case of adapt or perish. As an expression of their faith and appreciation, they adopted him into the tribe, an honor he prized above all others.

Grinnell accepted that tourists were now a fixture of Glacier. After all, the point of making it a national park was for the enjoyment of the public. But he would never consider himself a full-blooded tourist. On July 11 he and Elizabeth motored fifty miles to Many Glacier Hotel, yet another piece of the Great Northern Railway's ambitious design to turn Glacier into "America's Alps." Completed in 1915, the hotel sprawls along the eastern shore of one of the mountain lakes. The ride had been dusty and bumpy, and Grinnell could not help feeling somewhat unsettled by the recent human imprint on a wilderness that he had once allowed himself to call his own. Upon checking in at Many Glacier, whose veranda fronts the stupendous panorama of a pyramidal peak known nowadays as Grinnell Point, he groused at his noisy room and the careless clerks. "Somewhat annoyed," he wrote in his diary, "but hope for better things tomorrow."

Whatever had been nagging Elizabeth since Billings now kept her from venturing far from the hotel. On the morning of the thirteenth, Grinnell hired a horse and set out alone in the direction that he and Schultz had bushwhacked in 1885. Since the creation of the park, a trail had been opened for the hearty. "Rode up under my mountain . . . to my lake and return," he jotted in his diary. That is, to Mount Grinnell and Grinnell Lake, but not quite to Grinnell Glacier.

He resolved that the next day he would summon what was left of his strength and make it all the way to the ice, reckoning that he might never have another opportunity. Not that he believed the glacier was nearing extinction (although it was). Rather, it was he who was approaching the end.

From 1849, the year of his birth, to 1938, when his bones were buried in the family plot in the Bronx, George Bird Grinnell's life was a study in romanticism, evolution, and progressivism.

It was the first of these that induced him and his fellow Yale students to spend a summer out west with Professor Marsh. The trip reinforced the American dream—or perhaps American paradox—of the West as both a shimmering relic of a pristine past and a beckoning crucible of national and personal renewal.

Yet it was not romance but evolution—and its existential antonym, extinction—that informed the actual fossil digging. The Yale expedition uncovered more than one hundred prehistoric species; most impressive of all was the metacarpal of what Marsh concluded was a large "flying dragon"—the first pterodactyl to be unearthed in North America.

All the while, Grinnell's attention was drawn to a different aspect of evolution (and extinction) that was taking place before his eyes. Buffalo were already growing scarce. The Pawnees now had to travel far from the reservation to hunt the herds that once had carpeted the prairie. A comparable decline was true for other species as well. And the Indians themselves—it required little deduction to see the perilous direction they were headed.

Although the lesson of progressivism took a while to sink in, over time Grinnell resolved to do whatever he could to forestall, steer, and alleviate the sundering of his world. While many of his contemporaries, men of means and "good" families, had awakened to the realization that something must be done to address the problems caused by urbanization, immigration, industrialization, consumption, and corruption, Grinnell turned this same reformative urge—the so-called Social Gospel—toward other causes. He may not have been the very first American conservationist; but it was Grinnell and a like-minded cohort who paired conservation with progressivism, forming groups such as the Audubon Society (later expanded to become the National Association of Audubon Societies) and the Boone and Crockett Club (big-game hunters becoming big-game protectors). A shining demonstration of their financial, social, and political clout was passage of the first law to protect migratory birds, a precedent of federal rights over states' rights that would pave the way for a later pillar of environmentalism, the Endangered Species Act.

Recognizing that wildlife preservation demanded protection of wildlife habitat, Grinnell and company, including Boone and Crockett cofounder Theodore Roosevelt, established the first game refuges. They were so forward as to recommend that certain of the nation's newly created national forests be entirely off limits to hunting. The New York Zoological Society, the offspring of the Boone and Crockett Club, would delight millions who visited its menagerie at the Bronx Zoo; but what many have forgotten is that the Bronx Zoo was conceived also as a sanctuary where vanishing native species could repropagate. Buffalo raised at the zoo provided the breeding stock that helped keep this iconic beast from vanishing from the continent.

Grinnell, who had explored Yellowstone National Park in 1875, three years after Congress had designated it the *first* national park, not only grasped the precious uniqueness of this "pleasure ground," but also believed that the concept of a national park deserved to spread. Throughout his long working life, he was vigilant in defending Yellowstone from those who yearned to plunder, pollute, and privatize its precious assets, and his groundwork and activism were a central force in the creation of the National Park Service in 1916. Thereafter he lent a strong and respected voice to the debate on what national parks should be.

Grinnell's attitude toward Native Americans was likewise shaped by the potent compound of romanticism, evolution (in the form of Social Darwinism), and progressivism. He wished, idealistically, that Indian culture could be forever bathed in the sentimental sepia of an Edward Curtis photograph, unadulterated by outside fingerprints. But he also subscribed to the conventional wisdom shared by most reformers (not to mention eugenicists) that Indians lagged behind the curve of evolution and needed to catch up rapidly, or else face extinction. "The white race has had 2000 years in which to learn its lesson, while we are trying to crowd into two generations of Indian life the experience which we have been 60 or 70 generations in learning for ourselves," Grinnell wrote.

Indian advancement, he acknowledged, required the support and sympathy of whites and their government, but only to a degree. Indians, whom whites had forced into a state of dependency, must now find a way to lift themselves up and become self-sufficient again—by raising crops, herding livestock, and learning the white man's language and trades. On its face, this prescription of bootstrapping was empowering; yet its underlying assumption was that Indians were innately inferior. Self-determination and self-identity were worthy goals, but the ultimate goal of all Americans— indigenous or immigrant—ought to be assimilation. Grinnell's advocacy of Native Americans was sincere, steadfast, and second to none, but he had no doubt that their best chance for survival lay down the white man's road.

He toggled restlessly between two worlds: East and West, the nineteenth century and the twentieth, the wild and the tame, the entitled and the dispossessed, the "civilized" and the "savage." Only a generation earlier, Americans who went west took a long time getting there. Lewis and Clark required more than two years to reach the Pacific and return home. For travelers on the overland trails to California and Oregon, the crossing was an epic of survival. Grinnell came of age in an era when railroads made it possible to migrate—to commute, as it were—between East and West in just a few days. With each passing year, travel became less of a travail and more of a compulsion that fed upon itself, and toward the end of Grinnell's career, his hunger was almost hyperactive. The twain still did not quite meet, a notion that he would adhere to always; yet he came to appreciate that, with minimal exposure and measured expectations, he could live a back-and-forth life of his own design.

And another split in the story of George Bird Grinnell must not be overlooked. For all his curiosity about the external world, there was one realm he hesitated to explore, let alone share: He guarded his inner self.

A man's appearance, his deeds, his whereabouts, his friends and relations— all lend shape and shading to his profile. And if he leaves behind enough artifacts and the right sort of writing, these can shed light on his disposition—

mental, emotional, even sexual. With Grinnell we see whom he projected himself to be, how he wished himself to be regarded and remembered. "Those of us who have been trying to do something for the public welfare act as we do because we have the vision to see what ought to be done," he explained, "and, having seen this, self-respect demands that we do our duty as we see it."

This sense of decency and decorum was expressed best through sportsmanship. By the Boone and Crockett Club credo, which Grinnell codified and embodied, a good sportsman was encouraged to moderate his "natural impulse." In the gluttony of the Gilded Age, such self-control separated a gentleman from a robber baron or a "game hog."

Yet Grinnell hardly kept his lamp under a bushel. Although he shrank from giving after-dinner speeches and sat for formal photographs only under protest, he mixed well at clubs and banquets and around campfires, and he could be full throated in board meetings and congressional hearings. His fastidiously tended handlebar moustache suggested more than a little vanity. In New York and Washington, his public image as a doer, and as a man who "knew the Indian" and had gone west when the West was still up for grabs, meant a great deal to him.

Possibly Grinnell was simply too busy and proper to indulge in self-reflection. Or was there something he wanted to avoid reflecting upon? Within the unsaid, was there something unsayable? Be that as it may, he left behind more than a few clues to his nature.

Grinnell and Elizabeth had no children of their own, but, as the eldest of six siblings, he became the patriarch of the clan after his father died in 1891. The family lived side by side in Audubon Park and shared a farm in Connecticut. Small wonder, then, that Grinnell looked forward to extended sojourns in the West and immersed himself in native culture. By devoting so much time and attention to Indians, he might have believed that he was climbing out of one confining picture frame and into the expansive exoticism of another. Yet comparisons between the two spheres of his life—as well as the judgments he passed on each (if not on himself)—are revelatory.

This biography draws upon forty thousand pages of Grinnell's correspondence; some fifty diaries and notebooks documenting his western travels; thirty-five years of *Forest and Stream* articles and editorials; and much more. Then, too, we have his unfinished autobiography, seven autobiographical novels written for boys—the "Jack" books—and hundreds of other jigsaw pieces that accumulated until a heart attack invalided him in 1929.

What is missing? Grinnell was a diligent letter writer. He answered his mail punctually, for fear that he might fall behind. Even after he left *Forest and Stream* and moved his office to his library on Fifteenth Street, his routine was to dictate a letter to a stenographer, who typed it up, made a copy (by way of an often smudgy transfer process called letterpress), and bound it chronologically in a letter book after posting the original. Thus nearly fifty years of Grinnell's correspondence have been preserved.

In shorter supply are letters written *to* Grinnell and nearly all letters he wrote by hand when he was away from his office. (Pity, his penmanship is superb.) Alas, only a few letters between Grinnell and Elizabeth survive. Perhaps others were lost; perhaps she did not consider them worth including in the papers she donated to the Connecticut Audubon Society after his death; or perhaps she discarded them for more personal reasons. Her presence in the account that follows suffers from their absence.

Few deep secrets are overtly revealed in Grinnell's papers, but careful reading teases out several concealed memories and regrets that he was not inclined to utter aloud or express through a stenographer. Secrets from whom? His wife, his family, his peers, the public? Himself?

We can only build the dinosaur with the bones we dig up.

PART ONE

BOY
HUNTER

(1849–1876)

AUDUBON PARK

For George Bird Grinnell history began at home. As concerned as he would become about the fitful course of the continent, he would never doubt the place of his own forebears in the march of American civilization.

The first Grinnell, Matthew, arrived in New England in 1630. This was ten years after the *Mayflower* had set its passengers ashore, but it did not take long for the Grinnells to graft themselves to Pilgrim stock. Matthew Grinnell's grandson Daniel married Lydia Pabodie, a great-granddaughter of John Alden, whose name appears seventh on the Mayflower Compact. Their son George, born around 1686, was our George Bird Grinnell's great-great-great-grandfather.

In later years a murmur would circulate among family members, wondering if the first North American Grinnell had started out as a Frenchman of the Huguenot persuasion. (Not so; he was all English.) But nobody had any reason to question the family's Mayflower bona fides. Indeed, as generations progressed, and the population of the United States grew more diverse, the Grinnells' ancestry became a badge worn ever more conspicuously. One of George Bird Grinnell's brothers helped found the New York branch of the Society of Mayflower Descendants, to which George paid his dues faithfully. When a somewhat self-congratulatory volume entitled *Signers of the Mayflower Compact and Their Descendants* was published in 1899, George Bird Grinnell bought a half-dozen copies. An entire chapter therein is devoted to "Grinnell and Allied Families."

George Bird was equally proud of the bloodlines on his mother's side. Helen Alvord Lansing's forebears were Dutch Protestants; the first arrived in New Amsterdam, as New York was then called, around 1650. A couple of generations later the family seat was Lansingburgh, on the east bank of the Hudson River, north of present-day Troy.

Helen Lansing's father, Dirck Cornelius Lansing, was a man of abundant intellect and piety. After graduation from Yale College in 1804 and a stint at Boston's Park Street Church, he moved westward to Auburn, New York, where he became pastor of a Presbyterian congregation and helped found the Auburn Theological Seminary. His sermons inveighed on such sobering topics as "The Rejection of the Gospel—Criminal, Irrational and Dangerous" and "The Abuse of Divine Goodness as Evidence of Human Depravity."

The Grinnells were God-fearing, too, but they kept a firmer focus on the material world than on the celestial. As the nineteenth century gained momentum, various members—based in Newport, New Bedford, and eventually in New York—joined the American heraldry of merchant princes, launching a far-roaming fleet of whaling ships and building the fastest clipper ships and coastal packets in the glory decades of sail. One of those clippers, *Flying Cloud*, made a world-record passage from New York, around Cape Horn, to San Francisco in an astonishing eighty-nine days, eight hours. Perhaps more famously, two Grinnell-financed ships, *Rescue* and *Advance*, would valiantly probe the Arctic ice in search of the Franklin Expedition, lost in its search for the Northwest Passage.

George Bird Grinnell's branch of the family was only distantly related to the millionaire Grinnells, but they were every bit as resolute. His great-grandfather, another George, left Saybrook, Connecticut, a decade or so before the American colonies rebelled against Great Britain. As George Bird would recount, this exemplary antecedent "turned around at the top of the last hill and waved his hand to his mother, who was standing in the door, waving back to him." Off, then, to seek a new life.

The acreage George Bird's great-grandfather carved out near Greenfield, Massachusetts, would remain in the family for the next hundred and fifty years. "On this farm my grandfather was born," George Bird Grinnell would write with folkloric nostalgia in his unfinished and unpublished memoirs. "The country was wild then, and my grandfather has told me that in the days of his settlement there his father was troubled by bears, which used to come to the farm and carry off sheep and pigs. Tradition says that he used to look out of the window on moonlight nights and see wolves running around the sheepfield, trying to find a place where they could get in."

George Grinnell, Jr., son of the wolf-watcher and grandfather to George Bird, attended Deerfield Academy and then entered Dartmouth College. He was an able agriculturalist but, as the nation took shape around him, he was drawn to play a part beyond that of yeoman. He was elected to Congress as a Whig in 1829 and served for ten years until he could no longer afford to neglect his farming chores.

George Jr.'s son, George Blake Grinnell, was born in 1823. At the age of seventeen, instead of heading off to college, he accepted a position in a bank owned by a great uncle in Auburn; here he first laid eyes on the reverend's daughter, Helen Lansing. After three years George Blake relocated to Brooklyn, where he worked at his cousin George Bird's wholesale dry-goods firm. As fortune would have it, five years after his departure from Auburn, Reverend Lansing became pastor of the Clinton Avenue Church in Brooklyn. Grinnell was quick to join the parish and continue his courtship with Helen. Within a year the young couple was married. One day shy of nine months later, on September 20, 1849, Helen gave birth to a son, George Bird Grinnell.

Any avian eponym implicit in the boy's middle name was purely coincidental, though later in life "Bird" would become an apt fit. As a child and young man, he was always George Bird Grinnell, to distinguish himself from his father, George Blake Grinnell. But even after his father's death he continued to use it as a byline; and on occasions when space demanded elision, he would allow only Geo. Bird Grinnell, never George B. Grinnell or G. B. Grinnell.

A year after his first child was born, George Blake Grinnell became a full partner in George Bird & Company. The family lived its first years in Brooklyn to be near Helen's parents, and it was there that a second son, Frank Lansing Grinnell, was born in 1852. The following year, or thereabouts, the Grinnells moved to New York proper, renting a house on Twenty-First Street, west of Sixth Avenue.

New York, population half a million, was by far the largest city in the United States, more than twice as big as its closest rivals, Baltimore, Boston, and Philadelphia. Yet it was not yet the sprawling metropolis it would become later in the century. The Grinnells' house was at the northern fringe of development. Affluent New Yorkers lived below Fourteenth Street; the best addresses were in the blocks surrounding Washington Square. Present-day Madison Square, at Twenty-Third Street, was a "wholly unimproved lot surrounded by an old wooden fence" that served as a pasture for livestock, George Bird Grinnell would recall. "I have a distinct mental picture of an old nannie with her head through a hole in the fence, watching the occasional passerby on Fifth Avenue and Broadway." Looking north from his rear window, "there was nothing to interfere with [the] view of the wooded hills."

During those early years, young George was not allowed to wander far on his own, which only made the occasions when he ventured outward with his father all the more indelible. Often before the workday began, father George would seat his son beside him in the family carriage and head north on Sixth Avenue. "[A]s soon as 23rd Street was passed"—the end of cobblestones—"we were on a dirt road on which the horse could be driven at speed," George Bird remembered. "It must have been just about this time that Central Park was established, though for many years after, little or nothing was done in the way of its improvement. . . . It was then a wilderness of rocks and pasture land."

But not even a fast horse could outpace the city's galloping growth. During the 1850s, fueled by the California gold rush and Southern cotton and powered by railroads and steamships, New York ballooned. Millions of immigrants, chiefly Irish and German, disembarked at the welter of piers that ringed lower Manhattan. The majority of these new arrivals moved on, but many threw themselves into the city's farrago of flesh and toil. Not only was New York the nation's busiest entrepôt of trade, but by the mid-1850s it was the largest manufacturing city in the United States as well. This rapidly rising tide lifted many ships, including that of George Blake Grinnell's dry-goods concern, but it also clotted traffic and increased the congestion of tenements (a recent term) into which thousands of new New Yorkers squeezed together, sooty cheek by hungry jowl. Crime increased, most infamously in the Bowery and Five Points neighborhoods, and disease— smallpox, tuberculosis, and, most feared of all, cholera—went unchecked.

Anxious about the health of his family, George Blake Grinnell left New York in the winter of 1856 and relocated across the Hudson, in Weehawken, New Jersey. By this point two of George Blake's brothers, William and Thomas, had come down from Greenfield to join the firm of George Bird & Company. Uncle Will soon married the sister of another of the city's dry-goods merchants, Levi P. Morton, whose ambition would eventually make him governor of New York and vice president of the United States. Shortly after the Morton marriage, the Grinnell brothers combined their growing fortunes in the firm of Morton, Grinnell & Company. From dry goods they expanded to larger-scale trading, specifically cotton, and by all evidence they thrived during the years before the Civil War.

Young George Bird Grinnell, not yet seven, stored several memories from the six months spent in Weehawken. One was of his father walking so far out onto the frozen Hudson "that he became a mere speck, and finally vanished from sight." Another, and decidedly warmer, memory is of a visit to the Crystal Palace, erected in a vacant lot on Fortieth Street as the crown jewel of the Exhibition of the Industry of All Nations. The 123-foot-tall palace, clad in fifteen thousand panes of glass, stood for five years until it burned down in 1858. In a lifetime of adventures, Grinnell would collect hundreds of mementos and artifacts; one that he never gave away or put aside was the small porcelain figure of a French chocolate seller that his mother purchased at the Crystal Palace.

During the summer that the family lived in Weehawken, George and Helen Grinnell paid a visit to their friends the Wellington Clapps, who lived on the upper west side of Manhattan in the village of Carmansville. Several notables owned estates thereabouts—James Gordon Bennett, publisher of the *New York Herald*; James Monroe, nephew to a president; and the colorful Eliza Jumel, eventual bride of Aaron Burr. All of these grandees had bought property this far north in order to put a healthy distance between themselves and the gritty city. To them and to their less gentrified neighbors, Carmansville was unto itself and quite rural, still surrounded by farms and woodland.

Not long after the Grinnells' visit to Carmansville, for reasons now forgotten, Wellington Clapp agreed to lease them his house for three years. He would move downtown to Eighteenth Street, which was significantly closer to his place of work in lower Manhattan.

There are few turning points more crucial in the life of George Bird Grinnell than his father's decision to relocate to northern Manhattan, for the Clapp house, into which the Grinnells moved on New Year's Day 1857, was not in Carmansville itself, but, rather, on land immediately adjacent, a partially wooded property once known as Minnie's Land.

Minnie was the nickname of Lucy Bakewell Audubon, wife of the naturalist and artist, John James Audubon, whose eminence, if not fortune, had been assured by the publication of his magisterial *Birds of America* (1838). The son of a French plantation owner and his mistress, Audubon was born in Saint-Domingue (now Haiti) and raised and educated in France; in 1803, at age eighteen, he moved to the United States to avoid conscription in Napoleon's army. He readily adapted his European manners to American life, and in so many ways he came to embody the American ideal of virility, versatility, and derring-do. He could navigate rivers as confidently as most flatboatmen; he took to the woods and uplands of the American frontier like an Indian. He was a superb horseman and swordsman, not to mention a crack shot. Men stood in awe of his athleticism; women swooned at his good looks.

Unable to support his wife and two sons as a farmer or merchant, Audubon turned his full attention to the one activity for which he had unparalleled talent: observing, collecting, preserving, and drawing wildlife. On and off but always obsessively, over nearly two decades, while his debts mounted and his family at times nearly starved, he tramped and floated the Ohio and Mississippi river valleys and throughout the South, determined to identify and draw every species of bird in the United States. If this meant killing birds to study them, then he would do so. More practical than merciful, he often loaded his shotgun with mustard seed, so as not to muss the plumage of smaller specimens.

In 1826 Audubon packed up his illustrations, 435 life-sized watercolors, and set sail for Liverpool, in search of indulgent patrons and exacting printers. Dressed in buckskin, ruddy-cheeked from his years in the wild, he cannily advertised his frontier authenticity to gain entrance into favored clubs and drawing rooms and succeeded in opening enough wallets to ensure the publication of his life's work. The volumes of *Birds of America* were printed in Edinburgh and London and sold by subscription, earning enough to pay the most urgent bills and deliver a modest financial reprieve to the artist and his family.

Birds of America was a stupendous accomplishment, a pinnacle in the art of printing and a magnificent milestone in the culture of America as well. To turn the pages—especially at a time when most citizens lived along the Eastern Seaboard and knew little about the continent sprawling beyond the horizon—was to admire the country itself. *Birds'* bounty and diversity of species offer a gazetteer of generous, almost excessive providence: the ungainly pelican, the impish titmouse; the garish American flamingo, folded like a parasol to fit in the frame; Carolina parrots clowning in the branches of a cocklebur; petrels tumbling, doves kissing, woodpeckers pecking. *Birds of America* is art gallery and menagerie rolled into one. Audubon placed birds in their native settings, bobbing in the waves, soaring in the wind, fluttering about the branches and trees and nests of their natural habitats, eating the berries, bugs, seeds, fish, even snakes that are their survival—in sum, graphically telling the honest and enchanting story of their uninhibited lives. "It was a wild and poetical vision of the heart of the New World," declared an early reviewer.

In 1841 Audubon succeeded in securing a loan to purchase fourteen acres on the Hudson River side of Carmansville. Two years later he and his wife were able to add six more acres. The land was theirs—or hers, to be precise, for the artist registered the deed in Lucy Audubon's name to spare it from encumbrance by current or future creditors.

Secluded and quite overgrown, the plot was three interlocking rectangles, bounded on the east by the Bloomingdale Road—today's Amsterdam Avenue—which at the time was the principal thoroughfare running between New York and Yonkers. On the west the farm sloped downward to the Hudson, affording a splendid view of the water and the palisades of the opposite shore. Younger son, John Woodhouse, an artist in his own right, set to work building a house, a two-story, squat-roofed clapboard, "simple and unpretending in its architecture," remarked one visitor. The entire family—Audubon, Lucy, sons Victor and John, John's wife and his two young daughters—moved in on April 1, 1842. Adding to the procession were several cartloads of caged rodents. The kitchen was in the basement. The youngsters slept on a trundle bed in their grandparents' room.

A first-floor parlor became the artist's studio. "In one corner stood a painter's easel," journalist Parke Godwin observed, "with a half-finished sketch of a beaver on paper; in the other lay the skin of an American panther. The antlers of elks hung on the walls, stuffed birds of every description of gay plumage ornamented the mantle-piece; and exquisite drawings of field-mice, orioles, and woodpeckers were scattered promiscuously in other parts of the room, across one end of which a long rude table was stretched to hold artist materials, scraps of drawing paper and immense folio volumes filled with the delicious paintings of birds taken in their haunts."

John Woodhouse planted a garden and an orchard, and his evident aptitude for construction, not to mention the family's incessant need for income, motivated them to build several more houses on the property—to be rented at first, and then, when the market was ripe, to be sold. John also built houses for himself and Victor to accommodate their growing families. The arrival of the Hudson River Railroad, which began chugging noisily past the Audubon front porches seven years after the family moved in, foretold the future of Minnie's Land and the soon-to-be-not-so-outer reaches of the ever-expanding city to the south.

For a while longer, though, Minnie's Land remained a place where animals abounded. During Parke Godwin's visit, "Several graceful fawns and noble elk were stalking in the shade of the trees, apparently unconscious of the presence of a few dogs, and not caring for the numerous turkeys, geese and other domestic animals that gabbled and screamed among them." The children fed otters, martens, and muskrats, kept in cages. A buffalo bull, cow, and calf occupied their own pen, separate from the milk cow and pigs.

"[H]ow I wonder," John James Audubon remarked early on, "that men can consent to swelter and fret their lives away amid those hot bricks and pestilent vapors, when the woods and fields are all so near." Near, however, would work both ways.

George Bird Grinnell, to his regret, never met John James Audubon. The artist died at Minnie's Land on January 27, 1851, and was buried nearby in the cemetery of Trinity Church. Sales of Audubon books continued after his death, but the income was not enough to sustain the growing Audubon tribe, which eventually included more than a dozen grandchildren, plus servants and workers. The brothers speculated on a foundry and lost; John Woodhouse barely survived a disastrous foray to the California gold fields. The most obvious recourse was to keep on developing, leasing, and, in the end, selling that which they already owned. By 1855 the original Minnie's Land—which had come to be known by the more dignified and marketable name of Audubon Park—was diminished by several acres; it now comprised nine households, with a census of more than eighty souls, among them George Blake Grinnell's friend Wellington Clapp.

George and Helen now had four to watch over: Morton had arrived while the Grinnells were on Twenty-First Street; Helen, who was born in Wee-hawken, was a sickly baby. Their parents hoped that Audubon Park would prove more salubrious.

On January 1, 1857, George Blake Grinnell set off from New Jersey, fol-lowed by the rest of the family in a closed carriage driven by the family coachman. Baby Helen was carried in the arms of her nurse. Hector, a white mastiff, shambled alongside. They crossed on the Hoboken ferry, and as they turned north on the Bloomingdale Road, snow fell, and the road became thick with mud and slush. By Manhattanville the horses were jaded, and a new pair was hired for the final mile of the trip. Seven-year-old George's first recollection of Audubon Park was of looking out the window the next morning and seeing Hector stake his turf in a vicious battle with a black dog belonging to the nearest neighbor, the Smythes.

In the days that followed, Grinnell was delighted to discover that his domain was anything but hostile. Even better, he was allowed to roam Audubon Park with little supervision—a liberty not permitted at a younger age in more urban environs. He made friends with the Audubon grandchildren and several of the other children who lived nearby. Audubon Park was their own world. A fence ran around much of the perimeter, and there was an entrance gate at the upper end of the property that reminded visitors and residents that they were in, if not a sanctuary, then an enclave that was unique and self-contained.

To George Bird Grinnell, Audubon Park was Robin Hood's Sherwood Forest or Leatherstocking's Glimmerglass. Screech owls nested about the houses, oblivious to their human neighbors. Pine, oak, hickory, hemlock, chestnut, and dogwood bowered his memory. Grinnell would insist that "the notes of the thrushes of Audubon Park seemed to possess a clearer, more resonant quality than those of others of its kind."

North of the park the woods were deeper still, extending for a mile to Fort Washington. Within, springs fed small brooks that flowed to the river. Even the railroad, a noisy, smoky intrusion, provided benefits in a boy's life. In order to follow the straightest course, the tracks ran on an elevated causeway a short distance from the shore, creating a protected cove between land and railway embankment. Grinnell and his merry band fished for eels, "killies," and crabs. In winter the ice made for fine skating.

In hindsight, however, Audubon Park was a paradise to be lost. The Hudson was a seasonal flyway for many species of birds whose numbers would diminish, in some instances to nil, over the fifty years Grinnell was to call this home. "It was while we lived in the Clapp house," he recorded in his unpublished autobiography, "that one morning in autumn my mother, going to the front door before breakfast, saw that the dogwood tree . . . was covered with passenger pigeons feeding on the berries. She dodged back into the hall, caught me by the arm, and brought me to the door where I could see them. In later years there were regular autumnal flights [of these birds] up and down the bank of the Hudson River." The last seen were in

1873 or 1874, he estimated, then added: "The boys killed a few, shooting them from the roof."

Grinnell received his early education from various sources, none of them especially formal. The teacher he remembered most vividly was Lucy Audubon. Left on her own in Kentucky during her husband's years of rambling after birds, "Grandma" Audubon, as she was known to Grinnell, had fed herself and her children by teaching. Widowed and still impecunious thirty years later, she established a class of sorts in her bedroom. Grinnell was already an avid reader by the time he came under her tutelage, but he credited Grandma with teaching him the rudiments of arithmetic. He stated in his memoirs that he attended her informal academy for a couple of years, although the sessions were likely more intermittent. Regardless, Lucy Audubon made a profound impression. Tall, slender, always dressed in widow's weeds, she was "a most kindly, gentle, benignant woman," Grinnell remembered. "A little feared, for she had the repose and dignity of a great lady. . . . With the children she unbent far more than with older people, and they loved her dearly."

Grinnell's relationship with his own parents is more difficult to piece together. Very little correspondence between George and Helen Grinnell and their eldest son survives, and their presence in his memoirs, while central and sympathetic, is short on detail.

George Blake Grinnell was a busy man. His commute to downtown by train, from 152nd Street to Chambers Street and then by foot to his office on Park Place, took a couple hours out of every day, and work frequently required that he be away from New York. Four decades after George Blake Grinnell's death, George Bird Grinnell would reflect generously, "My father and I had always been intimate, bearing to each other the relation of close friends, rather than merely of father and son."

Helen Grinnell was an affectionate mother, but her tempered Christian upbringing inclined her not to boast about her brood. "I am very proud of my children, but I do not tell anyone so," she wrote in the diary she kept for son Frank. Yet the diary in itself was evidence of her doting nature. She kept a separate book for each of her children, jotting in them intermittently through their younger years. Thus far only the books for Frank and sister Helen have surfaced; none for George or Morton, nor for the last two of the six Grinnell children: William, born in 1858, and Laura, in 1859.

The diaries also show that she could be quite strict when her children went astray, which was often. She did not hesitate to whip them, the boys at least, when they were disobedient. On one occasion she tied seven-year-old Frank to a chair. When a child got out of line, one of the admonishments she used was "scapegrace," for she saw their mischievousness as a departure from God's ordained path.

The family attended the Church of the Intercession, which, though Episcopalian, not Presbyterian, had the virtue of being a short walk from Audubon Park, on 154th Street. The Grinnells had a pew in their name there and sometimes attended services twice on Sunday. At home George Blake Grinnell read aloud from the Bible. "My chief anxiety in life," Helen Grinnell stated, "is to have all my dear children good. I want them to grow up to be good and useful members of society; above all, meek and gentle Christians."

At times the parents must have felt that, despite their earnest efforts, they were raising a tribe of renegades. "[M]ost of the boys of Audubon Park . . . ought to have been sent to some reform school, for they were bad," George Bird admitted jocularly in later years. "They wanted excitement and were determined to have it. . . . So they used to beat the pigs, steal chickens for surreptitious roasting at fires in the woods, occasionally steal figs, fruit, or anything edible from the village grocery store, steal food of any kind from their mother's pantry, steal cigars from their father."

There were frequent scuffles between the boys of Audubon Park and those of Carmansville, whose fathers worked in a sugar mill just up the river. As is the way with all boys, rich or poor, clothes were constantly torn, muddied, and, to the greater consternation of parents, sometimes discarded entirely. One November day, with snow beginning to fall, Mrs. Grinnell discovered little Mort, stripped naked in the front yard by one of the older brothers, "to make an Indian of him." In the warm days of summer a favorite sport was diving from piers and pilings along the river—until prudish passengers on the passing trains complained. Young George and a companion were caught in the act and hauled into court for violation of a public ordinance requiring that all public bathers wear proper costumes.

When George turned ten a cousin gave him a pony. The first time he climbed into the saddle, his gift horse bolted under the low-hanging branches of a hemlock tree, unseating its uncertain rider. "I soon became more or less at home on the little horse and learned that to be thrown involves no great hardship," he later attested.

When he was twelve he received his first gun—a double-barreled shotgun—as a Christmas present from his Uncle Will. "Georgie is delighted," his mother wrote in one of the diaries, "and almost fancies he must be somebody else, the joy of possessing a gun being almost too much for him." In the early going at least, the birds he hunted were unharmed. "[A] woodcock one autumn made its appearance in our garden, near what would now be the corner of 157th Street and Broadway," he recalled, "and until forced to migrate gave me abundant shooting. Every morning before breakfast I sallied out, put up the bird, and shot at it. Often I found it again, later in the day. I never hit it, but it gave me much excitement."

By hunting birds Grinnell began observing them more carefully: green herons in the swamp east of the Bloomingdale Road; ruffed grouse on the steep hillside near the Institution for the Instruction of the Deaf and Dumb, west of present-day 165th Street; eagles and crows scavenging ice floes on the river in wintertime. And always he received encouragement from one of the Audubons. When he succeeded in shooting a small pigeon, he took it to John Woodhouse, who informed him that it was not a pigeon but a ground dove, common enough farther south, but rare to Manhattan Island. He later presented a small, greenish bird to Grandma Audubon, who by then had rented out her own house and moved in with son Victor. She identified the bird as a juvenile red crossbill and told him something about its life. "Then after a little talk," Grinnell recalled, "she and I went downstairs and out of doors, found the birds still feeding there, and set the captive free."

On his frequent visits to the Audubon houses, his eyes were filled with the specimens and accoutrements once belonging to the naturalist: deer and elk antlers, rifles, shotguns, powder horns, and ball pouches. "There were many trophies from the Missouri River," Grinnell observed, "a region which in those days seemed infinitely remote and romantic with its tales of trappers, trading posts and Indians." Of the Audubon paintings that hung on the walls, one was *The Eagle and the Lamb*, a breathtaking oil from 1828 depicting a golden eagle, its talons extended, wings rampant, poised on a mountain precipice as it delivers the *coup de mort* to its defenseless prey. Not long before her death Lucy Audubon would draft a handwritten note, bequeathing the painting to her favored Audubon Park pupil, who had been so transfixed by its violent and vital grandeur.

In the fall of 1859 the Clapps, from whom the Grinnells had been renting, announced that they wanted to return to their house in Audubon Park. Deliberations on where to move next were interrupted on November 12 by the birth of Laura Grinnell, the last of the children. A week later four-year-old Morton came down with scarlet fever, followed by seven-year-old Frank, then three-year-old Helen, and finally Willie, not yet two. Only George, now a skinny but hale ten-year-old, and newborn Laura were spared. For the next month the household was a hospital, while mother Helen lay in bed, recovering from her recent labor, and the children lay stricken, nursed by their governess, their grandmother Lansing, and, "our Heavenly Father," as Helen Grinnell recorded in one of her diaries. Finally, after New Year's, the pall that hovered over Audubon Park was lifted, as the children regained their health, mercifully none the worse for the scare.

If George Blake Grinnell had considered moving to another neighborhood or town, he abandoned the idea after the sicknesses, renting a different house built by John Woodhouse Audubon. To accommodate his large family, servants, and mother-in-law, he added a wing on the side toward the river, at his own expense. He named the husky, two-storied, bay-windowed residence the Hemlocks, for the tall conifers that shaded the property.

In the fall of 1860 George Blake made another move as well, ending his partnership with Levi Morton and forming one with cousin Jonathan Bird.

The other big excitement that season was the visit of the Prince of Wales to America, which included a stay in New York. George and Helen Grinnell somehow received an invitation to the grand ball for the eighteen-year-old future King Edward VII. ("Where the Prince was, there was the jam, and where the Prince was not, you could swing a cat around with comparative comfort," Helen reported.) George Bird Grinnell preserved his own memory of the prince's visit. Riding his pony, perhaps on Bloomingdale Road, "I was overtaken by a carriage," he recalled, "accompanied by several policemen on horseback, which contained Mayor [Fernando] Wood and a young man in a red coat whom I at once knew must be the Prince of Wales. I galloped my pony for a little way along the side of the road by the carriage and took off my cap, and the Prince of Wales waved his cap at me with a friendly grin."

A few days after the prince sailed for England, America elected a dark horse by the name of Abraham Lincoln as its next president. Three months later, on February 19, 1861, the president-elect's train passed by Audubon Park, en route from Springfield to Washington. George Bird Grinnell made no mention of seeing the Hudson River train or whether he was in the crowd of 250,000 that lined the route of Lincoln's carriage from the Thirtieth Street station to the Astor Hotel.

Lincoln's task could not have been less appetizing. He and his upstart Republican Party, elected on a pledge to halt the expansion of slavery, now had to find a way to abort the looming disaster of civil war. Yet his slim margin of victory was one of the wedges that widened the division between North and South. A month after Lincoln's inauguration, on March 4, 1861, the first salvos of rebellion were fired at Fort Sumter, South Carolina. Seven states seceded from the Union.

The echoes of those first cannonades rattled windows seven hundred miles away in New York. The city had grown, and grown rich, to a large extent as a trading center for southern cotton. Cotton flowed north from plantations, while goods manufactured in New York passed through New York warehouses and docks en route to southern economies in the holds of New York–built ships. (Which is partly why New Yorkers, mostly Democratic anyway, had voted against Lincoln in November.)

The shock waves from the sectional rift and anxiety over imminent blockade and large-scale disruption of trade had an immediate effect on a wide range of businesses, dry goods not the least. "Our country is in the most fearful state, war without doubt being just upon us, with all its attendant horrors," Helen Grinnell wrote on May 18, as four more states seceded. George Blake Grinnell's latest business partnership had failed, she announced. "We are to return to first principles." They would have to sell the carriage and the matched pair of gray horses and reduce the retinue of servants, which had grown to include coachman, gardener, governess, cook, and laundress—six of them Irish, plus "our French girl," Louise. "We expect to do all this and do it cheerfully," she pledged. "In fact, as far as I am concerned, I have felt very little unhappiness with regard to being poor, excepting for dear Papa, and I must say, I feel very unhappy for him. It is hard to toil for years for nothing." For the moment, thirty-seven-year-old George Blake Grinnell, father of six children under the age of twelve, was staring into the abyss.

But almost as quickly the pendulum swung in the other direction. War proved to be a boon for New York economically. Although cotton trading collapsed, all manner of military necessities—ships, grain, meat, horses, uniforms, shoes, medical supplies—were provided by city businesses taking advantage of federal contracts and protective import tariffs. By the fall George Blake Grinnell was still somewhat straitened, but the family had not been obliged to move from Audubon Park or, as Helen had fretted, to dismiss any servants. By the summer of 1862 George Blake had recovered his financial footing sufficiently to rent a house in Brattleboro, Vermont, twenty miles north of the Grinnell homestead in Greenfield, intending for his family to wait out the remainder of the national strife, which was now expected to continue for at least another year.

The war dragged on, however, its end no longer predictable, and with George Blake prospering apace. The family was back in the Hemlocks at Audubon Park by Christmas.

On July 9, 1863, George Blake again sent his family to New England, staying first in Greenfield and then renting a farm in nearby Gill, Massachusetts. The timing was fortuitous and perhaps not accidental; a few days after the Grinnells' departure from the city, rioting broke out in response to the Enrollment Act, which, to meet the latest draft quotas, dispatched federal marshals to enlist draft-age men and to punish shirkers and deserters. The act also allowed a draftee to pay $300 to have a substitute fight in his place—tempting to poorer workingmen, but also galling.

For four days the so-called Draft Riots raged throughout the lower precincts of Manhattan. The mob, mostly Irish, tore down telegraph poles, tore up railroad tracks, burned draft offices and the houses of the wealthy. Brooks Brothers was stripped of its wares; clerks at Lord & Taylor stood guard with loaded guns. The worst violence was inflicted upon the very portion of the populace on whose behalf the North was putatively fighting. Hundreds of African Americans were set upon, beaten, shot, and lynched. One especially heinous assault that spoke for the rest was the ransacking and burning of the Colored Orphan Asylum. Barely two weeks had passed since Union armies had repelled a Confederate invasion at Gettysburg. To New York's burghers, the Draft Riots were something nearly as alarming: an invasion from within.

George Blake Grinnell, who had remained in New York, was thankful that his wife and children were out of harm's way. Likewise he felt fortunate that Audubon Park and his business downtown had not been disturbed. His biggest inconvenience may have been the closure of the Hudson River Railroad. To get home, Grinnell had to cross over to the New Jersey shore, drive by coach to Fort Lee, and then hire someone to row him across the Hudson again.

The Grinnells were back in Audubon Park by September, in time for George to begin the first rigorous schooling of his life. Grandma Audubon, various tutors, and a short stint at the nearby Fort Washington French Institute for Young Gentlemen had hardly amounted to a full and formal education—and certainly not one that would propel him toward the goal that his parents had in mind for him: college.

Churchill Military Academy was in Sing Sing (today's Ossining), on the Hudson, twenty-five miles north of Audubon Park. Its founder, Marlborough Churchill, had graduated from West Point and wore the insignia of a colonel, although he was no longer in active service. While he did not expect all of his fifty or so students to matriculate as West Point cadets or embark on military careers, quite a few did. Churchill's most illustrious alumnus at the time was General Alexander S. Webb, who, two months before George Bird Grinnell arrived at Sing Sing, had stood firm at the Copse of Trees on Gettysburg's Cemetery Ridge and repulsed Pickett's Charge.

Even if their son was not headed for a career in uniform, Grinnell's parents reckoned that the drill of Churchill would stiffen him academically. "He needs the physical discipline as well as close mental application," his mother acknowledged. In his memoirs and throughout his life's correspondence, Grinnell made only passing mention of the three years he spent at Churchill, but apparently he fit in and applied himself satisfactorily. "He is very happy there," his mother noted in November. He and his parents must have liked the school well enough, for the following year twelve-year-old Frank joined his older brother. No transcript of George Bird's grades, honors, or demerits survives, and only one blemish is recorded in Helen Grinnell's diary. After a visit to Sing Sing in 1865, she wrote, "Hastiness and improper language had brought him into trouble."

When the boys came home for holidays, they found the mood at Audubon Park mixed. George Blake Grinnell's dry-goods business continued to thrive, but their cherished neighbors, the Audubons, were a fading presence. Brothers Victor and John Woodhouse Audubon had died, in 1860 and 1862, respectively, leaving their mother, Lucy, to live with a daughter-in-law and granddaughter in a house they no longer owned. Strapped for money, she was obliged to sell the original paintings for *Birds of America* to the New-York Historical Society. Finally, in 1864, Lucy sold everything else and moved to Kentucky, where ten years later, at age eighty-seven, she died.

Titles and mortgages, owners and tenants had shuffled continuously in the years since the Grinnells had first come to the park. Of all the residents, they would prove to be the most enduring. Sufficiently flush with wartime profits, George Blake Grinnell was finally able to buy the Hemlocks in 1864. For the first time he owned the roof over his family's head. As the Audubons took their melancholy leave, Audubon Park became a true home for the Grinnells. One or more of them would live there for the next forty-five years.

While George and Frank Grinnell marched on parade and studied tactics in the classroom, a very real war ground toward its finale. Sherman's March to the Sea and the fall of Charleston, Savannah, Petersburg, and Richmond are all recorded with mounting excitement in Helen Grinnell's diary, until April 10, 1865: "Today we have the splendid, glorious news of the surrender of Lee's entire army. Gen. Grant is a splendid man and able general. He has made for himself a name and fame that must live for ages."

Five days later her tone was one of misery and incredulity. "Alas! Alas! What crushing news!" she wrote, struggling to capture the darkness of the moment for her children's future comprehension. "Last night our good and most merciful and kind-hearted ruler, President Abraham Lincoln, was murdered: shot through the head in the most cold blooded, heartless manner. The nation is paralyzed by this awful blow. We do not know which way to turn or what is to become of us."

Lincoln was slain on Good Friday. George and Frank Grinnell were home in Audubon Park for Easter to attend services at the Church of the Intercession with their parents and younger siblings. On April 19, the day of Lincoln's funeral in Washington, the Grinnells filled the family pew once again, this time to memorialize the martyred president. On the twenty-first, a week after the assassination, a special train left the capital, wending toward Springfield, Illinois. After stops in Baltimore, Harrisburg, and Philadelphia, the casket was ferried across the Hudson and borne to New York's City Hall. After a half hour of ministration by an undertaker to repair the ill effects of its recent jostling, the body was placed on public view. More than half a million mourners pushed their way into the line that entered through the basement and then inched up a set of narrow stairs to the rotunda, where, finally, they could gaze for a moment upon the still-beneficent countenance of Abraham Lincoln.

On that Monday, April 24, George Blake Grinnell took his wife and sons George, Frank, and ten-year-old Morton into New York "to see the dead face of our good president." Through family connections, they were ushered into the Governor's Room, just off the rotunda, and permitted to view the president before the crowd began to file in. "The face was wan and shrunken," Helen Grinnell observed, "but we felt satisfied to have seen it."

George Bird Grinnell recorded his own memory of that day. "I . . . still remember the air of gloom that pervaded the whole city, the eagerness with which people purchased fresh editions of the newspapers, and the tears which rolled down the faces of women, and even of some men, as they walked along the streets." On April 25, for the second and final time, Abraham Lincoln's train rolled past Audubon Park, now headed homeward.

George returned to Churchill and graduated a year later. His parents had high expectations for their eldest, and it was determined that he should take the admission examinations for Yale College, where his grandfather Lansing had gone. His own expectations were not so effulgent: "I did not in the least wish to go, and tried to escape it, but my parents had made up their minds, and I was not in the habit of questioning my father's decisions. I had wasted my time at school, and I had been warned by Mr. Churchill and by Mr. E. L. Davenport, a Harvard man, who was the teacher of Latin, that I was not prepared to pass the examinations, and would be very lucky if I succeed in doing so."

But over the summer, he bore down. "I did work hard, but with no special intelligence, for I had never learned how to study."

Three years earlier, when he was preparing to enter Churchill, George Bird Grinnell had received a letter from his other grandfather, George Grinnell of Greenfield, the man whose own father, yet another George Grinnell, had stood at the top of the hill and waved farewell to his mother. In his letter to the latest namesake, the Greenfield Grinnell offered several paragraphs of advice to a young man whom he hoped was headed toward his own hilltop. He covered the usual ground, exhorting George to abstain from intoxicating drink, to "practice private prayer," and to avoid "unprincipled and immoral" companions.

The best of his counsel was more philosophical. "To a mere child," the letter continued, "home, under the parental roof is his world,—all the world he knows. The real world, in which he is to move and act the part of a man, he can hardly conceive of. But as he advances in years . . . it is all important that he should go out beyond his hived home . . . to pursue the higher course of education, to learn also manliness of character and deportment. A youth, so placed, will love home none the less or the inmates of home. But he will soon see & feel that he must go abroad . . . to act his part well [in] the theatre of busy life."

In a postscript he added: "Keep hopeful; look on the bright side."

In September 1866 George Bird Grinnell took a train to New Haven and sat for the entrance exams. To his amazement he passed all but Greek and Euclid (geometry). After six weeks more of concerted tutoring, he cleared these hurdles as well, and, having just reached his seventeenth birthday, joined the Yale class of 1870.

MEMBER OF THE CLASS

G rinnell loved Yale—remarkably so, given that the treatment he received during his time in New Haven was, at best, mixed and his performance poor. Due to being "conditioned" in two subjects, he was a month late in joining his hundred or so fellow freshmen.

Each day began with chapel, followed by lessons—Greek, Latin, algebra, Euclid. Then came recitations, in which students answered questions on the day's material. The school year was divided into three terms; students received a grade for each course and each term on a scale that ranged from 0 to 4. The latter was perfection; not even the class valedictorian attained it. An average below 2.0 was grounds for suspension, with the student advised to "cram up" under a private tutor until he was able to pass the necessary examination or recitations and rejoin his class. Grinnell's average his first year was 2.06—one nostril above water.

As a freshman Grinnell received his fair share of hazing. Initiations were customarily meted out by sophomores who had suffered them only a year earlier. Torments included pilfering personal items and "smoking out"—barging into a freshman's room, filling it with cigar and pipe smoke and prodding the victim to recite lessons or sing a song. One of the more extreme humiliations was known as "bringing down," in which the fresh-man was gagged, blindfolded, and bound and then taken to a secluded location away from campus. "The cutting off of hair is the commonest device," revealed Lyman Baggs, class of 1869, who was a sophomore when Grinnell was a freshman. "Perhaps they mark upon his cheek the numeral of his class, employing for the purpose some chemical that will remain for several days indelible; or strip him and smear his body with paint; or pour cold water upon him; or"—Baggs at last lends a moral fig leaf to his litany of torture—"practice certain things which cannot be named."

In his memoirs Grinnell declined to mention any such indignities during his first year at Yale; nor did he note his poor academic showing. "Little of interest happened," he wrote.

Sophomore year was a different story. "I had become so much at home in New Haven, and with my class, that I was perpetually in trouble. I took part in all the hazing and hat-stealing which was usual by Sophomores at that epoch. I was then barely seventeen years old, and quite without any sense of responsibility."

By now Grinnell had achieved his full height of five-feet-ten, but even as he entered manhood, he never filled out much beyond the skinny lad who had taken his first brave strides in Audubon Park. Big ears added to his ungainliness, and while his peers were in a hurry to sport beards, moustaches, and sideburns, his undergraduate cheeks remained smooth and boyish.

Early during his sophomore year he found a way to cut a larger figure, however. With two classmates as accomplices, he climbed the lightning rod of the Lyceum, the main classroom building, and advertised in red paint the number of their class on the face of the college clock. "There it remained for one or two days, to the enormous pride of my class," he would write thirty-five years later with a vestige of pride and prankishness. The names of the painters were kept secret—at least from upperclassmen and the administration. Had they been discovered, the perpetrators of such an "imbecile barbarism" (in Baggs's judgment) would have been severely punished, by college authorities formally and surely by some unspeakable application of sophomoric justice.

Yet redress came soon enough for George Bird Grinnell. Shortly after the clock-tower caper, he was "detected in hazing a Freshman" and suspended from Yale for a year. He never spelled out the specifics of his transgression, but it must have been particularly reprehensible, for, while hazing was against the rules, it was widespread and seldom led to banishment. Then, too, Grinnell's crime might have been one blot too many on a record already stained.

It did not occur to him—or to his parents, for that matter—to give up his education entirely. He spent his year of exile in Farmington, Connecticut, forty miles north of New Haven, tutored by Reverend R. L. Payne, a sympathetic Yale alumnus. "[W]e had a very good time, doing very little study," Grinnell confessed. "We took long walks, paddled on the Farmington River, and on moonlight nights in winter, used to spend pretty much all night tramping over the fields."

The reverend's leniency did not produce a more scholarly pupil. At the end of the year, Grinnell sat for exams at Yale and failed, obliging him to spend the fall and winter of his junior year, still nominally a Yale student, in Stamford, Connecticut, under the kindly but firmer guidance of a Dr. A. M. Hurlburt. Besides carrying on an active medical practice, the doctor had built an impressive track record of rehabilitating miscreants and underperformers from Yale College.

"Dr. Hurlburt was not only a good tutor, but a good handler of boys," Grinnell recalled. "While making his rounds, he took me with him in his chaise, heard me recite as we drove along, and made me study while he was paying his professional calls."

The medicine worked; after spending the first two terms of his junior year under Hurlburt's care, Grinnell returned to New Haven. He had not been a fully participating member of the class of 1870 since the first term of his sophomore year—a full year and a half in absentia. His grades for that year, while far from stellar, were the highest of his undergraduate career.

It is a measure of Grinnell's amiability that he was welcomed back so readily by his schoolmates. His friends now called him "Birdie," a term of genuine affection. At the end of the spring term of his junior year, two men, one a senior and the other an alumnus, rapped on his door with a two-foot-long key. They had come to announce his election to Scroll and Key, Yale's second-oldest senior society.

Two societies stood above all others in Grinnell's day: Skull and Bones, the elder, founded in 1832, and Scroll and Key, founded in 1841. Only a select few were chosen—fifteen in each "Key" class—and those so favored were regarded as "big men" on campus. Whereas Bones men tended toward the scholarly and literary, Key men were more of the "social element," observed one of Grinnell's contemporaries—meaning "men of ability if possible, but at all events congenial and, in the college sense of the word, gentlemanly."

Initiations and meetings were highly ritualized and secret. Members never spoke the name of the society, except to other members, and secret songs and a secret handshake were likewise integral to Scroll and Key mummery. Active Key men wore their badges, engraved with an eagle clutching a scroll and key, night and day.

For Grinnell, as with most senior society men, the link formed between fellow members was a higher order of loyalty than that to their alma mater. Over the next half century Grinnell diligently sustained a number of Yale friendships, but few more avidly than the cohort of Key classmates. Several wound up living in or near New York, while others who lived farther away made sure to look him up when they were passing through the city.

As a senior he had a coveted room in South College, overlooking the Green, and the year was "a very pleasant one," he recorded in his memoirs. His grades were still not good, but good enough. In a graduating class of 110, he tied for next to bottom—not that this seemed to bother him or the friends he now held so closely. "My career in college was a checkered one," he would reminisce at one of his reunions, "but I don't believe there is any-one here that loves the members of the Class more than I do."

If he had other pursuits, beyond friendships, while at Yale, they were few. His absence during sophomore and junior years precluded involve-ment in literary, dramatic, or debating societies. Other than a brief mem-bership in one of the sailing clubs, he showed little enthusiasm for the popular sports of his day: rowing, cycling, and baseball. Nor did he appear to expend much time and energy in the pursuit of women.

The Yale student body, of course, was entirely male; yet teas, regattas, and other social gatherings offered opportunities for Yale men to mingle with the opposite sex. Although he was not as athletic or as polished or as book-smart as some of his peers, Grinnell was a winsome enough bachelor. His mother had seen that he learn to dance, and she enforced good manners. Even so, in scores of letters exchanged with classmates over more than half a century, only once did he mention a girl as an object of collegiate desire. "You will be saddened, I think a little bit, to read the enclosure which tells of the death of Mary Trowbridge," he wrote to classmate Jim Russell in 1929, when both were approaching eighty. "Of course, many, many years ago, when we were in college, we were among her worshippers. She was a splendid girl, and I hope with all my heart she had a happy life." This was as wistful as he got about women. Discretion was a gentlemanly virtue that covered much.

THE YALE EXPEDITION

George Bird Grinnell's time at Yale was all too brief. He was twenty years old at graduation and unformed in his ambitions. Other classmates would commit themselves to law, medicine, ministry, brokerages, and banks. In the spring of 1870 he had no firm notion of what he might do next—unless it was to join his father in business, which hardly seemed like much of an adventure.

Lacking a plan, he at least had a direction. Just before graduation he learned of an expedition being formed by one of Yale's professors to dig fossils in the West. Grinnell understood next to nothing about fossils, and he had taken only one course in geology. He had yet to make the acquaintance of Dr. Marsh, Yale's professor of vertebrate paleontology; very few students had, as he taught no undergraduates. All that most of them knew was that Marsh was a bone collector.

The picture Grinnell had of the American frontier came mostly from novels. James Fenimore Cooper's Leatherstocking Tales—*The Deerslayer, The Last of the Mohicans, The Prairie*—had enthralled the boys of Grinnell's father's day and continued to do so for generations more. "Cooper is the American novelist *par excellence*," Grinnell would credit in *Forest and*

Stream in 1889. "Certain it is that many a youngster has imbibed from Cooper's chapters his early taste for roughing it."

Yet the novels of Scottish-born adventurer "Captain" Mayne Reid were in some respects even more enthralling to young readers because the best of them were written about and for boys. Grinnell liked to say that he was "brought up" on Reid's *The Boy Hunters*, which "told of lands that were far away, and of people that were strange, and of animals that all had heard of, but none had seen." The boys of the tale were "the best shots of their age, could ride a horse with any, could swim the Mississippi, paddle a canoe, fling a lasso, or spear a catfish, as though they were full grown men."

"[I]n all the range of boyhood literature there was nothing that could equal them," Grinnell attested. "Later in life, not a few of [Reid's readers], who had now become men, traveled to and fro over the earth and visited in person those distant lands . . . [and] wherever they went or whatever they saw, they found that the description given by Mayne Reid was essentially true to life."

Othniel C. Marsh was a bit of a storybook character in his own right. His chair and salary at Yale were underwritten by his wealthy uncle, George Peabody, the international merchant-banker whose endowment of museums and institutions in Baltimore, at Harvard, not to mention at Yale, made him the acknowledged father of American philanthropy—a generation ahead of Andrew Carnegie or J. P. Morgan.

Peabody, who never married and had no children of his own, saw a spark in his nephew. As a boy growing up in western New York, Marsh was a restive student, favoring hunting and fishing and rummaging through diggings from the nearby Erie Canal. He came late to formal schooling and did not enroll at Yale until he was twenty-four. Upperclassmen wasted no time nicknaming him "Daddy."

Marsh was a senior in 1859, when Charles Darwin's *On the Origin of Species* was first published, and Darwinism was only beginning to edge its way into academic conversations when he completed a master's degree and went off to Germany to study paleontology. The Darwin debate reached full fever during the three years Marsh spent in Berlin and Heidelberg, and he returned to New Haven in 1866 a thorough convert. At Yale he became the college's first professor of vertebrate paleontology, his chair underwritten by George Peabody, who at the same time also endowed a handsome sum for the construction of the Peabody Museum of Natural History. Marsh was not expected to teach; nor would he receive a salary. His job, it was understood, would be to fill the museum with fossils and bones.

Marsh was a man of appetites both coarse and cultivated. His rooms were strewn with journals, rocks, and fossils, while his taste in bric-a-brac ran toward Japanese scroll paintings and Chinese cloisonné. "He had a "naïve love of fine living," observed English paleontologist Arthur Smith Woodward. Burly of build and bulldog tenacious, he could be aggressively protective of his personal privacy and professional findings, especially in later years when engaged in the notorious "bone wars" with rival paleontologist Edward Drinker Cope.

To the extent that the subject of homosexuality ever entered polite conversation in the late-Victorian years of the nineteenth century, it was characterized as a perversity of nature, moral weakness expressed as feminine delicacy. Marsh was never questioned, at least not in print, by his peers or academic acolytes, although many who knew the professor at Yale could not help wondering why he had missed out on marriage. Most ascribed it to his obsessive pursuit of paleontology, but Yale president Timothy Dwight sensed something more elusive in "the deepest life of his manhood." Years after Marsh's death, Grinnell would observe: "Marsh was a peculiar man, and did not show his real self to those whom he casually came in contact."

Of the twelve Yale men recruited for the 1870 expedition, three were Scroll and Key brothers. All came from families of means, and nearly all would mature into men of substance. James Wadsworth, of the landed and patriotic Wadsworths of Geneseo, New York, would be elected to Congress. Charles "Gaff" Reeve would wind up as the first chief of military police of Manila and later as brigadier general. John Nicholson would become chancellor of the state of Delaware. Still others became manufacturers, and two would serve on the board of the Yale Corporation. Eli Whitney, whose grandfather invented the cotton gin, became president of the New Haven Water Company.

There was one other common denominator, Grinnell explained in *Natural History* fifty years later: "None of them except the leader had any motive for going other than the hope of adventure with wild game or wild Indians. . . . It was an entirely innocent party of 'pilgrims.'"

Not that Marsh was a seasoned veteran of the western wilds himself. He had dug for fossils in Nova Scotia, New England, and in the sediment along the Delaware River, but until 1868 he had never appraised the potential of the continent that lay beckoning between Ohio and the far Pacific. That summer Marsh and several other scientists accepted an invitation from the Union Pacific Railroad to travel to the end of the line, which at that point in its crawl across the country reached only as far as a work camp named Benton, in southeastern Wyoming. "It was my first visit to the far West, and all was new and strange," Marsh wrote. "I found myself . . . surrounded, as far as the eye could reach in every direction, reminding me of mid ocean with its long rolling waves brought suddenly to rest. It was in fact the bottom of an ancient sea . . . and I was not long in deciding that its past history and all connected with it would form a new study in geology."

That new study had not begun with Marsh, however. His knowledge of the American West and his anticipation of its scientific fecundity had been primed by a number of predecessors. Geologists had accompanied the military expeditions surveying possible routes for a Pacific railroad. Paleontologist Ferdinand Hayden had been collecting fossils along the Missouri River, deep into Montana Territory, since the early 1850s and had explored the Dakota Badlands and Black Hills, the Yellowstone and Powder rivers, and much of the Kansas-Nebraska plains. Hayden shipped many of his samples to fellow paleontologist Joseph Leidy in Philadelphia, who identified tantalizing evidence of ancient camels, elephants, rhinoceri, and horses, among others. More recently, in 1867, geologist Clarence King, a graduate of Yale's Sheffield Scientific School, had embarked on a government-funded survey of the Fortieth Parallel, and, as a protégé of Marsh, King kept the professor informed on his fieldwork. Quite possibly Marsh also knew of John Wesley Powell's anticipated expedition to the Green and Colorado rivers.

On the 1868 trip Marsh persuaded the conductor to stop at Antelope

Station, in southwestern Nebraska, where a well digger was said to have uncovered bones of "elephants and tigers." The train paused briefly for Marsh to look through the mound of earth dug from the well. "I soon found many fragments and a number of entire bones," he related, "not of man, but of horses diminutive indeed, but true equine ancestors." There was more. "Other fragments told of his contemporaries—a camel, a pig, and a turtle."

The conductor grew impatient, and Marsh could sift no further. But before the train pulled out, continuing toward Benton, he struck a bargain with the station agent to collect more bones and have them ready when he came back through. The eastbound train halted just long enough at Antelope Station for the agent to pass Marsh a "hatful of bones." Marsh's trained eye identified eleven long-extinct species. By far the most remarkable bones, he determined, belonged to a three-toed horse, perhaps three feet tall and more than three million years old.

Marsh named the creature *Equus parvulus*. Here was fossil proof of a prehistoric progenitor to a species that in its later iteration would not again run free in the Western Hemisphere until the arrival of the Spanish in the sixteenth century. Moreover, if *Equus parvulus* was indeed a forerunner of the horses being saddled and harnessed in the nineteenth century, then the doors of Darwin's cabinet had been thrown wide open in the great American outback, waiting for its contents to be examined, assembled, and catalogued. If Marsh had his way, the final repository for these treasures would be the museum that was to be built for him with his uncle's money in New Haven.

Indian unrest on the plains prevented Marsh from setting forth again until the summer of 1870 with his team of pilgrims. During the interim the transcontinental railroad had been completed, and Marsh, thinking expansively, planned to take it all the way to the West Coast, stopping at promising points to search for specimens.

The Yale party left New Haven on June 30, armed and provisioned to the teeth. In Chicago they fueled their courage in the saloons between station and hotel. On to Omaha, crossing the Missouri by stern-wheeler. By then some of the young men had buckled on their revolvers to be ready for the blood and thunder they expected at any time. At every station, Gaff Reeve "strode on the platform in his fruitless search for increasing wilderness and woolyness," Harry Sargent recollected drolly, "and was a puzzle to the peaceful tillers of the soil who classed us as a baseball club . . . while Marsh was sized up as a financial backer or possibly umpire."

In the open prairie a short distance outside of Omaha, Grinnell for the first time practiced firing his new repeating rifle. "I believed that now I was on the frontier," he quipped, "and I was not far wrong."

They left the Union Pacific at Plum Creek, the nearest station to Fort McPherson, built near the confluence of the North and South Platte rivers to protect overland travelers from attack by Indians. Marsh carried with him a letter from General Philip Sheridan, commander of the Department of the Missouri, directing military posts to provide escort and all possible courtesies along the expedition's route. At McPherson the travelers were aroused by the news that earlier that same day a group of antelope hunters from the fort had tangled with a small party of Indians, presumably Cheyennes. One of the hunters was wounded in the arm by an arrow, and one of the Indians was hit by rifle fire. The next morning a detail of army troopers was sent out in pursuit, led by a civilian scout, William F. Cody.

Grinnell and his Yale chums knew Cody from stories serialized in the *New York Weekly*, under the title "Buffalo Bill, the King of the Border Men." They were plainly smitten by the presence of "the most celebrated prairie man alive." He was "a tall, well-built, handsome man who wore his blonde hair long and was a striking figure," Grinnell observed. When Cody returned from patrol, carrying the moccasins of the Indian shot by the antelope hunters, "the newcomers from New Haven stared in wonder," Grinnell wrote.

When the Yale expedition left Fort McPherson on July 14, they were escorted by a troop of cavalry totaling nearly seventy. The civilians rode ponies captured from the Cheyennes in the battle of Summit Springs the previous summer; for several of them, it was their first time mounting a horse. Their baggage was carried by five six-mule wagons and one four-horse wagon. Buffalo Bill rode in front of the column, along with three other scouts: Major Frank North and two Pawnees, phonetically identified by Grinnell as Tucky-tee-lous and La-Hoor-a-sac. Presumably

THE YALE EXPEDITION | 49

as a nod of respect, Grinnell named his horse after Tucky-tee-lous, which he was told meant, "When he being alone meets a Sioux alone and they both shoot."

Cody returned to Fort McPherson after the first day, but Frank North and the Pawnees stayed with the group for the next two weeks, during which time Grinnell's estimation of these scouts grew to eclipse the wide-eyed esteem he had earlier afforded to Buffalo Bill. Unlike the showman Cody, the thirty-year-old North was "modest almost to diffidence, and it was with difficulty that he could be induced to speak of his own heroic achievements," Grinnell would write. Yet North's bravery and fortitude spoke for themselves.

Frank North was born in upstate New York and moved west as a teenager with his family, homesteading on the Nebraska prairie near Columbus, at the mouth of the Loup River. He learned to speak Pawnee while working on their reservation, and in 1864 he was hired to recruit a group of Pawnees to serve as scouts. One of the first trans-Mississippian tribes to make peace with whites, the Pawnees were ideal for the job; they were longstanding enemies of the Cheyennes, Sioux, and Arapahos—tribes that put up fierce resistance to overland immigrants and railroad surveyors invading their traditional hunting grounds. Throughout the 1860s North's Pawnee scouts played an invaluable role in protecting white settlements and railroad crews along the Platte River and its tributaries. In return the Pawnees received weapons and horses and were allowed to leave their reservation in eastern Nebraska and continue their annual buffalo hunts on the western prairies.

Under the leadership of Frank North, the Pawnees fought faithfully and fiercely, returning home each winter with the scalps of their enemies and the thanks of the United States government. "The secret of Frank North's success in commanding the Pawnees, who loved him as much as they respected him, lay in the unwavering firmness, justice, patience, and kindness with which he treated them," Grinnell would write in the scout's obituary, published on the front page of *Forest and Stream*.

Grinnell was similarly enchanted by the Pawnees, the first Indians he had ever met on their home ground. Once the expedition was under way, the Pawnees shed their military uniforms in favor of moccasins, breech-clouts, and blankets. "They wore their hair long and had their scalp locks braided and sometimes they would decorate them with a piece of bright colored cloth or a feather," Grinnell wrote to his parents. "They were jolly fellows, both of them, and would sing and dance for us frequently."

One night the Yale men reciprocated, donning blankets and marching, single file, to the Indians' tent, "where we sat in a circle and smoked the pipe of peace. . . . Then they sang the buffalo song and we sang some college songs."

Every experience was so new, every bend in the trail was a first for something, and he was eager to soak in all of it. "[T]he longest summer day isn't long enough for him to ask all his questions," Frank North said of Grinnell.

Grinnell began a diary at the first night's camp out of Fort McPherson—a habit he would continue on his western trips for the next fifty-eight years. As the expedition moved north across the Nebraska Sand Hills, headed for the Loup River, he recorded seeing antelope daily, and one morning a large herd of elk crossed the river below where he and the others were searching for fossils. The entire party opened fire at once, but only Jim Russell, a Kentuckian and a Scroll and Key man, managed to kill one. "I wish it had been me," Grinnell allowed.

He did shoot a rattlesnake, cutting off the rattles for his youngest brother, Willie. His diary identified many birds—great blue heron, sharp-tailed grouse, short-billed curlew, killdeer, phalarope—giving their binomial scientific names where he could. He described long, parched marches, advising in an aside to his brothers back in Audubon Park that they "can believe the descriptions of suffering from thirst that they read in Mayne Reid's books." A prairie fire nearly overran one camp. During a thunderstorm he drank rain out of his broad-brimmed western hat.

The country between the Platte and Loup rivers is a jumble of rolling, grass-covered dunes once inhabited by the earliest mammals, including camels, Marsh's tiny horses, and a large rhinoceros-like ungulate, perhaps eight feet tall and fourteen feet long, eventually to be named a brontothere.

After the party reached the Loup, the men fanned out among side canyons, bluffs, and cut banks. While soldiers kept a lookout for Indians, the Yale men hunted for bones, and, to Marsh's satisfaction, they found a great many.

The bones that excited Grinnell the most, however, were human. Just before reaching camp one evening, he and several others came upon a cluster of Indian burial scaffolds, identified by North as Sioux. The bodies were eight feet off the ground and wrapped in blankets, buffalo robes, and wolf skins, with bows and arrows by their sides. Nearby lay the skeletons of horses dispatched to join their owners in the afterworld. In his diary Grinnell expressed no misgivings for intruding upon these sacred grounds, or remorse for robbing the graves. "I took some beads from the remains and also a medicine bag, some cards, bracelets and moccasins."

After seventeen days of marching, hunting, and digging, the Yale party completed its rugged but rewarding circuit and arrived at North Platte City on the Union Pacific. "We created quite a sensation as [we] galloped up the street. We were all well armed and all dirty and our appearance was striking," he boasted.

For Birdie Grinnell, the initiation had been transformative. He was no longer a distant observer of the frontier he had been imagining since he was a boy. He was a full participant—a naturalist, a hunter, a plainsman.

And his attachment to his tent mates had increased steadily during the dusty days afield. On the last page of Grinnell's diary, which ended at Fort McPherson on July 30, he recalled a line spoken by Polonius in *Hamlet*: "The friends thou hast, and their adoption tried, / Grapple them to thy soul with hooks of steel." Shakespeare actually wrote "hoops," but Grinnell's meaning was heartfelt just the same.

The next phase of his baptism took place farther down the track in southeastern Wyoming. Detraining at Fort D. A. Russell, near Cheyenne, the Yale party headed south, again with cavalry escort, into the badlands that stretched along either side of Crow Creek into northern Colorado. The fossil hunting was good here—turtles, piggish oreodons, and an even larger brontothere, the titanotherium. From the badlands the expedition followed the stratigraphic formation northward to Antelope Springs, in southwestern Nebraska, where Marsh had collected his hatful of delights two years earlier. This time he was able to excavate further and discovered even more species of horse—"one of them a little fellow only two feet tall and having three toes," Grinnell remarked.

On August 20 the party camped on Horse Creek, a feeder of the North Platte. Hungry for fresh meat, Marsh agreed to let Grinnell and Jack Nicholson set out upstream to hunt ducks. The main party decamped, too, following a route more suitable for the heavily laden wagons, with the assumption that, by keeping to Horse Creek, the hunters would intersect with the column at the end of the day. No one, including the army captain in charge of the march, realized that the creek wandered in a direction away from the intended rendezvous.

Grinnell and Nicholson rode along the stream, killing a few ducks. After about fifteen miles, with no sign of the wagons, they began to grow uneasy; their anxiety increased with the discovery of another Sioux grave, this one more recent than the one on the Loup.

Alone in Indian country, armed only with light-gauge shotguns, and unsure of their whereabouts, Grinnell and Nicholson expected to be set upon, scalped, and murdered at any moment. The assault came in mid-afternoon, but not from hostile Indians. At first they reckoned the plume of smoke was a Sioux signal, but soon they realized that a prairie fire was charging directly toward them. "[W]hen the flames got within about half a mile from us," Grinnell narrated, "I got off my horse and fired the creek bottom; after doing this, as the flames seemed to advance slowly, we mounted and rode on, but after going a few hundred yards I thought it best to get off and set the grass ahead on fire. . . . The fire seemed about a quarter mile off when I dismounted, and I gave my horse to Jack to hold, and also my gun. I had set the fire going in two places and was lighting a match for the third when suddenly I heard Jack scream to me, 'Mount, Birdie, mount.' I knew by his tone that there was danger, so without looking round, I jumped on my horse and then turned to take my gun from him. At that moment the fire was not twenty feet from us, the flames were 5 or 6 feet high, and the air was so hot and filled with smoke that we could not breathe. As soon as I was on my horse, we both put spurs to the animals and galloped down into the bottom where it was burnt."

Slightly singed but otherwise intact, they decided that the best plan would be to backtrack along the creek until they reached the previous camp and from there follow the wagon tracks. At sunset they ate one of the ducks raw, fearful that a fire would attract Indians. They spent a sleepless night, shivering in Grinnell's poncho, their horses tied by lariat to their legs. The next day, drooping in their saddles, they finally struck the trail of the column. By afternoon they were reunited with the expedition.

"I am happy to say that, though there were scouting parties out after us all day, we made our own way into camp without any assistance from anyone," Grinnell wrote home five days later. "In a word, we paddled our own canoe."

The rest of the summer's trip was full of adventure, but none nearly so harrowing. Returning to Fort D. A. Russell, the Yale expedition proceeded westward by rail, disembarking this time at Fort Bridger in southwestern Wyoming.

Again protected by army escort but now carrying their camp on pack mules, the party struck southward along the Henry's Fork of the Green River, continuing upstream and flanking the formidable Uinta Mountains, until reaching the confluence of the White River. "We stood upon the brink of a vast basin, so desolate, wild and broken that it seemed like the ruins of the world," marveled Charles Betts, class of 1869 and patent lawyer in the making. The country ahead was rough and comparatively unexplored, but hunters and Indians had told of gigantic bones on the upper White, where it crossed into Colorado.

Marsh's trip into the region would indeed prove productive; the pack mules would return freighted with the bones of prehistoric tortoises, the horse-like eohippus, and a six-horned rhinoceros, named by Marsh dinocerata. Grinnell, too, seemed inspired—by the setting and the unusually rich prospects of the exposed Tertiary terrain. "I was eager to explore," he declared, "for I felt sure that entombed in the sandy clays . . . there must be hidden the remains of many strange animals new to science, long waiting to be brought to light, and to tell the tale of their life history."

Yet history, he also discovered, did not necessarily lie buried, like treasure, beneath the ground; a chapter of it was very much alive in the settlement of Henry's Fork.

Before the expedition left Fort Bridger, Grinnell had ridden over to Henry's Fork in search of a better horse for the rough trip ahead. "It was almost sundown when I . . . approached a little camp of three buffalo skin lodges standing close together along the stream," he recalled. He was invited to stay the night by three white men, Ike Edwards, John Baker, and Phil Mass.

Until arriving in their camp, Grinnell had assumed that the days of the mountain man were over. The trappers who had succeeded Lewis and Clark—men like Jim Bridger, Jedediah Smith, John Colter, Jim Beckwourth, Joe Meek, Hugh Glass—were the first to take the full measure of the American West, harvesting its bounty of furs and giving names to landmarks previously unseen by white men. They seemed motivated as much by wanderlust as by the desire to turn beaver skins into money. They lived a hearty, feral, devil-may-care existence, far from the fetters and footprints of the East. Grinnell knew their stories, and the fictions derived from their stories, and in later years he would write about them at length. On Henry's Fork, he glimpsed the last breathing remnant of a nearly extinct species.

"John Baker and Phil Mass each had a Shoshoni wife and each a large flock of children of various sizes," Grinnell observed. "Ike Edwards . . . gave me robes and blankets for my bed; then by the small lodge fire, which was needed for light only and not for warmth, we talked far into the night." Edwards, he learned, had a pedigree very much like his own; he claimed to be a direct descendant of the venerable New England theologian Jonathan Edwards.

In the morning Grinnell watched the men skin beaver, and he bargained for a colt from their horse herd. "The life in the camp was an ideal one," he wrote with dreamy reverence many years later. "There was plenty of food, plenty of covering, and plenty of shelter. . . . Their mode of life appealed strongly to a young man fond of the open, and while I was with them I could not imagine, nor can I imagine now, a more attractive—a happier—life than theirs."

The Yale expedition returned to Fort Bridger on September 28, after a strenuous but fruitful month in the field. Their impedimenta now included nearly two tons of fossils. For Grinnell his apprenticeship was essentially complete. The remainder of the trip he would be a tourist, with no further scientific obligations to Professor Marsh.

Writing in *Forest and Stream* three years later, he would bid adieu to this formative interlude in his early manhood. After a successful day of shooting sage grouse in the foothills of the Uinta Mountains, Grinnell, Jack Griswold, Jim Russell, and Jack Nicholson had returned to camp, content and weary: "[W]e sat around the fire, talking of the day and its incidents, of bygone years and future plans. From time to time, college songs, so well known 'neath the grand old elms of New Haven, but new to these regions, broke the stillness of the clear night and were echoed back from the mountains in a grand refrain. But at length the camp grew more quiet, the fire burned down, and, knocking the ashes from our pipes, we wrapped our blankets around us and one by one lay down to dream. . . ."

A week later they were in Salt Lake City, the Mormon capital, which, since the completion of the transcontinental railroad, had become a popular destination for "Gentiles" curious to observe polygamy on display. They found the city orderly, its streets broad and clean, its houses shaded by well-tended trees and surrounded by productive gardens and orchards, with snow-capped mountains and the great tabernacle looking down from above. Marsh, with Grinnell in tow, paid a call on the Mormon leader, Brigham Young, who was surely delighted to learn of the existence of prehistoric horses; similar creatures inhabit *The Book of Mormon*.

In an article Charles Betts submitted to *Harper's New Monthly* he declared: "[W]e flirted with twenty-two daughters of Brigham Young in a box at the theatre, and, overcome by the effort, immediately crossed the Sierra Nevada to San Francisco."

Having traversed the continent, Grinnell's thoughts now turned toward home. He had been away four months, although it felt like much longer. Before returning east, however, he took a side trip to the Yosemite Valley to see the Mariposa Grove of giant sequoias, the largest of which towered two hundred feet. Six years earlier Abraham Lincoln had signed a bill ceding the Yosemite Valley and the Mariposa Grove to the state of California. The grant consecrated Yosemite's natural wonders for "public use, resort, and recreation" and stipulated that these be protected "for all time." Though not the first *national* park—that designation would belong to Yellowstone, created in 1872—here nonetheless was the seed of the great American idea, one which Grinnell would help gestate and nurture throughout his working life.

In his memoirs Grinnell mentioned that, during his time in Yosemite, he made the acquaintance of two "persons of importance": Galen Clark, credited as the first white man to set eyes on the Mariposa Grove and one of the authors of the original Yosemite act; and James Hutchings, another of the valley's early promoters. He just missed meeting thirty-two-year-old John Muir, who recently had built a sawmill for Hutchings but left his employment in the summer of 1870 after becoming too intimate with Hutchings's wife.

Before leaving San Francisco, Grinnell had visited a photographer's studio on Montgomery Street and had his picture taken. Portrait photography had thrived in San Francisco during the gold rush and in the two decades since. New arrivals wanted souvenirs of their metamorphosis into argonauts.

He chose a tableau that would affirm his authenticity as a plainsman or scout—modeled on his new idols, Buffalo Bill, Frank North, Ike Edwards. He stands before a painted backdrop of a narrow trail wending into a grove of trees. It is impossible to say whether his outfit is his own or has been provided from the photographer's wardrobe. His buckskin shirt is theatrical in the excess of fringe decorating its collar, shoulders, and breast. His pants, too, appear to be buckskin. He stands still for the camera's long exposure with his left leg cocked forward slightly, almost coyly, showing off a double layer of beadwork: on the pant leg itself and, for good measure, on the chaparajos—or chaps—worn on top and gartered flamboyantly below the knee with a tasseled bow. If the chaps are not leather and perhaps made of fabric, then the beadwork could be embroidery. Either way, the pattern is floral, with a heart at the hem. On his feet he wears moccasins, though these look a lot like slippers. To prove he means business, Grinnell carries a revolver in a holster and holds at rest a rifle in a fringed scabbard.

Yet the boy hunter who stares into the distance, past the camera, is slight of shoulder, far from brawny. Indeed, the overall impression, amplified by his outfit, is implicitly feminine—not masculine, anyway. A wisp of fair hair falls across his uncreased forehead beneath his broad-brimmed hat. The strongest evidence that he has reached maturity during the long summer outing is the faint moss of moustache that has begun on his upper lip. Once grown, he will never shave it off.

Grinnell made the trip from San Francisco to New York with Jack Griswold, arriving in time for Thanksgiving. Others in the Yale party stuck with Professor Marsh, who was not quite ready to give up hunting fossils for the season. He and his reduced crew stopped briefly in southwestern Wyoming, where they collected the skeletons of ancient fish. On Marsh's next stop, in the Cretaceous beds along the Smoky Hill River in Kansas, he discovered the bones of two especially magnificent species. One, the mosasaur, was an enormous lizard-like reptile with paddles for feet. The other seemed unextraordinary at first.

Riding toward camp one evening, Marsh spied a six-inch-long fossil at the side of the trail. Quick examination showed that it was hollow, with a "peculiar joint." Giving it further study by firelight, Marsh suspected that it might be the tibia of a gigantic bird. "The only joint much like it that I could find in any animal, living or extinct, was in the wing finger of the Pterodactyle, or flying dragon, but these reptiles so far as known, were only diminutive creatures, not one-twentieth the size or one-hundredth the bulk this bone indicated," he was to explain.

The mystery of the bone continued to gnaw at Marsh. Finally he eliminated all other conclusions. "I made . . . a careful calculation of how large a Pterodactyle must be to have a wing finger corresponding to the fragment I had found, and ascertained that its spread of wings would be about twenty feet—truly a gigantic dragon even in this country of big things, where hitherto no Pterodactyle large or small had ever been discovered."

And there was one other bit of excitement that Grinnell missed by heading home ahead of Marsh. Of all the wondrous sights he had beheld in the West, the one that eluded him was perhaps the most emblematic of all: *Bison bison*—buffalo.

Many years later Grinnell would reminisce in a letter to Edward Nelson of the Bureau of Biological Survey, "In 1870, I think it was, I happened to be on a train that was stopped for three hours to let a herd of buffalo pass. We supposed that they would soon pass by, but they kept coming." Either he had the year wrong or this was a case of wishful memory. Nowhere in his diary, in letters home to his mother and father, in his memoirs, or in the narratives written by others in the Yale party, is there any confirmation of this story.

In 1870 vast herds of buffalo, millions of animals, still roamed the Great Plains. But somehow they never roamed within sight of Grinnell—or else he surely would not have left them out of his various accounts of the expedition.

Marsh, however, had better luck. As winter settled in on the prairie and he was finishing up the last of his excavating, he was invited to join a hunting party from Fort Wallace and, though relegated to a spectator's seat in an army ambulance, he succeeded in shooting two impressive specimens, one of which he declared a "monarch." The head, robe, and feet were added to the thirty-six crates of fossils that arrived in New Haven in December.

Around the time Marsh was chasing buffalo, George Bird Grinnell was fastening his collar and taking a seat behind a desk in his father's office at 36 Broad Street, as a clerk without pay. He had entertained a vague notion of pursuing medical studies upon his return, but his father's solicitations prevailed. "I found that he was anxious to have me go into business, to relieve him," Grinnell commented flatly. "This seemed the proper thing to do."

And yet he could not so easily set aside his recent experiences. His head was full of the open range, of Indians, of camp life, of the hunt, of men engaged in primordial pursuits. So much of it was fleeting, so much already buried. When the rest of his Yale chums arrived in New York at Christmas, they doubtless told him of the buffalo hunt. There was so much more to see and do.

Forty-five years later Grinnell would reflect on the summer of 1870 and the sense of duty that tugged at him: "I desired enormously to spend the rest of my life with these people, but, of course, the knowledge of the grief that this would give my parents pulled me back again."

CHAPTER 4

A WILD GALLOP

George Blake Grinnell did very well in the first few years following the Civil War. In 1866 he formed a brokerage firm that handled mostly railroad securities. Perhaps the biggest reason for the good fortune of the partnership was its principal client, Horace Clark, who, among his other distinguished credentials, was the son-in-law of railroad tycoon Cornelius Vanderbilt. Clark helped Vanderbilt consolidate the New York Central and Hudson River railroads, and he ascended to the presidency of the Lake Shore and Union Pacific railroads. "His speculations have been the most gigantic of Wall Street," the *New York Times* declared. Accordingly, the business that George Blake Grinnell conducted for Clark and Vanderbilt proved, as Grinnell's eldest son was to acknowledge, "large and profitable."

George Blake offered his son no pay at first; and only a pittance later, as he taught him the business of stocks and bonds. Whether or not he was destined to take over Grinnell & Co., George Bird knew that one day he would inherit responsibility for his father's affairs on behalf of his five younger brothers and sisters. And learning to handle finances prudently would serve him well even if he decided to pursue other interests. It certainly did not hurt to know the meaning of a dollar, especially since there were so many dollars pouring into his father's account. Even so, he squirmed in the seat assigned him in the stuffy office on Broad Street.

Of the dozen Yale men who had gone west with Marsh, Grinnell was the only one who remained drawn to the professor. Just a few weeks after returning to New York, Grinnell agreed to help Marsh collect specimens for the Peabody Museum. The bone hunting this time was not prehistoric. Instead Grinnell in his spare time made the rounds of taxidermists and menageries, looking for choice skeletons. Zoos, or zoological gardens, were rarities in America in those days, but circuses and exhibits of exotic animals were a popular form of amusement. P. T. Barnum's "Grand Traveling Museum, Menagerie, Caravan & Hippodrome" began touring in 1870, with elephants complementing the showman's signature display of human "freaks."

One of the principal suppliers for these traveling menageries was the Reiche brothers, in New York's Bowery. The Reiches had begun by importing canaries, many of which wound up, proverbially, in mines; they also sold monkeys to organ grinders. Soon they were dealing in elephants, hippopotami, lions and tigers and leopards, hyenas, giraffes, gnus, ostriches, and more. Not surprisingly, given the callous care shown these animals in capture, shipment, and custody, more than a few suffered and inevitably perished.

"I stopped in at a menagerie and after introducing myself as your assistant I told the manager what I wanted," Grinnell wrote Marsh in February 1871. "He was very polite to me, showed me all his beasts and birds free of charge, and said that he would be delighted to let me have such animals as died." Grinnell told Marsh that he had narrowly missed a chance to acquire skeletons of a zebra and a tapir, but he expressed optimism that a new shipload from Africa would produce richer rewards: "Among the larger beasts are a giraffe and a rhinoceros. Many of the animals will of course die on the voyage and perhaps I will be able to get some of them." He was likewise sanguine that two of the menagerie's bears—"one white (*U. maritimus*), the other black (*U. americanus*)"—were also on their last legs and "expected to die in a week or two and I can probably get them anyhow."

Yet Grinnell's efforts to please Marsh had limits. "I wish, Professor, that

I could get all these things and make them free gifts to the college, but I cannot," he wrote apologetically. "The only thing I can give you is my time and labour. That I do most freely give, and I beg you to call on me whenever you want anything done." Marsh gratefully sent Grinnell checks for his acquisitions; Grinnell dutifully sent Marsh a ledger of all purchases and their cost. Unable to get to New Haven, he invited Marsh to come to Audubon Park to discuss how he could better fulfill the professor's wishes. By this time Grinnell had been working in his father's office for less than three months. He signed the letter, "G. Birdie Grinnell."

Over the next year and a half, Grinnell worked faithfully to expand Marsh's collection, learning a great deal about anatomy along the way. The inventory of osteological delights reads like the passenger list for Noah's ark: sea turtle, seal, alligator, "flying fox," sharp-shinned hawk, snowy owl, eagle, weasel, moose, possum, armadillo, chimpanzee, anteater, warthog, "the shin bones of a giraffe," and "a Bengal tiger said to be perfect." He obtained a boa constrictor and a kangaroo, both of which had died in Barnum's show, and a coyote from the Central Park zoo. "I have the address of a man in Chicago who has two camels buried. . . . I know a man who is going to South America to collect on the banks of the Orinoco. . . . How was the skunk? High? . . . If you find that the sloth skull and tiger cat skeleton are too badly boiled up to be of any service to you, let me know and I will alter the account."

He gave Marsh little reason to complain about that account, as he grew increasingly skilled at driving a sharp bargain. He paid $150 for a full-grown elephant skeleton and could barely contain his good fortune when he bagged the bones of a black baboon (from the Celebes, today's Indonesian island of Sulawesi). "I have now to speak of a very rare skeleton that I have for you. It is a monkey (Cynocephalus niger), and it is the first, as far as known, ever brought to this country. A work on the quadrumana [a primate with hand-shaped feet] that I consult says that there is but one specimen in Europe." Alive the baboon was valued at $2,000. Grinnell procured its skeleton for $10. "I hope you will like him."

Marsh repaid Grinnell's dedication in ways that more than compensated for his labor and for any friction that arose over his clear preference for science over business. In May 1871 Marsh whimsically named one of his newly discovered fossils after his hard-working helper. "Many thanks for the honor you have done me," Grinnell responded. "I have shown the description of *Crocodilus Grinnelli* to several of my friends, and they look on me now as one of the greatest of created men."

And almost two years after the Yale expedition a crate arrived from New Haven containing a splendidly mounted buffalo head—a trophy from the Nebraska hunt that Grinnell had missed. He thanked the professor profusely and congratulated him on his "prowess on the prairie."

As much as Grinnell would have liked to accompany Marsh on forthcoming fossil-digging expeditions in the West, he had to turn down the invitations. Work would not permit an absence of so many months. Yet it would allow him a two-week vacation. In the spring of 1872 Grinnell wrote to Frank North, asking the scout if he could accompany the Pawnee Indians on their summer buffalo hunt, with North as guide. North demurred but said that his younger brother, Luther, might be interested.

George Blake Grinnell's best client, Horace Clark, president of the Union Pacific and Lake Shore railroads, provided sleeping-car passes free of charge. Grinnell left New York the first week of August, traveling "in most luxurious fashion," accompanied by Jim Russell, a Scroll and Key classmate and the one member of the 1870 expedition with an aim straight enough to kill an elk. Russell lived in Paris, Kentucky; Grinnell had visited him the previous summer at the time of the Bourbon County Fair, further sealing their friendship.

They were met at Plum Creek station, Nebraska, by Luther North, who soon proved to be every bit as impressive as Frank. "Lute North is a splendid fellow, and I don't know whether I like him or his brother best," Grinnell wrote Professor Marsh.

Lute North was short and slim, all sinew. He was twenty-six in 1872, three years older than Grinnell, and already had half a lifetime of hard work behind him. At fourteen he and Frank had begun hauling logs to the government sawmill on the Pawnee reservation. At sixteen he enlisted in the Nebraska cavalry. In 1866 he joined his brother to lead the Pawnee scouts, and by August 1872, when Grinnell and Russell stepped off the Union Pacific, Lute North had skirmished with his share of Indians, suffered the prairie privations of thirst and blizzard, and proven his grit and bravery many times over.

Nothing about Lute North would ever disappoint, unless it was the scout's reluctance to toot his own horn. For that he would have George Bird Grinnell.

The Pawnees were surrounded by many enemies—Sioux, Cheyennes, Arapahos, Osages, and Comanches. They were "true Ishmaelites," Grinnell would write. "They had no friends upon the prairies save those whom they had conquered and held by fear." Remarkably the Pawnees had never warred with whites; by allying themselves with the government, the tribe had found a way to negotiate two worlds better than most.

Their traditional homeland was along the Missouri and Platte rivers, where they had lived in earthen houses and grew corn, beans, and squash in the rich riparian soil. With the acquisition of horses, they ventured onto the prairies and enriched their diet and domain by hunting buffalo in present-day Nebraska and Kansas. But then, through a succession of treaties, they ceded ground to whites, and by 1859 their reservation was a ten-by-thirty-mile swatch along the Loup River, northwest of Columbus (where the North clan had settled). In payment for their conciliation, the government permitted the Pawnees to leave the reservation twice a year to hunt. "Now, for a little while," Grinnell observed, "they returned to the old free life of earlier years, when the land had been all their own, and they had wandered at will over the broad expanse of the rolling prairie."

Virtually the entire tribe—some four thousand men, women, and children—had left the reservation in mid-July 1872, heading southwest. Arriving at Plum Creek, Grinnell, Russell, and North, accompanied by an elderly teamster and a mule-drawn wagon, struck out to find the Pawnees.

"Many a time during my wanderings west of the Missouri," Grinnell wrote a year later, "had those hunts of the Indians been described to me with a graphic eloquence that filled me with enthusiasm . . . and I had determined that if ever offered I would take part in one."

He may well have been recalling Mayne Reid's description of the buffalo chase; or possibly James Fenimore Cooper's *The Prairie* (1827), in which the Trapper—a grizzled Natty Bumppo—savors the taste of roasted buffalo hump as "the culinary glory of the Prairies" and praises the Pawnees as a "valiant and honest tribe" who "set an example of courtesy blended with reserve that many a diplomat of the most polished court might have strove in vain to imitate."

Or more likely he was remembering Francis Parkman's *The Oregon Trail* (1849), which describes a buffalo hunt—"[E]ach horse sprang forward convulsively, and, scattering in the charge in order to assail the entire herd at once, we all rushed headlong upon the buffalo"—as well as the seasonal hejira of the Pawnee tribe—"Here every summer pass the motley concourse; thousands of savages, men, women, and children, horses and mules, laden with their weapons and implements, and an unruly multitude of wolfish dogs."

Thus primed with expectation, Grinnell rode into his own tableau of western history. "Bear with me for a moment . . . while I give you a brief description of the country through which we are to journey," he implored in one of his first submissions to *Forest and Stream*. "Far away to the north I would point out to you the faint dark line formed by the tall cottonwoods that fringe the Platte and by which its direction east and west may be traced as far as the eye can reach . . . Among the numberless bluffs that rise one after another like the waves of a tossing sea, the buffaloes can be seen by thousands; some peacefully reposing on the rich bottoms, others feeding on the short nutritious grass that clothes the hillsides."

Then he added, "[T]heir days are numbered, and unless some action on this subject is speedily taken . . . these shaggy brown beasts, these cattle upon a thousand hills, will ere long be among the things of the past."

Melancholy portent aside, Grinnell was exhilarated to be among so many of the beasts that had evaded him two summers earlier. Even more enchanting were the Pawnees, whose camp he and his companions came upon in the bottom of Beaver Creek, a tributary of the Solomon in northern Kansas: "The scene was one of bustling activity. The women and children were busily at work bringing water, chopping wood and cooking, while the men strolled about the camp smoking or talking or clustered together and gazed at us as we approached." Lute North was warmly welcomed by the Pawnee chief, Pí ta Le Shar, who called Lute "my son."

To Grinnell's lifelong delight and satisfaction, he, Russell, and North did not arrive too late for the buffalo hunt. Breaking camp, they joined "the spectacle of four thousand Indians on the march"—heavily laden ponies pulling travois and led by women, boys herding horses reserved exclusively for the buffalo chase, and out in front "the principal men of the tribe, all mounted on superb ponies, their saddles glittering with silver ornaments and their bridles tinkling with little bells." Hardly a firearm was in evidence; the Pawnees still preferred to hunt with bows and arrows, although now their arrow points were cut from sheet metal.

The buffalo hunt proved to be the most momentous, the most defining experience of Grinnell's eighty-eight years on earth. It was mythic; it was ecstatic. He was not the same afterward, and in the midst of it, he surely sensed that it might not repeat itself. He would tell the story many times, and it appeared in print at least twice, amply embroidered.

"The scene we now beheld was such as might have been witnessed here a hundred years ago. It was one that can never be seen again," he wrote in *Pawnee Hero Stories and Folk-Tales*, published in 1889, after the buffalo were gone and the remaining Pawnee had been relocated to a reservation in Indian Territory. "Here were eight hundred warriors, stark naked, and mounted on naked animals. A strip of rawhide, or a lariat, knotted about the lower jaw, was all their horse's furniture. Among all these men there was not a gun nor a pistol, nor any indication that they had ever met with the white men. For the moment they had put aside whatever they had learned of civilization. Their bows and arrows they held in their hand. Armed with these ancestral weapons, they had become once more the simple children of the plains. . . . Here was barbarism pure and simple. Here was nature."

Then the chase was on: "As we proceeded, the pace became gradually a little more rapid. . . . The plain was peopled with Centaurs. Out over each horse's croup floated the long black hair of his rider, spread out on the wings of the breeze. . . . Like an arrow each horse darted forward. Now all restraint was removed. . . . What had been only a wild gallop became a mad race."

More than an eyewitness to this magnificent drama, Grinnell was also a participant, a distinction that he would wear with a feigned casualness that could never quite mask his sustained elation throughout many years of circulation in the clubs and banquets of the East. "I put spurs to my horse and as soon as I got within easy distance, fire"—he carried a repeating rifle—"and the ball, entering near the root of the tail, ranges diagonally forward and comes out at the shoulder. The huge beast drops to the shot, and I pull up to examine my first buffalo. I marvel at his monstrous size and vast strength, and admire his massive horns and hoofs, which shine like polished ebony, and his shaggy head with its impenetrable shield of hair, hide and bone."

North and Russell also killed buffalo, and, gazing over the field of battle, Grinnell observed the Pawnees gathering meat: "Every ounce of this will be saved, and what is not eaten while fresh will be jerked and thus preserved for consumption during the winter."

Grinnell could not resist an editorial coda: "How different would have been the course of a party of white hunters had they the same opportunity. They would have killed as many animals, but would have left all but enough for one day's use to be devoured by the wolves or to rot upon the prairie."

In camp that night, Grinnell, North, and Russell joined in the Indians' rejoicing. "Some roast the delicious hump ribs, and some broil the heart and liver. Many stuff the intestines with fragments of the tenderloin and boil them, thus obtaining a most delicate soup, and others take the great marrow bones and greedily feed upon the luscious contents. And so the evening wears away," Grinnell concluded contentedly, "passed by our little party in the curious contemplation of a phase of life that is becoming more and more rare as the years roll by, and by the Indians in feasting and merriment, and when at last we seek our couches and drop off to sleep, the Pawnees are still pegging away at the buffalo meat quite manfully."

With that, the midsummer's dream was over. Grinnell was back in New York by August 18. "Altogether we had a good time, so good that I would like to repeat it," he wrote Marsh, adding that, shortly after his return, he had acquired the skulls of an elephant, a rhinoceros, and a large, tusked babirusa for the professor's growing collection. From buffalo to elephant—all in the short span of fifteen days.

On September 2, two weeks after he had been feasting on the fruits of the buffalo hunt, he told Marsh somewhat tepidly, "I have this day been received as partner in the firm of Geo. B. Grinnell & Co."

Yet, as he fitted himself more tightly into the harness of family business, there was one last interlude from his recent western trip that inhabited his memory. He could not find a place for it in either the *Forest and Stream* article or *Pawnee Hero Stories*; but he described it with some detail in his unpublished memoirs, dated 1915. After the hunt, riding back north to the railroad, "[W]e were attacked by about fifteen Indians," he wrote. They had sent the wagon ahead to cross the Republican River, near the mouth of Red Willow Creek, east of present-day McCook, Nebraska. "It was well on in the afternoon. The sun was hot, and we were more or less sleepy. No one, I think, except perhaps Lute North, was thinking of anything except the joy of reaching the river and getting to camp."

Grinnell happened to look up a side coulee and caught a glimpse of an Indian afoot, holding his horse. "What seemed likely was that the man . . . was an enemy—Sioux or Cheyenne—one of those who had attacked the Pawnee camp only a few days before and endeavored to run off the horses."

Soon a group of mounted Indians "streamed out from the hills and rode down upon us." With flight out of the question, North directed his untested companions to dismount and form a defensive triangle with their horses, "and we stood behind them ready to point our guns over the saddles." The Indians circled, narrowing their distance with each pass. "Two or three of them had guns, and from time to time they fired, the bullets usually knocking up the dust long before they reached us, but sometimes singing over our heads, and for a short time the song of each bullet created an extraordinary connection in my mind, and I experienced the sensation described as 'having your heart in your throat.' This soon passed off, however. . . . We had plenty of ammunition, and we wasted a little of it, shooting carefully at the men on horses that rode so fast about us. However, the distance was great, the targets moved rapidly, and while on two or three occasions we thought that one of us had hit a horse, only one animal was really crippled and that from a shot by North."

After a half hour or so, the Indians lost interest and withdrew: "They were poorly armed, and we had the best guns of that day." Grinnell, Russell, and North remounted and resumed their journey, unharmed.

In the years to come Grinnell would relive this brief skirmish and his narrow escape countless times. North remembered, too, but he also remembered far more perilous and violent scenes and thus made light of the hot afternoon on Red Willow Creek.

As for Jim Russell—he did not recall the occasion at all. After the summer outing of 1872, Russell assumed the life of a Kentucky gentleman, raising a family, growing tobacco, and enjoying the bourbon of Bourbon County. "I regret now, as I have for years, your failing memory," Grinnell joshed his old chum in 1917.

It became clear that, if this were going to be anybody's story, it would be Grinnell's alone. It mattered more to him than to Lute North or Jim Russell, if it mattered to them at all. They let him keep it, and it became part of who he was.

George Bird Grinnell spent the next year trading securities for Grinnell & Co. and living at home in Audubon Park; as a hobby, he kept a collection of specimens, birds mostly, which he had learned to preserve in the manner of the Audubons.

The markets, meanwhile, were booming, none more so than railroad stocks. The one interruption in the firm's galloping good tidings was the death of Horace Clark in June 1873, "a dreadful misfortune to my father, who admired and loved Mr. Clark," Grinnell wrote.

Admired, and also depended on him. With other partners and with his father-in-law, Cornelius Vanderbilt, never far away, Clark had continued to speculate heavily in railroads, the securities for which were carried on margin by Grinnell & Co. "Margin" meant that Clark bought stocks from Grinnell and also borrowed money from Grinnell to buy those stocks. Assuming that the stocks increased in value, Clark could sell them at a profit, pay back his loan, plus interest, and make money. If the value of those stocks should drop, Clark was expected to increase his margin—that is, pay more on the loan he had received from Grinnell for those stocks. This loop was all quite legal. In good times it worked as a nifty and lucrative slipknot for the parties at either end of the financial rope. In not-so-good times, however, the slipknot could too easily unravel.

Busy though he was, Grinnell continued scavenging bones for Marsh. Once again he had to turn down an offer to go west on a paleontological expedition. As consolation, he was able to squeeze in a brief elk-hunting trip with Lute North on the Cedar River northwest of Columbus, Nebraska.

Summer is not the preferred season for hunting elk, but the primary object, it seems, was to escape New York and spend time with North. "Lute—my *guide*, philosopher and friend, ah, how shall I describe you? What fitting words can I convey an idea of your genial spirit, your kind heart and generous disposition?" Grinnell wrote with unchecked admiration. If he and North never happened upon a single elk, Grinnell would have been satisfied to sprawl beside the campfire and listen to the scout tell stories of Indian fights.

Yet not all of their time together was harmonious. "Did we quarrel on the Cedar a hundred years ago?" North would write Grinnell in 1915. "Well, it is all right now, and I am awfully sorry to have hurt you even unintentionally."

"Yes, we quarreled," Grinnell replied. "It was all my fault."

In the end, trusty North got Grinnell within range of his prey, and Grinnell did the rest with his .50-caliber Sharps, the same rifle he had carried the summer before to hunt buffalo. "This was for me the supreme moment. As I stood over her, all the trouble and annoyance of the trip; all the worries and cares of every day life were forgotten, and I was absorbed in the proud contemplation of the graceful creature lying before me."

Worries and cares awaited Grinnell upon his return. On September 1, 1873, George Blake Grinnell announced the creation of a new firm, George Bird Grinnell & Co., capitalized at $900,000. Yet the old shingle, George B. Grinnell & Co., did not disappear; $13 million of ongoing trade remained on its books. And George Blake did not intend to step away entirely, at least not at first. He made his loyal cashier, Joseph C. Williams, a general partner in the new enterprise and listed himself as special partner. For all that, he made clear that the torch was being passed.

The torch exploded all too quickly, however. Less than three weeks after George Bird Grinnell became a principal in the firm bearing his name, the stock market crashed.

"The panic of 1873 came out of a clear sky," Grinnell would insist in his memoirs. Yet this was not quite so. The postwar boom in the United States had been driven largely by railroad expansion. The Grinnells, the Vanderbilts, and other speculators had benefited from government land grants and woven steel and stock into a latticework of consolidations that promised extraordinary growth. So long as investors were eager and the value of stock soared, lack of income from these investments was of minimal concern. But in the spring the bottom had fallen out of European markets, and throughout the summer foreign appetite for American securities tapered off drastically. Wall Street, meanwhile, continued to ignore the signals emanating from abroad, blinkered in its bullishness.

On September 18 Philadelphia financier Jay Cooke—who, during the Civil War, had sold the bonds that saved the Union and then had undertaken to build a second railroad across the continent, the Northern Pacific—could no longer meet his obligations and was forced to declare bankruptcy. The crisis of confidence was contagious. Dozens more railroads and thousands of businesses soon failed. On September 20 the New York Stock Exchange closed, and it remained closed for ten days. Grinnell & Co., which, up till then, had been able to count on Horace Clark for additional margins to cover the firm's exposure, was left standing naked in the storm.

In Grinnell's characterization of the dire events of 1873, his family and firm were among the victims of the panic, as indeed they were. But it is likewise true that they also played a pivotal role in precipitating the worst financial crisis in the country's history, thus far. Cornelius Vanderbilt controlled more railroad securities than any man in the United States, and Grinnell & Co., in its former incarnation and now in its new, had an active hand in making this mammoth engine go. For the Grinnells, as for Vanderbilt and his fellow financial travelers, the crash of 1873 was their own fault. Speculation fed on itself, until steam turned into so much hot air. "The Vanderbilt stocks, which are held at high prices, and which in ordinary times are regarded as among the safest of all investments, gave way shortly," the *New York Times* reported on September 20, "and a tumble of remarkable nature ensued."

Looking back, George Bird Grinnell would view the cataclysm as a betrayal. "Commodore Vanderbilt, who might have helped . . . was not very active in his efforts to procure the necessary securities," he griped bitterly. "Trusted officers of banks and corporations disappeared with the money of institutions; the stock market promptly fell to pieces, prices dropped almost to nothing."

Yet unlike thousands of other investors, bankers, and ordinary citizens who went broke or lost their jobs, the Grinnells were spared total devastation, thanks to George Blake Grinnell's adroit and, according to numerous contemporary observers, devious maneuverings. In the days following the collapse of the Northern Pacific and the closing of the New York Stock Exchange, a creditor, Henry Meyers, came forward to file suit against Grinnell & Co., thrusting the firm into involuntary bankruptcy and thereby freezing its assets.

Other creditors, as well as newspapers, smelled something foul. Meyers, described by one paper as a "farmer and horse-dealer" from Dutchess County, New York, was a minor creditor at best and a comparative stranger to the exchange. Many concluded that he had been put up—either by Grinnell & Co., or Horace Clark's widow, or various Vanderbilt interests—to create a legal moat around the firm to prevent the Grinnells from having to sell off assets to pay investors money they had earned on stocks up until the time of the crash.

George Blake Grinnell and Joseph Williams were called before the Governing Committee of the Stock Exchange to explain themselves. Because George Bird Grinnell was not a member of the exchange, he was exempted. George Blake and Williams declined to answer the pointed questions of the committee and were punished with revocation of their membership—a severe and rare rebuke that the *New York World* characterized as "an indelible form of disgrace." Still, there was method to their maddening silence. Their aim was to buy time—long enough for markets to find surer footing.

In addition to the public chastisement by the Stock Exchange, the Grinnells had to face the brickbats of other creditors who regarded the bankruptcy as a sham. The lawyer for one of these was no less than William M. Evarts, president of the bar association of New York City (and future secretary of state to Rutherford B. Hayes). "The conduct of George Bird Grinnell & Co. was well understood in the street," the *Times* reported in its paraphrase of Evarts's argument before a U.S. District Court judge. "[T]hey conspired under a scheme of bankruptcy to ruin others. It was well understood that a collusion and a fraudulent proceeding existed between the firm and the petitioner Meyers."

When the judge threw out the involuntary bankruptcy, George Blake Grinnell promptly filed for voluntary bankruptcy, buying still more time, though the press now used the term "alleged bankruptcy" to describe the firm's tactic.

Still the Grinnells would not budge until December, by which time the stock market had recovered sufficiently for the firm to emerge from legal protection. On Wall Street the move was received as a sign that the worst was over. "The trade in stocks was enlivened on Monday last," the *World* reported on December 15, "by the formal discontinuance of all proceedings in the Grinnell bankruptcy case. The relief universally felt at this issue of legal proceedings of more than two months' duration is due entirely to the liberation of $13,000,000 of money employed in the Grinnell loans."

All suits against Grinnell & Co. were dropped. "[O]ur customers took some of their stocks off our hands, and the concern resumed with money enough to pay all its debts, and to have a little capital remaining," Grinnell summarized a little too tidily in his memoirs.

A number of questions about the Grinnells' motives and conduct throughout the crash of 1873, including its approach and aftermath, will never be answered satisfactorily. Did George Blake Grinnell see the panic coming and make his son, who had no seat on the stock exchange, the head of a similarly named but separate business as a way to confuse hungry creditors? What was at the bottom of the bankruptcies? Was George Bird Grinnell a knowing participant in the entire affair? When approached by reporters during Grinnell & Co.'s turbulence, he pleaded ignorance and remained tight-lipped.

In the end, George Blake Grinnell prevailed; the family came through the panic more or less intact, financially anyway. Meanwhile, though, George Bird Grinnell had to endure the public pillory of not just the family name but *his own name* as well. Later he would insist, without substantiation, that his father was applauded by his peers for his hard-nosed perspicacity in the face of adversity. But regardless of George Bird Grinnell's degree of involvement, whether he had been complicit or unconscious, and regardless of George Blake Grinnell's intentions, there can be no question that the father had exposed his son—a novice who had turned twenty-four the very day of the panic—to tremendous unpleasantness and shame.

"The winter was one of great suffering," George Bird Grinnell recorded in his memoirs, and the cloud that enveloped the Grinnell family in 1873 was to cast an everlasting shadow. The fear and embarrassment of bankruptcy, of prodigality, of financial nonfeasance of any sort, large or small, would forge in him a conservatism—conservatism as conservation, as preservation, as *self*-preservation—that would shape his relationships with family members, friends, other authors, the various causes he embraced, and even the Indian tribes he strove to aid in their struggles for integrity and survival. He would always be proud to be a Grinnell, but after 1873 he also recognized that it was a name he had to defend and exonerate.

In February 1874, "having brought us safely out of the woods," as his son credited, George Blake Grinnell withdrew from business entirely, never to work on Wall Street again. Chagrined and singed, he retreated, renting out the family house in Audubon Park and moving to a farm in Milford, Connecticut.

George Bird Grinnell, who had never hidden his "settled dislike" for the business of stocks and bonds, saw his chance for escape as well. The avenue that presented itself most fortuitously was *Forest and Stream*.

"The Publishers . . . aim to merit and secure the patronage and countenance of that portion of the community whose refined intelligence enables them to properly appreciate and enjoy all that is beautiful in Nature," managing editor Charles Hallock pronounced in the first issue in August 1873. "It will pander to no depraved tastes, nor pervert the legitimate sports of land and water in those base uses which always tend to make them unpopular with the virtuous and good. . . . A practical knowledge of natural history must of necessity underlie all attainments which combine to make a thorough sportsman. It is not sufficient that a man should be able to knock over his birds dexterously right and left, or cast an inimitable fly. He must learn by study and experience the haunts and habits of the game or fish he seeks."

It was an editorial summons tailored perfectly for George Bird Grinnell. The *Forest and Stream* office turned out to be only a half-dozen blocks from Grinnell & Co. In its first months, Grinnell, using the pen name Ornis (bird), submitted two articles: "Elk-Hunting in Nebraska," followed by "Buffalo Hunt with Pawnees," an account of the 1872 trip with Lute North and Jim Russell.

Another avenue of escape was Professor Marsh. The firm of George Bird Grinnell & Co. was officially dissolved by the end of the year, and in the spring of 1874 Grinnell went to work full time in New Haven. Marsh could not pay his new assistant, but living on a small allowance from his family, as little as a dollar a day, was better than the drudgery and vicissitudes of stock trading.

THE BLACK HILLS

O thniel Marsh was a busy man in 1874. Construction had at last begun on the Peabody Museum. Each of the previous four summers, beginning with Grinnell's trip of 1870, he had taken a Yale group onto the plains to look for fossils; all the while, he had teams of freelance bone hunters digging around the West. Grinnell's contributions from the zoos and taxidermists in the East comprised a small, though welcome, fraction of the immense collection Marsh was amassing in New Haven.

With so much on his plate, Marsh had to decline two offers to accompany a military expedition into the unmapped Black Hills and badlands of Dakota, Wyoming, and Nebraska. One of those offers had come from his friend General Sheridan, who subscribed to the notion that the army could encourage science at the same time it was performing its more pressing chores of surveying railroads, protecting settlers, and policing Indians. Expressing his regrets to the general, Marsh volunteered Grinnell in his place.

Grinnell left New York on June 5 and stopped long enough in Chicago to receive orders from Sheridan. He then continued to St. Paul, where he met Lute North, whom he had recruited as his assistant. Together they proceeded to Fort Abraham Lincoln, on the western bank of the Missouri

River, near Bismarck, Dakota Territory. There they presented themselves to the commanding officer of the Black Hills Expedition, George A. Custer.

Custer was a bundle of contradictions. He had finished at the bottom of his class at West Point, as Grinnell had done at Yale. During the Civil War his gallant cavalry charges at Gettysburg and up and down the Shenandoah Valley had earned him the brevet rank of brigadier general by the age of twenty-five. In his campaigns against Indians in the West, his long hair and buckskin clothes equaled the sartorial panache of Buffalo Bill or Wild Bill Hickok. His daring won him fame, but his impetuousness and flouting of army regulations got him court-martialed and relieved of duty in 1867. He returned to the field a year later to pacify the Cheyennes on the southern plains, culminating in the infamous attack on Black Kettle's camp on the Washita River, where most of the casualties were women and children. In 1873 his Seventh Cavalry provided escort for Northern Pacific surveyors mapping a route from its temporary terminus at Bismarck westward along the Yellowstone Valley of Montana.

The official purpose of the Black Hills reconnaissance was to find a suitable location to build a military post from which to keep an eye on the Sioux. Custer, as usual, had his own ideas. If anything, the bankruptcy of the Northern Pacific in September 1873 had put him on even cozier terms with the railroad. As a favor to his West Point classmate and Confederate opponent Thomas Rosser, now with the Northern Pacific, Custer had authored a four-thousand-word pamphlet touting the fertile land and abundant minerals along the railroad's surveyed route—forecasting a rich and rosy future for the Northern Pacific once the indignity of bankruptcy was surmounted. The opening of the Black Hills, which by treaty still belonged to the Sioux, would certainly help the cause.

That treaty, ratified by Congress in 1868, gave the Indians as "permanent reservation" all of present-day South Dakota west of the Missouri River, including the Black Hills; and additionally declared land between the North Platte River of Nebraska and the Yellowstone River of Montana, westward to the Big Horn Mountains of Montana as "unceded territory," which no white man was allowed to settle on or even pass through. The route of the Northern Pacific Railway was one of the first and most brazen breaches of the agreement. And while Custer's Black Hills reconnaissance was technically permissible under the treaty—because he was an agent of the government—his presence, in such immense force, was another poke in the eye of Indian sovereignty.

Now thirty-four, Custer relished the pure adventure of commanding a mounted expedition into terra incognita—for the Black Hills, while thoroughly familiar and spiritually sacred to the Sioux, had been visited by few whites. From a distance, the hills are so unto themselves that they at first seem a mirage, wavering on the high-plains horizon; their blackness is actually the distant green of trees on its billion-year-old ramparts, which rise five thousand feet from the surrounding ocean of prairie—the tallest mountains between the Rockies and the Pyrenees.

For early travelers, who tended to skirt the hills before hastening toward safer country, it was not hard to imagine the Black Hills as an island of buried treasure. Rumors of "all the gold we could carry" had been seeping outward since the 1830s. With this in mind, Custer had invited two "practical miners" to join his reconnaissance. Fellow travelers included ten companies of the Seventh Cavalry, two companies of infantry, one hundred Indian scouts, many of them mere schoolboys from the Santee reservation in Nebraska; Custer's two brothers, a brother-in-law, and his black cook, Aunt Sally Campbell (the only woman on the trip); the president's alcoholic son, Lieutenant Frederick Grant; a sixteen-piece band mounted on white horses; three reporters and a photographer; Captain William Ludlow, chief engineer of the Department of the Missouri; geologist Newton Winchell and botanist A. B. Donaldson, both from Minnesota; and, in the capacity of zoologist-paleontologist, George Bird Grinnell, with Luther North to keep him company. Total: one thousand men and two thousand animals, not counting Custer's beloved pack of coursing hounds.

In later years, after Custer's death at the Little Bighorn, Grinnell would endeavor to be politic in his public depictions of the celebrated and (by most white accounts) martyred warrior. But even then Grinnell did not advertise himself as a Custer admirer. In his Indian books, weighed heavily toward the native point of view, he barely mentions Custer and never as a champion or hero. "Custer was a friendly, pleasant man, but gave one the impression of being intensely in himself," Grinnell qualified in 1927. Damning with fainter praise, he confided to fellow Indian historian George Hyde: "I have Custer's book, 'My Life on the Plains,' which I regard as quite unreliable. Custer knew nothing about Indians and was anyhow a harum-scarum fellow. He wanted a fight, and a victory, and he usually got it." That is, Grinnell added, "until the end came." First impressions, formed in the summer of 1874, went a long way.

Of the many versions of the Black Hills reconnaissance, recorded by news-papermen, chief engineer Ludlow, and various notetakers, letter writers, and diarists, Grinnell's leather-bound journal managed to cancel out the dust and din of an army marching, making camp, breaking camp. With no other obligations than as naturalists, he and North rode ahead or to either side of the column, looking for bones and wildlife.

On July 5, three days out from Fort Lincoln, Grinnell arose before dawn and started before the command was under way, carrying his shot-gun. "Secured several birds new to me," he recorded in his conscientiously penciled notes. "I found a nest of *Plectrophanes maccownii* [chestnut-shouldered longspur] with four eggs. . . . I saw the female distinctly and am positive that it was *maccownii*. In examining a tall butte for fossils I discov-ered a nest of some *Falco*, probably *lanarius*. It was placed in the cleft of a rock near the top of the butte and the rocks around were white with excre-ment. The nest contained three young about half feathered. . . . The young withdrew to the farthest corner of the hole when I made my appearance, but the female was furious at my invasion of her home. . . . I fired just as she was darting down and gave her the whole charge. The gun was loaded with small bird seed, and she flew off with a wavering and undecided flight to a point of rocks nearby. I tried to approach her but could not and so failed to secure her."

Somewhere on his celestial perch, John James Audubon was smiling.

All told, Grinnell identified more than one hundred species of birds, and he collected and preserved nearly two hundred bird specimens. His list of mammals numbered thirty-four. To his disappointment, he saw no living buffalo and picked up only one skull, of an old bull. Pronghorn antelope were in much greater evidence, and, of all the mammals, he admired these fleet creatures the most. "As we proceed," he wrote in his report to the army, "the antelope become more numerous, until finally there is no hour of the day when they are not to be seen, either running gracefully off over the prairie or curiously watching the command from the top of some distant bluff." The ubiquity of antelope in 1874 would lead Grinnell to postulate in later years that *Antilocapra americana* had once outnumbered even buffalo on the plains.

With the column moving every day, sometimes marching fifteen or twenty miles between camps, Grinnell had little time to dig for fossils. His pale-ontological report, filed with the geologist, Winchell, mentions a few shells and occasional bits of larger vertebrates. "[Even] if we were to find a cart-load, we could not get them [home]," he griped.

Other forms of hunting were more successful. In the company of North and the equally able scout Charley Reynolds, Grinnell killed a number of deer and antelope. He was less impressed with Custer's hunting skills. "On the plains General Custer did no shooting that was notable," Grinnell remarked with pointed frankness in *Two Great Scouts*, his 1928 tribute to the North brothers. "It was observed that, though he enjoyed telling of the remarkable shots that he himself commonly made, he did not seem greatly interested in the shooting done by other people. On one occasion when Luther North and I were traveling not far from the command, three deer frightened by its passage ran by us and North killed the three with three successive shots." Presenting a choice cut of deer to the general's tent, Grinnell bragged on North's marksmanship, to which Custer responded, "'Huh, I found two more horned toads today.'"

Later Custer came upon a group of ducks swimming in a small pond and announced, "'I will knock the heads off a few of them.'" Grinnell signaled to North, who dismounted and sat on the ground behind the general. "General Custer fired at a bird and missed it, and North shot and cut the head off one of the birds. Custer shot again and missed, and North cut the head off another bird. Custer looked around at him and then shot again and missed, and North cut the head off a third duck."

Another ambition of Custer's was to shoot a grizzly bear. On August 7 Custer, Ludlow, and the Arikara scout Bloody Knife spotted one on the side of a hill seventy-five yards away. Custer fired two shots with his Remington, one hitting the bear in the thigh and the second in another nonlethal spot. Ludlow and Bloody Knife fired next, and the bear at last fell; its life ended when Bloody Knife, living up to his name, severed the grizzly's jugular with his blade. Photographer William Illingworth took a picture of Custer with his trophy. "I have reached the highest rung on the hunter's ladder of fame," Custer wrote to his wife, Libbie. "I have killed my grizzly after a most exciting hunt & combat."

Grinnell, who was coming over the hill when he heard the shots, examined the specimen and wrote up his scientific observations: "It was a very old male, the canine teeth being mere broken stumps, many of the incisors gone, and the molars worn down almost to the gums. . . . The old veteran bore on his body the marks of many a conflict. On his back, just behind the shoulders, was a rugged scar ten inches long and 2 feet wide; his face was marked in several places, and his sides and thighs were disfigured in the same manner. These scars, I am led to believe, were the result of battles with some rival during the rutting season."

If there was one thing that Custer deserved credit for in the Black Hills, it occurred on July 30, when miners William Ross and Horatio McKay—whom Custer had brought along with designs neither military nor scientific— panned up a few grains of gold from French Creek, which flowed from the southeast flank of the Black Hills into the Cheyenne River. The command was camped in a grassy valley, promptly named Custer Park, and the general needed no further reason to lay over for several days.

The following morning, while Custer and Ludlow set out to climb Harney (now Black Elk) Peak—at 7,244 feet, the highest point in the Black Hills—Grinnell and Lute North devoted their time to observing and collecting birds. Others in camp took advantage of Custer's absence and played baseball; afterward Colonel Joseph Tilford hosted a champagne supper for several of his fellow officers, including the unquenchable Frederick Grant.

Meanwhile Custer's miners followed down the creek, looking for gold.

"There is much talk," Ludlow recorded on August 2. "I saw in General Custer's tent what the miner said he had obtained during the day. Under a strong reading glass it resembled small pin heads, and fine scales of irregular shape, thirty in number. The miners expressed themselves quite confident that if they could reach bedrock in the valleys at a favorable place, plenty could be obtained."

A few shining pinheads would prove to be enough to spark a stampede — a stampede that Custer ensured by hurrying the news of the discovery to the outside world.

On August 3 Custer divided his command. He led five companies toward the southwest; two more companies rode toward the southeast in the direction of the Cheyenne River badlands. The rest of the troops remained on French Creek. Each reconnaissance figured to be gone three days. Grinnell and North accompanied the second, smaller group, hoping for better fossil hunting. Rough terrain kept them from reaching the river, and they returned empty handed.

Riding with the other contingent was the guide Charley Reynolds, and at the end of the first day, Custer dispatched Reynolds alone, carrying a few bites of food, his rifle, and a sack of mail. His destination was Fort Laramie, some ninety miles "through a country infested with Indians," as Captain Ludlow described in his official report. Along with soldiers' letters was a report from Custer to General Sheridan, which ended with the incendiary announcement that "gold has been found in several places, and it is the belief of those who are giving attention to this subject that it will be found in paying quantities."

Hiding by day and riding by night, Reynolds reached Fort Laramie on August 5. His tongue was so swollen from thirst that he could not speak. But the messages in the mailbag spoke for him. Eight days later newspapers were bugling the news of "Rich Mines of Gold and Silver Reported Found by Custer." The *Inter-Ocean* of Chicago published a dispatch sent directly from the Black Hills by its reporter, William Curtis: "GOLD! . . . The Precious Dust Found in the Grass Under the Horse's Feet."

Because Grinnell was absorbed with his birds and absent from the main command for three days, his diary made no mention of gold or the excitement it was stirring among the soldiers. Only years later would he craft his own version of events, stating in an 1896 article in *Forest and Stream*: "When I heard that Charley was going to make this ride, I was extremely anxious to make it with him, believing that there was some danger in it; and knowing that two or three men could very likely go through where one could not. Charley was anxious to have Capt. North and myself go along."

No doubt Grinnell was basing his bona fides on the brave standoff that he, North, and Jim Russell had made two years earlier. Indeed, it seems plausible that Reynolds would have welcomed someone with Lute North's experience. But Grinnell? As Reynolds and Custer left French Creek, he and North had ridden in the other direction.

The rest of the Black Hills trip was comparatively uneventful. "Thus ends the expedition of 1874, as far as science is concerned," Grinnell wrote on August 23, with still a week's march to go. "I only lament that [the] country is so barren, for Lute and myself have, as far as we know, done just as Prof. Marsh would have done had he been along. . . . But as Lute sings, 'What is the use of repining?'"

The column marched wearily into Fort Abraham Lincoln on August 30, having covered eight hundred miles in sixty days. Even before Custer had dismounted and embraced his wife, prospectors were heading toward the Black Hills. The gold rush that followed would have staggering consequences—for the Sioux, who regarded the Black Hills as "the heart of everything that is," and for Custer, whose provocations and headlong aggression toward Indians protecting their homeland would lead to his own fatal reckoning.

For George Bird Grinnell the summer of 1874 was decisive as well. He had been the naturalist of record on the first trip, military or scientific, to penetrate farther than the foothills of the Black Hills. His zoological and paleontological notes were included in the *Report of a Reconnaissance of the Black Hills of Dakota, Made in the Summer of 1874*. He had worked conscientiously under harsh and hurried conditions, and although he had seen no buffalo and collected only a few fossils, it had been a trip of historic discovery nonetheless. Three years earlier Grinnell had told Marsh, "I shall work as hard as I can for the cause of science, in the hope that some time I

might be able to leave business and devote myself wholly to the study of it."
In the Black Hills of Dakota he had found an open book and left his mark,
workmanlike in his curiosity, tenacious in his pursuit.

And many of the men he traveled and messed with would also earn
a place in history. Lieutenant Edward Godfrey, interpreter Fred Gerard,
scouts Charley Reynolds and Bloody Knife, not to mention George Armstrong Custer, would ride with the Seventh Cavalry all the way to the Little Bighorn.

The following spring Grinnell received a letter from yet another friend
made in the Black Hills, William Ludlow, who invited him to join him on
a new reconnaissance, this one from the upper Missouri River southward
to Yellowstone National Park.

CHAPTER 6

A NATION'S PARK

T he Yellowstone plateau was hard to get to in 1875; it always had been. The first white man to lay eyes on the spouting geysers, steaming vents, bubbling pools, and stinking mud cauldrons was likely John Colter, a brave-hearted Virginian who had excused himself from Lewis and Clark's Corps of Discovery to do some trapping and exploring in present-day Montana and Wyoming. His five-hundred-mile trek in the early months of 1808 took him along the western shore of Yellowstone Lake and the headwaters of the Yellowstone River. Adventurers who followed sniffed the sulfur wafting from the earth and dubbed the region "Colter's Hell."

Those who doubted the reports of fire and brimstone, and those who believed them, came to see for themselves. In September 1870 a group of curiosity seekers, mostly merchants from the mining boomtown of Helena, accompanied by a small military escort, made a tour of the fantasia of the upper Yellowstone. They were led by Nathaniel Washburn, the surveyor general for Montana Territory, and Nathaniel Langford, a former federal tax collector who had been recruited by the Northern Pacific to share his Yellowstone experience in a series of lectures throughout the country. The Northern Pacific, once it resumed its crawl westward from Bismarck, would follow the route that Custer had helped map along the Yellowstone River, passing within sixty miles of the country the Washburn party was about to admire. As with the Black Hills, the more people who knew about the delights of Yellowstone, the better it would be for the railroad.

The concept of a national park had been gestating for years. Artist George Catlin, who reached the upper Missouri on the first steamboat in 1832 (though he never got as far as the upper Yellowstone), was among the first to ruminate on the subject: "[W]hat a splendid contemplation . . . when one (who has travelled these realms, and can duly appreciate them) imagines them as they *might* in future be seen (by some great protecting policy of government) preserved in their pristine beauty and wildness, in a *magnificent park*. . . . What a beautiful and thrilling specimen for America to preserve and hold up to the view of her refined citizens and the world, in future ages. A *nation's Park*, containing man and beast, in all the wild and freshness of their natural beauty."

Forty-three years later, lounging beside the Firehole River near Yellowstone's geysers—the most reliable of which Washburn named Old Faithful—one of those refined citizens, attorney Cornelius Hedges (a Yale man, class of 1853), was credited with a remark that would frame the debate on national parks long into the future. He was provoked by the greed of his fellow campers, one of whom suggested that "if there could be secured by pre-emption a good title to two or three quarter sections of land opposite the lower falls of the Yellowstone and extending down the river along the cañon, they would eventually become a source of great profit to the owners." Another member of the party thought that it would be "more desirable to take up a quarter section of land at the Upper Geyser Basin, for the reason that the locality could be more easily reached by tourists and pleasure seekers."

There it was, glowing in the campfire coals, a devil's design for Colter's Hell: private control of the nation's natural wonders in order to corner profits. But then Hedges put the devil in his place. According to Langford's diary, Hedges urged that "there ought to be no private ownership of any portion of that region, but the whole ought to be set apart as a great National Park, and that each one of us ought to make an effort to have this accomplished."

Hedges's wisdom prevailed, at least within his cohort. Back in Helena he and Langford dashed off glowing accounts of their extraordinary vacation, and Langford soon departed for the East to deliver the promised lectures that did the bidding of the Northern Pacific. "This is probably the most remarkable region of natural attractions," he gushed in one of his geysers of publicity, "and while we already have our Niagara and Yosemite, this new field of wonders should be withdrawn from occupancy, and set apart as a public National Park for the enjoyment of the American people for all time."

The next year brought more lectures, more glowing magazine articles, another government survey, and circulation of a series of breathtaking paintings of Yellowstone by Thomas Moran and photographs by William Henry Jackson, funded by the Northern Pacific. On March 1, 1872, President Ulysses S. Grant signed into law the "Act Establishing Yellowstone National Park." The park was "hereby withdrawn from settlement, occupancy, or sale . . . and dedicated and set apart as a public park or pleasuring-ground for the benefit and enjoyment of the people; and all people who shall locate or settle upon or occupy the same, or any part thereof . . . shall be considered trespassers." Yellowstone was placed under the control of the secretary of the interior, who would provide for "the preservation, from injury or spoliation, of all timber, mineral deposits, natural curiosities, or wonders with said park." Furthermore, the secretary would "provide against wanton destruction of the fish and game found within said park, and against their capture or destruction for the purposes of merchandise or profit."

The size of the park, which at first could only be estimated, was more than three thousand square miles. The boundaries were delineated in fairly general terms, since no surveyor had lugged his instruments near, much less seen, most of them.

In inviting Grinnell on the 1875 Yellowstone reconnaissance, Ludlow explained that he, not Custer, would be in command. Custer was in New York, puffing himself to reporters, playing the stock market, and writing a memoir that would appear the following year. Professor Marsh, too, was tied up, in the midst of testifying to the Bureau of Indian Affairs on the disgraceful treatment of the Sioux, whose displeasure over poor rations and white trespass he had observed firsthand during a recent fossil-hunting trip to Nebraska. Grinnell naturally thought of asking Lute North to come along, but North, needing to make a living, had gone into the livery and feed business in his hometown of Columbus.

Instead Grinnell invited Edward S. Dana, a Yale classmate. Dana was the son of James Dwight Dana, esteemed professor of natural history at Yale, and grandson of Benjamin Silliman, the equally august professor of chemistry and geology. After graduation he had gone abroad to study mineralogy at Heidelberg and Vienna, returning to New Haven in the spring of 1874 to complete a master's degree, at the same time that Grinnell was exiting New York to work for Marsh. Grinnell had been delighted to discover one old friend in New Haven, and a Scroll and Key man at that.

Grinnell was only two months older than Dana, yet he treated him more protectively than he did his younger brothers. In some respects, they even looked like brothers—fair, trim, with tidy moustaches. In a genteel, New England way, Dana was a hardy enough fellow; in his scientific inquiries, he had tramped the Alps and the glacial rubble of the Connecticut River valley. It was said that his only concession to New Haven winters was to wear a sweater under his suit coat.

To Grinnell, though, Ned Dana would always be a tenderfoot, and the trip they took in the summer of 1875 provided Grinnell with an opportunity to demonstrate how seasoned and self-sufficient he had become since graduation. In his memoirs Grinnell would write: "Dana had never been in the West and was as ignorant of its dangers as it was possible for anyone to be. I felt, therefore, that I must constantly look after him, to see that he did not through ignorance get into some trouble." Where once Frank or Lute North had kept greenhorn Grinnell from losing his way, now Grinnell assumed this role with the dude Dana. Grinnell would later remark, with a hint of self-satisfaction, "When I had parted from Mrs. Dana, Ned's mother, just as we were leaving New Haven, she said to me, as we shook hands, 'Good bye, Mr. Grinnell, take good care of my boy.'"

Traveling at their own expense, Grinnell and Dana reached Bismarck, still the terminus of the Northern Pacific, on July 3. There would be no sizable army escort this time. Besides the two Yale chums, the party that boarded the flat-bottomed steamer *Josephine* consisted only of Captain Ludlow, his brother Edwin, a Lieutenant Thompson, a civilian assistant named Wood, and, to Grinnell's great delight, Charley Reynolds, the scout whom he had befriended and so thoroughly admired during the Black Hills expedition.

The trip up the Missouri took three weeks, much longer than expected, due to a fever that nearly killed Edwin Ludlow and delayed the full party from assembling near Carroll Landing in Montana until July 27.

Montana was still a territory in 1875 (it would not achieve statehood until 1889), and most of its population clung to the young mining towns along the edges of the Rocky Mountains. The eastern three-quarters of the territory were still the domain, albeit an increasingly contested one, of Indians: Blackfeet, Gros Ventres, Assiniboines, Crows, Cheyennes, and Sioux. Until the completion of the Northern Pacific (still eight years away), the Missouri River provided the easiest, safest, if not the shortest, route to the mining camps, military posts, and territorial capital of Helena. Fort Benton, America's "innermost port," was more than two thousand river miles from St. Louis. Carroll Landing, 160 miles downstream from Fort Benton, was the starting point of the Carroll Trail, which lately had become the favored stage and freight route to Helena and farther south to the fertile Gallatin Valley and the farming and ranching hub of Bozeman. Ludlow's orders were to prepare a proper map of the trail. Yellowstone, sixty miles beyond Fort Ellis, the southernmost of the army's garrisons, would be strictly a bonus. Ludlow could continue his journey to the national park only if time permitted. Time was now short, but they were not going to miss Yellowstone.

For George Bird Grinnell the three-month trip in the summer of 1875 was the beginning of a fifty-year relationship not only with America's first national park but also with Montana. Besides New York and Connecticut, there is no state (or territory) in which Grinnell spent more days. The two Indian tribes he got to know most thoroughly and wrote about most extensively—the Blackfeet and the Cheyennes—are Montana tribes. The two national parks he helped to shape and defended most vociferously—

Yellowstone and Glacier—are Montana parks. (Or close enough; most of Yellowstone is in Wyoming, but the northern lip and its busiest entrance are in Montana.) And it is fair to say that neither the state of Montana nor Yellowstone would assume the identities that they enjoy today if it were not for the continuing influence of Grinnell, who early on recognized their beauty, their resources, their people, and their potential and committed himself to honoring them nationally in a manner that directly reflected his ideals of heritage and preservation. If his devotion to Montana ran deep, it was because his memories of Montana, beginning in 1875, were among his richest.

From Carroll Landing the group rode south into the badlands known as the Missouri Breaks, accompanied by a half-dozen infantry recruits. Ludlow reported them as unarmed, despite the threat of Sioux war parties, which had killed three soldiers along the trail a few days earlier.

Climbing from the steep, sage- and cactus-covered breaks, the mapping party entered a rolling, grassy prairie, with the timbered Judith and Moccasin mountains round-shouldered in the distance. In his memoirs Grinnell mentioned that "there were buffalo in the country, and plenty of antelope" but that they did little hunting. "As usual on such expeditions," he explained, "we were mounted on condemned army horses which were perfectly well able to carry us about over the prairie at a walk, but could not do much running." So, no roasted buffalo hump.

He was, however, able to boast of meeting, on separate days, two of Montana's most renowned frontier characters, John Jeremiah "Liver-Eating" Johnson and Luther "Yellowstone" Kelly—free spirits who happened to be passing through the country.

Not that Grinnell's companion, Charley Reynolds, paled in comparison. He was, as William Curtis had written in the Chicago *Inter-Ocean*, "the sort of man one doesn't expect to find on the prairies. He would adorn a drawing-room . . . for he is one of God Almighty's gentlemen." Curtis described Reynolds as short and stocky "with a shrinking blue eye and a face from which exposure has not yet effaced the beauty, a voice as soft as a woman's, a manner unobtrusive and gentle."

A doctor's son, college graduate, and Civil War veteran, Reynolds had drifted westward from Kansas, hunting, scouting, and surviving several close fights with Indians. Never settling down or forming close attachments, he earned the nickname he would carry to his grave: "Lonesome Charley." In Grinnell's eyes Reynolds was in some respects a more complete paragon than Luther or Frank North; he was an equally proficient plainsman but more polished and, if possible, even more self-effacing.

"In those days, it was not etiquette on the plains to ask a man about his past," Grinnell wrote many years after Reynolds's death, "and of course I never put any questions to Charley." Still, Grinnell recalled with open tenderness, "We hunted together frequently, and on the trip to the Black Hills rode together a great deal and became very intimate and, I think, fond of each other. . . . Life in camp draws men together, and it was so with Reynolds and I."

The connection formed in the Black Hills deepened on the Montana prairie. One afternoon, as they approached the army garrison of Camp Lewis, Grinnell and Reynolds—no mention of the whereabouts of protégé Dana or any of the others—came to Big Spring Creek, which can be precisely described by its name. "Charley and I were hot, dusty and tired from our long ride," Grinnell wrote in *Forest and Stream* in 1897, "and the rush of the cold waters which flowed down from the mountains and by the camp was very attractive to both of us." They had not forgotten that hostile Indians were still about; it was near here that the three soldiers had been killed. "But we had our rifles with us and thought that we could take care of ourselves. . . . It took but little time to strip and plunge into the sparkling water, and the pool was deep enough to swim in. It was delightfully fresh and cool, and we were swimming about, now and then dipping under like a couple of ducks—or perhaps geese—that had long been deprived of water, when suddenly on the bank above us a shot sounded, and we pulled for the shore and our guns. . . . There was no time for dressing, and with guns and belts in hand we crossed the stream, climbed up on the bank and peered over it on the other side."

They immediately caught sight of a procession of friendly Crows, returning from the successful pursuit of the Sioux who had recently been raiding through the country. "Galloping down the valley and flanked on either side by a man dressed in superb war clothing rode a naked Indian on a naked horse, carrying in his hand a pole to the end of which was tied a stretched scalp, the long hair of which blew out behind him in the breeze. His face was painted black and he was singing a song of war and triumph. The men who rode beside him were clad in shirts and leggings of white buckskin. Long war bonnets of eagle's feathers hung down behind them and blew out over their horses' hips. As they rode they sang, and as they sang they fired shots in the air."

Hurrying into their clothes, Grinnell and Reynolds watched as 150 Indians passed by, the second large group of Indians—after the Pawnees—Grinnell had observed in full dress, on their own ground, free-living, and unattached to whites. "The Mountain Crows [are] a stark and sturdy race, the men big and fine looking as any race I have ever seen," he remarked. "Their hair is long and often hangs down so that it rests upon the back of the rider's horse, and you can imagine that all these men attired in all their finery made a good appearance as they rode down toward us."

Even more memorable was the scene he witnessed after they arrived at the trading post at Camp Lewis. A number of Crows soon appeared; among them was the brother of Long Horse, the only Crow killed in the fight with the Sioux. "[W]e were still lounging at the store," Grinnell recalled with wide-eyed clarity, "when the young brother . . . strode into the store and, resting his left forefinger on the counter, chopped it off with his butcher knife and went away."

The final leg of the 250-mile trip to Fort Ellis was rich in scenery but absent of excitement. Ludlow was diligent in his surveying, and Dana filled notebooks with the geology of the route. Knowing that they had to return to the Missouri before the river was too low to carry steamboats, the party stayed only one day at Fort Ellis and set out for Yellowstone on August 11. At Mammoth Hot Springs they discarded tents in favor of simple tent flies, wrapped the chronometers and other surveyor's instruments in their bedrolls, abandoned the supply wagon, and proceeded onward with saddle horses and pack mules.

Three years after the founding of the national park, visitors had beaten a rough but recognizable path to the main attractions: Mammoth Hot Springs, the falls and canyon of the Yellowstone, Yellowstone Lake, and the geyser basins. Grinnell's journal, which since Bismarck had been limited to perfunctory jottings on wildlife, now awoke. "The country is beautifully diversified," he wrote as they rode deeper into the park. "Little open prairies, pieces of heavy timber, hill, mountain, and ravine succeed one another and form a new and charming landscape at each step." From the summit of ten-thousand-foot Mount Washburn, "We had the most magnificent view I have ever seen. All the surrounding country was spread out for us in a glorious panorama. The Yellowstone Lake, the Geysers, part of the Cañon, Mt. Sheridan and the Tetons all were seen with utmost distinctness." Superlative followed superlative. The view of the Upper Falls of the Yellowstone was "altogether the grandest and most beautiful that I have ever seen. It altogether beggars description." Yellowstone Lake was "a beautiful sheet of water, and one might spend a month or two exploring its shores with pleasure."

Curiously, he was more matter-of-fact in his appreciation of the park's geothermal wonders: "We laid two days seeing all the principal geysers except the Giant. The Beehive played 3 times, Giantess once, Grand once, Old Faithful regularly at intervals of 65 minutes and the Castle often."

All the while, Grinnell continued to observe and collect birds, and his zoological report—appended to Ludlow's general report of the reconnaissance—was the most thorough inventory of birds (and mammals) taken in Yellowstone to date. Of these hundred or so species, one in particular would become a lifelong favorite: the American dipper, also known as the water ouzel, found along and often beneath rushing streams. "Although tolerably familiar with the habits of the bird from books, I must confess to the most ludicrous feeling of astonishment the first time I saw the bird walk calmly down a flat stone until its head disappeared under the water," he recorded with unscientific glee. "It repeated this several times, occasionally coming to the surface as if forced up by the water and immediately down again. When carried down a few feet by the force of the current, it would fly a few feet upstream and dive from the wing. When standing, it kept bobbing up and down constantly."

Of the copious notes taken by Grinnell, Ludlow, and Dana, the most enduring—and foreboding—described the conduct of the other travelers they encountered. During their two days spent at the Upper Geyser Basin, Ludlow counted more than thirty other visitors and recorded ghastly evidence that "the rude hand of man" was defacing the "miracles of art" with axes. "To procure a specimen of perhaps a pound weight, a hundred pounds [of sculptured mineral formation] had been shattered and destroyed." He called for troops to be stationed in the park to protect the natural treasures—the germ of an idea that, over time, would evolve into the creation of a policing system run by national park rangers.

In his letter accompanying his zoological report, Grinnell expressed similar outrage at the loss of wildlife—both inside the park and on its perimeter. "It may be out of place here," he wrote, "to call your attention to the terrible destruction of large game . . . which is constantly going on in those portions of Montana and Wyoming through which we passed. . . . It is estimated that during the winter of 1874-'75 not less than 3,000 elk were killed for their hides alone in the valley of the Yellowstone, between the mouth of Trail Creek and the [Mammoth] Hot Springs," a distance of roughly forty miles. "Buffalo and mule-deer suffer even more severely than the elk, and antelope nearly as much."

Grinnell knew of what he spoke. During his western trips—this was his fifth—it had been impossible not to notice the decline in the buffalo herds. And what was unseen by his own eye he learned from the stories of men like the Norths, Buffalo Bill, Charley Reynolds, Liver-Eating Johnson, and Yellowstone Kelly. They all agreed that Indians were not to blame. Rather, the existential danger to buffalo, elk, and antelope came from trigger-happy hide-hunters and the proliferation of meat-hunters who fed hungry miners, soldiers, and homesteaders. "The general feeling of the better class of frontiersmen, guides, hunters and settlers," Grinnell wrote, intending his letter to reach a wider audience than the War Department, "is strongly against those who are engaged in this work of butchery, and all, I think, would be glad to have this wholesale and short-sighted slaughter put a stop to."

He concluded by issuing an unvarnished warning: "It is certain that, unless in some way the destruction of these animals can be checked, the large game still so abundant in some localities will ere long be exterminated." He called for stiffening game laws and, in agreement with Ludlow, employing the military to increase enforcement. This was by far Grinnell's most emphatic stance on conservation to date. If his tone was strident—well, he was only getting started.

The return from Yellowstone to Carroll Landing took three weeks. The trip downriver to Bismarck took another ten days; the Missouri was low, in places only eighteen inches deep, and the boat ran aground frequently.

The train ride from Bismarck to St. Paul was especially uncomfortable for Ludlow, who had received a telegram informing him that Grinnell's brother Frank had died. Rather than burden his friend en route, he waited until they arrived in St. Paul to share the grim news.

Rambunctious, mischievous Frank Lansing Grinnell. "You have done nothing but romp and play the livelong day," his mother wrote in his diary when he was six. Of all the Grinnell children, Frank was the most outgoing, the most graceful, the best athlete. "You dance beautifully, stand on your head till I am perfectly amazed and walk on your toes till I am astonished," his mother complimented when he was eight. "We shall see what kind of man you will make."

By adolescence he clearly stepped to his own beat. "Georgie has grown so staid," Helen Grinnell observed in January 1866, when both boys were home from Churchill for the Christmas holiday, "and laughter-loving Frank entertains us with his jollity."

It was his heedlessness that got him into frequent trouble. "Frankie got on the roof a few days ago in his nightgown and bare feet and padded around in the snow to see, as he said, 'how the little beggars feel without shoes,'" Helen Grinnell told daughter Helen, barely stifling her amusement. Although she whipped him more than the other children and occasionally confined him in "the closet of obedience," she always forgave him. And nothing seemed to dampen Frank's spirit. "Frankie, I must say you are a most affectionate, noble-hearted boy, generous and loving," his mother acknowledged. Plainly he was her favorite.

Frank had thrived at Yale, playing football and baseball, and in his senior year he was initiated into Scroll and Key. (Mort Grinnell, though three years younger, was precocious enough to be in Frank's class but paled in his brother's glow.) After graduation in June 1875 Frank joined his family in Milford. If he had a profession in mind, he had not embarked upon it by Tuesday, September 7. He was not a regular member of the Milford base-ball club but was filling out the roster as a substitute in a game played in nearby Bridgeport. While he was warming up with his teammates, a ball—soaked in water to give it extra weight and greater density—was thrown from centerfield and struck him behind the right ear. He was taken, uncon-scious, to the home of W. D. Bishop, president of the New York, New Haven and Hartford Railroad, where he died four days later. His funeral was held on the fifteenth at the Church of the Intercession, across from Audubon Park. On the day Frank Grinnell was buried in Woodlawn Cemetery in the Bronx, his older brother was floating down the Missouri River, a long way from home.

No diaries or letters survive to convey the shock inflicted upon the family by Frank Grinnell's sudden death. Whatever the magnitude of heartbreak, it was enough to drive George Blake Grinnell, his wife, and three youngest children from Milford. In December they departed for what they hoped would be the restorative climate of Santa Barbara, California.

In recent years Santa Barbara had gained a reputation as a "sanatorium city." In 1872 Charles Nordhoff (whose grandson of the same name would coauthor *The Mutiny on the Bounty*) published *California for Health, Plea-sure and Residence*, in which he pronounced Santa Barbara "the pleasantest of all the places" in California. "In Santa Barbara there were not a dozen days during the whole winter in which a baby I know of did not play on the seashore," Nordhoff testified. The completion of the transcontinental railroad put the once-isolated mission and presidio town within reach of easterners (though for the final stretch travelers still had to take a steamer from San Francisco or Los Angeles). By the time the Grinnells settled into the Arlington Hotel, Nordhoff was touting the city as "a cozy nest for New England and Western New York people, many of who originally came here for their health, and remain because they are charmed with the climate."

George Bird Grinnell did not join his parents right away; instead he resumed his work with Professor Marsh in New Haven, where construction on the new museum continued and the collection of bones and fossils was multiplying. After Christmas, however, Helen Grinnell confided to her son that "father seemed rather lonely" and implored him to come for a visit. George Bird's train was waylaid by snowdrifts in the Sierra Nevada, but eventually he arrived at Santa Barbara, where he was relieved to discover that the rest of the family, if not George Blake Grinnell, was having "a very good time." (Mort Grinnell was the only one who stayed home.)

Marsh had told Grinnell of some nearby archaeological sites, the ancient villages of nearly extinct California Indians. Grinnell collected some specimens, but mostly he allowed himself to be seduced by the salubrious atmosphere and "the February strawberries." His visit was short—barely a month—and by the end of February he was back at work in New Haven. Nevertheless, Santa Barbara was a place he would always remember fondly.

George Bird's visit doubtless did his father good. And by the fickle laws of fate, it most certainly saved Grinnell's life. Over the years, he would repeat the story of receiving a telegram from General Custer, inviting him to join the Seventh Cavalry on an expedition against the Indians during the summer of 1876—the expedition that would come to an abrupt halt on June 25.

No such telegram has ever been located. Grinnell had not seen Custer since the Black Hills trip two years earlier, and his relationship with the general had not been especially warm even then. But among Grinnell's papers is a letter from William Ludlow, dated March 29, 1876: "I congratulate you on your safe return from the Pacific Coast. . . . I am making preparations to go out again with Custer. Three expeditions will be in the field. One under command of Genl. Crook is already out, another under Genl. Gibbon has started from Ft. Ellis & Shaw, and Custer's will go about Apl. 15th or 20th. Each column will number 700–800 men, and the objective of so much hurried preparation is the taming or heading off of the well-known Sitting Bull. It is not the sort of trip that I presume would pay you. There will be a great amount of marching—and hardly any chance of your specialité & I have not invited anyone on that account. Nevertheless, if you should care to go, pack up & come out. You know how glad I should be to see you, and we will mess together & look out for our noble selves."

Obviously Grinnell declined.

June 25, 1876, was a Sunday. Grinnell left no account of where he was on that day, but most likely he was at Milford with his family, all of them having returned from California in the spring. Nor is there any record of his reaction when he heard the news of the Seventh Cavalry's shocking defeat on the parched ridges above the Little Bighorn. Yet it did not take him long to grasp that, if he had not taken time away from New Haven to go to California to be with his grieving, convalescing family, he might have been tempted to accept Ludlow's invitation. (Thankfully for Ludlow, he, too, was unable to join Custer's campaign.)

Grinnell would spend many days over many years interviewing participants in the Little Bighorn battle in an effort to piece together the sequence of events that might have included his own violent ending. "Every little ravine running down from the northwest side of the ridge, every little bunch of brush, was occupied by Indians who kept up a constant and galling fire, and the Indians were so many that the destruction among the troops was very great," he would write of Custer's last stand in *The Fighting Cheyennes*. "The Indians state positively that they did not kill the troops by charging into them, but kept shooting them from behind the hills. The final charge was not made until all the troops of the main body had fallen."

For Grinnell the death of Custer stung far less than that of his friend and trail mate, Charley Reynolds. A description of Reynolds's final moments was given to Grinnell by Billy Jackson, a scout who, like Reynolds, had been with Major Marcus Reno's battalion. Custer ordered Reno to cross the Little Bighorn at the upstream, or southern, end of the Indian encampment; after a brief skirmish, Reno's troops retreated back across the river and set up a defensive perimeter on a near hilltop. Billy Jackson was one of the hundred men in Reno's command who survived the day; Charley Reynolds and the Arikara scout Bloody Knife, who had also been on the Black Hills expedition, were among the forty who did not.

Grinnell would retell Jackson's account in a tribute he later gave to Reynolds: "Reno ordered the retreat. The soldiers started with more or less order, but the fire was terrible, and in a moment they became panic-stricken and crowded toward the ford. A body of 500 Indians was charging toward them down the valley. Charley called out to the scouts, 'Here, boys, let us try to stop these Indians and give the soldiers a chance to cross.' The scouts stayed behind and turned, shooting into the charging mass, a dozen men against 500, [and] the Indians came on like a whirlwind and struck. The soldiers crowded at the ford, they were killed like sheep as they struggled to get across. They made no defense. They were butchered with bullets, arrows, lances and clubs, or knocked off their horses with gun barrels."

Thus far, Reynolds was Horatius at the bridge—except Horatius held his ground, repulsed the Etruscans, and lived.

"Charley's horse had been killed at once. He shot an Indian who was charging toward him on a buckskin pony, and as the Indian did not at once fall off, he shot the horse, and Indian and pony rolled over together almost at his feet. He fired again, and then again. Bullets and arrows were flying thick. Suddenly Charley seemed to be hit in half a dozen places. He fell, raised himself on his elbow and fired another shot—his last. Then he sank back."

Grinnell's rendering of Reynolds's death, however sensational, was an honest expression of his respect and affection. "One of the bravest and best, a noble gentleman, though clad in the rough garb of a mountaineer, now sleeps in an uncared-for grave amid the yellow bluffs and desert solitude of the Little Big Horn," Grinnell eulogized in May 1877. "Dear Charley, we shall not look upon his like again."

For Grinnell the tragedy became sacred, canonical, to be treated with the greatest sanctity. In January 1887, when Buffalo Bill's Wild West show came to Madison Square Garden in New York, Grinnell was appalled that Cody would dare to reenact the still-raw events of 1876. "Buffalo Bill, who takes the part of the hero, wears an auburn wig and otherwise makes up to represent Custer," Grinnell reported in *Forest and Stream*. He had never swooned over Custer when he was living, but to have Buffalo Bill—who had never especially impressed him, either—impersonate a fallen national icon was insufferable blasphemy. "The death of the gallant Custer, ten years ago, has not yet become an incident of history so remote as legitimately to be made the subject of a circus show," Grinnell editorialized angrily. "If we are not mistaken, Mrs. Custer is now a resident of this city. Under these circumstances the Wild West performance is an outrage on decency."

His concern for the widow Custer was chivalrous, to be sure, but it was likewise apparent that Grinnell nursed his own deeply personal attachment to Little Bighorn—to what almost had happened to him, and to what had happened to men he knew and loved.

PART TWO

NATURAL HISTORIAN

(1876–1886)

CHAPTER 7

AGE OF SURPRISES

I n the fall of 1876, three years after Grinnell had published his first articles in *Forest and Stream*, publisher and editor Charles Hallock invited him to become natural history editor.

It was not an elegant-looking publication by any means; its type was small, and its black-and-white pages were sparsely illustrated. Throughout Grinnell's tenure, which was to continue for the next thirty-six years, he would always refer to it as a newspaper or journal, never a magazine. Yet *Forest and Stream* held itself in high regard, as did its owner and editor, Charles Hallock. He was another Yale man (though he finished at Amherst) and the son of the editor of the New York *Journal of Commerce*; he had fished and hunted from Labrador to the Caribbean and helped found Blooming Grove in Pennsylvania, regarded as the preeminent hunting and fishing reserve in the country.

The early issues covered a wide range of sporting activities. Columns included: "The Horse and the Course," "Woodland, Lawn and Garden," "Yachting and Boating," "Shotgun and Rifle," "Fish Culture," "The Kennel," and, not insignificantly, "Natural History." Attention was also paid to baseball, tennis, archery, and croquet. Many articles were contributed by freelancers with proven expertise in their fields; but a large percentage of each week's issue was written by Hallock himself.

Though Grinnell's pay was only ten dollars a week, he threw himself into the work. Natural history columns began appearing under playful titles: "The Domestic Life of the Brown Thrasher," "Audacity in Hawks," "Spare the Sparrow," "The Culture of Carp," "Sagacity of the Pickerel," and "A Word about the Flying Squirrel." He also drew upon his association with Othniel Marsh, reviewing scientific papers on extinct North American vertebrates, including odd reptiles called odontornithes—birds with teeth—which Marsh had dug from the ancient sea bed of the Kansas prairie. "We live in an age of surprises," Grinnell wrote. "[R]ecently our trust in that ancient simile, 'as scarce as hen's teeth,' has been overthrown."

Hallock welcomed Grinnell's infusion of enthusiasm and wanted more. *Forest and Stream*'s weekly deadlines robbed Hallock of time he would have preferred to spend fishing, and he sized up his new contributor as the man who could set him free. "Sometime—soon—I wish to meet with you and your father in consultation as to the future of the paper," he wrote Grinnell early on. He proposed that the Grinnells gradually buy out his interest, while allowing him to keep his name atop the masthead. When the paper announced on its front page that "George Bird Grinnell, Esq." had taken over the natural history department, it also mentioned that he had become a stockholder. With that, Grinnell began putting more into *Forest and Stream* than he was taking out.

But even as his involvement with the journal grew, Grinnell continued to live in New Haven and work for Marsh. Each week he mailed his natural history dispatches to New York. Ned Dana, meanwhile, had earned his PhD in geology and begun teaching mathematics, physics, and chemistry at Yale, while writing his *Textbook of Mineralogy*. He and Grinnell found time to collaborate on a short paper for the *American Journal of Science*, describing a prehistoric lakebed they had discovered on their Montana trip. Every day at five o'clock, Grinnell and Dana would take an hour walk around New Haven, two bachelors who now had much clearer notions of where they were headed.

Grinnell, though, always had at least one eye turned toward events in the West. In the months following the battle of the Little Bighorn, the army escalated its efforts to punish the Indians and to peaceably—or, if necessary, by force—bring them back to their reservations. Toward this end, General Sheridan asked Frank and Lute North to recruit one hundred Pawnees as scouts to aid in the pursuit of the Sioux and Cheyennes. Crazy Horse's Oglala Sioux were believed to be along the Powder River, and Dull Knife's Northern Cheyennes were tucked away somewhere on the eastern slopes of the Big Horn Mountains of Wyoming. Sitting Bull was reckoned to be in Montana.

A year earlier the Pawnees had volunteered to give up their reservation on the Loup River and relocated to Indian Territory (today's Pawnee, Oklahoma), a decision they came to regret. Hundreds perished from fever, and almost overnight the proud and mobile tribe of the prairie was dejected and impoverished. When the Norths arrived at the Pawnee agency in September 1876, they were shocked by the deplorable condition of their old friends. "They were miserably poor, nearly all of them had ague"—malaria—"and many of them were dying," Lute observed. When the Norths told them why they had come, the Pawnees "fairly climbed over each other" to enlist. Once warriors, they would be warriors again, fighting against their historic enemies.

On September 18 the Pawnees were formally mustered in at Sidney, Nebraska, and provided with horses, guns, uniforms, and blankets. They were attached to Colonel Ranald Mackenzie, Fourth Cavalry, under General George Crook.

Grinnell learned of the Powder River campaign of 1876–77 via the newspapers and a series of letters from Lute North. At dawn on November 24, the cavalry, led by the Norths and their Pawnees, as well as a number of other scouts from other tribes, surprised the camp of Dull Knife, Little Wolf, Wild Hog, and Black Hairy Dog on the Red Fork of the Powder River, west of present-day Kaycee, Wyoming. The wind was biting; the temperature was twenty below zero.

"I will tell you how it was," Lute wrote Grinnell. "F[rank] and I led the charge against the camp, and just at the edge of the village was a little clump of willows, which we had to pass. [An] Indian . . . had run into the bushes, and as I was coming straight toward him he jumped out in front of me, about twenty steps away, and raised his gun (an old muzzle-loader). I dropped my reins and swung the 'old long nine' around and we both cut loose. He fell and I passed on. Some time after, F[rank] and I happened around that way again and I took a look at [the body]. The shot had entered his right breast and come out under his left shoulder. . . . Of course everybody was shooting, and somebody else may have killed him, but I tried all the same."

Driven from the village, many of them barely clothed, the Cheyennes took up positions among the rocks of the surrounding slopes and sniped on the soldiers throughout the day. Try as they might, however, they could not prevent the capture of more than six hundred horses and the burning of 173 lodges, one thousand saddles, and all of their buffalo meat and robes. "I tell you they are the bravest people I ever saw," Lute volunteered. "I don't think there were more than three hundred warriors in the village, and we had about a thousand men, and were fighting them all day, yet did not succeed in driving them more than half a mile from the village."

North estimated that twenty-five Cheyennes were killed. (Six cavalry-men died as well.) The man Lute North shot at the start of the assault proved to be one of three of Dull Knife's sons slain in the battle. The Paw-nees removed their scalps and presented one as a prize to Lute. "I didn't take his scalp," North clarified to Grinnell. "Had one of the boys do that part of it for me. I will send it to you if you want it." Later in the same letter he reiterated, "If you want the scalp, tell me how I had better send it."

Evidently Grinnell was not put off by the offer, for two weeks later North wrote again: "Your good letter came this morning and I hasten an answer and will send this piece of scalp."

Three months after the fight on the Powder River, North exhorted Grin-nell to drop what he was doing in New Haven and join him for the remain-der of the campaign. Grinnell's letters in response are now lost, but North's side of their exchanges depicts fighting as thrilling sport. "How I would like to have you out with us this summer, for I know we will find Indians and you and I might get some satisfaction out of them," he wrote from Sidney in February 1877. A month later North coaxed Grinnell again: "We generally try to show up to the front in a fight. . . . [A]s to your being scared, why of course I know better than that but just come out and try it."

Grinnell never got the chance to test himself in battle—if he ever truly considered doing so. The attack on Dull Knife and Little Wolf's camp had delivered one of the last in a series of crippling, demoralizing blows to the Indians of the plains. The Cheyennes, the Sioux, and their allies were beaten; the survivors, not counting Sitting Bull's band, gone to Canada, had little choice but to return to their reservations. The Plains Indian wars, with the exception of a few desperate "break-outs," were history. The Pawnee scouts were mustered out in April 1877 and never fought for the army again. The same proved true for Frank and Luther North.

Once the fighting subsided, the North brothers wasted no time moving into the former stronghold of the Sioux and establishing themselves in the cattle business. The Sand Hills of Nebraska, a thousand square miles of undulating, grass-covered dunes, had, until recently, been prime grazing ground for buffalo. But the buffalo, like the Indians who hunted them, were now scarce, and opportunistic stockmen began filling the void with beef herds driven up the trail from Texas. Frank, Lute, and their other brother, Jim, formed a partnership with William Cody to establish a ranch on the Dismal River, which feeds the Middle Fork of the Loup, sixty miles from the railroad at North Platte. The headquarters was initially a couple of tents on the edge of an alkaline lake.

When Grinnell paid a visit in the summer of 1877, fifteen hundred longhorns were spread out across the Cody-North range. Buffalo Bill had come and gone by then, touring the East in a melodrama inspired by the 1857 Mountain Meadows Massacre of California-bound emigrants by Mormons disguised as Indians. The hard work of running a ranch he left to the North brothers.

Although Grinnell would later assert that he "worked for two or three summers" on the Cody-North ranch, his visits more closely resembled vacations, and, given his obligations to Professor Marsh and the Peabody Museum, which had just opened in July, his stay the first year was likely no more than a couple of weeks. And he timed that stay between the spring and fall roundups, so that he and Lute could enjoy hunting antelope in the hills.

Yet the brevity of his time on the Nebraska range did not keep Grinnell from embroidering his memories of those excursions. "In the old days, when I punched cows," he wrote in 1916, "most of us could drop down out of the saddle and pick up a hat, handkerchief, or whip pretty much every time." No doubt he was an accomplished horseman by the time he joined the Norths at Dismal River; he had ridden many hundreds of miles of rough trail, forded swift rivers, and acquired most of the skills of the wrangler repertoire. Even so, he did not do a great deal of cowpunching—or trick riding, for that matter. In *Jack the Young Cowboy*, one of the books Grinnell would write for boys, Jack Danvers, a New Yorker who spends his summers on a western ranch, wonders "what some of those eastern pilgrims, who had talked to him of the romance of the cowboy's life, would think of that life if for one day they had to do the work that the cowboy has to do every day." To be honest, in 1877 George Bird Grinnell was still part pilgrim.

The following summer Grinnell did not go directly to Dismal River but continued farther west to Como, a station and siding on the Union Pacific just east of Medicine Bow, Wyoming, to check on Professor Marsh's latest bone bonanza.

A year earlier two railroad employees living at Como, William Carlin and William Reed, had written to Marsh, exclaiming on the extraordinary fossils they had stumbled upon. Marsh suspected that they were from the Jurassic period, 150 million years old. He immediately put Carlin, Reed, and a trusted deputy, Samuel Williston, to digging.

When Grinnell stepped off the train at Como in August, he saw crate upon crate of fossils stacked on the platform, awaiting shipment east. Over the next ten years the bone beds at Como Bluff would come to be described as quarries, so bountiful were the treasures unearthed there. The most famous, and largest, discovery was the fossilized skeleton of a gargantuan Jurassic reptile that measured more than sixty feet long and twelve feet tall and weighed perhaps fifteen tons. Marsh named it brontosaurus—"thunder lizard." Another prize was the jaw of a dryolestes, acknowledged to be the first Jurassic mammal found in North America.

After inspection of the diggings and a week of hunting, Grinnell went on to the Dismal River, where the North brothers continued to make improvements, including a snug log house with gun ports, in the event that the Sioux might leave their reservation and pay an unfriendly visit. At the end of his stay, on the three-day ride to the railroad at North Platte, Grinnell was stricken with a violent fever. Somehow he managed to get back to Milford, where he collapsed into the care of his mother and father. For seven weeks, he recalled, "I was out of my head at night, and my delirium always took one form. I imagined myself riding about the cattle, saw great banks of clouds coming up in the west with thunder and lightning, and then the cattle would break away, and of course we would all ride after them as hard as he could." In his dreams, at least, he was a full-fledged cowboy.

Slowly, at first with the use of a cane, he was able to resume work at Yale. Fossils continued to pour into the Peabody Museum from Como and other Marsh-sponsored sites across the West. Grinnell's job was to uncrate and sort them, though at first Marsh was not inclined to assemble his ancient skeletons and display them for the amusement of the general public. To Marsh, paleontology was a competition, a colossal card game, and he preferred to keep his most precious findings to himself. "What I have, I hold," he asserted.

Yet Marsh did not withhold from his assistants, and during the six years that Grinnell worked under Marsh, the professor gave him a thorough education not only in the forensic field of paleontology, but also in the discipline of osteology—bone anatomy. With Marsh's help and encouragement, Grinnell published in the *American Journal of Science* two different papers on fossils in the Yale collection. (It didn't hurt that Ned Dana was now an editor of the venerable journal.)

All the while, Grinnell was writing prolifically for *Forest and Stream*, and editor Hallock was happy to give his understudy all the space he wished. In the fall of 1879 Grinnell published—under the nom de plume "Yo"—an account of his recent hunting trip in the Medicine Bow Mountains, south of Como. "That Americans, as a people, devote too much time to their work and too little time to their recreation is a proposition that needs no demonstration," he began.

In the final paragraph of ten installments, he took a deep breath and shifted his message from one of refreshment to one of depletion: "As I look back on the past ten years and see what changes have taken place in these glorious mountains since I first knew them"—he meant the Rockies generally—"I can form some idea of the transformations which time to come will work in the appearance of the country, its fauna and its flora. The enormous mineral wealth contained in the rock-ribbed hills will be every year more fully developed. . . . Towns will spring up and flourish, and the pure, thin air of the mountains will be blackened and polluted by the smoke vomited from the chimneys of a thousand smelting furnaces; the game, once so plentiful, will have disappeared with the Indian; railroads will climb the steep sides of the mountains and wind through the narrow passes, carrying huge loads of provisions to the mining towns, and returning trains will be freighted with ore just dug from the bowels of the earth; the valleys will be filled with fattening cattle, as profitable to their owners as the mines to theirs; arable land will be taken up and cultivated, and finally the mountains will be stripped of their timbers and will become simply bald and rocky hills. The day when all this shall have taken place is distant no doubt, and will not be seen by the present generation; but it will come. In the destruction of the noble forests that now clothe these majestic hills lies a great danger. Water is scarce enough anywhere in the West at present, but in the mountains, at least, there is plenty of it. Should the timber, however, be destroyed with the wantonness that has recently prevailed, the region may become as arid as in Arizona; and in that event the streams which water the great plains would be sadly diminished in volume, if not quite dried up."

But even then he was not quite finished. "[This] subject is one that demands, and will receive, I hope, greater attention in the future than it has in the past; and before long I hope to be able to set forth some of its more important features in the columns of *Forest and Stream*."

He soon got his chance. In recent months it had becoming increasingly apparent that Charles Hallock was losing his grip. "[He] had become more and more eccentric, drinking heavily and neglecting his duties," Grinnell was to recall in his memoirs. By then the Grinnells, son and father, were majority stockholders. At the annual meeting in May, they and the company treasurer, Edward Wilbur, asked Hallock to step down, and George Bird Grinnell took over as president of the Forest and Stream Publishing Company and publisher of *Forest and Stream.*

The offices were moved from Fulton Street to a "spacious suite" in the New York Times building on Park Row. "With new and better arrangements for work," a front-page editorial announced, "*Forest and Stream* is prepared to add to its excellence and usefulness, and to keep pace with the participation in healthy and manly sport which is so rapidly increasing throughout this country."

The time had come for Grinnell to leave New Haven. With Professor Marsh's guidance, and surely with his blessing, Grinnell prepared for and passed the PhD examinations in osteology and vertebrate paleontology. His dissertation was a rather dry and painstaking morphology of the roadrunner, a species of cuckoo native to the American southwest and Mexico. It was a peculiar choice; Grinnell had likely never seen a roadrunner in the flesh. On the other hand, he had spent his time at Yale working with the fossils of "flying dragons" and "birds with teeth." Why not study a bird that races across the land and seldom flies? "The ground cuckoos and their nearest allies constitute a curious outlying group in which adaptation to a life upon the ground as opposed to arboreal habits has reached a high degree of development," he wrote in the introduction to his thesis.

Upon receiving his degree, Grinnell departed New Haven "with keen regret" and moved to New York to devote himself full time to *Forest and Stream.* And surely it was no coincidence that the assumption of his new titles and the completion of his doctorate occurred at the same time that his family decided to move back to the city and resume residence at the Hemlocks, in Audubon Park.

CHAPTER 8

THOROUGH SPORTSMAN

Under Charles Hallock's editorship, *Forest and Stream* defined what it meant to be a sportsman. He was a person adept with rod and gun, able in camp, and knowledgeable of the habits and haunts of game and fish. "Manliness" was an essential component, and Hallock preached that fresh air and outdoor exercise could transform a boy "narrow in the chest" to a condition of hearty vigor.

Yet not every man of sport deserved to be called a sportsman, he clarified. A proper sportsman was also expected to be someone of self-discipline and high-minded decency—a gentleman, in the English sense of always demonstrating good form. Such conduct spoke for itself, Hallock assured. Adherence to the moral code of sportsmanship was like recognition of God's grace: proof thereof and insurance therein.

Along with the physical and moral qualifications, high on Hallock's list of sportsman's criteria was a third quality: the aesthetic. "A keen lover of nature must he be, drinking in all her sublime changes; finding a pure delight in watching the various little minutiae of the varying seasons."

George Bird Grinnell bought into Hallock's notion of sportsmanship wholeheartedly. Hunting on Manhattan Island as a boy and then in New England, he absorbed the principle that the hunt by fair chase mattered more than the number of birds in a day's bag. Birds ought to be shot on the wing, not on the water. One did not shoot birds in the nesting season or shoot any species of songbird. And ignorance of the code of conduct—a breach often committed by foreigners—was no excuse.

Indeed, under Grinnell's editorship, *Forest and Stream* would aim frequent criticism at "pot-hunting" immigrants, accusing them of roaming the outskirts of eastern cities, shooting small birds as they had once done with impunity in the old country. An article headlined "Aliens and Guns" reported: "Five song bird killers, captured last Sunday near Bronx Park, in the upper part of the city, were of Italian extraction. . . . In their possession were found twenty-nine robins, two indigo birds, five thrushes, a grosbeak and a cat bird; and evidence seemed to show that they had regaled themselves on several other birds, cooking them over a fire kindled in the woods."

Yet *Forest and Stream* did not find fault strictly with hungry newcomers or the commercial hunter. Men of means and standing were often just as guilty. Another editorial asked: "[W]hat can be said of a class of men whose station, birth, fortune and associations in life are the best, yet who deliberately and with premeditation violate the game laws in their letter and spirit, and who further violate the laws of humanity and common decency by the wantonness and cruelty of their acts? To some the term *noblesse oblige* seems to be meaningless. Rank, station, fortune and character are but means to a life of sham respectability. . . . A gentleman is a gentleman at all times, and a sportsman is a gentleman."

When it came to the hunting of bigger game, one of the most despicable methods was deer hounding, a practice common in the Adirondacks, in which dogs chased deer into ponds and lakes, where they could be easily killed. Grinnell decried hounding as "unsportsmanlike and brutal."

He himself never hunted deer or other mammals by any method in the East, but after he went west and was initiated by Frank and Lute North, Charley Reynolds, and the Pawnees, he grew to honor the "nobility" of big-game hunting and enjoyed the thrill as much as the next man. He did not give into greed, however. For him the alarming disappearance of the buffalo taught a stark lesson in the importance of sportsmanship in the pursuit.

Of course there were exceptions to the code of killing prescribed by *Forest and Stream.* One was killing for the sake of science, to collect specimens. Another was the killing of species that preyed on domestic animals: wolves, coyotes, cougars, eagles, bears. "I have no sympathy with the bears," Grinnell allowed in an early editorial. "They are vermin, and the sooner they are destroyed the better."

Yet another exception, harder to justify but accepted just the same, was the longstanding tradition of personal collecting—trophy hunting—which was done not for meat, not always for science, nor for protection of other species, but strictly for pleasure and, in the case of bears, cougars, African lions, and Asian tigers, as proof of having bested a beast higher than man in the food chain.

Though other sportsman's journals called for protection of fish and game, beginning in the spring of 1880 no publisher took on the cause of regulation and conservation with more determination than George Bird Grinnell. His editorials advocated laws restricting hunting seasons, bag limits, commercial sale of game, and cruel and otherwise unfair practices such as netting ducks or trap-shooting live pigeons, not to mention deer-hounding.

Forest and Stream would continue as avidly as ever to publish authentic, first-person stories of turkey hunts in Texas, shad runs on the Delaware, duck shooting in the Carolinas, elk camps in Wyoming; lively discussions of dog breeds, gun models, powder, bait, decoys; and the results of the latest field trials, shooting competitions, and regattas. But gradually the perspective shifted with the new masthead. While the interests of the hunter or fisherman continued first and foremost, more and more space was given to stories on habitat, migration, and game and forest preserves. The journal became a forum in which readers from around the country could learn of game management and legislative efforts in states not their own.

If there was a turning point when the editorial balance of Grinnell's *Forest and Stream* tipped unmistakably from hook-and-bullet diversion to conservationist urgency, it was reached in April 1882, in the form of a front-page jeremiad: "Every right-minded man detests the brute who 'crust-hunts' deer [pursuing deer in snow] when they are his almost helpless victims, and even their hides are worthless; who kills brooding birds and their half-grown young for market or the tickling of his wolfish palate; and catches fish any way he can, the fish that are spawning or guarding their fry. He is a nuisance, that should be abated by any means within the law, or even by straining the law a little."

It was the sheer vehemence of this harangue and the ones to follow that declared the journal's new momentum. Under the headline, "Loose Moose Morals," Grinnell snapped: "It is high time that offenders against the [New York] game laws should stop boasting of their exploits. There is enough game left in this country yet to enable every man to get his share of it honestly. And one had better go without it than to steal it."

On the topic of saving the Adirondacks from poachers, commercial hunters, and also—a new and increasingly worrisome target of his contempt—rapacious loggers, he growled: "This is another age of the Vandals; not the barbarians of old times who overthrew the cities, but ravagers of a new type, who would destroy to the last vestige the grand forest preserves of the East and the West." By Grinnell's evolving definition, a sportsman should not hold his tongue when nature was being so violently offended.

Yet Grinnell, like Hallock, was not one to let editorial duties keep him from the field. He worked out a routine in which he, business manager Edward Wilbur, and his young managing editor Charles Reynolds (no relation to the guide, Lonesome Charley Reynolds) took their vacations in shifts. Wilbur and Reynolds would go away for the early part of summer, leaving the latter part and the early autumn to their boss.

Grinnell was not able to slip away from New York in 1880, but in the summer of 1881 he negotiated free rail passage to the Pacific Northwest, a junket so generous that he was able to bring along Ned Dana and the husband of a cousin, Edward Landon. Grinnell repaid the railroad's courtesy with a long series of articles, "Bye-Ways of the Northwest," that celebrated the comforts of Pullman sleeping and dining cars. After stops in Como, Salt Lake City, Lake Tahoe, and San Francisco, the trio arrived by steamer at Victoria, British Columbia, where the real objective of the cross-country journey was to commence.

Over the next two weeks, they and their Indian guides traveled by canoe among the wild inlets at the mouth of the Fraser River. They had entered one of the greatest fisheries in the world, but they had come not to feast on salmon or shellfish, but to hunt the mammals of the steep, densely wooded shore. Grinnell succeeded in shooting at least one deer and a black bear, his first.

Back at *Forest and Stream*, reinvigorated by his recent outing, it was inevitable that Grinnell would turn his attention once more to Yellowstone National Park, which was increasingly stalked by predators of the commercial variety.

Even before the Northern Pacific had completed its main road across the nation, it began surveying the route of a branch line from Livingston, Montana, southward fifty miles to the northern entrance of Yellowstone. Quietly the railroad also contemplated a continuation of its line within the boundary of the park; and not so discreetly it had encouraged the formation of the Yellowstone Park Improvement Company to develop hotels, stage lines, and other amenities for the tourists that the Northern Pacific intended to deliver to the nation's Wonderland.

On September 1, 1882, an agreement to grant a contract was struck between the Department of the Interior and the Improvement Company, creating a monopoly on the business development of the park. At a token rate of two dollars per acre, the company would for ten years control seven tracts, 640 acres each, surrounding the most popular destinations in the park. To provide hot water for its guests, the Improvement Company could divert the geysers and geothermal springs as it wished. The commercial enterprise that had been foreseen, and then rejected, by Nathaniel Langford and Cornelius Hedges in 1870 was now a very real possibility.

By pure chance, on the very day that the Park Improvement Company was given preliminary approval of its monopoly, General Philip Sheridan happened to be making an inspection of Yellowstone. Like Grinnell seven years earlier, he was disturbed to learn of the wholesale slaughter of the park's elk strictly for their hides. And at the conclusion of his trip, upon reaching the Northern Pacific Railway, he was informed of the arrangement between the federal government and the new concessionaire. "I regretted exceedingly to learn that the national park had been rented out to private parties," he wrote in his official report of his summer travels. He condemned the Interior Department for caving in to commercialism and made a series of bold proposals to protect Yellowstone. To provide greater refuge for "our noble game," he recommended increasing the eastern and southern boundaries of the park by more than three thousand square miles. Realizing that regulations to protect the park were useless without enforcement, he reprised Grinnell and Ludlow's suggestion that federal troops be stationed in Yellowstone as a police force.

Meanwhile, the Park Improvement Company had begun constructing a sawmill to erect a large hotel next to Mammoth Hot Springs and had recruited local hunters to provide twenty thousand pounds of meat for its workers—to be harvested from the park's population of elk, deer, bighorn sheep, and buffalo.

Sheridan and Grinnell had met only briefly, but the general was quite aware of the editor's participation in the Black Hills expedition of 1874 and Ludlow's reconnaissance of Yellowstone in 1875. And as a sportsman, he surely was a reader of *Forest and Stream.* So it was that over the coming winter Sheridan turned to Grinnell, encouraging him to publicize his campaign. Not that Grinnell required much prompting.

On December 14 Grinnell published the first shot in a determined defiance of the interests threatening the national park and its wildlife. "For many years we have hunted and traveled and fished and mined and fought Indians over the length and breadth of the great West," he stated. "We have seen it when it was, except in isolated spots, an uninhabited wilderness, have seen the Indian and the game retreat before the white man and the cattle, and beheld the tide of immigration, once small, like a tiny mountain stream, move forward, at first slowly, and then, gathering volume and strength, advance with a constantly accelerated power which threatens before long to leave no portion of our vast territory unbroken by the farmer's plow or untrodden by his flocks."

"There is one spot left," Grinnell concluded, "a single rock about which this tide will break, and past which it will sweep, leaving it undefiled by the unsightly traces of civilization. Here in this Yellowstone Park the large game of the West may be preserved from extermination."

For the next three months *Forest and Stream* devoted a portion of every issue, usually the front page, to deriding and derailing "the Park Grab."

December 21: "[T]his project is neither more nor less than a barefaced attempt to use this government reservation for the purpose of enriching a few speculators."

January 11: "The people are a little tired of having the public domain given away with a lavish hand."

January 18: "It is the duty of this journal to do all in its power to protect the interests of the people, to guard against any invasion of their rights, and to sound the note of warning and alarm when these rights are threatened."

Rallying to the guidon was George Vest, once a Confederate congressman and now a United States senator from Missouri. Sheridan had reached out to Vest at the same time he was recruiting *Forest and Stream*. Five-foot-six and lean as a jockey, Vest proved to be one of the most stalwart, if unsung, champions of conservation of the day. He had yet to lay eyes on Yellowstone, nor been anywhere near it, but as a man who had grown up in a wilder day and, moreover, as chairman of the Committee on Territories, he took it upon himself to abort the Park Improvement Company's sly deal with Interior.

Alas, his bill incorporating Sheridan's recommendations went nowhere. Undeterred, Vest attached a rider to the Sundry Civil Appropriation bill, prohibiting "exclusive privileges or monopolies" on park concessions. With help from Representative Anson McCook of New York, he lifted language from his earlier bill authorizing the secretary of war "to make the necessary details of troops to prevent trespassers or intruders from entering the Park for the purpose of destroying the game or objects of curiosity therein." A bigger park budget also allowed for ten assistant superintendents to be added to the force.

Again Vest met opposition; he and his allies were not successful in expanding park boundaries or in driving the Improvement Company from Yellowstone entirely, but the 4,400 acres originally allotted by the Interior Department for private franchise was reduced to ten, and no structure could be built within a mile of the geysers or Yellowstone Falls.

On March 8, five days after passage of the appropriation bill that included the Yellowstone section, *Forest and Stream* thanked Senator Vest and celebrated the measured victory over the dark forces that had sought to sell off the pleasure ground of the people. Yet with congratulations came a warning. "The Park is at present all our own," Grinnell wrote. "How would our readers like to see it become a second Niagara—a place where one goes only to be fleeced, where patent medicine advertisements stare one in the face, and the beauties of nature have all been defiled by the greed of man?"

It was an alarm Grinnell would have to sound over and over. Already a corporation was forming to build a railroad deep into the park. And more tourists were coming. The Northern Pacific's road from St. Paul to the Pacific was completed in September 1883, and its branch line was approaching the town of Gardiner, Montana, just outside the park's north entrance. Within the park the Improvement Company was proceeding with construction of the 250-room National Hotel at Mammoth Hot Springs. (It was only half finished when President Chester Arthur, with an entourage that included General Sherman, Senator Vest, and Secretary of War Robert Lincoln, toured the park in late August.) Tent hotels sprang up around the main attractions.

Yet the fight that *Forest and Stream* had waged against the "raid" on the park's treasures had altered awareness of Yellowstone's worth to the American public. Grinnell's editorials had caught the attention of other newspapers, especially in the East, where most *Forest and Stream* readers, and most park visitors, lived.

"It is only a matter of right that the Yellowstone National Park, which is coming to the front as a leading natural attraction, should be protected in the interests of the public," the *New-York Commercial Advertiser* proclaimed.

"The Park is for the people and should be managed in the interest of the people rather than the interest of speculators," echoed the *Tribune*.

Scolded the *Herald*: "Our monopoly-cursed country will look to Congress to protect the great National Park so perfectly that one can visit it without being at the mercy of a single person, firm, or 'combination of capitalists.'"

Grinnell had done a good deed by defending Yellowstone. Along the way, he established himself as the leading voice in American conservation. Ten years old in July, *Forest and Stream* had an impressive circle of allies and an ever-widening circulation of readers.

Grinnell was by no means a purist, however. For example, he could pub-licly curse the ravenousness of railroads even while accepting free tickets on their lines, and he owned several different railroad stocks. Similarly, in British Columbia he had shot a bear presumably for no other purpose than to shoot a bear.

Another seeming contradiction was Grinnell's enthusiasm for ranch-ing. He would never cease to lament the disappearance of the buffalo and the diminishment of the wide-open West by settlers and stockmen. Yet the romance and business opportunity of raising cattle, first fanned by his visits to the Cody-North ranch in Nebraska, were too seductive to resist. In the spring of 1883, immediately after the Yellowstone Park tempest had calmed, Grinnell purchased a thousand-acre ranch north of Medicine Bow and west of Como Bluffs, Wyoming. He had looked the country over with Wil-liam Reed, one of the fossil hunters he had met in 1878, and he bought the ranch with the agreement that Reed would manage three thousand sheep in the harsh high country of the Shirley Basin.

Reed was plenty capable and trustworthy. Born in Connecticut, he had grown up on a Nebraska homestead and served as a civilian scout for the army before finding employment with the Union Pacific and then with Othniel Marsh. But no amount of experience could prepare him for the severe winters that followed. The ranch sat on the northern slope of the Shirley Mountains. The acres owned by Grinnell were watered by a good creek, which irrigated enough ground to winter-feed a few horses. Sheep, however, had to forage for themselves in the dry, exposed, sagebrush uplands. At an elevation of more than seven thousand feet, snow covered the ground early and melted late. In his memoirs, Grinnell described the Shirley Basin as "one of the most attractive spots in the country." As sheep country, it proved not so appealing.

He never pictured himself as a *sheep* rancher. Like thousands of absen-tee investors from as far away as Europe, Grinnell was eager to join the cattle boom that had swept across the West with the completion of more railroads, the disappearance of the buffalo, and the containment of the Indians. True, there were far more sheep than cattle in Wyoming in 1883, but Grinnell and Reed had other ideas. Their aim was to sell their wool and sheep and switch to raising cows. The decision was made easier when roughly a third of the three thousand sheep did not survive the winter. Grinnell sold off the remainder and replaced them with cattle and horses.

But already he was too late. Due to overstocking, the price of beef was falling. Almost before he got started, he was looking for a way to get out, a goal he would not accomplish for another sixteen years.

Grinnell may have paid a brief visit to his Wyoming ranch in the summer of 1884, though no diary or letter says so. His memoirs, too, come to an abrupt halt at about this time. Regardless, his true destination that August was Yellowstone.

The federal appropriations bill of the year before had failed to expand the park boundaries; now Senator Vest, with support from Grinnell and others, was pushing a new bill to finish what they had started. Toward this end, Grinnell joined a party led by Arnold Hague of the United States Geological Survey to take the measure of the wilderness south of Yellowstone Lake and north of Jackson Hole. Its natural beauty was an obvious asset, as was its importance as a game reserve. The point that Hague and Grinnell wanted to drive home above all others was the region's extraordinary value as the headwaters of two great rivers: the Yellowstone, which flows toward the Gulf of Mexico and the Atlantic Ocean, and the Snake, which flows via the Columbia River into the Pacific. Both of these streams begin within a stone's throw of each other in a wide meadow known as Two Ocean Plateau.

Grinnell and Hague rode for two weeks, often following no trail, doing more admiring than mapping, and the following winter, while Vest pushed the park expansion bill in the Senate, Grinnell published a fifteen-part series in *Forest and Stream*, extolling the richness and grandeur of this rarely seen but eminently vulnerable territory.

Once again Vest's bill did not pass, and once more the boundaries were not enlarged. Still, Grinnell declared in consolation, "It is satisfaction to know that the public interest in the Yellowstone National Park is now greater than it has ever been, and we believe that the efforts to be made for its protection will have the support of all the best classes of the community."

In the *Forest and Stream* series, he wrote with optimism but also with a sense of melancholy. In the nine years that had passed since his previous visit to Yellowstone, the park had become a playground full of people. As he gazed upon the geyser basins of the Firehole River, his eyes widened: "The scene in the valley below is one of life and activity. Horses and cattle are browsing on the flat. . . . Two or three stages move briskly along the roads. . . . Men are chopping wood, building fires, and hobbling and picketing out their horses. There are houses—one, two, three, a dozen. It is the old spot, but how changed by the lapse of a few years. . . . Here at our feet in this valley [is] going on just what is now taking place all over the West, only it [is] a little more concentrated. If from some lofty station in the sky one could obtain a bird's eye view of the vast area between the Missouri River and the Pacific Ocean he would see, but on a vastly grander scale, and spread out over a territory measured by miles, where this contains inches, just such scenes as were taking place before me here. From the British line south to the Mexican boundary, and from the great river west to the ocean, wherever there is wood, water and grass, there the settler, earnest, industrious and much enduring, has passed in and erected his little cabin, has broken up his bit of prairie, planted his crop, turned out his few head of stock, and made for himself a home in the wilderness."

CHAPTER 9

NO TENDERFOOT HE

fter Yellowstone, Grinnell was looking for some new, less-traveled country to explore, and he chose as his guide James Willard Schultz. Ten years younger than Grinnell, Schultz had grown up in Boonville, New York, on the edge of the Adirondacks, the son of a prosperous grocer. When he was not hunting, fishing, or rambling in the woods, he practiced the violin. He shared his parents' love for classical music and opera and often accompanied them to New York to hear the Philharmonic.

But then the strings snapped. His father died. Military school was not for him, and in 1877, while visiting an uncle in St. Louis, he somehow talked his mother into sending him the money to buy passage on a steamboat headed up the Missouri River as far as Fort Benton, Montana. Enough opera—a grander performance lay before him. "The love of wild life and adventure was born in me, yet I must have inherited it from some remote ancestor, for all my near ones were staid, devout people," he would write of his renunciation and conversion in *My Life as an Indian*, published in 1907, with an introduction by George Bird Grinnell. "How I hated the amenities and conventions of society; from my earliest youth, I was happy only when out in the great forest which lay to the north of my home, far beyond the sound of church and school bell, and the whistling locomotives."

The Indians in question were Piegans, the southernmost band of Blackfoot, who, since long before Lewis and Clark trespassed on their homeland, had dominated the buffalo country from the Yellowstone River north into southern Canada, westward to the Rocky Mountains, eastward to the Sioux lands of the Dakotas. Over the years, through treaties, the depletion of buffalo, and the subterfuge of whiskey traders and corrupt agents, the Piegans' reservation had been shrunk to the northern brow of Montana, above the Missouri.

Soon after landing at Fort Benton in the spring of 1877, Schultz went to work at Blackfeet trading posts, where he married a Piegan woman and took the name Appekunny, which derives from *Pikani*, the Blackfoot origin of the word *Piegan*, meaning, "spotted robe," as in a poorly tanned hide. Schultz himself was smooth-faced with large, dark eyes, and jug handles for ears. He never considered living in the East again, but he reckoned the East ought to hear from him. His first story appeared in *Forest and Stream* in October 1880, and then in the fall of 1883 he submitted a series of ethnological sketches of Blackfeet habits, language, and folklore. They were the longest pieces on Indians the journal had run to date, and they really had nothing whatsoever to do with hunting, fishing, or outdoor recreation—unless one considered the Blackfeet way of life a manual of rustic sportsmanship.

Perhaps what convinced Grinnell to run the series was Schultz's vivid depiction of a people whose proud past, while receding, remained within reach. "Bands of the ancient inhabitants are still yet to be seen—small remnants of a once mighty nation," Schultz wrote in the introduction to "Life Among the Blackfeet." "Still camping where their forefathers were wont to pitch their lodges, some of them preserve their native dignity and hold to their ancestral customs as sacredly as ever." Grinnell knew a bit about the Blackfeet from his previous trips to Montana, but he had never encountered any, and he had yet to travel beyond Montana's southern tier.

It was a later article by Schultz that piqued Grinnell to see the Blackfeet country for himself. In late October 1884 Schultz, in the company of two other white men and a Piegan identified as Man Who First Took His Gun and Ran Ahead left the agency on Badger Creek for a month-long trip to the St. Mary Lakes, the long, glacial gouges penetrating inward to the raw dorsal of the Continental Divide. (Today it is the route of the Going-to-the-Sun Road in Glacier National Park.) Schultz described catching lake trout so large and so plentiful "that it is no pleasure to fish." It took only a brief stroll to shoot a half-dozen grouse. Nearly everyone in the party killed a bighorn sheep. The country Schultz described was equally boastworthy. "Never in my life have I beheld such grand scenery," he wrote of the view from a mountain above the upper St. Mary Lake. "Below us several thousand feet, lay the lake (about twelve miles long), its unruffled surface dotted with several small islands. . . . Beyond the head of the lake is a long, wide, densely timbered valley, and on the upper left-hand side of this valley is a mountain, the top of which is a true glacier. With the glasses it appeared to be at least 800 feet thick." (He seemed to be describing what today is known as Blackfoot Glacier.) "All in all," Schultz concluded, "we had a pleasant trip, plenty of fish and game for camp use, and above all, a sojourn among the pines and lakes so like those of our boyhood days."

This was enough for Grinnell. In the spring of 1885 he wrote to Schultz, asking his correspondent to guide him into the country described in the recent article (which Grinnell had in hand but for some reason did not publish until the end of the year). Schultz was happy to oblige. Grinnell left New York in mid-August and, thanks to the efficiency of the Northern Pacific, was able to spend a week in Yellowstone before continuing on to Helena, from where he traveled by stage to Fort Benton and finally to the Blackfeet agency.

"He arrived on the mail stage," Schultz recalled of their first meeting, "a slender quiet, fine-appearing man of medium height, in outing clothes that showed much use; his baggage a canvas-covered bedroll, a war sack, a Sharps .45 caliber rifle, and a fly rod. No tenderfoot he."

The next month exceeded Grinnell's expectations. Schultz had discovered that the St. Mary Lakes could be reached by wagon, allowing them to carry a sheet-iron cook stove, a ten-by-ten wall tent, considerable bedding and provisions, plus a fourteen-foot-long skiff for trolling on the lakes. Completing the party was twenty-eight-year-old Charles Rose, also called Yellowfish, the son of a Piegan woman and a white man who once had worked for the American Fur Company. All three men took along saddle horses as well. Grinnell's described his as "an old buffalo horse, tough and wiry."

The fourth day out, September 4, they caught their first glimpse of the lower of the two St. Mary Lakes, "which the Indians call the Walled-in Lakes," Grinnell wrote in his diary. It had snowed during the night. "Dimly through changing mist clouds we thought we could see a long way up the Upper Lake, and recognized, or thought we did, the stern black faces of tremendous escarpments which rose from the water's very edge. Now and then a soft veil of mist would drop down from the overhanging clouds and float from the upper end of the lake to the lower, now concealing and revealing the beauties of the scene."

Grinnell's affinity for this new realm was immediate, as if it were the destination he had been looking for all his life. Yellowstone was extraordinary and exquisite, to be sure, yet its charms were already shared by many. By comparison, and certainly in Grinnell's eyes as he approached the Rocky Mountain Front that thirty years later he would help to consecrate as Glacier National Park, the Walled-in Lakes and the soaring, alpine wilderness that enveloped them were virtually unblemished country. A few landmarks bore white man's names: St. Mary was credited to a passing priest; Schultz had stuck "Flattop" on a mountain on his 1883 trip; the colossal, stand-alone sentinel thrusting its Precambrian helmet five thousand feet above the prairie to the north of the St. Mary Lakes was already known as Chief Mountain. And the Indians—Blackfeet on the east, Kootenais and other tribes from the western slope of the range—had their own names for a great many of the features. But to George Bird Grinnell, these imprints were minor. Here before him, on the reflective waters of the lakes and on the open faces of the peaks, he beheld tabula rasa, or as close to it as he would ever get.

Foul weather did not dampen his spirits, nor the fact that they did not have the country entirely to themselves. Historically the bellicose Blackfeet had kept outsiders—native and white—wary and at bay, but in recent years, as the military and the Bureau of Indian Affairs imposed their will, and disease, whiskey, and starvation sapped their strength, the Blackfeet were no longer able to defend their homeland with their former forcefulness.

A week into the trip, Grinnell, Schultz, and Yellowfish encountered a group of emboldened Kootenais who had followed the ancient trail over the mountains to hunt bighorn sheep, elk, moose, bear, and beaver.

Tough hunting only made the trip more worthwhile. Fish and birds were easy pickings, as Schultz had promised. The main attraction, bighorn sheep, was anything but. "The life of a sheep hunter is not one of luxurious ease," Grinnell related. "He must breast the steepest ascents and must seek for his game over ridges, along precipices and up peaks, and follow it to its home among the clouds. . . . The sheep hunter must have good lungs, tough muscles, a clear head and an iron nerve. . . . Sheep hunting is no boy's play."

It was a lesson learned firsthand. On September 10 Grinnell and two Kootenais climbed a steep ridge on the west side of the upper St. Mary Lake. He could not keep pace with his companions and was quickly left behind. "Soon it began to snow and blow and was so very cold," he wrote in his diary that night, "and I performed my customary operation of sitting on a rock and shivering."

After a while he heard a bighorn sheep snorting on the steep rock wall above, but the snow was so thick he could not make it out. He resumed his climb, and then, pausing to look upward, he spied the head of a sheep just visible over the ridge top. He sank behind a rock and waited. When he next looked up the slope, the sheep had moved closer. "Twice it stopped, once at about 200 yards and once at 100. . . . I tried to shoot but the snow blew so thickly that I could not see." The sheep continued farther across the slope and stopped a third time, behind a pile of rocks 150 yards away, leaving only its head and neck exposed. "I knew that it was now or never, for if it once got fairly by me, it would not stop within shooting distance. So I fired. The wild bound that the animal gave and the fact that it started at headlong speed down the hill assured me that my shot had told."

Grinnell followed the blood trail. "There is something rather horrible in the wild and savage excitement that one feels under such circumstances; the mingling of exultation over the apparently successful pursuit, tempered by the doubt about securing the prey, and then the fierce delight, temporary of course, when the capture is assured," he confessed in the account of the hunt he published in *Forest and Stream*. "It seems shocking that a respectable civilized and well-ordered being, such as a person of ordinary cultivation in the nineteenth century may be supposed to be, should, under any circumstances, indulge in such brutal feelings. It shows how thin is the veneer of civilization which hides the brute in our nature and how easily this veneer is rubbed off."

He found the sheep, a yearling ewe—"probably the best and sweetest meat I could have killed." The .45-caliber bullet had struck three inches below the head and ruptured the windpipe and one of the carotid arteries.

Now the harder work began. Gutted, the sheep weighed eighty pounds, possibly more, and to reach his horse, Grinnell had to lug the animal back up the rocky slope down which he had pursued it, some 1,500 vertical feet, then along the rough face of the mountain, and finally downhill for half a mile. "I am a little man, slight, and rather feeble . . . and usually find my own weight enough to carry," he humbly informed his readers. Indeed, he probably outweighed the sheep by only forty or fifty pounds. But pride, and the anticipation of fresh meat in camp, spurred him on. After a few fortifying pulls on his pipe, he lifted the sheep onto his back and, clutching his rifle, retraced his steps. At first he doubted he could make it one hundred yards, but by pausing every few feet, he found he was able to continue. He fell once on the sharp talus, "and it seemed to me as if a dozen holes had been punched in my ribs and my legs and arms broken." Finally he stumbled to his horse and packed the sheep across the saddle. That night in camp he shared his adventure with his companions. After he finished, Schultz said, "That mountain shall be called Singleshot Mountain from this day forth, in memory of your single shot."

And so it was. The mountain flanking the upper St. Mary Lake, to the north of the Going-to-the-Sun Road, continues to bear the name Singleshot.

On the fourteenth Grinnell, Schultz, and Yellowfish left the St. Mary Lakes and turned up Swiftcurrent Creek, the next corridor leading into the mountains to the north. The following two days would be another of the defining episodes in Grinnell's long career, for not only would the experience make a permanent impression on his memory and imagination, but, reciprocally, he would leave his signature on the geography that he took in at the head of Swiftcurrent.

They turned off the wagon road at St. Mary River and bundled a tent, blankets, bacon, bread, and frying pan on a single packhorse. In his diary Grinnell noted that the color of the creek was "pale greenish, and its aspect led me to suspect the existence of glaciers near the head of the stream." Passing a series of cascades, they reached what Grinnell called the "fifth lake" (today's Lake Josephine). From its shore, Grinnell admired a great triangular mountain looming above the western shore, and from a slope above the lake he could see a sixth lake farther along, above which he could make out a glacier on the high mountain headwall.

"I estimate this glacier is at least a mile in width, where visible," he observed. "The thickness of this mass of ice can scarcely be less than 100 feet and may be much more." Figuring that there would be no grass for the horses higher up, they made camp in a patch of green below the fifth lake. Nearby they found a recent Indian camp strewn with the bones of bighorn sheep and mountain goats. "We pitched our tent and after a good supper went to bed with high hopes for tomorrow."

In the morning they split up—Yellowfish to hunt, Grinnell and Schultz on foot to find a way to the glacier. Working their way through thick timber, loose rock, and blasts of wind, rain, and snow, they climbed nearly to the top of the mountain, and, as Grinnell recorded, "[A]t length [we] found ourselves on the upper edge of a great rocky amphitheatre. . . . Down through the midst of this great basin . . . foamed a great torrent, the sum of a thousand springs which flowed from the rocks and as many rivulets which crept out from beneath snowbanks."

From their position on a south ridge above the valley, they were not able to see the full scope of the glacier above them and so could not be sure if two glaciers or one hung from the headwall of the Continental Divide. They had viewed the southern portion of the glacier earlier, and now they could see only the northern portion. "In character it is very similar to the one to the south of it," Grinnell noted. "Like it, it falls over a cliff which shows through it, but it seems thicker. . . . I should take it to be 150 to 200 feet thick." Later, in writing up his narrative for *Forest and Stream*, he allowed, "It is quite possible that these two apparently distinct ice masses may be merely the two extremities of one glacier of great size." This point could only be clarified, he added, "by someone who shall visit this interesting country properly equipped with a pack train, so as to reach the ice." He vowed that he would be that person.

For he was smitten, dazzled, and deeply touched, like a wayfaring mendicant in a Renaissance cathedral. In his diary he endeavored to coax paint from his pencil: "The mountains today were spread out before us in a wonderful way. Never have I seen anything like them for raggedness and apparent inaccessibility. They seem to be all knife edges or pyramids or cones, and it is unusual to see one about these lakes that is square or round-topped. Up here the foliage has changed. . . . The rocks are of all hues, from gray through green and pink and dark red and purple, and the green of the willows, the yellow of the aspens and cottonwoods, the red of the mountain maple and ash, . . . the green and blue of the water, the fields of snow, the foaming cascades with their whirling mist, the dull green ice, and over all the leaden sky made a mass of color bewildering yet beautiful."

His name was not yet upon Grinnell Lake, Mount Grinnell, or Grinnell Glacier. But his spirit already was.

Descending from the glacier, exhausted and hungry, he and Schultz found that Yellowfish had reached camp ahead of them, but with no meat to show for his day of stalking sheep and goats. After another day of unsuccessful hunting, the trio started for the St. Mary Lakes, where they retrieved the wagon and headed for the Blackfeet agency, arriving on September 21.

Grinnell had never before spent time on an Indian reservation. At the beginning of the trip with Schultz, he had looked in at the Blackfeet school and was delighted by what he saw. "The children read quite nicely and write remarkably well," he wrote in his diary. "They seem bright and intelligent and are extremely interested in their work." Back at the agency three weeks later, Schultz arranged for Grinnell to witness a Thunder Pipe ceremony— Grinnell called it the "Bear Pipe"—performed by Red Eagle, the uncle of Schultz's wife. This was a special opportunity, for the pipe was normally unwrapped only during the medicine lodge, or sun dance, in July, but a number of Piegan horses had been stolen in recent days, and the pipe was to be lit to protect the warriors who were setting out in search of the horse thieves, presumed to be Crows.

While waiting for the ceremony to begin, Grinnell sat down on a log and began to make friends with the small children, "who were nearly as numerous as the dogs," he wrote. "There was one little fellow about two years old who quite won my heart by his genial smile and general air of cordiality. His clothing consisted of several strings of beads, a buckskin thong about the neck to which was attached a medicine stone, and an extremely abbreviated shirt, which came down just to his lower ribs. The rest of his person was covered only by a thick coating of mud. . . . This young savage marched up to me in the most confiding way, and after shaking hands in a matter-of-course, quite as if we had been equals, clambered up on my knee, and, having inspected my watch and chain and notebook until satisfied, sat there watching the antics of his seniors."

What sympathy Grinnell had developed for Indians during his hunt with the Pawnees thirteen years earlier was rekindled this day at the pipe ceremony, and his skill of observation and of recording those observations, honed as a naturalist, now transferred to recording the customs and rituals of the Piegans. Much of the spiritual subtlety of the ceremony undoubtedly went over his head, but the seating positions, the singing, the burning of sweet pine, and finally the ritual unwrapping of the sacred pipe found their way into his notebook with studious care. Schultz was not much good as a translator; for that, they were accompanied by Joe Kipp, owner of the trading post where Schultz worked.

Grinnell described Red Eagle as "a medicine man of great power, old and blind, gray hair, a massive face and a majestic presence." The pipe was "a handsome stem, about four feet long, wrapped for a part of its length with large, handsome beads, and profusely ornamented with white weasel tails and feathers," Grinnell jotted. "Near the lower, or pipe [bowl] extremity was a spread plume of twelve tail feathers of the war eagle, each one having its extremity wrapped with red or yellow horse hair, which hung down in a long tuft. Below this plume the stem was tied with red, green and yellow ribbons, and again below this was a cluster of brightly burnished hawks bell."

Red Eagle raised the pipe slowly to his face and made a cooing sound, then pressed it to his lips and raised his sightless eyes heavenward, as if to penetrate the skin of the lodge with his entreaty. After a while he moved the pipe over his arms, shoulders, and head and began to sing a song of supplication to the sun. Turning to his left, Red Eagle passed the pipe to Schultz, who spoke a few words and handed it to Grinnell, who held it to his face and made a short prayer to it, before passing it to an old blind warrior on his left. The old man offered his own prayer to the pipe and handed it to his neighbor. And so it was passed around the circle, while Red Eagle shook a rattle made from the scrotum of a buffalo bull and continued to sing.

The following morning at Joe Kipp's trading post, Grinnell struck up a conversation (Kipp interpreting) with Four Bears, whom Grinnell identified as the "camp orator." Four Bears asked where Grinnell came from, and Kipp explained that he "came from the end of the world, the edge of the salt water." As they talked further, Four Bears offered to give Grinnell a Blackfoot name.

"Four Bears stepped up to me and took me by the hand, led me out into the sunlight and faced me toward the sun," Grinnell described in his diary. "He took off his cap and I my hat. Then he prayed, 'Oh, Sun, oh, Old Man, look down. Have pity. Look on this man and me. Let us live. Many years ago, when I was a young man, I went up onto the top of the Sweet Grass Buttes, where all the Indians are afraid to go and staid there long, and while I slept, my medicine said to me, take the name *Pe-nut-u-ye-is-tsim-o-kan* (Fisher cap, i.e., cap made from the skin of a fisher). For many years I had that name, but now I am getting old, and before long I must die. I do not longer need this name, and now I give it to this, my son. Pity him. Give him long life. Keep him from all danger of every kind. When he goes into battle, let all the bullets miss him, or if any of them must hit, let them glance off from his body. Care for him and let him live. Make him strong. Let his children live very long and have abundance. Hear, Sun. Hear, Old Man. Pity, pity.' As he began his prayer he spat upon his hand and passed it over my head on either side and down over my shoulders, arms, and breast. Then he said to me, 'That is what you are called, *"Pe-nut-u-ye-is-tsim-o-kan."*'"

In return for his new name, Grinnell gave Four Bears a plug of tobacco, but it is not implausible that the exchange of gifts occurred in the opposite order. Either way, Grinnell and Four Bears each felt he had struck a fair bargain.

When he wrote up an abbreviated version of the naming ceremony for *Forest and Stream*, Grinnell titled it "A Christening." He had always been more a man of allegiance than of devotion. He was Scroll and Key for life, but despite his regular attendance at the Church of the Intercession when he was in New York, he was not especially faithful. However, something about Four Bears' gesture moved him in an entirely different way: Never before had anyone offered him a different identity.

Before boarding the stage that would take him homeward, Grinnell met with R. A. Allen, the government agent of the Blackfeet reservation, and received an overview of the tribe's condition. Allen assured him that the Indians were doing well, but, for all the Piegans' resilience, it was quite evident to Grinnell that they were still reeling from the catastrophe of two winters before, known thereafter as "the famine winter."

Up until 1883 the Piegans had been able to find enough buffalo on the northern plains to supplement the thin rations they received from the government. But by the fall of that year the buffalo were gone, and through the incompetence and underestimation of Allen's predecessor, John Young, there were too few rations on hand to feed the two and a half thousand Piegans on the reservation.

When Allen arrived in March to take over the agency, he visited a number of Piegan lodges to assess the disaster. Out of twenty-three lodges, he found a rabbit stewing in one pot and a steer hoof boiling in another. The other twenty-one lodges had no food at all. By spring, when more rations finally arrived, an estimated six hundred Piegans had died of starvation or the afflictions fed by hunger—one quarter of the tribe's population. Eighteen months later, in September 1885, the Piegans had not yet rebounded, and in certain respects never would.

The damage done the Piegans, and their ongoing plight, struck a chord in Grinnell. Ten years earlier he had watched Othniel Marsh advocate on behalf of the Sioux of the Red Cloud agency. Marsh had gone to Washington and presented samples of inedible rations to Commissioner of Indian

Affairs E. P. Smith and to the Board of Indian Commissioners and then aired his charges to the national press. He did not quit until President Grant consented to appoint a commission to investigate abuses on the reservation. Ultimately Marsh succeeded in having the agent at Red Cloud removed, and his concerted campaign to call attention to the corruption of the Bureau of Indian Affairs contributed to the less-than-voluntary resignation of Columbus Delano, Grant's secretary of the interior.

Shortly after Grinnell's return to New York, articles began appearing on the front page of *Forest and Stream* advocating for a better ration system, more and better schools for Indian children, and increased agricultural and industrial training for Indian adults. "It is quite certain that with a white man's training the Indian will make a good citizen," Grinnell stated. *Forest and Stream*, once strictly a sportsman's journal, was entering new territory.

The Montana trip had one final, unexpected byproduct. One Friday in mid-December an expressman appeared in the Forest and Stream offices on Park Row, announcing that he had a delivery for that address and insisting that it was too unwieldy to bring into the building. When Grinnell got down to the street, he found a crowd of pedestrians gaping at a large crate occupied by two grizzly bear cubs, approximately the size of Newfoundlands. Grinnell needed no paperwork to know the identity of the sender. The cubs had belonged to Joe Kipp, who had gotten them from a Piegan named Cut Bank John, who had shot the mother grizzly and captured her offspring. Kipp had kept them confined in a log stable behind his trading post, which is where Grinnell had last seen them. Whatever intimation he might have made to Kipp that the bears would be welcome in New York was now moot. And the reason why Kipp was willing to relinquish possession of the bears and go to the trouble of expressing them across the country was now manifest.

"Grizzly bears are healthy animals," Grinnell wrote with droll understatement in *Forest and Stream*. "They have good constitutions, and from cubs they all too soon develop into Old Ephraims"—a western term of respect, if not endearment, for the species. "Col. Kipp, with an interest not altogether unmixed with solicitude and apprehension as the expansion of girth and the muscular development of his interesting pets, began to envy the man who had lost a bear. It was probably with strangely mingled emotions, prompted by his embarrassment at the possession of the growing bears and his high regard for the *Forest and Stream*, that the Colonel finally decided to inclose the incipient monsters in a secure receptacle and ship them."

Grinnell, at least in the pages of his paper, was not one to look gift bears in the mouth. "It is needless to say that the *Forest and Stream* appreciated the gift," he continued by way of gratitude. "Our Bear Editor has lugged his rifle many a weary mile, looking for bears, and it was glorious good fortune to find two grizzlies right at hand, without even the necessity of crossing a ferry to get within range of the game."

Passersby on Park Row seemed to be equally grateful to have grizzly bear cubs in their midst. Some fed them loaves of bread. Little boys poked them with sticks. "The bears took it all in good part," Grinnell noted. "They also took in a collection of hats, cuffs and shreds of garments."

The cubs' visit to downtown Manhattan was short-lived, however. After brief negotiations, they were delivered to the zoo at Central Park, where at first they seemed to settle in satisfactorily. One lasted less than three years, dying of pneumonia, its hide preserved by a New York taxidermist. The other lived until 1893. Both received tender eulogies in *Forest and Stream*. "She was, as bears go—or more truly, as bears do not go—a creature of sweetness and light," read the send-off for the second. "All that a savage and ferocious bear of the wilderness should be, she was not. All that a civilized and polished bear of the town should be, she was."

In the fifteenth and final installment of "To the Walled-In Lakes," published in *Forest and Stream* in March 1886, Grinnell wrote: "Each year it is harder for me to turn my back on all that is left of the happy, free life of the olden time. The return to civilization is like the return to his dungeon of a prisoner who has been shown a glimpse of freedom."

But if he honestly felt imprisoned by work or family, it did not show. Nor was anything in his immediate circumstances an obvious cause for brooding. He missed his brother Frank and had mourned when Frank North had died the previous spring, of complications from a fall while riding for Buffalo Bill's Wild West. Other than that, Grinnell's life appeared robust and relatively cloudless. And lately two new acquaintances had made it even fuller. One was a man, nine years younger, to whom his name would be attached forever: Theodore Roosevelt. The other was a man, two years younger, whose friendship Grinnell would cherish deeply but never divulge entirely to anyone: George Gould.

DEAR PARTNER

B y 1885 George Bird Grinnell was *Forest and Stream,* and *Forest and Stream* was George Bird Grinnell. As much as he cared about amusing, engaging, and educating the American sportsman, thus expanding his readership, he gradually abandoned any pretense of comprehensiveness with respect to geography or subject matter. In every issue there still would be stories on, say, "Black Bass in Lake Champlain," "Rambles Through Newfoundland," or "Minnesota Duck Shooting." But more and more, *Forest and Stream* focused on the regions of the country Grinnell knew personally and the issues that he himself cared about most. Once he became interested in Indians, *Forest and Stream* became interested in Indians—though not all Indians, just the tribes he'd had contact with. Over the years, readers learned a lot about the Blackfeet and Cheyennes; next to nothing about Indians of the Southwest. When Grinnell grew concerned about Yellowstone, Yellowstone became an obsession of the journal; Yosemite or the Grand Canyon got shorter shrift. And so it went.

Some of this favoritism could be attributed to limited resources. Every week Grinnell, with the help of managing editor Charles Reynolds, worked to fill an issue with freelance submissions and field reports from a stable of irregular columnists who, though they may have been seasoned as sportsmen, were unpolished as journalists. Necessarily the editors had to write a good deal of the copy themselves, and in doing so, they tended to cover the ground they knew best.

New voices in the field of outdoor writing were always welcome, of course, provided they held to Grinnell's high standards of veracity and sportsmanship. In the issue of July 2, 1885, under the heading "New Publications," Grinnell offered a review of *Hunting Trips of a Ranchman*, written by twenty-six-year-old New York assemblyman Theodore Roosevelt, who was in his third term representing New York City. The book was printed on large, rich pages with spacious margins, handsome engravings, and a gold-stamped cover in a limited edition of five hundred. "Luxurious books upon the better class of field sports are certainly more highly appreciated now than they used to be," Grinnell wrote admiringly.

He likewise complimented the author's reputation as a public servant. "The excellent work which he has accomplished at Albany shows him to be—if nothing more—a person of exceptionally well-balanced mind, and calm deliberate judgment," Grinnell opined.

The Roosevelt family—well-to-do and philanthropic—was far more deeply established in New York society than the Grinnells. None of which kept Grinnell from critiquing the young Roosevelt's merits as a hunter, rancher, and naturalist. "I knew enough of Theodore Roosevelt—if only from his course in the New York Legislature—to feel that in all that he wrote he wanted to know the truth," Grinnell would explain after Roosevelt's death.

As the 1885 review continued, Grinnell declared with a note of avuncular condescension, "[His] experience of the Western country is quite limited, but this very fact in one way lends an added charm to his book. . . . Where Mr. Roosevelt details his own adventures he is accurate, and tells his story in simple, pleasant fashion, which at once brings us in sympathy with him."

But, Grinnell added, Roosevelt still had a great deal to learn. "We are sorry to see that a number of hunting myths are given as fact, but it was after all scarcely to be expected that with the author's limited experience he could sift the wheat from the chaff and distinguish the true from the false."

Theodore Roosevelt was not one to suffer a pat on the head or a cuff on the ear. Upon reading Grinnell's review in *Forest and Stream*, he called at Grinnell's office, red in the face from the midsummer heat and with his famous teeth bared. He was surely a *Forest and Stream* reader by then and ought not to have been surprised by the confident demeanor of the slim, pipe-smoking editor who greeted him and calmly announced that he was the author of the unsigned review. "He at once saw my point of view," Grinnell said of the meeting, "and after we had discussed the book and the habits of the animals he had described, we passed to the broader subject of hunting in the West."

They indeed had a lot in common. Like Grinnell, Roosevelt had grown up in New York—although in Roosevelt's case he had been born in the city proper, near Union Square. He, too, had witnessed Abraham Lincoln's funeral parade. Severely asthmatic—by his own admission "a sickly boy, with no natural body prowess"—young "Teedie" was bullied by boys of greater strength and stamina. He found escape in books, including those of James Fenimore Cooper and John James Audubon; none made a more lasting impression than the adventures of Mayne Reid. His brother Elliott was more beloved by their mother and was the better natural athlete in the family.

Trips to the country provided scant relief for Roosevelt's shortness of breath but aroused his curiosity for wild things and wild places. Birds were a beguiling abstraction until he turned fourteen and was fitted for eyeglasses; at the same time, he was also presented with his first shotgun. He learned taxidermy and filled a home museum with the specimens he killed. As an adolescent, his father took him aside and gave him the advice that changed, if not saved, his life: "Theodore, you have the mind but you have not the body, and without the help of the body the mind cannot go as far as it should. You must *make* your body."

Yet even after Roosevelt added muscles to his frame through weight-lifting and boxing and became a hale Harvard man, he could not retool his squeaky high voice or banish his near-sighted squint. The nicknames "Four Eyes" and "Storm Windows" followed him into adulthood, and when he reached the brutal arena of the New York Assembly in January 1882, at twenty-three its youngest member, he was pummeled with worse: "Young Squirt," "Punkin-Lily," "Jane-Dandy." Sizing up Roosevelt's gold-rimmed spectacles, hair parted down the middle with Edwardian sideburns, and tight trousers belled at the bottom, more than one wag took to calling him "Oscar Wilde," after the prissy English poet who was lecturing in America during the winter Roosevelt made his legislative debut.

Roosevelt's first trip to the frontier West, in September 1883, put such slanders behind him for good. Brother Elliott had recently returned from a trip to India, bearing skins and horns and thrilling tales from his big game hunts there. Roosevelt wanted his own trophy—a buffalo preferably, before they were all gone. With guides and hired horses, he rode among the sagebrush-covered buttes and coulees and across the vast, short-grass prairie of western Dakota Territory, until at last, after several misses, he succeeded in killing a large buffalo bull.

Not only had he secured his trophy, but before returning to New York at the end of the month, he also had invested $14,000 in a cattle ranch on the Little Missouri River, named Chimney Butte, its brand an eight-point Maltese cross. Earlier that same summer George Bird Grinnell had bought his own piece of the dream in the Shirley Basin of Wyoming, five hundred miles to the southwest.

Roosevelt returned for the winter session of the New York State Legislature, full of swagger from his Dakota conquests. Then in February, with no warning, he was knocked to his knees by the deaths of his wife, Alice, during childbirth, and, on the same night, in the same house, his mother, from typhoid fever. "The light has gone out of my life," a ruined Roosevelt managed to scribble in his diary for February 14—Valentine's Day.

Leaving his infant daughter, named for the mother she would never know, Roosevelt took his sorrow to the lonesome badlands of the Little Missouri in June 1885, throwing himself into ranching and hunting. He established a second ranch headquarters, Elkhorn, and in August he ventured westward into the Big Horn Mountains of Wyoming. This time his prizes included buffalo, antelope, elk, bighorn sheep, and bear. He described the destruction of buffalo as "a veritable tragedy of the animal world," but then declared that their extermination was "the only way of solving the Indian question." He acknowledged that elk were "doomed to extinction," then shot an elk near his ranch, "probably the last of his race that will ever be found in our neighborhood. . . . Such a chance was not to be neglected." He shot not one but three grizzlies, including a cub. Of the first kill he wrote: "[I]ndeed, it was over so quickly that the grizzly did not have time to show fight at all or come a step toward us. . . . I felt not a little proud, as I stood over the great brindled bulk."

In New York that winter he wrote up his exploits and placed the manuscript in the hands of G. P. Putnam's Sons. Reviews of *Hunting Trips of a Ranchman* were generally kind, as was Grinnell's—except in the places where it wasn't.

In the end, it was hard for Grinnell not to recognize some of himself in the double life of the spirited gentleman who strode into the *Forest and Stream* office. For the photograph on the frontispiece of his book, Roosevelt had worn an outfit similar to the one Grinnell had donned in the picture taken in a San Francisco studio in 1870. Roosevelt stands before a painted backdrop of ferns and flowers, dressed in fringed buckskin shirt and pants. Cinched around his waist is a broad belt fastened with a silver buckle, holding many cartridges and a large hunting knife in an engraved silver scabbard, said to have been made by Tiffany & Company. Like Grinnell in the 1870 photo, Roosevelt sports an almost manly moustache.

Grinnell's mixed review of *Hunting Trips of a Ranchman* was born of skepticism in Roosevelt's triumphs and trophies; Grinnell himself had never been so trigger-happy or so successful in a single season in the West. And there was another bone between them. As a staunch Republican, Roosevelt had worked hard to elect James G. Blaine in November 1884. Grinnell was not especially active in politics at that point, but he was among the Mugwumps—Republicans with their "mugs" on one side of the fence, their "wumps" on the other—who had shifted party allegiance and given the presidency to New York governor Grover Cleveland.

But any doubt, jealousy, or rivalry was quickly dispensed with, and over the years, with one or two exceptions, common ground marginalized any differences of personality between them. They were never together anywhere besides in the East, but they would spend many hours in each other's company in New York, Washington, and at Roosevelt's summer home on Long Island, where they conversed energetically and at length on their shared passions of ranching, hunting, and conservation. They were more like fellow travelers, complementary in their strengths, respectful of each other's unwavering good intentions and individuality.

Grinnell forged another relationship in 1885, this one harder to define. The first indication of it—the first indication that survives—comes in a series of poems, the first published in the May 21, 1885, issue of *Forest and Stream*. In keeping with the journal's custom, its author used a nom de plume, H. G. Dulog—an anagram for G. H. Gould.

George Huntington Gould was the younger brother of Grinnell's classmate Charles Winthrop Gould. Like the Grinnells, the Goulds had deep New England roots. Charles and George, banker's sons, grew up on Madison Square in New York. Inspired by Grinnell's stories of the Yale expedition with Professor Marsh, Charles Gould spent the summer of 1871 with the second team of Yale bone hunters in the West. After admission to the bar, he entered practice on Wall Street, not far from the *Forest and Stream* offices. He and Grinnell did not exactly chum around, but their paths crossed often. At some point during those first years after Yale, Charles introduced Grinnell to his brother George.

One of the reasons why so little is known about how the two Georges first met is because Grinnell did not keep a diary while he was in New York. His letter books do not begin until August 1886. Even then, the letters to George Gould are few and, by the less-than-private conditions of their dictation—to a stenographer in a busy office—they are cautious in language and sentiment. No handwritten letters from Grinnell to George Gould have surfaced so far.

What can be pieced together is that George Gould went to Harvard instead of Yale. A classmate who ran into him some years after their graduation in 1872 described Gould as looking "exceedingly vigorous and as strong as in the days when he rowed on our class crew." A photo of Gould, taken later in life, reveals broad shoulders and a handsome, healthy countenance—firm cheeks, solid jaw, rich moustache, and confident, engaging eyes.

His energy and range of intellectual curiosity are evident in his early movements after Harvard. He did not last as a civil engineer on the New York Central and Hudson River Railroad. He spent a year in Paris at the prestigious École Libre des Sciences Politique, returning to New York to earn a law degree. He then went to work for the Mutual Life Insurance Company, a confinement that did not suit him for long. In 1881 his Harvard class correspondent reported that Gould was "now prospecting in the mining regions of Mexico." The notice also mentioned, "Is unmarried."

Gould made several extended trips to Mexico, and in the fall of 1883 he went to Dakota Territory on another mining matter. None of these forays made him rich, although, with the death of his father, accumulating a new fortune was never a paramount ambition. In early 1884 he went to Santa Barbara, likely not for the first time, to visit his brother Fred, a doctor who had self-prescribed Pacific air and sunshine for his frail health. By then George Gould knew George Grinnell well enough to send him several poems.

Like the Indian stories Grinnell had been publishing in *Forest and Stream* of late, "Santa Barbara in Spring" and "The Bull Fight" were not a natural fit for "A Weekly Journal of the Rod and Gun." But who was to tell Grinnell otherwise? In the first poem, Gould salutes Santa Barbara for its "fruitful farms," "plumed shafts of verdant pine," and canyons "hung with bloom." The second poem is a romantic paean to the pageantry of the Mexican bullfight, as witnessed by the poet—H. G. Dulog—in an amphitheater "whose sands/Had reeked for years with bloody sacrifice." He describes the performance of the matador as high art, a passion play for the sensualist heart.

Careful he stands spreading his scarlet flag
On the stretched point of his red-hilted sword
And swerving always from the lumbering charge
Till chance be given for the fatal blow.
Even then for once he fails—the ill-aimed blade
Slips on the shoulder, glancing on the bone,
Comes bent and bloody from the ragged wound
That serves but to enrage; and now at length

With better nerve he points the mortal steel
Right where the crested withers leave the neck,
And leaning forward drives the weapon in
Up to the quivering hilt. . . . .

Grinnell published Gould's poems under the ready rubric, "The Sports-man Tourist," with no note of explanation. Three months later, in the middle of the seventh installment of "To the Walled-in Lakes," he contrived an excuse to run yet another of Gould's poems. While ruminating on the spiritual beliefs of the Kootenais, Grinnell's train of thought digressed to "some lines written in the shadow of an old Spanish mission by my friend H. G. Dulog":

In Orient old; in states yet new,
Whose broad foundations scarce are planned;
In crowded towns; where far and few
The settlers' rough-hewn cabins stand;
On Arctic ice or tropic stand;
Where holy church has work to do
God's servants find their native land.

At least a bullfight could be loosely considered outdoor sport. This last poem was pure indulgence, a public gift to a special friend.

Reading between the lines, it is impossible to discern whether Grinnell at this point recognized that Gould was homosexual; few men dared advertise themselves as such in the late nineteenth century. Certainly nothing in the poems suggests so, except maybe the image of the bullfighter plunging his blade up "to the quivering hilt."

Neither in 1886 nor during the forty years of friendship that followed would either of the men drop a clue that they desired or, for that matter, consummated sexual relations. Yet over time it would become apparent, in their encounters and correspondence, that their attraction belonged in a different category, one that they perhaps dared not articulate out loud and surely did not wish to explain to others. In his letters Grinnell usually addressed Gould as "Partner"—a play on the western salutation, "Howdy, pardner," and one that he used for no other man in his life. This is a small detail that, in and of itself, proves nothing. Even so, it is one of many.

On the other side of the ledger there is also evidence of Grinnell's interest in women at this time. At the end of August 1886 he set out for Yellowstone, his third trip in as many summers. In his diary for September 4, written from Old Faithful, he confided, "Passed a wretched night either sleepless and worrying about F. or dreaming about her." The identity of F. is not revealed, nor probably will it ever be. At the end of the trip he wrote again in his diary that he had telegraphed "F. B. M." A few pages later a poem appears—in Grinnell's familiar handwriting, with several changes indicating it was an original work in progress.

> She is gone and my aching heart is torn
> With a grief time can never erase

Several more stanzas follow, not entirely legible but equally mawkish and mournful.

> I dream then that time has backward flown
> I treat [?] once more in her honeyed tongue
> And she whom I loved is all my own
> As when hope was strong and my love was young

Later, in the same notebook but in ink instead of pencil, an afterthought:

> Fare the[e] well my darling, wherever thou art
> Fondly I loved thee and trusted thee too.
> You've shattered my faith and you've broken my heart,
> Never again can I think woman true.

With that, Miss F. or F. B. M. passed from his life, with the exception of one final exhalation of despair, which came in a letter to Lute North four months later: "Since I saw you, I have had lots of money troubles and have lost the girl that I loved better, I think, than I did my life, but I have borne it all pretty well, because I have kept constantly working."

The nature and object of Grinnell's romance can only be conjectured, but it seems mildly coincidental that he was moved to try his hand at verse so soon after publishing George Gould's poems. At any rate, Gould was also on his mind. On the same day that Grinnell wired F. B. M., he sent a telegram to Gould, confirming their plans to meet up in Shirley Basin later in the month.

"He is a very good fellow; a thorough gentleman and a man of great cultivation," Grinnell would say of Gould. "Like everyone else, he has his peculiarities, but to me they are not unpleasant ones."

Grinnell also invited Lute North to join them in Wyoming. Gould and North had never met, and it had been a while since Grinnell had seen either of them. Gould had recently made up his mind to settle in Santa Barbara. But before making the move, a hunting trip guided by Grinnell was not to be passed up. Lute North, meanwhile, had also changed addresses. The Norths and Bill Cody had sold their Nebraska ranch in 1882, and after Frank's death, Lute had taken a job as a federal tax collector in the Black Hills. Ever since Grinnell had bought his own ranch, he had been wanting to show it to North and get some advice from his old friend.

They had no luck hunting elk on the mountain above the ranch, and so they switched to the sagebrush flats below. For all of Lute North's reputation as a marksman, it was Gould who won the day. "After dinner took light wagon and went out north toward Dry Creek after antelope," Grinnell recorded in his diary on October 2. "Gould killed 4. L.H.N. & G.B.G. none." Regardless of the score, the threesome got along famously. Before going their separate directions, Grinnell suggested that next year they make a trip to the St. Mary Lakes of Montana.

PART THREE

PRESERVATION, RESERVATION

(1886–1897)

CHAPTER 11

THE AUDUBON SOCIETY

G rinnell's complaint to Lute North that he was "kept constantly working" likely referred to a cause that had demanded a growing portion of his time over the past couple of years: the excessive killing of birds—and not just game birds, but also species whose feathers were used to adorn women's hats.

"We must realize how important this matter is, and must realize it now," Grinnell had written in *Forest and Stream* in the summer of 1884. "The number of birds killed every month for millinery and other purposes is immense, and the number of people engaged in their pursuit is constantly increasing. We shall lose all our small birds unless something is done." Songbirds, he lectured, were critical to agriculture, because of the number of harmful insects they ate. Besides, he added, "we must reflect on the pleasure we all derive from the presence of birds. It is a great delight not only to hear them but [also] to watch them, and to understand, as we can by careful observation, their ways and life. When we consider the enjoyment they have given us and the good they are constantly doing, should we not make some effort to prevent their extermination?"

Subsequent issues of the journal exposed "the industry of slaughtering birds for their feathers"—butchery for the sake of bonnets. Finally, on February 11, 1886, *Forest and Stream* issued a manifesto.

"Very slowly the public are awakening to see that the fashion of wearing the feathers and skins of birds is abominable," began the rallying cry. "There is, we think, no doubt that when the facts about this fashion are known, it will be frowned down and will cease to exist. Legislation of itself can do little against this barbarous practice, but if public sentiment can be aroused against it, it will die a speedy death."

Grinnell directed his attention away from the hunters of endangered birds and away from the men who sold them and turned to the consumers of the ill-gotten feathers—women. "The reform in America, as elsewhere, must be inaugurated by women, and if the subject is properly called to their notice, their tender hearts will be quick to respond."

He announced the formation of "an association for the protection of wild birds and their eggs." For its name he suggested that of someone near and dear to him. "In the first half of the century there lived a man who did more to teach Americans about birds of their land than any other who ever lived. His beautiful and spirited paintings and his charming and tender accounts of the habits of his favorites have made him immortal, and have inspired his countrymen with an ardent love for the birds."

The new association would be called the Audubon Society.

The rules of the Audubon Society were threefold. Grinnell called for an end to killing of any wild bird not used for food; an end to the destruction of nests and eggs of all wild birds; and an end to "the wearing of feathers for ornaments or trimming for dress." (Ostrich feathers were specifically exempted.) To become a member of the Audubon Society, one simply had to sign a pledge to adhere to the rules. In return, a member received a certificate bearing a portrait of John James Audubon. Children were welcomed; admission was free.

The idea for the society had not sprung fully formed from Grinnell but had been inspired by several other forces that had gained momentum in recent years. In 1873 the Nuttall Ornithological Club had been formed by a group of bird-loving friends in Cambridge, Massachusetts. Ten years later several of its members attended a convention of ornithologists held at the American Museum of Natural History in New York, at which a plan for an organization of more national scope took hold: the American Ornithologists' Union. Grinnell was an early joiner.

One of the AOU's first efforts was to conduct a thorough inventory of American birds. The data collected by the AOU Committee on Migration and Distribution was vast; letters poured in from lighthouse keepers and thousands of amateur observers responding to notices in magazines and newspapers (including *Forest and Stream*). The study was so fruitful that in 1885 the AOU was able to persuade Congress to appropriate $5,000 to continue the work begun by the union, particularly as it related to the benefits of birds to agriculture. A year later Congress voted more money and created a new Division of Economic Ornithology and Mammalogy, under the direction of thirty-year-old C. Hart Merriam—AOU member, zoologist, medical doctor, Yale man, and friend of George Bird Grinnell. (Merriam, in turn, would expand his portfolio into the Division of Biological Survey, the grandfather of today's U.S. Fish and Wildlife Service.)

Grinnell was active on a different AOU Committee, this one focused on how best to *protect* North American birds. One of its first tasks was to quantify the devastation of native populations. The numbers were shocking: forty thousand terns killed in a single month near Philadelphia; seventy thousand birds from a single village in Long Island supplied to New York dealers in a mere four months. The committee's report estimated that in one year five million birds had been killed for the millinery trade. Many were shipped to Europe, where the vogue of feathers had reached baroque extremes. (The term "milliner" comes from the Italian *Milano*.)

Grinnell participated in the drafting of a series of "model laws," which proposed legislation, tailored for specific states, to halt the destruction of birdlife. Accordingly, in his initial announcement of the creation of the Audubon Society, he declared that the society's work would be "auxiliary" to that of the AOU and would "further the efforts of the A. O. U. committee" on protection. Defining the problem was only a start; Grinnell grasped that the solution lay in educating and mobilizing the public.

Throughout the spring of 1886, *Forest and Stream* banged the drum for the Audubon Society. Nearly every issue carried a letter from a distinguished voice, decrying the destruction of birds and endorsing the society, among them poets Oliver Wendell Holmes and John Greenleaf Whittier, newspaper editor Charles Dudley Warner (coauthor, with Mark Twain, of *The Gilded Age*), and the American Humane Society. Henry Ward Beecher sermonized against the "slaughter of the innocents." Because women created the demand for feathers, the reverend wrote, "it rests upon them to stay this wanton destruction." Nature writer John Burroughs seconded Beecher: "It is barbarous taste which prompts our women and girls to appear on the street with their head gear adorned with the scalps of our songsters."

An even more effective volley was fired by a young man named Frank Chapman, who, at the time, was employed in the collections department of a New York bank. He had been one of the first to volunteer for the AOU's bird survey. Yet it was another, more impromptu survey that he conducted on his own that had the greatest impact—if not as science, then as agitprop.

"The streets of New York City do not offer a productive field for the ornithologist," Chapman would write in *Autobiography of a Bird-Lover*. Nevertheless, on two consecutive afternoons he decided to walk along Fourteenth Street, then the busiest shopping street in the city, and count the species of birds whose feathers ornamented women's hats. "It is probable that few if any of the women whose headgear formed part of my record knew that they were wearing the plumage of the birds of our gardens, orchards and forests," he remarked.

Chapman's results were tabulated in *Forest and Stream*: robin, four; bluebird, three; Wilson's black-capped flycatcher, three; waxwing, twenty-three; golden-winged woodpecker, twenty-one; snow bunting, fifteen; blue jay, five; scarlet tanager, three; Baltimore oriole, nine. This was just a sampling of the forty species he could identify positively; many other feathers he could not name. But of seven hundred hats observed, 77 percent had feathers.

Surprisingly, Chapman's list did not include a single egret. Few birds were in greater demand than egrets—two species specifically, the snowy egret and the great egret. Their coveted feathers—the most perfect of which could command more than their weight in gold—are at their lushest during the breeding and nesting season, which meant that hunters who shot egrets in the swamps, bays, and barrier islands of the South killed not only the adult birds but doomed the eggs and baby birds of the egret rookery. Perhaps it was a fluke, a seasonal aberration, that Chapman saw no egrets on Fourteenth Street. But already egret feathers were becoming scarce, and the concern of Chapman, Grinnell, and those sympathetic with the causes of the AOU and Audubon Society was that the elegant egret would go the way of the great auk, the Carolina parakeet—or the once-prolific passenger pigeon, whose population, like that of the buffalo, had gone from impossible to estimate to impossible to find.

The shaming did its job. Membership pledges deluged *Forest and Stream*. By June the Audubon Society boasted ten thousand members; by the end of the year that number had nearly doubled, with more than three hundred local chapters. "The movement is confined to no one section of the land," Grinnell announced. "From Maine, from Florida, from Louisiana, from California and from Canada come assurances that our hands will be upheld to the work which we have undertaken." The Society for the Prevention of Cruelty to Animals, actually a federation of state societies, the first of which was founded in New York in 1866, lent its wholehearted support. Especially encouraging was the formation of branch societies by female college students. Women wrote of stripping feathers from their hats and burning them. They began calling hats without feathers "Audubonnets."

The contagion of the Audubon movement was a mixed blessing for Grinnell and managing editor Charles Reynolds, who had to field the flood of letters, keep track of hundreds of society branches, and issue certificates of membership, in addition to putting out a weekly edition of *Forest and Stream*. In January 1887 they added further to their workload by publishing *Audubon Magazine*, issued monthly to exhort the disparate branches under one banner. The first eight numbers carried a biography of Audubon written by Grinnell. Tips for bird watchers and profiles of different birds were regular fare, many of them provided by female contributors. The price was six cents a copy, which hardly covered the expense of composition and distribution.

Meanwhile, the feather and fashion industry, in Europe and North America, was full-throated in its attacks on the Audubon Society, the AOU, and *Forest and Stream*. It was patent hypocrisy, the opposition argued, for *Forest and Stream*, a magazine for men who killed birds for sport, to stand against the shooting of songbirds.

Grinnell refuted the charge in a front-page editorial: "There is nothing inconsistent in the attitude of *Forest and Stream*," he asserted. "Simply because a man pursues and kills game birds and animals which, so far as we may reason from analogy, were created expressly for men to hunt and kill, it does not follow that he is bent on the foolish and wicked extermination of other birds who were created to gladden the world with their beauty and song and to wage their warfare against the noxious insect hosts. As a matter of fact, the average sportsman recognizes more fully than the average non-shooting man the economic value of such as the Audubon Society is concerned with. The sportsman, through his clubs and journals, has secured many of the best bird protective laws now in force."

Forest and Stream's readers were not disconcerted by the suggested incongruity. By the end of 1886 the journal announced that it was "enjoying the support of a wider circle of friends than at any former period in its history." Four months later it was able to increase its pages from twenty-eight to thirty-two. The formula was working: In addition to maintaining its position as "the chosen exponent of those who seek recreation with gun or rod, rifle, canoe, or yacht," *Forest and Stream* had succeeded in purveying the notion that there was no more effective steward of wildlife and its habitat than the sportsman—that is, the class of sportsman defined and encouraged in its pages.

With the Audubon Society Grinnell had shaped the voices of a sympathetic citizenry into a chorus. Once roused, however, this chorus proved difficult to manage. By 1889 membership in the society would reach nearly fifty thousand; yet, with membership free and the magazine nearly so, *Forest and Stream's* losses were directly proportional to the movement's success. Finally, in January 1889, Grinnell would confess that the magazine required "a great deal more labor than our busy staff can well devote to it." Reluctantly he announced to his readers that publication would cease forthwith.

And so the Audubon Society lost its binding agent. Lacking central leadership, individual societies flickered and faded. Still, public concern for songbirds and efforts to protect them—furthered by the AOU and in the pages of *Forest and Stream*—persisted, even as the feather trade continued to tickle the fashion fancy of a majority of American women. In 1896 two wealthy Boston women, Harriet Hemenway and her cousin Minna Hall, would found the Massachusetts Audubon Society "to discourage buying and wearing for ornamental purposes the feathers of any wild bird, to otherwise further the protection of our native birds." Other states soon followed their lead, and in 1905 Grinnell's original idea of a confederation of bird defenders was reborn as the National Association of Audubon Societies, which continues today as the National Audubon Society, one of the most respected and effective forces for conservation and education in the country, if not the world.

CHAPTER 12

THE ROCK CLIMBERS

As the Audubon Society had proven, Grinnell was energetic, but not tireless. "You ask me to tell you about myself," he wrote to Jack Fannin, a naturalist he had befriended during his trip to British Columbia. "I am neither married nor dead. . . . I do not get ahead very fast and have not succeeded in accumulating either wealth or fame to any considerable extent. My health is not good because I am always overworked."

The heavy workload was self-inflicted, and it was almost as if he burdened himself with so many tasks and causes in order to heighten the relief that came when he was finally able to escape westward. Throughout the early part of 1887 he wrote frequently to Lute North and George Gould, promoting their next outing, this time to the Walled-in Lakes of Montana. "Really it begins to look as if we might go, and if we do, what a good time we will have," he told North. "We will just live on the fat of the land. . . . You will pursue the ferocious grizzly to his lair, and single handed conquer him, and bear your bleeding trophies back in triumph to the camp; Gould will chase the wary bighorn from crag to crag, and I will painfully scramble up the mountains after white goats. . . ."

"My dear old man"—North was three years older—"it will be the grandest country you ever saw."

Lute North seldom answered promptly, and his erratic correspondence was a chronic source of frustration to Grinnell, who allowed that North, for all his charms, "was not at home with the pen." In January Grinnell wrote, "[T]he arrival of your letters are so like angels' visits that I try never to waste any time in replying."

A month later Grinnell was unsettled by an ambiguous remark North had made in one of his irregular communications. "You said that something had happened," Grinnell replied to North, "and that you did not know whether you should ask me to congratulate [you or] not, and I took it for granted that you were going to be married. It scared me so that I haven't got my breath back yet, and—although you may not have intended to alarm me—I cannot help feeling that I should like to thwack you a few times with a stout young club."

Marriage of course would prevent North from joining Grinnell and Gould in Montana, but it would also be a betrayal of their bachelor brotherhood. As it turned out, no wedding bells rang—not yet.

Gould was a more reliable mark. He had outshot his companions the previous summer, although his enthusiasm was less for stalking game than for the enjoyment of good fellows in a new country. In response to Gould's query about who would be included on the Montana trip, Grinnell assured his friend that he had invited no one besides him and North, with James Willard Schultz as outfitter. "Four or five men have asked to go, but I have strongly told them that our party was [filled] up last Oct., and that I could not dare to suggest any additions."

In closing he thanked Gould for his kind invitation to visit him in Santa Barbara, before or after the Montana trip. Gould had recently purchased forty acres in the nearby coastal community of Montecito, where he was to live until his death, without ever returning to New York. One of Gould's Harvard class reports would provide a brief glimpse of the life he made for himself there: "He has his law office on the sunny side of State Street, and his home in Montecito [is] approached by a lovely winding drive through the live oaks. Here he lives with his books and his Chinaman and is as devoted as ever to his favorite Gibbon"—Edward Gibbon, author of *The*

History of the Decline and Fall of the Roman Empire—"whose ponderous periods he still can freely and affectionately quote."

"How I should like to [join] you. . . . But I can't do it," Grinnell replied to Gould's invitation to California. This was the first of many bids to be with Gould that Grinnell would decline over the years. He much preferred to pick the time and place of their meetings, and, for a few years in the late 1880s, he was the more successful persuader.

In mid-July Grinnell made a hasty but necessary trip to Wyoming to check on his ranch. The previous winter had been epically brutal. Livestock, already weakened by drought, died by the tens of thousands. Come spring, some ranchers found not a single living animal carrying their brand. Fair-weather investors lost their stomach and abandoned the market, never to return. "Well, we have had a perfect smashup all through the cattle country," Theodore Roosevelt wrote to Henry Cabot Lodge in the spring. "The losses are crippling." Roosevelt described the range as "a mere barren waste; not a green thing could be seen; the dead grass eaten off till the country looked as if it had been shaved with a razor." Thereafter he would spend little time on his Dakota ranch.

Grinnell did not hear much from his man, William Reed, during the winter of "the Big Die-Up," as it came to be called. The Shirley Basin had been stricken by its share of blizzards and weeks of sub-zero temperatures, but Grinnell's ranch was stocked mostly with horses, and evidently there was grass and hay enough to keep nearly all of them from starving. Still, he felt he was losing his shirt. "There is something wrong," he complained to Reed in April. "The bills are too heavy and the improvements not enough."

He went to Wyoming in a foul humor—exacerbated by "digestive difficulties" and "facial neuralgia" that impaired his eyesight. Like Roosevelt, he derived little satisfaction from ranching anymore, and he determined to either sell or lease his Shirley Basin holdings. "[F]or a couple of weeks I had as bad a time as I think I ever had," Grinnell wrote Lute North upon his return to New York. In the end, he succeeded in leasing the ranch and its livestock for three years. Even then, he did not break even. "My ranch project proved a financial failure," he would write in his memoirs.

As the date of the fall trip to Montana neared, Grinnell refused to give up on Lute North. "You must do it, Lute," he exhorted. "You and I are very old. . . . Together we have seen the prairies change from deserts to farms; together we have seen the mountains fill up with white men. The men with whom we [rode], where are they? . . . Who is now left? . . . Come, will you go with me?"

North never said no; he simply did not answer the stream of letters Grinnell wrote, right up to his departure from New York at the end of September. That left Gould, who traveled by ship from Santa Barbara to Vancouver and on October 1 met up with Grinnell and Schultz at the Canadian Pacific depot at Lethbridge, just north of the border and some seventy miles from the St. Mary Lakes.

In his published account of the month-long adventure, titled "The Rock Climbers," Grinnell referred to his camp mates pseudonymously. Schultz went by his Blackfoot name, Appekunny. Gould, or H. G. Dulog, was the Rhymer. Grinnell was Old Yo. And two weeks into the trip they were joined by a new man, J. H. Monroe, whom Schultz had recruited to help with the guiding and camp-tending.

Jack Monroe was two years younger than Grinnell, with a sketchy background and colorful recent history. Census reports suggest that his parents came west with the Mormon migration. Monroe received little formal schooling and paid even less attention to the teachings of the Latter-Day Saints. When he first arrived in Montana is not clear, but he soon established a reputation as hard-working and self-sufficient, but also with a wild streak. Like Schultz, Joe Kipp, and quite a few other white men who lived along the border, Monroe had seen gainful opportunity in running whiskey from Montana to the native reserves in Canada, where sale of spirits was strictly outlawed. The North-West Mounted Police had been established a decade earlier in an effort to stem this forbidden traffic along the Whoop-Up Trail, as the bootleggers' route was known. At some point Monroe had been wounded in a scrape with the Mounties and placed under guard in the hospital at Fort Macleod, west of Lethbridge. Before he had fully healed up, he managed to escape and made his way back across the border to the St. Mary Lakes. He had regained his rugged health by October 1887, when he joined Grinnell, Gould, and Schultz. But he remained a wanted man in Canada.

Over the next few days, the foursome paired off, Grinnell with Schultz, Gould with Monroe, to hunt for goats on the ridges above upper St. Mary. Flattop, Singleshot, Goat, and Red Eagle mountains were familiar land-marks from two years earlier. "When I started out I could not get thirty yards up the hill without stopping and panting as if I were going to die right there," Grinnell wrote to Lute North. Gradually he found his legs and his wind, but game was scarce. The weather grew colder, the wind worsened, and winter sent more snow. Grinnell killed a couple of mountain goats and a lynx that was robbing their camp, but Gould shot nothing besides a few ducks—and at a bear, which he missed.

Gould was a good sport, if somewhat less than a dedicated sportsman. They all shared a tent, and one morning Grinnell awoke to find a few lines of doggerel the Rhymer had scribbled on one of the canvas walls. Three of the eighteen installments of "The Rock Climbers" would bear the byline H. G. Dulog. The first was a Dickensian send-up of his trip from Vancouver to Lethbridge on the Canadian Pacific. His second contribution to the series is adventure in verse, with prefatory apologies to Wordsworth:

> Hark! The report. The mountains ring.
> There speeds the ball that spoils the spell,
> Far Kootenai is answering,
> And Singleshot rolls back the swell,
> Good news, good news the echoes bring
> When cracks the rifle of Grinnell.

By October 26 Gould had had enough of mountain life and departed for Lethbridge. "I was sorry to see Gould go," Grinnell wrote in his diary. In a letter to Lute North he elaborated: "Gould left me because we had bad weather, very cold and snowy . . . and because he had bad luck hunting and hadn't killed anything. Moreover, he is somewhat of an invalid and has to take some of his whiskey, and his stock of that ran out, and so he went in." Grinnell was surely exaggerating Gould's invalidism; by all evidence, Gould got around as nimbly as any of the others in the party.

Three days after Gould's departure an unexpected visitor rode into camp. Lieutenant John H. Beacom was commander of mounted troops at Fort Shaw, on the Sun River, west of the newly minted town of Great Falls. Grinnell's diary does not mention Beacom's official reason for roaming through the foothills of the Rocky Mountains, but perhaps he and his small detachment of soldiers were on the lookout for whiskey traders. At any rate, Grinnell and the thirty-year-old Beacom took an immediate liking to each other, and Grinnell encouraged Beacom to accompany him to the Swiftcurrent valley. Caching most of their outfit and leaving the rest of the soldiers in camp at St. Mary, Grinnell, Beacom, Schultz, and Monroe, with three pack mules and a week's worth of grub, headed up the trail that led to the ladder of lakes Grinnell had ascended in 1885 and, ultimately, to the glacier above them.

En route to Swiftcurrent they spotted a group of Indians coming from the mountains. "Then a sadness fell upon the four," Grinnell wrote, "for if a lot of Indians had been hunting on the head of Swift Current, it would not be easy for [us] to get any game there. Schultz said that they were probably Piegans, for it was too late in the season for the Kootenais to be about the lakes, and—here came a supposition that would shape the future of the region—he suggested, optimistically, that "the Piegans are notoriously poor mountain hunters and do not penetrate far into the frowning rock cañons, nor climb on the jagged icebound peaks."

Grinnell had no such hesitancy. On November 1 he and his companions worked their way through an inhospitable maze of timber, the pines so close together that they were forced to lead their saddle horses and mules. They arrived in camp at the head of the fifth lake with packs askew and clothing torn. "Altogether it was a most vexatious ride, and I used more profanity than I usually do," Grinnell admitted in his diary.

Both Grinnell and Beacom carried cameras and took pictures of the glacier looming above them. Grinnell had very little experience with the delicate plates and sensitive shuttering, and his photographs would prove a disappointment. Fortunately Beacom was better skilled, and several of his images yet survive, revealing a husky, glowering glacier—an ominous benchmark that would measure the dramatic retreat forthcoming over the next century and a half.

In "The Rock Climbers," published upon his return to New York, Grinnell assigned no names to the geographic features at the head of Swiftcurrent, other than "Fifth Lake," "Sixth Lake," and so on. The glacier above the lakes was simply "the glacier." In his diary, however, he took greater liberty. On October 31, for instance, he wrote, "Up before light, breakfast by 7 and started for the glacier at head of 6th lake (Grinnell's lake) or rather to find out if it is accessible." The next day's entry reads: "Packed two mules and started for Grinnell's lake, as we have named the one that flows into 5th Swift Current Lake."

Yet when it came to naming the glacier, he avoided taking credit. "Camped at head of lake, intending tomorrow, if fair, to try to make the glacier. Beacomb [sic] proposes to call this Grinnell's glacier. I protested and he may not carry out his intention."

On November 2 they ate breakfast by moonlight and before daybreak began the scramble to the ice—all except Beacom, who decided that an "old hurt" would impede his climbing and that he ought to be getting back to his soldiers. Grinnell had come this far in 1885; from here on, he was breaking new ground.

They followed the stream that empties into the head of the Fifth Lake, crossed a side creek (today's Cataract), and reached the shore of the Sixth— henceforth Grinnell—Lake, which they estimated to be a mile in diameter, its water green and slightly milky. Looming above on the south side of the lake was "the solid wall of a peak which we named Monroe's Peak," Grinnell recorded in his diary. Further along, at the head of Grinnell Lake, "There rises a thousand feet of precipice over which plunges the water fall from the glacier," the diary continued. And to the north "Grinnell Mt. rises abruptly in a series of rocky ledges to a great height." With little ceremony and less modesty, he claimed another landmark in the name of Grinnell.

The main attraction, needless to say, was the glacier itself, which hung above them like a "white waving line of foam," Grinnell would write in *Forest and Stream*. The lip of the glacier was split in the middle by a tumbling torrent, "dashing itself to spray in its fall." For a few moments the mountaineers stood in awe.

Schultz carried Grinnell's camera on his back; Monroe carried a shotgun; Grinnell carried his rifle, in hopes that he might happen upon a sheep or goat on the ice. But first they had to find a way up. "The mountains did not invite ascent," Grinnell wrote. "[T]hey seemed rather to defy it; to smile coldly and say in their voiceless speech, 'Untrodden by white man's foot we have stood since the foundations of the world were laid. If you can surmount us, do so.'"

The most promising approach appeared to be the grooved channel carved by the glacier's spillway. "Slowly and carefully they climbed upward," Grinnell recounted, "often crossing the stream from one side to the other, clinging with tenacious grip to each little spruce twig, thrusting their fingers into the crevices in the rock, and fitting their feet on every knob or projecting splinter or roughness that would aid them. Sometimes holding on with elbows, knees, calves, yes, even with their chins . . . inch by inch and foot by foot they made their way upward."

Getting from one side of the cascade to the other was a test of courage. "The boulders which lay in it were smooth as glass, and the fine mist which rose from the falling waters froze on them, making them very slippery. Long jumps from one to the other had to be made and often in places where a slip would ensure a fall of forty or fifty feet sheer on to rough rocks below."

Two-thirds of the way up, they came to a series of ledges, grassy slopes, and snowdrifts that made the rest of the way less arduous and considerably less perilous. At last they came to the northeastern flank of the glacier itself, bracketed by a lateral moraine of boulders that the ice had plowed into a ridge fifty or sixty feet high. Grinnell, Schultz, and Monroe did not dare venture very far onto the ice. They had not thought to bring ice axes or rope. Nor did they carry any surveying instruments. Grinnell's best estimate was that the glacier encompassed a basin two miles wide by three or more deep, and it comprised "two principal masses, the lower of these covering a great extent of ground and running up into the little ravines and gorges of the mountains on either side." The upper mass—known today, in its shrunken state, as the Salamander for its slinky, horizontal profile—"rests on a ledge which runs far back among the peaks, and in its slow motion is constantly falling over the cliff and uniting with the lower mass." He calculated that the thickness of the lower ice was seven hundred feet; the upper ice perhaps three hundred. Later, studying the entire glacier through a telescope, he guessed that it occupied some three thousand vertical feet of the mountainside. (Or so he stated in "The Rock Climbers"; in his diary he estimated "1500 or 2000 feet.")

They paused for a lunch of bread and cheese at the foot of one of the morainal ridges. Grinnell puffed on his pipe with satisfaction. Tracks of either goats or sheep led up a snowy side canyon, and soon the men were in pursuit. Schultz was first to spot a large bighorn ram two hundred yards away, outlined against the sky. Grinnell dropped to one knee and fired, aiming for the neck just below the throat. The ram ran, but Monroe dashed to the spot where the animal had stood. "'Blood on the snow, and lots of it,'" he announced.

They followed the blood trail downhill, and it was Monroe who found the fallen animal. "'[Y]ou've killed the best piece of meat in the mountains,'" he congratulated when Grinnell caught up.

"He was indeed a beauty," Grinnell agreed proudly. "Five years old, his horns were not very large but were perfectly symmetrical and unbroken; his coat was perfection, thick, smooth and glossy, dark brown with its pure white rump patch. He was short of limb, strong of back, sturdy and stout, plump and round as a bull elk in early September, in fact, a picture such as one seldom has an opportunity to look at." Dressed, it weighed between 250 and 300 pounds, they figured. They built a fire and roasted and ate several ribs on the spot. Even then there was far more meat than they could carry, and Grinnell wanted the head as a trophy. They decided to leave the carcass and to bring the pack animals as near as they could the following day.

From where the sheep had died, they could see a better way off the mountain, following down the north flank of the precipice they had climbed with such difficulty that morning. By the time they reached their campsite, darkness had fallen.

The next day, while Schultz and Monroe led two horses up the somewhat less risky route by which they had descended the previous evening, Grinnell stayed in camp, updating his diary and studying the birds of the upper Swiftcurrent—Canada jay, Steller's jay, banded three-toed woodpecker, Franklin's grouse, and his friend, the water ouzel. Schultz and Monroe returned at dusk, in the end having lowered the ram over the ledges above the lake by rope. The following morning they packed up and headed for the St. Mary Lakes.

They found Lieutenant Beacom and his soldiers still camped at the lower lake, and Grinnell told him all about "the ice in G's Basin." He also gave Beacom a rough sketch of the upper Swiftcurrent, similar to one he had drawn in the back of his diary. It showed the outline of the fifth and sixth lakes and a wiggly line representing the stream connecting the uppermost lake to "Ice/Glacier." Several other landmarks were named on the map. A ridge running parallel to the lakes was called "Appekuny's Mt." The map also identified "Grinnell Mt." on the north flank of the glacier and "Monroe Peak" on the south. And finally, demarking the headwall of the glacier, above and beyond Monroe Peak, was "Gould Mt."

He sent a similar map to George Gould. Writing to his friend upon his return to New York, Grinnell explained, "Gould Mountain and Grinnell Basin"—evidently this map included Beacom's designation of the basin at the head of the valley—"will probably appear on the map of the St. Mary's region, which is to be made by a young army officer who was with us for a day or two above the Lakes. He went up Swift Current with [me] and from afar saw the glories of my glacier. . . . The reason I possess a basin and a glacier is because this young man insisted in naming both after me. I, having secured these pieces of property, could do no less than sprinkle the names of the other members of the party . . . over the adjacent territory."

Most of the names stuck—with the exception of Monroe Peak, which is now Angel Wing. Appekunny's Mountain is today Apikuni Mountain, and the two peaks that face each other, north and south, across the glacier, their brows touching the Continental Divide, still bear the names Mount Grinnell and Mount Gould.

The first installment of "The Rock Climbers," appeared in *Forest and Stream* on December 29. George Gould's long poem, "The Cliff Dwellers," was the fifth segment, published in the February 2 issue. Grinnell wrote to Gould, deprecating his own efforts in the serial and apologizing for any typographical errors that might have marred Gould's verse.

Gould responded with thanks and compliments; although the letter is now lost, apparently he also had teased Grinnell about becoming too familiar with the stenographer who prepared his correspondence.

Grinnell answered his tent mate: "It is well for you to indulge in fancies, to weave . . . a romance in which a charming female and I are to have the parts of heroine and hero, but unhappily there is not the slightest basis of fact for this last one. I long for pretty stenographers, but I have none and the hand that wrote my last to you was that of . . . a boy."

Presumably this was welcome news to Gould.

CHAPTER 13

FAIR CHASE

In mid-December 1887 Grinnell attended a dinner at the home of Corrine Robinson at 422 Madison Avenue, the address at which her brother Theodore Roosevelt preferred to hold social gatherings. Since first meeting Grinnell at the *Forest and Stream* offices in July 1885, Roosevelt had been characteristically busy. He had published numerous magazine articles and a biography of Thomas Hart Benton; run for mayor of New York (unsuccessfully); built a summer residence on Long Island (naming it Sagamore Hill, from the Algonquin word for "chieftain"); married his childhood sweetheart, Edith Carow; and done a great deal of hunting.

It was this last occupation that prompted the dinner. The Big Die-up had taught a harsh lesson. The West was more fragile and less resilient than romantics like Roosevelt had allowed themselves to imagine, and during the years he had spent on the high plains and in the mountains, the game he enjoyed stalking had become steadily more scarce.

He and Grinnell had mulled this worry many times. "We regretted the unnecessary destruction of game animals," Grinnell was to recall in 1923, "but we did not know all it meant, nor had we the vision to look forward and imagine what it portended. So, though we discussed in a general way the preservation of game, it must be confessed—in the light of later events—that we were talking about things about which we knew very little. We wanted the game preserved, but chiefly with the idea that it should be protected in order that there might be good hunting which should last for generations."

At the New York dinner they agreed to form the Boone and Crockett Club, named for two of Roosevelt's frontier heroes. Fish already had the American Fisheries Society, founded in 1871. Forests had the American Forestry Association (1875), and, more recently, the American Ornithologists' Union and the Audubon Society had come to the aid of birds. In 1887 the Boone and Crockett Club became the first organization of national scope dedicated to "the preservation of the large game of this country."

Also at the founding dinner were Roosevelt's brother Elliott, his cousin J. West Roosevelt, and six gentleman sportsmen, all New Yorkers, including Archibald Rogers, yachtsman, polo player, master of the hounds, heir to a railroad fortune; Rutherford Stuyvesant, descendant of New Amsterdam's founders, landlord to their real estate; and J. Coleman Drayton, a southern scion who had married into the Astor family. "The members of the club, so far as it is developed, are all persons of high social standing," Grinnell wrote in *Forest and Stream* shortly after the gathering, "and it would seem that an organization of this description, composed of men of intelligence and education, might wield a great influence for good in matters of game protection."

The first proper meeting of the club occurred in February 1888 at Pinard's Restaurant on Fifteenth Street. The constitution approved that night limited core membership to one hundred; no one was eligible who had not "killed with the rifle in fair chase, by still-hunting and otherwise, at least one individual of one of the various kinds of American large game"—that is, bear, buffalo, bighorn sheep, caribou, cougar, musk ox, white (mountain) goat, elk, wolf, pronghorn antelope, moose, and deer. Fair chase was defined—and here the hand of Grinnell was plainly visible—by what was *not* fair: no "killing bear, wolf, or cougar in traps, nor 'fire-hunting,' nor 'crusting' moose, elk, or deer in deep snow, or killing game from a boat while it is swimming in the water."

Joining the founding class were Albert Bierstadt, western adventurer and celebrated artist of American landscapes; William D. Pickett, Kentucky railroader and Wyoming bear hunter; William Hallett Phillips,

Washington attorney and advocate of Yellowstone preservation; Clarence King, mountaineer, geologist, and first director of the U.S. Geological Survey; and Arnold Hague, companion of both Grinnell and Roosevelt and the Geological Survey's man in Yellowstone. Roosevelt was named president and Archibald Rogers secretary.

Almost as an afterthought, realizing that certain worthy men might not qualify, the Boone and Crockett constitution further stipulated that "associate and honorary members" could be elected in addition to the blooded regulars. To further increase collective heft, the club added as associate members two former secretaries of the interior, Carl Schurz and Benjamin Bristow, and two generals, William Tecumseh Sherman and Philip Sheridan. The generals, of course, commanded the troops stationed in Yellowstone.

The rest of the bylaws were succinct, and several issues were not touched upon at all, perhaps because the founders and their fellow members took them for granted. For instance, there was no mention of how trophy hunting fit into the sportsman's ethos. Grinnell, in his diaries and in the pages of *Forest and Stream*, emphasized that he killed for meat—food for himself and for his camp mates. Or else he killed to collect specimens, as John James Audubon had done in good conscience. For the Boone and Crockett Club, the sheer thrill of the hunt and the reward of heads, horns, and hides as proud keepsakes were desirable goals that went without saying.

The club did very little in its first year, other than urge members to set a good example as sportsmen. "Among the members of the Boone and Crockett Club are a number of men whose large wealth enables them to indulge to the fullest extent their fondness for hunting," Grinnell wrote in a *Forest and Stream* editorial that was equal parts congratulation and caution. "In the past the worst enemies that the great game of the West has had, excepting, of course, 'skinners' and the meat hunters [who slaughtered game in large quantities for commercial use], have belonged to just that class." Let it be known, Grinnell warned, that the Boone and Crockett Club "discountenances the bloody methods of all game butchers without regard to occupation, wealth or social status, and no man who is guilty of slaughtering game can expect consideration from, or friendship with, its members."

———

Grinnell was not so absorbed by club matters that he considered cancelling his return to the St. Mary country and "my glacier." He hoped that this time Lute North would come along. He was counting on George Gould even more. At the end of May he wrote the latter: "Your delightful letter of ten days ago, my dear Mr. Gould, has so filled my heart with rejoicing that I want to write to you at once to tell you how glad I am that you will try to go off with me somewhere this fall."

When Gould reminded him of how dreadful the weather had been the previous year, Grinnell applied warm encouragement to his friend's cold feet: "What [if] we do freeze by day and dry up in the smoke by night? Have we not glorious appetites? Do we not sleep well? Does not our circulation [recharge] itself? Go to! We will become dirty and pro[fane] . . . and will enjoy life."

Grinnell rode by train as far as Great Falls, one hundred miles from the Blackfeet agency. His diary does not mention where he rendezvoused with Gould and North, but both arrived as promised, and by October 1 all were headed into the mountains, accompanied and provisioned by James Willard Schultz. Grinnell was delighted that Jack Monroe could join them, and Schultz had recruited a young Piegan known as Brocky—easier to utter than his Indian name, Tail Feathers Coming over the Hill.

They proceeded directly to Swiftcurrent and Grinnell Glacier. Again camp was made at the head of the valley, and on October 7 they climbed to the lateral moraine on the north side of the ice.

This would be the consummation of George Bird Grinnell's courtship with Grinnell Glacier. On his two previous trips into the Swiftcurrent valley, he had stood on its threshold in admiration and awe. And on numerous occasions, well into his old age, he would renew his acquaintance with the glacier on which his name was permanently imprinted. But in October 1888 he gave himself to Grinnell Glacier as a suitor at last embracing the object of his desire.

On his previous visit the temperature had been colder, with winter farther advanced, and the glacier was sluggish as it settled itself for hibernation. This time, though, the ice was fully awake, and in Grinnell's descriptions, published two years later in *Forest and Stream*, it seemed almost a living, sentient organism: "The glacier was vocal with the sound of running water. The musical tinkle of the tiny rivulet, the deep bass roar of the dashing torrent, the hiss of rushing water, confined as in a flume, fell upon the ear, and up through the holes and crevasses in the ice came strange hollow murmurs, growlings, while the whole ice mass seems to shake and quiver from the concussion of the masses of water that are rushing along beneath it."

They were braver now, venturing farther onto the ice. They had thought to bring along a rope from one of the pack animals, and they tied themselves together as they skirted the seemingly bottomless crevasses. On his own, Grinnell then ascended the steep slope of the glacier's west arm. "This was the most difficult and dangerous climb I have ever done," he admitted in his diary.

Lacking an ice ax, he used his rifle for balance. To lose his footing would have meant a long slide to certain death. "Yet this particular mode of going out of the world did not seem especially alarming," he reflected, "for it was certain if [I] started to slide down this slope [I] would be dead before [I] reached the crevasses, since the rock fragments that dotted the ice would have stripped all the flesh from [my] bones before [I] had reached the end of the slope, and only [my] skeleton would fall into the crevasse."

But at last he reached the top of the glacier, without mishap, and from a narrow saddle he was awarded a magnificent view of the entirety of the glacier and the sequence of Swiftcurrent lakes that cupped the glacier's melted riches before spilling them downstream. To his right, looking southward, he could admire the dark and rugged profile of Mount Gould. At his left shoulder, much nearer, rose the softer brow of Mount Grinnell. And from his lofty perch he could see far to the west, "to a beautiful park country of open grassy meadows with here and there a little lake and clumps of pine timber—a real paradise."

He recognized that he was astride the Continental Divide and that the lakes and streams he looked upon flowed westward to the Pacific. The contrast was stunning: "[I] had come from surroundings of snow and ice and cold gray rocks, and now [I] looked down on a scene which held only freshness, verdure and beauty."

The heart-pounding climb and breathtaking vistas did not deprive him of his wits, however. Grinnell had brought along a barometer, with which to determine elevation, and a compass, allowing him to make more precise estimates of the glacier's scale than he had done the year before. He figured that the ice was three miles at its widest; depth from front rim to rear wall, one and a half to two miles; rise in elevation, 1,850 feet.

With parting glances at the balcony of ice above, the group left Swift-current and moved on to the St. Mary Lakes. The weather there was not much better than it had been the year before, but the hunting was. Gould and North both killed mountain goats, firsts for them, and Grinnell killed a bighorn sheep on Singleshot Mountain. While carrying the carcass to the horses, he wrenched his back, which grew more painful in the days that followed. "I thought when I plunged into that hole and the sheep came down on top of me that I was broken in two," he groaned in recollection.

Grinnell's aches and pains notwithstanding, camp life was quite cozy. Their tent this time was a traditional Indian lodge, with an open fire in the center, a smoke hole at the top. "This is our home," he wrote in a sketch of the trip that appeared in *Forest and Stream.* "[H]ere we spend our time laughing at the storms of rain, sleet and snow, which daily burst upon us from the mountains." As usual he used nicknames for his tent mates: the Outlaw (Jack Monroe), Appekunny, Brocky—and, then, "Yo is the next man, sitting, pipe in mouth, on his bed and doing something. . . . [N]ext to him comes the Small Chief"—the Pawnees addressed Lute North as Little Chief—"that ancient . . . warrior who has been companion in so many scenes of happiness and of hardship. Once more the same blanket covers their lean and sinewy forms, and the bald head and the gray now rest again on the same pillow. Next to them . . . is the stalwart form of the Rhymer, who, with his moccasined feet stretched out toward the fire and dainty cigarette held between his lips, is perhaps composing a poem, but more probably is dropping off to sleep."

After Lute North departed for the railroad on October 21, Grinnell and Gould left the others at the St. Mary Lakes and rode up Red Eagle Creek in search of moose. They pitched their tent in a meadow of willows, alders, and enough grass for the horses. Snow fell during the night, and in the morning they continued farther into the mountains, coming upon tracks of moose, but also of elk, sheep, bobcat, lynx, and fox.

Back at camp that evening, Grinnell's sore back rendered him useless.

"Gould kindly did all the work and I sat and watched him," he recorded in his diary, adding, "Pity we could not have seen the moose."

The next morning they awoke to find their tent covered in eighteen inches of fresh snow. They spent another night in the Red Eagle camp, the snow too deep for hunting.

Throughout the trip, Grinnell and his companions had shot and trapped a variety of animals, from small birds to mice and weasels, which were intended for the American Museum of Natural History. Near the Blackfeet agency, they acquired another specimen, this one quite alive. A Piegan named John Takes Gun in the Night had captured a young bighorn sheep, and, rather than fatten it for the pot, he was willing to sell it to Grinnell, who figured that, if two grizzly cubs could survive a train ride across the country, then so could a sheep.

Grinnell arranged to have it crated and shipped, collect, to Washington, to the attention of William T. Hornaday, the renowned taxidermist who had recently been appointed curator of the Department of Living Animals at the Smithsonian, the precursor to the National Zoo. Grinnell wrote to Hornaday, assuring him that the ewe was in "the very pink of condition" and thriving on a diet of potato peels and crackers. "You would smile if I were to try to tell you how attached I became to the little creature," he added. "I had to keep her one night in a barroom where I slept, and she manifested a disposition to eat the stumps of cigars and cigarettes which were strewn on the floor, so I had to keep by her side and watch her until she lay down for the night."

From here onward, though, there was little to smile about. The final pages of Grinnell's 1888 diary are filled with the testimony of Indians reciting the sins of their agent, Marcus Baldwin.

Since Grinnell's first visit to the Blackfeet reservation in 1885, conditions had gone from bad to worse, as more whites settled in Montana. Cattlemen scoffed at government regulations and turned their herds loose on the high plains where buffalo once had grazed. Gold miners trespassed with impunity upon the Sweet Grass Hills, on the northern edge of the reservation. The devastating winter of 1886–87 only increased stockgrowers' appetite for Piegan grass. Individual Piegans were forbidden to own cattle; out of hunger, they killed the animals owned by whites and in the agency-controlled herd. They were urged to till the soil, but their land was dry, the growing season was short, and for hundreds of years the Piegans had been hunters, gatherers, and warriors—not farmers. At the end of 1885 a reservation with a population of two thousand planted a mere twelve acres of potatoes.

Meanwhile, their agents were consistently corrupt, incompetent, and, as political appointees, more beholden to their patrons in power than to the Indians they were sworn to serve. Whereas once the tribe had been mobile and mighty, living in cooperative bands, families now hunkered in painful poverty along the southern boundary of the reservation to be closer to the meager government annuities that they were now dependent upon for survival.

Under pressure from Montana cattlemen, Congress authorized a commission to persuade the Piegans, as well as the territory's Sioux, Assiniboine, and Gros Ventres, to relinquish "so much of their land as they do not require." The commissioners arrived on the Blackfeet reservation in February 1887, with snow deep on the ground and the temperature far below zero. The Indian delegation was led by Three Suns, also known as Big Nose, leader of the Grease Melter band, and by White Calf, leader of the Skunk band, keeper of the sacred Beaver Bundles and regarded as head chief of all the Piegans. Both men had hunted buffalo, stolen many horses, and counted coup on their enemies.

But the Piegan people were without food and clothing, and so they agreed to sell off a hefty piece of their homeland. The initial asking price was $3 million. The commissioners wore them down to $1.5 million, to be paid out over ten years in the form of livestock, clothing, tools, schools, medical assistance, mills, blacksmith shops, a new agency, and other means of furthering the tribe's "civilization, comfort, and improvement." Due to the severe weather, only two hundred Piegan men "touched the pen" to the agreement, which Congress approved on May 1.

White Calf would refer to the winter of 1887 as the time "when we sold the Sweet Grass Hills," but they had relinquished so much more. For a ten-year lifeline, the Blackfeet of Montana allowed their reservation to be decimated—from 17 million acres to 1.7 million. Once they had roamed and raided almost at will; now they found themselves backed into a box, the Canadian border to the north, the Rocky Mountains to the west, Birch Creek to the south, and Cut Bank Creek to the east.

Agents came and went on the reservation, and the latest, Marcus Baldwin, was perhaps no worse than most. A devout Democrat, he had been practicing law in Ohio when President Grover Cleveland appointed him to superintend the Piegans. Whatever Baldwin's intentions may have been, he soon proved himself a man of poor judgment and shady scruples. His official reports to Washington took credit for strides the Piegans were taking toward self-improvement and self-sufficiency, even while he was allowing cattlemen and miners to ride roughshod over Piegan land. Opaque bookkeeping could not quite obscure chronic embezzlement. At one point he overestimated the amount of beef available for rations by 100,000 pounds. He shortchanged the Piegans, lined his own pockets, and looked the other way while whiskey traders poisoned his wards.

By the time Grinnell, Gould, Schultz, Monroe, and Brocky rode into the Badger Creek agency on November 6, 1888, the Piegans had lost all faith in Baldwin; yet they had no power to send him packing. Their nickname for him was Agent Tomorrow, reflecting their doubt that he would ever get around to listening to them.

"On my way back to the Agency, I learned that White Calf, the head chief of the Piegans, and a number of head men wanted to talk to me," Grinnell wrote Lute North. "The agent was not there, and they talked very freely and made a great many complaints. I think I got enough material to have the agent removed."

By 1888 most Piegans lived in log houses and wore a combination of traditional and white man's clothing—trousers, shirts, and dresses provided by the agency, along with beaded moccasins and handmade ornaments. They wrapped themselves in trade blankets, and nearly all still wore their hair in braids.

But even as the Piegans bridged two worlds, very few spoke English. As a rule, Grinnell's interpreters were trustworthy, dependable, and nuanced; nevertheless, something inevitably got lost in translation. "I am not in a position to swear that the Indians said these things," he would allow, "but I can swear that the interpreter said that [they] said them."

Be that as it may, there was never an Indian to whom Grinnell felt closer than White Calf, chief of the Piegans. With Billy Russell, of white and Piegan parentage, interpreting, Grinnell listened and jotted notes as White Calf spoke for his people and beseeched the white man known as Fisher Cap to intervene on their behalf in Washington. "I will tell you a true tale," White Calf began. "Lose it not but portray all to the Great Father."

Grinnell also made a point of transcribing his reply to White Calf's opening remarks: "I come from the East, a private man. My business is to write. Many thousands hear my words, more people perhaps than live in all Montana. I know the [Piegans]. I know the hardship of their past & I hope they will have a better future."

He continued: "Their agent is a servant of the government who should do what is right for them. If I learn that he does not do right, then I will tell all to the Great Father & the Commissioner of Indian Affairs & they will make a change if things are not right. I will write out all that the people say & many people in the East will be interested in the [Piegans]."

Then followed page upon page of transcribed testimony, from White Calf, but also from Running Rabbit, Eagle Flag, John Takes Gun in the Night, Brocky, and others—every one of them damning Baldwin. They wished only that the government honor its treaties. "The road made for us is straight & the agent covers it up & disturbs it. He makes it so we cannot follow it," White Calf explained. Even in translation, White Calf's message was vivid and profoundly personal. "Our body is the reservation," he said.

Grinnell and Gould left two days later, vowing to press the Piegan case against Baldwin, whom they did not meet during their time at the agency. Both wrote letters to Commissioner of Indian Affairs John H. Oberly. Gould's message, not surprisingly, was the more poetic. The Indians were like imprisoned felons under a corrupt warden, with little hope of reprieve, he averred. "They feel that they are not sliding but are being pushed towards a pit of helplessness. Their revenues are stolen, their rights are insolently disregarded, even their feelings are needlessly wronged."

Grinnell was more methodical and more persistent. His first letter, dated November 20, described the results of his "personal investigation conducted on the ground." Baldwin was "systematically untruthful and so distrusted by white, half breeds and Indians alike." He kept no promises he made to the Indians. He refused to see the Indians or hear their complaints. He offered no assistance, ignored their rights, neglected to issue rations, and allowed white men's cattle to graze on the reservation.

Pressed by the commissioner for more specifics, Grinnell prepared a twenty-eight-page brief elaborating on the charges enumerated in the first letter. Then in mid-December he took the train to Washington at his own expense and gained an audience with Indian Commissioner Oberly and his superior, Secretary of the Interior William Vilas. The Piegans were being mistreated, he told them, face to face. Baldwin had to go.

Still he was not done. For a change, he did not air his case in the pages of *Forest and Stream*. In February he gave a long interview to the New York *Evening Post*, describing the "invasion" of the Blackfeet reservation by white ranchers, going so far as to list the brands of the trespassing cattle. "The cattlemen push onto the reservation as if they owned it, and never so much as say by your leave." The Piegans, he explained, his indignation rising, "have been crowded in on all sides, their reservation has been made smaller and smaller, and after every reduction in size the white men come up to the borders of the reservation and want more land. . . . Is it strange that they feel that they are ill-used or that they have lost confidence in a Government which permits such acts?"

His grievance expanded as it warmed: "It seems to me a monstrous thing that outrages of this kind should be possible. I do not think that anyone who knows me is likely to call me a sentimentalist. During the last twenty years I have spent a considerable portion of each year in the far West. I have been a cattleman and know how cattlemen feel. I have met Indians on the warpath, and have hunted and lived with them for months at a time, and I think I understand Indian character as well as almost anyone. Any man with a spark of feeling hates to see oppression, and when those who are ill-treated are utterly helpless and have absolutely no recourse, it makes it ten times worse."

And finally his anger boiled over, a rarity for Grinnell. "To take advantage of people who have no means of protecting themselves is opposed to the Anglo-Saxon idea of fair play," he vented. "If the American people want the Indians killed off, let the army do it—it is perfectly practicable at small cost. [B]ut when it is pretended that we are trying to civilize them, we ought to keep the agreements that we have made. I have seen Indians swindled and imposed on until I am fairly sick and tired of the whole subject, and it makes me ashamed to live under a government where such treatment is possible."

In the end, it was the politicians and officeholders who precipitated Baldwin's removal. In March, Benjamin Harrison, a Republican, was inaugurated as president, and it was his turn to dispense the spoils of office. Baldwin resumed his law practice and became a pillar of the burgeoning town of Kalispell, no worse for his time among the Indians.

George Bird Grinnell, too, turned a new page. Until recently, his relation to Native Americans had been mostly one of fascination. From here on out, though, he would come down firmly, unequivocally, on their side. It was a position he would expand and never apologize for. "We are too apt to forget that these people are humans like ourselves," he would soon write, "that they are fathers and mothers, husbands and wives, brothers and sisters; men and women with emotions and passions like our own."

His was not a lone voice by any means. He had joined a chorus of reform that had been growing over the previous decade, now that nearly every Indian tribe had been placed on a reservation. The Women's National Indian Association and the Indian Rights Association, both founded in Philadelphia, and Boston's Indian Citizenship Committee led the national campaign for reform of Indian policy and elevation of the Indian from "savagery" to "civilization." Helen Hunt Jackson, a member of the Boston group, had published her incendiary A Century of Dishonor in 1881 with the intention, she said, to "do for the Indian . . . what Uncle Tom's Cabin did for the Negro." And every year since 1883 a group of church leaders had been convening at Lake Mohonk Lodge in the Catskills to coordinate efforts to aid and educate Indians.

Grinnell was aware of this movement, and his views certainly were in concurrence, but in 1889 he was just beginning to find his way as an advocate. While he was generally quick to join and, in the instances of the Audubon Society and Boone and Crockett Club, to found organizations that furthered the causes he believed in, he was not yet inclined to attach his name to any association for the defense and uplift of Indians. For the moment, his allegiance was directly to the Indians themselves.

CHAPTER 14

GHOST DANCE

Grinnell's expanding interest in Native Americans next took him to the Pawnee reservation in Indian Territory. Over the years, Lute North had told him one Pawnee story after another, most recently around the campfire in Montana. Grinnell was forever pestering him to put his words to paper; short of that, North consented to accompany Grinnell to the reservation and act as interpreter while his friend interviewed tribal elders. "I ought to live with the tribe a year or two to get it all," Grinnell confessed to North. "However, we will do the best under the circumstances."

They stayed less than a month, but it was long enough for Grinnell to collect a book's worth of material. He worked on the manuscript in the evenings and on weekends and published it under the Forest and Stream imprint in time for Christmas sales. Its full title was *Pawnee Hero Stories and Folk-Tales, with Notes on the Origin, Customs and Character of the Pawnee People*. Several chapters also ran in *Forest and Stream*.

More than a volume of stories—for example, "The Boy Who Was Sacrificed" and "How the Deer Lost His Gall"—it is a primer on why Indians deserved to have their history and culture preserved, and why whites ought to care. "The entire ignorance concerning Indians, which prevails among the general public, can be dispelled only by letting the public understand something of the ways of life of the wild Indian," Grinnell lectures.

Yet the Pawnees were more than a case study. "Once the Pawnees were a great people," he vouches. "They were undisputed masters of a vast territory. They had everything that heart could wish. . . . They roamed over the country without let or hindrance. In peace they were lighthearted and contented; in war cunning, fierce and successful."

Since relocating from Nebraska to Indian Territory in 1875, the tribe had shrunk from three thousand to eight hundred, and Grinnell was anxious to record its lore from the lips of the oldest Pawnees, before they were gone. He sensibly grasped that the proper approach should be one of minimal intrusion. "The task I have set for myself is one of recorder," he writes in his introduction. "No attempt has been made to give a literary color to the hero stories and folk-tales here written out. I have scrupulously avoided putting into them anything of my own. . . . The Indians themselves are talking. They are stories of Indians by Indians."

He would let his readers form their own opinions. "The Indian is neither a fiend nor a saint," he emphasizes. "There are good ones and bad ones."

But then, even as he suggests that whites ought to treat Indians with an open mind, he himself slips into the prevailing prejudice of better-educated Americans. "As a rule [Indians] try to act up to their ideas of what is right, but the standard of a race of barbarians cannot be the same as that of a civilized people, and in judging of their character we must make allowances for this difference. The standard of right and wrong among civilized people is a growth, the product of the experience of thousands of years. The Indian races have not been through a like experience."

Nowhere in his letters, diaries, or published writings did George Bird Grinnell acknowledge having made a serious study of evolutionary theory, though he received a practical introduction to Darwin during his years with Professor Marsh. Yet, regardless of Grinnell's formative learning, Darwin and Marsh had mainly concerned themselves with the evolution of animals. Grinnell had to look elsewhere for the latest ideas on human progress.

In 1877, eighteen years after *On the Origin of Species* shook the world, industrialist-turned-anthropologist Lewis Henry Morgan published *Ancient Society*, which put a human face on Darwinism. Morgan formulated a rigid hierarchy of the evolution of man. He graded human development from Lower Status of Savagery to Middle Status of Savagery to Upper Status of Savagery, continuing upward to similar gradations of Barbarism, until reaching the apex: Civilization. According to Morgan, only those with European—Aryan—heritage had reached the top. Native Americans, he declared, had yet to evolve past Middle Barbarism.

When Grinnell, in his introduction to *Pawnee Hero Stories and Folk-Tales*, refers to Indians as "a race of barbarians," he clearly is acknowledging at least an indirect acceptance of Morgan's theory. He presumes that he is being reasonable and fair. His perspective is paternalistic and indeed racist, yet he nonetheless feels that he stands confidently on the scientific and moral high ground. This was the view of enlightened, progressive thinkers of the day: Indians still had a long way to go. It would be a shame if they were to become extinct before they climbed the ladder to Civilization.

Reviews of *Pawnee Hero Stories and Folk-Tales* were generally flattering. The *New-York Tribune* commended it as a "collection of decided value and original flavor, a really precious contribution toward anthropological science." For his part, Grinnell called the Pawnee book "my baby—a squally brat that has caused me an infinity of trouble."

Forest and Stream's review was hardly more objective. It was written by one of Grinnell's Scroll and Key classmates, lawyer and occasional fiction writer John Elliott Curran. "This book is from a loving hand," Curran pronounced, "and that being so, there is a deeper philosophy in it than any cold pedant could possibly give. . . . In this book of Mr. Grinnell's we get near to the Indian as he *is* (no, let us say in shame, as he *was*). We get near his heart and soul."

No less indulgent was a book review in verse that appeared in *Forest and Stream* a few issues later:

Here one has woven from a hundred shreds
Of myths' and legends' many-colored threads
The stately robe a vanished nation wore.

The poet was H. G. Dulog.

Pawnee Hero Stories did well enough that Forest and Stream Publishing decided to issue a second printing. Henry Henshaw, editor of *American Anthropologist*, admired the book and invited Grinnell to join the esteemed Anthropological Association of Washington. Later in the year he would be elected to the American Folk-Lore Society, whose membership included academic eminences such as Franz Boas, Mark Twain, and Joel Chandler Harris, author of the Uncle Remus stories. Over the course of a few months, Grinnell had gained a reputation as an ethnologist.

By 1889 Grinnell's pursuit of Indian stories had begun to equal, if not to replace, his hunger for stalking wild animals. The summer after completing *Pawnee Hero Stories*, he rode the eastern boundary of Yellowstone with Arnold Hague and canoed the rugged interior of British Columbia with George Gould, collecting specimens of sheep and goats for the Smithsonian. Grinnell enjoyed the country and companionship as much as ever, but his enthusiasm for killing—regardless of purpose—was not what it once had been. After shooting a bear in Wyoming, he wrote: "He bawled just as the bullet hit him and then moaned as he flopped about. . . . It wasn't even a grizzly of the smallest size, but just a plain, simple, ordinary, common black bear. . . . I confess a sneaking regret that I had killed the poor fellow."

His diminished appetite for blood and heightened desire to preserve human history were fueled at least in part by his own aging. He had entered his forties, and back troubles had hampered his mobility on recent pack trips. City life and unrelenting work were hardly restorative. He worked seven days a week and most evenings, commuting by elevated train and street car between Audubon Park and his offices at 318 Broadway, where *Forest and Stream* had been obliged to move in 1888 upon the demolition of the Times building on Park Row.

The sudden death of Jack Curran in May further shaded Grinnell's mid-life reflections on mortality. Curran had given up the security of a law practice to devote himself to writing. He had contributed a few pieces to *Forest and Stream*, including the review of *Pawnee Hero Stories*, and had recently published his first novel. Grinnell was at Curran's bedside when he died and afterward enlisted their classmates to set up a fund to pay for the schooling of Curran's three young children. (Grinnell would keep the fund going until both sons had graduated from Yale and the daughter from Barnard College.)

A month after burying Curran, Grinnell joined more than fifty classmates for their twentieth reunion at New Haven, accepting an invitation to stay with Ned Dana. Grinnell was glad to see so many familiar faces and enjoyed the barbed toasts and friendly ribbings at the class supper. Still, the weekend left a slightly bittersweet aftertaste. Half the men had brought wives. Most, including Dana, were raising families. When it came to marriage, Grinnell had long since made up his mind. In a letter to the class correspondent, he reported tersely, "I am not married and do not expect to be."

Grinnell arrived at the Blackfeet agency the last week of August. George Gould would join him later, but first Grinnell wanted to give his full attention to the Piegans.

He had already made up his mind to avoid James Willard Schultz. As a guide, Schultz had proven himself a shirker, too inclined to sit around camp and not keen to keep up in the high country. As a writer, he was no more reliable. Grinnell had encouraged Schultz to expand his *Forest and Stream* series, "My Life among the Blackfeet," into a book, but Schultz kept coming up with excuses for not completing the manuscript. First his wife was sick; then his eyes troubled him. The real explanation was that Schultz drank too much. Grinnell had never paid Schultz very much—for his stories or his guiding—but finally he concluded that he would take the Blackfeet matter into his own hands. Frustrated by Schultz and also inspired by the success of the Pawnee book, Grinnell set out to gather more stories, with the intention of completing the book himself.

One of the first people he interviewed was Hugh Monroe (no relation to Jack). Monroe was white, born in Quebec in 1798. He had gone west with the Hudson's Bay Company, married a Piegan woman, and since the 1820s had lived as a member of the tribe. As an English speaker, he would prove to be an invaluable source in Grinnell's endeavors to piece together the history of the Blackfeet. Monroe's grandson Billy Jackson was likewise a treasure trove, but in another respect. One-quarter Piegan, Jackson had served as a scout for the Seventh Cavalry, alongside Grinnell's old friend Charley Reynolds. Unlike Reynolds, Jackson had survived the Little Bighorn, and his eyewitness account of that bloody day would fill many pages of Grinnell's notebooks.

An even more valuable Piegan source was Wolf Calf, also known as Pemmican, who was approaching one hundred years old. "When I first heard of whites, I was a young man," Wolf Calf began (with Billy Russell interpreting).

Wolf Calf had been among a group of Piegans who came upon several white men near Birch Creek. He remembered the spot well; it was just south of the present reservation boundary, where a saloon now stood. "Chief of the little war party was Sidehill Calf," Wolf Calf related. "He said to his son, look out for the best horse these white men have and steal him." The Piegans tried to run off three of the horses, and in the ensuing confrontation, one of the Piegans was stabbed, and the leader of the whites shot Sidehill Calf.

The date of the encounter was July 26, 1806, and, as Wolf Calf and the Piegans would later learn, the killer of Sidehill Calf was Captain Meriwether Lewis, who had led a small party to explore the Marias River, a promising tributary of the Missouri, while Lieutenant William Clark and the rest of the Corps of Discovery continued their homeward journey to St. Louis. If Grinnell required any greater imperative for collecting the stories of Piegan elders, here seated before him was a man who had come of age before whites had entered his world; who had borne witness to the portentous and now-infamous confrontation between Lewis and the Indians; who on the eve of the twentieth century could remember what Piegan life had been like at the end of the eighteenth.

To Grinnell's great delight, George Gould caught up with him on September 10. In place of Schultz as guide, Grinnell recruited the vastly more capable and convivial Jack Monroe. They camped on the lower Swiftcurrent; from there, instead of riding all the way to the final lakes below Grinnell Glacier, they turned up the northern tributary of the stream. They did not give their full attention to hunting, although Grinnell shot three goats on the slope of Mount Wilbur (named for *Forest and Stream*'s business manager). On the ride out of the valley, his horse fell, pinning his leg in a tangle of downed timber and bruising it badly.

Two days later he was able to get around well enough, and, leaving Gould to his leisure in camp, he and Monroe rode to the head of today's Boulder Creek and climbed what, from the description in his diary, was most likely ten-thousand-foot Mount Siyeh, named for one of several Piegan chiefs Grinnell had interviewed a few weeks earlier. "A most superb prospect before us," Grinnell wrote in his diary. They could see across the summits of the surrounding mountains, north beyond Mount Gould and Mount Grinnell to the headwaters of the Belly River and farther still to Chief Mountain; west to the pass called Going to the Sun, and southwest to a glacier that, even from a distance, appeared to dwarf Grinnell Glacier. He named it Blackfoot Glacier; the mountain above it, Blackfoot Mountain. By the time they got back to camp, it was dusk and their moccasins were worn through. This time Grinnell made note of his birthday: "41 years."

They parted a week later—Gould and Monroe headed down the Missouri, Grinnell to introduce himself to a new tribe, the Cheyennes. The two "partners," Grinnell and Gould, said goodbye without any inkling that it was the last time they would see each other.

Grinnell's intention was to engage with the Cheyennes as he had with the Blackfeet and the Pawnees. But his first foray in the fall of 1890 had a different outcome than he anticipated. "I saw something of the Cheyennes but could not get very much out of them because they were all so much excited over the Christ dance," he wrote when he got back to New York. "Most of the people were dancing all the time, and those who were not dancing were by no means inclined to talk, so I can call my trip there pretty near a failure."

Today the "Christ dance" is better known as the ghost dance. The previous year, in 1889, a Paiute shaman from Nevada named Wovoka had undergone a transformation that sent shock waves through Indian country. During an eclipse of the sun he had a vision in which he "went to heaven and saw God and all the people who had died long ago." As a boy, Wovoka had lived with a white family, who introduced him to Jesus Christ. Wovoka's vision borrowed heavily from the Bible. He promised that if Indians hewed to their traditional ways, worked hard, conducted themselves honorably, and danced a special dance that God had shown especially to Wovoka, then their world would be right again: All of their ancestors would come back to life; whites would be swept from the earth; the buffalo would return; and Indians would live happily and wholesomely for eternity.

Word of Wovoka's paradisiacal prophecy took hold among western tribes otherwise deprived of hope and confined to land of little use to them. Many had not seen a buffalo in a decade, much less eaten one. Emissaries set out for Nevada to absorb Wovoka's teachings firsthand and to learn the "ghost dance."

After the Blackfeet reservation, Grinnell spent several days at Fort Keogh, on the Yellowstone River in southeastern Montana, where a number of Northern Cheyennes were living. From a Cheyenne named Porcupine, who had been to see Wovoka, he received a vivid account of the origin and spread of the ghost dance. As an indication of his initial skepticism, Grinnell headed his notes, "False Christ."

But even while he gave no credence to the potency of the movement, he sympathized with the Indians anyway. "This is only what any of us will do if we get hungry," he reasoned. His only real complaint was that excessive dancing kept the Indians from the more important work of farming, looking after livestock, and pursuing industries that would advance them on the road to civilization.

Grinnell did not see an actual ghost dance performed until he reached the Southern Cheyenne reservation in Oklahoma in mid-October, but he would be one of the very first to give a full description of the phenomenon to the eastern press. "The dancing usually lasts for four nights, beginning a little before sundown and continuing until any hour the next morning," he explained with ethnological precision in an interview with the *New-York Tribune*. "The Indians, men, women, and children, form a circle, probably one hundred feet in diameter, standing shoulder to shoulder, close together.

All, of course, face inward. Several men take their places in the circle and start the dance by singing a song. . . . They move slowly to the left, one foot at a time, keeping in unison with the music. The scene is extremely weird when the moon is up. The Indians clad in white sheets look like so many ghosts."

The more the Indians danced, Grinnell was told, the sooner "the world would be turned upside down and the white people spilled out." He was not especially discomfited by the ominousness of such a prediction, but, on the other hand, as he allowed in a letter to Lute North, "It is quite possible that the Indians might be frightened into killing someone." More likely, however, "Some crazy-headed settler, or body of settlers, will attack the Indians and kill some, and if they do, they may start a war . . . and if a war is started now, it will be worse than the Custer massacre ever was."

Grinnell's concern that the ghost dance might lead to violence proved prescient. Soldiers, agents, missionaries, and other whites who lived near Indian reservations became increasingly alarmed at the dancers' fervor. Every tribe had its own variation of the ritual. The Cheyennes tended toward introspection and peace. Their neighbors, the Sioux, were decidedly more militant in their desire to see whites wiped from the earth. The army responded by beefing up its presence in Sioux country. On December 15, Indian policemen, led by agent James McLaughlin, attempted to arrest the venerable and influential Sioux holy man Sitting Bull, who, if not an actual leader of the ghost dance, was plainly one of its proponents. Sitting Bull was shot dead before he could be taken into custody.

Fearful of further retribution, three hundred or so of the most devout practitioners of the Sioux ghost dance left their stronghold in the northwestern corner of the Pine Ridge reservation and headed for the relative safety of the agency. On December 29, twenty miles shy of their destination, on Wounded Knee Creek, in the year-old state of South Dakota, they were surrounded by troopers from the Seventh Cavalry, Custer's old command. Regardless of who first provoked whom, in the ensuing barrage of bullets and artillery an estimated two hundred Sioux were killed, along with thirty soldiers.

Grinnell was right: Wounded Knee was as bad as the Custer massacre, or nearly so. "It is rather pitiful to think of the Indians being shot down, men, women, and children, in this way," he wrote two days after the massacre and only three weeks after his dark forecast, "but it is the old story over and over again, and it does not do any good to think about it." Adding to the sting of the tragedy was the news that among the army casualties was Captain George Wallace, an old acquaintance from the 1874 Black Hills expedition. And then, ten days after Wounded Knee, Grinnell learned that Lieutenant Edward Casey had been murdered on Pine Ridge by a young Sioux named Plenty Horse. Grinnell and Ned Casey had been schoolmates at Churchill Military Academy.

"Both [Casey and Wallace] were fine fellows and good soldiers," Grinnell eulogized in *Forest and Stream*, and then said bitterly, "No feature of these so-called Indian uprisings is more deplorable than the fact that men like Casey and Wallace must be sacrificed to the irresponsibility of Congress and the bad system of the Indian Department."

CHAPTER 15

SACRED RANGE

T he news from the West was disturbing, to be sure, but Grinnell began the New Year with raised spirits. "When I came in from the mountains . . . I was as tough and strong as any man could be." His mood elevated further in the spring, when Congress enacted a conservation measure that Grinnell, *Forest and Stream*, the Boone and Crockett Club, and nearly every advocate for wilderness and wildlife had been pushing for many years.

In expressing its commitment to preserve big game, the club's constitution pledged "to further legislation for that purpose and to assist in enforcing the existing laws." So far as Grinnell was concerned, the most pressing legislation concerned protection of the country's first game reserve, Yellowstone National Park. He had been in the thick of the fight between commercial and conservationist interests since 1875, when he expressed alarm over the thousands of elk slaughtered in the Yellowstone River valley, just outside the park's northern boundary. A great stride was taken in 1883, when Senator George Vest, with the support of Grinnell, *Forest and Stream*, and lobbyist William Hallett Phillips, had narrowly passed a bill that reined in the Park Improvement Company and provided troops to deter destruction of game and the park's natural curiosities.

Yet the railroad had not been cowed. Every year Vest introduced a bill calling for expansion of the park to protect the range of buffalo, elk, and other game that migrated seasonally from the higher ground of the Yellowstone Plateau to the winter grounds that surrounded it. And every year railroad interests, going by one name or another, directed their congressional minions to amend the legislation, authorizing a railroad across the northern rim of the park.

The tug-of-war grew both nasty and petty. Funds for the park administration and policing were cut. Proposals were introduced to eliminate Montana's piece of the park entirely. More soldiers were sent to patrol the park but were given no clear policy of enforcement and were backed by no judicial authority. Meanwhile, tourists, vandals, and poachers tromped through Wonderland, pouring soap into geysers to stimulate eruptions, starting wildfires, and picking away at the last remaining herd of wild buffalo in the United States.

In the pages of *Forest and Stream*, Grinnell took the long view. "Every sportsman desires to have the great game which inhabits this Park saved from the extinction which is so surely impending for each species, unless rigid protection is afforded it here," he had written in March 8, 1888, less than a month after the founding of the Boone and Crockett Club. For Grinnell, survival of the game that he and his peers loved to hunt made obvious sense. In Yellowstone he saw the opportunity to make this point graphically clear. Here, in this treasured spot, he would take a stand and never back down. Not only did he write editorials and devote columns to Yellowstone legislation week after week, month after month, but also for the first time in his career he waded deeper into the fray, traveling from New York to Washington to press his cause directly to lawmakers.

In 1891 he made a tactical decision to hold the Boone and Crockett Club annual dinner in Washington, using the chummy, fraternal occasion as an opportunity to bring certain men of authority into the fold. At the Metropolitan Club on January 14, Theodore Roosevelt—Boone and Crockett president and, since 1889, commissioner of the United States Civil Service—commanded the head of the table. On his right sat Secretary of War Redfield Proctor; on his left Speaker of the House Thomas Reed. Grinnell anchored the other end, flanked by Secretary of the Interior John Noble and Secretary of the Smithsonian Samuel Pierpont Langley. Interspersed among the club's members were several congressmen, whose ears were bent and votes seduced, from the first slurp of soup to the last puff of cigar. Besides big game, the topic that dominated the evening's discussion was Yellowstone.

Grinnell, for one, left the room in an optimistic mood. "We showed [Speaker Reed] that the railroad people were trying to use our good bill, to which there is no objection and everybody is anxious for, to carry through their private scheme for monopoly," he wrote Archibald Rogers, who was absent from the dinner. "I think we excited a real interest and feel more hopeful than I have for two or three years."

Still the logjam could not be broken. In the end it took not only the arm-twisting of Boone and Crockett sportsmen but also the cooperation of the American Forestry Association. Beginning in 1889, with the inauguration of Benjamin Harrison, leaders of the Forestry Association and two of Yellowstone's most knowledgeable and dogged champions, William Hallett Phillips and Arnold Hague, went to work on Secretary of the Interior Noble, urging him to (a), consider withdrawing from sale all publicly owned forest lands and (b), creating strictly controlled forest reserves similar to those in Europe. Grinnell of course knew Noble through his Indian activism; the secretary oversaw the Bureau of Indian Affairs.

The influence from all sides bore fruit in February, when Noble attached a rider to the tail end of a bill otherwise intended to clean up the Timber Culture Act of 1873. The bill's now-celebrated Section 24 stated: "The President of the United States may, from time to time, set apart and reserve, in any state or territory having public land bearing forests, in any part of the public lands, wholly or in part covered in timber or undergrowth, whether of commercial value or not, as public reservations." The rider snuck through at the close of the session, and President Harrison signed the bill to which it was attached on March 3. Thus, in a hush, the seed of the country's future system of national forests was planted.

Hague and Phillips wasted no time nurturing it. A dream they had been pursuing for years, repeatedly stymied by the railroads, was now within reach. If they could not expand the actual boundaries of Yellowstone, then they could effectively buffer them. They approached Secretary Noble with a proclamation; Noble got with the president; and on March 30 Benjamin Harrison issued an executive order setting aside a million and a quarter acres—roughly five hundred square miles—of forest on the eastern and southern boundaries of Yellowstone, the same country Hague and Grinnell had ridden through in past summers. Not only was Yellowstone the first national park; now the Yellowstone Park Timberland Reserve, as it was officially called, became the country's very first national forest.

"I feel that the whole country owes you and Phillips, and, of course, afterwards Secretary Noble, a debt of gratitude for getting this thing put through," Grinnell wrote to Hague on April 6. He next wrote Phillips, expressing similar gratitude and urging that no time be wasted in having "printed notices stuck up on the borders of the forest reserve warning people off." He was well aware that hunting in the new reserve was not yet regulated. Nor did the new law and forest boundaries do anything to deter the railroad from carving a route through the park itself.

As much as Grinnell would have liked to be in Yellowstone that fall, he could not make time. He was making good progress on the Blackfeet book, and he was eager to gather enough stories to finish the manuscript. He asked Gould to join him, but something about the trip down the Missouri with Jack Monroe the previous summer had soured him on Montana.

Instead Grinnell took along two young Yale men: Henry Stimson and William Seward. They had graduated together in 1888, and both were just starting law careers. Seward had the more lustrous heritage; Stimson would have the brighter future. Seward's grandfather, of the same name, had been governor of New York before serving as Abraham Lincoln's secretary of state. Stimson would one day serve as secretary of state to Herbert Hoover and secretary of war to both William Howard Taft and Franklin D. Roosevelt.

Stimson and Seward each killed mountain goats, but Grinnell shot "nothing on the whole trip larger than a goose." He spent most of the time, accompanied by guide Billy Jackson, climbing the mountains he had seen from Mount Siyeh the year before. "The country up there was absolutely virgin," he told Gould. "I do not think I have ever been in any place where I felt so sure that no white men had ever been before. . . . [T]here was no sign of previous passage by human beings: no chopping, no fires, no sign of horse."

Previously untrod, but no longer unnamed. With every trip, Grinnell affixed more labels to the landmarks of a world he had come to regard almost proprietarily: Grinnell Glacier and Grinnell Lake; Mount Gould, Monroe Point, Appekunny's Mountain. There was no North Mountain; instead there was Little Chief, Lute North's Pawnee honorific. On this latest trip with Seward and Stimson, Grinnell added a slew more. Since Edward Wilbur already had a mountain, it was time managing editor Charles Reynolds got one; each wound up with a creek in their name, as well. The peak and enormous glacier at the headwall of St. Mary became Mt. Jackson, after Billy Jackson, below which crept Jackson Glacier. Stimson was awarded a mountain (though it later became Mount Logan). Seward's name stuck to Mount Seward, and his sister Cornelia Seward Allen was immortalized on Mount Allen. The mountain on which Stimson and Seward fired so many errant shots at goats became Fusillade—an oblique acknowledgment of Grinnell's earlier marksmanship on Singleshot Mountain.

After a month of hunting and exploring, Grinnell returned to the Blackfeet reservation and gathered one more notebook of stories. The trip was productive, and he was once again invigorated. Yet he had not quite been able to re-create the wonder and excitement of old. The country may have been virgin still, but after guiding two neophytes into its folds, he felt almost as if he had violated a trust of intimacy. "Our investigations this fall make me regard the St. Mary's country as a sacred range," he explained to Gould. "I know that I have no especial desire to see anything more of it, and so it is not likely that I shall again write you imploring you to visit it with me." Then, wistfully, he wrote, "If you had been with me this year, I think you would have had a good time."

Yet his pledge of withdrawal made little difference. The lower country of rivers and lakes was growing more populous every year. The Great Northern Railway already reached the Blackfeet reservation and would soon cross the entire West from St. Paul, Minnesota, to Seattle, Washington. This would mean more settlers, miners, cattlemen, and tourists.

What would become of Grinnell's "sacred range"? The recent success in protecting Yellowstone had planted an idea—as had the establishment of Sequoia and Yosemite as the nation's second and third national parks a year earlier. "How would it do to start a movement to buy the St. Mary's country, say 30 × 30 miles, from the Piegan Indians at a fair valuation and turn it into a national reservation or park?" Grinnell asked his diary on September 17, 1891. "The Great Northern R. R. would probably back the scheme and T. C. Power [U.S. Senator Thomas C. Power from Montana] would do all he could for it. Mr. Noble would favor it, and certainly all the Indians would like it. This is worth thinking of and writing about."

He arrived home at the beginning of November, his head full of possibilities. The Blackfeet book was all but done. A delegation of Piegans was coming east to meet with the commissioner of Indian affairs, and Grinnell intended to be on hand to help them convey their concerns. "I have the welfare of this people very much at heart," he told their agent, George Steell, "and I am not speaking too strongly when I say that I will do almost anything to benefit them."

The trip to Washington was not to be. On December 19 George Blake Grinnell died of pneumonia at home in Audubon Park. He was sixty-eight years old. George Bird, his eldest son, was an executor of his estate. Moreover, he was now the chief of the Grinnell tribe.

STANDING MENACE

At the time of George Blake Grinnell's death, Audubon Park was still very much the family seat, but the tide of an expanding city now lapped at its doorstep. The population of Manhattan in 1891 exceeded a million and a half people, more than double what it had been when the Grinnells first moved to its northern shore in 1857. The nearby village of Carmansville had once been working-class, but Washington Heights, as the neighborhood centered on 155th Street was commonly known, was becoming increasingly more gentrified—middle class supplanting working class, row houses and apartment buildings replacing freestanding frame houses. The elevated train, the streetcar, and improved streets pumped population into the city's ever more robust extremities.

After the crash of 1873, George Blake Grinnell had retired to Audubon Park and, as the *Times* reported, "lived quietly." Nearly all the obituaries mentioned his bankruptcy, making no comment on its unseemliness and instead taking on faith that, in the end, he had paid off his creditors. His comeuppance and exoneration were the episode in his career that the public remembered most, and few New Yorkers had heard much about him since.

Yet he was not exactly inactive in the eighteen years that followed. He had managed his investments with prudence; railroad, telegraph, and industrial stocks dominated a stout portfolio. He bought more property in Washington Heights, and he maintained his farm, named Beaver Brook, in Milford, Connecticut, on Long Island Sound, seventy miles from New York. There he raised produce and kept a few cows and pigs, enough to supply the kitchens of Audubon Park with vegetables, butter, and bacon.

Also in Milford he invested in an old mill on the waterfront. One of his tenants manufactured straw hats. Another tenant was a company in which George Blake Grinnell was the largest investor: Bosworth Machine manufactured and leased (and also owned patents on) sewing machines built especially for stitching harnesses. He had many contemporaries who were wealthier, but George Blake had made sure that, if his heirs managed their inheritance wisely, they would live comfortably.

No one benefited from the father's largesse more than George Bird Grinnell. After the embarrassment of 1873, as Grinnell chose a course that led him first to the tutelage of Othniel Marsh and then to *Forest and Stream*, his father's blessing and backing never wavered. Grinnell did not make much as an editor or author. His annual trips to the West were surely paid from the family purse, at least in part. Guides, guns, grub, and train fare added up, as did membership in the Union League, Metropolitan Club, Century Association, and eventually an exclusive duck-hunting club in North Carolina; all were possible, thanks to George Blake Grinnell. Then, too, bed and board at Audubon Park were free.

None of Grinnell's siblings wandered far from the fold, either. In 1882 Helen had married William Page, a lawyer in Frank and Mort Grinnell's class at Yale. Four years later Laura married another member of the Yale class of 1875, Newell Martin, likewise an attorney. Both sisters and their families lived side by side in houses George Blake Grinnell had built for them at Audubon Park. Mort Grinnell was a surgeon for the New York Police Department; he and his wife, Natalie, moved into the Hemlocks at first, along with the two bachelor brothers, George and William. Eventually, though, Mort and Natalie moved downtown to Twenty-Sixth Street and later lived full time at Beaver Brook Farm.

George Bird Grinnell was fortunate to have two lawyers in the family, and they would prove to be helpful in managing family affairs. But after his father died, it was he, the eldest son, who immediately assumed responsibility for Audubon Park, the Connecticut farm, Bosworth Machine, and other holdings. And it was he who devoted the most attention to his mother, his sisters being preoccupied with their growing households.

The shock of her husband's death sent Helen Grinnell to her bed. Four months later she was unable to walk and barely able to sit up. George Bird, who was long accustomed to spending his evenings at home, began to feel trapped. He had to inform White Calf and the Piegans that he could not join them in Washington. He regretted that he could not accept Ned Dana's invitations to New Haven. He missed the annual Boone and Crockett dinner. In turning down an opportunity to address the Anthropological Association he explained with a shade of self-pity, "[M]y mother's health is so unsatisfactory that I do not feel like being absent from the house even for a night."

With George Gould, whom he had not seen in a year and a half, he struck an even more melancholy tone. "I do not say much about your frequent invitations to Santa Barbara, but I cannot come now and probably not for many years," he wrote in February.

A month later Gould sent him a card advertising the Santa Barbara flower show; the images stirred Grinnell's memories of his visit in 1876. "[I] look back on Santa Barbara as an earthly heaven," he replied to Gould. "As things stand now, however, I am more busy than ever, for I have on my shoulders my fathers affairs, some of which are in a bad state of entanglement."

So long as his mother was alive, he feared he would never again be able to go west, and, consciously or not, he conflated the passing of his own life with the passing of the West's glory days. Anchored to office and home, Grinnell peered into the past the way a retired ship captain looks seaward. Before putting the finishing touches on the Blackfeet book, he worked on an article for *Scribner's Magazine* about buffalo, which turned into an extended exercise in nostalgia.

"On the floor, on either side of my fireplace, lie two buffalo skulls," he began, describing a winter evening at Audubon Park—with his mother bundled in her bedroom on the floor above. "They are white and weathered, the horns cracked and bleached by the snows and frosts, and the rains and heats of many winters and summers. Often, late at night, when the house is quiet, I sit before the fire, and muse and dream of the old days; and as I gaze at these relics of the past, they take life before my eyes."

He conjured the immense herds that once covered the prairies and the Indians who hunted them. Yet the article was less a sentimental journey than a dirge for the dead. Where once the species was so abundant that the country was "one robe," it had now "passed into history." The North American population of buffalo that had numbered in the millions—the number may have been thirty million or more—had by 1892 dwindled to fewer than one thousand. The article was titled, "The Last of the Buffalo."

When it came time to submit his Blackfeet manuscript, Grinnell naturally chose the house of Charles Scribner's Sons, whose magazine had welcomed the buffalo article. "These are the Indians' stories and are not worked up by me," he explained to William Brownell, who also edited the prose of sophisticates like Matthew Arnold and Edith Wharton. "I want them to appear just as they were told by the Indians."

So far, Grinnell had published only under the Forest and Stream imprint or in anthropology and folklore journals. He doubted his chances of placing his work alongside that of belletrists. He apologized to Brownell for the "drier portion" of the manuscript on Blackfeet customs and beliefs but hoped that the stories would hold readers' interest. Lest Brownell dismiss him as another teller of tall tales, he stated, "I am an adopted member of the [Piegan] tribe of Blackfeet, and this manuscript represents the material which I have collected during several seasons of close intercourse with the people." He chose to say nothing about James Willard Schultz's role in the endeavor.

Lately he had been wearing his tribal membership as a badge of honor. In January he had told anthropologist Franz Boas, "Have been a member of the tribe for years and can do with them more than any other white man." Whites took him at his word, though just what Grinnell meant by "member" is not clear. His diaries offer little help, other than to describe the less-than-formal naming ceremony performed by Four Bears outside Joe Kipp's trading post in 1885. The only other evidence of Grinnell's adoption is expressed in the salutations he used when addressing the Piegans. They were "brothers," and shortly after the death of George Blake Grinnell, George Bird wrote to White Calf, "I feel as if you and all your people were my close relations." Henceforth he would greet White Calf as "My Father." Clearly family was something that had taken on broader and deeper meaning.

To Grinnell's surprise, Scribner's accepted the manuscript, and it appeared in the fall as *Blackfoot Lodge Tales: The Story of a Prairie People*. To his further satisfaction, Scribner's agreed to bring out a new edition of *Pawnee Hero Stories*. Along with "The Last of the Buffalo" in *Scribner's Magazine*, 1892 was proving to be a productive year.

The first and last chapters of *Blackfoot Lodge Tales* are written by a man confident of speaking on the tribe's behalf—and by someone to whom the tribe evidently deferred. "During my annual visits to the Blackfeet reservation, which have extended over two, three, or four months each season, I see a great many of the men and have long conversations with them," Grinnell declares, although, in fact, he had never spent more than a couple of weeks at a time with the Piegans. "They bring their troubles to me, asking what they shall do, and how their condition may be improved. They tell me what things they want, and why they think they ought to have them."

Writing, as he was, for white readers and not to the Piegans directly, he did not in this context refer to them as brothers, as equals. Instead, "I listen and talk to them as if they were so many children," he clarifies. "If their requests are unreasonable, I try to explain to them, step by step, why it is not best that what they desire should be done, or tell them that other things which they ask for seem proper, and that I will do what I can to have them granted."

Despite his categorical condescension—his paternalism, his embrace of contemporary evolutionary theory, his casual use of the word *savage*—he vouches for the humanity of the Blackfeet and Indians in general, and he condemns white civilization for its conduct toward them. The very first paragraph of *Blackfoot Lodge Tales* reads: "The most shameful chapter of American history is that in which is recorded the account of our dealings with the Indians. The story of our government's intercourse with this race is an unbroken narrative of injustice, fraud, and robbery. Our people have disregarded honesty and truth whenever they have come in contact with the Indian, and he has had no rights because he has never had the power to enforce any."

Among Grinnell's contemporaries, notwithstanding other friends of the Indian, this was a radical charge. Few members of the Boone and Crockett Club were inclined to shoulder the white man's burden, or the guilt. Certainly Theodore Roosevelt, the one-time Dakota cowboy, did not share Grinnell's shame at the American empire's transgressions against its native population. "I don't go so far as to think that the only good Indians are the dead Indians, but I believe nine out of ten are, and I shouldn't like to inquire too closely into the case of the tenth," Roosevelt told a New York audience in 1886, borrowing a remark attributed to future Boone and Crockett member Philip Sheridan.

In *Blackfoot Lodge Tales* Grinnell took a somewhat more enlightened position. Indians make willing workers, open to progress "toward civilization," he asserts, when given honest, steadfast, trustworthy guidance by men and women with "no private interest to serve, but [who] wished to do the best that he could for [the] people." Guidance, that is, provided by someone like Grinnell.

Reviews of the Blackfeet book praised Grinnell for his authenticity and authoritativeness. The highest compliment was paid by James Mooney of the Smithsonian's Bureau of Ethnology, then engaged in a comprehensive study of the ghost dance: "The author has that rare combination of scientific accuracy with attractive literary style which makes all that he writes a reference dictionary to the ethnologist and [a] pleasure to the folklorist and the popular reader."

As he had anticipated, Grinnell was unable to go west in the summer of 1892, his first absence in twelve years. If anything, though, this hiatus served to redouble his dedication to preserving the West's natural assets. Now more than ever, Yellowstone was under siege.

The creation of the forest reserve on the east and south side of the park had done nothing to deter the ambition of the railroad to run a line from Gardiner, at the north entrance, through the park, to the mining town of Cooke City, just outside the northeast boundary and not included in President Harrison's 1891 forest reserve proclamation.

If and when Congress agreed to charter the Montana Mineral Railway, as the latest Yellowstone venture was called, the presumption was that the Northern Pacific would step in and buy the line. The pro-railroad lobby was relentless, and Senator Vest, one of the park's staunchest defenders, had grown weary to the point of capitulation. He calculated that if the railroad were granted its right-of-way and if the northeast portion of the park—everything north of the Yellowstone River, more than three hundred square miles—were "segregated," then perhaps his antagonists would be appeased and "those of us who are aesthetic and sentimental" about Yellowstone might at last succeed in stiffening the rules to protect the vast remainder of the national park. Addressing his fellow senators, Vest rationalized that "there are not many objects of great curiosity in that portion of the reservation" anyway. (This was hardly so: the country considered for segregation included the valley of the Lamar River, a tributary of the Yellowstone that today is regarded as critical buffalo, elk, and wolf habitat and is one of the most popular tourist destinations in the park.)

Grinnell, too, began to flag. "I am sick of fighting for the National Park," he complained in February, while cursing the lobby as a bunch of "sharks." But by May he dug in once more. "The Park is threatened by serious dangers," he wrote in *Forest and Stream*. "There are selfish influences pressing upon it [from] every direction, and the very people who should have its interests at heart, that is the inhabitants of the surrounding States, are the ones most intent upon accomplishing its destruction."

In December he marshaled his full arsenal of arguments against segregation in a virulent broadside, "A Standing Menace: Cooke City vs. The National Park." It appeared simultaneously in *Forest and Stream* and as a sixteen-page pamphlet. Writing to William Hallett Phillips a week later, Grinnell declared with renewed resolve: "[This] is one of the cases where [we] cannot very well stop fighting."

"A Standing Menace" doubted the value of the Cooke City mines. Grinnell insisted there was a better way (via the Clark's Fork River) to reach

Cooke City that would not invade the park. He warned that the boundary and railroad proposed in the segregation bill would provide poachers with even easier access to the park's wildlife. And granting a right-of-way for one railroad would set a precedent for further invasion by others. In his conclusory thrust Grinnell took umbrage with pro-segregationists who argued that progress was being impeded by a small group of sentimentalists.

"The National Park *is* founded on sentiment," he asserted. "It is a legislative recognition of the existence in human nature of something higher than the sordid love of gain—than the mere question of dollars and cents. . . . To all that class who unblushingly place their little interests above a great public interest, who without scruple would inaugurate measures which must lead to the ruin of the National Park, Congress should oppose but one answer, and that should be written in distinct and permanent characters on every border of the Park: 'Thus far thou shalt come and no further.'"

Grinnell made sure that the "Standing Menace" pamphlet was circulated throughout Washington. He published testimony by the president of the Northern Pacific that the Cooke City mines were actually worthless and that a railroad there would be senseless. He encouraged Yellowstone Superintendent George Anderson, a battle-tested West Pointer, to testify against the railroad before Congress, and he received strong support from Theodore Roosevelt, who had toured Yellowstone in 1890. "[A]ll public-spirited Americans should join with *Forest and Stream* in the effort to prevent the greed of a little group of speculators," Roosevelt beseeched.

Yet despite all these noble efforts, the railroad appeared to be winning the war. The bill passed the Senate and steamed onward to the House. Smelling victory, the bill's advocates pressed the speaker of the House to put the bill to a "suspension vote," a parliamentarian ploy that allowed a bill to be hurried through without amendment or protracted debate. Grinnell got wind of the suspension tactic and attacked it on the front page of *Forest and Stream* as a "trick" and a "fraud."

Evidently swayed by this eleventh-hour offensive, the speaker chose to let the Yellowstone bill languish, and the session came to a close without a vote. The railroad lobby would come back one more time, a year later, but by then the Panic of 1893 had cooled Congress's ardor for speculation, and segregation became a dead letter. This was one Yellowstone battle that George Bird Grinnell would never have to fight again.

For all that, there remained the pressing matter of how to give teeth to the park's existing regulations. Since taking over as superintendent, George Anderson had continuously asked his superiors in Washington for more manpower and authority. In the summer of 1893 he had only one civilian scout, Felix Burgess, patrolling the entire park. With two more, Anderson thought he could get a grip on the poaching, which was increasing at an alarming rate. "This will be a very small sum for a nation to pay for the preservation of its rapidly disappearing wild animals, and no similar expenditure would contribute so much to the end for which the park was created," Anderson wrote Secretary of the Interior Hoke Smith, a Georgian appointed by newly inaugurated (for the second time) Grover Cleveland. He wrote again in the fall, warning, "As winter approaches, I hear of preparations to make raids on my buffalo. It would be a crying shame if the Govt. were to permit this last remaining herd to be destroyed."

Anderson finally did get a small reinforcement of scouts, and *Forest and Stream* also played a crucial role in ensuring the long-term safety of the park's wildlife.

Of the few buffalo left on the continent, the largest remnant lived in Yellowstone. Taxidermists and their clients paid poachers more than $300 (roughly $10,000 today) for a hide, along with its woolly head and horns. The worst danger, not unexpectedly, came from Cooke City, known to be the roost of several poachers, the wiliest of whom was Edward Howell.

Winter was the best time of year to rob Yellowstone of buffalo. The animals could not run through deep snow, and their robes were at the thickest. Also there was less chance of getting caught—or so Howell thought.

In February 1894 a scout spotted the track of a toboggan near Soda Butte Creek, along the route a poacher would take between Cooke City and the buffalo wintering grounds on the north side of Yellowstone Lake. Anderson sent Felix Burgess and a sergeant named Troike in pursuit. In mid-March they traveled on ten-foot-long skis, balancing and pushing themselves by a single pole. Eventually they came upon fresh tracks, presumably those of

Howell and his toboggan, and, through a fierce snowstorm, followed the poacher over windswept Specimen Ridge to frozen Astringent Creek in the Pelican Valley on the north side of the lake.

First they came upon six buffalo hides and heads, wrapped in burlap and strung from tree limbs, out of the reach of wolves. Burgess and Troike skied on, drawn by the sound of gunfire. From the timber they spied Howell absorbed in the labor of skinning a buffalo. Four more lay nearby.

Armed with only a .38 revolver but with the wind in his favor, Burgess, a veteran of the Indian wars, crossed four hundred yards of open ground, every moment expecting Howell to raise his head and reach for the repeating rifle leaning against a nearby buffalo carcass. But the brim of Howell's hat limited his view, and his shepherd dog, curled by his side, never caught the scent of the unexpected stranger, allowing Burgess to slip between Howell and his gun before ordering the butcher to raise his hands and drop the knife. Burgess and Troike then escorted their prisoner eight miles to the Yellowstone Lake hotel, occupied for the winter by a caretaker and his wife. "I expect probably I was pretty lucky," Burgess said later. "Everything seemed to work in my favor."

Grinnell learned of Howell's capture by way of a telegram from park headquarters. He hastened an editorial into print, decrying the Yellowstone slaughter and the lack of authority to punish "miserable scoundrels" like Howell. As the law stood, park officials could do no more than confiscate the meat and hides and escort poachers to the park boundary. "Such a condition is not only an anomaly under our form of government," Grinnell lectured, "but a disgrace to every American citizen. . . . Congress, by its continued neglect, encourages the evil-minded to believe that they may penetrate even here and destroy the last remnant of a race long nearly extinct. . . . At this rate it will not be long before the last shall have been shot down." Grinnell was determined to wave Howell's bloody knife under the nose of Congress until at last he had closed the legal loophole that endangered the big game for which he had worked so hard to provide sanctuary.

From Yellowstone Lake Howell was taken to the guardhouse at Fort

Yellowstone, pending instructions from the secretary of the interior—instructions that were slow in coming.

By sheer coincidence, another special visitor was in the vicinity just then. *Forest and Stream* correspondent Emerson Hough had recently arrived to write a serial on the park's winter wonders, to appear under the heading, "Forest and Stream's Yellowstone Park Game Exploration." Hough was Grinnell's jack-of-all-trades in Chicago, where he covered sporting news from the Midwest and West. A lawyer by training, he was self-motivated and highly ambitious, and in March of 1894 Hough was in the right place at the right time. Grinnell could not have been more pleased with their mutual good fortune.

When George Anderson sent out a detail to recover the hides and heads that Howell had been in the act of plundering, Hough asked to join them. His own "expedition" was guided by Thomas Elwood "Billy" Hofer, who over the years had escorted Grinnell, Theodore Roosevelt, President Arthur, and sundry other swells through the wilds of the park. Hofer was raised in New Haven—though not the Yale side of New Haven—and had gone west as a boy, knocking about Colorado mining camps before finding his way to Yellowstone in the 1880s. His dispatches from the park appeared regularly in *Forest and Stream*.

The third member of Hough's party was Frank Jay Haynes, who parlayed his services as official photographer for the Northern Pacific into a thriving career selling pictures and postcards to Yellowstone tourists. For Grinnell's purposes, they made a crack team. Hofer taught Hough how to ski and led the way, and Hough's colorful on-scene retelling of the capture of Howell, accompanied by Haynes's photographs of the carnage, produced a sensational effect. Other papers picked up the story, and each episode of Hough's serial in *Forest and Stream* was introduced by an editorial written by Grinnell, denouncing Howell's wholesale butchery and Congress's shameful delinquency and encouraging readers to demand that the government protect the property "which belongs to those whom it represents."

Three days after Howell's crime against nature was posted in *Forest and Stream*, Representative John F. Lacey introduced a bill to place Yellowstone under "the sole and exclusive jurisdiction of the United States."

Victor Audubon, *View of the Hudson River*, from below Minnie's Land, c. 1845.

n James Audubon.

Lucy Bakewell Audubon with granddaughters Lucy (left) and Harriet.

George Bird Grinnell as
a Yale undergraduate.

The Hemlocks,
Audubon Park.

Grinnell's study and bird
collection, the Hemlocks.

illiam F. "Buffalo Bill" Cody, 1870.

Frank North.

Luther "Lute" North.

"Lonesome" Charley Reynolds.

Yale College scientific expedition, 1870. Grinnell stands second from left; O. C. Marsh stands at center; and Jim Russell sits at far right.

George Armstrong Custer (center) with grizzly bear, 1874.

Theodore Roosevelt, portrait for *Hunting Trips of a Ranchman*, 1885.

George H. Gould.

Edward S. Dana.

James Willard "Appekunny" Schultz and son, Hart Merriam Schultz.

Grinnell Glacier, 1885.

Terms, Five Dollars a Year. }
Ten Cents a Copy. }

NEW YORK, THURSDAY, DEC. 25, 1873.

{ Volume 1 Number 20.
{ 103 Fulton Street.

Forest and Stream,
December 25, 1873,
featuring Grinnell's
"Buffalo Hunt with
the Pawnees."

From Harper's Weekly, 1871.

THE GOBBLER'S CHRISTMAS CAROL.

AH! hungry reader! gourmandizer!
How bless your lot, how foul is mine!
Pray realize [l—realize, ah!,
Mine 'tis to die that you may *dine.*

When from the natal shell I bursted
To fledging life and parent hen,
That precious life I little trusted
Would be so soon *shelled out* again.

Amid the barn-yard's rare attractions,
Strutting the feathered herd among,
I little dreamed such fowl eggs-actions
On Christmas holidays were wrong.

I never troubled the Hereafter;
The present was sufficient bliss—
Alas! 'tis no cause for laughter
To find our necks *twirled* short in this.

Yet 'twas for this betimes I fattened,
For this alone so fully fed;
Trust when a Christmas day next happened
My rein should not in cost be bled.

For this I proudly strutted, hobbled:
I dreampt not of this bitter cup.
Long time I gobbled, gobbled, gobbled,
But now at last I'm gobbled up.

Say, reader, am I justly treated?
Should that which is *a?right* my meat?
Be freely out to strangers meted?
Confess it now, I beg, entreat!

Regard my end with melancholy—
Drawn and quartered, basted, sauced—
And when you sing the yule and holly
Contemplate, too, the holocaust.   CHARLES HALLOCK.

Buffalo Hunt with the Pawnees.

THE sun pushing aside the misty curtains of the east commences to renew his daily course, bringing again light and life to all animated nature. It touches the more elevated bluffs with flaming light and suffuses the whole heavens with a ruddy glow. The leaves of the low willows, frosted with a coating of tiny dew-drops, glisten in his light, and each silvery globule that hangs from the high grass reflects his image like a polished mirror. The waters of the Republican, dark and turbid as they always are, seem to become purer as they are touched by his beams, and flash and gloam as they whirl along toward the Missouri. The mellow whistle of the meadow lark is heard from the prairie, the short cry of the migrating blackbird falls from on high, a flock of ducks on whistling wing pass over us on their way to those genial climes where frost and snow do not penetrate, and where the rigors of winter are not felt.

The quiet beauty of the prospect is enchanting, but I desire to introduce you to more stirring scenes. Bear with me for a moment, however, while I give you a brief description of the country through which we are to journey —of the land of the buffalo. Could we attain the heights traveled by the feathered travelers that are continually passing, a magnificent view would meet our eyes. Far away to the north I would point out to you the faint dark line formed by the tall cottonwoods that fringe the Platte and by which its direction east and west may be traced as far as the eye can reach. As far to the south and scarcely to be discerned save by the keenest sight, another low dark line marks the course of the Solomon, and between these two we see many lesser streams, some flowing north and some south, each bearing its share of alluvium to swell the deltas of the Mississippi. Besides these the plain is intersected by innumerable ravines running in all directions. These serve to carry off the surplus water in times of rain, each emptying into some large one, and that in turn into one still larger, until finally a stream is formed which joins into the main river. On the borders of such streams feed the deer and elk; along their grassy bottoms stalks the wild turkey, resplendent in his bronzed plumage; among

the tangled thickets that grow upon their banks lurks the great white wolf; and amid the topmost branches of some lofty cottonwood the white-headed eagle rears her gigantic brood. Among the numberless bluffs that rise one after another like the waves of a tossing sea, the buffaloes can be seen by thousands; some peacefully reposing on the rich bottoms, others feeding upon the short nutritious grass that clothes the hillsides. The calves play clumsily about, and the old bulls from the tops of the bluffs grimly watch over their uncouth families.

Rarely are these scenes disturbed save when the prowling Sioux, returning from some foray upon the luckless settlers, halts for a brief period to rest his worn out animals and to eat his hasty meal, or when a squadron of cavalry with rattle of arms and clink of spur hurries along upon the trail of the dusky robber, all too late to recover his booty or avenge his crimes. A few hunters or a party of surveyors occasionally pass through this region, but except by those and by the Indian it is rarely visited.

We are standing upon the northern border of the present range of the buffalo. A few passing beyond the Republican advance as far north as the Platte, but rarely cross that river. South of the former, however, they still abound; not in such numbers indeed as in former years, but still often sufficiently numerous to blacken the plains and to become an easy prey to whoever will hunt them. But their days are numbered, and unless some action on this subject is speedily taken not only by the States and Territories, but by the National Government, these shaggy brown beasts, those cattle upon a thousand hills, will ere long be among the the things of the past.

Jim. R— and myself had left New York a week before, and meeting Lute at Plum Creek, had there obtained horses and a team and started off to overtake the Pawnees, who with their families and all their *impedimenta*, had set out from their reservation three weeks before for a grand buffalo hunt. Many a time during my wanderings west of the Missouri, had these hunts of the Indians been described to me with a graphic eloquence that filled me with enthusiasm as I listened to the recital, and I had determined that if ever the opportunity offered I would take part in one. The time had at last come, and we were now on our fourth day out from the rail road, having traveled over one hundred and twenty miles, and hoping before nightfall to catch up with the Indians.

Nor were we disappointed in this hope, for when we crossed the Republican and turned southward, the trail which we were following became fresher and gave evidence of having been made only the day before. Soon we passed their last night's camp, the ashes of the fires still warm and the fresh buffalo bones not yet dried by the sun. Encouraged by these signs we urged forward our horses, and a short time [...] sight of the broad bott[...]

There w[...]
over four [...]
few Ponca[...]
the lodges [...]
as we after [...]
tered that a [...]
them for se[...]
Of course [...]
tunity wou[...]
stock and [...]
tended to p[...]
not being n[...]

The scen[...]
girls were b[...]
and cooking [...]
ing and tall [...]
gazed at us [...]
lage we had [...]
to see old F[...]
received us [...]
him "my s[...]

as he sat by his side. The old man told us that the hunt so far had not been very successful, that the buffalo were not plenty north of the Republican as they used to be when he was a young man, but tomorrow, he said, a grand surround would be made, as his young men had reported plenty of buffalo about twenty miles to the southward. Pleased with this intelligence we left him and after a stroll through the Indian camp returned to our own, and were soon enjoying the deep and dreamless sleep that follows a hard day's march.

But alas for our anticipations. When we rose next morning we were dismayed by the sight of a dark mist which hung over the valley, sometimes lifting for a few moments so as to disclose the bluffs beyond, and then settling down again heavier than before. It was evident that the scouts sent out by the Indians to look for buffalo would be unable to see through the heavy fog, and so our prospects for a hunt on this day were very poor. We started from our camp soon after the Pawnees moved out, and before long our doleful thoughts were dispelled by the interesting spectacle of four thousand Indians on the march.

At the head of the column walked eight men, each carrying a long pole wrapped round with red and blue cloth and fantastically ornamented with feathers, which fluttered in the breeze as they were borne along. These were the buffalo sticks, and were religiously guarded at all times, as the success of the hunt was supposed to depend largely upon the respect shown to them. Immediately after these came thirty or forty of the principal men of the tribe, all mounted on superb ponies, their saddles glittering with silver ornaments, and their bridles tinkling with little bells. Then followed a motly assemblage, consisting of the squaws of the tribe, each of whom as she walked along led one or two ponies heavily packed. A moderately loaded pony would carry, first the lodge, with the poles tied on each side of the pack, the ends dragging along on the ground, next a pile of blankets and robes a foot or two in height, around which are tied pots, tin cups, and other utensils, and on top of this heap are perched from two to five small children, each of which holds in its arms two or three young puppies. Loose horses without any burdens, and half-grown colts, each with a little pack on his back, run at large among the the crowd, and their shrill neighings mingle with the barking of the dogs and the incessant clamor of the women. Along the outskirts of this strange concourse ran half a dozen well grown boys engaged in playing a game in which they seemed intensely interested, and on which as I afterward learned, they were betting. Each held in his right hand a slender stick about four feet long, and one of them had also a ring of plated raw hide three or four inches in diameter. As the latter ran he threw this

Grinnell with Piegans and notebook, 1891.

Grinnell (center left) and Billy Jackson (center right) talking sign language.

The poacher Edward Howell (right) with his captors, 1894.
PHOTOGRAPH BY FRANK JAY HAYNES.

Buffalo heads recovered, Yellowstone National Park.
PHOTOGRAPH BY FRANK JAY HAYNES.

The *George W. Elder* in
Glacier Bay.
PHOTOGRAPH BY
EDWARD S. CURTIS.

The Two Johnnies: John
Burroughs (left) and John
Muir.
PHOTOGRAPH BY EDWARD
S. CURTIS.

The Harriman Alaska Expedition at an abandoned Tlingit village; Grinnell standing at
center in dark vest and light cap. PHOTOGRAPH BY EDWARD S. CURTIS.

John Lacey was another unlikely (and under-sung) hero of the American conservation movement. Born and raised in Oskaloosa, Iowa, he worked his way from soldier to lawyer to legislator to judge, and finally to the U.S. House of Representatives. His enjoyment of the outdoors took him to Yellowstone in 1887, where, immediately after crossing the park's northern boundary, he and his fellow stagecoach passengers were robbed by masked men. Lacey grasped, better than most, how badly Yellowstone needed law and order.

Lacey's bill raced through the Committee on Public Lands and less than two weeks later was passed by the formerly hostile House, without debate. The momentum carried onward to the Senate, where Senator Vest chaperoned it through the Committee on Territories. Word reached Washington that Howell had been released from the guardhouse, underscoring the necessity of stiffer enforcement. For once the railroad lobby did not butt in. With Grinnell and *Forest and Stream* enfilading from New York, William Hallett Phillips and Theodore Roosevelt worked the Capitol trenches. "I have seen half a dozen Senators about it already," Roosevelt wrote Superintendent Anderson at the end of March. "I haven't got the least idea whether we will be successful or not."

He need not have worried. The Senate passed the bill on May 2, and President Cleveland signed it on May 7.

Anderson would call the capture of Howell "the most important arrest . . . ever made in the Park." The legislation it precipitated, titled the Yellowstone Park Protection Act but commonly known as the Lacey Act, was every bit as momentous. Park regulations henceforth would be determined by the secretary of the interior; violations of these regulations would be adjudicated not by the courts of the three surrounding states—Wyoming, Montana, and Idaho—but by a federally appointed commissioner and one or more deputy marshals appointed by the commissioner. At last Yellowstone was entirely its own entity: in land (national park), in administration (U.S. Army), and now by law.

And the law was very specific and firm. It forbade "all hunting or killing, wounding, or capturing at any time of any bird or wild animal, except dangerous animals, when it is necessary to prevent them from destroying human life or inflicting any injury." Fish could not be taken from park waters by seines, nets, traps, or explosives. Even the frightening of wildlife was proscribed. Further, the secretary of the interior was authorized to issue regulations "for the preservation from injury or spoliation of all timber, mineral deposits, natural curiosities or wonderful objects." Anyone caught violating these rules could be fined as much as $1,000 and sentenced to two years in prison.

"I believe the days of poaching in the Park are nearly at an end," Anderson stated optimistically.

Or so he hoped; poaching, vandalism, and other insults to the natural sanctity of Yellowstone would never cease completely. But with the Lacey Act on the books and with punishments for violations posted publicly, those who had labored for so long to ensure Yellowstone's preservation had drawn a line that miscreants would be much more hesitant to cross. The park's buffalo would now have a fighting chance to rebound; so, too, would the species as a whole. And soon the framework that now girded Yellowstone would be adopted by the three other national parks so far in existence: Yosemite and California's "big tree" parks, Sequoia and General Grant.

Grinnell was quick to congratulate all those who had fought for the Lacey Act—Lacey, Vest, Roosevelt, Phillips, Anderson, Hoke Smith—but he reserved a hefty portion of credit for himself and *Forest and Stream*. "It is not too much to say that the passage of this bill is due directly to the agitation of the subject by the *Forest and Stream*," he crowed in the issue of May 12. "The *Forest and Stream* was the first newspaper to urge protection for the National Park, the first to announce last winter's bloody work, and to point out the inevitable consequences unless Congress took immediate action; and it looks with satisfaction on its record in this matter, for it has become known far and wide as the champion of the Park."

Grinnell did not go west in the summer of 1893, either, his second absence in a row. "My mother is no better than she has been, and there seems no prospect of her recovery," he wrote to his tenant on the Shirley Basin ranch, explaining why he was unable to get out to Wyoming. Nor was he one of the millions who made their way to Chicago to see the World's Columbian

Exposition; instead he had to be satisfied with Emerson Hough's dispatches from the fair.

The closest he came to a western adventure during this two-year hiatus was to arrange for George Gould to visit Yellowstone. "He is a man of whom I am very fond," Grinnell wrote Billy Hofer, by way of introduction. Grinnell vouched for Gould's hardiness and experience but added, "he likes to be fairly comfortable in camp."

Gould wrote a droll account of his trip for *Forest and Stream,* under the customary byline, H. G. Dulog. Evidently, however, he had not been entirely pleased with Billy Hofer as a guide. In a letter to Gould, Grinnell stood up for Hofer as "a good packer and a pleasant camp companion," but he also sensed that Gould would have preferred the company of a different "partner," whom he had not seen since 1890. "If ever I get out to take another hunt, I shall try harder than ever . . . to persuade you to go with me," Grinnell wrote after Gould returned from Yellowstone. "One may have five or six men in the lodge every night and still be alone, and this is the way I have felt for the last two years."

In the meantime, Grinnell had to be satisfied with other partners. Not long after completing *Blackfoot Lodge Tales,* he teamed with Theodore Roosevelt to edit the first of what would become a series of Boone and Crockett anthologies, *American Big-Game Hunting,* which included Grinnell's "Last of the Buffalo" (under the title "In Buffalo Days") and noble stories of stalking written by Roosevelt, Owen Wister, Archibald Rogers, and other club members.

He also joined the City Club, founded in 1892 by a group of upstanding citizens (among them Yale classmate William Gulliver) to fight the venalities of Tammany Hall. Through the City Club's initiative, Good Government Clubs formed in most assembly districts—including the Twenty-Eighth, where Audubon Park was located—and Grinnell was named to the executive committee of the citywide Good Government Convention.

He likewise became a member of the more exclusive Committee of Seventy, joining the likes of J. P. Morgan, Carl Schurz, Elihu Root, and Jacob Schiff. The Committee's organizational circular proclaimed: "It is believed that the people of the city are tired of the burden of inefficiency, extravagance and plunder, and understand that a city, like a well-ordered household, should be managed solely in the best interests of its people, and to this end should be entirely divorced from party politics and selfish personal ambition or gain." It was a goal that suited Grinnell entirely: Well-ordered households were of great concern to him.

Yet despite his desire for betterment, he was not one to wear partisanship on his sleeve, even while surrounded by so many Republicans. In 1894 the City Club, the Good Government Clubs, and the Committee of Seventy were backing Republican William Strong for mayor. Levi Morton, Republican Benjamin Harrison's vice president—and George Blake Grinnell's old business partner—was running for New York governor. Grinnell supported both Morton and Strong, yet in 1892 he had declined to vote for Harrison's reelection and instead had cast his ballot for Grover Cleveland. Cleveland was a Democrat, but he was a "good Democrat," Grinnell wrote George Gould.

If any label fit George Bird Grinnell, it was "goo-goo," the nickname given to the good-government activists. Reform was the watchword of the day—whether in the precincts of New York or in the West.

Finally, though, the bonds that had tethered him to home and hearth since the death of his father were loosened. Helen Lansing Grinnell died on August 23, 1894. The funeral took place at home in Audubon Park, and, with her passing, George Bird Grinnell and brother William Milne Grinnell were the last remaining occupants of the many-roomed manse they still called the Hemlocks. Their mother's will named both as executors of her estate.

Almost immediately Grinnell arranged to return to the Blackfeet and Northern Cheyenne reservations. Apparently he had forgotten about his remark to George Gould, made in a moment of melancholy three years earlier, that he did not care to see the mountains of the Walled-in Lakes again.

CHAPTER 17

THE CEDED STRIP

G rinnell stepped onto the platform at Blackfoot station on October 22, 1894. A great deal had occurred since his last visit three years earlier, as evidenced by the bustle at the station itself. The Great Northern Railway was now complete from St. Paul to Seattle, and its tracks passed through the heart of the reservation. Construction of a new agency was under way on Willow Creek, six miles to the west, to make it easier for supplies to reach the Indians.

Yet the railroad also made it easier for non-Indians to gain access to the reservation. Prospectors had begun poking around, illegally but none too secretly, in the Swiftcurrent valley. Thus far there had been no big strikes, but early hints of copper were tantalizing, and Grinnell was anxious to inspect for himself. Talk of "opening" the reservation to mining and settlement had been circulating since 1892. Already there were whites of great financial and political influence who referred to the portion of the reservation along the eastern slope of the Rocky Mountains—St. Mary, Swiftcurrent, Two Medicine, Chief Mountain—as "the mineral strip."

The Piegan people were slightly better off than when Grinnell had last been among them, living more settled lives and raising their own cattle on the high plains. However, they were still very much at the mercy of whites.

Agent George Steell had done an effective job slowing the whiskey traffic, but he himself was a morphine addict. As harsh as he was on whiskey traders, Steell was selectively lenient toward trespassing cattlemen. More shamefully, he grazed his personal herd on Indian grass and hired Piegans to tend it—paying them with government money (vouchers, actually) redeemable only at the agency store, whose suppliers were his cronies.

Finally, with the election of Grover Cleveland, Steell had been replaced by Captain Lorenzo Cooke, an army officer. Steell was only marginally inconvenienced; he simply moved his cattle south across the reservation boundary and resumed ranching. By the time Grinnell arrived in Montana, Captain Cooke had been on the job a year but had already earned a reputation as a closed-minded disciplinarian.

During his absence from the Blackfeet reservation, Grinnell had received intermittent reports on the copper diggings. Back in July he had written to Steell, whose past sins he did not dismiss but whose eyes and ears he still found useful, sharing his expectations for the so-called mineral strip: "I had hoped that it might be practicable to set off the mountain part of the Piegan reservation as a national park, or a forest reserve." But, he added anxiously, "If the minerals actually exist . . . there is no hope that my plan can be carried out."

His concern was that a copper strike would spark a stampede that would ultimately shred Indian ownership. He remembered all too well what had happened after a few grains of gold were discovered during Custer's reconnaissance of the Black Hills in 1874. The Sioux, believing they were protected by a treaty ratified by Congress and signed by the president, had seen their homeland invaded and taken away. The same had happened to the Nez Percés in Idaho and to any number of other tribes. In every case the government had backed the miners, and the Indians took the hindmost.

Grinnell envisioned a middle way, one that would benefit the Piegans and the nation both. If the government acted promptly, an agreement might be struck whereby the Piegans ceded the mineral strip for a satisfactory sum before their land was occupied at the point of a pick and shovel—by which time their leverage would be negligible.

All the while, he nursed a second, or perhaps it was a third, option: If the mining boom did *not* materialize, maybe the Piegans could be persuaded to sell the strip anyway.

Steell had led Grinnell to believe that the Piegans might be open to such a treaty and sale, although Grinnell would have been more skeptical if he had been able to attend the 1891 meeting in Washington between the Piegan delegation and the commissioner of Indian affairs, at which White Calf had stated emphatically: "We wish you would give us a key to lock up the reservation; we think Congress or somebody else will cut this reservation down again. We want . . . to lock it so nobody can get in there."

Grinnell remained sympathetic to the Piegans' wishes, but he also knew that, realistically, they should prepare themselves for the inevitable. The treaty ratified in 1888, in which the tribe had "sold the Sweet Grass Hills," brought them $150,000 annually for ten years. Six years on, the money was nearly gone, and the tribe was still a long way from self-sustaining, with most living on shared land, dependent on rations and communal lifeways.

Grinnell hinted that he might be willing to participate in negotiations between the Piegans and the government. "I desire to see the mountain part of the reservation sold," he wrote to George Steell, "providing the rights of the Indians can be protected in all respects."

Steell had no such loyalty to the Indians and was eager to have the reservation opened as soon as possible, for as little as possible—and by whatever means necessary. At one point he even tried to bend Grinnell to his ambition by cutting him in on a claim in the mineral strip. To which Grinnell responded indignantly: "If I were to accept your offer, every man who might hear of me doing so would believe, and justly enough, that whatever influence I have [was] purchased for this interest. . . . The only thing that can influence me in this matter is the good of the Indians, and no other interest can enter into my view of the case."

For some reason he did not regard his dream of a national park, one that contained a glacier named for him and dozens of landmarks named by him, as a conflict.

Yet it was already more than a dream. The day before leaving New York, he had written to F. J. Whitney, an official of the Great Northern who had provided him with free tickets. He and Whitney arranged to meet when he passed through St. Paul. "I am anxious to converse with you on the subject of the attractions of the St. Mary's Lake country and its adaption for a public park and pleasure resort," Grinnell announced to Whitney. "I presume you are familiar with the St. Mary's Lakes. I am sure that Mr. Hill is, for I remember a year or two ago having quite a long talk with him on the subject." Mr. Hill was James J. Hill, founder and president of the Great Northern.

Grinnell arrived at the Blackfeet reservation bearing a letter from Secretary of the Interior Smith that gave him permission to tour all parts of the reservation, including the area where copper was said to be located, although the letter invested him with no authority to broach the subject of a treaty. He spent a week inspecting the sites of Swiftcurrent, including several seams that, to his untrained eye, appeared "very rich."

On November 4 he met with a group of twenty or thirty Piegans—including White Calf, Siyeh, Brocky, and Little Plume. This was the first extended meeting he'd had with tribal leaders in three years, and they had a lot on their minds. For nine hours the Piegan chiefs recited their grievances against Agent Cooke. The agent did not issue enough rations or show sufficient respect to the chiefs. The agent worked the Indians too hard on agency roads, ditches, and buildings. The agent had banned the annual medicine lodge, or sun dance, and jailed Piegans for building sweat lodges.

"A long and tiresome council," Grinnell wrote in his diary. "I tried to explain the bad things and praised the good. . . . The air was horrible and I went to bed with a headache."

Before Grinnell departed the reservation, Bear Chief, an old friend, presented him with a war shirt, headdress, and stone pipe. "The shirt and headdress are very sacred, and in old times very greatly valued," Grinnell noted in his diary. "Now, since things have changed, they have no longer any value, [and so he] gives them to me."

Afterward he wrote to the secretary of the interior: "While considerable dissatisfaction exists among some of the Indians . . . my personal inquiries [lead] me to believe that, as regards actual progress toward civilization and the protection of the rights of the Indians, matters there are in satisfactory condition."

Given the respect Grinnell now commanded among Indian experts, and indeed among Indians themselves, it was only fitting—and perhaps inevitable—that Secretary Smith would ask him to serve on a commission to treat with the Piegans over the sale of the western strip of their reservation. Grinnell had not thrust his own name forward, but his affinity for the Piegan people and, moreover, for the idea of turning the St. Mary country into the next Yellowstone was no secret. "The appointment which you offer is not one which I covet but one which I should feel like accepting if I thought that by so doing I could help these Indians on toward self-support and civilization," he replied to Smith. "I do not know whether your Department would expect the members of this commission to drive as hard a bargain as possible, or whether it wishes to have a fair price paid for the territory ceded."

In closing he added, "I assume, of course, that you wish to have justice done." And then he agreed to be on the Blackfeet reservation the following September.

Grinnell left New York at the first of August 1895, to allow time among the Northern Cheyennes before continuing on to the treaty talks at Browning. He invited his brother Mort to accompany him, hoping a change of scenery would distract Mort from his grief. For the past year Mort's wife had been failing, and he had given up his medical practice and moved her to Connecticut. She died at Milford on July 10.

Mort was now the second of the Grinnell siblings to lose a spouse. Helen Grinnell's husband, William Page, had collapsed in his law office two years earlier. Of the six Grinnells, one was dead (Frank), two were bachelors (George and William), two were widows (Mort and Helen), and only the youngest was married (Laura). After William Page's death, Helen and her five children had moved back into the Hemlocks, joining George and William, plus five servants to feed and look after them. Laura and Newell Martin, with three children, continued to live in their own house in Audubon Park.

Grinnell and Mort detrained at Rosebud, Montana, and rode by stage sixty miles to the Cheyenne agency at Lame Deer, where they were quartered in the schoolhouse. Bedbugs drove Grinnell from his cot on the first night, and he slept on the floor for the rest of his time at the agency.

Roughly one thousand Northern Cheyennes lived on the Tongue River Indian Reservation, as it was officially named at the time of its formation in 1884. Many of them had been among the Cheyennes who had been forcibly relocated to Indian Territory but then escaped north in 1878. Now they occupied three hundred thousand acres of dry, rolling uplands between Tongue River and Rosebud Creek.

"I don't know anything about the Cheyennes now," Grinnell had told Lute North the year before, "although I have seen something of them at one time and another, but, then, nobody else knows anything about them, so I don't see why I have not as good a chance as anybody to do the work."

As with the Blackfeet, it was impossible for Grinnell to gather material on their history and their way of life without also hearing their complaints about current conditions and past injustices. A talk with White Bull—interpreted by William Rowland, a white married into the tribe, and recorded by Grinnell's nimble pencil—described early encounters between the Cheyennes and persuasive traders.

"They brought many guns and showed them how to use them and told them they would be better than bows and arrows, that they could shoot the buffalo dead and need not run up close to them. Some men did not want to take guns, they said if we killed them like that we will kill all the game too quick and then we will be a poor people and will starve. . . . The best thing [they could] do is to give them the furs that they want . . . and tell them not to come back here any more. The trader told them it was good to take these goods and trade for them and that he would bring a lot more and build a house for a trading post. He said that if you get poor and all the buffalo should be killed, we will bring out white men's buffalo and give them to you."

The cascade of seduction continued:

"Then they"—whites—"will begin to tell you about their great chief who sent them out here. Then they will tell you that you must throw away your lodges and will tell you to build houses. . . . When the white men get thick, they will make roads through your country. It will make no difference how big the mountains are, they will go over them and through them. They will come to be numerous, will marry your women, and then go off and leave their children poor. . . . By and by they will want your children taken away and teach them to write on paper. You like your children and don't want to part with them. You all know that if you find a bird's nest and take the young birds, the old one flies all around you trying to get them back. When they ask for the children, tell . . . them that they have got everything you had and made you poor. Now if you give them your children, say [they] must pay for it."

This was not what Grinnell had come looking for precisely, but he wrote it all down, patiently and faithfully. Eventually, having won their confidence, he was able to gather the stories of the tribe's origin, of their migration westward from the Great Lakes, their battles against other tribes, their customs of birth, marriage, burial, and, as best he could, their beliefs. "The bad spirits or powers that shoot arrows of disease at people are not the ghosts of persons, but are like malignant fairies," he jotted with the uncertainty of an outsider. "It is hard to explain." Like James Willard Schultz, Grinnell struggled to translate the Indian sense of the supernatural into his own language.

He was more successful in conveying his aspirations for the Cheyennes to the authorities in Washington. In a letter to the secretary of the interior, written upon his return to New York, he explained that the reservation was too dry for crops and that the only hope the Cheyennes had of achieving self-sufficiency was through grazing cattle—cattle that the government would be wise to provide. "Physically and mentally these Indians stand very high," Grinnell assured. "Ever since they have been known to the white men they have been noted for their courage, their determination and their steadfastness of purpose. The same qualities which gave them preeminence in warlike pursuits will, if wisely directed, make them successful in the paths of peace. They are worth saving from pauperism and extinction. From the point of view of mere dollars and cents, it is worth the government's while to make them self-supporting."

The Cheyennes' talent in war was also something Grinnell was learning a great deal about. It had been only nineteen years since the Custer fight, and there were still plenty of Cheyennes alive who had been at the Little Bighorn. Grinnell had not yet been to the battlefield, which was less than fifty miles west of Lame Deer, but he could already picture it. He had heard the story from surviving soldiers and scouts; but very few whites—certainly very few white historians—had heard the story directly from the lips of an Indian combatant. White Bull had been at the Little Bighorn, and so had the Cheyenne chief American Horse, who was nineteen on June 25, 1876.

"[S]ome old man harangued in village that soldiers [were] going to charge the camp from both ends, upper and lower," American Horse recalled to Grinnell. "Then every one that had a horse mounted it, but most were afoot. . . . They charged to meet the troops. Reno . . . charged down into the flat where there is a bunch of timber. When [Reno's soldiers] got . . . out into the open flat, S[ioux] & C[heyennes] charged and troops ran for the river. They rode right out to them, knocked some off their horses. . . . It was like chasing buffalo, a grand chase."

Grinnell's admiration of Custer had been lukewarm ever since the Black Hills reconnaissance, but in later years, as Custer was increasingly lionized by the public, Grinnell had been careful not to cast even the slightest aspersion on the fallen general's reputation. But after hearing the accounts of men like White Bull and American Horse, it was even harder for him to champion Custer. "While it seems ungracious to cast reflections on the dead," he confided in his diary, "it seems evident, in the light of recent testimony, that . . . Custer had no business to attack this camp, the size of which had been many times reported to him. Having decided to attack it, he should not have divided his command."

Finally, after three tiring but fulfilling weeks among the Northern Cheyennes, measured by many new friends and many thousands of words of notes, Grinnell and Mort left for the Northern Pacific in time to meet their appointment with the Piegans on September 1.

In the decade since he first set eyes on the mountains that spanned the western horizon of the Blackfeet reservation, George Bird Grinnell had come to believe that he cared more about them than did the Indians, a supposition he had initially expressed in "The Rock Climbers," published in *Forest and Stream* in March 1888.

It was a perception inherited from James Willard Schultz, who had married into the tribe and purported to know the people well. "The Blackfeet disdained that sort of life," Schultz wrote, explaining why so few Piegans spent time beyond the range of the buffalo. "[T]hey would not hunt that which they could not ride to or near." Schultz went so far as to assert that the Piegans were afraid of the mountains. "'My people seldom venture into them alone,'" he quoted his wife, Natahki. "'[G]hosts live in these long, wide, dark woods. . . . Some men, it is said, have even seen these ghosts peering at them from behind a distant tree. They had terrible, big, wide faces, and big, wicked eyes.'"

Later Grinnell would write to Robert Sterling Yard, publicist for the National Park Service, explaining the genesis of the idea to create Glacier National Park. "In the year 1891 I made an entry in my notebook, September 17, suggesting—only to myself, of course—that it might be a good idea for the government to buy the mountains about the St. Mary's Lakes and turn the region into a national park. These mountains were then a part of the Blackfeet reservation, but I felt sure that the Blackfeet would be willing to sell the mountains to the government, for the Blackfeet had always been a prairie people and had never been mountain hunters."

Yet while it was true that the Blackfoot—the Bloods and Blackfoot of Canada and the Piegans of Montana—had survived and thrived as buffalo hunters, they did not avoid or even turn their backs upon the mountains that formed the border of their homeland. Hundreds of years before Grinnell climbed the slopes of the Continental Divide, the Blackfoot had exploited the most accessible routes across the Rockies—today's Marias, Two Medicine, Cut Bank, Piegan, Gunsight, Logan, and Swiftcurrent passes. These they used when raiding their enemies, the Pend d'Oreilles (Kalispel), Flatheads (Salish), and Kootenais. And the west-slope tribes followed the same routes when "going to buffalo," hunting the great herds on the high prairies on the east side of the divide. The Blackfoot name for the mountains that separated east from west was *Mistakis*—the Backbone—and they had names for many of its vertebrae, ribs, and appendages—names that Grinnell never learned and soon replaced.

The Blackfoot went to the mountains for other reasons as well. In the foothills they cut trees for lodge poles and, in later years, for firewood and houses. In spring they dug camas root and prairie turnip; in summer they picked serviceberries and chokecherries. Here they also gathered tobacco and dozens of species of plants used for food and for medicinal and ceremonial purposes. At higher elevations they quarried stones to make their pipes.

Above all else, the Backbone was a spiritual realm. It was where the Blackfoot captured eagles for their potent feathers. Wind Maker, the creator of the waves that made the wind blow, was one of the spirits who lived in the upper St. Mary Lake. Chief Mountain was the home of Thunder, who presented the most sacred of the medicine pipes, the Long-Time Pipe, to the people. Many a Blackfoot made the perilous climb to the summit of Chief Mountain for his vision quest. (The war shirt that Bear Chief presented to Grinnell was "visioned" on Chief Mountain.) Other mountains along the front range were used for vision quests as well, and medicine lodges were conducted at Two Medicine Lake—hence the name.

Schultz's translation of his wife's claim that there were ghosts in the mountains was clumsy at best. To the Blackfoot every supernatural being, every human, every creature, every natural object possessed an animate spirit, and every one of these spirits was sacred and essential to the native world—a belief dating back to the beginning of Blackfoot history. For Grinnell, the assumption that he was the first white man to set foot on certain mountains and glaciers of the Walled-in Lakes may well have been accurate. But his presumption that the Blackfoot considered the mountains a region of little worth that they would readily cede to the government revealed two things: his outsider's understanding of the nuances of Blackfoot lodge tales and, more tellingly, his own wishful thinking.

Grinnell and Mort arrived on the Blackfeet reservation the same day as the two other commissioners appointed by Interior Secretary Smith: William Pollock of the Bureau of Indian Affairs and Walter Clements, a Georgia lawyer with no Indian experience but with home-state ties to Smith. Piegan leaders had already voted in favor of pursuing the possibility of selling the mineral strip.

The commissioners rode from the station to the newly constructed agency at Willow Creek—soon to be named for Commissioner of Indian Affairs Daniel Browning—and were greeted by none other than George

Steell, who earlier in the year had won back the job of agent after the dismissal of Lorenzo Cooke for misuse of funds and his inability to keep prospectors from the reservations. Grinnell had lobbied for Steell's return, and his good word evidently had carried some sway.

Grinnell was the only commissioner the Piegans knew, and they were heartened by his presence. He had gone to bat for them before—working to get agent Marcus Baldwin dismissed—and they were confident that he would represent them fairly. "Saw many of the people," Grinnell wrote in his diary the day he arrived, "all of them cordial."

The next order of business was to make an inspection of the land in question. The party was a large one, perhaps a dozen men, including the Grinnell brothers, Jack Monroe, agency engineer Ross Cartée (to help with mapping), Pollock of the Indian Bureau, and several Piegans. (Commissioner Clements had been thrown from a wagon shortly after his arrival and spent his entire time on the reservation laid up with a bad knee.)

For the next two weeks they covered much of the country Grinnell had been exploring since his first visit in 1885. And in a way the trip resembled one of those familiar fall hunts. The weather was its usual inhospitable mix of rain, snow, and bitter wind. They shot prairie chickens on the prairie, and, once they reached the mountains, they went after bigger game. They saw more grizzly bears than usual, and on the fifth day out, Mort and Jack Monroe came upon a sow with cub. Grinnell's diary does not specify whether Monroe fired his rifle before the bear charged, or vice versa; either way, the bear kept coming, undeterred by the bullet or Monroe's harassing dogs. "Mort shot her the last time, so that she fell at Jack's feet," Grinnell wrote. "A most exciting and dangerous scrimmage."

After inspecting several mine sites in the Swiftcurrent valley, they assembled in the new hospital at the Blackfeet agency on September 20. Grinnell, who was the man most trusted by both sides, at first did little talking. Before leaving New York he had confessed in a letter to Billy Jackson, "I do not like the job at all because I think, however it may turn out, the Indians will be dissatisfied and will think that I have not done what I ought to do. At the same time, it seems to me that I can do more for the tribe by being on the commission than I can by being off it."

White Calf, the head chief, opened the proceedings by acknowledging the Piegans' disadvantage in negotiating with the powerful government of the United States. "I do not have it in my mind to refuse the counsels of the Great Father," White Cloud declared, "for it is to him that we look to for assistance."

He also announced that the Indians had enlisted the advice of Joe Kipp, George Steell, and Charles Conrad. Why the Piegans regarded Conrad, a wealthy businessman, as an honest broker is hard to explain. He was familiar to the older tribal members as a freighter who had once delivered needed supplies to the reservation from Fort Benton; but more recently he was known, by whites at least, to be working in concert with Great Northern president James J. Hill, who saw nothing but profit in opening the reservation to white miners and settlers. Conrad was also the principal developer of the town of Kalispell, on the Great Northern, west of the reservation.

As for Steell, whatever his economies as an agent might have been, he had a history of reaping personal financial advantage from his appointed position. And Joe Kipp had any number of black marks on his record. Like Steell, he was married to a Piegan and indeed was part Indian (Mandan) himself. But he would always be remembered as the man who had led the army to a camp of sleeping Piegans on the Marias River in January 1870, resulting in the massacre of two hundred men, women, and children, many of them sick with smallpox. Over the years at his various trading posts, Kipp had poisoned the Piegans with whiskey, and in 1873 he had ordered the murder of Blood chief Calf Shirt. Nevertheless, the Piegans did not see, or chose not to see, these white men as foxes in their henhouse.

The Piegans, though, were hardly passive. Little Bear Chief pressed Pollock to explain why the commissioners had come. "The government is pleased at the progress of the Indians along the white man's road," Pollock answered. "They are still unable, however, to take care of themselves. . . . You have a large tract of land which you cannot use. The better plan is for the government to buy this land that you may be provided for when your treaty [of 1888] expires. You must do this or the government will be obliged to support you; which thing I believe the Piegans do not wish."

The rub came when the two sides got specific on the boundaries of the strip to be ceded and the price the government would pay for it. Two lines— the Canadian boundary on the north and the Continental Divide on the west—were easy enough to agree upon. Using a map engineer Cartée had made with the aid of one Grinnell had been working on for years, the commissioners drew the eastern line from the point where the Great Northern Railway crossed the Two Medicine River (not far from present-day East Glacier), northwestward across Lower Two Medicine Lake, between the two St. Mary Lakes, to the east of Divide Mountain, through Chief Mountain, until reaching the Canadian border again. The commission wanted the southern boundary to be where the railroad cut across the reservation, or alternatively, even farther south at Birch Creek, which was the existing reservation boundary. For the smaller of these two designations—Canada to the railroad—the government was prepared to pay $1 million; if Birch Creek were added, the offer was $1.25 million.

The Piegans did not want to give up any grazing land, and initially they stated that they would not give up any land south of Cut Bank Creek, some ten miles north of the railroad, designating a much smaller strip than delineated in either of the government's requests. For it they demanded $2 million. Then, after further deliberation, they said they would sell from the railroad north for $3 million.

"Those mountains will never disappear," Little Dog said. "We will see them as long as we live. Our children will see them all their lives, and when we are all dead, they will still be there. This money will not last forever. I knew that you would be afraid when I told you our price, so I will rest a while and let you consider it, as we do not intend to retreat or go back. You must not forget that we have wives and children; it is for them that we ask this money. Those mountains will last forever. The money will not."

When Grinnell finally spoke, he asked the Piegans, "Do any of you wish to say more?"

Little Dog replied, "We are waiting for you to speak."

"We want to see the Indians get as much as possible," Grinnell began, "but don't want to make fools of them. You have asked three times as much as we think those mountains are worth."

He explained that, even if he and his fellow commissioners agreed to the $3 million price, Congress would not approve it. "For many years I have known the Piegans," he continued, "and many times have I thought of you and your little ones who were going to school. I want you to grow fat and rich, and your children to be happy. . . . The price that we have offered you for the land north from the railroad will give you yearly, for ten years after the present treaty expires, two thirds of what you are now getting, and if you want to sell from Birch Creek up, it will give you more; almost as much as you are now getting. In that time you will get rich and your cattle will fill this reservation with fat herds. Otherwise, if you stick to your proposition, we will have to return to the East, and you will have gained nothing. . . . If you don't want to trade with us, we must get on the train and go. . . . I hope you will not send us away, for we can help you. If you think you have enough for three years and then can look out for yourselves, that is for you to decide. Your people have done so well in the last seven years; have become so rich, and have improved so much from being a savage people, that I want to see you go on and become self-sustaining. If you are helped for ten years more by another agreement, you will then not want any more help. You will be able to go alone like the white man; the only difference will be the color of your skin. Try to think of these things carefully and let us know whether we are to go or to stay."

Both sides proved adept at brinkmanship; each declared its willingness to walk away from the negotiation. When the commissioners argued that the "rocky ridges" were of little use to the Piegans—"that they never furnished you houses; nor fed your cattle nor fed you and clothed you"—the Piegans took a different view. "I think you have placed too small a price on the mountains," Four Horns responded. "The watches you have in your pockets cost many dollars. The same kind of metal that they are made from is in the mountains." (Traces of gold and silver had been found, along with copper.) "Two of you went into the mountain and saw the rock. Now you have set too small a price."

When the Piegans suggested that they might bypass the government and sell the land directly to whites, Grinnell replied crisply: "It cannot be done now."

Discussion continued for five days until, at last, on September 25, acting on the advice of Agent Steell, trader Kipp, and builder-baron Charles Conrad, the Piegans agreed to a government offer of $1.5 million for the largest of the three proposed strips—from Birch Creek north—more than a thousand square miles total.

White Calf spoke most eloquently for the Indians. His foremost concern was for the future well-being of his people. Yet he also wanted to emphasize the Piegans' deep attachment to the past and to their homeland. "You whites came across the water," he said. "We always lived here. This is our land." More than that, he explained, "Chief Mountain is my head. The mountains have been my last refuge." The terms of the agreement called for the boundary to slice across the eastern face of Chief Mountain, severing it from the reservation.

Even so, White Calf was willing to complete the transaction: "[W]e will make a good treaty, but in the future we don't want our Great Father to ask for anything more." He requested that the Piegans be allowed to cut timber and hunt and fish on the ceded strip. And in closing he told the commissioners, so that there would be no ambiguity, "I shake hands with you because we have come to an agreement, but if you come for any more land, we will have to send you away."

That evening Grinnell wrote in his diary, "In the afternoon [the offer] was accepted and tonight everybody was glad. Many Indians made good speeches to me, thanking me."

Over the next three days, Piegans came into the agency to "touch the pen," and ultimately 305 names were signed to the agreement, well above a majority of adult males on the reservation. James Willard Schultz acted as recording secretary. "Not a dissenting voice," Grinnell noted proudly.

The final treaty, ratified the following winter by Congress, included further benefits to the Piegans besides granting them access to the ceded strip for grazing, hunting, and fishing. Indians were to be given preferential treatment in employment on the reservation, and because the reservation was deemed unfit for farming but suitable for raising cattle, it would continue as a "communal grazing tract," and not be divided up in allotments, as was occurring with many other tribes.

One phrase embedded in the treaty appeared quite innocuous but would one day have enormous consequences. The Indians' right to enter the ceded strip was valid *"so long as the same shall remain public lands."* From the time of Grinnell's first visit to Yellowstone in 1875, no one had argued more volubly that national parks belonged to the American public. But in 1910, fifteen years after negotiating the purchase of the Ceded

Strip (as it became widely known), the United States would construe an entirely different meaning to the term *public lands* in order to create Glacier National Park and so divest the Piegans of the visitation rights promised by treaty.

Grinnell never intended to secrete any such betrayal in the language of the agreement he and his fellow commissioners hashed out. On the other hand, during the days of discussion with the Piegans in September 1895, he did not bring up the subject so dear to his heart: a national park.

Yet his gold watch was ticking. Congress declared that the strip would not be "thrown open to occupancy by the whites" until after its boundaries had been surveyed and marked. That might take a year, possibly two—certainly no more. The lessons learned in Yellowstone had taught Grinnell that the Walled-in Lakes and the gateways to his glaciers would need more than a treaty to protect them.

There was one other task the commissioners had to accomplish before they could return home. Once the Piegan treaty had been signed, Grinnell and Pollock left the reservation and traveled on the Great Northern two hundred miles to Harlem, Montana, on the edge of the Fort Belknap reservation. (Mort Grinnell left before the Piegan treaty sessions, and Clements left immediately afterward.) Fort Belknap had been carved from former Blackfoot lands in 1888 to provide a home for the Gros Ventres and Assiniboines. The Gros Ventres, or Atsinas, are distant relations of the Arapahos and, after being pushed westward in the eighteenth century, eventually aligned with the Blackfoot. The Assiniboines share their ancestry with the Sioux, and they too were pushed from the Great Lakes onto the prairies, most of them to Canada, with some bands ending up in northern Montana.

By 1890 prospectors had found gold in the gulches of the Little Rocky Mountains on the southern border of the thousand-square-mile reservation. Two mining camps, Zortman and Landusky, were filling out. The scenario was similar to that of the Piegans. Payments from an initial treaty were nearing an end; whites were invading the mineral land; the government sought to embrace the inevitable.

Grinnell measured off the parcel to be ceded, a thirty-square-mile bite out of the lower end of the rectangular reservation. The tribes, however, were divided over whether to sell; the Gros Ventres were more reluctant than the Assiniboines. Grinnell and Pollock, their negotiating skills honed after a week with the Piegans, listened dutifully but bore down firmly. "This land which some of you are ready to sell is not used by anybody," Pollock asserted. "There is no timber there. There is no grass there. There is no place that you could plow and sow oats or wheat. You can grow nothing there."

Grinnell was more severe: "I see that some of you people are quite blind—you can't see far. . . . You think that because for seven or eight years you have had plenty to eat and have lived well, and for the next year or two you are going to have plenty to eat, that it will always go on like that? That is not true. It is not going to last. . . . Two years from now, if you don't make any agreement with the Government, you will first have to kill your cattle, and then you will have to starve." He expressed doubts that the mines would ever be worth anything, but one thing he was certain of: "You people can't use it for anything. It is no good for you."

In the end he and Pollock were successful, but only barely. Of the 334 adult males on the reservation, 190 signed the agreement—57 percent. Only one-quarter of the Gros Ventres assented. The price this time was $360,000.

Among the Piegans, Grinnell bore the honorific Fisher Cap. At the end of his ten days on the Fort Belknap reservation, his nickname was simply Gray Clothes. And he was wrong about the potential of the land that he had persuaded the Indians to relinquish. Over the course of the next century the diggings at Landusky and Zortman would produce well over a billion dollars in gold.

He arrived back in New York in mid-October, contented but also relieved at the work accomplished, especially on the Blackfeet reservation. "I myself think the treaty a liberal one on both sides," he wrote Billy Jackson. "I was well satisfied with the way things came out at the last, and all the Indians seemed to be so, too. Some of the people at first when I got there thought that I had left the road and was walking on a different trail from that which I had followed in earlier years, but I think that now they see that I am traveling along just in the same direction that I have kept ever since I began to work for these people."

A PLANK

H e left no doubt which way he leaned in *The Story of the Indian*, a volume in the popular "Story of the West" series published by D. Appleton & Company. Grinnell finished writing it before going to the treaty conference at Browning and read the last of the page proofs while on the Cheyenne reservation. "No narrative about any people can do them justice," it begins, "if written by one who is not in some degree in sympathy with them, and acquainted with their ways of thought and with the motives which govern them."

Those who purported to understand the Indian as well or better than Grinnell applauded his knowledge and insight. "We know in advance that anything written by the author of 'Pawnee Hero Stories' and 'Blackfoot Lodge Tales' is at once accurate and interesting," affirmed Frederick Hodge of the Smithsonian's Bureau of American Ethnology. Charles Lummis, editor of the California journal *Land of Sunshine*, proclaimed, "Mr. Grinnell has drawn a clear, just and rather comprehensive picture of the Indian. . . . It is a book every thoughtful man and woman will be wiser and better for reading."

Most pleasing was the letter he received from George Gould. "Dear

Partner, Your book is a good one," Gould wrote in one of the rare letters to Grinnell that survives. "You have put a good deal of yourself in [it], even though it was written to order, and there is no one else who can talk about Indians with the same union of sympathy and full critical knowledge that you have."

Grinnell answered Gould on Christmas Eve. "Dear Partner," he replied, "A number of pleasant things have been said about the Indian book but nothing so gratifying as what comes to me in your letter of the 15th. I value it because of my confidence in your critical judgment and my faith that you would call attention to anything in it which seemed to you false or worthless."

For the umpteenth time, he regretted that he could not accept Gould's invitation to come to the West Coast.

Grinnell had another book out that winter. The second Boone and Crockett anthology, *Hunting in Many Lands*, was nominally edited by Grinnell and Theodore Roosevelt, but most of the polishing was done by the former. It begins with a summary of the club's achievements over the previous two years, notably the Yellowstone National Park Protection Act and an act by the New York State Legislature to incorporate the New York Zoological Society, with officers and managers drawn largely from Boone and Crockett membership.

The hunting stories are boundless—in both geography and appetite. Roosevelt's chum Winthrop A. Chanler—the A was for Astor—stalks hippopotami, rhinoceri, cape buffalo, zebras, waterbucks, and hyenas in East Africa. His readers learn that the best way to stop an elephant is to fire the first ball into a front knee. Madison Grant, foremost in founding the Zoological Society (and a soon-to-be founder of the eugenics movement), also kills moose, and after the head of one of them is home and mounted, he observes, "His nose showed none of the Jewish characteristics which taxidermists are fond of."

The subject of killing predators prompts neither apology nor debate among the Boone and Crockett brethren. Such species destroy livestock and the wild game that human hunters hunted, and thus they are adversaries to be eliminated. In the pages of *Hunting in Many Lands* Casper Whitney kills a cougar, Alden Sampson shoots a grizzly, William Rockhill bags bears in Tibet and China, and Theodore Roosevelt's brother Elliott stalks an Indian tiger. As a member of a Russian expedition comprising twenty-two train cars, seventy fox hounds, sixty-seven greyhounds, and a legion of beaters, drivers, and hunters, Henry T. Allen helps to vanquish the "dreaded and accursed" wolf.

The most appealing piece, to Grinnell anyway, was "To the Gulf of Cortez," by George Gould. "About a year ago, my brother [Fred], who is a very sagacious physician, advised me to take the fresh liver of a mountain sheep for certain nervous symptoms," Gould's contribution begins. "None of the local druggists could fill the prescription, and so it was decided that I should seek the materials in person."

Gould, whom Grinnell had once half-jokingly called an "invalid," evidently was none too nervous for a strenuous adventure in the mountains of Mexico. In a wry tone familiar to readers of Mark Twain's *Roughing It* or *Innocents Abroad*, he recounts his quest for a cure as if he were on a gentleman's junket to the mineral baths of the Continent. Of his pack mule he writes: "Its sex was female, but its name was Lazarus, for the overwhelming necessity of naming animals of the ass tribe either Lazarus or Balaam tramples on all distinctions of mere sex."

Gould's aim proved to be every bit as sharp as his wit. After returning to Santa Barbara, he sent Grinnell the best of his bighorn trophies; its horns were sixteen inches around the base and forty inches in length, among the biggest ever seen in the East. Grinnell displayed the magnificent specimen in the Boone and Crockett exhibit at the Sportsmen's Exposition at Madison Square Garden and had its profile embossed on the cover of *Hunting in Many Lands*.

Yet even while the membership of the Boone and Crockett Club—and likewise the editors of *Forest and Stream*—continued to espouse the philosophy of hunting as manly, conscionable sport, they also insisted that hunting, as practiced by their adherents, was becoming more refined. "Have the sportsmen of today reached a higher and better sportsmanship than that of their predecessors of a few generations ago?" the journal asked in August 1895. The answer was yes: In years past, "killing was the sport, but now killing is but an incident of the real enjoyment."

Grinnell and *Forest and Stream* also reminded that the hunter who hunted for the sake of hunting had a "trivial" effect on game supply. The real culprit had always been "the skin hunter" and the "market shooter," who supplied wild game for the butcher shop and the restaurant table. Several years earlier *Forest and Stream* had made an example of Delmonico's, one of the most fashionable dining establishments in New York, for serving woodcock, a bird once prevalent in surrounding states but increasingly scarce. Such shaming encouraged Delmonico's to change its menu, and *Forest and Stream* and its Boone and Crockett coreligionists now pressed further for the "utter abolition" of the sale of game.

In February 1894 *Forest and Stream* published "A Plank," laying out its case for prohibition. "We have just been celebrating the four-hundredth anniversary of the coming to this continent of men equipped with firearms," the editorial began. "For four centuries, from the time of Christopher Columbus to that of Charles Delmonico, we have been killing and marketing game, destroying it as rapidly as we know how, and making no provision toward replacing the supply. The result of such a course is that for the most part the game has been blotted out from wide areas, and today, after four hundred years of wanton wastefulness, we are beginning to ask one another how we may preserve the little that remains, for ourselves and our children."

The Plank made clear that hunting for sport should continue—under prudent regulation. Hunting for profit, however, must end.

Grinnell drummed on the Plank week after week. Legislation was slow in coming, and he discovered that resistance was linked to the stubborn stereotype of the sportsman as a gentleman of privilege who wished to preserve game for his own hunting pleasure. "[I]f anyone shall assume from the fact that game protective laws are devised in the interest of a class, or that they operate to the advantage of one class, and not of all classes, he falls into grave error," he retorted. "They are made up of all classes, and of every class, high and low. . . . Good game laws are for the advantage of the sportsmen; but that is only another way of saying that they are for the benefit of the community at large."

Still, it was hard to read the roster of Boone and Crockett members and not see high society dressed in hunting habit. Many of them had indeed furthered the cause of game protection, but their credentials as big-game stalkers were not impeccable. Senators George Vest and Henry Cabot Lodge had made the cohort of one hundred, as had attorney Elihu Root, a consummate New York insider, and Carl Schurz, former secretary of the interior and a fierce but not necessarily bloodthirsty civil-service reformer. When it was discovered that the guide of Albert Bierstadt, and not Bierstadt himself, had killed the moose that qualified the distinguished landscape artist for membership, the club welcomed him anyway. As of 1895 Grinnell's architect brother, William, was listed as a member, although he was a man more inclined to the boulevard than to the backwoods. The Boone and Crockett Club may have been for the people, but it was hardly of the people.

At least as worrisome as the commercial sale of wildlife was the commercial threat to habitat, specifically forests. After passage of the Forest Reserve Act of 1891 and the subsequent creation of the Yellowstone Park Timber Land Reserve, Grinnell and other conservationists began to campaign for a more comprehensive policy to protect and superintend the nation's timber. Several states had their own forestry divisions to oversee state forestland, but as yet the federally owned forests had no agency with the funds, manpower, and legal mandate to look after them. For too long the Agriculture Department's Division of Forestry had been essentially one man, Prussian-born Bernhard Fernow, a wise and practical forester, but he was hardly able to watch over national reserves, which in four years had increased to 17 million acres.

In early 1896, at the same time that Congress was ratifying the treaty to purchase the western portion of the Blackfeet reservation, the secretary of the interior authorized a special commission to study federal timberlands and make recommendations on how they ought to be used and managed. The commission's members included Charles Sargent of the Arnold Arboretum in Massachusetts, Yale botanist William Brewer, Harvard naturalist Alexander Agassiz, Grinnell's friend Arnold Hague of the Geological Survey, and an energetic thirty-year-old forester by the name of Gifford Pinchot, who, after graduation from Yale and a year studying the science of forestry abroad, had applied Europe's rigorous management principles to the wooded Vanderbilt estate in North Carolina, the Biltmore. In the summer of 1896 he and his fellow commissioners went west to look over the national forests.

Pinchot arrived on the Blackfeet reservation in June. In his autobiography, *Breaking New Ground,* he acknowledges that the three weeks he spent in the mountains above the St. Mary Lakes were not strictly devoted to the work of the forestry commission. Guided by Billy Jackson, he did what Grinnell had done on his own early visits: he hiked and hunted. But also, "We learned the lay of the land, and why this was the place for a Forest Reserve," Pinchot would recall.

In mid-July he arrived at the Great Northern station in Belton, Montana, on the west side of the mountains from the Blackfeet reservation. There he rendezvoused with Sargent, Brewer, and Hague. Also joining the commission was John Muir, who four years earlier had founded the Sierra Club. It was the first meeting between the two men who soon would emerge as the pole stars of American conservation—Pinchot the practicing utilitarian, Muir the pure preservationist. Pinchot would remember Muir a half century later: "In his late fifties, tall, thin, cordial, and a most fascinating talker, I took to him at once. It amazed me to learn that he never carried even a fishhook with him on his solitary explorations. He said fishing wasted too much time."

For the rest of the summer the commissioners toured the forest reserves of the West, from Montana to the Cascades and Sierra Nevada, from California to the Grand Canyon, from New Mexico to Colorado. The report they submitted to the secretary of the interior in January 1897 recommended the creation of thirteen new reserves, totaling more than twenty-one million acres—among them the Black Hills in South Dakota, the Tetons in

Wyoming, Mount Rainier in Washington, and two in Montana: the Flathead Forest Reserve and the Lewis and Clark Forest Reserve, which bordered the Blackfeet reservation and Ceded Strip on the south and west.

A month after receiving the report and only two weeks before he left office, President Grover Cleveland issued a proclamation creating precisely the reserves proposed by the commission. With a stroke of the pen, the amount of preserved forestland in the United States more than doubled. Western timber states attempted to override Cleveland's order through legislation, but the incoming president, William McKinley, and his interior secretary, Cornelius Bliss, mollified them with several concessions. An amendment to the Sundry Civil Bill ratified the thirteen new reserves by stipulating that some amount of timber could be harvested from them and assuring that the reserves would remain open to mining—all subject to the regulation of the secretary of the interior. Thus was laid the foundation of federal forest management for the next century and more. National forests would be preserved, but they would also be porous. Today the U.S. Forest Service operates under the slogan, "Land of Many Uses," an apt expression of the terms of the compromise struck in 1897.

By chance 1896 was one of the years that Grinnell did not visit the Blackfeet reservation and the mountains to its west, and so he missed making the acquaintance of Gifford Pinchot during his foray into St. Mary.

Grinnell had several excuses for his absence that summer. *Forest and Stream* had moved to new offices in the New York Life Building at 346 Broadway. At about the same time, business manager Edward Wilbur fell gravely ill. Then the barn and several other buildings at the farm in Connecticut burned to the ground. The Bosworth Machine Company was struggling; orders for harnesses were down, which Grinnell blamed on the rising popularity of bicycles.

Besides, Grinnell didn't need to go to Montana to see the Piegans. In March he invited Bear Chief, his wife, Young Antelope Woman, and their daughter to occupy *Forest and Stream*'s "Indian camp" at the second annual Sportsmen's Exposition held in Madison Square Garden. Billy Jackson came along also, as interpreter. The camp included a skin lodge furnished with bows, arrows, medicine bundles, and a sacred pipe, and nearby a willow-framed sweat lodge. "It is very important that the people you send should know that they are coming to be looked at," Grinnell wrote Jackson beforehand, "and [that they wear] their Indian clothes and keep themselves painted up." In 1896 most easterners expected neither more nor less from Native Americans.

Bear Chief was a gracious guest. "It will be an abiding satisfaction that our representative Native American Hunter was a man of such worth and bore himself with such never-failing dignity and good breeding," Grinnell wrote. He reciprocated by acting the thoughtful host. Although he did not invite the Piegans to stay at Audubon Park, he took time to show them around the city. He set up a tour of one of the Cunard steamships—"the iron that floats on the water"—berthed in lower Manhattan, and he hosted a dinner for Mr. and Mrs. Big Chief in a private dining room at Muschenheim's Arena restaurant on West Thirty-First Street. "Very little wine will be needed, perhaps five bottles of some inexpensive table claret," Grinnell specified. "Besides that there should be plenty of seltzer, or vichy, or else apollinaris."

He also arranged for the Piegans to return home by way of Washington, where they met with Commissioner of Indian Affairs Daniel Browning. "If we could write down Bear Chief's impressions of what he saw from the time he left the reservation until his return, what a volume it would make," Grinnell reflected after the Indians left town. "It is needless to say that every moment of that time in New York was improved in seeing the strange and wonderful sights of this 'place of many houses.'"

Meanwhile, Grinnell had not lost sight of the Ceded Strip. It too was becoming a place of many houses, or at least one of many mines and settlers. The treaty with the Piegans forbade "throwing open" the strip until after it had been properly mapped, but prospectors were already working claims on the streams of the upper Swiftcurrent. "[T]he charms of this country are soon to disappear," Grinnell lamented in September 1896. "It has been a place where one could go with little danger of meeting anyone, but now that the mineral deposits have been discovered and the Piegans have sold the mountain portion of the reservation, it will soon be overrun by miners, and the few of us who used to visit it will have to look for another camping ground."

His anxiety was legitimate, yet he was by no means giving up. In December, as the forestry commission prepared its report to the secretary of the interior, Grinnell wrote to Arnold Hague, calling attention to the Ceded Strip. He and Hague had ridden for weeks in Yellowstone and spent many hours discussing the value of that country as a preserve for wild game; now he stressed the point that he knew would have broad economic and political appeal in Washington: watershed protection. The streams that began in the mountains of the Ceded Strip fed two great rivers, the Missouri and the Saskatchewan. The Milk River and Cut Bank Creek were two vital sources of the former, and the St. Mary River flowed northward across Montana to join the latter in Canada. "[O]n the gentler acclivities and towards the heads of many of these narrow valleys, there is a great deal of small pine timber which ought not to be destroyed because of the work which it does in the spring in retarding the melting of the snows," Grinnell emphasized. His concern was that, once the region was open to miners, "unless it is protected, much of the timber will be burned off, and if this should take place, I do not see what the [downstream] settlers will do for water, either for themselves or for their stock."

Grinnell urged Hague and his fellow commissioners to include the Ceded Strip in one of the forest reserves. Hague needed no convincing; nor did Gifford Pinchot, the one commissioner who had seen the Ceded Strip.

So it came to be. In the proclamation signed by President Cleveland two months later, the Ceded Strip was incorporated in the Lewis and Clark Forest Reserve. At the very least, Grinnell had bought time until he could find a way to consecrate his land of glaciers as a national park. Here, anyway, were all the parts—if no longer quite so pristine as they once had been, then at least still intact and under the watchful control of the federal government.

On the other hand, Grinnell was neither so single-minded nor so idealistic that he did not hedge his bet. Shortly after the treaty to purchase the Ceded Strip was ratified, Jack Monroe wrote to him, seeking his backing in a min-

ing venture. A year earlier Grinnell had indignantly rejected a similar proposition from George Steell; he now said to his trusty guide, "I do not care to
have my name on a location anywhere in that country." Yet he wasn't necessarily averse to signing on as a silent investor, and he told Monroe that he
would talk over the idea with brother-in-law Newell Martin. "I am a good
deal like other men, I suppose, in being anxious to make what money I can
in a decent way," he explained.

Grinnell wrote again a month later, informing Monroe that Martin was
good for $500. The letter also inferred that he would put some of his own
money into Martin's stake.

But the deal was never struck. Monroe became impatient and found
other partners, leaving Grinnell to lament his missed opportunity. "I certainly should have been glad, and so would Mr. Martin, to have come to
the front with the stake money," he wrote Monroe in November. "I am very
much disposed to believe that there is something in the St. Mary's country,
but it is a big country, and whether we could find, or could have found, anything there, is perhaps open to question." He wished Monroe luck. "I trust
you will make a good big [strike] for yourself even if I am not in it."

This and his previous letters to Jack Monroe are quite strange. For one
thing, they flew in the face of Grinnell's regret that St. Mary was filling
up with people. For another, they darkened his dream for a national park.
What is more, the letters unabashedly encouraged Monroe to begin prospecting in an area that, until mapping was completed, was strictly proscribed by law—a law that Grinnell had helped to write and enact.

It was no great surprise that Jack Monroe needed money. Perhaps Grinnell needed money, too—more than he was letting on. If anybody was going
to strike it rich in that country, why shouldn't it be the men who knew it
better than almost anyone?

In April 1898, when the Ceded Strip was at last opened to miners and
settlers, a land rush occurred on the upper tributaries of the Swiftcurrent.
The mining camp of Altyn flourished at Cracker Lake, at the foot of
Mount Siyeh, its population mushrooming to nearly one thousand by 1900.
Another camp was named St. Mary's City. "About 200 enthusiasts of the
worst kind have started a town . . . between the [St. Mary] Lake and Divide
Creek," Jack Monroe wrote Grinnell two months after the opening. "There

is no way they can produce anything, and they will in time, like Kilkenny cats, eat each other up completely. I will bet you an alpine stock that we can make hay in the streets and stable our horses in a gambling hell . . . inside of two years."

Monroe's prediction came true. By 1902 the boom had gone bust—no copper worth digging, even less gold and silver—and virtually all the prospectors quit the country. It was just as well for Grinnell, as a preservationist and almost-investor, and also for Jack Monroe, who in the end filed a claim—gold this time—not on the Ceded Strip but in the Sweet Grass Hills, one hundred miles to the east.

The following summer Grinnell went to Montana earlier than usual. In the past he had scheduled his trips to the Piegans and St. Mary in the fall, when the hunting was better (and so as not to coincide with the summer vacations of office mates Edward Wilbur and Charles Reynolds). But by 1897 his enthusiasm for hunting big game had faded. Indeed, he had not killed anything except birds since his last hunt with George Gould in 1890. Lately he had satisfied his passion for shooting with annual trips to a gentlemen's duck club established by a group of fellow New Yorkers on Currituck Sound in North Carolina. He usually went in January, when winter storms held the migrating ducks in the protected waters inside the barrier of the Outer Banks. The worse the weather, the better the shooting.

He arrived on the Blackfeet reservation at the first of June, while the prairie grass was still green. Almost immediately he and Jack Monroe headed into the mountains—now the Ceded Strip—with the aim of climbing ten-thousand-foot Mount Jackson, by Grinnell's estimation "probably the highest peak in that section of the Rocky Mountains." Crossing the upper St. Mary River, they and their horses were swept downstream and "soused about in the tumultuous waters," Grinnell wrote, "sometimes right side up and sometimes wrong, until at last we had drippingly crawled out on either shore and counted up our bruises."

"For the rest of the day we were, of course, very wet, and matches and tobacco pretty well soaked, so that we could not smoke, which was deprivation," Grinnell recounted to George Gould. It took them seven hours to reach the summit of Mount Jackson.

On his return to the reservation, he found the Piegans "camped in the circle, getting ready for the Medicine Lodge." The medicine lodge, as the Blackfeet called their interpretation of the sun dance, was a five-day ritual held shortly after the summer solstice, at the time of the ripening service-berries, an essential food source that the Indians mixed with buffalo to make pemmican. It was an occasion for the gathering of the various bands, involving sweat lodges, fasting, singing, praying, opening of sacred bundles, and cutting of the central cottonwood pole. On the final day of the ceremony, the leader of the medicine lodge, always a woman, distributes morsels of food (in earlier times buffalo tongue) to every man, woman, and child of the tribe. The warriors repay their answered prayers of the previous year by recounting their deeds and then performing the sacred sun dance. "Slits are cut in the skin of the breast, ropes passed through and secured by wooden skewers, and then the men swing and surge until the skin gives way and tears out," Grinnell writes in *Blackfoot Lodge Tales*. "This is very painful, and some fairly shriek with agony as they do it, but they never give up, for they believe that if they should fail to fulfill their vow, they would soon die."

Although he had written about the medicine lodge with great care, Grinnell had yet to witness one in person. In recent years a succession of agents, including George Steell, had tried to ban this practice outright, and Grinnell had some doubt that the ceremony would be allowed in 1897. But a week before he arrived on the reservation, Steell had resigned (again)—shamed and stained by his leniency toward miners and white ranchers and by the suspicious increase of his own cattle herd. In the end, even Grinnell had damned Steell as a man merely more bearable than his drunken, thieving predecessors. "[T]here seems to be something about the business of Indian agent which saps the morals of every man who takes the position," Grinnell observed to Herbert Welsh of the Indian Rights Association.

Steell's replacement was the former editor of the Fort Benton *River Press*, George McLaughlin, a Republican appointee. If nothing else, the new man seemed ambivalent, if not oblivious, toward the medicine lodge.

Preparations were under way when Grinnell returned from climbing Mount Jackson on June 15. He was invited by White Calf to pitch his tent among the people.

Grinnell gathered many new details about the medicine lodge, presumably from talks with White Calf, whom, as he noted in his diary, "is almost the only one that knows all the old songs and the old ceremony." Once again, however, Grinnell did not observe the final dance. "[I]t rained in torrents the whole time and ultimately our lodge blew to pieces," he told James Willard Schultz. After four days he left for Wyoming, to check on his ranch.

Yet his brief stay with the Piegans had been rewarding nonetheless. On his last day, as he related to George Gould, "I was highly honored by being promoted to the head chieftainship of the tribe, being saluted as the Father of the People."

The idea of being named chief may well have been broached by Grinnell. Or quite possibly it was White Calf's way to express gratitude for his past work on behalf of the tribe and to encourage its continuation in the future. Regardless, Grinnell wrote to Schultz, "I was greatly touched by the speech that White Calf made when he told me that I had been chosen, and was so entirely astonished that I had nothing to say in reply."

To Jack Monroe he confided: "This last trip onto the Blackfoot reservation was the best one that I ever made there. I had more satisfaction out of it. I do not expect to make so good a one again."

This would not be his final visit to the Blackfeet, and he would take the responsibility as chief seriously in his ongoing efforts on behalf of the people. He had been awarded a credential that he would value as highly as any medal or honorary degree. He cared just as much about the tribe's future as he did about its past. Yet his ascent to the rank of chief was in a way a benchmark that he could not expect to surpass. He would now seek fresh, unturned soil; the Cheyennes awaited him.

Then, too, there were destinations he realized he might never reach. His brother Mort had recently remarried and taken his bride on a honeymoon abroad. "I sometimes wish that I had a lovely wife and were traveling in Europe," Grinnell told Jack Monroe, "but I don't wish that always."

When George Gould informed him that his brother Fred had also married, Grinnell responded with a different degree of wistfulness: "You and I have missed much in life by remaining old bachelors, but no doubt we have each of us done the best we could to overcome the blemish in each existence."

If he could not claim the title of husband, he would always be "Dear Partner"—and now, at the age of forty-eight, he was Father of the People.

DIVERSE VOICES

George Bird Grinnell was a man of worthy causes, which is not to say that he lived his life according to a grand plan. He continued to labor and lobby on behalf of Native Americans, forest reserves and national parks, wild birds and big game. He had *Forest and Stream* to run, and there was rarely a week that he did not contribute an article or editorial of his own. He wrote for *American Anthropologist* and the *Journal of American Folk-Lore*. He continued to plug away on the Cheyenne book, and in 1897 he edited, with Theodore Roosevelt, a third Boone and Crockett collection, *Trail and Camp-Fire*, contributing a fifty-page article, "Wolf and Wolf Nature." That same year, as a member of the board of managers of the New York Zoological Society, he played a central role in planning the 261 acres granted by the city for the zoo in Bronx Park, and his expertise was called upon in the selection of the species of North American quadrupeds—including buffalo—to be raised, bred, studied, and protected there. On top of that, he paid careful attention to the Bosworth Machine Company and the Milford factory where the sewing machines were manufactured. Not to mention, he tended to his own portfolio of stocks and real estate and that of his mother's and father's estates, as an executor.

He awoke each morning with the intention of working hard and doing good deeds, yet he took on so many tasks all at once that there hardly seemed enough hours in any given day to accomplish even a fraction of what he intended. Not surprisingly, by the end of most winters his doctor was urging him to get away from the hectic demands of New York. That he could go directly from a harried, desk-bound routine to climbing ten-thousand-foot mountains was a measure of his grit, willpower, and innate resilience. He was simply too driven to rest, at home or afield. The only relaxation he allowed himself was shivering in a duck blind one week a year. On the occasional weekend at the Connecticut farm, he was always up early, tramping the fields and marshes or supervising upkeep of the buildings, livestock, and orchards. On trips to his Shirley Basin ranch, he was often in the saddle from daybreak to dark.

At forty-seven, he had no premeditated ambition to be famous. Unlike Theodore Roosevelt—who had ascended from assemblyman to civil service commissioner to police commissioner and, with the election of William McKinley, to assistant secretary of the navy—Grinnell neither conceived nor pursued an Arthurian arc to his career. He did not set out to be president—of a corporation or the country. He would have been gratified if *Forest and Stream* or any of his books made him rich, but he did not embark on these enterprises with that end foremost in his mind. (And thus he was never disappointed.) The esteem of his social and professional peers, of other sportsmen, of the Indians he befriended, and of western men like Lute North, Jack Monroe, Billy Jackson, and Billy Hofer mattered to him, but he did not court their approval. He was a prolific correspondent, often dictating to his stenographer several thousand words in a day, but he was not a garrulous conversationalist. "I have not the gift of gab," he confessed to William Hallett Phillips. He attended many meetings—Boone and Crockett Club, the New York Zoological Society, various Good Government committees—sometimes several a week; he volunteered his knowledge and point of view freely, but he preferred not to preside over the proceedings, and he avoided public speaking wherever possible. "I was induced to make a speech over in Brooklyn before a club of people presumed to be literary and had a disgusting time over stage fright for the two or three days preceding the event," he told George Gould. "I am not cut out . . . for an orator."

Perhaps his most underappreciated talent was as a listener. He seemed most content when he was gathering the stories of others. His Indian books are enduring evidence of his talent as auditor and reporter. Similarly, his ear for diverse voices made him a superb editor. Most of the contributors to *Forest and Stream* and the Boone and Crockett anthologies were amateurs. "The Boone and Crocketters are not particularly strong on the literary side," he confided to Gould. He would comb the tangles from their prose before presenting their submissions to the reading public. In the case of the alcoholic James Willard Schultz, Grinnell's editorial tolerance was stretched to the breaking point and beyond. He eventually gave up on Schultz as a reliable contributor, yet he never stopped encouraging him, occasionally sending a few dollars, despite his better judgment, and exhorting him to quit drinking. He was not a pushover by any means, but he took no satisfaction in wielding authority just for the sake of it. "My nature is such a gentle one," he allowed in yet another admission to Gould.

It wasn't so much that he didn't have time for a private life as he didn't seem to *allow* himself a private life. He lived in a house with his brother William, his sister Helen and her children (when they weren't traveling or at the Connecticut farm), and a staff of servants. He rode by cable car and elevated train from Audubon Park to the *Forest and Stream* office every morning and rarely left during the day. He kept up his membership in several clubs but rarely visited them except for meetings. He drank modestly, an occasional glass of wine or dram of gin. His one un-reined indulgence was his pipe. He never seemed to take it from his mouth, which may explain why he talked so sparingly.

In August 1897 Grinnell wrote to Dr. Washington Matthews, an army surgeon and self-educated linguist who had made a systematic study of several Indian languages. Grinnell asked Matthews what sort of phonograph might be best for recording. "I know you have had experience in the use of this instrument. . . . How long would it run? Did you have [one] of the large horns, perhaps three feet long, for the people to sing into? Have you any idea how many cylinders it would be well to take [with] such an instrument? . . . I am told that the cylinders will hold about 600 words each."

At the end of September Grinnell went west, for the second time that summer, carrying, in place of a hunting rifle, a Graphophone, an adaptation of Thomas Edison's patented phonograph, and a forty-inch horn made from a substance called leatherette that he had purchased from the Columbia Phonograph Company on Broadway. He also packed eight or ten dozen wax cylinders.

Over the course of a month, first on the Northern Cheyenne reservation and then on the Blackfeet, he filled nearly eighty cylinders, recording more than one hundred songs. In his diary for September 22 he wrote: "Explained graphophone to Two Moon. He sang soldier song into it. . . . On 2nd cylinder Two Moon sang doctoring song and wolf song. Soldier song singer addresses followers: 'Brothers, when we fight we must all stick together. None of you must run away.' . . . Wolf Song words are by a woman who talks, 'I am getting old. I do not know whether you would marry me or not. You see me and you can do as you like. If you were to marry me, I don't think you would love me.'"

Grinnell had William Rowland along to interpret, but the translated words did not readily convey the sacred significance of the songs. For instance, Two Moon's "doctor song" was a prayer for help from He amma wihio that begins, "'I am grandfather (i.e., of the people) that you hear singing. That's me.'"

Earlier Grinnell had admitted, "I cannot get at the significance of the word [wihio]." But through repeated listening, he at last gained insight. "The great spirit, white man, and spider are all called wihio because they are smarter than their fellows and can do things that others cannot," he wrote in the notes that followed Rowland's translations of Two Moon's singing. "[Because] the spider spins a web and goes up or down, it is more able than other insects. The idea of superior ability or intelligence is conveyed in the word. They know more than others. When the white man first came he seemed to know more than the Indians and taught them things."

The doctor song, then, was a song of humility, of recognition of higher authority, a petition made by the tribe's most powerful medicine man to his people's holiest spirit, He amma wihio—the Wise One Above.

The following day he recorded a chorus of four men, Owl Bull, Lone Bear, Dives Backward, and Ridge Walking. They sang war songs, sun dance songs, courtship songs, and a "triumph" song. On another night he recorded singing and dancing until two o'clock in the morning. In many cases Grinnell transcribed the Cheyenne words phonetically, and he did the same when he arrived on the Blackfeet reservation on October 14. White Calf sang for him the "Smoking Song of Beaver Medicine" (cylinder 45), the "Lizard song and rainmaking song" (cylinder 47). He translated a Piegan woman's song as, "I married him at the Medicine Lodge when I might have married him at any other time. Now I cannot put my head out of the door and am always sitting down crying." Songs of rocky romance, it seems, are the same in any language.

Miraculously quite a few of the wax cylinders have survived into the twenty-first century, and thankfully they have been preserved digitally by the Archives of Traditional Music at Indiana University. Some of the cylinders are too scratchy to be intelligible, much less enjoyable; but others sound like snatches from a distant gospel station picked up late at night on a car radio. Shrieks punctuate the liveliest songs; drums thump like heartbeats. And the Indians' voices are high-pitched, harmonious, and, as they carry across a century and more, energetic and enchanting.

Grinnell went to great effort to transport the fragile recording device by train to Montana, and he seemed quite satisfied with the results, although once he got the Graphophone and the wax cylinders safely back to New York, he was uncertain what to do with them. "Some day they may electrify the world," he wrote George Gould, "but hardly this year."

Yet as time passed, the recordings would prove of great value—not only to ethnologists eager to study authentic native music but also to anyone curious about the sound of George Bird Grinnell's voice, for he can be heard making brief introductions to the recordings. His voice is a lean tenor, like those of the Indian singers, and he has the slightly nasal, upper-class accent that linguists call Mid-Atlantic English, similar to that adopted by actors during the early years of talking pictures. To listen to the brief utterances of Grinnell, one hears precisely the voice one expects: deliberate, assured, proper.

Grinnell had traveled to the Montana reservations in the fall of 1897 to try out his new machine, to collect stories, and to listen to the concerns of the people. On the Cheyenne reservation he received an earful of the latter. Earlier in the year, a white sheepherder on a ranch that bordered the reservation to the east was found murdered. A committee of armed whites stormed the reservation, demanding that the Indians surrender the killers. Many Cheyennes took to the hills for safety. The anxious agent, Captain George Stouch, called for army troops to keep the peace. Newspapers seized on the commotion by reporting a "breakout" on the reservation. Before an ugly confrontation erupted into something worse, the sheriff of Custer County rounded up several Cheyennes and brought charges against Little Whirlwind's Voice—known also by the name given to him as an army scout, David Stanley—and two brothers, Spotted Hawk and Little Whirlwind (no relation to Stanley). In November Stanley and Little Whirlwind were found guilty of second-degree murder and sentenced to life in prison at hard labor (though Stanley's charge was later reduced). Spotted Hawk was found guilty of first-degree murder and sentenced to hang. The judge and jury in Custer County had not been swayed by revelations that Stanley, at the time of his arrest, had confessed to killing the herder on his own; only later had he implicated the other two.

The case was symptomatic of a larger friction between Cheyennes and neighboring white ranchers. Conditions on the Northern Cheyenne reservation were far worse than on the Blackfeet reservation or on the closer reservations of the Crows and Sioux. Cheyenne land was arid and unsuitable for growing hay and other crops, except in the reservation's few stream bottoms. Because the Cheyennes had been assigned to their reservation later than most Plains Indian tribes—as of 1897 the reservation boundaries had yet to be officially surveyed—they were much further behind in settling into permanent homes and building up herds of cattle. The ranchers, meanwhile, had been grazing their stock on the best Indian land for years and were eager to exploit the recent unrest in order to dispossess the impoverished Cheyennes of their tribal lands and push them westward toward the Crow reservation.

In conversations with the Cheyennes and their agent, Grinnell was convinced that a tremendous injustice had been done, and upon his return to New York, he rolled up his sleeves and brought to bear all his credibility as an Indian authority. "Recent developments in association with the case go to show, as stated by Capt. Stouch, that only one individual was concerned in the murder," he informed Herbert Welsh of the Indian Rights Association in Philadelphia. "The boy Spotted Hawk has been, as stated, convicted on the testimony of Stanley, the self-confessed murderer, Stanley's effort being to save his own life at the expense of that of Spotted Hawk."

He did not hesitate to put himself forward as a character reference: "I have known Spotted Hawk for several years, and knew well his father, and now know his mother and brothers. They are all good people, and I am convinced that the young man who has been convicted is entirely innocent of the murder and had no knowledge of it until long after it was committed."

He asked the Indian Rights Association to help pay for an appeal. (Little Whirlwind had been tried separately, and his case was not as dire as that of his brother, who faced imminent execution.)

Through Grinnell's prompting, the Indian Rights Association agreed to put up $250 to appeal Spotted Hawk's case to the Supreme Court of Montana. Moreover, the IRA was able to persuade Secretary of the Interior Cornelius Bliss to raise another $250. To represent Spotted Hawk, they hired former United States senator Wilbur Sanders of Helena. They reasoned that if they could get Spotted Hawk's sentence overturned, then the governor might be induced to pardon Little Whirlwind.

Grinnell could have dropped the matter once it was in the capable hands of Sanders and the Indian Rights Association, but he would not give up on Spotted Hawk and Little Whirlwind. He wrote frequent letters of encouragement to their local lawyers and he formed a strong alliance with Wilbur Sanders.

It took a year and a half, but Sanders finally succeeded in getting the Supreme Court to reverse Spotted Hawk's decision, after which Custer County declined to retry him. Surprisingly, however, Governor Robert Smith would not pardon Little Whirlwind. Not until 1901, four years after the killing of the sheepherder, was the Cheyenne liberated by Governor Smith's successor, Joseph Toole.

Grinnell stuck by both young men till the end, even visiting Little Whirlwind in the state penitentiary in Deer Lodge. Just before his release, Grinnell wrote to him: "I have not forgotten you, nor have I stopped trying to do what I could to set you free. . . . Governor [Toole] said that he would look into the case and do what was right. . . . Nevertheless, if anything should happen to prevent you from being turned loose this time, we shall have to try it again and keep on trying as long as you are shut up." (On the other hand, he cared nothing for the fate of David Stanley, who died in prison of tuberculosis in October 1899.)

As a token of gratitude for Grinnell's steadfast faith and support, Little Whirlwind sent him a fancy bridle he had woven of horsehair. The compensation that mattered more to Grinnell came when finally he was able to greet Little Whirlwind and Spotted Hawk as free men on the Cheyenne reservation.

Another unexpected reward from the Spotted Hawk and Little Whirlwind ordeal was the friendship that developed between Grinnell and Hamlin Garland, the celebrated author of the American prairie.

Garland had grown up on a succession of homesteads in Wisconsin, Iowa, and South Dakota. Seeking to replace a life of hard labor with a life of the mind, he moved to Boston; there he caught the attention of the city's lion of letters, William Dean Howells, who urged him to about-face and write about the gritty realities of the American West. Garland's first book, *Main-Traveled Roads* (1891), won him a place at the literary table shared by Howells, Theodore Dreiser, Frank Norris, and other plain-speaking voices of progressive reform. He was particularly drawn to the struggles of American Indians, and in July 1897 he made a trip to the Northern Cheyenne reservation to report on the ongoing troubles.

He arrived in time to witness the arrest of David Stanley, and, fair to say, his sympathies lay entirely with the Cheyennes. "A simple murder case magnified by hate and greed," he wrote in his notebook. "It is well, under the circumstances, that the whole nation can have something to say about the invasion of the Cheyenne territory by a mob of interested ranch men, rustlers, husky men and local political candidates for county offices. If a bloody struggle had been precipitated that day, it would have been due to these whites and not to the Cheyennes. . . . It is the self-interest and local barbarism of the whites which keep the Indian continually alarmed, suspicious and revengeful. . . . There is but one thing to do and that is to fence in these reservations. Keep the whites off the Indian's land and the Indian on his own land."

Garland was sufficiently aroused by what he had witnessed on the Northern Cheyenne reservation to write a novel, *The Captain of the Gray-Horse Troop*, based on the 1897 murder. The protagonist, Captain George Curtis, is a fictional double for agent George Stouch, and the novel's polemical message echoes the published opinions of George Bird Grinnell. "'The older I grow the less certain I am that any race of people has a monopoly on the virtues,'" Captain Curtis declares. "'I do not care to see the 'little peoples' of the world civilized in the sense in which the word is commonly used. It will be a sorrowful time to me when all the tribes of the earth shall have cottonade trousers and derby hats. . . . If I could, I would civilize only to the extent of making life easier and happier. . . . The tragedy of their certain extinction overwhelms me at times.'"

Garland had left the Cheyenne reservation before Grinnell arrived at the end of September, but Grinnell learned of Garland's travels from agent Stouch and others. "I am exceedingly glad to think that you have visited my children," Grinnell wrote to Garland. "I am sure that if you and I can form an alliance, we can do very much to awaken public interest in these Indians and perhaps to help them along more speedily on the road to civilization and self-support. . . . What I have done for these Indians is the one thing in my life that I am satisfied with and proud of, and very naturally the more I do for them, the more I want to do."

Soon after his return to New York, he invited Garland, who lived downtown at Gramercy Park, to come to Audubon Park for dinner and the night so they could discuss the Spotted Hawk case and other matters of common interest. "[W]hen he asked me to visit him at his house on West 156th Street, I was glad of the opportunity," Garland would reminisce. "I especially wished to see him in the light of his own fire."

Garland's diary entry the day after the visit records: "His house is a joy. . . . Its dusky, wide, mysterious rooms are such a child would remember with shuddering delight. Savage weapons are on the walls, wolf and bear skins on the floor, and in the corner bookshelves stand volumes filled with pictures of red men and animals."

He described Grinnell as "a singular mixture of the staid Manhattan citizen and the old borderman"—a high compliment from a man who referred to himself as a son of the Middle Border. "No one would suspect, as they see him going about the streets of Harlem, that he is honorary chief of several tribes."

Between the two, Garland was more widely published, but he was self-educated and for that reason more self-conscious. Grinnell was eleven years older, a patrician easterner; he was also, as Garland acknowledged, a bona fide chief. These differences mattered little, however, and on many more occasions during the coming years, in correspondence and in conversation, they would pool their knowledge and sympathies in an effort to advance the cause of Native Americans. A current that would draw them even closer was their mutual friendship with Theodore Roosevelt, who was, if not an avowed friend of the Indian, nonetheless a border man at heart.

PART FOUR

AMERICAN ANTHROPOLOGIST

(1897–1902)

ECLIPSE OF MEMORY

T he winter that followed was, as usual, one of stress and distraction. Grinnell's schedule included frequent meetings of the New York Zoological Society to plan the grounds and buildings of the Bronx Zoo, on which work was to begin in the spring. Spotted Hawk and Little Whirlwind remained much on his mind. He was upset by reports of increased drinking on the Blackfeet reservation, and the Ceded Strip was due to open (legally) to miners in April.

More time-consuming than anything else, however, was the merger of Bosworth Machine with a Boston firm; the new company would be named Campbell Bosworth, and negotiations of stock valuation and capitalization were protracted and delicate. An agreement was struck to cease the manufacture of the sewing machines in the Grinnell-owned factory in Milford and thereafter make them in Boston. Grinnell acknowledged that he would not have been able to manage the transition without the legal help of his brother-in-law Newell Martin.

His brothers, Mort and William, on the other hand, were no help at all. William continued to live at Audubon Park, but more and more he led a life that did not include his family. His architecture practice was well established by the 1890s; two of his signature buildings were the Queen Anne–

style Washington Heights Athenaeum on 155th Street and the seven-story Excelsior Power Company building on Gold Street in lower Manhattan. His other passion was collecting Oriental art, and he traveled abroad often to the Middle East and Asia in search of more treasures.

Mort, too, liked to travel. He and his new wife, Jennie, had honeymooned on the Nile and spent the winter of 1897–98 at the Hotel del Coronado in San Diego. He had given up his medical practice entirely and now fancied himself a writer. In March he sent a short story and a novel to George for his thoughts.

If Mort was expecting his older brother's approval, he received quite a shock. Grinnell deemed the short story unsalvageable. He regarded the novel as a professional and, for that matter, personal insult. "The trade of writing for publication is one that, like most other trades, has to be learned and requires a great deal of practice before a man can hope to accomplish very much at it," he lectured Mort.

More than sibling rivalry fueled Grinnell's dismay and disgust at Mort's new choice of occupation. Mort was nominally a coexecutor of their father's estate, but rather than mind his own inheritance and those of his siblings, he conducted himself more as a prodigal son—a dreamer who lived beyond his means. It fell to brother George to handle the family finances and keep Mort from insolvency. "It is extremely unpleasant for me to say these things because I think that they will perhaps be unpleasant for you to hear, but they must be said," Grinnell wrote after reading Mort's manuscripts. "I am inclined to think that if you will work at this trade, and work hard, you can do something at it, but it is first necessary to disabuse yourself of the idea that all that is required is to provide yourself with paper, ink and pen. It takes grinding toil to make anything that people will pay for."

Two months later he was even more blunt: "As for trying to earn a living by writing for pay, you had better try to earn a living by laying bricks."

Whether Mort followed his brother's suggestions for revision is not known. The following year the novel, entitled *An Eclipse of Memory*, found a publisher in Frederick A. Stokes, a Yale man who had graduated a couple years after Mort. To most readers, *An Eclipse of Memory* was a memory deserving of eclipse, noteworthy only for its clichéd frivolousness: a marriage, a mistress, a shipwreck, a second marriage, another voyage, the reappearance of the first wife, not drowned after all.

Yet for Grinnell to insist that the characters were not "real people" was to deny the opposite. The leading man, Jack Oswald, is clearly Mort. He is raised in an "atmosphere of refinement," grows up to love nature, goes to college early (Mort entered Yale at sixteen), becomes "a follower rather than a leader," and slides by on his athleticism and amiability. Then, as a grown man, he turns irresponsible: "He felt that he could do something creditable, but he also knew that he never would. . . . He was a combination of generosity and selfishness. Of money he knew not the value."

George Bird Grinnell could not have written a more frank assessment of his brother if he had wanted to.

Somewhat less blatant but transparent nonetheless is the description of fellow traveler Billie Brown. "'You know Billie,'" a shipmate remarks, "'not a very heavy intellect, but a good boy who will run errands for the ladies and dress for the whole party.'" Answers another: "'Yes, I know him. He is what you might call a pretty boy.'" Billie later appears on deck dressed in "a bicycle suit of rather loud check with a cap to match." Quips a sarcastic admirer: "'Quite like a fashion plate, Billie, but where did you get that cravat; it would make Joseph's coat blush with envy.'" Billie takes the jibe in good sport: "'Oh, that's the latest London agony. You can put me on the bow at night for a headlight if you want—for ten dollars per night.'"

In 1899 novels did not declare characters homosexual—not in so many words. But by naming Billie after his younger brother William—called Willie but in family letters also called Billy—Mort left little to guesswork. In a later chapter he has Billie fall for a "harmless" girl named Margaret, but this is thin cover for what anyone who knew William "Billy" Grinnell already suspected, even if they were too well-mannered to say it out loud or wished it weren't so.

Unlike many—most—of his contemporaries, William did not go to elaborate lengths to repress or otherwise mask who he was, much to the discomfort of his immediate family. After William's death in 1922 and the settlement of his will, the *New York Times* would run a brief item reporting that "James A. Scott, a retired policeman, now in charge of safe deposit vaults at 41 West Thirty-fourth Street and living at Forest Hills, L. I., received

$70,000 from the estate of his friend, William Milne Grinnell, whom he met while playing handball on Washington Heights many years ago." The *Times* described Scott as "the most intimate friend of Mr. Grinnell."

Grinnell was far more enthusiastic about another piece of writing that had recently come his way. In the summer of 1897, while passing through Nebraska, Lute North's brother Jim had shown him a manuscript entitled, "A Quarter Century on the Frontier, or The Adventures of Major Frank North, the 'White Chief of the Pawnees,'" written by Omaha newspaperman Alfred Sorenson. A condensed version had appeared in the *Platte Valley Times* in 1896.

When Jim North got hold of the full narrative, he naturally thought of Grinnell, who in turn looked it over and told Jim that it had the makings of "a capital book" but that its "literary quality" needed improving. With Jim North's consent, Grinnell submitted it, unedited, to the publishing house of F. Tennyson Neely. Neely responded that he would be delighted to issue the book, provided the Norths would contribute to the cost of production. Jim North declined the offer—which gave Grinnell an idea he felt would work to everyone's benefit, the Norths and his own.

The North brothers, Frank and Lute, were by now recognized, especially among Nebraskans, as heroes of the frontier. Nobody, however, thought more highly of them than Grinnell. They were his visceral and emotional connection to the wild West. For more than twenty years he had worked on Lute North to record his memories, but Lute was not at ease as a writer. Getting him to answer letters was hard enough. "If it were not for the members of your family and for old time's sake, and for the affection I bear you, I would certainly stop off at Columbus the next time I went west and kill you," Grinnell griped jovially after one of Lute's recent crimes of postal silence. "You are no good at all, and I am indignant at you because you never let me hear from you."

Reluctantly he accepted that the Sorenson manuscript was his best chance for a North book. He was tempted to tackle it himself, but then he thought of George Gould.

Eight years had passed since Grinnell and Gould had seen each other.

Yet correspondence between them had not slowed. As ever, they kept to topics of history and hunting and nature. Gould's interests tended to focus more narrowly on the Pacific Coast. In April Grinnell published a two-part article by Gould on the first whites, members of Coronado's expedition, to set foot in California. Grinnell praised it as "a splendid thing."

Gould had begun growing olives on his Santa Barbara estate (today's Olive Mill Road in Montecito runs alongside Gould's former property), and each year he sent Grinnell a sample from his orchard. To Gould's latest invitation to inspect the groves of Santa Barbara in person, Grinnell sent his usual kind regret: "If I were a gentleman of elegant leisure, I should, I think, migrate to Southern California . . . but there are papers to be gotten out, real estate business to be carried on, sewing machines to be manufactured, and books and articles to be written, and besides that, a family of comfortable size to be supported."

In lieu of setting out for the Pacific, Grinnell proposed a way to reel Gould closer. Gould's writing was disciplined, elegant, entertaining; he was so picky about words that it was Grinnell who usually had to apologize for errors that appeared in Gould's *Forest and Stream* articles. In June he wrote to Gould, asking him to read Sorenson's biography of North with the idea of "licking it into shape."

Gould's response was, in some respects, even harsher than Grinnell's deprecation of Mort Grinnell's novel. The original Sorenson manuscript was 206 typewritten pages. Gould slashed it by more than half, omitting a "vast amount of useless detail" and recasting Frank North's escapades as leader of the Pawnee scouts in "less garrulous form." Even the passages he kept were barely worth saving. "The dry & disjointed style led me to expect an accuracy that would inspire reliance," Gould wrote Grinnell, but "[t]he stuff is full of contradictions, inaccuracies and statements which though they must contain a basis of truth appear like the grossest of falsehoods. . . . A band of 27 Indians exterminated is called Sioux in one place & Cheyenne in another. . . . We are told that the Pawnees rode bareback & naked 180 miles for 27 hours on end . . . without food or rest & spent the next night in dancing. . . . As a general thing the distances given for Indian marches are next door to fable."

Gould took no pride of authorship in the revisions. He instructed Grinnell, "Don't let . . . my small amount of work done stop you from burning this whole business if you think best."

Grinnell did not disagree, but he was deflated by Gould's severe editing. Even if Grinnell were to write a supplementary chapter or two on the Pawnees, there still would not be enough material for a book. "It will make a pamphlet and a small one at that," he conceded. His plan to honor Frank North and to knit together a triad—of himself, the Norths, and Gould— had fallen short.

And then came a letter from Lute North that upset him even more. At the age of fifty-two, North had at last married. Her name was Elvira Coolidge; she was recently widowed and thirteen years younger than her new husband. North had first met her during his ranching days on the Dismal River (where, during a friendly shooting match, it was said that she had outshot Buffalo Bill Cody).

"My dear Lute," Grinnell responded on August 6, "It [is] not well to express to a newly married man all the sentiments of my heart. Never mind, my fast friend; I will get even with you." He was joking—sort of.

The news was indeed disconcerting, for it put Grinnell on the spot. As a bachelor, he had taken some comfort in knowing that two of his dearest friends, North and Gould, were bachelors also. "I will take a horrible revenge," he warned North. "The first chance I have, I will get married myself. Then how will you feel?" Realizing the implausibility of this threat, he added: "It may be some time before this opportunity occurs. During my study of women for the last 48 years, I have found them pretty able to take care of themselves and altogether too smart to be caught by me." Softening further, he announced, "I want to see your wife. I hope that she will like me, and I hope that she will be patient with me."

With George Gould, whose bachelorhood was inviolable, he commiserated on North's marriage: "It was a great shock to me. . . . [I]t seems melancholy that an old fellow like this, after having traveled the prairie for so many years—for he is older than I am—should at last be roped, thrown and tied. However, he seems to feel no mortification over it and writes me quite cheerfully. I do not, therefore, venture to offer him my sympathy, but I feel for him deeply."

Grinnell's tongue was in his cheek, but his nerves were somewhat shaken.

The nation's nerves had been rattled as well during the first months of 1898, beginning with the sinking of the USS *Maine* in Havana Harbor on February 15, a provocation that led to a congressional declaration of war against Spain two months later. Grinnell, like many Americans, had little doubt that the United States held the moral high ground and would prevail in delivering Cuba from colonial oppression, but he remembered how his father's affairs had suffered at the outbreak of the Civil War. "I am somewhat uneasy over this war talk, which I fear may have a depressing effect on business," he wrote to brother Mort in March. But on calmer reflection, he next recalled how robustly his father had rebounded once armies mustered and the demand for materiel increased. "As a matter of fact," he continued to Mort, "I suppose that the probabilities are that a war would make business active"—by which he surely meant an upsurge in the manufacture of harnesses and a consequent demand for harness-sewing machines. He also entertained hopes of selling the horses on his Wyoming ranch to the army.

At forty-eight, Grinnell ought to have been too old to consider enlisting, but he was not immune to the contagion of patriotism that was stirring hundreds of thousands of Americans to volunteer for military service. On April 23, two days before Congress officially declared war, Grinnell reached out to Theodore Roosevelt, who was already planning his resignation as assistant secretary of the navy in order to form a volunteer cavalry known as the Rough Riders. "My dear Roosevelt," he wrote, "Ever since the war talk began, I have been thinking more or less about what I should do in the event of actual hostilities and want now to make a confidential suggestion to you. I have thought that a regiment of mounted Indians might be very useful for scout duty and outpost fighting if any force lands in Cuba."

He did not mention Frank and Lute North, or the Pawnee scouts, but they were surely not far from his thoughts. "I should not care to take there any Indians from the high, dry plains," he continued sensibly. "It would be a waste, for as soon as they landed, they would have to go into hospital and would be for a time useless. However, the Indians from the south would be more easily acclimated and would, I feel sure, do good service, just such work, in fact, as some of them used to do in the days of the Indian wars about thirty years ago. I believe that among the southern tribes I could raise such a regiment, and, if desired, I would be willing to do so, and to take charge of them in Cuba."

Grinnell was anticipating not only what Indians could do for the country, but also what the country could do for Indians. Here was a chance to reinstate them as warriors, to win them the respect of a nation that had come to think of them as useless and ungrateful. And to lead such a regiment would be no small feather in Grinnell's cap.

"It might be said that it would [be] more economical to enlist such a force from among the native Cubans," Grinnell reasoned. "Such people would not need to be acclimated and would know the country. There is force in this." On the other hand, "I myself do not know how those dagoes fight, nor how much dependence is to be placed in them, whereas I know that Indians could be trusted."

For the time being, he asked for Roosevelt's discretion: "I do not care to be published as having made such a suggestion as this, but if you think well of it, let me know, and I can draw up a brief letter which I may ask you to submit to the proper authorities in Washington."

Grinnell's idea went nowhere. Roosevelt informed him that formation of a regiment of Indian scouts would require an act of Congress, and even if Grinnell had dropped everything, as Roosevelt had done to create the Rough Riders, the Indians could not have been trained in time. Grinnell had predicted that the war in Cuba (and Puerto Rico) would last years; it was over by August. (The insurgency in the Philippines would last far longer, however.)

The press and the public gave much of the credit for the Caribbean conflict's quick resolution to Theodore Roosevelt and his Rough Riders. U.S. ambassador to England and soon-to-be secretary of state John Hay described the four months of resounding military victories as a "splendid little war," and Grinnell concurred entirely. "I have watched, as you may imagine, with the greatest interest the splendid work done by you and your command in Cuba," he commended Roosevelt. "This did not surprise me, but it pleased me greatly. . . . You were the very man for the work, and, of course, you did it well."

Instead of going to war, Grinnell went west. He skipped the Shirley Basin, which was by now an annoyance he could not bear to face straight on. His horses proved to be too heavy for the army's purposes, even if the war had continued. Then his tenant, William Collins, left on short notice, apparently to join the "cowboy cavalry of Wyoming," absconding with $1,000 he had collected selling Grinnell's cattle. Grinnell wrote to a lawyer in Laramie, conceding that he was ready to sell "at almost any sacrifice." He hoped he might get $6,000 for the thousand acres and $20 for each horse. The following year, to his great relief, the deal was done and the financial millstone was at last removed from his neck.

He arrived on the Blackfeet reservation in time for the medicine lodge— his first complete one, having been rained out the year before. He did not write of his experience, other than to mention that he spent eight or nine days in the summer encampment. His presence there showed that he was not one of the many whites who frowned upon the ceremony, although in a letter to Rides at the Door later on, he admonished against excessive dancing in general. "[I]n summer, when they have the hay to put up and their cattle to look after every day, they ought not to dance at all."

After the medicine lodge was over and the Piegans had dispersed, Grinnell and Jack Monroe set off to climb Blackfoot Mountain. The previous fall Monroe had tried to scale the peak with Gifford Pinchot, but, to Grinnell's private relief, they had not succeeded. "[U]ntil somebody goes up that," Grinnell told Monroe, "I shall still regard myself as the chief of the St. Mary's country."

This time they took more care crossing the upper St. Mary, well above where they and their horses had been upended a year earlier. Blackfoot Mountain stands to the southeast of Mount Jackson, and though not as tall (9,500 feet), it girds itself with a more formidable ice field. Grinnell and Monroe began their climb at daybreak, under a cloudless sky. They carried ice axes and a coil of rope and blackened their cheeks with charcoal to prevent snow blindness. The hike across the glacier was slow but presented only a half mile or so of real danger, where the ice slope fell away steeply. "If one had slipped on the traverse, he would have brought up in another state of existence," Grinnell remarked with a wink of graveyard humor. In a few places they were obliged to cut steps with their axes, but by midday they were on top. "Jack, who was in advance, with a fine courtesy and a thoughtfulness that would be matched in few companions, stopped, turned to me and motioned me to go ahead," Grinnell wrote in *Forest and Stream*. "It was a touch of delicate generosity which gave an insight into my friend's character; for, as I have already suggested, to me it did mean a little something to place my foot first on the summit."

A moment later Grinnell's heart sank, as he noticed a huge stone that had recently been overturned. "Could it be that other people had been here, and had begun to build a monument on the summit?" he asked himself. "A second glance, however, served to show that the stone had been turned over by a bear in his search for mice."

That same summer, Grinnell went to Omaha to take in the Trans-Mississippi and International Exposition.

By nearly every measure, the Chicago World's Fair of 1893—the World's Columbian Exposition—had been a marvel beyond all precedent and expectation. Yet, for the most part, it had celebrated the industrial growth of the East. Civic leaders in the West, feeling somewhat slighted, set out to celebrate the progress taking place in the vast expanse of the continent between the Mississippi and the Pacific. They transformed a bluff of the Missouri River into a prairie Eldorado of garish arches and colonnades, a Venetian lagoon, and faux neoclassical temples to manufacturing, mining, agriculture, and fine arts. The Spanish-American War had turned the nation's gaze outward, as the United States contemplated its new station as a Great Power; nonetheless, the appetite for another world's fair drew two and a half million visitors to Omaha during the exposition's five-month run.

Grinnell had missed the Chicago fair, and he might not have been inclined to take in the Omaha spectacle if it had not included the Indian Congress, organized by James Mooney of the Bureau of Ethnology and sanctioned by the Bureau of Indian Affairs. "It is the purpose of the proposed encampment or congress to make an extensive exhibit illustrative of the mode of life, native industries, and ethnic traits of as many aboriginal American tribes as possible," the BIA stated in a letter distributed to Indian agents across the country. The organizers wished to show off the advances that Indians had made since they had quit warring with whites twenty years earlier. Yet to lure the curious public, the Indians were expected to live in "tepees, wigwams, hogans," and other traditional dwellings on the four acres reserved for them on the north side of the exposition grounds. Furthermore, "the encampment should be as thoroughly aboriginal in every respect as practicable, and the primitive traits and characteristics of the several tribes should be distinctly set forth."

The Piegans and the Southern (but not Northern) Cheyennes were among the thirty-five tribes to attend the Indian Congress. Of all the lodges erected in the Indian encampment, the Piegans' drew the most attention as one of the few made from buffalo hide and painted with old-time hunting scenes.

Grinnell arrived at the fair on September 24 and spent only one day, part of it in the lodge of his Piegan friend Mountain Chief. He did not record which of the Indian events he took in, but a favorite of fairgoers was a reenactment of the ghost dance. Another was described as a "dog feast." Buffalo Bill's Wild West, while not officially connected with the Indian Congress, concluded each of its Omaha performances with a dramatization of the battle of the Little Bighorn.

Perhaps the most popular Indian event was a "sham battle" between Blackfeet and Sioux enacted before a grandstand and an audience of many thousands. "Up and down the field the contending forces fought, first one side having an advantage and then another," reported the Omaha *Evening Bee*. "Every protuberance upon the ground and every tree had its Indian and his gun behind it and whenever a head appeared, it was shot at . . . causing scores of Indians to bite the dust." (Bows and arrows would have been more authentic, but they were not practical for mock combat.)

In the short time that Grinnell spent among the Indians at the Omaha fair, he made the acquaintance of photographer Frank Rinehart and his assistant, Adolph Muhr. As a young man in Denver, Rinehart had mastered the technical complexities of photography while in partnership with William Henry Jackson, famous for his field images chronicling western expansion. In 1885 Rinehart established his own studio in Omaha and was the obvious choice for official photographer of the Trans-Mississippi Exposition. He was the only photographer permitted in the Indian encampment.

In addition to taking pictures of Indian life at the fair throughout the summer, Rinehart took more than five hundred formal portraits. Never before had a single photographer compiled so comprehensive a gallery of Native Americans. He posed nearly all of his subjects against a painted backdrop, wearing their finest and most representative regalia—headdresses, beadwork, jewelry, and moccasins. Some have fur and feathers in their hair. Some hair is roached; some is braided. Some Indians pose with sacred pipes, others with eagle-feather fans, still others with bows or rifles.

The names Rinehart wrote at the bottom of the eight hundred eight-by-ten glass plates read like poetry pressed into pictographs: Touch the Cloud, Yellow Smoke, Afraid of Eagle, Running Deer, Kicking Bear, White Swan, Yellow Magpie, Black Otter, Poor Dog, Many Horses, Dust Maker, Goes to War, Kills Alone, Left Behind, Buried Far Away. He also photographed Apache chief Geronimo and Lakota chief Red Cloud. There is nothing forlorn in the countenance of Rinehart's Indians. They stare directly into the camera, calm, poised, and, in a few instances, a little defiant.

Native dignity notwithstanding, Grinnell was haunted by the gulf between the dazzle of the white man's world's fair and the evanescence of the Indian campfires: "When I walked through the Omaha Exposition grounds one hot day in September of 1898, on my way to the encampment of the Indian Congress, I found it difficult to realize that only fifty years before, the ground where Omaha now stands had been a camping place for Indians; and that only twenty-five years ago, Nebraska, one hundred and fifty miles west of Omaha, had been a country dangerous to pass through, because [it was] the home and hunting ground of hostile tribes. . . . In its display of science and art, of invention, machinery and product, the Exposition stood for the bounding present; it marked the swelling tide of the progress of an expanding people. . . . And over against all this, pathetic in the contrast, was the Indian in his skin lodge, clad in primitive dress, and typical of a diminishing race—a people to which the century had brought an utter obliteration of the old life . . . so complete and so momentous that the white man cannot conceive it."

Grinnell's reputation as an expert on Indians was underscored still more firmly by publication of two articles in the *Atlantic Monthly*. In the first, entitled "The Wild Indian," Grinnell explained, "We cannot deal with the Indian of today unless we know the Indian of yesterday. . . . I say this with the more confidence because for many years I have lived with the plains people in their homes, engaging in their pursuits, sharing their joys and sorrows. . . . I have thus learned to live and feel as an Indian thinks and feels, and to see things as he sees them."

He condemned the tendency of most Americans "to despise those who in appearance or by birth or tradition are different from ourselves,—the feeling which leads many a white man to speak with contempt of negroes or Chinamen." He also disparaged the lingering characterization of Indians as enemies. The Indian was a fighter, he acknowledged, but "like any other human being, he is many-sided, and he did not always wear his war paint."

As enlightened as this sounded, Grinnell still hewed to the prevailing anthropological wisdom that Indians were only midway up the ladder from savagery to civilization and that they possessed "the stature of a man with the experiences and reasoning powers of a child." He also fell into the high-brow habit of referring to Indians, plural, as "the Indian."

The editor of the *Atlantic*, Walter Hines Page (who would later become Woodrow Wilson's ambassador to England), wanted to call the second article "The Tame Indian." Instead Grinnell titled it "The Indian on the Reservation." In the previous *Atlantic* piece, he had exercised liberal forbearance toward Indians in transition; now he criticized those in charge of that transition for their misfeasance, inconsistency, and indifference. The only high marks Grinnell gave were to military men placed in charge of agencies.

He damned with faint praise the work of the "friends" of the Indians who devised plans "which should at once transform the Indian from a rover and warrior to a sedentary laborer." He did not question their earnestness, "[B]ut . . . they had no personal knowledge of the inner life of the people they were trying to help."

He repeated the frustration he had expressed for many years to the Indian Bureau in Washington: It wasn't that Indians were lazy and unwilling to work; rather, they wanted to work, but there was little paying work to be found on reservations. He then explained that too many Indian reservations "were situated in the land of thirst" and thus were unsuitable for crops. Stock raising was the best chance for Indians to make a living and to become independent of government support. Next he railed against the "rings" of whites that robbed Indians of their land and annuities.

Rousing his readers, he made the case that Indians were integral to the national fabric and were not going away anytime soon: "Interest in the Indian is steadily increasing. Many thoughtful people are coming to recognize that he possesses qualities that are worth studying. Writers take him for their theme, sculptors model him, and painters use for subjects scenes from his old wild life. Intelligent people who study him wish to know more about him, and soon learn his true character and give him his true place, demanding for the race the consideration which it ought to have."

The *Atlantic Monthly* articles, published in January and February of 1899, were the voice of a man who had won the unqualified respect not only of "the Indian," but also of his white peers. Among men of influence and discernment in the East and West Grinnell had earned deep deference. He possessed a catalog of knowledge and experience that few contemporaries could match.

In April, when his friend Clinton Hart Merriam drew up a list of the most eminent experts in the fields of natural history and ethnology to join a scientific expedition along the coast of Alaska, there was no question that Grinnell would be invited as one of the passengers.

At first he demurred, insisting he was too busy to get away, but in the end he accepted, flattered to sail with such a pantheon.

THE ALASKA EXPEDITION

A rich man goes on a bear hunt. That, anyway, was the original idea behind the Alaska expedition.

In the spring of 1899 Edward H. Harriman was exhausted. Over the past year he had taken control of the Union Pacific Railroad, and after seating himself as chairman of the board, he decided that he owed himself a change of scenery. His friend Daniel Elliot of the Field Museum in Chicago suggested that, given Harriman's predatory nature and love of the outdoors, he might enjoy shooting the largest bear known to man, the Kodiak.

In March Harriman showed up, unannounced, in the office of Clinton Hart Merriam, head of the Department of Agriculture's Division of Biological Survey. He had chosen wisely, for it was Merriam who first identified the Kodiak as a subspecies of Alaskan brown bear. Merriam, however, was not so quick to identify his visitor as one of the most powerful railroad men in the United States. The stranger explained that he was planning a trip along the coast of Alaska, and, in addition to his ambition to kill a Kodiak, he wanted to take a party of scientists to keep him company and to give the voyage the gravitas of an "expedition." After some hasty checking and a second visit from Harriman, Merriam climbed aboard enthusiastically.

Harriman asked Merriam to put together a list of passengers who would sail from Seattle on the steamship *George W. Elder*, which the railroad tycoon was having refitted for its purposes of research and Gilded Age recreation. Harriman would be accompanied by his wife and five children (including seven-year-old Averell Harriman, the future diplomat and governor of New York), plus his wife's brother, William Averell, and Averell's wife and daughter. Like Noah, he preferred that his other shipmates come in twos—two zoologists, two botanists, two geologists, and so on. "When I raised the question of cost, remarking that few scientific men were financially able to meet the expense incident to such a trip," Merriam recalled, "he promptly put my mind at rest by replying that all the members of the expedition would be his guests."

Merriam's protean curiosity had made him an expert in a variety of interlocking disciplines. His father had done well on Wall Street and lived as a gentleman farmer (and two-term congressman) in the foothills of the Adirondacks. (Small world: James Willard Schultz was a boyhood friend, and Schultz would name his only son Hart Merriam Schultz.) Merriam was precocious in his study of bugs, birds, and taxidermy, and in 1872, not yet seventeen, he so impressed Smithsonian curator Spencer Baird that he was named a naturalist on a government survey of the newly created Yellowstone National Park. While still at Yale, he published his first book, *A Review of the Birds of Connecticut*. As a medical student in New York, his enthusiasm for anatomy was unbounded. He dissected a seal in his rented room on West Twenty-Second Street and became so engrossed in his inspection of "2 uncleaned human skulls, 1 pelvis + 1 arm" that he took them home in his trunk for Christmas. He practiced medicine for a few years, but his love of the natural world led him far afield. He served as a surgeon on a sealing expedition. In 1883 he helped found the American Ornithologists' Union. In 1888 he was one of the thirty-three founders of the National Geographic Society. He published regularly in a number of journals, including *Forest and Stream*, and traveled widely, from Death Valley to Alaska.

The Biological Survey had grown out of the AOU's committee on bird migration. Initially it was called the Division of Economic Ornithology and Mammalogy, and Merriam was named its first chief in 1886. Government employment did not crimp his portfolio in the least. Having begun as an ornithologist, Merriam would, in the course of a long and distinguished career, identify more than three hundred species and subspecies of wild animals. Several would eventually carry his name: Merriam's canyon lizard, Merriam's pocket mouse, and Merriam's turkey. At forty-three, he himself looked like a hybrid of creatures, with his woolly buffalo hair and unruly walrus moustache.

Merriam knew, if not as a friend, then at least by reputation, every man chosen for the scientific party of the Harriman Alaska Expedition. Many were fellow members of Washington's Cosmos Club. The first two scientists he tapped were well-traveled geologist Grove Karl Gilbert and biologist William H. Dall. Dall was an authority on mollusks but better known for his extensive travels to Alaska and Siberia and as author of the indispensable *Alaska and Its Resources* (1870).

The list that followed was a legion of honor, including several veterans of groundbreaking western surveys. Botanist Frederick Colville had been with Merriam in Death Valley; geographer Henry Gannett had been on the first survey of Yellowstone in 1871; ornithologist Robert Ridgway had been a member of the transcontinental Fortieth Parallel survey; botanist William Brewer had been on the forestry commission of 1896. To this roster was added Bernhard Fernow, recently retired chief forester and current dean of Cornell University's College of Forestry; William Trelease, director of the Missouri Botanical Gardens; William Ritter, president of the California Academy of Sciences; Wesley Coe, professor of anatomy at Yale; and George Bird Grinnell, listed in the official report of the expedition as "Editor, Forest and Stream."

Also included in the scientific party were the "two Johnnies," as they would be affectionately called once the expedition was under way: seventy-two-year-old nature writer John Burroughs and seventy-one-year-old protector of Yosemite, champion of wilderness, and Sierra Club president, John Muir, listed as "Author and Student of Glaciers."

Yet there were more, many more, besides these twenty-five men of science. Harriman invited three artists: Louis Agassiz Fuertes, who specialized in birds; landscape painter R. Swain Gifford; and Frederick S. Dellenbaugh, a veteran of John Wesley Powell's exploration of the Colorado River. Of the two photographers recruited, Duncan Inverarity would be forgotten by history; the other is today all but immortal, as are his photographs.

In 1899 Edward Sheriff Curtis owned a storefront photography studio in Seattle. He supported his family by taking portraits of the city's burghers and also of adventurers en route to and from the goldfields of the Klondike. The previous year several of his pictures of local Indians had been chosen for an exhibition by the National Photographic Society, and an article bearing his byline, "The Rush to the Klondike over the Mountain Passes," had run in *Century*—although the seven photos that accompanied the story were actually taken by his brother Asahel.

Curtis was a very able alpinist and had led parties to the summit of Mount Rainier and other peaks of the Cascades. In the summer of 1898 he encountered a group of "scientificos" on the slopes of Rainier. "A couple of times they got lost," he recalled, "[and] I managed to get them to my camp [where] I thawed them out and bedded [them] down." One of the men he rescued was C. Hart Merriam.

Merriam was impressed by Curtis's combined abilities as photographer and outdoorsman and felt he was just the man to document the Harriman Alaska Expedition. Curtis was informed that the *Elder* would be fitted out with a darkroom, but the invitation did not cover the cost of his plates, chemicals, and other photographic gear. The best Merriam could offer was the possibility that his scientists might wish to purchase some of Curtis's photographs. (Even so, the copyright for those photos would belong to Harriman, and none could be published without his consent.)

Grinnell did not receive his invitation from Merriam until the middle of April. The ship was scheduled to leave Seattle at the end of May and was expected to be at sea at least two months but perhaps even longer. He said no at first, citing the pressure of work. "[B]ut so many good men are going that I finally was persuaded into joining the outfit," he told George Gould.

Once he made up his mind, he did not wait for Harriman's special train of palace cars to leave New York on May 23. Instead he threw his kit together and paid his own fare west, first stopping off on the Blackfeet reservation on May 17. He spent a week there, accomplishing little, other than renewing old acquaintances and absorbing their chronic grievances. He arrived in Seattle on May 29, a day ahead of the Harriman train. At his hotel the only face he recognized was that of Yellowstone Kelly, once a scout for generals Custer and Miles during the Indian wars. Grinnell recruited his old friend as one of the Harriman expedition's hunters.

The *George W. Elder* left Seattle on the last day of May. The Harriman family, their servants, the scientific party, photographers, and artists totaled forty-four. To attend them were two doctors, a nurse, a chaplain, two stenographers, and eleven hunters, packers, and camp hands. Sixty-five officers and ship's crew brought the number of souls aboard to 126.

The 250-foot-long ship was stuffed full as it steamed northward. Secured to its deck were a steam launch and two smaller launches powered by naphtha engines. Canoes, camping equipment, and all manner of surveying and scientific instruments were stowed below. Space was also made in the hold for what John Burroughs described as "a farmer's barnyard": eleven steers, a flock of sheep, chickens, turkeys, a milk cow, and a team of horses. The ship also had a well-stocked library.

From a scientific standpoint, there was no master plan; nor did Harriman have any particular route in mind, other than one that put him within shooting distance of a Kodiak bear. "The ship had no business other than to convey the party whithersoever it decided to go," Merriam explained. An executive committee had been formed on the train, with Harriman as chair; Grinnell, Muir, and Curtis were named to it in absentia. Next came committees on Routes and Plans, Steam Launch and Small Boats, Music and Entertainment, Lectures, and Library, among others. Grinnell was assigned to the Committee on Big Game, along with Harriman's personal physician, Lewis Morris, and seventeen-year-old debutante daughter Mary (who two years later would found the Junior League of New York).

The *Elder* cruised smoothly through the Inside Passage, protected from Pacific swells by Vancouver and Queen Charlotte islands. The ship paused at several spots so the scientists could rehearse their respective trades. "Steamer stopped . . . and a dozen people went ashore," Grinnell wrote in his diary on the third day out. "The botanists & geologists gathered specimens and came off after being gone 2 ½ hours." Each evening after dinner one of the scientists gave a lecture. "Dr. Dall was our Alaska specialist,"

John Burroughs explained. "In John Muir we had an authority on glaciers, and a thorough one—so thorough that he would not allow the rest of the party to have an opinion on the subject."

Grinnell appreciated being in this august company, but, as an ethnologist, if this was to be the sphere of interest he assigned himself on the trip, he was by himself. Short stops in uninhabited bays were rich fodder for the other scientists, but for Grinnell to observe natives, as he had done in the lower states, he needed to spend time among them. Over the two months of the Harriman expedition, these opportunities were rare and all too brief.

On June 4, however, the *Elder* stopped at the Anglican Mission at Metlakatla, on Annette Island, where Scottish-born missionary William Duncan had built a church and an orderly community for the indigenous Tsimshians. Grinnell did not have time to learn much about the history, language, or customs of these natives—the first he encountered—but he was immediately struck by how much better off Metlakatla was than any Indian reservations he was familiar with. "The houses of the people are comfortable in appearance and roomy," he noted. "There are 4 stores, a sawmill, cannery &c. They have among them blacksmiths, carpenters, shoemakers, tailors. [They] are absolutely self-supporting and do not owe a dollar to anyone."

Grinnell and his shipmates happened to arrive on a Sunday morning in time for church services. "It would be hard to imagine a more decorous and attentive audience," he commented. As for the Tsimshians' appearance, "Except for their color, and for their peculiar gait, which seems to be common to all these fishing Indians, these people and their wives and children could hardly be told from any civilized community of a thousand souls anywhere in the country."

By noon the *Elder* was under way again, but Grinnell had stayed long enough to glimpse the blueprint that he wished for the Blackfeet, Cheyennes, and every tribe in the American West.

Between anchorages, he and his fellow passengers had little to do besides admire the scenery of the rugged coastline, thickly timbered to the water, with snowcapped mountains and glaciers tiering to the horizon. "Toward evening a great range of snowclad peaks came in sight," he wrote after leaving Metlakatla, "and after sunset the afterglow . . . was so beautiful that it broke up the hymn-singing in the saloon."

Turning up Lynn Canal, which is not an actual canal but a long fiord, on June 6, they reached Skagway, the jumping-off point for the Klondike. A few months before, gold seekers had been obliged to heft all their necessities from the waterfront to White Pass, three thousand vertical feet nearly straight uphill, in order to penetrate the upper Yukon. Now Harriman and company were carried courteously to the boundary between Alaska and Canada on the newly completed, twenty-mile-long White Pass & Yukon Railroad. Grinnell's eye was drawn to the muscular gouges made by the retreating glaciers and to the delicacy of the berries on the white heather. As the narrow-gauge train crept higher, he was delighted to see that the Audubon's warbler and white-tailed ptarmigan were still in breeding season.

Then, noticing the carcasses of dead horses as he neared the summit, he was struck by "the pathos of the trail . . . where men were turned to beasts." The railroad went no farther, and in a ragged tent Harriman and his retinue were served a hearty lunch.

The next day the *Elder* entered Glacier Bay and steamed to within two miles of Muir Glacier, explored by (and named for) John Muir twenty years earlier. Even before the ship anchored, its passengers were greeted by explosive thunder as cathedral-sized shards of ice calved from the colossal edifice of the glacier and crashed into the sea. Muir estimated that the glacier had receded more than two miles since his first visit. Dislodged bergs floated in the bay "like huge monsters," John Burroughs noted. "Nothing we had read or heard had prepared us for the color of the ice, especially of the newly exposed parts of the berg that rose from beneath the water—its deep, almost indigo blue."

John Muir was not the only member of the Harriman expedition who had a glacier named for him, and Grinnell listened with keen interest as Muir described his earlier experiences on the ice fields of Alaska. But instead of joining the party of scientists who set out to take a closer look at Muir Glacier, Grinnell went ashore on a different launch and with a hunting party made up of Harriman, Merriam, the two physicians, Morris and Edward Trudeau, Yellowstone Kelly, and seven packers. Their intended destination was Howling Valley, twenty miles to the south and east of Muir Glacier, touted by Muir as a likely spot to find bears.

With no appreciable nightfall to hamper their movement, they left at 7 p.m. and hiked up the moraine of a glacier that bore the unappetizing name of Dirt, pitching camp on its ice at midnight. "Slept fairly well," Grinnell recorded, "though the cold of the ice penetrated the sleeping bag and made the hip & shoulder cold." They were off again by 4:30, climbing still. Once the snow reached above their knees, they roped together as a precaution against hidden crevasses. When they reached the ridge from which they could at last see into Howling Valley, they were forced to concede that the snow was too deep for the packers to continue. Reluctantly they turned back. They limped back aboard the *Elder* by late afternoon, wet, cold, and exhausted, and Grinnell was sound asleep by 5:30. "Mr. Muir talked on glaciers," he mentioned, "but I did not hear him."

The next morning Grinnell was stiff but otherwise no worse for wear. Parties that had been dropped off at Muir Glacier returned one by one, bearing birds, rodents, insects, plants, algae, rocks, dredged seabed samples, and ebullient tales of their escapades.

Grinnell made several more hunting forays, but the game he came upon was too small to shoot. Finally on June 15 he went ashore on Biorka Island, near Sitka, with Merriam, Mary Harriman, Yellowstone Kelly, and several others. Shortly after midnight a blacktail doe emerged from a thicket of ferns close to Grinnell and Mary Harriman. "I told her to shoot, she did so once and missed, [and] deer paid no attention," he wrote in his diary. "At a second shot which also missed, deer raised its head and looked. Then M[erriam] shot and deer turned and ran quartering toward Miss H. who fired again and deer dropped." On examining it, Merriam concluded that it had been hit only once. "This showed that Miss H's last shot did the business," Grinnell concurred.

At Sitka, once a Russian trading settlement and now the capital of Alaska, Grinnell wandered about like any of the tourists who had already begun frequenting this picturesque village. He complained that the prices of the native "curiosities" were too high but bought two whalebone knives, a spear thrower, and several baskets.

Later George Emmons, a naval officer who had retired to Sitka, escorted

Grinnell and Harvard mineralogist Charles Palache on a tour of the nearby Tlingit village. "At the house of Chief Tentlatch we were received with some ceremony. . . . I was offered the seat of honor," Grinnell wrote. Indian etiquette was not so different here than in Montana.

That evening Grinnell and his shipmates dressed in their best and were received by a different order of chief: territorial governor John Brady, by chance a Yale man (class of 1874). Tentlatch and several Tlingits attended as well, wearing white shirts and suit coats. One of the scientists—Grinnell possibly, though he did not mention it—had the Indians sing into a Graphophone and then let them listen in wonderment as their voices chorused back to them. The following morning, as the *Elder* pulled away from Sitka harbor, a Tlingit brass band marched down to the wharf and performed "Yankee Doodle" and "Three Cheers for the Red, White and Blue."

At Yakutat Bay, the expedition's next port of call, Grinnell at last got the immersion into native life that he had been hoping for. At the head of the bay they came upon a cluster of camps, where three or four hundred Tlingits were busy hunting seals. Many in the Harriman party were disgusted by the carnage and stench of the outdoor abattoir. Seal carcasses were strewn across the gravel beach, rotting among the weathered bones of previous slaughters. The rocks were greasy with seal oil. Grinnell, who had participated in the prairie version of this seasonal harvest, the buffalo hunt, was thoroughly fascinated.

The native men hunted from canoes among the ice floes in the bay, killing the seals with rifles and spears; the women took care of the rest. Grinnell noted that the process of butchering seals "absolutely reverses the method common in other regions," and he marveled at the surgical efficiency of the entire operation. Using crescent-shaped knives of steel or sometimes of stone, the women cut off the flippers, legs, ribs, and loins and set them aside. The skin was then carefully removed with the blubber intact. (The fat of aquatic mammals is attached to the hide; fat of land mammals is attached to the flesh.)

"When a woman has removed half a dozen seal skins," he observed, "she kneels on the ground behind a board which she rests against her knees, and, spreading the hide, hair side down on the board, rapidly strips the blubber in one large piece from the hide, which, as she draws it toward her, is rolled up by a twisting motion into a thick rope. The great sheet of pinkish-white blubber is then cut into strips and put to one side, to be tried out a little later." During his time at Yakutat, Grinnell counted the skins of more than five hundred seals. The only food evident in the camp was seal meat; flippers were a menu favorite.

Grinnell also made a close study of the Tlingit shelters. Some natives dwelled in canvas tents, much as Plains Indians had begun doing after the buffalo were gone. But a few seal hunters still built temporary wooden structures covered with spruce bark. Frames of drying sealskins were propped against the exterior walls and covered the roofs. In the center of each shelter was a stone fireplace, in which blubber was heated to separate, or try out, the oil. The oil, used as both food and fuel, was commonly kept in cans and barrels, although Grinnell noticed that some natives still used the snug, intricately decorated wooden boxes of an earlier day. He was likewise gratified to spy a few kettles made of laced sealskin, much like those he had seen of buffalo paunch on the plains.

Besides Grinnell, the member of the expedition most interested in the seal camp was Edward Curtis. During the first three weeks of the voyage, he had taken a great number of pictures of mountains, glaciers, and his fellow passengers, but at Yakutat, he, like Grinnell, had his first chance to view natives in their natural environment. "The Indian women frowned upon our photographers and were very averse to having the cameras pointed at them," John Burroughs noticed. "It took a good deal of watching and waiting and maneuvering to get a good shot." But Curtis was patient, polite, and as unobtrusive as possible, and thus he succeeded in photographing several scenes of camp life. His images were authentic and artistic, a combination he would perfect in his multivolume *The North American Indian.*

The next major point of interest was Prince William Sound. The area had yet to be thoroughly explored—a revelation that stirred the school loyalties of the Harriman expedition. At the head of nearly every bay or inlet stood a magnificent glacier, none with a name. And so the scientists agreed to call one of them Columbia, after the New York college. The *Elder* next steamed up the Port Wells arm of Prince William Sound and into a fiord where glaciers perched on either side like trophies waiting to be claimed. "[G]laciers to right of us, glaciers to left of us, glaciers in front of us, volleyed and thundered," Burroughs wrote, summoning his best Tennyson. They named this passage College Fiord and dedicated its glacial side chambers to various alma maters: Harvard, Yale, and Amherst; and because the women aboard also had a say, Radcliffe, Smith, Bryn Mawr, Vassar, and Wellesley also got their due.

The biggest discovery, however, awaited in a separate arm of Port Wells that branched off just before the entrance to College Fiord, pinched by the palisade of Barry Glacier. Against the captain's caution, Harriman ordered the *Elder* to steam into this blind alley. Grinnell estimated that it was twelve or fifteen miles long and a mile wide at its narrowest. Where the inlet ended he could see a grand glacier flanked on either side by numerous smaller glaciers. "Some of these are like broad, gently sloping rivers with many tributaries flowing down from far back in the mts," he remarked in his diary. "Others are like cascades and waterfalls coming down the steep rock slopes."

The *Elder* halted about two miles from the glacier's towering front rim. "The purity of the mountain tops, the black of the slate rocks which form their mass, and the pale green water make a picture which was curiously weird and awe inspiring," Grinnell wrote. They named this aisle of ice and the glacier at its head after their patron, E. H. Harriman.

If this panorama was not glorious enough, a pod of killer whales breached nearby as the ship sailed slowly up the sound, "to blow very deliberately the toll for [our] appearing [here] first," Grinnell delighted. The payment of that toll turned out to be a propeller blade, which the *Elder* sheared off on ice or rock as it exited Harriman Fiord. Repair required laying over a day at low tide in Orca Inlet. That evening it was Grinnell's turn to lecture to the other passengers. He chose to talk about the natives he knew best, the Blackfeet.

After a brief inspection of Cook Inlet, where the city of Anchorage now lies, the *Elder* turned toward Kodiak Island. The forest thinned along the shore, and the weather grew milder. On July 1 Grinnell, with four heavily armed shipmates, plus four packers, and, as guide, a supervisor from the Pacific Steam Whaling cannery on the island, took a launch up a promising stream on Uyak Bay. Over the next three days they found abundant bear sign but saw only one live bear, too small and too distant to pursue. They did not return to the *Elder* until July 5. Only then did they learn of Harriman's hunting success.

Accompanied by Merriam, Yellowstone Kelly, daughter Mary, niece Elizabeth Averell, and a local Russian guide, Harriman had set off in a different direction from Grinnell's group. On their second day out, the tycoon finally got what he had come to Alaska for. As Kelly later recounted for the benefit of Grinnell's diary, "They saw the bear a long way off and, approaching, came within 75 yds. The bear was eating grass. Mr. H. fired and Kelly immediately afterward." Kelly gallantly testified that the bear was dead before his own bullet hit home. Then with a second shot Kelly killed the cub.

The hunters arrived back at the ship, jubilant and triumphant, and immediately the expedition's taxidermist was dispatched to retrieve the prizes. When John Muir saw the animals being brought aboard, he was not impressed. For a Kodiak, the mother bear was actually rather small, though perhaps Muir's muttered disparagement was drowned out by the Fourth of July celebration that continued into the pale Alaskan twilight.

With his bear secured, Harriman declared a new ambition. He wanted to set foot on Siberian soil. The *Elder* followed along the Alaskan Peninsula, pausing briefly at Dutch Harbor on the Aleutian island of Unalaska and then at St. Paul, one of the Pribilof Islands in the Bering Sea. Passengers not stricken by seasickness went ashore to inspect the once-robust fur-seal rookeries. Merriam, who had served on a federal commission to take stock of the devastation, explained that the seal population was but a fraction of what it had been twenty years earlier. Grinnell could not help thinking of the North American buffalo, once so ubiquitous and now, like the seals of the Bering Sea, woefully diminished.

Leaving St. Paul in a dense fog, the *Elder* had its one serious brush with disaster. Just after dinner was served on July 9, the ship's hull struck a series of unseen rocks. Grinnell described it as "a bump, then a rattling & grating which shook the whole ship." Then again. And again. The *Elder* came to a full stop. Despite the steward's assurance that there was no danger, the diners raced on deck—except for Grinnell and Dr. Edward Trudeau, who calmly finished their meal. The ship cautiously reversed engines and soon resumed its course, evidently undamaged. "The affair was now regarded as a joke," Grinnell wrote in his diary later that night, "and furnished talk for the rest of [the] trip."

On the eleventh, with no further interruption, they entered Plover Bay, today better known as Providence Bay, on the Chukchi Peninsula of Siberia. The ship was greeted by several walrus-skin umiaks paddled by natives, who, as Grinnell soon learned, subsisted on walruses, seals, whales, and reindeer. The thirty or so Eskimos of this weather-beaten hinterland were eager to trade skins, walrus ivory, and harpoon points for tobacco, knives, and sugar.

"The women are very short; one by whom I stood came up to my nipple," Grinnell observed. "Men are larger and stout as to their bodies [and] on the whole pretty well formed and strong. All are dressed in reindeer skin clothing, the men's parkas, or shirts, usually with collars of bear fur. . . . Both sexes wear sealskin mukluks, which reach to the knee."

As at Yakutat, Grinnell was intrigued by the native houses. Summer huts and more substantial winter dwellings stood close by one another; the latter reminded Grinnell of the dirt lodges of the Pawnees. On closer inspection, he noticed that the sides of many were constructed of whale ribs.

For all the Siberian Eskimos' resilience, having survived for centuries under the harshest Arctic conditions, they had not been able to withstand the ravages of American whalers, who had, as John Burroughs lamented, corrupted them "with bad morals and villainous whiskey." Burroughs saw little to admire in these people. To his alien eye they looked like "grotesque dolls."

The Americans remained only a few hours at Plover Bay, repulsed by the Arctic wind and the odor of oil and offal. Yet in the brief time ashore, Grinnell saw enough to fill ten pages of his notebook. He, for one, was not in a hurry to get away.

The next day the *Elder* called at Port Clarence, on the American shore of the Bering Strait, the northernmost point on the summer's journey. Here they found a dozen whaling ships tucked behind a long spit of gravel and tundra. Port Clarence was a boreal caravanserai, a nexus of contact between far-flung peoples—and not so distant from where an ancient land bridge had once led human beings from one continent to another. For untold generations, natives from both shores of the strait had been coming to this sheltered harbor to trade and mingle. Similarly, whalers waiting for the pack ice to recede so they could hunt the bowhead whales that lived at the top of the world chose this harbor to rendezvous with supply ships from San Francisco and Seattle.

Soon after the *Elder* dropped anchor, it was surrounded by umiaks filled with men, women, and children eager to barter. Grinnell was impressed by the vigor of these Eskimos: "[They] were a fine looking lot, stout, strong and healthy."

And naturally he was curious about every aspect of their lifestyle. Once again he took copious notes on their clothing, dwellings, implements, and diet. "These people were well provided with food," he remarked in his diary. "They had some fresh salmon . . . smelts, and some other fish that I did not recognize. A good-looking girl offered me some of this last, and I ate it raw. It was rather tough and stringy and had an aftertaste of rancid oil."

Curtis, meanwhile, was busy with his camera, taking portraits of these gregarious travelers, many of whom had paddled a hundred miles or more to partake of the seasonal celebration.

The only shadow cast on this sunny scene was the drunkenness of the natives, who paid for whalers' whiskey with sealskins and other precious possessions. Worse still, "All the officers on the whalers are supplied with Eskimo women whom they take with them on [their summer] cruise," Grinnell noted. "The women are said to refuse to rear their half-breed children. They kill them."

The season was shortening, and on July 13 the *Elder* turned south toward home. The ship passed by St. Lawrence and King islands but not Point Nome, where a gold rush was in full eruption. Over the summer, while the

Harriman expedition was touring the Alaskan coast, thousands of fortune-seekers had stormed the beaches of Norton Sound, a hundred or so miles southeast of Port Clarence. Unwittingly or intentionally, the *Elder* steered well clear of the latest stampede of rapacity and mayhem.

On July 26, having retraced much of their outbound route and taken on coal at Juneau, the ship cruised along the inside passage of the Alaska Panhandle. South of Wrangell they pulled close to shore at a place marked on the chart as Foggy Bay, where they had been told they might find an abandoned Tlingit village. Grinnell counted nineteen totem poles and fourteen houses. Yet not a soul was in evidence. The village appeared to have been abandoned several years before, for reasons unknown to the passengers and crew of the *Elder*, who proceeded first to admire it and then to loot it.

In the houses they found oil boxes, masks, and other painted ceremonial items. "A grave to [the southwest] of village bore on a railed platform the figures of two bears sitting up," Grinnell observed. "Nearby was another grave with a flying heron on it." The Harriman party wasted no time deliberating. "It is purposed to take some of the totem poles and other figures for museums," Grinnell wrote. They anchored for the night to allow the crew to remove five totem poles—two each for the California Academy of Science and Chicago's Field Museum, one for the University of Michigan. They also came away with the carved façade of a house and the two bears from the cemetery. Merriam removed a pair of woven Chilkat blankets from a grave.

The Harriman Alaska Expedition docked in Seattle early on the morning of July 30. During two months it had covered nine thousand miles. The *George W. Elder*, its officers, and crew had acquitted themselves ably, accomplishing dozens of landings on difficult shores; dangerous tramps on treacherous glaciers; and the scattering of scientific teams in various, untracked directions, with not a man or woman lost or gravely injured. Edward Harriman had proven to be a cordial, indulgent, and intrepid host. "It is pleasant to recall," he would write graciously, "the spirit of harmony and good fellowship which prevailed throughout the voyage, and to remember that whether in the field of research or in the line of service, all showed a willingness to cheerfully carry out the duties which fell to their lot."

The final days at sea had been full of reminiscence and appreciation. In the evenings there were speeches and toasts. After one night's round of tributes to Harriman, Grinnell remarked with droll affection, "A great deal was said but perhaps not too much." The scientists inventoried and packed their many samples; Curtis did the same with his photographic plates. The various subcommittees met and issued reports. The executive committee recommended publication of a book containing various technical papers and a general account of the expedition. Burroughs would write the main narrative; Muir would write on glaciers; Fernow on forests; others on birds, geology, geography, climate; Grinnell would contribute "The Natives of the Alaska Coast Region." Ultimately their submissions would fill thirteen volumes.

Grinnell's ethnological observations were rich in their specificity but sobering in their conclusions, similar to his prognosis for Indians of the American West. "Hitherto they have been well cut off from civilization," he would write in his official report. "But change has come for the Eskimo, and this year of 1900 has already witnessed a melancholy alteration in their condition. The rush to the coast gold fields has brought to them a horde of miners, who, thinking only of themselves, are devoid of all feeling for others. . . . White men, uncontrolled and uncontrollable, already swarm over the Alaska coast, and are overwhelming the Eskimo. They have taken away their women and debauched their men with liquor; they have brought them strange new diseases that they never knew before, and in a very short time they will ruin and disperse the wholesome, hearty, merry people whom we saw at Port Clarence and at Plover Bay. Perhaps for a while a few may save themselves by retreating to the Arctic to escape the contaminating touch of the civilized, and thus the extinction of the Alaska Eskimo may be postponed. But there is an inevitable conflict between civilization and savagery, and wherever the two touch each other, the weaker people must be destroyed."

Before leaving Seattle, Grinnell bought several baskets from Edward Curtis, and he encouraged Curtis to pursue his photography of Native Americans. During their two months together, Grinnell's enthusiasm for native culture had proven infectious. Curtis had heard Grinnell lecture on the Blackfeet; Grinnell probably said something about getting together at the Piegan medicine lodge the following summer. At any rate, they promised to keep in touch.

Grinnell rode by train to Portland, accompanied by the Harriman family, Merriam, and several others from the scientific party. From there he continued up the Columbia River, onward to Salt Lake City and Denver. At Columbus, Nebraska, he stopped to see Lute North, but somehow they missed each other. "I walked about the station, looking for you," he wrote to North a week later. "I wanted very much to have you go to Omaha [with me] on the train, but I could not hear of you or reach you. It was a great disappointment."

And so to Chicago and finally New York, which he reached on August 9. "It was the most delightful excursion I have ever made and was the first absolute vacation that I have had for a dozen or fifteen years," he reported to George Gould.

Grinnell had been only a twenty-four-hour train ride from Santa Barbara, but he dared not tarry from work any longer. In his place he sent Merriam, who knew of Gould only through Grinnell. "I hope you saw Merriam," Grinnell wrote Gould, "and if you did, I am sure you liked him. He is a good fellow, able, but no more free of peculiarities than the rest of us."

Later, when Grinnell learned that Merriam had not stopped over in Santa Barbara after all, he wrote again to Gould: "I suppose the fact is [that] Santa Barbara is not on . . . one of the main-traveled roads. It is, however, as I remember it, the most charming place in all California, and I still live in the hope that before many years I may sit on your piazza, eat your dinner, and drink your gin."

INDIANS OF TO-DAY

G rinnell turned fifty on September 20, 1899, a month after his return to New York. He now needed eyeglasses, and he complained that his legs lacked their old spring. Yet he had held up better than most of his fellow travelers, including many younger men, and his one complaint about the recent trip was that there had been "very little hard work about it."

Before setting out for Alaska, he had found time to work on two different books. One was conceived as a field guide to North American Indian tribes. The idea had been pitched to him by Chicago publisher Herbert S. Stone, who told Grinnell he wanted a suitable text to accompany fifty-five of Frank Rinehart's Indian photographs from the Omaha world's fair. Although Grinnell dismissed the finished product, titled *The Indians of To-day*, as "a hack book," not everyone agreed. Charles Lummis, editor of *Land of Sunshine*, deemed it "a large, rich and dignified folio. . . . There is no maudlin sentimentality, no poetic vagueness, no brilliant inaccuracy. Mr. Grinnell only speaks 'right on'; soberly, coolly and with the experience and study of a lifetime."

The second book Grinnell wrote was a gift to his nephews. Having no sons of his own, he doted on those of his sisters. In 1899 Grinnell Martin and Frank and Rutherford Page were entering adolescence—two were thirteen, the other twelve—and Grinnell determined to provide them with an education in novel form, borrowing blatantly from Mayne Reid, most especially *The Boy Hunters*.

He told the story of fourteen-year-old Jack Danvers, who lived in New York: "Jack was not a very strong boy. He was slim and pale and spent most of his time reading. . . . [H]is parents were often anxious about his health. They had thought several times of moving to the country to live, so that Jack might have an out-door life all the year round, but Mr. Danvers' business was so confining that he was obliged to be in town constantly, and Mrs. Danvers was not willing to leave him."

At a doctor's suggestion, Jack's Uncle Will takes him to live on his Wyoming ranch for the summer. "[A] few months of rough life in the open air would do him more good than all the medicines in the world." The location is unmistakably Shirley Basin, "walled in by mountains on every hand, and 7,500 feet above the level of the sea." Jack befriends a boy a couple of years older from a neighboring ranch who is Lute North in all but name.

Under the instruction of an old-timer named Hugh Johnson, Jack learns to ride, rope, brand, shoot, and hunt. He is given his own gun and kills an elk, an antelope, then a coyote, a mountain lion, a bear, and two deer with one shot. Although the story is intended for young boys, graphic details of death and dying are not spared. When a colt breaks its shoulder, a ranch hand dispatches it with a hatchet. One of the book's illustrations, by Grinnell's friend Edward Deming, is of an elk with blood pouring from its mouth.

Jack also receives a running tutorial in natural history: the geology of the Wyoming basin ("once the bottom of a big bay"), the teeth of antelope (none on the front of the upper jaw), the law of the wild ("it ain't no more cruel for a coyote to kill an antelope than it is for an antelope to take a bite of grass").

"'I have seen quite a few Pawnees in my time,'" Hugh tells Jack, "'and . . . they're good people, no mistake about that. They are kind, and they give you the best they've got; and they're brave. I don't want to be with better people.'"

At the end of summer Jack returns to New York a very different boy than the one who left in the spring. His mother is shocked by the change. "Then he was white, slender and listless; now he was brown, broad-shouldered and boisterous."

Grinnell meant for *Jack, the Young Ranchman* to be the first in a series of "Jack" books. For its publisher he chose Frederick A. Stokes, who had also taken on Morton Grinnell's hapless novel, *An Eclipse of Memory*. Grinnell worked on the manuscript at night and on weekends and was able to give copies of the book to his nephews for Christmas.

Another writing project took shape that winter. Grinnell's promised account of the Harriman expedition ran in *Forest and Stream* in fourteen installments, beginning in February and was later adapted for the first volume of the *Harriman Alaska Series*, edited by C. Hart Merriam. The *Forest and Stream* articles included twenty or so photos by Edward Curtis. The images of Muir Glacier, Tlingit totem poles, native houses, seal rookeries, and the mountains of the Alaskan coast were the largest presentation of Curtis's work to a national audience thus far.

And a less pleasant task also awaited Grinnell's return from Alaska. His brother William was anxious to separate himself from the family. For the time being, he continued to live in one of the family-owned houses at Audubon Park, but he wanted out, financially at first and, in the end, entirely.

Newell Martin, married to Laura Grinnell, devised a legal strategy to give William his piece of the pie without the family having to carve up Audubon Park. To do so required William to file suit against the other heirs of George Blake Grinnell and Helen Lansing Grinnell—that is, William's siblings and their children. The suit was not necessarily acrimonious—at least not in any way the public could see—but nonetheless complicated. In order to settle, the defendants would be required to auction off seven lots of Audubon Park property, though not the Hemlocks and its immediate grounds. The income from this sale would then be divided five ways between the five siblings, thereby giving William Milne Grinnell his share and, of course, his leave. Meanwhile, the other four—George, Morton, Helen, and Laura—would form the Lansing Investment Company and with their money from the sale buy back the lots.

Finally the lots were auctioned, for a total of $245,000, and each of the Grinnells received $49,000. At the end of November a judge gave his blessing to the deal and henceforth most of Audubon Park belonged to the Lansing Investment Company. The Census for 1900, taken in June of that year, would list William Milne Grinnell, architect, as a resident of Audubon Park, suggesting that he maintained a modicum of civility with his next of kin.

Soon, though, he would leave their fold entirely, and rarely, if ever again, figure in their lives. Thereafter, whenever Grinnell heard from old friends from the Audubon Park days and filled them in on the doings and whereabouts of its former denizens, he was generally full of good-natured gossip and proud announcements. But not once did he mention what had become of brother William Milne Grinnell.

At the first of July, a week after the final installment of the Alaska travelogue ran in *Forest and Stream*, Grinnell was back on the Blackfeet reservation, in time for the medicine lodge. Before leaving New York, he had written Edward Curtis, urging him to attend. Curtis realized that Grinnell could provide ideal entrée to the Piegan people. "It is wild, terrifying and elaborately mystifying," he would write of his experience at the medicine lodge. "The first time I witnessed it I sat in the hallowed lodge with my friend George Bird Grinnell, who was called the 'Father of the Blackfoot people.' It was at the start of my concerted effort to learn about the plains and to photograph [the Indians'] lives, and I was intensely affected."

Indian agents had authority to ban any ceremony that they regarded as overly savage or that inflamed tribal unrest. The Piegans, who were never caught up in the ghost dance movement, wisely tied the medicine lodge to the Fourth of July—their nod, as it were, to the national holiday. "I am by no means sure that the Medicine Lodge is a good thing for the Indians," Grinnell wrote to James Willard Schultz, "but on the other hand, these people must have some pleasure in life, something to give life an interest. They can't travel; they can't read or write or go to the theatre, and we don't want them to get drunk. Is it not better to let them have their Medicine Lodge once a year than to stop it altogether."

Grinnell spent the week camped in the "circle." Oddly his diary made no mention of Curtis, although the proof of the photographer's presence is unmistakable. While on the Blackfeet reservation, he made formal portraits of White Calf, Double Runner, Little Plume, Yellow Kidney, and other head men. He shot various stages of the medicine lodge (although not the final "dance"). And he posed a number of Piegans in natural settings— beside a river, seated in a lodge, on horseback. His conscientious treatment evoked a golden age, not quite past but nearly so.

"The results which Curtis gets with his camera stir one as one is stirred by a great painting," Grinnell would write. He recognized the historic impor- tance of Curtis's photographs, for both men understood that, while the images might be permanent, the subject matter was transient. "What will [these pictures] be a hundred years from now when the Indians shall have utterly vanished from the face of the earth?" Grinnell wondered. "They will tell how the Indian lived, what were his beliefs, how he carried himself in the various operations of life, and they will tell it as no word will ever tell it."

Yet while Grinnell would later vouch that Curtis's photographs were "not like those which anyone has seen," *The Indians of To-day*, which showcased the portraits of Frank Rinehart, had been published a few months *before* Grinnell met Curtis in Montana. Curtis must have known of it, and perhaps Grinnell even showed him a copy. Grinnell's disaffection toward his con- tribution to *The Indians of To-day* aside, the book is a broad compendium of Plains Indian tribes. Curtis's decision to devote his career to photograph- ing North American Indians surely had been gestating for a while before his week with the Piegans, but it was not until after he joined Grinnell, and after *Indians of To-day*, that his commitment to the endeavor gained momentum.

The first volume of Curtis's *The North American Indian* would appear in 1907, the twentieth volume in 1930, and today the oeuvre of more than two thousand images is regarded, deservedly, as a towering achievement in art and ethnography. "The pictures speak for themselves, and the artist who has made them is devoted to his work," Grinnell would remark as Curtis's port- folio was expanding, tribe by tribe, reservation by reservation. "To accom- plish it he has exchanged ease, comfort, home life for the hardest kind of work, frequent and long-continued separation from his family, the wearing toil of travel through difficult regions, and finally the heart-breaking strug- gle of winning over to his purpose primitive men, to whom ambition, time and money mean nothing, but to whom a dream or a cloud in the sky, or a bird flying across the trail from the wrong direction means much."

After leaving Montana in July 1900, Curtis returned to Seattle, stopping briefly before going on to the Hopi reservation in Arizona. His brother Asahel had opened his own studio and no longer served as Curtis's assistant. In his place Curtis hired Adolph Muhr, who had helped Frank Rinehart photograph his impressive Indian gallery in Omaha the year before. How Muhr and Curtis first met is not known; that they would come together is not surprising. Surely the link between *The Indians of To-day* and *The North American Indian* was not coincidental. One led to the other, and the usher, it seems, was George Bird Grinnell.

Grinnell, too, had more tribes to see that summer. After the medicine lodge, he went north into Canada and spent several days among the Blood Indians, who were members, along with the Piegans, of the Blackfoot confederacy. Returning to Montana, he visited the Assiniboines and Gros Ventres on the Fort Belknap reservation and then finished up at Lame Deer, conducting more interviews for his Cheyenne book.

Somehow he also found time to complete a second Jack book. *Jack Among the Indians* begins with a letter written to "My Dear Nephews and Nieces": "You listened attentively to the story of 'Jack, the Young Ranchman,' and I hope that you will like to learn what Jack did the next season, when he spent the summer with the buffalo eaters of the Northern Plains, hunted their game, fought their enemies and lived their lives." This prefatory note is signed, "Your affectionate Uncle" and dated September 1, 1900—three weeks after Grinnell got back to New York.

Jack returns to his uncle's Wyoming ranch but soon sets out for the Blackfeet reservation with Hugh Johnson, "the smartest mountain man there is." They take a month getting there, and along the way Hugh has plenty of time to fill Jack in on the old days, when the West was "anybody's country." They dodge hostile Indians and do plenty of shooting: wolves, buffalo, and also a heron—just to get a better look at it. They arrive at the reservation in time for the medicine lodge, which Hugh describes as "'kind o' like Christmas, when everybody gives presents and everybody prays. . . . It's a mighty solemn time, I tell you.'"

Jack and Hugh are welcomed by the Piegans, and Jack is taken with the "simple savage life" of the camp. "'Everybody . . . is always kind and pleasant and smiling, [and] they don't seem like the Indians I have always read about,'" he realizes.

He makes friends with an English-speaking Piegan boy called Joe, who teaches him how to use a bow and arrow. When Jack wonders if there are any bighorn sheep left in the mountains to the west, Joe exclaims: "'Pooh! These Indians don't hunt in the mountains, they hunt on the prairie, they kill buffalo, but they don't go much into the mountains, nor into the timber; they're afraid of bears.'"

By the end of his time with the Piegans, Jack is wearing moccasins and buckskin leggings and killing buffalo with arrows. Although only fifteen, he becomes a full-fledged warrior after shooting an Assiniboine horse thief. "[H]e had never expected in all his life he would kill a man. . . . He wondered what the people at home would say if they were to know what had happened, and he wondered, too, whether it would be best for him to tell them."

Yet at home Grinnell had fewer people to tell anything to. By the autumn of 1900 he was the sole resident of the Hemlocks, not counting two or three servants. His brother William had moved elsewhere. Only widowed sister Helen Grinnell Page and her five children remained at Audubon Park, in their own house.

In November he went to New Haven to visit his old Scroll and Key classmate Ned Dana. "I wish these occasions came more often, since at our time of life men should not allow themselves to be closely confined," he wrote Dana afterward. He took his own advice and returned to New Haven two weeks later to watch the Yale football team complete its undefeated season by drubbing Harvard. "It was highly exciting," he told George Gould, "and for a brief period the fervor of youth was in my head, heart, and muscles."

He was also encouraged by the recent election. William McKinley had won a second term, with Theodore Roosevelt as the new vice president. When Roosevelt was nominated back in August, Grinnell had told him, "I was not particularly cheered by the news . . . for, like many of your friends, I wanted it to come a little later and for a different office."

But now that Roosevelt had helped McKinley vanquish William Jennings Bryan for the second time, Grinnell was as satisfied as any erstwhile Mugwump could be. "I do not particularly object to a democracy as it used to be understood when Cleveland was president," he wrote Yellowstone Kelly, who, after the Harriman expedition, had gone to the Philippines with the army, "but a democracy with Bryan at the head would be in my view an unmixed evil."

After Christmas Grinnell set off on his annual duck-hunting trip to the Narrows Island Club in North Carolina, but this year his enthusiasm was tepid at best. To Gould he talked about reaching "our time of life." To James Willard Schultz, he lamented that life was growing "rather too short."

More and more he felt the burden of bachelorhood. He did not relish going home to an empty house. "I am usually at work from 9 in the morning until 10 at night, with intermissions for meals," he confessed to Ripley Hitchcock, a fellow editor. And during the few hours he did spend at Audubon Park, he had trouble sleeping.

He referred to his nephews and nieces as "my families," but this was his tacit acceptance that he would have no children of his own. In 1899 Jack Monroe and his wife had named their fourth child George Grinnell Monroe. Grinnell sent a Christmas present to his "noble namesake" but struggled to get into the holiday spirit. "We elderly people . . . would be glad to forget Christmas altogether if we could," he wrote Monroe. "I am sure that I would."

Then in the spring he began an exchange of letters with George Gould suggesting that neither bachelor welcomed the notion of growing old alone. "I have not forgotten the attractions of that delightful place, and your residence there tends always to draw me thither," Grinnell wrote to Gould in Santa Barbara, "but there arises before me the specter of duty and the great amount of work that has to be done in the few short weeks of my remaining years. . . . If only one had income enough, he could probably make time, but the grinding here to earn bread and shoes for the children, and a new alpaca dress for Mrs. G occupies 10 or 11 months of the year."

Gould's reply to Grinnell (like so many) is not preserved in Grinnell's archives, but evidently Gould failed to recognize the facetiousness in Grinnell's remark about children and especially in his mention of a missus. In his surprise and alarm over "Mrs. G.," Gould must have asked Grinnell if he had acquired a "cook."

"I have not been engaging a cook," Grinnell assured Gould, "but time is sliding swiftly by and the days are coming when cooks may decline to be engaged by you and me at any rate of wages."

Grinnell's letter continued even more enigmatically; he dared not speak frankly through his stenographer. "The troubles of yours that you enumerate in the last paragraph of your letter strike me as being so serious that I decline to match them with any grief of my own. I do however—but entirely from the standpoint of an outsider—recommend you engaging a cook," he advised Gould.

Later in the summer Grinnell revisited this worn and, by now, transparent euphemism. Gould perhaps had said that a drink or two in the evening was better than the company of a cook. "To go back to your earlier letter, I cannot agree with you on the question of cooks," Grinnell replied. "It is true that devotion to the bottle may often postpone the need of a cook, but inevitably the day comes when the bottle ceases to cheer or even inebriate. When the time arrives, the system calls loudly for a cook. This statement is fact and not theory. You are perhaps too young to realize this truth"—Grinnell was two years older—"but I who have lived longer have my weather eye wide open now, looking around for a cook."

Grinnell closed with his usual longing: "It would be delightful if you and I could make another hunt together. I really never expect to kill anything again, but I should like to get up on the top of a reasonably tall hill and sit there through the day and then at night hear you relate your adventures."

It went without saying: the word that neither could bring himself to utter was *wife*, because neither could allow himself to picture the other with a wife. "Cook" was code for someone who would fill the *role* of wife.

In referring to each other, however, they did not mince words. Their preferred salutation remained "Dear Partner," though they hadn't laid eyes on each other for ten years.

Even so, Grinnell had resolved to look around. He would never forsake— never forget—George Gould, but he did not want to be by himself forever.

CHAPTER 23

WINNING OF THE WEST

In October 1901 Grinnell tried one more time to lure George Gould from his olive grove overlooking the Pacific. "If you thought you could endure a week or ten days among the mountains of the St. Mary's and the Swift Current . . . it would be a joy to me," the New Yorker wrote the Californian. "You and I could take . . . comfort together as we crouch over the smoldering fire and tug our grey beards, lamenting the days that have been." Once again Gould declined the invitation.

Grinnell had been to the medicine lodge on the Blackfeet reservation the previous summer, but it had been four years since he had ventured into the mountains. During his absence, the Ceded Strip had been opened to miners, and he was anxious to assess the changes and to reacquaint himself with the landmarks of the Walled-in Lakes.

He would describe his autumn outing as a pleasure trip. More accurately, it was a pilgrimage to a country that meant at least as much to him as home. A month before he set off, an article he had written years earlier was finally published in the *Century*. In it he called his beloved destination "the Crown of the Continent."

He left New York on October 8 in the company of brother-in-law Newell Martin and Ashbel Barney, the teenage son of wealthy cousin Charles

Barney, president of the Knickerbocker Trust Company. Jack Monroe met them in Browning, and they rode directly to the lakes.

Grinnell showed little interest in hunting big game, but he encouraged Martin and young Barney to shoot bears (they missed three) and mountain goats (one billy for Barney). For once the weather cooperated. They ascended to Blackfoot Glacier and to Gunsight Pass, from which they were afforded magnificent views of the basins and valleys to the west—a side of the world that Grinnell had yet to explore. And to the northeast of Chief Mountain they could make out the Sweet Grass Hills, rising from the prairie one hundred miles distant.

Next they made their way up Swiftcurrent, passing through the mining camp of Altyn, which had boomed briefly but was abandoned just as rapidly when copper came a cropper. Grinnell was alarmed to see so many man-made scars on a once-pristine valley. "Country defaced by buildings, prospect holes, stumps, etc.," he recorded in his diary. The tops of felled trees lay strewn about like sheaves of straw. In a letter to Gifford Pinchot, chief of the Division of Forestry, Grinnell complained, "[A] good bit of the forest between the head of McDermott's Lake [today's Swiftcurrent Lake] . . . and the lower lake on my stream was in such condition that the careless throwing of a match or a cigarette might have burned the whole country."

If Grinnell could not have the companionship of George Gould, then the next best thing would be to climb Mount Gould. At daybreak on October 23 he and Newell Martin set out from Grinnell Lake, clambered up the cliff over which Grinnell Falls tumbles, and then skirted the north edge of Grinnell Glacier. "My ice as beautiful as ever," Grinnell wrote. They labored upward along the southern shoulder of Mount Grinnell to the Continental Divide, following the route Grinnell had first scaled in 1889. From here they took advantage of a goat trail that hugged the outside of the amphitheater that shaped the cirque of Grinnell Glacier. (Today this precipitous western face is known as the Garden Wall.) They picked their way another two miles until the ridge angled steeply higher. "Climbed Gould with infinite difficulty, reaching summit at 6:45," Grinnell jotted in his diary. On the summit, at 9,550 feet—nearly a vertical mile above their campsite—they piled a cairn of stones to prove that they had been there and immediately began their descent, guided by a gibbous moon.

They finally reached camp at 8 a.m., twenty-five hours after starting out. "I confess that I was tired," Grinnell wrote Gould after his return to New York, adding, "I wish that you might have been with us."

From Montana Grinnell went south to the Southern Cheyennes in Oklahoma. The man he was most eager to meet was George Bent, who was said to know the tribe's recent history as well as any man alive.

Bent was born in 1843, the son of trader William Bent, a white man, and Owl Woman, a Cheyenne. William Bent was from a prosperous St. Louis family, and in the late 1820s he and his brothers developed the trading route between Westport, Missouri, and the bustling Mexican outposts of Taos and Santa Fe. Bent's Fort, on the Arkansas River, a midway point on the Santa Fe Trail, soon became a commercial hub in its own right.

George Bent spent his early years at Bent's Fort, raised by Owl Woman and then, after her death, by his mother's sisters, whom, in the Cheyenne custom, William Bent had taken as secondary wives. When he turned ten, George was sent to white schools in Missouri. Not yet eighteen when the Civil War broke out, he joined the Confederate State Guard, which became the First Missouri Cavalry. In 1863 he fled the white man's war and went to live with the Cheyennes on the buffalo prairie of Kansas. In due time he grew out his hair, traded boots for moccasins, and resumed speaking the language taught to him by his mother's people. His immersion in tribal life was guided by Black Kettle, one of the six chiefs of the Southern Cheyennes. Bent's first fight as a Cheyenne warrior was against a small group of Delawares on the Solomon River. And then came Sand Creek.

On the morning of November 29, 1864, George Bent was camped with Black Kettle's band on a tributary of the Arkansas River in southeastern Colorado. Earlier that year, while the rest of the nation was absorbed in the Civil War, territorial governor John Evans had issued a proclamation encouraging citizens to attack and kill any Cheyennes deemed hostile. Black Kettle had demonstrated repeatedly that he wished peace; in a series of parleys with Evans and the army, he was led to believe that no harm would come to his people if they camped in designated locations under the watchful eye of the military. He was gravely mistaken.

Cheyenne women, astir at dawn, at first believed that the mounted troops were buffalo, so dense was the steam from the horses' breathing. When at last the alarm was sounded that soldiers were approaching, Black Kettle raised an American flag from a lodgepole with a white flag beneath it. "Don't be afraid!" he exclaimed. "There is no danger! The soldiers will not hurt you!" With that, two regiments of cavalry—more than six hundred soldiers, most of them short-term home guard volunteers—led by former Methodist missionary Colonel John Chivington, charged the village.

The Cheyennes defended themselves courageously, but they were too few and too poorly armed. Some dug rifle pits in the creek bank; others were able to catch horses and escape. Too many had no chance at all. Women and children were not spared, their bodies scalped, mutilated, and dismembered. A pregnant woman had her fetus slashed from her womb.

The fighting lasted through midday. The Indians in the rifle pits fared better than the rest, and quite a few were able to get away once darkness fell. George Bent was shot in the hip but survived. Black Kettle also lived, as did his wife, although she was wounded nine times. (Both would be killed by Custer's Seventh Cavalry on the Washita River four years later.)

Received in Denver as a hero, Chivington boasted that his men killed five hundred Indians that day. George Bent estimated that the number was closer to 150, two-thirds of them women and children.

Sand Creek was one of the many stories that Grinnell hoped to mine from George Bent's memory, if not during his visit to the Southern Cheyennes in 1901, then in subsequent interviews.

When Grinnell stepped down at the depot of Bridgeport, Oklahoma, thirty miles west of the Cheyenne-Arapaho agency at Darlington, he found a tall, broad-shouldered, dark-skinned man of fifty-seven. Bent's mouth was all but hidden by a thick moustache, and, like many Cheyennes and many more men of mixed blood, he dressed in store-bought shirt and trousers. In the years following Sand Creek, Bent had remained with the Cheyennes, at times fighting as a Dog Soldier, at others serving as an interpreter and negotiator between Cheyennes and whites. In 1866 he married a daughter (actually an adopted niece) of Black Kettle, and when the Cheyennes and Arapahos were at last defeated and confined to a reservation along the North Fork of the Canadian River, Bent went with them.

He was now living with his third Cheyenne wife, Standing Out Woman, but in recent years he had done more for whites than for Indians. Specifically, he had been paid by whites to persuade the Indians to lease their reservation for cattle grazing. He had also coaxed the Cheyennes and Arapahos to embrace the 1887 General Allotment Act, which apportioned 160 acres to each man, woman, and child but also opened the door for whites to buy up the unassigned remainder.

The results of allotment were immediately apparent to Grinnell. Unlike the Montana reservations with which he was familiar, there was no longer a Southern Cheyenne reservation per se—that is, a dedicated, uninterrupted expanse of ground on which Indians could live communally in some vestige of the old way. When the General Allotment Act was implemented, most Cheyennes and Arapahos had chosen land along the Canadian and Washita rivers, where they made a go as farmers and ranchers. Whites bought up the rest. By 1892 the reservation was a checkerboard, with Indians totaling only 10 percent of the population of the six counties that now encompassed it. For Grinnell, this meant that he could not sit in one location—the agency at Darlington, for instance—and expect elders and other informed sources to come to him. He would be obliged to move about—from El Reno to Cantonment, to Bridgeport, to Weatherford, to Colony.

Grinnell had been striving for years to get his arms around the Cheyennes, but thus far he had reached, at best, halfway. The Southern Cheyennes and Northern Cheyennes were one people, separated by a thousand miles and several generations. During his visits to Lame Deer on the Montana reservation, he had learned a great deal about Cheyenne culture and history, but, as he told George Stouch, agent for the Southern Cheyennes, "I have squeezed the Northern Cheyenne pretty dry, so far as information about old time things go, and I want to talk to a new set of men."

He began with George Bent, who spoke good English and, better yet, wrote it. Grinnell's diary does not indicate how long he spent with him, but upon his return to New York, he sent Bent a copy of *Pawnee Hero Stories* and offered to find buyers for some Cheyenne artifacts—a dress, a shield, a lodge lining—that Bent was looking to sell. "It is a great pleasure to hear from you," Grinnell wrote Bent, "and I hope that you will write to me from time to time. I am working away at my Cheyenne notes and very likely shall often want to ask you questions."

Bent replied in a very legible hand, thanking Grinnell for the book and promising, "When you come out in spring we can get lots of things . . . that you never got before."

Grinnell arrived back in New York on November 26. From the Hemlocks he could hear the shuddering of steam drills digging the subway along Broadway. The nation was still suffering from its own case of jitters after the assassination of William McKinley, who had been gunned down in Buffalo on September 6 and died eight days later. "We are all troubled and very sad," Grinnell had written two days after Theodore Roosevelt was sworn in, "[but] the new President is a good man, and he will take care of the country."

Shortly after the assassination and just a week before leaving for Montana, Grinnell had taken a train to Washington and lunched with Roosevelt. Grief and etiquette notwithstanding, it was hard for Grinnell to suppress his optimism at the sudden turn of events. The president of the Boone and Crockett Club was now the president of the United States. A sportsman in the White House could make a tremendous difference. In an editorial in *Forest and Stream,* Grinnell would praise the contributions that Benjamin Harrison and Grover Cleveland had made to preservation; but Roosevelt stood in a class by himself. "President Roosevelt is a hunter of big game," Grinnell observed, "and [w]hen one goes in for big game there is apt to be something doing pretty nearly every minute." What better preparation for the job at hand?

For the past year the Boone and Crockett Club and *Forest and Stream* had been pressing for the creation of game refuges in the national forest reserves. "Within the boundaries of these reserves, if properly protected, almost all the large game of North America could flourish forever, just as it used to exist in the Old West, before the white man—greedy for dollars— penetrated the unknown fastnesses," Grinnell asserted. "We have already the example in such a game refuge in the Yellowstone National Park."

With President Roosevelt behind federal legislation, refuges could at last become a reality.

On the Native American front, Grinnell likewise allowed himself a measure of optimism, although thus far Roosevelt had been anything but effusive in his admiration of the country's indigenous residents. In the first volume of his series, *The Winning of the West*, published in 1894, Roosevelt had laid out the imperative of "race expansion," by which "English-speaking peoples" were destined to dominate "the world's waste spaces"—including an American continent occupied but, in his view, never firmly owned by Indians. Four years later, shortly after prevailing in Cuba and winning the governorship of New York, Roosevelt echoed this imperative more emphatically: "The continent had to be won. We need not waste our time in dealing with any sentimentalist who believes that, on account of any abstract principle, that it would have been right to leave the continent to the domain, the hunting ground of squalid savages. It had to be taken by the white race." This bias followed him to the White House.

Nevertheless, Grinnell wrote to Hamlin Garland: "Roosevelt is a man of very strong common sense. I have not talked with him especially on the Indian question, but . . . he is a fair man, as you say, and a good American, and a man with ideals. He does not sympathize at all with sentimentality about the Indians. However, he can be made, I feel quite sure, to do the right thing, and I am persuaded that he can do a great deal of good in the matter of appointing proper agents. He is absolutely a free man, his own boss and is under no obligations to anyone."

Grinnell, meanwhile, needed no guidance from above to press on with his work on behalf of Indians, and over the coming winter his labors would precipitate, in a roundabout way, the biggest change in his life since he had gone west with Professor Marsh thirty years earlier.

Until stock raising and farming could provide sufficient income and sustenance, Indians would remain on government rations. The only other assets they possessed—the only ones that whites would pay for—were traditional items: clothing, moccasins, headdresses, tepees, bows, arrows, pipes, drums, and implements of everyday living. Grinnell had purchased quite a few of these artifacts over the years, and the things he gathered on the Harriman expedition further stimulated his appetite for acquisition—not only for himself but also for institutions and individual collectors as decoration for their drawing rooms, libraries, and country houses.

During the Piegan medicine lodge with Edward Curtis, he had contracted with a Piegan identified as Mrs. Big Nose to make a buffalo skin lodge for Franz Boas. Grinnell had first met Boas when the acclaimed anthropologist was an editor at the *Journal of American Folk-Lore*. As curator of ethnology at the American Museum of Natural History, Boas recognized in Grinnell a trustworthy source of Indian specimens. He agreed to pay $100 for the Piegan lodge. Many more items would follow, with Grinnell serving as middleman. He had no other desire than to see these valuable relics saved for posterity, while putting money into the hands of the Indians who had few other means of getting it.

With railroads putting more tourists in contact with Native Americans and with the view of Indians as quaint heirlooms of the old West expanding, the appeal of Indian handiwork grew accordingly, as Grinnell noticed during his recent trip to Oklahoma. At Colony, southwest of Bridgeport, Presbyterian missionaries Walter and Mary Roe had started a cottage industry, employing Cheyenne and Arapaho women to make buckskin beadwork—ornamenting everything from moccasins to change purses, tobacco pouches, and napkin rings. These items were sold at trading posts and, in the East, through missionary societies and other friends of the Indian. Grinnell was thoroughly impressed. "Mr. and Mrs. Roe received me most cordially and seem to be about the sweetest and most earnest people I have ever met," he wrote in his diary.

The Roes called their enterprise the Mohonk Lodge, after the annual conference of Indian advocates held each year at the resort of the same name in upstate New York. They informed Grinnell that Indian women were earning as much as eighty cents a day and that the previous year the Mohonk Lodge at Colony had made more than $1,300. If this model worked for the Cheyennes and Arapahos, why couldn't it also work for the Piegans, the Northern Cheyennes, and all the other western tribes? What was needed was a national network to promote the idea and to market the merchandise.

At the same time, another Indian organization of national scope was also taking shape—this one organized by Charles Lummis, whose Los Angeles–based journal *Land of Sunshine* would soon change its name to *Out West*.

Lummis was nearly as energetic as his Harvard classmate Theodore Roosevelt. In 1884 he had walked from Ohio to California to take a job at the *Los Angeles Times*. Ten years later he took over as editor of *Land of Sunshine* and turned a chamber-of-commerce organ into an erudite literary journal, courting contributors such as Joaquin Miller, John Muir, Jack London, and Mary Austin.

Lummis had a deep affinity for the natives of California and the Southwest, and in 1901 he took up the cause of the Mission Indians. Some three hundred of them—so famously romanticized in Helen Hunt Jackson's 1884 novel, *Ramona*—were being evicted from the vast Warner Ranch in eastern San Diego County, where they had lived since before colonial days. In November a group gathered at Lummis's home to form a league to intercede on behalf of the Mission Indians but also with the ambition of "remedying—and keeping remedied" neglect and abuses of Indians generally. In a letter to Grinnell, Lummis explained, "We are really launching a far reaching and generic movement for which this acute case in Cal[ifornia] . . . makes a good introduction and appetizer."

A number of similar organizations already existed, including the Indian Rights Association of Philadelphia. But Lummis insisted that his new league would be different and better: "Instead of fighting the Bureau [of Indian Affairs] and getting in such bad odor that it hates to see us coming— as the Indian Rights Association has done—we must make ourselves so useful that the Bureau will find our way the line of least resistance. We can give it authentic and disinterested information; we can keep an eye on the field. . . . [Our] gospel is to be actual knowledge, common sense, Patience and Steady Pressure." He assured Grinnell that President Roosevelt, Secretary of the Interior Ethan Allen Hancock, and Commissioner of Indian Affairs William Jones had endorsed the new group.

Lummis asked Grinnell to serve on the league's executive committee. "The psychological moment has come, my dear Grinnell," he entreated.

"Let's pile in; soberly, patiently, tactfully, but like good Out-Door men who know about what we want, and together can devise how to get it."

Lummis's enthusiasm was contagious, and Grinnell accepted immediately, as did Hart Merriam and Hamlin Garland. Merriam was still with the Biological Survey in Washington, but he had begun spending his summers in Lagunitas, California, where he became a student of the tribes of the Pacific Coast and a serious collector of their basketry. Lummis's list of nominees for the league's advisory board included John Wesley Powell, Phoebe (Mrs. Randolph) Hearst, Stanford University president David Starr Jordan, Frederick Hodge of the Smithsonian, and Francis La Flesche of the Omaha tribe ("to have one real Indian"). Grinnell added Walter Roe of Oklahoma, "a missionary, to be sure, but one so different from all other missionaries that he has changed my views of the class." He also recommended Mrs. Frank Doubleday, née Neltje Blanchan DeGraff, wife of the wealthy book publisher and author of several books of her own on birds and gardens. Hamlin Garland had advised Grinnell that Mrs. Doubleday could "secure for the league all the money that it needs."

The name Lummis settled on was the Sequoya League, for the Cherokee who created the first Indian alphabet. During the winter, while Lummis drafted a constitution, Grinnell, Garland, and Merriam gathered support in the East. In January Grinnell introduced himself to Mrs. Doubleday. "She is a woman of great force, and can do a great deal of good," he informed Lummis. "Of course, her point of view is to some extent industrial and artistic." Yet as a New Yorker, she did not know any Indians; nor had she ever had any contact with them, other than the things they made that she and her friends collected.

In March Grinnell wrote to Lummis, informing him that Mrs. Doubleday was eager to start a New York chapter of the Sequoya League before she and her friends left town for the summer. The first order of business for the new branch, Grinnell reported, would be "finding a market for the things that the Indian can make at present and for which he can receive immediate payment." For this purpose, Mrs. Doubleday contributed the generous sum of $2,000.

The first meeting of the New York Council of the Sequoya League was held on March 20 at the Doubleday house on East Sixteenth Street, with more than eighty in attendance. "Everybody seemed to have a good time, and everybody seemed to be more or less interested," Grinnell told Lummis.

Novelist and Indian activist Constance Goddard DuBois talked on her work with the Warner Ranch Indians, and archaeologist George Pepper discussed his findings in the ruins of Chaco Canyon, New Mexico. Hamlin Garland and his wife were at the meeting, as were several western artists: De Cost Smith, Charles Schreyvogel, and Frederick Dellenbaugh.

And finally, it seems highly probable, although her name was not mentioned, that a young photographer, Elizabeth Williams, was present that night.

PART FIVE

MR. AND MRS. GRINNELL

(1902–1911)

THE CAPTURED WOMAN

This was not the first time she and Grinnell had met. The evidence is a letter Grinnell wrote to Jack Monroe, who had come to New York in February and stayed at Audubon Park. "Nothing special has happened since you went away," Grinnell wrote Monroe on March 13, a week before the Sequoya League gathering. "Mrs. Williams has spent a day or two at the house, photographing Cheyenne things, and I have seen her once."

Elizabeth Williams was twenty-five years old in March 1902. George Bird Grinnell, at fifty-two, was twice her age. He was well known; she was a recent widow with little professional reputation and few connections. She was in need of a lifeline, and he was looking for a "cook."

If a romantic spark was struck initially, it is not revealed in Grinnell's dictated correspondence, and precious few letters of Elizabeth's are included in his papers. Yet she must have impressed him, for by the first of April he was making arrangements for her to go out to Oklahoma "to take a lot of photographs for me." He wrote to George Bent, alerting him of her arrival. "If you see her, I wish that you would help her if you can. She wants to take pictures of people doing the regular things that they all used to do in the old times. She wants to see the women dressing hides and packing

wood and water, and putting up the lodges, and packing the horses. . . .
These photographs I hope will go in my book of the Cheyennes when it is
finished."

She was born Elizabeth Kirby Curtis on October 30, 1876, at the family
homestead in Charlton, New York.

Once the American Revolution had ended and upstate New York was
again safe for settlement, Seth Kirby moved from Connecticut and carved
out a farm in the southwest corner of Saratoga County, a mile from the
village of Charlton. At least three generations of Kirbys would be buried in
the village cemetery. The Elizabeth Kirby Curtis whom George Bird Grinnell was to meet was named for Seth Kirby's granddaughter. This Elizabeth
Kirby married Frank Curtis, of nearby Ballston Spa, and the couple took up
residence on the Kirby farm, Locust Hill.

By all appearances, the farm prospered under Curtis's management. An
1868 article in *The Saratogian* painted a tableau of pastoral gentility. Curtis was not one to dirty his hands by cultivating the clay loam soil. Instead
he raised Ayrshire cattle, Cheshire hogs, Merino sheep, and thoroughbred
horses. His barns and stables were showplaces of order and efficiency. The
orchard produced choice varieties of grapes, apples, and pears. "Among
the shrubbery in his garden," *The Saratogian* reported, "we saw two small
cedars from Mount Vernon, also two weeping willows from slips taken from
near the tomb of Napoleon at St. Helena."

The house was described as "roomy and pleasantly arranged for comfort and convenience." Books, magazines and newspapers gave "evidence
of taste and culture." A bathroom showed that "the luxury of cleanliness is
appreciated." And a cord from the kitchen to the belfry in the woodshed
allowed the cook "to summon laborers from any part of the farm, without
a moment's delay."

The aspect of farming that Frank Curtis liked best was talking and writing about it. He had been a correspondent for the *Troy Times* during the
Civil War, and afterwards, wearing the inevitable rank of colonel, he contributed to agricultural journals, *Country Gentleman*, and the *New-York*

Tribune. He was active in the New York State Agricultural Society and frequently away from home, lecturing.

Elizabeth Kirby Curtis (the elder) died childless in 1874, leaving Locust Hill to her husband. A year later Frank Curtis married Deborah Smith, called Delle, whose family farm was in Glenville, five miles to the west of Charlton. She was twenty-two; he was forty-four. She came with a distinguished pedigree; her great-grandfather was European-trained artist John Vanderlyn of Kingston, New York. A protégé of Aaron Burr and student of Gilbert Stuart, Vanderlyn painted portraits of Burr, James Madison, Andrew Jackson, and Zachary Taylor, and also *The Landing of Columbus*, commissioned for the Capitol Rotunda in Washington.

Delle Smith was precocious and vivacious. She entered Vassar College at fifteen. How she met Frank Curtis can only be speculated, but their families must have been acquainted, and their shared love of horses shrank their universe even smaller. Curtis was an organizer of the Saratoga County Fair, where young Delle won many ribbons for riding and driving.

A year after becoming Frank's second wife, she bore a daughter, whom they named for the first wife. Two years later she had a son, whom they named for him.

When Elizabeth Curtis was fourteen, her father died. It was bad enough that he left no will. Even worse, as his wife and young children soon discovered, he left them deep in debt. The showplace had been a sham. Many of Locust Hill's unpaid bills were for oats and corn and hay—crops that Frank Curtis had declined to grow—to feed the prized livestock on whose virtues he so avidly propounded. To appease creditors and attorneys, Delle Curtis was obliged to mortgage Locust Hill. She moved the family to Glenville and later Saratoga Springs, where she and her children depended on the rent she collected from the farm's new tenants.

There was no money to send Elizabeth to Vassar. She likely attended the Charlton Academy, closely associated with the village's Freehold Presbyterian Church and only a fifteen-minute walk from Locust Hill. By 1899 she was living in New York City, where she met and married Emery Leverett Williams of Boston, an ambitious but struggling artist, three years older. The Census gives his father's profession as carpenter. Emery took his first drawing lessons at fifteen and soon after moved to New York, where one of his instructors, perhaps at the Art Students League, was William Merritt Chase.

The rest of Emery Williams's brief story comes from an article in the *New York Herald* of September 30, 1900. The paper reported that in the spring of 1899 Emery and Elizabeth "abandoned the pleasant Bohemian life they were leading in New York and started for the west with a total capital of $75." Their goal was to "live among the Indians and reveal them as they were to the world," as so many eastern artists had begun doing. They detrained in Bismarck, North Dakota, where Elizabeth persuaded the local newspaper to let her cover a performance of Buffalo Bill's Wild West.

The show included a mock attack on the Deadwood stagecoach by a band of Indians. Buffalo Bill liked to recruit members of the audience as passengers. Elizabeth Williams consented readily. In this instance, "an unexpected bit of realism" was introduced, the *Herald* recounted. "A stalwart red man flung his arms about Mrs. Williams' waist, dragged her from the stage, placed her on a horse and galloped off with her to the Indian camp, where she was received with shouts of welcome. A few hours later her husband, who had witnessed the episode with real alarm, arrived at the camp and rescued her." The article also noted, "Mrs. Williams was ever afterward known as 'Wa-ya-ha-wea,' or 'the captured woman.'"

From Bismarck the Williamses walked and rode to a subagency of the Standing Rock Sioux reservation, located at the junction of the Cannonball and Missouri rivers. There they moved into an abandoned log cabin and settled in for the winter. "With their Indian neighbors Mr. and Mrs. Williams soon established close relations of friendship," the *Herald* story continued. "Mr. Williams would go familiarly among bucks and squaws, posing and sketching them. They in return would frequently call at the log cabin and gaze in wonder upon such mysteries of civilization as were there unveiled to them. With a frankness unusual among these reticent people, they would talk about their grievances, describe their difficulty in obtaining the money guaranteed to them, and complain bitterly about the surveillance to which they were subjected. In fine, Mr. Williams and his wife soon came to know, to admire and to love the companions among whom fate had thrown them."

Before leaving New York, Emery Williams had received encouragement from publisher Robert Howard Russell and occasionally sent him some of his drawings from North Dakota. But soon "the hardships incident to life in the wilderness during a long siege of winter proved too much for his delicate frame." Elizabeth got him to the agency hospital at Fort Yates, but to no avail. He died before spring arrived.

A widow at twenty-three, she returned first to Saratoga County and then to New York, carrying the drawings and text for her husband's book, *An Alphabet of Indians*, which R. H. Russell published later in the year.

It is a book for children; the illustrations are like those in a collection of nursery rhymes, although the *Herald* was convinced that Williams's depictions were "real Indians, not mere manikins in blankets and moccasins." The text evokes very little of Williams's experience with the Sioux of Standing Rock, other than his obvious sympathy for Indians in general. A is for Apache, B for Blackfeet, C for Crow, and so on, to Z for Zuni. The chapter "N is for Navajo"—a tribe Williams had never seen—begins, "The Navajo Indians are one of the oldest tribes, living in a beautiful part of the country, neighbors to the ancient Pueblos. Many live to a great age, often more than a hundred years. They are a peaceful people, for Indians."

Elizabeth did what she could to promote her late husband's *Alphabet*, but if it had not been for Emery Williams's death, his little book might not have received any notice at all. Elizabeth was not too stricken to share their star-crossed story with the *Herald*. "Love and youth are the two most beautiful things on earth. Pity they cannot last forever," the paper sighed mawkishly. "Art has recognized this, and so, instead of the commonplace ending of the old fairy tale, 'They were married and lived happily ever after,' art sometimes calls in the aid of death to give her lovers an immortal perch in the memory of readers."

Many years later Elizabeth would recall that, as a teenager, she had read Grinnell's "The Last of the Buffalo" in *Scribner's*. At least one source mentioned that she gave him a copy of *An Alphabet of Indians*. Maybe this was how he had made her acquaintance before the Sequoya League meeting. Where and when she learned photography is not certain, but she must have convinced Grinnell of her skill with a camera. He decided to give her a chance, first by photographing his Indian things at Audubon Park and then by sending her to Oklahoma. He seems also to have been willing to underwrite her work. Photographic equipment was not cheap, and a letter written on April 2 indicates that he was paying for her reflex camera and plates.

For all Elizabeth's enthusiasm for taking pictures, there are no extant photographs of her from her early years. Later pictures of her reveal a trim, fair-haired woman with a broad mouth and firm jaw. On a passport application she would give her height as five-foot-six. Her eyes were gray, similar to Grinnell's. She was athletic, an able horsewoman, like her mother. It is difficult to imagine her in a corseted gown, though she doubtless owned and wore her share. In one of the few pictures of her she wears trousers, high-laced boots, and a necktie.

Any semblance of courtship that spring in New York was necessarily brief. On April 12 Elizabeth departed for Oklahoma, traveling in the company of Mary Roe's sister, Elizabeth Page, a fellow missionary of the Reformed Church. Grinnell intended to follow in mid-May, but his plan was interrupted by a summons from the one man he could not ignore: President Theodore Roosevelt.

The trouble lay in, of all places, the Standing Rock reservation, where Elizabeth Williams had spent her final year with her husband. The Bureau of Indian Affairs had recently leased most of the reservation to two white cattlemen; the Sioux consented to the arrangement only under pressure. The Indian Rights Association sounded the alarm on this abuse, and a series of damning articles in the *Outlook* by George Kennan (future biographer of E. A. Harriman and distant relation of the diplomat George F. Kennan) drew the attention of the president.

Roosevelt immediately called upon Grinnell to get to the bottom of the difficulties. "Can you go? I earnestly hope you can," he beseeched. "Do say you will go. I really think it your duty. Pray, come on here and let me see you first."

"I have been in absolute misery," Grinnell confided to Hart Merriam, "but made up my mind last night that my private matters would have to go by the board and that I would go to Standing Rock." He calculated that by reporting to Roosevelt on the Sioux situation he might increase the president's interest in all Indian matters. "The Indian Bureau pot is boiling vigorously," Grinnell wrote to Emerson Hough, "and I have been invited to assist at the cooking."

Before heading to Washington to meet with the president, he wrote another letter to George Bent, reminding him of Elizabeth's imminent arrival. "I want you to be kind to Mrs. Williams and help her all you can," he implored. "If she needs an interpreter, you will go with her and help her, and I will pay you just the same as if I were there myself."

Grinnell arrived at Standing Rock on May 13, accompanied by old friend James McLaughlin, an inspector for the Bureau of Indian Affairs and formerly the agent at Standing Rock. (In 1890, during the time of the ghost dance, McLaughlin had infamously ordered the arrest of Sitting Bull, who was then killed in a confrontation with Indian police.) In three days of interviews and councils they were able to reach a compromise between the Indians, the ranchers, and the agent.

As promised, Grinnell used the occasion to stir the pot of Indian policy with considerable force. In a twenty-five-page report, he accused Commissioner of Indian Affairs William Jones and Standing Rock agent George Bingenheimer of coercing the Sioux to lease their land. "The whole trouble with the leasing of the lands of the Standing Rock Sioux," Grinnell wrote, "seems to have arisen from blundering ignorance on the part of the Indian Bureau, confirmed and assisted by blundering ignorance on the part of the agent at Standing Rock. . . . This whole lease matter might have been settled one year ago without the slightest friction, dissatisfaction or disturbance if the Commissioner had taken the trouble to acquaint himself with local conditions and had exercised patience, tact and discretion."

As for Agent Bingenheimer, "He is a local politician, of Mandan, N.D., an able man, but a political worker, pure and simple, a money getter, and not interested in Indians." More egregiously, "He is a man of suspicious nature, and very short tempered. . . . The autocratic position has been too much for him, and he is overbearing, domineering and tyrannical. . . . I recommend that he be not re-appointed."

A year earlier, when Roosevelt had attained the White House, Grinnell had sensed an opportunity to reform the uneven and too often corrupt method of appointing Indian agents. Standing Rock was as good a place as any to make his case to the president, a longtime champion of civil-service reform (if not of Indians). "The practice long in vogue of permitting western senators to nominate Indian agents for the agencies within their own states is a most unfortunate one," Grinnell insisted. "No local man—above all, no local politician—should be appointed Indian agent. Such men have too many affiliations. However good their intentions, the pressure to assist friends and to pay political debts by giving positions or granting favors of various sorts is too strong to be resisted."

His report found its way to Roosevelt, who was vacationing at Sagamore Hill. He thanked Grinnell for his hard and thorough work and agreed that Bingenheimer should go. However, he was somewhat shocked by Grinnell's harsh appraisal of Commissioner Jones. "I think him an absolutely honest man," Roosevelt replied.

Roosevelt then chided Grinnell for his categorical cynicism toward political appointees. "Remember always," the younger schooled the elder, "it is wholly a false idea to treat our government as a government of politicians who misrepresent us. In the long term, politicians exactly represent the people, their good qualities, their bad qualities, and their indifference. In flagrant individual cases of wrong it is always possible, and often profitable, to disregard local sentiment entirely and do something which it is not prepared to accept. But in the long run the success of a governmental policy under our institution, that is, of representative government, must depend upon the native good will of those sections of the people who take the greatest interest in the matter. As regards the Indian service, this means the senators and congressmen from the far west. Wise eastern philanthropists can do a good deal, but many of the eastern philanthropists are anything but wise; and these are in the aggregate very harmful."

Roosevelt did not necessarily mean to lump Grinnell with the aggregate of eastern philanthropists, yet he did not hesitate to point out the practical pitfalls of Grinnell's principles. "I will be supported, for instance, if I say I will turn out every unfit man and appoint no man whom I have not good reason to believe is fit," the president argued. "But if I announce that I will not appoint any man from the locality I will unite all the honest as well as all the dishonest people of the State against me. . . . If I take [a man] from some other State I may be able to get him confirmed, and may escape with only the result of violently angering two senators, who will not for a moment believe that my motives are not what I represent them, and will watch a chance to get even. If I continue it as a policy, I shall probably bring the entire Indian system of appropriations and management to an abrupt halt."

Grinnell acknowledged the realpolitik of Roosevelt's remonstration, but he did not soften his own brief. "I believe absolutely in Commissioner Jones' honesty," he answered. "I do think, however, that he is a man of very short memory, [and] I feel strongly that Agent Bingenheimer—who is a pleasant fellow to be with, and amusing—is not the man for Indian Agent at Standing Rock or anywhere else." In response to Roosevelt's request that he suggest a successor, Grinnell remarked, "I would hesitate to recommend the angel Gabriel for the position of Indian agent, a place where temptation, opportunity, worriment and insufficient pay combine to break a man down."

After each man had made his point, they moved on. Roosevelt recognized that he could count on Grinnell as an informed and decisive counsel on Indians, and Grinnell knew that, at the very least, he would have the president's ear the next time "the Indian question" arose. Even so, he needed no further reminder that, in Indian matters, Roosevelt was inclined to give the white man the benefit of the doubt, in the interest of civilization and "race expansion."

Four months later Grinnell would be flattered, honored, and perhaps a trifle surprised when Roosevelt asked him to draft the passage on Indian policy in his annual address to Congress.

"The officials who represent the Government in dealing with the Indians work under hard conditions, and also under conditions which render it easy to do wrong and very difficult to detect wrong," Roosevelt declared, echoing Grinnell. "Consequently they should be amply paid on the one hand, and on the other hand a particularly high standard of conduct should be demanded from them, and where misconduct can be proved the punishment should be exemplary."

Grinnell attended to one other important matter while at Standing Rock. His diary for May 14, two days after his arrival, mentioned: "Went to Mr. Williams' grave, now marked by a cross but no inscription." He was paying his respects on Elizabeth's behalf, a gesture that indicated she felt comfortable sharing her recent past with him.

From North Dakota, he went by way of St. Paul to the Southern Cheyenne agency at Darlington, arriving on May 31. "No wagon," he wrote in his diary. "Slept on platform, cool, clear night, but cows, hogs, dogs, chickens and freight train broke my rest." The next morning he walked to the agency. "Mrs. Williams has been here and working hard," he noted. "A pleasant day."

And again on June 2: "Pleasant day with Mrs. W."

That night he left for Bridgeport to see George Bent. For the next month he moved from one Cheyenne settlement to another—west to the Washita River, south to Colony, where the Roes ran the Mohonk Lodge, and finally back to the agency at Darlington to observe the medicine lodge. Throughout his ramblings, Grinnell was accompanied much of the time by Bent, who made introductions and served as interpreter.

Elizabeth Williams's whereabouts are not mentioned until July 8, when Grinnell's diary notes: "Ret'd to El Reno & met by Mrs. Davis and Mrs. Williams." The following day he packed up the Indian articles he had bought during the trip and arranged to ship them to New York. "Pleasant day sitting about with Mrs. W. & Mrs. Davis," he jotted. Two days later he said goodbye and departed for home.

On Thursday, August 21, George Bird Grinnell and Elizabeth Curtis Williams were married at St. Patrick's Cathedral. Elizabeth had been raised a Protestant but had converted to Roman Catholicism presumably at the time of her marriage to Emery Williams. Grinnell had been raised in the Episcopal Church, although his attendance was spotty at best. Several New York papers ran perfunctory announcements, the *Sun* noting that the marriage had been "by dispensation, Mr. Grinnell being a Protestant." If anyone else witnessed the ceremony, their names do not appear in the notices.

The *Times* stated that the couple would start soon on "a long wedding tour," but the following Wednesday Grinnell was back at *Forest and Stream*, dictating letters as if nothing much had changed in his life. On August 28 he wrote to brother-in-law Newell Martin at his office on Broad Street, reviewing stocks in the Lansing Investment portfolio—no mention of his marriage or of his wife.

Six days later to James Willard Schultz—no mention of marriage.

To George Bent, who knew Elizabeth and had seen the two together—nothing.

To Jack Monroe—nothing beyond, "Give my love to Carrie and the kids and shake hands for me with all my friends."

To Luther North in November: "I am glad to hear that things are going so well with you, barring the chickens [250 had vanished]. . . . I hope to get out in the spring to see you all, but I do not feel at all sure that I shall do so. My plans are never made very far in advance. . . . Also my old occupation of fighting the wolf that lives outside our front door keeps me busy."

Shortly after returning from Oklahoma, Grinnell had written a long, chatty letter to George Gould, filling him in on the Sequoya League, Standing Rock, and the Cheyenne medicine lodge. "I am back here now to remain for an indefinite period, and I hope during this winter to get the material for my Cheyenne book more or less in shape," he said. "I am slowly reaching a point, however, where I object to work, and if I could let go of the various things that are on my hands, I think I should do so. I feel as if I should like to spend my time in California, sitting in the shade, or the sun, as the temperature might indicate, smoking many pipes and talking ponderously with someone about my own age, or perhaps two years younger. . . . I have not outgrown my desire to make a trip with you down into old Mexico, but I have almost outgrown the hope that I shall ever do so."

Not a word about Mrs. Williams, though the prospect of spending the rest of his years with someone far younger than himself, or than Gould, was plainly on his mind.

Grinnell did not write again to Gould until January 1903, by which time Gould would have heard about the marriage from his brother Charles in New York. Yet Grinnell could not bring himself to broach the subject. "There is little with me that is new," he told Gould. "Life flows on in a more or less placid stream."

His first mention of Elizabeth in his correspondence did not appear until February 20, six months after he had brought his bride home to Audubon Park. The superintendent of Yellowstone National Park, John Pitcher, and his wife had seen the Grinnells in New York and invited them to tour Yellowstone on their next trip west. "If I had the time, there is nothing that would give my wife and myself more pleasure than to be with you for a couple of weeks," Grinnell replied, adding, "Mrs. Grinnell intends to write to Mrs. Pitcher before long."

The Pitchers were not the only western friends to make a trip east that winter. A delegation of Piegans led by their head chief, White Calf, with Joe Kipp along as interpreter, came to Washington in mid-January to hash out a proposed lease of reservation land to white cattlemen—a case that, to Grinnell, sounded uncomfortably similar to Standing Rock. He postponed his duck-hunting trip to help facilitate negotiations.

The first order of business was a visit to the White House, where the president shook hands with the chiefs and gave them a rousing Rooseveltian welcome. Talks with Commissioner of Indian Affairs Jones went awkwardly. "The Indians . . . did not talk to the point and wandered greatly, making many loose complaints and wearying the Commissioner with matters that he did not, and could not, understand," Grinnell related to Charles Aubrey, the government farmer on the reservation.

In the end he got all parties to agree to keep the white ranchers' cattle off the reservation, but he could do little to dissuade the Piegans from presenting their petition requesting allotment. Grinnell argued that keeping outside cattle off Indian land was essential to the tribe's self-sufficiency; so too was keeping the reservation an open range for Piegan cattle. The total, he was convinced, was greater—and more sustaining—than the sum of many 160- or even 320-acre parts.

After the talks, Grinnell went back to New York but then returned to the capital for the annual Boone and Crockett dinner at the Metropolitan Club, Theodore Roosevelt presiding. "Many of the diners were puzzled by one dish served to them," *Forest and Stream* reported. "It proved to be a fat and juicy mountain lion," sent from Wyoming by Grinnell and Roosevelt's favorite Yellowstone guide, Billy Hofer.

The Piegans stayed the week in Washington, long enough for White Calf to come down with a fever. He was taken to Providence Hospital, where he died of pneumonia on January 29. "White Calf while here went about town and refused to so clothe as to withstand the damp air, dressing much as he would in his native dry mountain country," the New York Times reported. The obituary also noted that doctors had marveled at the number of scars on White Calf's body. "The old chief fought the whites many years to hold his country against them."

Grinnell wrote his own obituary for White Calf, who would be regarded by history as the last supreme chief of the Piegans: "He was a man who was great in the breadth of his judgment . . . but greatest of all, in the devotion he felt for his tribe, and the way in which he sacrificed himself for their welfare. Buffalo hunter, warrior, savage ruler and diplomat; then learner, instructor, persuader and encourager in new ways; he was always the father of his people."

Margaret Kipp, who had accompanied her husband with the Piegan delegation and had stayed with White Calf to the end, wrote Grinnell from the reservation after the chief's burial on Cut Bank Creek: "He truly loved you as his own son. . . . In his last hours he often asked of you, wanting to know, 'When is he coming, have you heard from him,' and I would put him off by saying you would come soon."

Meanwhile, Grinnell did not shirk his commitments to the other Indians he had pledged to support. The New York chapter of the Sequoya League met over the winter, with special speakers invited to each session. As chairman of the executive committee, Grinnell invited Charles Eastman, a Santee Sioux physician educated in Boston, whose recent memoir, Indian Boyhood, made him the nation's most lustrous exemplar of Indian self-improvement.

At another meeting Hart Merriam talked about a project that he, Hamlin Garland, and Grinnell had been working on to bring order to Indian names. Whites had habitually thrust upon Indians Christian names such as Tom or Pete, or insisted on approximate translations such as Tail Feathers Coming Over the Hill, Stands at the Door, or, less elegantly, Scab, Guts, and Big Nose. From the white man's point of view, renaming simplified tribal registration and accelerated assimilation. More recently, with the spread of allotment and the assignment of individual title to parcels of reservation land, clear identification of family lineage became crucial: the government needed to know, preferably by first and last name, who was related to whom. Yet for Indians, names and, moreover, naming ceremonies, were integral to cultural esteem.

Hamlin Garland advocated standardization—that is, anglicization—of Indian names, but Grinnell argued that Indians should be allowed to retain at least this vestige of their heritage. "I feel as if present names, untranslated, ought to be adopted," he told Garland. "Of course many of these present names are unpronounceable in present shape, but some abbreviation of them might be used, and I think it better to do that than to saddle a family with Side Hill Calf, Boss Ribs Hunter, or something of that kind. Why should an Indian name necessarily mean anything to a white man? When I pronounce the name of my friend Smith, I do not think of a blacksmith or locksmith or tinsmith. His name is merely a verbal label by which he can be identified."

The search for a workable and dignified solution would continue for years—and would never be entirely resolved—but in the meantime it made for lively discussion among the good citizens of the Sequoya League.

Beyond stimulating talk and a resolve to do what was best for Indians, however, the New York branch had little to show for itself after its first year. Grinnell had enlisted the help of a Mrs. Kohlenberg on the Northern Cheyenne reservation to start a version of the Roes' Mohonk Lodge, with a promise from Mrs. Doubleday that she could get New York shops to carry the Indians' beadwork. So far, though, business was slow. "I have shown your samples to several people who have been at the house since they arrived and feel sure that I can sell myself a number of these things," Grinnell encouraged Mrs. Kohlenberg. "For example, my sister wishes one large scissors case with white beads, lodges on one side, dragonflies on the other. . . . A friend would like a few belts, a small doll cradle or two, and so on."

In June Grinnell took Elizabeth west to show her some of his favorite haunts. The morning before they left New York, he dashed off a letter to George Gould, apologizing for his uncharacteristic failure to keep in touch. "I am the criminal now," he said submissively, "and my only excuse is that your letter got covered up on my desk and hidden, and I have been under so great a drive for some months that I have done few of the things that I ought to have done. . . . I am taking the train in a very few minutes for Montana, for Indian work of different kinds, but expect to be back here toward the latter part of July. . . . I shall hope before I reach the Northern Cheyennes to let you hear from me again," he concluded, before hurrying to board the Pennsylvania Railroad.

"*I* am taking. . . . *I* shall hope before *I* reach. . . ." For all Gould knew, Grinnell was traveling alone.

The great "drive" that had consumed Grinnell over the winter and spring was his Cheyenne book, which he sent off to Charles Scribner's Sons before leaving town. "I should be greatly obliged to you if between now and, say, the 15th of July, you could have it read and let me know whether your people would care to publish it," he wrote to his old editor, William Brownell, who had been kind enough to publish *Blackfoot Lodge Tales* and the second imprint of *Pawnee Hero Stories*. As a title, he suggested *The Cheyenne Camp Circle*. The 200,000-word manuscript was the culmination of fifteen years of research, cinched at last by his sessions with George Bent in Oklahoma. "This is in many ways a better book than the others," he assured Brownell, "but, of course, I recognize that you may not think so."

The first stop on their trip was in Nebraska so Grinnell could introduce Elizabeth to Lute and Elvira North. They then spent three weeks among the Northern Cheyennes. "All seemed glad to see us," Grinnell noted in his diary, at last acknowledging Elizabeth's presence. She took a number of photographs, and together they observed the first government herd of cattle distributed among the Cheyennes, a project that Grinnell had been advocating for some time. "There was great excitement among the people," he reported. In his diary he proudly made note of Elizabeth's horsemanship: "All day in the saddle. Elizabeth had a narrow escape from a mad cow which she tried to turn and which almost caught her horse." But it didn't. Grinnell was not the only cowpuncher in the family.

They arrived on the Blackfeet reservation in time for the medicine lodge and were joined there by John J. White, Jr., and his wife, Grace, whom Grinnell had met at the first Sequoya League meeting, if not earlier. Jay White called himself a "broker," which really meant that he kept an eye on his inherited wealth. Lately his main interest was collecting Indian artifacts, many of which were sold to him by Grinnell. With no profession of his own, White desired to emulate Grinnell—someone who divided his life between East and West, the engaging indoors of the former and the rugged outdoors of the latter.

The relationship took on an added dimension once Elizabeth entered the picture. Grace White was born in Africa, the daughter of an Episcopalian missionary, and she and Elizabeth Grinnell were similarly strong and self-confident. Outside of his siblings and their spouses, Grinnell had never forged a friendship with another couple. The Whites, for better or worse, were his first foray in that direction. By their ages alone—Jay White was forty-three in 1903, Grace forty-two—they provided a bridge between an older husband and his much younger wife.

After the medicine lodge the Grinnells and Whites headed for the mountains, guided by Jack Monroe and another old hand, Billy Upham, who had been with Grinnell on at least one earlier trip. On July 9 they pitched their tents—one for the men, a smaller one for the women—at the base of nine-thousand-foot Chief Mountain. The following morning they rode around to the west side, and from there struck out on foot, climbing upward through strata of loose rock that at times demanded the use of hands as well as feet. "The women climbed with extraordinary pluck and facility," Grinnell noted in his diary. "At the very first, they had a little difficulty, but in a very few minutes Elizabeth came to understand how to walk and balance."

The tour continued the next day. They rode up Swiftcurrent, past the lower falls and lakes that Grinnell knew by heart and was now anxious to share with Elizabeth. "Climbed to pass above my glacier," he wrote. "The way was long and hard. The women did splendidly."

Neither Grinnell nor White had brought along guns and thus did not disturb the forty or so mountain goats they spotted. Jack Monroe, however, had packed a rifle for protection's sake. Grinnell used it to kill a golden eagle. "This is a bird I would not have shot at except in the mountains," he reasoned to Lute North, "but they destroy, in my belief, a great many young sheep and goats and therefore ought to be killed."

Grinnell had never been in these mountains so early in the year, and he marveled at the abundance of wildflowers—purple clematis, dog's-tooth violets, and three colors of columbines. On the ride back to Browning, they stopped at the inlet between the upper and lower St. Mary Lakes, where the Whites had good luck fishing. Elizabeth was too ill to join in—though Grinnell discreetly withheld her symptoms from his diary.

Perhaps it was coincidence, but shortly after the Grinnells arrived home, an article entitled "Women in the Field" appeared in *Forest and Stream*: "For many centuries the position even of civilized women was that of an inferior. Unable, owing to lack of physical strength, to fight for the things she desired, she was obliged to take second place. . . . Happily this is now largely ended, and woman's position in civilization, and above all in America, is constantly improving. More and more she is coming to share men's pleasures."

The piece was unsigned; regardless, it bore Grinnell's stamp of approval: "For many years *Forest and Stream* has believed that there is no reason why woman should not share with man those sports of the field which bring humanity more and more in contact with nature. And the result of the doctrine that it has consistently preached is seen today in the constantly increased use by women of the fishing rod and the rifle, the shotgun and the golf club, the saddle horse and the canoe. There are even women who sail their own yachts, and often do it quite as well as men sail theirs. Yet it is to be remembered that to most women all this outdoor life is new. . . . Nothing is more important, therefore, than that the woman undertaking this new pursuit should be taught by someone who is competent. This instructor is likely to be a brother, father, or husband, and he cannot devote too much care and effort in starting his charge just right."

For all that, Grinnell was still not ready to name names. "My little trip to the mountains was interesting in a number of ways," he wrote to George Gould on August 21, which happened to be his one-year wedding anniversary. "I enjoyed showing my companions the country over which you and I have scrambled. . . . I took a man and two women up to the top of Chief Mountain, where I suppose no woman has been before. Of course, the climb was not a difficult one, but it was rather a feat for the women."

His own footing, he quickly learned, was not so sure, either. Awaiting him on his return to New York was a letter from William Brownell. Scribner's had turned down his manuscript. "I am sorry that you cannot see your way clear to publish the Cheyenne book," Grinnell wrote Brownell, "but the commercial side of the question is obvious enough, and, as you suggest, I have few illusions as to the popularity of folk-lore."

The next day he sent the manuscript to Doubleday, Page and Company, whose publisher and wife he regarded as allies and friends. Three weeks later, after Doubleday's rejection, he sent it to Macmillan, with the same result.

TEMPORARY SOJOURNERS

A s certain things were coming together for George Bird Grinnell, others were coming apart. He had arrived at a vantage point from which he could see the horizon forward and backward—the life already lived and the home stretch approaching. This is the common lot of most men in their fifties, but in 1904 it was especially true for him.

"I came back from the west feeling like a fighting cock," Grinnell wrote to Ned Dana shortly after he and Elizabeth reached New York, "and I believe that I shall pull through the next nine or ten months without trouble. I propose to gradually ease up on work."

This was before the Cheyenne book was turned down three times in a row. He next offered it to the Smithsonian's Bureau of Ethnology, at no charge, but even as an academic monograph, no one was interested. He had worked on it for fifteen years, anticipating—hoping, at least—that he had done sufficient justice to the subject. He had other projects he was eager to tackle—there would always be other projects—but the rejections he received for the Cheyenne manuscript now meant that he would have to keep at it and bear down until it saw the light of day. The past was yet prologue; the final chapter remained elusive.

And something was not right with Elizabeth. A month after Grinnell's "fighting cock" boast to Ned Dana, he wrote to him again: "We had a great time in the West, but I am sorry to say that she has not held [her] strength." Since their Yale days, he and Dana had shared each other's sundry aches and pains, but Grinnell was not inclined to reveal details of his wife's condition.

In December he informed another classmate, Jack Nicholson, "Mrs. Grinnell is up and about again, and I hope she will continue to grow strong." But by February he updated Dana, "Mrs. Grinnell has not been quite up to the mark." In none of these communications did he make any inference of morning sickness or pregnancy, unless it was to mention that Elizabeth was spending many days in bed with the expectation that she would be "about again" soon.

Life at Audubon Park was changing under their feet, almost literally. The subway beneath Broadway was nearing completion, and by the end of the year Grinnell could ride from 157th Street—"practically at our door"—downtown to the *Forest and Stream* office in about twenty minutes. Meanwhile, construction of Riverside Drive was under way, its route bending through the very heart of Audubon Park. In May Grinnell complained that the motorway had divided his property, cutting off the house from where he pastured his two milk cows. In July he shared his gripes with sister Helen Page, who was passing the summer in Switzerland. "We have our ups and downs; our seasons of stress and storm . . . and then our periods of drought," he joked thinly, "when the Riverside Drive contractor drops an unusually large stone on the water supply pipe, and we are unable to take a bath or clean our teeth for days at a time." To Ned Dana he grumbled, "I am awakened at 7 o'clock in the morning by the sound of . . . steam engines and the chattering of Dagoes."

He did not relish the idea of automobiles passing by his front door—or anywhere else, for that matter. "When properly used, the automobile has all the essentials of a public benefaction," he allowed in *Forest and Stream*. "But as commonly used in the city streets by reckless drivers, it is largely a public nuisance and public menace." He liked being an automobile passenger even less than being an endangered pedestrian. "I have done so little riding in those machines that when they go at all fast, my heart is in my mouth," he told John Pitcher.

With traffic closing in on Audubon Park and apartment buildings springing up around it, Grinnell and Elizabeth sought escape in Connecticut. "I have recently purchased a few dirty acres at Milford," he informed Ned Dana shortly after returning from Montana. The property bordered Beaver Brook Farm, now owned by his sisters, who, as their children grew and went off to school, were spending more time there. Brother Mort and his wife lived year-round in a house next door. Over the coming years Grinnell would add a succession of parcels—five acres here, eight there—eventually stitching together a hundred-acre farm of fields, orchards, woodlot, and marsh that reached westward from the outskirts of Milford to the Housatonic River. From New York he and Elizabeth could get to Milford station in two hours.

At first they had no house of their own and stayed at Beaver Brook or with Mort. By the end of 1903 they were spending as many weekends as they could in the country. During weekdays in the city they suffered "blasts going off on every side, stones, logs, and rocks flying in all directions," Grinnell told Dana. "I do not suppose it is quite like being in Port Arthur"—referring to the Russian-held port in Manchuria then under bombardment by the Japanese—"but still one gets considerable practice in dodging flying missiles."

He was so distracted that he was not sure if he and Elizabeth could get away that summer. Edward Wilbur, the business manager and treasurer of *Forest and Stream* who had been with Grinnell for the past twenty-four years, fell ill in the spring and worsened over the summer. Grinnell was obliged to assume Wilbur's responsibilities. "As you know, I do not take lunch, and, as it happens, I have been for a couple of weeks—and still am— pretty nearly alone in the office and so greatly driven," he told Madison Grant, secretary of the New York Zoological Society.

Besides having to fill in for Wilbur, Grinnell carried a hefty load of writing and editing. He had by no means given up on the Cheyenne book, keeping up an intermittent correspondence with George Bent and publishing an excerpt on the medicine lodge in *American Anthropologist*. And over the previous fall and winter he had browbeat Boone and Crockett members into submitting articles for a third anthology, to be titled *American Big Game in Its Haunts*. With Theodore Roosevelt otherwise occupied, Grinnell had to edit the volume single-handedly. Grinnell's contribution was a seventy-eight-page survey of "The Mountain Sheep and Its Range," a topic on which he had been collecting data and anecdotes for years.

Interspersed with bloody tales of killing bears, moose, and sheep, *American Big Game in Its Haunts* is weighted with sober pieces on wildlife protection, game refuges, and forest reserves. In a companion statement published in *Forest and Stream* at the time of the annual Boone and Crockett meeting, Grinnell explained that the club's purpose was no longer merely to "bring together a number of big-game hunters for social intercourse." The club sought to become more than "an association of persons who enjoy hunting and killing of wild animals." Indeed, Grinnell asserted, "A considerable portion of its members now never hunt wild animals, but, looking to the future, are endeavoring to preserve for this country a reasonable stock for its indigenous wild creatures, which will be beautiful and historic objects for succeeding generations to admire." (Even the trigger-happy Roosevelt had spared a bear cub during a 1902 hunt in Louisiana, inadvertently launching the Teddy bear craze.)

An unsigned article in *American Big Game in Its Haunts*, likely written by Grinnell, reiterated what he, *Forest and Stream*, Roosevelt, and many others had been urging for years: federal legislation authorizing the president "to set aside portions of forest reserves as game refuges, where no hunting should be allowed." Thus far, no such legislation had made it through both houses of Congress, but it was not for lack of trying—or for lack of support from the White House.

Since taking office in September 1901, Roosevelt had been on a tear. In 1902 he had helped establish Crater Lake National Park in Oregon; the following year, Wind Cave National Park in South Dakota. During this same period he had been even more aggressive on forest protection, dedicating more than fifty new reserves, from Puerto Rico to Alaska, encompassing more than sixty million acres. And in March 1903 he figured out a way, if not to overcome, then to skirt the reserve-as-refuge impasse by issuing an unprecedented executive order that rendered a three-acre bird rookery off limits to hunters. Overnight, federally owned Pelican Island, on Florida's Indian River, became the country's first national wildlife refuge. By the end of his time in office, Roosevelt would consecrate another fifty such sanctuaries.

Grinnell and the Boone and Crockett Club were bolstered by Roosevelt's actions, and as the 1904 election approached, they worked hard on his behalf. They could never wish for a more effective ambassador for their agenda.

Grinnell's relationship with Roosevelt still had its ups and downs, however. He never neglected to remind Roosevelt of his admiration and loyalty, yet he did not hesitate to speak his own mind, as demonstrated at Standing Rock. In the spring of 1903 Grinnell managed to get under Roosevelt's skin again, this time with an editorial in *Forest and Stream*.

The paper had waded into what would later be dubbed the "nature faker" controversy, a tempest in a teapot stirred up by John Burroughs in the March 1903 *Atlantic Monthly*. Burroughs's piece, "Real and Sham Natural History," lit into popular nature writers Ernest Thompson Seton and the Reverend William J. Long for humanizing and sentimentalizing wild animals—making up stories of a porcupine rolling down hill, for instance, or of a fox riding on the back of a sheep to throw dogs off its trail—and committing the unforgivable sin of suggesting such tales were true. Burroughs mocked Seton's *Wild Animals I Have Known* as "make-believe" and asserted that Long's *School of the Woods* was written by "a man who has never really been in the woods, but who sits in his study and cooks up these yarns from things he has read in *Forest and Stream*." (Another eventual target of the nature faker police was Jack London; Rudyard Kipling was exempted because he made it obvious that *The Jungle Book* was fiction.)

Forest and Stream ran a snide rebuke of Burroughs by a longtime contributor who wrote under the byline Hermit. Hermit did not endeavor to counter Burroughs's criticism of Seton, Long, and their fellow fabulists; rather, he suggested that much of the natural history in Burroughs's own writing was "false."

As Grinnell well knew, Burroughs and Roosevelt were good friends; by coincidence, the two were camping together in Yellowstone National Park when Hermit's affront appeared in *Forest and Stream*. The president was shown the article at the end of the trip, when he arrived at Gardiner, Montana, to lay the cornerstone of the arch at the park's north entrance. Perhaps recalling the critical treatment that *Hunting Trips of a Ranchman* had received from Grinnell in 1885—when Grinnell had questioned Roosevelt's credentials as a naturalist—Roosevelt dictated a stern, six-page rejoinder to the "utter nonsense" published by "a paper of the standing of the Forest and Stream." He demanded that *Forest and Stream* print an apology. It was the longest letter Theodore Roosevelt ever wrote to George Bird Grinnell.

Hermit did not apologize; nor did Grinnell—not explicitly. "I am very glad to have your letter of April 24," he answered the president in as cordial a tone as he could summon. "I thank you for it because—like any other man who is trying to do his job as well as he knows how—I welcome intelligent criticism. You and I of course look at this matter from somewhat different standpoints. I imagine that you take the view that Mr. Burroughs should not be criticized at all, because of your affection for him; while I feel it is more important to get at the truth than to spare his feelings."

Grinnell stressed that he, too, respected Burroughs and had "hearty sympathy" for the *Atlantic Monthly* article. On the other hand, he pointed out, Burroughs had made "many statements which you and I and many others believe were incorrect." Grinnell disclosed Hermit's real name—M. A. Walton, "an old man, an ex-politician, and an ex-editor" from Cape Cod— even while he continued to stand by him: "I believe that this article has done and will do a great deal of good. . . . Out of the whole thing there will finally emerge a certain amount of unquestioned fact, a certain amount of discredit to the constantly growing army of natural history fakers, whom we should be glad to see wiped off the face of the earth."

Roosevelt's kettle cooled quickly enough, as he dedicated the Roosevelt Arch and then went on to California to hike through Yosemite with the other "Johnny" of the Harriman Alaska Expedition, John Muir.

Grinnell made amends by publishing the text of Roosevelt's Yellowstone speech (which the president delivered on the same day he wrote so fiercely to Grinnell). Here was a topic on which they agreed wholeheartedly.

"The creation and preservation of such a great natural playground in the interest of our people as a whole is a credit to the nation," Roosevelt told his audience. "It has been preserved with wise foresight. The scheme of its preservation is noteworthy in its essential democracy. . . . This Park was created, and is now administered, for the benefit and enjoyment of the people. . . . [I]t is the property of Uncle Sam and therefore all of us. The only way that the people as a whole can secure to themselves and their children the enjoyment in perpetuity of what the Yellowstone Park has to give is by assuming the ownership in the name of the nation and by jealously safeguarding and preserving the scenery, the forests, and the wild creatures."

A year later Grinnell would publish Roosevelt's account of his 1903 tour of Yellowstone in *American Big Game in Its Haunts*. He also included as the anthology's opening chapter a rosy tribute to Roosevelt as sportsman, naturalist, and preservationist (adapted from an essay that first had appeared in *Forest and Stream*). As head of the Boone and Crockett Club's editorial committee, Grinnell made sure that copies of *American Big Game* were sent to every member of Congress. If this was fealty, it had its purpose.

Others received Grinnell's accolades as well. Coincident with publication of *American Big Game in Its Haunts*, he began a series in *Forest and Stream* under the rubric, "Trails of the Pathfinders." The thirty-four segments that began in February 1904 and ran intermittently for the next year and a half saluted western explorers, traders, trappers, and missionaries, prompted by the Louisiana Purchase Exposition, which opened in St. Louis in April. Grinnell's cavalcade included Lewis and Clark, Zebulon Pike, John Frémont, Alexander Mackenzie, and several lesser-known but no less worthy wanderers. "The articles which are to follow contain much of history which is old, but which to the average American is new," Grinnell wrote in his introduction. He had kept booksellers busy for years, tracking down old histories and diaries, and he now distilled them for the edification of his readers. Whether he intended so or not, this was his version of Roosevelt's *Winning of the West*, published in four volumes between 1889 and 1896, which was not only a survey of early American expansion but also a treatise on national character.

"If ever any set of men played their part in subduing the wilderness and plowing the ground to receive the seed of settlement and to rear the crop of civilization which is now being harvested, these men did that work, and did it well," Grinnell wrote of *his* winners of the West. "Through hard experience these pioneers had come to understand life. They possessed a due sense of proportion. They saw the things which were essential; they scorned those which were trivial. If judged by certain standards, they were rough and uncouth; if they spoke a strange tongue, wore odd apparel, and lived narrow lives, they were yet practicing—albeit unconsciously—the virtues—unflinching courage sturdy independence and helpfulness to their neighbors—which made America what it is."

As if he did not have enough of his own ground to plow already, Grinnell somehow managed to knock out another Jack book. This one was called *Jack in the Rockies: A Boy's Adventure with a Pack Train*. As usual, young Jack Danvers goes from east to west: "Often when he was in New York, walking through narrow city streets, looking up at high buildings, hearing the roar and rattle of the passing traffic, and watching the people hurry to and fro, each one absorbed in his own business, it was hard to realize that away off somewhere, only a few days' journey distant, there was a land where there was no limit to the view, where each human being seemed absolutely free."

Soon Jack joins his old pathfinder, Hugh Johnson, and together they steam up the Missouri to Fort Benton, and from there ride over the route Grinnell had taken with the Ludlow reconnaissance in 1875, southward through Judith Basin, Gallatin Valley, to Yellowstone. The year is approximately the same, too—before the railroad, before tourists tamed the park, and before hunting in the park was proscribed. They shoot buffalo, a mother grizzly, and her cub. Hugh gives Jack a lesson on how to decapitate a moose (". . . stick the knife into the moose's head immediately behind the horns, split the skin down on the nape of the neck . . ."). Jack also receives lessons on what *not* to shoot. "'I don't want you to act like the rest of these pilgrims that come up the river, and to be shooting at everything you see that's alive,'" Hugh admonishes.

Hugh warns Jack that, unless laws are passed to restrict the hunting of elk in Yellowstone, soon there will be none left.

"'And if I should have a son and ever want to bring him out here and show him the things that I saw when I was a boy, he could not see them?'" Jack asks Hugh incredulously.

Hugh replies: "'[E]very fellow that comes out into the mountains, he's just like you and me; we think the other fellow oughtn't to kill game, but we ought to kill it. We claim that we don't kill anything more than what we want to eat, and these other fellows claim, maybe—if they're buffalo skinners or elk skinners—that they don't kill any more than they want to skin. Each man thinks that what he'll kill won't do any harm; but when they're all at work killing as hard as they can, the upshot of it is that there's no game left.'"

Grinnell chose Yellowstone as his own destination in the summer of 1904. Elizabeth was back on her feet, finally recovered from whatever had been ailing her for the past year, and he wanted to introduce her to "all the wonders of the park." If he kept a diary of the trip, it is not among the others.

For some reason they did not visit St. Louis on the way west, even though *Forest and Stream* had an exhibit at the world's fair, which celebrated the one hundredth anniversary of the Louisiana Purchase.

The Grinnells arrived in Yellowstone the second week in September. They were pampered by Superintendent Pitcher and his wife, and they made the grand tour of geysers, waterfalls, and wildlife. "Mrs. Grinnell had never been there before," Grinnell informed Ned Dana, "and she had a joyful time."

From Yellowstone they went to the Northern Cheyenne reservation. "Mrs. Grinnell alternately took photographs of Indians and galloped over the hills," her husband wrote afterward to George Gould. Two years after his marriage, this was the first time Grinnell mentioned her name to his never-forgotten friend in Santa Barbara.

While Elizabeth amused herself outdoors, Grinnell confined himself to the agency headquarters at Lame Deer. "I had it impressed on me . . . that there is no fool like an old one," he groused to Ned Dana. "Instead of going into camp and pottering about and having a good time, I took an interpreter"—the reliable William Rowland—"and sat at a table and worked for eight or ten hours a day, in the [effort] to do something with the Cheyenne language."

In the fall, after the Grinnells returned from Yellowstone and Lame Deer, Elizabeth announced that she would like to join her husband on his bird-shooting outings. The Narrows Island Club, his duck-hunting getaway in North Carolina, did not allow women as guests, never mind as members, but there were plenty of opportunities for shooting closer to home. Wood-cock lived in the thickets around Milford, and rail were plentiful along the New York and Connecticut shore. In late November Grinnell and Eliza-beth made a trip to Ocean County, New Jersey, to shoot quail, pheasant, and ducks, a variety that gave her an enjoyable initiation to shotgunning. Evidently she took to it quite eagerly; in the coming seasons she was often afield and seldom as a mere spectator. "[F]or many years I used to drag my wretched wife through fields and woods and over stone walls and through tangled swamps," Grinnell would write to John James Audubon's grand-daughter Harriet, "until at last she got to like this sort of thing as well as I." And she came to shoot nearly as well, too.

Over the years, Grinnell owned a series of hunting dogs, which he boarded with the guides at Narrows Island, in Milford, or with trainers out-side New York. One exception was a setter named Dewey, named no doubt for Admiral George Dewey, the hero of Manila Bay. Grinnell brought him to Audubon Park shortly after he and Elizabeth were married. "I want him as a dog to sleep in the house and be about with the members of the family," he explained to Dewey's breeder on Staten Island. "There are two or three acres of ground . . . so the dog will have plenty of room." At first Dewey seemed quite "biddable"—the highest compliment Grinnell paid any dog. He and Elizabeth took him along while horseback riding in Central Park, and Dewey lay politely at their feet in the evening. But six months later Grinnell shipped Dewey back to Staten Island after he "snapped at mem-bers of the household and on at least two occasions . . . actually attacked guests," Grinnell informed the breeder.

From then on, all the dogs lived in kennels. Grinnell's favorites were Wick, Shot, Breeze, Yale, and Grover. The latter, a Chesapeake Bay retriever, was named for Grover Cleveland—the second time Grinnell memorialized the former president and New York governor. (The first was

Mount Cleveland, at 10,479 feet the tallest mountain in the northern Rockies.) So esteemed was Grover, the retriever, that Grinnell devoted an entire chapter to the Chesapeake breed in *American Duck Shooting*, a book he pulled together for the Forest and Stream Publishing Company.

Throughout his adulthood, regardless of the purpose of his various outings, Grinnell never ceased observing and identifying native birds. His diaries are treasures for their ornithological notes alone. And even after his reluctant but necessary discontinuation of the first Audubon Society, he did not quit advocating for wiser sportsmanship and more effective legislation to protect birds—plumed birds, songbirds, game birds, and especially migratory birds. For years *Forest and Stream* had called for prohibition of the sale of wildfowl, for prudent bag limits, and for a halt to spring shooting. "The time is coming . . . and it cannot be long delayed when gunners will be obliged to make a choice between having no shooting at all, or giving up some portion of the season that is now open," Grinnell wrote in *American Duck Shooting*.

The Lacey Act was not exactly a radical step; nonetheless, it was a step in a radical direction. Congressman John F. Lacey, of Iowa, who earlier had sponsored the law to protect Yellowstone (called the Lacey Act also), spent several years pushing another bill to strengthen the federal government's role in protecting wildlife. In the latter decades of the nineteenth century several states had enacted laws restricting profligate hunting and hunting for profit. The new Lacey Act, finally passed in May 1900, did not aim to overrule these state laws; rather, it sought to strengthen them by ensuring that anyone who violated a state game law could be punished by federal law for transporting illegally killed game to another state for sale; and likewise it forbade the purchase of any game killed illegally in another state.

On its slow march toward enactment, Lacey's legislation met with stiff opposition from those who regarded it as a threat to states' rights. *Forest and Stream* did its part to rebut these objections. "Nine men out of ten honestly enough believe that once they have captured their game, it is theirs absolutely to do what they will with it, any restrictive statutes to the contrary notwithstanding," the journal commented skeptically, "and the usual appeal from the operation of the law is to the Constitution of the United States, an instrument which is believed in some occult way to guarantee the individual full license to do as he will with game killed."

What Grinnell called the "constitutional rights delusion" was precisely that—a delusion—since the courts had already determined that interstate commerce could and should be regulated by the federal government. "The trend of opinion . . . is in the direction of restricting the transportation of game," *Forest and Stream*'s editorial concluded. "The expedient is wise and effective. Game export should be forbidden, and the traffic should cease."

At the same time the Lacey Act was taking effect, the larger movement to protect bird life was growing considerably stronger and far better organized. Grinnell's *Audubon Magazine* was succeeded by a new journal, *Bird-Lore*, founded by Frank Chapman, the man whom *Forest and Stream* had enlisted to count the different species of bird feathers decorating the hats of women on Fourteenth Street. Individual Audubon societies sprang up by state, beginning in Massachusetts, and by 1900 there were more than thirty. They originally formed to discourage the selling, buying, and wearing of ornamental feathers, but they then worked diligently for passage of the Lacey Act and the so-called model laws drawn up by the American Ornithologists' Union. In 1901 alone, nine states and the District of Columbia passed some version of an AOU-inspired bird protection law. The various Audubon societies and the AOU, as well as groups like the League of American Sportsmen, also rallied in support of Roosevelt's decision to create the Pelican Island refuge in 1903. That same year North Carolina passed a law authorizing the state to appoint wardens to enforce its wildfowl regulations—said wardens to be chosen by the Audubon Society of North Carolina, led by T. Gilbert Pearson, a persuasive and indefatigable biology professor from Guilford College.

At the end of 1904 William Dutcher, the head of the AOU's game protection committee, convened a meeting in New York to discuss bringing all the Audubon groups under one umbrella. On January 5, 1905, the National Association of Audubon Societies was founded. Dutcher became president, T. Gilbert Pearson secretary, Frank Chapman treasurer; the board of directors was a who's who of the nation's best-known proponents of bird protection, not least of them George Bird Grinnell.

Within a month, *Forest and Stream* ran the full text of "An Act to Protect Migratory Game Birds in the United States." In its intent to overlay federal regulation on top of state laws, it was the offspring of the 1900 Lacey Act. But the Shiras bill, named for its author, George Shiras III, a Republican congressman from Pittsburgh, went even further by proposing that federal regulation of migratory birds should *supersede* state law. Nonmigratory birds—birds that lived their entire lives within a state—were already subject to state jurisdiction. Migratory birds, however, such as ducks, geese, wild swans, woodcock, snipe, and rail, ought to be in a different jurisdictional category, *Forest and Stream* averred. These species "breed in districts beyond the State boundaries in the north and pass, after a temporary stay, into other districts out of the State boundaries to the south, and thus being only temporarily and transiently in the limits of the State, they are not properly under its jurisdiction, nor may be efficiently protected by it."

"In practice the protection of wildfowl by the States has proved ineffectual," *Forest and Stream* continued. "If the migratory species are to be preserved, they must have the protection which only the Federal Government can give. The experience of the last quarter-century of game protection has convinced us all of the futility of striving to secure uniformity of protection for ducks. If it shall be attained at all, it must come through the intervention of Congress. All technical considerations dismissed, and fine-spun theories of State and Federal jurisdiction aside, the true consideration of public advantage supports this measure of Mr. Shiras."

George Shiras III was ten years younger than Grinnell but cut from a similar vintage of cloth. His great-grandfather George had moved to Pittsburgh after the American Revolution and was said to have launched the first steamboat on the Ohio River. All the Shiras men loved the outdoors; George III's grandfather established a camp on Lake Superior as early as 1849, where the succeeding generations of Georges spent many contented days hunting and fishing, when they were not practicing law. George Shiras, Jr., father of George Shiras III, was appointed to the U.S. Supreme Court by Benjamin Harrison and served until 1903. His son took his undergraduate degree from Cornell and law degree from Yale, and in 1902 he agreed to run for Congress on the condition that, if elected, he would serve only one term. By the time he introduced the migratory bird law, he was a lame duck.

Shiras had long since lost interest in shooting in favor of wildlife photography. Borrowing from the shameful (and illegal) practice of "jacklighting" deer at night, he developed a technique that switched on a flashlight and released a camera shutter simultaneously. Sometimes he used a stationary camera rigged with a tripwire; sometimes he approached wildlife stealthily by canoe. In time, his work inspired a new category of articles in *Forest and Stream* on "Hunting without a Gun" and "Hunting with a Camera." "[H]unting without a gun appeals chiefly to those whose minds are cast in a mold of great refinement, to whom the spoils of the chase do not constitute the most important part of their outing," one column posited. "The work of photography calls for the best qualities of the hunter. Is it difficult to creep within shot of the shy mountain sheep? It is still harder to approach within focusing distance." So successful and prolific was Shiras that *National Geographic,* in which much of his work was published, declared him "the father of wildlife photography."

Forest and Stream trumpeted the Shiras bill throughout the congressional session of 1904–1905 and gained many supporters. On February 18 the journal devoted its entire front page to Shiras's defense of the bill's constitutionality. "In the migratory game bill I did not attempt to declare ownership [of birds by] the National Government," Shiras was quoted, "for many of these birds are international, wintering in the southernmost part of South America and breeding beyond the Arctic Circle in northern Canada. The bill gives the Government *control of the shooting season* and puts the migrants in the 'custody' of the country at large whenever they tarry long enough to need our protection."

These qualifications notwithstanding, never before had a piece of conservation-minded legislation attempted so boldly to impose the will of the federal government upon that of individual states.

Even with the endorsement of President Roosevelt, the Shiras bill went nowhere. As promised, Shiras served only one term and was a private citizen by March. Yet his idea for federal regulation of migratory birds would not be so fleeting. Grinnell, *Forest and Stream*, bird lovers, and an increasing number of sportsmen recognized its merits and would not let it die. The federal migratory bird act would require another decade, but George Shiras's radical idea would finally take wing and would provide a model for more such legislation— carrying forward seventy years to the Endangered Species Act of 1973.

Meanwhile, Theodore Roosevelt never quit pressing on behalf of national forests, putting increasing confidence in the vision of Gifford Pinchot, chief of the Bureau of Forestry. It was Pinchot, for example, who likely authored the section in Roosevelt's first address to Congress, declaring: "[T]he fundamental idea of forestry is the perpetuation of forests by use. Forest protection is not an end in itself; it is a means to increase and sustain the resources of our country and the industries which depend on them."

Pinchot summarized his philosophy as "Forestry Is Tree Farming." The job of the government, he said, "was not to stop the ax, but to regulate its use."

Such emphasis on pragmatism and commercial gain, as chorused by Pinchot and Roosevelt, stood in sharp contrast to the priorities of John Muir, who believed that wilderness was not to be conquered by man but to be worshipped. Theodore Roosevelt, on his 1903 trip to Yosemite, had been smitten by Muir's "delightful innocence and good will." Yet while he admired Muir's holy asceticism, as demonstrated by his reverence for Yosemite as the most sacred of temples, he could not embrace Muir's holier-than-thou idealism. Muir, meanwhile, made no secret of his disdain for Roosevelt's appetite for killing. He believed that boys ought to grow out of their "blood-loving savagery" and that grown men—to wit, members of the Boone & Crockett Club—ought to respect "the rights of animals & their kinship to ourselves."

Pinchot, on the other hand, was an unapologetic hunter and a Boone and Crockett member in good standing. Unlike Muir, who grew up humble, hungry, and hard-used, Pinchot was well educated and well connected. Whereas Muir was a loner and an aesthete, Pinchot was outgoing and put himself forward as a man of science. (In 1900 Pinchot used family money to found the Yale School of Forestry, which was initially located in O. C. Marsh's former house.) And for all his experience in the field, Pinchot was even more accomplished in the arena of politics. He had famously wrestled with Roosevelt one evening in the New York governor's mansion, and since then they had come to see eye to eye on what was best for the nation's natural resources.

Roosevelt and Pinchot were in complete agreement that the Bureau of Forestry ought to be transferred from the Department of Interior to the

Department of Agriculture, and in February 1905, on the eve of Roosevelt's inauguration to a second term, Congress finally approved the transfer, with Pinchot continuing as custodian of sixty-three million acres of forest reserves. In July Pinchot changed the name of his agency to the United States Forest Service; two years later the Forest Service's reserves—with dozens more added to the list—would be officially renamed "national forests," because, in Pinchot's view, they were more than mere reserves.

Another milestone was reached in 1906, when, again through the able leadership of John Lacey, Congress passed the Antiquities Act, initially conceived as a law to deter looting and destruction of prehistoric ruins on federal lands. But, in its final provisions, it authorized the president "to declare by public proclamation"—that is, by executive order—"historic landmarks, historic and prehistoric structures, and other objects of historic or scientific interest that are situated upon the lands owned or controlled by the Government of the United States to be national monuments." Immediately Roosevelt put the act to work, making national monuments of the Montezuma Castle cliff dwellings and the painted badlands of the Petrified Forest, both in Arizona; the inscription-covered rocks of El Morro in New Mexico; and the igneous colossus of Devils Tower in Wyoming. Before he left office he would stretch the definitions of "landmark" and "historic and scientific interest" to protect another eighteen unique and precious sites— including the Grand Canyon and Muir Woods.

Grinnell applauded Roosevelt's—and Pinchot's—shrewd gains in protection and preservation. He was particularly pleased with Roosevelt's renewed commitment—expressed in his annual address of December 1904—to set aside certain forest reserves as game refuges. When the president called for more national parks, Grinnell used the occasion to nominate one of his own. "Besides the parks recommended by the President," Grinnell wrote in *Forest and Stream*, "may be suggested the main divide of the Rocky Mountains, from the Great Northern Railway north to the Canadian boundary line, and from the western border of the Blackfoot Indian Reservation west over the mountains beyond McDonald Lake and creek. This is the famous St. Mary's country, so well known to many of our readers."

Grinnell was also encouraged by Roosevelt's improved handling of Indian affairs. After Standing Rock, the president had heeded his advice to get rid of several unsatisfactory agents, beginning with the latest corrupt Blackfeet agent, James Monteath, followed more momentously by the replacement of Commissioner of Indian Affairs William Jones. As his new commissioner, Roosevelt chose Francis Leupp, an old friend, although Grinnell was not shy about taking credit for the appointment. "I managed to suggest to the President Mr. Leupp's name," Grinnell told a Canadian acquaintance, "and my reasons for appointing him appealed to the President so strongly that he induced him to take the job."

Roosevelt had not needed any persuading. He had first met the fellow New Yorker when Leupp worked for the National Civil Service Reform League and edited its official organ, *Good Government*. Later they renewed their acquaintance when Leupp moved to Washington as correspondent for the New York *Evening Post*; he also served as the Washington agent for the Indian Rights Association. In 1904 he wrote a campaign biography entitled *The Man Roosevelt*, which he described unabashedly as "a labor of love." Roosevelt invited Leupp to join his administration as the news of Jones's resignation hit the newspapers.

Grinnell also had known Leupp a good while. Both had been Mugwumps, Republicans pulling for Grover Cleveland, and they crossed paths when Leupp was with the Indian Rights Association. Grinnell was delighted when, at Roosevelt's suggestion, the association had sent Leupp to investigate agent Monteath in the fall of 1904. "You sized up Major Monteath just about as I did," he wrote appreciatively.

Thanks to Leupp, Grinnell's rapport with the Bureau of Indian Affairs was restored and indeed was better than at any time since he first thrust himself into Indian matters twenty years before. In January he went to Washington and had dinner with the new commissioner; and when Leupp came to New York later in the spring, Grinnell invited him to spend the night at Audubon Park. "I think Mr. Leupp is an admirable man," he pronounced, "and I know he is ten times as good a man for the place as I would have been."

Leupp had more faith in the General Allotment Act than did Grinnell, but they shared the same progressive views on education and self-sufficiency, and both professed leniency toward Indian customs, dress, and long hair. Likewise Grinnell was heartened by Leupp's enlightened grasp of cultural equivalency and his well-reasoned belief in the resilience of Native Americans. "If, a few centuries ago, an absolutely alien people like the Chinese had invaded our shores," Leupp posed in the pages of the *Outlook*, "and driven the white colonists before them to districts more and more isolated, destroyed the industries on which they had all subsisted, and crowned all by disarming them and penning them on various tracts of land where they could be fed and clothed and cared for at no cost to themselves, to what condition would the white Americans of today be reduced? In spite of their vigorous ancestry, they would surely have lapsed into barbarism and become pauperized. No race on earth could overcome . . . the effect of such treatment. That our red brethren have not been wholly ruined by it is the best proof we could ask of the sturdy traits of character inherent in them. But though not ruined, they have suffered serious deterioration, and the problem now before us is to prevent its going any further."

Come summer, Grinnell was eager to be back among the Cheyennes. But with business partner Edward Wilbur still ill and getting worse, he did not dare leave New York for long. In the meantime, he worked out a long-distance arrangement with George Bent, who was now living in Colony, Oklahoma, to gather stories from the Southern Cheyennes. "I don't know exactly how one should pay for a thing of this kind," he queried Bent in March, "but suppose the best would be to pay a little for a short story and a good deal for a long story; for example, a short story might be worth 50 cents, while a long one might be worth a great deal more, perhaps $5."

Bent sent along several stories of Cheyenne fights, written painstakingly on lined tablet paper. "These old war stories are good, and I like them," Grinnell responded. He asked Bent to dig deeper: "[T]here are also many stories of curious things that happened a long time ago, things that maybe you and I do not believe to be true but that the Indians believe used to be true."

The Cheyenne book, regarded as complete two years earlier, continued to expand. Still wanting more material, Grinnell asked Jay White to go to Colony on his behalf. White went cheerfully, spending several weeks interviewing Bent. White was more determined than ever to follow in Grinnell's every footstep; lately he had taken to addressing him as "Chief." Grinnell was aware that White lacked patience with the Indians; mostly, though, he was gratified to have engaged the assistance of someone so eager to please him. "I read your letter this morning with the enthusiasm of a young lover who has just received a long and delightful epistle from his girl," the Chief told his eager protégé.

Edward Wilbur died on July 30. "I feel badly to have lost him, for I was very fond of him," Grinnell wrote Lute North. "[W]e have sat together in the same room for about twenty-five years, and in all that time there never has been a particle of friction or dissatisfaction and hardly a difference of opinion between us."

At first Grinnell was not sure whether Wilbur's death would permit him greater freedom or demand greater confinement. Regardless, on September 1 he and Elizabeth left for Montana to spend a month among the Northern Cheyennes. Afterward he wrote to agent John Clifford: "We had a delightful visit with you. . . . Though it was short, this year's trip was a great deal better than last year's, for the reason that we spent so much more time out of doors."

Being home in Audubon Park was not so enjoyable. Excavation on Riverside Drive continued; the explosions were so violent that rocks were flung onto the lawn, and one stone flew so high that it put a hole in the roof of the house. "We all of us feel we are mere temporary sojourners on the property," Grinnell wrote Hamlin Garland earlier in the summer. Developers had begun making offers to buy the land on which the Audubons and Grinnells had once lived in arcadian tranquility. It was only a matter of time before the Hemlocks would be replaced by apartment buildings.

Immediately on his return to the city, Grinnell stepped up his acquisition of acreage in Milford. By November he had added a piece that included a house and barn—nothing genteel but, after a few repairs, habitable—and he soon hired a man to live on the place and look after it. Over the course of the fall he and Elizabeth had furniture and china delivered, and they began spending nearly every weekend there.

Elizabeth's family was on the move, as well. Her mother and brother, Frank, had relocated at least once since Elizabeth had married, and now they were obliged to move again due to straitened finances and Frank Curtis's difficulty holding a job. No one in the family had yet put a name to his problem, but, at twenty-seven, he gave all indications of suffering from what today would be called bipolar disorder.

In the spring of 1905 Delle Curtis had gone with Frank to a farm owned by a relative in Missouri. Frank worked picking strawberries, and at Elizabeth's suggestion, Grinnell began sending him and his mother regular checks to carry them along. "Frank seems to be doing well," Grinnell wrote Delle in June, forwarding thirty dollars. "I believe now, as I have always believed, that the very best medicine that he can take is constant occupation. That, after all, is the best thing for any of us."

A month later Delle and Frank had moved on, to a ranch in the Texas Panhandle. Grinnell sent money to buy Frank's "outfit" and again offered words of encouragement, by way of his mother: "The outdoor life, the variety of work, and the association with a lot of self-reliant men ought to do wonders for him. . . . Please give my remembrances to Frank when you see him and congratulate him on the situation in which he finds himself. I could find it in my heart to envy him his work, which is much of the kind I did a good many years ago."

By October, though, Frank had failed at ranch work, and Delle was desperate. Next stop, Caldwell, Kansas, where Delle had another relative and some hope of finding yet another job for Frank. Grinnell sent more money and more advice. "[I]t appears to me of very great importance for Frank's health that he should not spend time loafing about the town," Grinnell counseled at the end of November. "No man can be in a healthy condition if he is an idler." A week before Christmas Grinnell sent enough money for them to come home, but even after they reached the family farm at Glenville, the pattern continued. Grinnell would continue to support them in some fashion for the rest of his life.

Grinnell's own brother Mort had been, if not a burden, then at least a source of exasperation for most of his adult years. While Grinnell had shouldered responsibility for the family's finances, with steady help from Newell Martin, Mort and his second wife, Jennie, had taken expensive trips abroad and to California. His foray as a novelist had been, in Grinnell's view, time misspent; even more embarrassing was Mort's second book, *Neighbors of Field, Wood & Stream*, a collection of saccharine animal sketches—Stilts the Great Heron, Scramble the Grey Squirrel, Dart the Spider, and so on—that might as well have been a field guide to nature-faking.

Mort was forever finding new ways to lose money on his farm in Milford, and Grinnell inevitably extended loans to keep him solvent. Still, they got along, through thick and thin, and with Frank long dead and William out of the picture (and the family corporation), Mort was the only brother left in Grinnell's life.

Until he, too, was gone. At the end of October Mort went to New York to see Jennie off on a trip to Europe. He came home to Connecticut with a cold that, over the next month, descended into pneumonia. Grinnell was with him at Milford on December 9. "That day he went downstairs and walked around with me, talking, laughing and joking," he related. "At 9 o'clock at night he went to bed, and when I left him he said that he felt quite exhausted and did not know when he had been so tired."

Mort Grinnell did not survive the night. He was buried beside his parents and brother in Woodlawn Cemetery in the Bronx. He had lived to be fifty-one years old.

Grinnell, ever the responsible older brother, was on the pier two weeks later to greet Jennie's ship and break the news of her husband's death. "It was a sad errand," he told Jack Monroe.

After the funeral and the holidays, he wrote also to George Gould, informing him of Mort's death: "I am feeling his loss deeply, for he was almost the only man of those that I greatly care for whom I saw at frequent intervals."

In his next letter to Gould, he expressed his customary wistfulness, but this time it was tinged with an extra dose of opportunity lost. "One of the things I have longed for many years is a journey into the southern country in your company"—Gould had again invited Grinnell to join him in Mexico—"but the prospects of my getting so near the west coast as that seem less now than ever before."

Instead he went duck hunting.

CHAPTER 26

PULVERIZING ENGINE

M ost editors spend their careers anchored to a desk, living vicariously through the eyes, ears, and experiences of authors and cor-
respondents. Grinnell saw himself as an exception. His annual
western outings, going back thirty-five years, to 1870, refreshed him physically, mentally, and spiritually and strengthened his knowledge and credibility as a naturalist and ethnologist. They also provisioned him with fodder
with which to flesh out his books and feed the hungry pages of *Forest and
Stream*. But inevitably, as he aged and was more restricted by responsibilities, he found himself increasingly dependent on far-flung hunters and
gatherers to bring the world to him.

Grinnell had always welcomed a good yarn. *Forest and Stream* was
seasoned with the firsthand escapades of outdoorsmen who were accomplished in the field if not always in syntax. These contributors lent freshness
and authenticity to the journal; it was up to Grinnell, along with managing editor Charles Reynolds, to comb out the kinks. Even the Boone and
Crockett anthologies, whose tables of contents bore the names of educated
men, would not have been nearly so readable without the strict attentions
of its editor.

From coarse ore came the occasional gem; Emerson Hough was a shining example. From Chicago he covered the West energetically and eloquently for *Forest and Stream*, most sensationally in his account of the capture of the buffalo butcher Edgar Howell in Yellowstone in 1894. In his spare time Hough wrote for himself—so vigorously that the duties of *Forest and Stream* began to chafe, and his arrogance would eventually oblige Grinnell to cut him loose. Hough's novel, *The Mississippi Bubble*, was a national bestseller in 1902, followed by a skein of successful books, culminating with the now-classic western *The Covered Wagon* in 1922. After reading one of Hough's early novels, *The Girl at the Halfway House*, Grinnell confessed to his star employee, "It is something that I should have been proud to have done. . . . The reading of such a book as this makes one long to possess the creative power that you have."

A rougher diamond was James Willard Schultz, whose early dispatches to *Forest and Stream* had enticed Grinnell to visit the mountains of western Montana. Grinnell eventually gave up on Schultz as a guide and was disappointed (though undeterred) when Schultz failed to hold up his end on *Blackfoot Lodge Tales*. Still, he continued to accept Schultz's colorful and not entirely honest tales of life among the Indians and printed them after a brisk touch-up with his blue pencil. Schultz drank up whatever money Grinnell sent him, and no matter how much or how often he wrote, it always seemed that he (Schultz) owed more to *Forest and Stream* than was owed to him. And so he kept on writing.

In 1905 Schultz was in exile in California. His Piegan wife, Natahki (Fine Shield Woman), had died two years earlier; shortly afterward Schultz guided newspaper heir Ralph Pulitzer on a hunting trip into the Montana mountains to shoot bighorn sheep out of season. Schultz fled the state with the game warden on his heels. One of his first stops was Santa Barbara, where he attempted to throw himself on the charity of George Gould, whom he had guided with Grinnell in bygone years. "You do not, of course, need any warning against that amiable but more or less feeble person," Grinnell wrote Gould. "Schultz is not a cheerful companion either drunk or sober, and I hope that you will not have too much of him."

Gould sent Schultz on his way, to drift elsewhere. Spurred by nostalgia, grief, and the chronic need for money, he set about writing a memoir of his years with Natahki and sent the first segment to Grinnell in March

1905. "I have not got far enough yet to know whether it is the actual story of your life or whether it has no foundation in fact," Grinnell replied. Nevertheless, he encouraged, "It is good so far as it goes, and I advise you to keep on with the tale."

More pages followed. "You make good stuff as long as you are simply telling about what happened from day to day," Grinnell suggested in June. The first installment of "In the Lodges of the Blackfeet" ran in *Forest and Stream* in November, not under the byline James Willard Schultz or even under his Indian name, Appekunny, but under a pseudonym, Walter B. Anderson. "I would not allow his name to be signed to the stuff because his reputation is so villainous," Grinnell told Gould, even while vouching that "his present series is the best thing that he has ever turned out." To Jack Monroe he confided: "I have a certain pity for Schultz, much as I might have for an idiot or a criminal."

As ever, Schultz was his own worst enemy. In December he drank himself into the hospital before he had completed the memoir. "Of course, you are coming to a point now where, if you keep on drinking, you come more or less soon to the end of your tether and will go to the Sand Hills," Grinnell admonished, referring to the Indian afterworld. Grinnell's sympathy was born of self-interest. In the same letter that included ninety dollars to help with Schultz's medical bills, he cautioned: "[I]f the manuscript is not finished, it is of little value to us." To have the *Forest and Stream* series end prematurely would be an embarrassment to both editor and author. On the other hand, Grinnell exhorted, if Schultz could stay sober long enough to carry the project to conclusion, "it will go far toward rehabilitating you."

Somehow Schultz pulled himself together and completed the task, though the final, whiskey-soaked chapters were unreadable and had to be sent back for revision. The thirty-fourth and final installment appeared in *Forest and Stream* on July 21, 1906. By then Schultz had sought refuge at a school for Pima Indians in Arizona, deeper in debt than ever. Prudently Grinnell had paid him only incrementally. "I got tired of being used as a bank and told him that I would send him no more money except as he earned it," he explained.

In the end Grinnell paid Schultz $500 for "In the Lodges of the Blackfeet." More generously, he persuaded Doubleday, Page & Company to publish the series under the title, *My Life as an Indian: The Story of a Red Woman and a White Man in the Lodges of the Blackfeet*, and bearing the author's real name, J. W. Schultz. He also blessed the book in a one-page foreword: "It is a study of human nature in red. The author has penetrated the veil of racial indifference and misunderstanding and has got close to the heart of the people. . . . Such an intimate revelation of the domestic life of the Indians has never been written."

Publication of *My Life as an Indian* did more than merely rehabilitate Schultz. It made him famous and extended his writing life another forty years. Between 1907 and his burial on the Blackfeet reservation in 1947, Schultz published scores of stories in *Youth's Companion, American Boy,* and *Boy's Life,* many of which were bundled into books. *My Life as an Indian* is still in print. Never mind that Schultz's stories played loose with historical and autobiographical fact; generations of boys, held captive by civilization in the towns and cities of modern America, took to James Willard Schultz with much the same enthusiasm that Grinnell and Theodore Roosevelt had for Mayne Reid. Grinnell's Jack books sold well enough— better than any of his other books—but they would never be as popular as Schultz's stories. And for all Grinnell's deprecations of Schultz's untrustworthiness and dissipation, it must be said that, of all the writers whose work appeared in *Forest and Stream,* James Willard Schultz was its greatest success. "Good books about the American Indian are few, particularly those which make it possible to see him as a human being," J. Donald Adams, editor of the *New York Times Book Review,* pronounced in 1945. "One of the best is . . . *My Life as an Indian.*"

Another character whom Grinnell found himself relying on more and more was John J. White, Jr. The friendship between the Grinnells and the Whites had been cemented during their 1903 trip to Montana and the ascent of Chief Mountain. Since then, Jay White had put himself at Grinnell's virtual beck and call. In early 1905 he made two more research trips to Oklahoma on Grinnell's behalf.

Upon returning from the second, White and his wife repaired to their house at Bar Harbor, Maine. Elizabeth Grinnell accepted an invitation to

join them there in August, while Grinnell stayed home. When both couples were in New York, the Whites came to dinner at Audubon Park, and
the Grinnells dined at the Whites' sumptuous townhouse at 103 East Fifty-
Seventh Street. In the summer of 1906 the Whites begged the Grinnells to
join them in Europe. Elizabeth was excited by the prospect of her first trip
abroad, but Grinnell demurred. West was the only direction he ever looked.

In a letter to Indian Commissioner Francis Leupp, Grinnell testified, "I
have known Mr. White for a long time, and he is an honorable and excellent man." Yet there were some things about White that Grinnell preferred
not to dwell upon. For one, he was compulsively peripatetic, always on the
move—New York, Bar Harbor, Europe, Montana, Oklahoma, and eventually Africa. "He is a very nice fellow but suffers woefully because he has
no occupation," Grinnell told Jack Monroe. "I sometimes fear that if he
keeps up this do-nothing business for a few years longer, he will become an
invalid." Grinnell knew plenty of wealthy people, but White seemed to be
too rich for his own good.

Grinnell's concern was born out a year later. On September 19, 1907,
White was at home on Fifty-Seventh Street, sick in bed from "nervous pros-
tration," according to newspaper accounts. Margaret Carter, described as a
"French widow," knocked at his door and insisted that she be allowed in to
see White; she carried with her a small package that she wished to give to
him in person. Grace White was away in Bar Harbor.

White's physician, Dr. G. V. Foster, would tell the authorities that he
(the doctor) had been summoned to the White house by a phone call from
Mrs. Carter, saying that White was having another one of his "spells."
When the doctor got there, he found Mrs. Carter at Jay White's bedside.
An hour later White's nurse, a Mr. Cleeland (the *Tribune* spelled it Clel-
land), arrived; he told a conflicting story to the coroner, insisting that Mrs.
Carter had *not* been admitted to White's bedroom and that it was he who
had summoned Dr. Foster. Both Cleeland and Foster, however, agreed that
Mrs. Carter was highly agitated. Eventually they succeeded in showing her
to an adjacent room, where they coaxed her to lie down, still in her over-
coat. Mrs. Carter remained there until early the following morning, when
the nurse was startled by a gunshot. He rushed in, found her dead, a bullet
hole in her temple, a .22 revolver at her side. The package Mrs. Carter was

carrying revealed a $100 Treasury note and a pair of cuff links—*whose* cuff links it was not clear.

Jay White was deemed too ill to answer questions from the police or the coroner, but Grace White, who arrived back in New York later that day, was cooperative. She said that she had met Mrs. Carter some years earlier when both were engaged in "missionary" work. The *New York Times* noted that Mrs. Carter "took pleasure in feeding and petting the tramp dogs of the street" and had installed a drinking fountain for horses on Wall Street. Grace also revealed that she and her husband had helped Mrs. Carter financially from time to time; and on previous occasions when Grace was out of town, Mrs. Carter had "waited upon" Jay.

Asked if Mrs. Carter had contemplated suicide before, Grace said that the woman had been "slightly demented" for some time. And when asked bluntly, "Was there any strong affection between Mr. White and Mrs. Carter?" Grace answered, "Oh, no; she was just his good friend, just as she was mine."

The incident made the front page of several New York newspapers, but like many such scandals involving members of polite society, it was soon swept under the carpet. The *Tribune* observed that John J. White, Jr., had "no particular business . . . and is reported to be very wealthy."

The Grinnells were out West at the time, but they surely gleaned the details when they got home. It would have been indelicate for them to bring up the subject in conversation with the Whites—much less to broach it in a letter. But from then on, the intimacy that had developed between the two couples cooled. Grinnell would remain in close contact with Jay White, and Elizabeth with Grace White. But talk of further adventures together ceased. Indeed, after the events of September 1907 the Whites seemed rarely to spend much time with each other. Soon they would rent their New York house and move to Washington.

Grinnell and Elizabeth endured their own travails that year. In June 1906 Elizabeth suffered what Grinnell described to Ned Dana as "a sharp attack of illness." Again he did not spell out her symptoms, but her doctor thought it best that she take a rest cure at a quiet inn in Gloucester, Massachusetts, accompanied by a nurse. She was well enough to return home after a month, but, as Grinnell updated Dana, "She is now not especially robust."

For the cause of her condition, she needed look no farther than her family. In February Elizabeth had gone to St. Louis to be with her mother while brother Frank was examined by a specialist in nervous disorders. Once more Grinnell footed the bill. Afterward Delle Curtis and Frank returned to the farm in Glenville, New York, where Delle's two brothers lived. Throughout the spring Grinnell and Elizabeth looked around New Jersey and the Hudson Valley for a few acres on which Frank could make a cautious start at farming on his own. "This is less a business matter than a matter of health," Grinnell wrote to one prospective landlord. He and Elizabeth cast the net wide but could not find a suitable place. The search and the uncertain future of her relatives took a toll on her own nerves.

Grinnell had suffered as well. "I have been sick for a number of weeks with a bad pain in my eyes which makes me blind," he wrote George Bent in May. Still, he refused to slow down. "As I grow older, I have more and more work to do and less time to do it in," he told Jack Monroe." He agreed to tackle a fourth Jack book, drawing from the notes and memories of trips he had taken to the Pacific Northwest in 1881 and 1888.

In September, once Elizabeth had completed her rest cure, Grinnell and she went once again to the Northern Cheyennes, filling more notebooks and taking more photographs. Afterward they went on to the Blackfeet reservation, where allotment was finally coming to a head. Grinnell continued to oppose allotment in principle, and for the Piegans in particular. "I regard allotment as the greatest misfortune that can come to the Indians, and an absolute bar to their progress toward civilization," he wrote to Mrs. Doubleday, his Sequoya League confederate. On reservations where land had already been allotted, Indians "have been permitted to lease their lands [to whites] and from payday to payday [they] live in lodges in the old fashion, not working and not improving but instead continually sinking a little lower in helplessness and inefficiency."

He persisted in his pessimistic view that, even if the Piegans were obligated to live on the land allotted them, they could not make a living by farming on small tracts. "The Blackfeet Reservation is dry, cold and snowy," Grinnell lectured Montana Congressman Joseph M. Dixon, who was pushing an allotment bill. "The annual precipitation is about 20 inches, of which 12 inches comes from melted snow. . . . The reservation consists of high plateaus formed of glacial drift, land that is fit only for the growing of wild grasses on the prairie." Potatoes, he explained, did not yield a crop more than once in five years, and oats seldom ripened.

In the treaty to purchase the Ceded Strip, signed by the Piegans in 1895 and ratified by Congress in 1896, Grinnell had made sure that it included an article stipulating: "Since the situation of the Blackfeet Reservation renders it wholly unfit for agriculture . . . it is agreed that, during the existence of this agreement, no allotments of land in severalty shall be made to them, but that this whole Reservation shall continue to be held by these Indians as a communal grazing tract, upon which their herds may be fed undisturbed; and that after the expiration of this agreement, the land shall continue to be so held until such time as a majority of the adult males of the tribes shall request in writing that allotment in severalty shall be made of their lands."

But the stipulation that the land could not be divided without a vote of the tribe had been undercut by the 1903 *Lone Wolf v. Hitchcock* decision, in which the Supreme Court, in ruling on a case involving allotment of the Kiowa, Comanche, and Kiowa Apache reservation in Oklahoma, determined that Congress had "plenary authority over the tribal relations of the Indians." In effect the courts gave the government permission to ignore existing treaties and do as it wished—with regard to allotment and anything else.

With or without *Lone Wolf*, the ten years of payments on the Ceded Strip treaty were nearly up, and Montana's congressional delegation, pushed by Montana cattlemen, was eager to take the next step. Many, perhaps a majority, of the Piegans seemed inclined to comply, not so they could become yeoman farmers, but rather, as Grinnell had warned, so they could turn around and lease their allotted land to whites.

Grinnell lobbied hard to get the best possible terms for the Piegans. He pressed Congressman Dixon, Montana senator Thomas Carter, and Indian Commissioner Leupp to give 640 acres to each individual, knowing this was a pipe dream. They countered with a proposal that allotted either 320 acres of grazing land per individual or 80 acres of irrigable farming land. "I think that the people have got all that they could have hoped for and ought to congratulate themselves," Grinnell wrote Jack Monroe, "just as they ought to have congratulated themselves on the good price that they got for the strip of mountain territory that was bought in 1895."

In June 1906 the Blackfeet allotment passed both houses of Congress and moved to the president's desk. Grinnell knew better than to protest allotment per se, well recalling Roosevelt's nationalistic belief in the 1887 act as "the mighty pulverizing engine to break up the tribal mass." Instead he alerted Roosevelt to the question of unresolved water rights; the courts had yet to uphold claims of surrounding white ranchers who wished to siphon off the best streams before they could be channeled to Indian ground. Roosevelt vetoed the allotment bill. Here the matter stood when Grinnell and Elizabeth arrived in Browning in September. Allotment was coming; precisely when was still up in the air.

Not coincidentally, as Congress, cattlemen, and Indians all anticipated the "opening up" of the Blackfeet reservation and the land rush that would likely ensue, Grinnell's thoughts turned to a subject dearer to him than almost any other: the Ceded Strip and the adjoining mountains, forest, and lakes to the west of the Continental Divide. "I am inclined to think that it might be possible to get a bill setting aside this tract as a national park introduced by Congress," he wrote to François Matthes, topographer for the U.S. Geological Survey. "The region's chief value, so far as I know, is that of a great storage reservoir." Water, he understood, was a wedge in nearly all policy decisions in the West.

Writing a few days later to Roswell Lawrence of the influential Appalachian Club of Boston, he took a slightly different angle: "I have written more or less about the region and 12 or 15 years ago suggested that it ought to be set aside as a National Park. It contains some of the most wonderful scenery in the world and a great number of glaciers and is the natural home of many wild animals. . . . Does the Appalachian Club care to lend its influence to support such a bill if it is introduced?"

This was a form of allotment he believed in wholeheartedly. Matthes, the topographer, responded to Grinnell, suggesting approximate boundaries for the refuge under consideration. "The Park proposed would contain roughly 1500 sq. miles, containing upward of 50 ice-bodies and over 200 lakes," he said. "It might fitly be called Glacier National Park."

On the Blackfeet reservation in September 1906, allotment was upstaged by a more immediate disruption. The U.S. Reclamation Service had begun digging a thirty-mile-long canal from Swiftcurrent Creek, a tributary of the St. Mary River, to the Milk River. The St. Mary flowed from the mountains into Canada; the Milk likewise flowed into Canada but then had the good manners to turn south and empty into the Missouri. If water could be rerouted from the St. Mary to the Milk, more of it could be used to irrigate farms and ranches in northern Montana, after giving the Canadians their fair share, of course. Indians would also be beneficiaries—not just in water but in wages earned digging the canal.

When Grinnell and Elizabeth arrived, they learned that the Piegan workers had gone on strike, demanding fifty cents more a day to wages that ranged from $1.50 for scraper holders to $3 for men with teams of horses. Grinnell rode immediately to the work camp and addressed the ditch crew. "I preached to them somewhat in the old-time fashion, telling them to go to work and stay with their job, or, if they did not, they would lose it entirely," he later related to James Willard Schultz. The canal's chief engineer, Cyrus Babb, came in and, needing little persuasion, granted the raise. "As the meeting broke up, the men rushed out cheering and ran to the pile of scrapers and began to drag them away," Grinnell wrote in his diary. "It was pathetic and delightful."

Grinnell had worried that his influence among the Piegans had waned—due to the death of White Calf and other tribal leaders who had once lived freely and independently and to the rise of a younger generation born to annuities and immobility. He came away from this impromptu council with his confidence revived. "I regarded it as quite 'Providential' that I should have been on the ground at the very moment when the trouble came," he told Francis Leupp.

From the work camp Grinnell and Elizabeth, with Jack Monroe, proceeded to the St. Mary Lakes. The season was right for ducks, and in his diary Grinnell noted that Elizabeth shot a gadwall on the wing. She also had good luck fishing, landing several handsome cutthroat trout. Then the weather worsened and so did Elizabeth's health. Grinnell later joked to Jack Monroe that she had merely foundered from eating too many of his flapjacks, yet she felt badly enough that Grinnell agreed to cut the trip short.

They returned home via Canada, stopping briefly on the Blood reserve in Alberta, and arrived in New York at the end of October. They found conditions at Audubon Park only slightly more comfortable; construction on Riverside Drive had damaged the gas line to the house, and for several evenings they were obliged to feel their way around the house in the dark.

At the *Forest and Stream* office, calm was in short supply as well. Managing editor Charles Reynolds, who had been with Grinnell since the beginning, announced his retirement at the first of December. "To his newspaper work," Grinnell wrote in an appreciation, "Mr. Reynolds brought qualifications seldom united in one man: rare literary taste and judgment, keen intelligence, wise foresight, devotion to the right, and unflinching courage."

With Reynolds now decamping for Florida and Edward Wilbur dead, the weight on Grinnell's shoulders was greater than it had ever been in the twenty-six years since he and his father had bought *Forest and Stream*. To Ned Dana he described the departure of Reynolds as "a great misfortune. . . . I feel quite lost without him."

Elizabeth's family was another problem that grew more vexing. Delle Curtis had finally gone too far in her entreaties for support. Two days after Christmas Grinnell wrote her a letter devoid of holiday spirit. "I am unable to supply the large sum of money required for such an investment," he stated coldly. Perhaps she had asked him to buy the Curtis farm in Glenville. "I am now doing all that I can," he insisted. "It is my purpose to continue, so long as I can do so, to supply you with funds at the rate of $1,000 a year. I should prefer to send you a check on the first of each month."

And then his tone grew chillier still. "I must ask you hereafter not to write depressing letters to Elizabeth. Her physical condition is such that she

is very easily upset, and when troubled or excited by the receipt of a complaining letter from you, or by a disagreeable interview, it takes her a long
time to recover. I beg you to keep this matter in mind and to avoid commu-
nicating with her on matters that trouble her."

By March Elizabeth was feeling so poorly that her doctor again recommended a change of scenery, preferably a sea voyage abroad. Grinnell had
disappointed her by not agreeing to the European trip with the Whites a
year earlier; this time he was amenable. He reserved a stateroom on the
La Lorraine to leave New York on April 4, destination France. His only
previous trip to Europe had been with his mother while he was still at
Yale, thirty-eight years earlier. He made it clear that he was going strictly
for Elizabeth's health and with no desire to partake of the *beau monde*. "In
Paris my purpose is to go to some small French hotel and to shun the big
caravansaries where Americans and English gather together," he informed
Jay White, who was en route to Africa on safari.

To George Gould he explained, "There was no one else to take her."

They were gone seven weeks. Grudgingly he admitted that he enjoyed
himself and that the change did both of them good. "Mrs. Grinnell is very
much better than she was," he told Jack Monroe, "and, as for me, I gained
twelve pounds in weight. Nothing to do and plenty to eat for two months
fixed me up in great shape."

He saved his most amusing account of the trip for the Piegan chief Little Plume—part field note, part children's story: "Pita ke"—Elizabeth's Piegan name, translated as Medicine Bear Woman—"was sick and the doctors
said that the best thing for her to do was to take a long trip on a big boat, so
I took her across the salt water. We were going seven days in a boat that went
about as fast as a railroad train and at last we reached the country on the
other side of the salt water and landed. [W]e saw many strange things. . . .
In [France], for example, many men and women wear shoes cut out of
blocks of wood. They are pretty heavy, and they make a loud noise as one
walks along the stones. If you had a pair of shoes like that one, you never
could creep up close to your enemy."

Before sailing for Europe Grinnell had hastily written the next Jack book—
Jack the Young Trapper. Lessons in the strenuous life and the theme of para-
dise lost are much the same as in the previous Jack tales, this one set in the
Shirley Basin of Wyoming and the mountains of northern Colorado, where
Grinnell had roamed and hunted in 1879.

And as he was completing this Jack installment, Grinnell's Cheyenne
book took an unexpected turn. George Bent had written out various Indian
stories at Grinnell's request, and Jay White's interviews had also advanced
the research—although White and Bent had gotten along none too cordially. Writing to Grinnell during his visit to Oklahoma in November 1905,
White called Bent "too d[amne]d lazy. . . . I would like to knock him on the
head with an axe."

Yet Bent had not been lazy at all. He had begun collaborating with an
unassuming but rather determined amateur historian from Omaha named
George Hyde.

Hyde's eyes had been opened to Indians when he visited the Indian Congress at the Trans-Mississippi Exposition of 1898, at the age of sixteen. His
fixation only increased after he was struck deaf and almost blind by scarlet
fever. From then on, his avenues of inquiry into Indian life and history were
through the books and articles he found in the Omaha public library—
which he absorbed painstakingly with the aid of a magnifying glass—and
through correspondences with anyone he could locate with interests similar to his. He and George Bent began exchanging letters in 1904, and by
1905 Hyde had edited several of Bent's letters into a series of articles titled
"Forty Years with the Cheyennes," published in an obscure, short-lived Colorado journal. What is more, Hyde agreed to help Bent shape these and
other letters into a proper book.

Despite his remarkable self-motivation and self-education, George
Hyde was unable to carry the job to fruition. He was poor, virtually house-
bound, and without contacts in the greater publishing world—that is, until
he sought aid from Grinnell in late 1906. Protective of his own franchise,
Grinnell responded coyly to Hyde's inquiry: "It would be impossible to
say, without looking at the manuscript, what, if anything, could be done

with the Bent matter. I should suppose that possibly there might be in it a great deal that is interesting, and yet I have very little notion that the Forest and Stream [Publishing Company] would want to print the whole matter as a book."

Then, less candidly and more cunningly—without disclosing the Bent stories he himself had already acquired and making no effort to explain that he was the final arbiter for all Forest and Stream acquisitions—Grinnell said: "You understand, of course, that these things are commercial propositions, and while all Bent's writings would be of great interest to me personally, the Forest and Stream would look at the whole matter from a cold-blooded point of view as to whether they would get their money back." He invited Hyde to send the manuscript and promised to "have it looked over and pronounced upon as soon as possible."

Hyde mailed the first few chapters, leading Grinnell to write George Bent: "I am sure the story as you have written it is true, but our people here seem to think it would not do to print in Forest and Stream. . . . I want to look it over again, and then I may send it back to Mr. Hyde."

In July 1907, six months after receiving the manuscript, he finally returned it, dashing Hyde's hopes without snuffing them out entirely: "I do not clearly see any way for getting Bent's book published. I feel pretty sure that no one would tackle it in its present shape as a commercial venture. What [ought] to be done, if one had the time, would be to get hold of Bent, take the stuff up chapter by chapter and get him to fill in outlines and give details which would give some life to the story he has told. At present it is about as dull as anything can be."

Grinnell's assumption was that Hyde was not up to the task and thus would defer to him. "I think you wrote me once that you were quite deaf. . . . Am I right in inferring that it is difficult or impossible for you to talk with people on account of your infirmity?"

At least at first Grinnell honestly felt that the Bent memoir had a legitimate chance to stand on its own—as he had once wished for Schultz's Blackfeet tales. For more than thirty years he had been recasting other people's stories, in books and in the pages of Forest and Stream. He had tried (and, for the time being, had failed) to do this with Frank North's memoir. In 1905 Forest and Stream Publishing had dressed up My Sixty

Years on the Plains, the autobiography of wild and woolly Montana fron-
tiersman W. T. Hamilton (with illustrations by "Cowboy Artist" Charles M.
Russell). A year later Grinnell turned his hand even more deftly to Schultz's
My Life as an Indian.

Yet, in the event that the Bent-Hyde collaboration could not be salvaged,
Grinnell had other designs on it. With the consent and cooperation of its
unpolished author and handicapped editor, he would splice their work into
his own. He wrote both men, promising that he would make a trip to Oklahoma the coming summer. In the meantime, he allowed that he might like
to read Bent's letters to Hyde. "I certainly would not ask you to retype them
for me," he assured Hyde. "I know Bent's hand well." On second thought,
he wrote later, he wouldn't mind if Hyde retyped the letters. Hyde, who
had nowhere else to turn, sent the letters, typed, along with a sheaf of other
material he had gathered over the previous three years.

Grinnell had been chipping away at his own Cheyenne research for
more than fifteen years, revising and expanding his manuscript, and he had
grown understandably fatigued by the slow trek into a realm whose boundaries, ethnographically speaking, seemed to have no limit. And like the
Bent-Hyde manuscript, Grinnell's book had been rejected by publishers.
But now, with the Bent-Hyde trove before him, he was reinvigorated and
newly inspired. "My idea, after looking over this narrative again and the
notes which Mr. Hyde has gathered would be to attempt something much
more ambitious than a mere story about George Bent," he shared with Jay
White. "I should like to attempt a war history of the Cheyenne, running
from about 1830 to 1880." He outlined the high points in rapid fire, from
intertribal battles with the Pawnees onward through Sand Creek, Little
Bighorn, and the flight and recapture of Dull Knife and Little Wolf.

The big Cheyenne book, his *grand oeuvre*, could wait. First he would
write a book of action, valor, and victory, culminating in proud surrender.
"[I] want to tell the story so that those who read the book can see the Indians riding around and shooting, and the soldiers charging, just as if they
were looking at a picture," he told Bent. In other words, plenty of blood
and thunder.

In the months that followed, Hyde began supplying bits of research and
revisions to fill in the blanks in the Bent narrative. "There is no reason

why I should not reimburse you for the time you have taken," Grinnell wrote Hyde, enclosing a check for sixteen dollars. Like George Bent before, George Hyde was now on the payroll.

In May 1908 Grinnell and Elizabeth went to Colony, Oklahoma, and spent three weeks with Bent. For the first time he took with him a stenographer, a Miss Farley, so that he could better concentrate on his interviews. Before leaving New York he had written Bent, asking him to arrange lodging other than the tent that Jay White had occupied on his visits. He also alerted his host, "Mrs. Grinnell and I can eat almost anything, but my stenographer is new to the west, and she might not like dog."

At the end of August the Grinnells went west again, this time to the Northern Cheyenne reservation. Of the scores of notebooks Grinnell filled over more than fifty years of western travel—hundreds of interviews—none is more exemplary of his acuity and diligence than the leather-bound diary of September 1908. It is certainly one of the most carefully studied by scholars of the Indian wars, for, rather than allowing his interviewees to ramble from subject to subject—from ancient rituals to current complaints—Grinnell held men like John Two Moon (nephew of "Old" Two Moon), Black White Man, Little Hawk, White Shield, and Bobtail Horse to linear, chronological recollections of the fights in which they had participated. Grinnell had applied similar rigor in the past, but never before had he born down so conscientiously in fleshing out the "war history."

For example, here, as transcribed by Grinnell, is John Two Moon's account of the army's attack on Dull Knife's camp on the Red Fork of the Powder River in November 1876 (in which Lute North may or may not have killed Dull Knife's son):

"He mounted his horse and rode down through the center of the camp. The shooting was quick. He did not quite reach his friend Crow Necklace but saw him dressed in a w[ar] b[onnet] and riding a pinto horse. C[row] N[ecklace] rode across on the s[outh] side of camp & T[wo] M[oon] turned and went on [the] n[orth] side. He was dressed in a w[ar] b[onnet] whose tails reached the ground. . . . He charged across the camp to the s[outh] side, and as he reached the gulch where most of the people had gone up, he saw none of the people. He was ahead of the soldiers who were coming in file toward the camp. He kept on up the gulch and at a little knoll he overtook three men, One Stump [perhaps Stump Horn], Redwing Woodpecker and Split Eye. Another man overtook them (Brave Bear). There they dismounted. . . . Way back the soldiers had now fallen in line, the gray horse co[mpany] in center, charging toward the camp at a lope. Another company was marching toward the knoll where these 5 men were and firing at them. The gray horse co[mpany] hit the mouth of [the] gulch up which [the] people had gone and the C[heyennes] who were in it then fired at them. A soldier fell from his horse. Two C[heyenne] men jumped out from the gulch and took his gun and belt. The co[mpany] fell back and dismounted and began to fire into the gulch as fast as they could shoot. The deep gulch ran up to the hill and opened out to a wide flat. The gray horse company stood at the mouth of [the] gulch while the black horse co[mpany] watched the flat above. T[wo] M[oon] thought, 'My friends are in a very bad place. They will all be killed, I fear.' Yellow Nose was the only man on horseback in this deep gulch. He went up on the flat to the top and turned his horse s[outh] and came out just above where the five men were. When he came to the top of the hill, 3 of the 5 joined him & T[wo] M[oon] and Brave Bear charged down toward the soldiers."

And on and on, breathlessly and vividly, the recollection continued for several more pages in Grinnell's strong hand, the Cheyennes fighting bravely and paying dearly.

The climax of Grinnell's trip was a visit to the Little Bighorn battlefield, accompanied by Bobtail Horse and several other Cheyennes who had defended themselves against the attack of the U.S. Cavalry thirty-two years earlier. Unlike the withering heat of June 25, 1876, the weather on September 27, 1908, was a mixture of rain and snow, and the road from the Cheyenne agency at Lame Deer forty-four miles west to the battlefield, was relentless, wheel-locking gumbo.

"'It was not long before noon when I first saw Custer,'" Bobtail Horse recalled. "'The night before, [the Cheyennes] had had a war dance and danced all night, and I was sleeping when the rest of the people set out to fight Reno.' After he"—Grinnell's notes switch to the third person—"had mounted his horse and prepared to go to Reno, he looked up toward the hills and saw a body of soldiers coming down a little dry cr[eek]; not in it, but following down by it. He struck across to meet these soldiers and 4 C[heyennes] joined him."

Still more Indians met the charge, and the soldiers turned and retreated up the hillside. Here one can imagine Grinnell's guides pointing across the dormant landscape to the very route described.

"By the time the [soldiers] reached [the] hill beyond [the] steep gulch, they stopped and fought hard, but now there were many more Ind[ian]s in front of them. All at once sold[iers] turned and ran . . . and then the Ind[ian]s all ch[arge]d. He went too but the dust was so thick they could not see soldiers or each other. . . .

"All at once the Ind[ian]s gave a loud shout and charged up the ridge. The sold[iers] backed away . . . and the fight did not last long enough thereafter to fill a pipe."

By then, Grinnell and his eyewitnesses would have climbed to the granite obelisk marking the spot where Custer and his men had perished. The fingers holding his pencil would have been nearly numb, and the raw wind would have made it difficult for him to keep his own pipe going.

Grinnell arrived back in New York in time to vote in the November election. He was going to miss Theodore Roosevelt, who announced that he would embark on an African safari after leaving office. Roosevelt and Grinnell were never knockabout chums—there is no record of them riding or hunting together even once—but they knew each other's mind and shouldered the same wheel. They had not quite succeeded in turning national forests into game refuges, but the five national parks, eighteen national monuments (courtesy of the Antiquities Act), four national game preserves, fifty-one bird sanctuaries, and 150 national forests—a total of 230 million acres in federal land—that Roosevelt consecrated during his seven years in the White House exceeded the wildest expectations of all reasonable preservationists. Not the most momentous of these, but a satisfaction nonetheless, was the 18,000-acre National Bison Range in Montana, signed into law by Roosevelt in May, the result of a campaign initiated by Grinnell, *Forest and Stream*, and the Boone and Crockett Club, and, more recently by the American Bison Society, to save the North American buffalo from extinction.

Grinnell voted enthusiastically for Roosevelt's anointed successor, Secretary of War William Howard Taft (Yale, class of 1878), but like most Roosevelt men, he anticipated that the passed torch would burn less hotly. "It is, in my opinion, an entire mistake to think that Taft is the same kind of man as Roosevelt," Grinnell wrote to Lute North, "or that Taft is going to manage the country in the same way that Roosevelt has." On the other hand, he continued with reefed optimism, "Taft is a level-headed, quiet man, of judicial mind, who thinks a long time before he speaks. If the Roosevelt policies are continued under Taft, you can be sure that the good that is in them will be retained and the bad rejected, and whatever is done will not be done with a brass band."

In particular, Grinnell was counting on Taft's support for another of his causes that had been gestating for many years: Glacier National Park. A bill to establish the park had been introduced a year earlier but thus far had made little headway.

Glacier had another champion in Louis W. Hill, who in 1907 succeeded his father as president of the Great Northern Railway. In its route from St. Paul to the Pacific, the railroad passed through the Blackfeet reservation and ran along the southern boundary of the envisioned national park. The elder Hill had understood that railroads thrived on industry, mining, logging, and agriculture. Son Louis, who might have been an artist if he had not attended Yale's Sheffield Scientific School and been raised under his father's firm thumb, had a love of nature and grasped its attraction to a growing population of travelers. As a young boy he had toured Yellowstone, reached by the Northern Pacific Railway. He pictured Glacier as the Great Northern's Yellowstone, or the Santa Fe Railway's Grand Canyon.

Curiously, there is no extant correspondence between Louis Hill and George Bird Grinnell in which a national park is discussed. Yet assuredly each was aware of the other's efforts. Many years later Grinnell would state, "Important men in control of the Great Northern Railroad were made to see the possibilities of the region." Hill, who played a vital role in the Montana economy, had influence with Montana's two senators, Thomas Carter and

Clinton Hart Merriam.

Chief American Horse, Sioux.
PHOTOGRAPH BY FRANK RINEHART.

Edward S. Curtis, self-portrait.

White Calf—Piegan.
PHOTOGRAPH BY EDWARD S. CURTIS.

The Three Chiefs
(Piegan).
PHOTOGRAPH BY
EDWARD S.
CURTIS.

George Bird and Elizabeth Grinnell,
shooting in the Adirondacks.

George Bird and Elizabeth Grinnell on
Grinnell Glacier, 1925.

Honeymoon camp, Chief Mountain, 1902.
PHOTOGRAPH BY ELIZABETH GRINNELL.

Grinnell with Northern Cheyennes, Lame Deer, Montana.

Grinnell with Two Moon, Lame Deer, Montana.

Little Wolf (left) and Dull Knife.

Northern Cheyenne woman. PHOTOGRAPH BY ELIZABETH GRINNELL.

George Bent.

Charles F. Lummis.

Hamlin Garland.

George Shiras III, whom *National Geographic* called
"the father of wildlife photography."

Charles Sheldon.

John Bird Burnham.

William T. Hornaday.

Stephen Mather.

Gifford Pinchot.

John F. Lacey.

eorge Vest.

Grinnell (left) on Grinnell Glacier, with Mount Grinnell beyond, 1926.

Grinnell and Lute North, Little Bighorn, Montana, 1926.

Thomas Elwood "Billy" Hofer.

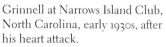

Grinnell at Narrows Island Club,
North Carolina, early 1930s, after
his heart attack.

newly elected Joseph Dixon, and Dixon's successor in Congress, Charles Pray. Hill's clout at least equaled that of the timber and mining men who did not care to see more land, federal or private, set aside as scenery.

Throughout 1908 Grinnell did his part. He wrote to Senator Carter, urging him to usher the bill to a vote. He had the Boone and Crockett Club pass a resolution supporting the park legislation. He also turned the next Jack book into an extended paean to the wonders of a country he had been visiting for more than thirty years.

Jack and his old trail mate, Hugh Johnson, set off to explore the mountains above the St. Mary and Swiftcurrent lakes, along the way noting that "Indians of the plains never tried to pass beneath these gloomy walls." Jack and Hugh predict that the Piegans will eventually be "crowded out of the most of this country by the white folks." Pity, Jack remarks, because "these Indians are so kindly and generous and hospitable that I feel a personal sympathy for each one of them that, of course, I don't feel for the inefficient people back east."

Jack and Hugh surmise that they are two of the very first white men in these mountains, and they hunt to their hearts' content. They shoot sheep, goats, and a wolverine. Jack also shoots a bear (grizzly or black not specified), explaining to Hugh, "'He looked so handsome standing there on the hillside that I couldn't help taking a shot at him.'" He delights in the bird life, identifying harlequin ducks, gray jays, Steller's jays, three-toed woodpeckers, juncos, and one of Grinnell's favorites, the water ouzel.

Jack grows rapturous as he reaches the headwall above the last of the Swiftcurrent lakes, a scene that "was perhaps the grandest and most beautiful that Jack had ever beheld." Observing the rubble at the foot of the glacier, Hugh comments, "'I expect if no more snow fell up here this piece of ice would just melt away and leave nothing but the hole that it's laying in.'"

Grinnell ends *Jack the Young Explorer* with an elegiac afterword. "There is a wonderful fascination in penetrating a new country, in placing one's foot where perhaps the foot of civilized man never trod before," he writes. "A century ago there were many such places in the United States, fifty years ago there were still not a few, twenty-five years ago there were hardly any, and it is no wonder that Hugh and Jack wished to explore these valleys and the mountains that walled them in."

Grinnell's postscript moves ahead to the present day and describes Senator Carter's bill to create Glacier National Park. The Carter bill had not passed by the time that Grinnell wrote *Jack the Young Explorer*; nor had it passed by the time the book was published in the fall of 1908. The best Grinnell could do was wish it Godspeed. "If the measure shall become law," he writes hopefully on the book's final page, "this most beautiful country, with its wonderful glaciers, its rushing rivers, its broad forests and its abundant game supply, may remain forever as a pleasure resort and playground for the benefit of the whole people of the United States. Valuable as it will be in this respect, its economic worth to the United States will be not less great. It will be a mighty reservoir, from which for ages an unfailing supply of water may be drawn to give drink to those thirsty plains, which need only moisture to yield a generous return to the farmer."

At the end of November, Audubon Park was sold. The Grinnells had anticipated this day for quite some time and had been selling off parcels of the original estate even before formation of the Lansing Corporation. Apartment buildings and row houses now encircled it, and Riverside Drive, which would not be completed until 1910, bisected it. In 1904 Archer M. Huntington, the only son of Collis P. Huntington, whose Central Pacific Railroad had made him one of the wealthiest men in America, had purchased the section of Audubon Park between 155th and 156th streets, west of Broadway; there he constructed the Hispanic Society of America to house his extraordinary collection of Spanish and Portuguese art and literature. Huntington also donated land on 155th Street for construction of the American Numismatic Society.

The New York *Real Estate Record and Builders Guide* reported that the Audubon Park sale comprised some eighty-three lots. The purchase price mentioned was $1.5 million. The new owners were Adolph M. Bendheim, Sonn Bros., and Max Marx. "You will be sorry to learn that the old place at Audubon Park, where I lived pretty nearly all my life, has been sold," Grinnell wrote Lute North two days before Christmas. "The Jews have got it, and shortly the place will be, I suppose, covered with apartment houses.

I have no idea where I shall go to but must soon begin the melancholy task of house hunting."

In sharing the news with George Gould, Grinnell's tone was even more forlorn. "Since writing you last, I have suffered a misfortune which I never weary of lamenting," his New Year's greeting began. "I had cherished the hope that before the time for moving out had come, I should be reposing in Woodlawn [Cemetery]. Disappointment is the lot of man. If you should think of me during the next two or three months, imagine me climbing the stairs of 'walk-ups' and inspecting apartment after apartment, consisting of six rooms and a bath. We talk of liking to have space enough about us to swing a cat, but in most of the New York tenement houses, there is not room to swing a mouse."

STUYVESANT SQUARE

T he sale of Audubon Park did not take Grinnell by surprise. Yet, until it happened, he did not give much thought to where he and Elizabeth would go next. In a way, he was like the Indians he knew so well: For generations they had ranged seasonally, to hunt, to trade, to raid, but eventually they returned to the safety and familiarity of their home ground. To be pushed off one's land was more than an inconvenience; it was an affront to one's very identity. At least this was how Grinnell chose to frame his situation at the beginning of 1909. "I was turned out and became a wanderer on the face of the earth," he told Yale classmate Lewis Hicks. To George Bent, who knew a thing or two about rude eviction, he explained, "I . . . have been in great trouble because the old place where I have lived all my life has been sold, and I have to get out of it and find another place to live in. It is like pulling up an old tree by the roots and trying to plant it somewhere else."

The terms of the sale allowed the Grinnells to remain at the Hemlocks until the new owners were ready to develop the property. Sister Laura Martin and her family had already moved to East Thirty-Eighth Street, and the other sister, Helen Page, lived at Beaver Brook Farm in Milford, when she was not taking long trips abroad. Brother William was already long gone from Audubon Park and the family.

Grinnell complained about the encroachment of the clamorous city upon his boyhood idyll; however, when he began searching for a new address, the only direction he looked was deeper downtown. He considered a place on East Fifty-Seventh Street, near where the Whites used to live, but was put off by the price. Then in early February 1909 he found something that suited his needs and budget, even if it did not meet his every ideal of gentrified living.

The brick, vaguely Italianate townhouse at 238 East Fifteenth Street had been built for a ship chandler. It was four stories—five, counting the basement. Its front rooms faced Stuyvesant Square, just west of Second Avenue. Grinnell agreed to pay $48,500 to owner Edward Page, a textile merchant (no relation to Grinnell's brother-in-law). "I now think that I have found a place which is so much better than the average uptown New York house that I should be very well satisfied with it," he told Ned Dana. "It is down in a little forgotten corner of this big town, just on the edge of a pretty tough neighborhood and about a rifle shot from the abodes of the rich and the great who live on Washington Square."

Stuyvesant Square was no Audubon Park, yet its four blocks of flower-beds, shade trees, and fountains, surrounded by a cast-iron fence, provided decorous respite from the surrounding urban commotion. The square had been the gift of Peter Gerard Stuyvesant, great-great-grandson of the first director-general of the Dutch colony of New Netherlands. Its residents, despite Grinnell's joking remark that they hunkered in the shadow of the Bowery, were upstanding and well-to-do. Two doors down from the Grinnells, at 234 East Fifteenth, celebrated landscape painter William Merritt Chase lived with his wife and daughters. Across the street, on the west side of the park, was the Friends Meeting House and Seminary. One block farther north, on Sixteenth Street, stood St. George's Episcopal Church, where J. Pierpont Morgan, the wealthiest of America's wealthy, sat on the vestry. Its rector, the Reverend William S. Rainsford, was a renowned sportsman. As if the snugness of New York society needed better illustration, it so happened that Rainsford's recent book, *The Land of the Lion*, was dedicated to none other than John J. White, Jr., who had accompanied him on safari in 1908.

Grinnell spent most of the spring dividing up family furniture, shipping his horses and milk cow to the country, and preparing the new house for occupancy—papering, painting, repointing bricks, and wiring for electric lights. The only fixtures he took from the Hemlocks were two mantelpieces, "so that there will be there a little bit of the old house," he explained to niece Sylvia Page. With loving care he also packed up his collection of mounted heads, stuffed birds, and tanned animal skins; an assortment of Indian bows, beadwork, headdresses, parfleches, and baskets; several photographs by Edward S. Curtis; an original Double Elephant Folio edition of *Birds of America*, bound in red morocco; and his most prized possession, *The Eagle and the Lamb*, the oil painting bequeathed to him by Lucy Audubon.

In early June Grinnell, Elizabeth, and three servants spent their first night on Fifteenth Street—and just in the nick of time. "I have not been back [to Audubon Park] since the moving," Grinnell wrote Ned Dana a week later, "but I understand that all the old trees in which I used to climb as a small boy have been chopped down and that the . . . wrecking of the old house has begun. Of course I do not wish to go back there until the place is so changed that it is wholly unrecognizable."

It took them the rest of the summer to settle in. The kitchen, laundry, and furnace were located in the basement. Steep stairs from the street opened into a vestibule that in turn led to the first-floor parlor and dining room. On the second floor Grinnell built a library for himself. A letter from Grinnell to Steinway & Sons indicates that Elizabeth's old piano or perhaps a new one was delivered to Fifteenth Street.

"We are becoming more or less accustomed to life in the city, though we are still without many of life's comforts," he wrote Jack Nicholson at the end of July. "We have no light in the house and no cushions on the furniture, but at least we have a place to eat and sleep, shelves for our books. We have also a telephone, the number of which is Stuyvesant 2971."

He accomplished little else during the months of transition—not by his normal standards of prodigious productivity. For *Forest and Stream* he churned out a four-part reminiscence on goat and sheep hunting in British Columbia, using his old pen name, Ornis. He put the finishing touches on a history of Bent's Fort, written over the previous summer, which would run in *Forest and Stream* as a four-part series entitled, "When Beaver Skins Were Money." He wrote to President Taft, urging him to retain Francis

Leupp as commissioner of Indian affairs. (Taft did, but Leupp resigned any-way, citing exhaustion.) He also helped an old friend, Indian agent James McLaughlin, find a publisher for his memoir, *My Friend the Indian*. Mean-while, he had to confess to George Bent and George Hyde that, aside from the tangential Bent's Fort articles, he had done little work on either of his Cheyenne projects—the "big" book and the "war" book. On weekends he and Elizabeth escaped to the peace and quiet of Milford.

They worried at first that they might not be able to go west that sum-mer, but at the end of August they packed their trunks and headed to the Northern Cheyenne reservation and then to the Piegans and the moun-tains beyond. They invited Jay White to join them, but he was amusing himself in Bar Harbor. And so, on the morning before departing New York, Grinnell contacted another friend, wondering if there was any chance he could make the trip.

"I wish that there were hope that we might meet you out there. The trip will be one for invalids, children and weak women, and there will proba-bly not be excitement enough to appeal to you," he wrote wryly to George Gould. "I shall like, if I can, to see once more the snow-capped mountains and craggy peaks of the upper lakes and river, but I shall hardly be in shape to climb either for the mountains' scalp or for that of any animal making its home high up among the rocks."

Arriving in Browning in mid-September, Grinnell and Elizabeth spent four days visiting old friends, including Brocky and Little Plume, last of the chiefs from the buffalo-hunting days. Both had aged noticeably in the three years since the Grinnells had last been on the reservation. "The first [was] quite blind, [the] 2nd quite sick," Grinnell noted in his diary.

They then headed into the mountains. Grinnell was not interested in exploring new country, preferring to pay his respects to favorite haunts. Jack Monroe was off working his mining claim in the Sweet Grass Hills and not available to guide them, and they were disappointed to learn that they had just missed Edward Curtis's latest visit to the reservation.

They rode the familiar and, by now, well-traveled trail to the St. Mary Lakes, but almost immediately Elizabeth took sick. This time Grinnell blamed the altitude, though the elevation of the lakes is less than five thousand feet. Leaving her in camp, he and his packer, a man named Abbott, rode farther on, to Gunsight Lake, at the foot of Gunsight Pass, on an ancient trail over the Continental Divide to Lake McDonald. They might have pressed on, but the snow above them was already deep, and, besides, Elizabeth was "still sick and anxious to get out." The weather turned cold and windy, with intermittent rain. "This is the third night [Elizabeth] has been sick," Grinnell wrote on September 17, "and for these three nights I have had no sleep."

As they had done on their previous trip to these mountains, the Grinnells decided to cut their camping short. On September 20 they started back for Browning. "E[lizabeth] happened to remember my birthday," he remarked. He was sixty years old.

When they reached New York they found the city caught up in the parades and pageantry of the Hudson-Fulton Celebration, commemorating the three-hundredth anniversary of Henry Hudson's discovery of the Hudson River and the centennial of Robert Fulton's first successful steamboat ride.

A few days later it was Grinnell's turn to break down. Something was lodged in his eye. For most of a week he was obliged, on orders from an oculist, to "sit with closed eyes while someone read or talked to me." Regrettably he had to give away his tickets to the Yale-Harvard football game. (Yale won, 8–0, completing an undefeated season in which no opponent scored even a point.) Grinnell was, at best, an erratic follower of the sporting fortunes of his alma mater, but his fortieth reunion was coming in June, and school spirit was swelling among his classmates; a number of them, including Ned Dana, had urged him to run up for the game.

In the New Year, after a successful duck hunt in North Carolina with nephew Frank Page, Grinnell gave his attention to one issue above all others. The bill to create Glacier National Park was once again before Congress, and he was confident that this time it would pass. "There can be no objection to the bill on any ground," he editorialized in *Forest and Stream* in early March. "Here is an opportunity to establish a grand reservoir and game refuge—to accomplish one of the objects for which the readers of *Forest and Stream* have been working for many years. Let everyone now put his shoulder to the wheel and push."

The park bill passed the Senate easily and then moved to the House, where it was shepherded through the Committee on Public Lands by Montana congressman Charles Pray. Grinnell left no stone unturned. He called upon his Boone and Crockett brethren to lobby their representatives. He took a train to Washington and met with Pray, who impressed him as "a frank, downright man, not at all like a politician." He saw to it that Pray, along with Montana's two senators, was invited to the upcoming Boone and Crockett dinner and he recommended that Senators Carter and Dixon be elected associate members. Perhaps needlessly, but just to be sure, he reminded A. C. Harvey, tourist agent for the Great Northern, that "this bill, which if it becomes law, must be of great value to the . . . Railroad."

His perseverance paid off at last. The Glacier bill passed the House on April 13, after being amended to cut any appropriation to pay for the park's maintenance. Grinnell was not dismayed by this slight and remained optimistic that a conference committee, required to resolve the differences between the House and Senate versions of the bill, would present no further obstacles.

By this point, anybody who knew anything about the proposed Glacier National Park was cognizant of its paternity. Grinnell's passion was impossible to ignore. "This has been a 'baby' of mine for pretty nearly twenty-five years," he declared proudly.

Even while Glacier was the prize he most desired, Grinnell recognized that it was not the only national park that needed him. It was impossible, for instance, to ignore the controversy over the proposed damming of the Hetch Hetchy Valley of the Tuolumne River within the boundaries of Yosemite National Park. Grinnell had a sentimental attachment to the park and to California in general. He had glimpsed the wonders of Yosemite and the groves of giant redwoods during his first trip west in 1870. And he had fond memories of his visit to Santa Barbara in 1876—feelings animated by his correspondence with George Gould.

The Hetch Hetchy dam on the Tuolumne was, literally and figuratively, a watershed moment in American conservation. In multiple iterations of the story, to the point of near-mythological simplicity, it pitted "aesthetic conservationism," as embodied by John Muir, against "utilitarian conservationism," as embodied by Gifford Pinchot. Muir, the purist, vituperated against those who would allow a magnificent segment of a national park to be turned into a reservoir for the city of San Francisco, damning the dammers as "temple destroyers, devotees of ravaging commercialism" who "instead of lifting their eyes to the mountains, lift them to dams and town skyscrapers." Pinchot, meanwhile, saw little harm in drawing upon the earth's resources for "the good of man," if done prudently. In Grinnell's words, Pinchot admired nature "through economic spectacles."

Pinchot's official portfolio never grew beyond that of chief forester, but his expansive ego would take credit for "the birth of conservation" as government policy. Moreover, he had the full confidence of President Roosevelt—who admired Muir but deferred entirely to Pinchot on Hetch Hetchy. Pinchot had actually never set eyes on the Hetch Hetchy Valley, but he had no doubt that a dam was justified. "Injury to Hetch Hetchy by substituting a lake for the present swampy shore of the valley . . . is altogether unimportant, when compared with the benefits to be derived from its use as a reservoir," he pronounced.

The debate over Hetch Hetchy raged through the final years of the Roosevelt administration, into Taft's term, and it was at high volume while Grinnell was midwifing the birth of Glacier National Park. He had lost touch with Muir since the Harriman Alaska Expedition; Pinchot, on the other hand, he had come to know well—through Roosevelt, through their mutual interest in national forests, and as fellow members of the Boone and Crockett Club. Many of Grinnell's fellow conservationists in the East—Boone and Crockett men among them—were, if not muted, then at least muffled by Pinchot's persuasive personality. "Pinchot, of course, is popular, and his opinion carries some weight," Grinnell acknowledged to naturalist William Brewster.

But there was more at stake here than popularity and clubby consensus.

The long campaign to protect Yellowstone from the railroad had made a lasting impression on Grinnell, and his willingness to join the battle to save Yosemite stemmed as much from his desire to defend national parks as sacrosanct and inviolable as it did from any particular affinity for the Hetch Hetchy Valley. To this end, he agreed to become a director of a new organization called the Society for the Protection of National Parks, and he bravely took a stand against the policy of "highest possible use" espoused by Pinchot. "It is an unfortunate thing when the greatest city of a great State endeavors to seize upon and divert from its purpose something that belongs to the whole people of the United States," he wrote in *Forest and Stream*, decrying the dam. To Grinnell, highest use meant something quite different from the qualified version of conservation professed by Pinchot.

And then he warned: "If this scheme can be carried through, it is evident that no one of our national parks is safe. . . . If the Hetch Hetchy Valley is to be destroyed, we may look after a while to see power houses built in the Grand Cañon of the Yellowstone and the water of the falls used to run factories in the National Park."

By the spring of 1910 Gifford Pinchot was out of office—fired by President Taft essentially for insubordination. John Muir was seventy-two, worn out by his years as Yosemite's high priest and palace guard. Grinnell, however, was still going strong, and the national parks had no stauncher friend than he. The Hetch Hetchy battle would not be resolved for another three years—with Woodrow Wilson signing the bill that authorized construction of a dam—but the issues raised and the lines drawn in Yosemite would never recede. And Grinnell's alarm that the ripples caused by Hetch Hetchy might one day threaten his beloved Yellowstone would prove cannily prescient.

At the moment, though, he had much to be thankful for. Over the previous three weeks, the Glacier bill had received the final blessing of Congress and was duly delivered to the White House. On May 13, as Grinnell arrived at the Forest and Stream office, he received a telegram from Charles Pray, informing him that President Taft had put Glacier National Park on the map.

In its next issue *Forest and Stream* celebrated the news with hearty fanfare. "*Forest and Stream,* in whose columns was first described the region now the Glacier National Park, has for years urged the desirability of protecting this region and its wild inhabitants by setting it aside as a National Park," Grinnell preened. "It is a great satisfaction that this good end is at last accomplished and to feel that in the case of the Glacier Park, as twenty years ago in the case of Yellowstone Park, we have been able to assist in bringing about legislation which will be of lasting usefulness to the country at large."

Perhaps sensing that he had exceeded his customary bounds of modesty, he concluded his self-congratulation with a brief homily: "To receive credit for good work well done is pleasant, but a reward far higher than any praise that can be given is the deep satisfaction that comes from the consciousness of having served the public well, of having had a part in bringing about results whose value will long outlast our brief time and our petty activities."

He had lost Audubon Park, but he had gained a national park. His Walled-in Lakes, his Crown of the Continent, not to mention the Ceded Strip, were complemented by a comparable expanse of wilderness on the western side of the Continental Divide—in total, more than a million acres of majestic mountains, seven hundred lakes, three thousand miles of rivers and streams, two dozen glaciers, with many of these landmarks bearing names he had given them. Glacier National Park was his baby indeed.

Grinnell arrived in New Haven on June 20 in high spirits. He had attended previous reunions of his Yale class, but the fortieth was regarded as special. He had kept up with a number of classmates over the years; he saw Ned Dana more than most, and he occasionally ran into George Gould's brother Charles, who worked on Wall Street, as did Robert de Forest, who managed the money of some of New York's richest philanthropists and served on the board of the Metropolitan Museum of Art. Jack Nicholson, who had been on the Marsh expedition in 1870 and afterward had risen through the legal ranks of Delaware to preside over the state's Court of Chancery, was an occasional guest of the Grinnells in New York. (Nicholson came around less often after he borrowed $1,000 from his old fossil-digging companion.)

Throughout the winter, Grinnell had done his part to stoke interest in the gathering, cajoling men he had not heard from in a long time with coarse campus endearments. "My dear Belf," he wrote in February to Charles Belford of Mauch Chunk, Pennsylvania, "You have been as dumb as an oyster now for many years, but won't you let me hear from you." To Edward "Ned" Lewis, a physician who lived in Englewood, New Jersey, he chaffed jovially: "How can I bring myself to write to a miserable wretch, who for six or seven long years has never shown his face to me, not announced by the scratch of a pen that he is living? . . . Let us go to New Haven next June and see there the chaps that we have loved for so many years."

The chap he wished to see perhaps more than any other was Jim Russell, who had been on the Marsh expedition and also on the buffalo hunt with Grinnell and Lute North in 1872. "The Lord only knows whether it is fifteen, twenty, or twenty-five years since I have seen or heard from you," Grinnell wrote Russell, "but I should like to stick a prod in you which would cause you to holler out, even if the language was profane."

Russell still lived on the family farm near Paris, Kentucky, and continued to enjoy the lifestyle of a country gentleman, raising horses and growing tobacco, although by now he was widowed and his children were grown. When Russell wrote back that he would come east for the reunion, Grinnell replied: "I think you can understand how it warmed my heart to see your handwriting once more and to feel—what of course I know from my own experience—that the old love which subsisted between us is unchanged. . . . I think it is usually so, if men have been close to one another during the years of college life, time and distance do not affect their feelings." Grinnell invited Russell to stop in New York on his way to New Haven. "I will meet you at the train and guide your tottering footsteps to our door."

There had been some discussion among the reunion organizers whether to invite wives. Grinnell thought it a "dangerous thing," suggesting that "men have rather different standards from women, and if any wife was taken there and for any reason had a bad time, her bad time would make her husband suffer." In the end, wives were included, and Elizabeth accompanied Grinnell to New Haven, where they were guests of Ned Dana and his wife, Caroline.

Fifty-four of the seventy-seven surviving members of the class returned, including every living Scroll and Key man, save one. They headquartered at the Book and Gavel Society of the Yale Law School, dubbed "Camp

'70," under the command of classmate Charles "Gaff" Reeve, an honest-to-goodness major general.

The festivities led off with a luncheon at the Lawn Club, followed by the Yale-Harvard baseball game (won by Yale), and were capped off by a banquet, at which many glasses were raised and wives were not welcome. Grinnell sat between Jim Russell and Belf Belford and laughed and groaned through a succession of merry reminiscences and tender ribbings.

No one enjoyed himself at the reunion more than Grinnell—unless it was Elizabeth, who, as a trim thirty-three-year-old woman among a crowd of sixty-year-old gentlemen of good cheer, was surely showered with compliments. Elizabeth was no teetotaler—if the orders of spirits and wines to the New York house are any indication—and she had long since demonstrated her ability to handle herself in mixed company. She once turned to a male dinner companion and, according to Grinnell, "knocked the man . . . senseless by alluding to Pithecanthropus erectus by name. It was quite entertaining."

Afterward Grinnell gushed to Ned Dana: "Our meeting at New Haven was far and away the best one we ever had. . . . Mrs. Grinnell . . . declares that she never had so good a time in her life, and I believe it is true."

As he left New Haven, he vowed that he would not allow revived friendships to fall dormant again. In July he and Elizabeth spent several days near Boston with Scroll and Key brother George Huntress and his wife, and he assured Jim Russell that he could think of nothing more delightful than to visit him in Kentucky. "Thank the Lord, our old affection for one another has not changed in any degree," he wrote Russell. "We ought to be grateful for that." Looking at the photograph taken of the class at the Lawn Club—straw boaters doffed to reveal gray or balding heads—Grinnell flattered Russell, "[Y]ou stand out as one of . . . the most beautiful individuals of the group."

They did not make it to Kentucky that summer. Nor did they make it out West. They had contemplated another tour of Montana and mentioned swinging farther west to California, but in August wildfires swept across the northern Rockies, burning more than three million acres of forest. As the winter of 1886 had earned the gallows moniker, the Big Die-up, the summer of 1910 would be remembered forever as the Big Burn. Before it was three months old, Glacier National Park lost one hundred thousand acres—ten percent of its timber. Grinnell was relieved to learn that most of the destruction occurred on the west side of the park, but he called off his trip just the same.

He made good use of the time. He wrote *Brief History of the Boone and Crockett Club* and sent the manuscript to various members for review and emendation, apologizing for exerting so much control over the narrative. He need not have worried, for the membership was more than happy to have Grinnell do the hard work as chairman of the club's editorial committee.

The book came to seventy-two pages; two thousand copies were printed, enough to distribute to every member of Congress, the governor of every state, and several hundred newspapers. The club's achievements—on behalf of Yellowstone, the New York Zoological Society, forests, and wildlife—told an admirable story, and in his conclusion Grinnell describes an evolution that he was enormously proud of and for which, implicitly, he deserved perhaps more credit than any of the club's founders, including Theodore Roosevelt.

"[S]ince its establishment in 1888, the purposes and activities of the Boone and Crockett Club have wholly changed—[and] it might be said, have been reversed," Grinnell emphasizes. "Beginning as a club of riflemen, apparently concerned only with their own recreation, it early discovered that more important work was to be done in the field of protection than in that of destruction. No sooner had the Club been organized and begun to consider the subjects that most interested it, than it became apparent that . . . the selfishness of individuals was rapidly doing away with all the natural things of this country, and that a halt must be called."

Grinnell gave Roosevelt his fair share of ink in *Brief History*, but he was even more fulsome in a review of *African Game Trails*, Roosevelt's account of the eleven months he spent on safari in Africa after leaving the White House. All told, Roosevelt, son Kermit, and their party killed or trapped several thousand animals, including eleven elephants, seventeen lions, seven cheetahs, three leopards, nine hyenas, ten buffalo, eleven black rhinos, and nine white rhinos. Before his departure Roosevelt had insisted that this would not be a "game-butchering" excursion, but a scientific expedition to collect specimens for the Smithsonian. All the same, some of the choicest trophies ended up at Sagamore Hill.

Grinnell's notice of the book, which ran in *Review of Reviews* in October, stressed the nobler intentions of his Boone and Crockett cofounder. "One might suppose it is a mere hunting story, but it is much more than that," he stated. "From the book may be learned much natural history hardly to be found in other works, not a little ethnology, excellent lessons in game protection, and the very latest information as to the progress that civilization is making in Eastern and Central Africa."

Grinnell could not have wished a more generous characterization of one of his own books.

But as usual, with respect to his editorial work, he gave more than he got. During the past year he had begun soliciting articles for another Boone and Crockett anthology, and they were predictably slow in coming and mixed in their merits. The task was all very wearisome, and in December he complained to Madison Grant, the club's secretary, "Personally I am wondering whether I had better not resign from the Boone and Crockett Club, as its various activities seem to be taking up most of my time."

PART SIX

PRINCIPLED
PRAGMATIST

(1911–1919)

CHAPTER 28

BREAK THE OLD HABIT

G rinnell was beginning to feel the same way about *Forest and Stream*. To George Gould he confided, "If some kind person would come to New York and take away from me *Forest and Stream* and send me off in the country to live, I might be able to do a few of the things that I should greatly enjoy." He had yet to replace Edward Wilbur or Charles Reynolds, and while *Forest and Stream* was not in the habit of printing a proper masthead, it is safe to say that its ranks, always thin, were now thinner.

By early 1911 Grinnell had had enough. On April 15, with no forewarning, at least not to friends and family, he transferred controlling interest of *Forest and Stream* and Forest and Stream Publishing to Charles Otis, the thirty-eight-year-old president of Dow Jones & Company, publisher of the *Wall Street Journal*. The details of the transaction revealed the degree to which the weekly had struggled during Grinnell's ownership.

As it turned out, Grinnell had been covering the company's chronic losses out of his own pocket; up to 1911 he had contributed more than $150,000 (equivalent to $3.5 million today). In acquiring two-thirds of Forest and Stream (Grinnell keeping one-third), Otis was not required to pay Grinnell a cent; he simply pledged to keep the journal going. At the time of the transfer, Grinnell agreed to put an additional $5,000 into the

Forest and Stream account. Should there be any profits in the future, they would go, in part, to paying down the debts Grinnell had accumulated in the journal's name over the years. According to a memorandum drafted by Grinnell's brother-in-law and family attorney, Newell Martin, the alternative to such starkly lopsided terms would be to close down the paper outright.

The new owner was no sportsman, but Grinnell did not hold this against him. "Otis has made a great success with the *Wall Street Journal* and believes that he can do the same with *Forest and Stream*," he told classmate George Huntress. "I do not see why he may not, though, to be sure, a weekly is not a daily." The relief he felt was immediate. "At all events," he continued to Huntress, "this arrangement takes the business responsibility off my shoulders and is likely to leave me very much more free than I have been for many years."

For the time being, until Otis learned his way, Grinnell agreed to keep his hand in. But in the summer, he promised, "I mean to go away for some little time."

Elizabeth was sick that spring. Three days before the Forest and Stream transfer, she had undergone surgery—apparently something to do with her teeth or an infected jaw, for Grinnell, in reporting her rapid recovery, informed Jay White that she was "getting to look a little more like herself, not so one sided as she did."

They took a few days at Long Branch, New Jersey, walking on the beach and collecting shells. A week later Grinnell was writing Jack Monroe, planning a trip to Montana. Given Elizabeth's recent setback and remembering her difficulties during the previous two excursions in the mountains, he advised Monroe, "I am inclined to think that we had better make arrangements to go with as much comfort as may be possible, to have a cook, tents, reasonably good food, and generally somebody to do the hard work. It is some years since I have been in the hills, and while I used to be able to do my share of the work, I do not think I can do so any longer."

Before Grinnell could take his leave, however, a controversy arose that would eventually change the course of conservation.

Earlier in 1911 Grinnell had been appointed chairman of the Boone and Crockett Club's Game Preservation Committee. One of its first projects was to have a small group of pronghorn antelope shipped from Yellowstone National Park to the National Bison Range in Montana and another group to the Wichita Mountains Wildlife Refuge in Oklahoma as nuclei for new herds. The club had paid for this endeavor, and, anticipating similar preservation projects, Grinnell had reached out to the president of Remington Arms & Ammunition, George W. Jenkins, inquiring whether his company might care to help out financially. "Your company is directly interested in such preservation," Grinnell reasoned to Jenkins, "for it is obvious that [if] the game [is] gone, the demand for your arms will grow less." Furthermore, he continued, "I believe that the advertising you would receive in connection with such a subscription would be of value to your company. Such [dedication] to the cause of game protection would be [an effective] reply to attacks that have been made on you and on your methods."

Neither Remington nor any other gun manufacturer was inclined to take Grinnell up on the offer, but less than a month later Remington, the Winchester Repeating Arms Company, and several more gunmakers broached a similar proposal to the National Association of Audubon Societies, on whose board Grinnell also sat. As reported in the *New York Times* and other newspapers, the manufacturers offered the Audubon board of directors $125,000, to be paid over five years, to aid the National Association's effort "to prevent bird and game destruction."

There would be no strings attached to the offer, the gun consortium assured; they would expect no representation on the Audubon board. Gilbert Pearson, who had taken executive charge of the Audubon Societies after founder William Dutcher suffered a stroke, recognized that the contribution would double his annual budget. He put the matter before his nine board members. Grinnell was one of six who voted aye.

Public reaction was explosive. Bird lovers accused the Audubon board of selling out to the manufacturers, whose pump and "automatic" shotguns were capable of firing five shells in two seconds. Heretofore conservationists had opposed the sale of such lethal weapons. "It is this sort of gun that plumage hunters and market game hunters most use," railed the president of the New York State Forest, Fish and Game League.

The following day Pearson issued a statement defending the Audubon vote: "[T]he association reserves the right to take any measure at any time against the use of any kind of ammunition or make of gun which it considers to be a serious menace to the wild game."

It was not enough. Objections were so shrill that the Audubon board reconvened two weeks later and reversed its decision, rejecting the gun manufacturers' offer. Grinnell went along, but under gritted protest. A lifelong bird hunter, he took the position that there was nothing intrinsically malevolent about the guns that bird shooters used; the real problem was regulation and enforcement. The funds offered by the manufacturers might have helped pass the migratory bird bill first introduced by George Shiras in 1904—a bill that had been reintroduced in every session of Congress since then but had yet to find sufficient votes to become law. Grinnell believed that, if marshaled wisely, the joint self-interest of conservationists and gun manufacturers could make the difference.

When it came to Hetch Hetchy and Yellowstone, he had been more of a Muir idealist; now, in his conviction that unlikely bedfellows could forge a productive marriage, he was back to showing a streak of Pinchot pragmatism (although, perversely and impulsively, Pinchot, who sat on the advisory board of the Audubon Societies, had opposed the gunmakers' overture). "It is no doubt partly true the manufacturers are striving to protect the game in order to preserve targets for the persons who purchase their arms," Grinnell accepted, "but so long as the game is protected and increased, the aim [of the gunmakers] is of no great importance."

Neither the Shiras bill nor the gun manufacturers' offer was dead yet, however. Come fall, the manufacturers would take their money and incorporate a new organization, the American Game Protective and Propagation Association, and, under the guidance of another Bird—John Bird Burnham—who had once been a protégé of George Bird Grinnell at *Forest and Stream*, it would help pass one of the most influential conservation laws of the century. Grinnell would stand behind Burnham and the AGPPA all the way.

The Grinnells got to Browning on July 3, in time for the medicine lodge.

As usual Elizabeth took photographs and Grinnell took notes, but they were not as admiring of the Piegan proceedings as in years past. "They continue to degenerate," Grinnell complained of the medicine lodge ceremonies in a letter to James Willard Schultz.

Grinnell and Elizabeth stayed on the reservation only three days and then took the Great Northern, following the southern boundary of Glacier National Park, over Marias Pass, to the station at Belton, the entry point to Lake McDonald and the west side of the park, country Grinnell barely knew at all. There they met the park's first superintendent, William Logan, whose previous posting had been as Indian agent at Fort Belknap.

By 1911, one year after Glacier's founding, Logan's small staff and meager budget had cleared only a few miles of roads and trails in the park. The Great Northern had completed only one hotel, a Swiss-style chalet at Belton, in keeping with the railroad's promotion of Glacier as "America's Alps." Grander hotels were coming—at Midvale (today's East Glacier), Swiftcurrent (today's Many Glacier) and on Lake McDonald, but visitors were already abundant.

At Lake McDonald they met two other couples, the Reeds, of Chicago, and the Murdoughs, of Portland, Oregon—"pleasant seeming people," Grinnell remarked. Together they rode hired horses along the east shore of the lake to Avalanche Basin. Grinnell remarked at how different the west side of the park was from the east: The forest was thick with larch, cedar, and hemlocks and the undergrowth verdant with ferns. Gazing upward through the clouds, he thought he could make out Sperry Glacier, which he reckoned to be on the west side of Gunsight Pass.

The next day they returned to Browning—actually Jack Monroe's ranch at nearby Blackfoot—and then, joined again by the Reeds and Murdoughs, spent several days camping on the upper St. Mary River. Elizabeth bore up well. Perhaps it was coincidence, but she never complained when women were along. The most serious mishap this time out was to a porcupine that got into their grub and had to be dispatched by Grinnell with a club.

Before departing Browning on the twenty-third, Grinnell took a deci-sive step: In front of witnesses, he applied for an allotment on the Blackfeet reservation. His justification was that White Calf, as head of the council of chiefs, had inducted him into the tribe years before. Grinnell wanted to build a house on Indian land at St. Mary, just outside the boundary of the national park.

President Roosevelt had signed the Blackfeet allotment bill in 1907; each tribal member was given a choice between 320 acres of grazing land or a combination of 280 acres of grazing land and forty acres of irrigable farmland—less than Grinnell had hoped for. The process of surveying, appraising, and dividing the reservation was proceeding slowly—and would not be completed until 1912—but with the creation of Glacier, Indians has-tened to claim the land that bordered it (even though grazing was better on the grassy plains to the east).

Released from his duties at *Forest and Stream*, Grinnell envisioned spending more time in Montana, and he and Jack Monroe contemplated becoming neighbors. Monroe's four children by his Piegan wife (who died in 1908) were each entitled to an allotment, and he had his eye on parcels near Lower St. Mary Lake, where he aimed to build a hotel for guests who wished to camp in the mountains and climb to the glaciers. Monroe had already asked Grinnell to consider backing his scheme.

Grinnell's application for allotment was turned down five days after he departed the reservation. Jack Monroe was crestfallen, not only because he was losing a business partner, but also because he regarded the rejection as a betrayal of one of the tribe's truest allies. "The basest of all the crimes is ingratitude, and these people are ingrates," he wrote Grinnell, breaking the news of the council's decision. "I fear these people have lost more than one good friend by this day's work. To write this letter to you is one of the hardest tasks of my life."

Grinnell was likewise bruised. Monroe had told him that most of the mixed-blood members of the tribal council had voted in his favor but that "the Indians"—that is, the full bloods—had voted against him. Most of the old-timers were gone, and the younger generation felt neither obliga-tion nor loyalty toward the aging white man who called himself Fisher Cap. "Their memories are so short and their experiences are so limited that they do not comprehend all the thought and work that I have put forth on their behalf," Grinnell wrote Monroe. "One does not feel [indignant] with them," he added, "because they are just like children, but it does seem that the men of today [ought to] understand my motives as did the men of a dozen years ago."

From Browning, Grinnell and Elizabeth went west, passing through Vancouver, Victoria, and Seattle. Turning eastward finally, they stopped briefly to inspect the National Bison Range near Dixon, Montana, where Grinnell was pleased to learn that the herd had doubled in size in the three years since the refuge had been first stocked. Sadly, however, the eleven antelope brought from Yellowstone, with the Boone and Crockett Club's help, had dwindled to eight.

They finally arrived on the Northern Cheyenne reservation on August 4 to observe the medicine lodge and the massaum, also known as the animal dance, buffalo dance, or crazy dance. The self-torture of the sun dance was still discouraged by the Indian Bureau, and the Northern Cheyennes had not performed these deeply spiritual rituals for several years. The current Cheyenne agent, J. R. Eddy, either was not aware, or else he didn't mind. As interpreter, Grinnell enlisted Willis Rowland, son of William Rowland, and his Cheyenne wife, who had been so helpful in years past.

Over the next three weeks the attention Grinnell paid to the ceremonies was more intense than during any previous visit. So methodical, meticulous, and thorough are his notes that today they read like a virtual manual. For example, this passage on the preparation of a medicine lodge dancer:

"The instructors knelt at his right side and with charcoal marked upright parallel lines on the skin on the right breast to indicate where the knife should enter and where come out. Then one instructor took the skin in his fingers above the marks and the other below the marks, and pinching up the skin they thrust in the knife at the marked place on the right, and it came through at the marked place on the other side. Before using the knife, it had been rubbed down with a piece of charcoal. The left breast was pierced in the same way. . . . When the right breast was pierced, the instructors, assisting each other, passed a small straight stick, the length of a finger, through the slit, and to this skewer tied the strings on one of the ropes. After the left breast was pierced, a similar skewer was passed through that slit and tied.

"After the strings had been tied, the instructors raised [him] to his feet and supported and directed him as he walked over to the middle of the sage-covered path. Then the instructors pulled four times on his breast to straighten out the ropes. They moved his body toward the east and then toward the west; again toward the east and again toward the west—four times. Then they took hold of his right leg and moved it four times forward, and at the fourth movement he began to walk to the west end of the sage-covered trail. . . . He was constantly trying to break loose, but the skin of his breast did not break; it only stretched."

Step-by-step descriptions such as these would fill more than one hundred pages in the big Cheyenne book.

While at Lame Deer, Grinnell was also able to add more detail to the story of the Dull Knife flight, the first pieces of which he had gathered from Black Horse two years earlier. This time it was Big Beaver who told of the capture of Dull Knife and 150 Cheyennes and their imprisonment at Fort Robinson, Nebraska, in December 1878. (Little Wolf's band had earlier split off from Dull Knife's and hidden from the army until surrendering in March 1879.)

"Now the officers began to persuade them to go back s[outh], but D[ull] K[nife] refused," Big Beaver recalled. "'No, he said, I am here on my own ground and I will never go back. You can kill me here, but you cannot make me go back there.' Then the rations were stopped and from that time there was suffering."

When the Cheyennes could stand no more, they resolved to break out of the cramped, unheated barracks at any cost. Before they had been captured, the Indians had disassembled several guns—some of the parts hidden under women's clothes, others worn in plain sight, disguised as ornaments. Armed with these few weapons, the Cheyennes forced their way out of the barracks and fled as best they could into the frigid January night.

"The bullets were flying past," Big Beaver remembered. "When they came to White R[iver] they followed up on the ice and then turned up into the hills. Now and then a person would drop. The firing was continual. . . .

One bunch was ahead and the soldiers who had saddled up and gone around came in between the leading party and those behind them. . . . The troops made a circle and came back in front of them and dismounted & Indians all dropped to the ground. There was a little washout with a few rocks about it, and just as the people dropped here the troops fired on them. Almost all were killed, but some of us jumped out and ran to and through the line of soldiers 10 or 12 feet apart and so escaped."

More than sixty Cheyennes died during the breakout; more than twenty were wounded; and in the end all the survivors, including Dull Knife and Big Beaver, were recaptured. Their long, valiant resistance was over, but even then they managed to snatch a measure of victory from miserable defeat. For the next five years, Dull Knife's and Little Wolf's Cheyennes were allowed to live among the Sioux on the Red Cloud Agency in South Dakota. In 1884, a year after Dull Knife's death, they were at last assigned to their own reservation on the Tongue River of Montana, in country they had known and hunted upon for generations. Little Wolf lived until 1904, long enough for George Bird Grinnell to know him well.

Grinnell was not enthusiastic about returning to the Forest and Stream offices. After being back in New York for just three weeks, he resigned entirely. He immediately notified the post office that henceforth he would receive his mail at 238 East Fifteenth Street.

When Lute North got the news, he wrote back glumly, "I was very much surprised to hear of your leaving the Forest and Stream. I don't think it will interest me so much now. I always thought of you first thing when it came."

Jack Monroe was more cheerful. "Take a good rest," he advised Grinnell, "and don't go to work until the spirit calls you *hard*. I believe to drink a little whiskey to break the old habit of hard work would be wise and help break the high tension under which you have been living so long."

Monroe again brought up the matter of going into the hotel business together. Grinnell demurred on Monroe's partnership offer. "I have been trying now for a dozen years to free myself from worries and anxieties," he explained. But he was interested in leasing five acres or so on the allotment of Monroe's daughter Mabel and volunteered to send a $100 down payment. "Then would you be willing to have a house and stable built for me?" he asked. "Of course the land would have to be on some stream and should have a view of the [St. Mary] lake." He promised to come out the following summer to select a spot.

The remainder of the fall Grinnell tried to wean his thoughts from *Forest and Stream* by taking three-day weekends at Milford, and at the end of October he and Elizabeth went bird hunting in the Adirondacks. "Mrs. Grinnell made a particularly fancy shot, killing a bird that [started] from out of a tree top," he boasted to Jay White, whose latest address was London. "This is regarded as one of the [most difficult] shots at partridge."

For the time being, Elizabeth's mother and brother were posing no further difficulties. Elizabeth occasionally visited them in upstate New York, without Grinnell. Delle Curtis occasionally came to New York to see Elizabeth, but she was never invited to stay at Fifteenth Street.

Grinnell spent the first months of 1912 tending to odds and ends. Charles Scribner's Sons was pleased enough with *Trails of the Pathfinders*, which had appeared the year before, that Grinnell pulled together more pieces and submitted them under the title *Beyond the Old Frontier*. He also whittled down and annotated an ungainly manuscript by William D. Pickett, "Memories of a Grizzly Hunter," for the next Boone and Crockett book. Pickett wrote proudly of killing twenty-three grizzlies in a single season, four in a single day. In his introduction to *Hunting at High Altitudes*, Grinnell would describe Pickett, a railroad man who had served in the Confederate army before moving west, as "a keen sportsman, a lover of outdoor life, and a Southern gentleman [who] represents the ideals of the Boone and Crockett Club." Bears were still not part of the conservation conversation.

Free from his daily and weekly obligations to *Forest and Stream*, Grinnell could now make trips without having to plan far ahead. In early March he went to Louisiana at the request of Yale classmate Robert de Forest, who represented the Russell Sage Foundation, established by Margaret Sage, widow of the railroad tycoon. The foundation had been contacted by Edward A. McIlhenny, of Avery Island, Louisiana, who, when he was not manufacturing Tabasco sauce, devoted his energy and resources to the protection of the wildfowl that rested and nested on the barrier islands of the Louisiana coast. To stop the slaughter of birds by market hunters—McIlhenny's cause célèbre was the snowy egret—he and Charles W. Ward, who had made his fortune growing carnations, established a 13,000-acre wildlife refuge on Vermilion Bay of the Gulf of Mexico and made a down payment on 75,000-acre Marsh Island, just to the east. With the deadline on their option approaching, McIlhenny reached out to the Russell Sage Foundation and De Forest, who knew just the man to evaluate the proposition.

Grinnell spent three days at Marsh Island, guided by McIlhenny. In a detailed report he strongly recommended that it be purchased and protected as a wildlife refuge. He was particularly struck by the importance of the island as a way station for birds completing their long migratory flights over the Gulf. "Many of the birds reach here exhausted," he noticed. "On landing near Chenier la Croix we found on the beach two dead warblers that had apparently reached the shore too exhausted to search for food. Just after our boat had left its anchorage, a weary Wilson snipe alighted on deck and stood there with half closed eyes and drooping wings until frightened away. A tired purple martin, resting on a stake, refused to move when a boat-tailed grackle tried to alight on the same stake. The grackle attacked the martin, seized it and so injured it that it fell into the water and died."

Grinnell's in-depth memorandum, his reputation as a naturalist, and his graphic evocation of the fragility of the birds proved decisive. Mrs. Sage purchased Marsh Island, and today the Marsh Island Wildlife Refuge is regarded as one of the more vital sanctuaries in the United States.

The subject that Grinnell seemed to focus on least that winter and spring was his Cheyenne work. It was not that he suffered from writer's block. On the contrary, as his letter books show, he was as prolific as ever. A stenographer came to the house several times a week to take dictation and type up his many letters.

Bad news was partly to blame for his distraction. On January 22, 1912, nephew Rutherford Page, who had graduated from Yale two years earlier, was killed while racing a biplane in Los Angeles. Three weeks before the crash, Grinnell had written to Jay White: "A nephew of mine has gone out west and is trying to become an aviator. He was still alive at last report and has made a number of flights, going up to 200 or 300 feet, with hopes of ascending much higher. He will die when his time comes, and not before."

Ten days after Page's death, the end came for the Whites' only daughter, Louise. At fifteen she had married Walter L. Suydam, Jr., described in one newspaper as a "Long Island sportsman." Seven years later she forsook Suydam's millions to run off with a plumber, and, after obtaining a divorce, married her lover and set up household on East Twelfth Street. The couple was found on the morning of February 4, having argued, opened the gas jets on the stove, and ended their lives.

Jay White was out of reach in Africa; Grace White was in New York. "As you know, our hearts went out in sympathy to you and Mrs. White in the sad circumstances," Grinnell wrote White a month later, somewhat stiffly. He then switched to a subject more comfortable to both: "I . . . congratulate you on having acquired an elephant. That it had only one tusk is disappointing but rather interesting."

Grinnell found one more excuse for not turning his attention to the Cheyennes. He started another—and, as it turned out, his last—Jack book, *Jack the Young Cowboy*, which he set in a western roundup. After a few chapters, however, he bogged down and sought Lute North's assistance. "I have worked more or less with cattle in my time, as you know, but in that time nothing ever very startling happened and very little that is worth telling about," he confessed. "[I]t is so long ago that I feel a little bit shaky about many matters. . . . I want you to help me correct my blunders."

North was ready and willing to critique the pages Grinnell had written so far. "I was in four or five stampedes in the years that we had cattle," he answered, "and two of them were exciting enough, especially the one where my horse fell almost in front of three thousand head of cattle. . . . I suppose you couldn't make a trip out here and talk the thing over."

Grinnell thought this a capital proposal, and at the first of April he took a train to Omaha and spent a few days with North, who was working there in a whiskey distillery. Over samples of North's merchandise, the two friends discussed the Jack story while reliving old times. The North brothers and the ranch they ran with Buffalo Bill Cody are given their due in *Jack the Young Cowboy*, and Jack's close call in a stampede is clearly Lute North's. Jack passes a delightful summer—like Grinnell's, his western sojourns were seasonal—riding, roping, hunting, and when the day comes for Jack to leave, "his heart-strings were stretched when he shook hands with his friends and took the passenger for the Atlantic coast."

Grinnell felt the same when he left Omaha. "I look back with great pleasure on our visit. We did have a very good time together," he wrote North in thanks. Before parting, they made plans to meet that summer in Montana, accompanied by their wives. "It hardly seems possible that we should be going to make another trip into the mountains together," Grinnell wrote later in the spring. "I shall hardly believe it until I see you astride a horse and dragging or driving a pack animal."

For once Grinnell felt no urgency. He could leave for the summer and stay away for as long as he wished. He would go to all his favorite places and visit cherished friends. And he would let nothing interfere with his plans. In April he politely told Yale that he could not accept an honorary master's degree because it meant he would have to be in New Haven on June 19 to receive it. By then he expected to be in Oklahoma.

He and Elizabeth left New York on May 31. They intended to stop in Kentucky to see Jim Russell, but, as Grinnell apologized in his diary, "This we did not do," blaming "bad connections, delays & changes." He left Elizabeth in Oklahoma City, where she was to rendezvous with her mother, and proceeded on to Colony, Oklahoma, where George Bent took him in. It had been four years and many letters since they had seen each other. Three days later Elizabeth arrived unexpectedly; her mother had not been able to join her, after all. "I was sitting in my room, writing," Grinnell told his diary, "when I saw the mule-drawn buggy pass and recognized first the trunk and then E[lizabeth] sitting with the driver."

For the next two weeks, he talked with Bent, and, with Bent acting as interpreter, interviewed a number of Cheyennes—on marriage customs and memorable battles, horses and hunting, the meaning of the medicine lodge, the sacred arrows, and the sacred buffalo hat. "All prairie Indians thought it honorable to be eaten by wolves after he had been killed by his enemy," reads one matter-of-fact entry.

From Oklahoma Grinnell and Elizabeth went north to Colorado, touring the Garden of the Gods, Manitou Springs, and the capitol in Denver. They then continued on to Eatons' Ranch in the foothills of Wyoming's Big Horn Mountains. The other guests, like the Grinnells, were well-fixed easterners. Grinnell had gotten to know Howard Eaton on his visits to the East—Roosevelt was a mutual friend—but this was his first visit to the ranch. Every summer the Eaton brothers guided guests through Yellowstone, and Grinnell pictured Jack Monroe doing the same from the hotel he intended to build at Glacier.

From the nearest station at Ranchester, Wyoming, it was only an hour or so by train to Crow Agency, the jumping-off point for the Northern Cheyenne reservation on Tongue River.

The month Grinnell spent among the Northern Cheyennes was undoubtedly worthwhile, but his interviews and observations seemed more random, less focused, compared to the year before. He had already spent three weeks with the Southern Cheyenne and perhaps could finally accept that he had enough material for the books he intended to write. Elizabeth had begun to tease him about the repetition of their visits by substituting the name *Lame Deer* for *taxes*—as in, "There is nothing certain in this life except death and Lame Deer."

For the first time Grinnell was driven over parts of the reservation in an automobile. As an indication of how much had changed since his trips of a decade earlier, and how at ease the Grinnells were on this latest visit, each morning they played a set or two of tennis on a newly built court at Lame Deer. Grinnell complimented Elizabeth on how well she was picking up the game, although he failed to mention whether the Cheyennes had taken to it as avidly.

They reached Browning on August 6. Over the years, Grinnell had tried to get Lute North to join him on another trip to the Walled-in Lakes, but, with the exception of 1888, North had always found reasons to renege. This time, though, he held true. He and Elvira stepped off the train the following day. Jack Monroe appeared a few hours later. They rode out of Browning, following a new automobile road, still under construction. At St. Mary Grinnell picked a site for the cabin on the allotment assigned to Monroe's daughter, and Monroe pointed out where he intended to build a hotel.

Grinnell and North left their wives at Monroe's camp and set out to climb Singleshot Mountain for old time's sake. On the ride along the shore of the St. Mary Lakes, they passed three horsemen. "The leader spoke," Grinnell wrote in his diary, "and asked if this was Mr. Grinnell's party and if I was Mr. G[rinnell]." The man introduced himself as Louis Hill, president of the Great Northern Railway. His first impression of Hill was of "a very bright, energetic and determined fellow. He will do well for the Park."

During the next week they made the rounds—Swiftcurrent, Iceberg Lake, "my glacier"—camping, looking for game, and, as best they could, avoiding "that dangerous animal," the tourist.

The Grinnells stayed another ten days after the Norths departed, then headed west to Spokane, down the Columbia River to Portland, and south to San Francisco. On September 2 they crossed the bay to Lagunitas, in Marin County, and stayed two days with Hart Merriam and his wife, Virginia.

In 1910 Merriam had been liberated from his duties at the Biological Survey in Washington by a generous endowment from Mary Harriman, the widow of E. H. Harriman, whom Merriam had impressed on the Harriman Alaska Expedition. Merriam was given carte blanche to conduct research of his choosing for the rest of his days. He continued his pursuit of mammalogy, specializing in grizzlies and Alaskan brown bears.

And like Grinnell, he had expanded his passion for natural history to include ethnology. Merriam's *The Dawn of the World: Myths and Weird Tales Told by the Mewan Indians of California* became a shelf-mate of Grinnell's Pawnee and Blackfoot books. After he moved to the West Coast full time, he became deeply interested in the early, and in some cases extinct, Indian tribes of California. (Only a year earlier, a Yahi Indian named Ishi had been discovered foraging in a slaughterhouse in Oroville, California.

He was currently living on the campus of the University of California at Berkeley, where anthropologists studied him minutely as "the last wild Indian in North America.")

Also like Grinnell, Merriam cared deeply about the protection of wildlife, wilderness, and national parks. The two Boone and Crockett members talked about Alaska; commiserated over James Willard Schultz, whom Merriam had known since boyhood; and wondered at their friend Theodore Roosevelt's campaign for president as a Bull Moose. They hiked up Mount Tamalpais and through the nearby redwood groves. "We had a fine time," Grinnell wrote Merriam afterward, "and enjoyed every minute of it."

Because this was Elizabeth's first ever trip to California and Grinnell's first in more than thirty years, they could not miss Yosemite. They spent three days sightseeing—El Capitan, Bridal Veil, Cathedral Spires, Sentinel Rock, Yosemite Falls, Vernal Falls, Royal Arches, and Glacier Point. In the Mariposa Grove, Grinnell was awestruck by the giant sequoias. "[They] are perhaps the most beautiful things I have ever seen," he effused. He thought it appropriate that the trees honored great men and institutions: Grant, Sheridan, Lafayette, Longfellow, Mark Twain, John Muir, Harvard, and, not least of all, Yale.

On September 13—Friday the thirteenth—Grinnell wrote in his diary: "Rose at 6 and took 8 A.M. train for Santa Barbara. Rode all day through beautiful country. Hotel Potter good but expensive. . . . Tried . . . to find Geo. Gould, but without success."

The following day's entry was even shorter: "G. H. G. absent, can learn nothing of him. Rode out to mission. Took 11:05 train to Los Angeles."

Before leaving New York, Grinnell had written Jim Russell of his intention of coming to Kentucky. Before arriving in San Francisco, he had telegraphed Hart Merriam. Nearly every time he knew he was going to pass through a town where he hoped to see an old friend, he had the forethought to send word. In this instance, though, he made no such effort to get in touch with George Gould, whom he had been longing to see for the past twenty-two years. His stopover in Santa Barbara was not by necessity; he went there intentionally to see Gould. And yet he could not bring himself to ensure he would be there. Gould's law office was not far from the train station, and anyone could have directed Grinnell to his house on Olive Mill Road in Montecito.

Instead he and Elizabeth continued onward, to Los Angeles, east to the Grand Canyon, then to Colorado and the site of Bent's Fort, and finally homeward, arriving at Milford on September 22, nearly four months after leaving New York.

Awaiting Grinnell was a letter from Gould, which, like so many others, is not among the papers that Elizabeth saved after her husband's death. But Grinnell's reply survives.

"Dear Partner," he wrote, "Among the mail which I found here on my return a week or two ago was your letter of September 16th which really came near squeezing a few tears out of my old dry eyes. I feel it a great misfortune that I should have missed you. We stopped in Santa Barbara only one night and left Los Angeles for the east on Sunday morning. If I had been able to learn that you were likely to return in two or three days, I should have waited for you."

He did not give an explanation for why he had not given Gould advance notice of his visit. "I feel rather as if you and I, who have shared many joys and sorrows, ought not wholly to lose sight of one another, and I hope that now and then you will let me hear from you."

What sorrows did he mean? In a letter he could never convey all that he felt. And to do so face-to-face was evidently too much to contemplate.

CHAPTER 29

UNDUE DESTRUCTION

George Bird Grinnell's oldest friends remained his dearest: Yale class-mates, Boone and Crockett members, fellow travelers Lute North, Jack Monroe, Billy Hofer, Hart Merriam, many Indians, a few sol-diers, and, in a category all alone, George Gould. Fifty years after the Audubons had left Audubon Park, Grinnell still kept up with family members. "I believe that many of us think often and with affection of our old friends," he wrote to Audubon's granddaughter Maria, "but because we do not hear from them we are disposed to believe that they have forgotten us. People who have had a real affection for one another—unless their intercourse has been interrupted by a quarrel—never, I believe, lose the old feeling."

Yet it is also fair to say that Grinnell made very few new friends in his later years. For instance, Grinnell's relationship with Jay White had its moments, but for all White's desire to impress, he never sank his teeth into anything beyond hunting big game and collecting Indian artifacts. "You should make heroic efforts to get something to do that will really engage your attention," Grinnell admonished the wandering dilettante; but White never did. When White gave Grinnell a lion skin as a gift, Grinnell thanked him but advised that it would "probably have to go on the floor."

Grinnell never considered putting White up for membership in the Boone and Crockett Club.

Two exceptions to his reticence toward new friends stand out: John Bird Burnham and Charles Sheldon. Both were nearly young enough to be Grinnell's children; both were exemplars of a new generation of conservationist; and both would step to the fore at just the right time.

Like Grinnell, Burnham had a wiry build, with a chiseled jaw and well-tended moustache; he, too, smoked a pipe. Born in Delaware in 1869, he was a descendant of early colonists and two signers of the Declaration of Independence. In 1891, upon graduation from Trinity College in Hartford, he was hired by *Forest and Stream*, at first on the business side but then pitched in as a writer of short pieces and even as an illustrator. After a thrilling but otherwise unrewarding year in the Klondike gold fields, he moved to a farm on the Adirondack side of Lake Champlain, converting it into a private game preserve. Grinnell and Elizabeth were guests of Burnham, his wife, Henrietta, and their three daughters during more than one grouse-shooting season.

Burnham's alarm over widespread violation of game laws won him appointment as chief game protector of the New York Forest, Fish and Game Commission, and by 1911 he was acting commissioner. As a sportsman and an authority on game regulation and legislation, he was the sensible choice to found and direct the American Game Protective and Propagation Association, sponsored by the gun manufacturers recently spurned by the National Association of Audubon Societies. Burnham's longstanding association with Grinnell made the fit that much more logical. "I am a warm friend of Mr. Burnham and have the highest regard for him," Grinnell assured H. S. Leonard, vice president of Winchester Repeating Arms. "I want him to succeed."

Immediately upon formation of the AGPPA, Grinnell lent his name to its letterhead, staking his reputation on the association's good intentions and pragmatic approach and endorsing the common goal of passing the Shiras migratory bird law. Furthermore, Grinnell assured Burnham in December 1911, "The Boone and Crockett is altogether disposed to support your association."

But even with the backing of Grinnell, the Boone and Crockett Club, and the gunmakers, Burnham's fledgling group still did not command sufficient firepower to win the battle. The Shiras bill had failed repeatedly. The most recent version, renamed the Weeks bill, after its latest sponsor, Congressman John W. Weeks of Massachusetts, had fallen flat in March 1912. More help was needed.

In April Grinnell was succeeded as chairman of the Boone and Crockett's Game Preservation Committee by forty-one-year-old Charles Sheldon, whose credentials as businessman, outdoorsman, and conservationist were impeccable. As a boy "Billy" Sheldon, as he was called, roamed the Green Mountains of Vermont, an appetite not suppressed by four years at Yale. After Sheldon graduated in 1890 (twenty years after Grinnell), a classmate pulled strings and got him a job on the Lake Shore Railroad, where he quickly rose to division superintendent. Capable, self-confident, and charismatic, he went to Mexico as general manager of the American-owned Chihuahua and Pacific Railroad. His adroit diplomacy with the Mexican government and the region's landowners helped make the railroad a success and, more fortuitously, gained him a percentage in one of the richest mines in Mexico. In 1903, at the age of thirty-five, he retired a wealthy man and devoted the rest of his days to wild nature.

While in Mexico, Sheldon had made a number of excursions into the rugged Sierra Madre in search of bighorn sheep and the not-yet-extinct Mexican grizzly, of which little was known by American naturalists. (On one of his hunts, he was said to have crossed paths with the future revolutionary Pancho Villa.) Sheldon's interest in mountain sheep eventually led him to look up the preeminent expert on the species, Edward Nelson of the Biological Survey in Washington, who promptly enlisted him to undertake the agency's fieldwork in an even harsher quarter of the continent.

At Nelson's behest but at his own expense, Sheldon spent the next five years on the northern Pacific coast and along the upper Yukon River, hunting and collecting Dall sheep, caribou, brown bears, grizzlies, and a variety of smaller mammals for the Biological Survey and the Smithsonian. His assiduous field notes from these trips are as valuable as the specimens he brought back, and his published accounts of his exploits, *The Wilderness of the North Pacific Coast Islands* and *The Wilderness of the Upper Yukon,* reveal Sheldon as a thorough sportsman in the very best sense.

Tough and nearly tireless, Sheldon spent three of his years in the north pursuing his prey across the never-before-explored flanks of Mount McKinley, which he reverently called by its native name, Denali. (Sheldon's masterpiece, published posthumously, is titled *The Wilderness of Denali*.) In stark contrast to the man-versus-beast histrionics of the pulp press, his descriptions of his adventures never hint of sensationalism or self-flattery. His hunting stories are vivid yet matter-of-fact, and he understood conservation as only a hunter could. "We go back to the wilderness, and the more primitive it is, the more strongly we feel its charm," Sheldon explains. "But the wilderness must include the animals. Our active sympathies, developed by civilization, extend also to them. We feel them along with their wilderness environment. We learn to know and love them. They become inseparable from the mysterious emotions aroused by mountains, valleys, woods, and waters."

However, he continues, "They also arouse, kindle and set glowing the primitive instinct to hunt and kill. The pursuit leads us to nature which in turn leads us to pursuit. We cannot deny that this must react on our race. Endurance, strength, skill, boldness, independence, manliness are the qualities produced."

To pursue nature as a goal in itself—in the manner of, say, John Muir, whom Sheldon did not know or name—was a pale substitute for a more primordial way of engagement, he writes. "The time may come when most of us will undertake to work, endure, and suffer the hardships of the wilderness, prompted only by love of it for its own sake. But to many of us, in our present stage, hunting prevents the mere contemplative in the beautiful from producing"—and here Sheldon invokes the unthinkable—"effeminateness."

Shortly after Nelson introduced him to Theodore Roosevelt, Sheldon was welcomed into the Boone and Crockett Club. Roosevelt would praise his new friend as a "wilderness wanderer who, to the hardiness and prowess of an old-time hunter, adds the capacity of a first-class field naturalist." Grinnell met Sheldon at one of the annual dinners in Washington, encouraged his writing, and recognized in him the strong blood that could pump life into the club's increasingly unstrenuous, hearth-bound membership.

And then in May 1909, at age forty-two, Sheldon married thirty-year-old Louisa Gulliver, the daughter of one of Grinnell's Yale classmates, William Gulliver. Grinnell attended the ceremony and assured Jack Nicholson, who had not yet met the groom, "Sheldon is one of the very salt of the earth." Soon Sheldon became part of Grinnell's greater family, for Bill Gulliver died two weeks after the wedding; thereafter Grinnell and other members of the class of 1870 took it upon themselves to keep tabs on his widow and children.

Like their husbands, Elizabeth Grinnell and Louisa Sheldon took to each other immediately. They were roughly the same age and equally athletic. In August, after the wedding, Sheldon took Louisa to Admiralty Island, on the coast of southeastern Alaska, to hunt brown bears. Sheldon wrote of her first encounter with *Ursus arctos horribilis*, "Glancing at Mrs. Sheldon, I saw that she was perfectly cool; the rifle was at her shoulder. . . ."

When Sheldon took charge of the Boone and Crockett Club's Game Preservation Committee in the spring of 1912, he worked energetically to create refuges for pronghorn antelope and also concentrated on the latest legislation before Congress to regulate the hunting of migratory game birds. In addition to the Weeks bill, a similar version had been introduced by Connecticut senator George P. McLean. The Boone and Crockett Club, initially an organization focused on big game and its haunts, had come to regard all creatures, great and small, as deserving of its attention.

Over the years, opposition to the migratory bird bill—regardless of whose name was on it—had come from three sources: market hunters who wanted no limits on the birds they killed and sold; sportsmen who wanted the longest possible season and largest possible bag limits; and those who thought the legislation represented an unconstitutional infringement of states' rights. "This is . . . the most revolutionary, the most far-reaching legislation, in its possible and probable effect on our system of government," one western congressman exclaimed in protest. "Pass this bill and every barrier standing against the assertion of Federal police control in every line and with regard to every act and activity of the American people is broken down, and we no longer have a Government of self-governing States, but are well on our way to an empire governed from this Capitol."

More recently, however, conservationists had found themselves faced with a nettlesome threat from within their own ranks.

William Temple Hornaday had not always been against the killing of wildlife. In fact, he had once made his living off slain animals, and he had done his share of shooting. Raised on a farm in Iowa, he became by his early twenties the preeminent taxidermist in the United States. In search of specimens for his employer, Henry Augustus Ward's Natural Science Establishment of Rochester, New York, he spent two years in South Asia, bagging all manner of beasts, including crocodiles, tigers, elephants, and monkeys and gibbons galore. In Borneo he shot forty-three orangutans, ten in a five-day spree. All these triumphs he celebrated in bloody detail in his book *Two Years in the Jungle*. His skill at mounting his trophies advanced him to the position of chief taxidermist for the National Museum, as the Smithsonian was called in its early years.

At the National Museum Hornaday continued his hunter-gatherer ways. In the fall of 1886, aware that North American buffalo would soon be extinct, he traveled to Montana and through luck and determination succeeded in killing twenty remnants. Six of these specimens he mounted in a lifelike tableau, which he displayed at the National Museum so that, at the very least, Americans could be reminded what buffalo looked like.

"I am really ashamed to confess it, but we have been guilty of killing buffalo in the year of our Lord 1886," Hornaday wrote in *Cosmopolitan*. "Under different circumstances, nothing could have induced me to engage in such a mean, cruel, and utterly heartless enterprise as the hunting down of the last representatives of a vanishing race. But there was no alternative. The Philistines were upon them, and between leaving them to be killed by the care-for-naught cowboys, who would leave them to decay, body and soul, where they fell, and killing them ourselves for the purpose of preserving their remains, there was really no choice. Perhaps you think a wild animal has no soul, but let me tell you it has. Its skin is its soul, and when mounted by skillful hands, it becomes comparatively immortal."

The demise of the buffalo cooled his blood lust, and in the coming years he came to prefer his wild animals alive rather than stuffed. Through his impassioned persuasions, Congress provided funds for a national zoo-logical park, a public version of the private zoos that existed in Europe; Hornaday was named the first superintendent of the Department of Living Animals of the United States National Museum—today's National Zoo in Washington's Rock Creek Park. In 1895, when a committee of the Boone and Crockett Club succeeded in passing legislation to incorporate the New York Zoological Society and to establish a zoological park in the city, the new board—which included George Bird Grinnell—chose William T. Hor-naday as founding director.

Grinnell and his fellow board members were fully in favor of Bronx Park as a site for the zoo. "It possesses the essentials of abundant water, abundant shade and sufficiently diversified topography," Grinnell wrote Hornaday in May 1896, "and besides this, the woodland and open grass lands are so admi-rably mingled that sites for the different buildings and enclosures could be selected with but little interference with existing natural conditions."

Yet once the location was decided on and the city signed over the land, it was Hornaday's vision that prevailed. He oversaw the layout of the grounds, the architecture of the Lion House, Reptile House, Monkey House, Flying Cage, and other structures. He championed the mission of the Zoological Society to provide a free park for "the enjoyment of the general public, the zoologist, the sportsman and every lover of nature." Additionally Hornaday called for the "promotion of zoological science" and cooperation with other organizations "in the preservation of the native animals of North America and encouragement of the growing sentiment against their wanton destruction."

The New York Zoological Park—Hornaday detested the name "Bronx Zoo"—opened its gates to the public on November 8, 1899, and thenceforth Hornaday ruled it as a fiefdom, answering to his board but never bowing to it. He worked at a frenzied pace and expected the same dedication from his employees. And with increasing intensity he turned his attention beyond the animals in his care to those that enjoyed no such sanctuary. He pub-lished a lengthy alarum on "The Destruction of Our Birds and Mammals" and used the *Zoological Society Bulletin* to advocate for the Lacey Act and other game-protection laws. In 1905 Hornaday founded the American Bison Society to promote "the permanent preservation and increase of the Amer-ican Bison," and, toward that end, the following year the New York Zoological Society sent seven buffalo from its herd of thirty-two to the Wichita Mountains Wildlife Refuge.

With funding from Mrs. Russell Sage, Henry Ford, and Andrew Carnegie, Hornaday created the Permanent Wildlife Protection Fund in 1911; it gave him a platform, independent of the Zoological Society, from which to launch his attacks on the perceived enemies of wildlife. In all of these causes, Hornaday garnered the appreciation of Grinnell and the Boone and Crockett Club, which welcomed him as an associate member in 1909. Eventually, though, the rapport between Hornaday and Grinnell's camp was stretched to the breaking point.

The rift between Hornaday and John Bird Burnham in particular had been building since the latter's time as state game commissioner; Hornaday had pronounced Burnham's efforts on behalf of wildlife "a lamentable failure." His disdain reached an even shriller pitch after Burnham took the helm of the American Game Protective and Propagation Association and bedded down with the gunmakers. Hornaday was convinced that the $125,000 offered by the manufacturers was a bribe, pure and simple, to get conservationists to withdraw their protests against the manufacture of pump and automatic shotguns.

Hornaday had been protesting the introduction of these more efficient firearms for nearly a decade. "A new engine of great destructive power has appeared in the field to aid the forces at work in the extermination of our game," he warned in 1904. In the strongest rhetoric, he likened automatic shotguns to the seining and dynamiting of streams and demanded that such instruments of wholesale destruction be outlawed.

On principle, but also out of spite, he was anxious to see the early versions of the migratory bird law fail. He preferred a law that protected *all* migratory birds, not just game birds; but almost anything that bore the fingerprints of Burnham and his devious "protective" association did not deserve to see the light of day. He even fought to keep Burnham from being elected to the Boone and Crockett Club.

Throughout the controversy, Grinnell counseled Burnham to shrug off Hornaday's provocations. In the hope of keeping channels open, Grinnell found it easier to communicate with the zoo director via Madison Grant, who served as secretary of both the Boone and Crockett Club and the New York Zoological Society.

(Grant and Hornaday weathered more than one storm together. History would remember Hornaday for many things but none darker than his decision in 1906 to exhibit a Congolese Pygmy by the name of Ota Benga in the Monkey House—a popular attraction until outraged African-Americans halted the degrading spectacle and removed Ota Benga to the Colored Orphan Asylum. Similarly, Madison Grant would have his reputation as a conservationist eclipsed by *The Passing of the Great Race*, his pseudoscientific treatise on white supremacy that became a clarion for the eugenics movement.)

Early in 1912, shortly after the gun manufacturers made their offer to the National Association of Audubon Societies and then to the AGPPA, Grinnell was moved to digress on the pettiness and potential destructiveness of Hornaday's conduct toward the migratory bird bill's proponents. "I am not . . . disposed to quarrel with Hornaday, whom I like," he wrote Grant. "He is a good fellow and a useful man, so long as he works at his own job. It is when he goes outside of his own job that he blunders and stirs up trouble. . . . We may properly be deferentially tactful with people who have bees in their bonnets, but we should not carry our tact to the point of getting our friends or ourselves in trouble."

Formerly Hornaday's ally, Grinnell now called him "unsafe" and feared that his disruptions endangered not only the bird bill, but also the greater movement of conservation. "The history of game preservation," Grinnell wrote Grant, "appears to me to show that many of the most promising movements have failed to accomplish results because game protective organizations have committed an extraordinary error. They have expended their time, money and effort in fighting each other about nonessentials, instead of getting together and working shoulder to shoulder. . . . As it used to be, and perhaps often still is, with the sects of the Christian religion, everyone who believes differently from those of each little group is wrong and must be damned."

The sectarian wounds between purists and pragmatists ran deep and, to a degree, would never heal. Much of the blame belonged to Hornaday. "He delights in a row," Grinnell told Grant, a characterization that Hornaday did not reject. Looking back on his career, Hornaday would proclaim, "I am positively the most defiant devil that ever came to town."

Yet a rapprochement was cobbled together long enough to give the migratory bird bill the nudge it needed. On the evening of September 18, 1912, a group of conservationists gathered for dinner at the Century Association in New York. Hornaday was there, as were Grant and the president of the Zoological Society, Henry Fairfield Osborn. T. Gilbert Pearson represented the Audubon societies; Grinnell represented the Boone and Crockett Club; Charles Sheldon seems to have been absent. Burnham, the hired gun of the American Game Protective and Propagation Association, attended, undoubtedly chewing on his tongue. Someone—Hornaday took credit—proposed that the language of the Senate version of the bill be altered to read: "All wild geese, swans, brant, wild ducks, snipe, plover, woodcock, rail, wild pigeons, and other migratory birds and insectivorous birds which in their northern and southern migrations pass through or do not remain permanently the entire year within the borders of any State or Territory, shall hereafter be deemed to be within the custody and protection of the Government of the United States and shall not be destroyed or taken contrary to regulations hereinafter provided for."

The difference was the phrase, *and insectivorous birds.* The bill now gave protection not only to migratory *game* birds but to *all* migratory birds, in order to court congressmen from farm states, who, thanks to efforts by the Bureau of Biological Survey, grasped the crucial role birds played in mitigating crop-destroying insects. The list of species now covered songbirds—robins, martins, and others beloved by not only sportsmen but also the greater public.

The rewording made that night came to be known among conservationists as the "the dickey-bird amendment." In due course the Weeks bill in the House was rewritten to echo McLean's in the Senate.

Everyone did his part. Grinnell published a rousing editorial in *Forest and Stream.* Hornaday distributed ten thousand copies of a circular, "Slaughter of Useful Birds: A Grave Emergency." Copies of his book-length polemic, *Our Vanishing Wildlife,* were delivered to every congressman. Hornaday also incited the membership of the Camp-Fire Club of America, of which he was a cofounder, to pepper Congress with letters. Audubon societies from every state did the same. Meanwhile, Sheldon and Grinnell leaned on the influential friends of the Boone and Crockett Club, and Burnham and his paid associates worked the halls of the Capitol.

The Senate's version of the bill passed first and then the House's. President Taft signed the Weeks-McLean Act into law on his very last day in office, March 4, 1913.

Although Hornaday would insist that "our 'song bird' issue rolled up far more support than their 'game' [issue]," Grinnell spread congratulations equally between the Zoological Society and the AGPPA. "To my mind," he wrote Madison Grant, "even more important than the passage of this bill . . . is the fact that harmony which I have so long advocated seems now to prevail." He dictated almost the exact same letter to Burnham.

Yet the campaign begun by George Shiras nine years earlier was not yet over. The Department of Agriculture, through the agency of the Biological Survey, still had to determine how the Weeks-McLean Migratory Bird Act would be implemented. Details such as length of hunting seasons, demarcation of hunting zones, and enforcement were left to a committee. Grinnell, Burnham, Hornaday, Pearson, and Shiras were among its fifteen members. While the committee deliberated, two district courts challenged the law's constitutionality. And since many of the birds that migrated across state lines also migrated across the international boundary with Canada, Congress was obliged to negotiate a treaty with Great Britain, which had dominion over America's northern neighbor. Not until 1918, after all the snarls were untangled and loose ends tied up, would the Migratory Bird Treaty Act, as it was officially called, become the permanent law of the land—and the flyways above it.

The long and trying ordeal revealed much about the evolution of the conservation movement and the internal friction between compromisers and idealists. But where others, like Hornaday, chose to see fault lines, Grinnell chose to see only growing pains. In 1911, as the migratory bird law was struggling to be born, he had written to Allen Chamberlain, president of the Appalachian Mountain Club: "The general conservation idea . . . is growing day by day, and I believe that I shall live long enough to see vast changes for the better."

CHAPTER 30

FIGHTING CHEYENNES

The rest of the winter and spring of 1913 was not nearly so hectic. "I fritter away much time," Grinnell told one of his former stenographers, but his notion of idleness was not one anybody would find fault with. He published three books that year: *Jack the Young Cowboy*, *Beyond the Old Frontier*, and a collection of folk tales for children, *Blackfeet Indian Stories*. The latest Boone and Crockett anthology, *Hunting at High Altitudes*, which included William Pickett's bear-killing reminiscences and reprinted Grinnell's history of the Boone and Crockett Club, also went to press. As for the Cheyenne books—he was working on them.

No longer tethered to an office, Grinnell gave more attention to the farm in Milford. Over the years he acquired several more parcels of land as they came up for sale. Thirty of his one hundred acres were under cultivation—alfalfa, millet, corn, potatoes, and vegetables. The remainder was wooded. He kept horses, a milk cow, pigs, and chickens. On weekends he and Elizabeth detrained at Naugatuck Junction, one stop west of the village of Milford, where they were met by a hired man in a two-seated rockaway. The road to the farm followed northward for a mile along the flats of the Housatonic River. The house, painted white, and the barn, painted green, sat on a low rise.

Help came and went, however. "Perhaps I am too finical," Grinnell admitted to Lute North after one of the all-too-frequent changes of staff that continued through the years. In January 1913 he responded to an advertisement in *New England Homestead*, placed by a couple seeking work. "I wish to get a man and his wife, without children," he stated. "The man should be able to take care of the general farm work. . . . The farmhouse is small, and a part of it is occupied by Mrs. Grinnell and myself when we go to Milford from Friday until Monday morning. In a wing are sleeping quarters and sitting room for anyone taking care of the place. The wife would be expected to keep house and cook the meals for my wife and myself. . . . She must be a good cook, not necessarily a fancy cook, but must give good, clean, plain food."

The summer began with lowered expectations. "The West has become so extraordinarily commonplace that one gets tired of it," Grinnell wrote to George Huntress as he and Elizabeth prepared to leave New York. The previous summer's sightseeing had dragged on too long; this year's itinerary would not be so ambitious. They wanted to spend a few days with the Eaton brothers in Wyoming but were disappointed to learn that the ranch had no more room for dudes. The next stop was to be Glacier, but Grinnell lamented in advance that the park had been "turned into a pleasure resort" crowded with tourists. Over the winter he had given up his plans to build a house on Jack Monroe's allotment at St. Mary; the cost was prohibitive. Monroe, too, had abandoned the idea of building a hotel for tourists. The Great Northern had beaten him to the punch, opening lodges and camps throughout the park.

Yet Grinnell could not stay away. "The force of habit keeps me still going to that dear place, though reasons for going there grow constantly fewer," he wrote Charles Reed, the Chicagoan he and Elizabeth had camped with in 1911.

On July 30 they checked into Glacier Park Lodge at Midvale, completed only a month before. The days of requisite roughing it were over. The lobby alone was two hundred feet in length, supported by thirty pillars of Douglas fir, fifty feet tall, three to four feet in diameter, some of them estimated to be more than five hundred years old. On his early trips Grinnell had carried his own bedroll, slept in a tent or on the floor of a trading post. This time his diary mentioned: "Good room with bath. . . . Good night & good breakfast."

To talk to Piegan friends, he did not need to stop in Browning. "A number of these Indians are camped up close to the big hotel at Midvale and come into the hotel every night and dance and make speeches," he wrote James Willard Schultz. "They are featuring old Frog Mouth as the oldest Indian in America. . . . [A]s a matter of fact, he is little over 67."

Grinnell and Elizabeth rode by automobile to St. Mary. "Trip made in about 2 hrs. and comfortable," he remarked. Again there was no need to camp; they took a room in the St. Mary Chalet and rode up the lake in a sixty-five-foot steam launch. Everywhere they went they ran into tourists. Along the shore they noticed two men shooting motion pictures.

For a few days they were able to distance themselves from the throng by riding up Red Eagle Creek and camping at the foot of Red Eagle Glacier, guided by one of the original settlers of the Walled-in Lakes, Henry Norris. (Jack Monroe was not available.) Grinnell spotted bighorn sheep and mountain goats but did not give chase. Then, almost on cue, Elizabeth became sick with indigestion, ending the outing. They spent the rest of their stay in the park, not venturing far from their hotel.

Later Grinnell would commiserate with Billy Hofer, with whom he had spent many weeks in the untracked wilderness of Yellowstone: "There is still quite a little room in the Glacier Park that has not been invaded by the tourists. Of course, when you go along the main-traveled routes, you are pushed off the trail every few minutes by the multitude. . . . You and I have been out West when it was reasonably lonesome. We ought to be thankful for the memories that we have of it, and not grumble too much about the crowds we see at present. Most of them regard themselves as explorers and have a fine time. That, after all, is what national parks are for."

After Glacier, Grinnell and Elizabeth headed south and passed a perfunctory week on the Northern Cheyenne reservation before continuing on to Denver and Santa Fe. They got as far as the ancient pueblos and cliff dwellings of Frijoles Canyon (in present-day Bandelier National Monument), whereupon, as Grinnell wrote to Jay White, "Mrs. Grinnell gave out again."

They were back in New York on September 13, sooner than Grinnell anticipated. "Mrs. Grinnell worked a little too hard in the mountains and got sick, and I had to bring her back, which I did not much like," he wrote in another letter to Billy Hofer. It was clear that Elizabeth had not so much suffered from indigestion as she had lost her appetite for the menu of western excursions. If the West was becoming commonplace to Grinnell, it was enervating to Elizabeth. She had given up photography a year or so before, and she had never been keen on sitting around a campfire with men only. Her symptoms, always vague, abated once she arrived home. A few weeks later she was fit enough for a bird-shooting trip to the Burnhams in the Adirondacks.

Grinnell was plenty fit, too, and in the fall he finally ran out of excuses for not bearing down on the first of the Cheyenne books—the "war" book. And yet he hesitated still. Instead he drafted a story, really a series of stories, about a Cheyenne boy named Wikis—not someone Grinnell knew, but a composite. The narrative, roughly thirty thousand words, follows Wikis (Cheyenne for wind) from the age of four to early manhood. The project was a detour born of apprehension; publishers had rejected his previous Cheyenne offerings for lack of commercial appeal.

He sent "The Boyhood of Wikis" to Ripley Hitchcock, who had published Grinnell's *The Story of the Indian* and was now with Harper & Brothers. He explained that it was told "in Indian fashion, simply, without any particular dressing up." And he braced for disappointment. "If . . . you feel that the public is not yet advanced enough to read with interest anything that does not talk about 'painted savages,'" he leveled with Hitchcock, "just tell me so, and I will leave the matter for my executors to attend to."

When Hitchcock suggested to Grinnell that he take creative liberties with "Wikis" and expand it into an entire book, Grinnell replied stubbornly: "You know that I am cranky and insist on dealing with facts. . . . I should not care to go back on the things about which I know or which have happened within the recollection of men that I know."

At that, Wikis went into a drawer, and Grinnell accepted that it was time to buckle down to the work he had been putting off for too long.

Moreover, he had come to realize that, given the prevailing political winds, the best service he could perform for his Indian friends just now was as a historian. With the change of administration in Washington— the departure of "strenuous Theodore" and the election of "psychological Wilson," as Grinnell quipped to Ned Dana—Grinnell's influence with the Indian Bureau fell off drastically.

In January 1914 he went to Washington, where so recently he had enjoyed ready access to Indian Commissioner Francis Leupp and his successor, Robert Valentine. Wilson's new man, Democrat Cato Sells, gave Grinnell the cold shoulder, as did Interior Secretary Franklin Lane. "I left word for Mr. Lane that if he wanted to talk with me about any Indian matters, I would be at his service during the two days of my stay," Grinnell wrote J. R. Eddy, the agent at Lame Deer. "I did not hear from him."

When he paid a visit to the Indian commissioner's office, "Mr. Sells was very pleasant but gave me the impression that he believed that he knew all about the Indian Office and Indian matters. . . . The Commissioner seems very confident of his ability to carry on his own office without assistance or suggestion, and so long as this is his attitude, one does not care to proffer anything in the way of advice."

Grinnell would forgive Lane for his slight, but his grudge over Sells's disrespect and arrogance intensified as his term continued. A year later Grinnell would write a letter to the *New York Times* accusing the commissioner of knowing "less about Indians and Indian matters than almost anyone connected to the Bureau."

Grinnell resolved to present his own superior fund of knowledge, and once he got busy on the Cheyenne war history, he found that the chapters came steadily. Summoning his years of research, interviews and correspondence with George Bent, assistance from George Hyde, and, to be thorough, close reading of military accounts of the Cheyenne wars, the book—which he began calling *The Fighting Cheyennes*—took shape.

The more he wrote, the more he came to admire his subject matter. When sculptor and Boone and Crockett member A. Phimster Proctor asked Grinnell to suggest worthy models for his work, Grinnell recommended the Northern Cheyennes. "These people are fifty or sixty miles from the railroad, and in certain ways have been less contaminated by white contact than any people that I have met. . . . I regard the Northern Cheyennes as the finest types physically that I know of."

In March he began planning yet another visit to Lame Deer and to several battlefields he wished to describe in the book. Elizabeth, however, announced that she would not join him. Her preference was to take a house in Woodstock, Vermont, to be near Charles and Louisa Sheldon. Grinnell consented and found a place to rent from late June through September. Milford would have sufficed, he explained, but "the attraction of Woodstock is the Sheldon family. Mr. Sheldon I know very well and like exceptionally. . . . His wife is . . . an extraordinarily strong and attractive woman whom we all think a great deal of. They are crazy about Woodstock."

Woodstock was fifteen miles west of the Connecticut River, with a village green, stately steeples, covered bridges, and a census of noteworthy citizens. It happened to be the birthplace of Charles Perkins Marsh, author of *Man and Nature* (1864), the seminal text of a philosophy and scientific discipline that one day would be known as ecology. ("[M]an is everywhere a disturbing agent. Wherever he plants his foot, the harmonies of nature are turned to discords," Marsh cautioned.)

Woodstock was also the current home of Frederick Billings, who, in the midst of founding and building the Northern Pacific Railway, purchased Charles Perkins Marsh's farm and reforested it according to the principles of stewardship that Marsh had encouraged in his book. Beyond the picturesque, Woodstock was a town of well-meaning wealth—an ideal fit for Charles Sheldon, railroad man turned conservationist.

Grinnell stayed a week in Woodstock before heading west. He and Sheldon spent an enjoyable day together, climbing four-thousand-foot Killington Peak; Grinnell's esteem for his young friend increased with every stride. In recommending Sheldon for membership in the Century Association later in the year, he would describe his nominee as "a man of splendid courage and endurance . . . a delightful fellow, possessing great personal charm, to which is added hard common sense and an admirable balance."

Grinnell arrived on the Northern Cheyenne reservation on July 8. After making the rounds of old friends, he was driven by automobile to Sheridan, Wyoming, with Willis Rowland, as interpreter, and White Elk, who was the same age as Grinnell, as guide.

They spent a day looking over the site of the so-called Fetterman Massacre, named for Captain William Fetterman, who on December 21, 1866, led a detachment of eighty infantry and cavalry from Fort Kearny to aid a party of woodcutters under attack by Indians. In so doing, they fell into a trap ingeniously set by Lakota Sioux chief Red Cloud. A small group of Cheyennes, Sioux, and Arapahos, including a young Crazy Horse, lured Fetterman's men over a ridge, out of sight of the fort, whereupon they were swarmed by a force of more than one thousand Indians. Every last soldier was killed, their bodies stripped and mutilated, to avenge the atrocities committed against Cheyennes and Arapahos at Sand Creek in 1864. So resounding was the defeat and the formidableness of the alliance of tribes defending their traditional hunting grounds of Wyoming's Powder River Basin that two years later the U.S. Government abandoned Fort Phil Kearny, closed the Bozeman Trail to whites, and by treaty guaranteed Sioux ownership of the Black Hills and hunting rights to a vast area of Dakota, Wyoming, and Montana territories. This was the treaty that Custer would disrespect and, by his discovery of gold, demolish during his reconnaissance of the Black Hills in 1874—with George Bird Grinnell and Lute North along for the ride.

"I went over the Ft. Phil Kearny battle ground and heard the story of the fight from a man who was in it, and it was quite a stirring time," Grinnell wrote Billy Hofer. "I was in the back seat with White Elk, who talks a very few words in English, but as we drew near the place, he pointed out and by words and signs told me what had happened in one place and another, and as we went on farther, he became more excited and began to sing to himself a little triumph song." Doubtless it was the same song White Elk sang over

Fetterman's fallen soldiers in 1874 and again two years later after he shared in another great triumph at the Little Bighorn.

When Grinnell's train pulled into New York on August 2, Elizabeth was there to greet him. Two developments had occurred while he was away: War had broken out in Europe, and Elizabeth had taken up golf. On July 28 Austria-Hungary declared war on Serbia, and within a week Germany invaded Luxembourg and Belgium, inciting Great Britain to declare war on Germany. "The European war is a most appalling thing, and no one knows what it will come to," Grinnell wrote to a cousin in England. "As things look at the present, the United States is the least likely of any of the powers of the world to be drawn into the war."

After a few days in New York, Grinnell and Elizabeth returned to Woodstock. He was not inclined to pursue golf himself but amenably joined Elizabeth on her outings, on which, as he joked to a niece, "I carry Elizabeth's clubs about and find fault with her playing."

They stayed through September, seeing the Sheldons frequently and enjoying the cool mountain air. Later in the fall Grinnell would boast to Jay White in London that Elizabeth was "so robust that when you come back here again, you will probably not know her. This summer, if I recollect aright, she gained ten pounds, and nowadays when we are out walking or shooting, she seems to keep up with me without any difficulty. I suspect that the time is close at hand when she will walk me down, and perhaps will soon herd me along by means of a stick, as we have all seen robust Indian women doing their feeble husbands."

He had just turned sixty-five.

Grinnell did not devote all of his time in Vermont to caddying. He had brought along or rented a typewriter, and it can be assumed that he hired a secretary, since he did not know how to type. On September 11 he wrote to George Hyde, with whom he had not been in touch for some time, informing him that he had completed a rough draft of a dozen chapters of the

Cheyenne war book and inquiring whether Hyde would be willing to look them over for inaccuracies.

Hyde replied that he would be very glad to help out. "My deafness and bad sight keep me in the house most of the time, and my one amusement is reading about the plains," he explained. "I am at it early and late and have collected a great amount of new material."

Over the next year Grinnell wrote letters to a number of other authorities and eyewitnesses, seeking clarification on specific Cheyenne engagements. "No one, I suppose, knows who killed the . . . son of Dull Knife," he posed to General W. S. Schuyler, who had been a young lieutenant during the attack of November 1876. "Capt. North never [claimed] to have killed him. He said that many people were shooting, but that when he and the boy shot at each other—almost at the same time—the boy fell. It was my inference that North's shot killed the boy. I am greatly interested in all that you say about this fight."

To General Edward S. Godfrey, who had survived the Little Bighorn and written about it authoritatively for *Century,* he broached a more delicate matter: "The Cheyennes who were at the Custer battle tell me a story . . . that [seems] too incredible, yet I cannot doubt that they tell it in good faith, and I want to ask you whether you can or are willing to throw any light on it. The Cheyennes tell me that they believe one reason for their victory is that the soldiers were drunk."

Grinnell also reached out to George Bent from time to time, but his queries reaped diminishing returns. "He has the best memory of any man I have ever met, and is the laziest man I ever met," Grinnell complained in exasperation to Billy Dixon, an old plainsman and Indian fighter.

For Bent's part, he had good reason for losing faith in Grinnell after so many years with so little to show. "I am getting tired of him," he admitted to George Hyde. Grinnell kept promising to make another trip to Oklahoma to see Bent, but he never quite got around to it, and, indeed, never saw Bent again after their visit in 1912.

For better or worse, the man he always came back to was Hyde, who lived with his rheumatic mother and worked for two dollars a day—the cost of typewriter ribbons, paper, and postage included. In early December

Grinnell sent Hyde a package containing fourteen chapters. "I should like to have you go over it, verify all the references, note any errors of fact or conclusion, and pin or paste your comments on the sides of the sheets," he instructed and then added: "I do wish to give the Indian side fully, just as they tell it, because the Indian side of the story has never been told."

Hyde was generally satisfied with what he read, but he was not afraid to point out Grinnell's sins of commission and omission. In the chapter on the Sand Creek massacre, he noted twenty-eight mistakes, and "most of them are bad ones," he told Grinnell. "I believe it would take no more time to rewrite the chapter than to attempt to correct it." Grinnell wrote back contritely: "I would rewrite the chapter, if I were you, and shall be glad to have you do so."

The chapter that received the most scrutiny, naturally enough, was the account of the Custer fight. Grinnell had researched this event more rigorously than any other in the annals of Cheyenne warfare, and Hyde deferred to his superior knowledge. "I suppose the idea I had gained that the Indians charged up and began fighting on horseback at once came from the fact that all accounts of the battle tell the story in that way and that we never had a really detailed account from trustworthy sources before now," Hyde conceded.

And so it went, Bent making corrections and suggestions, Grinnell incorporating them (or not)—and on occasion welcoming Hyde's offer to rewrite chapters entirely.

Strangely, although George Hyde and Lute North both lived in Omaha, they did not meet; nor did Grinnell encourage them to meet, perhaps because of Hyde's physical limitations. "He is a very young man, quite crazy about plains history," Grinnell told North. "Unfortunately, he is almost blind and stone deaf, so that he can only be communicated with by writing." Rather than arrange an introduction, Grinnell sent a separate set of chapters to North.

He took time off during the winter to shoot ducks in North Carolina, to enjoy weekends at Milford, to attend the annual Boone and Crockett dinner in Washington and the Sportsmen's Exposition at Madison Square Garden, and he and Elizabeth even went to the theater "for the first time in a year or two." But most days and a great many evenings were devoted to the Cheyennes. By the end of April the manuscript stood at 180,000 words, and Grinnell summoned his courage to test the market one more time. "I shall take my bundle under my arm," he told Lute North, "and shuffle round from publishing house to publishing house, trying to persuade them with tears in my eyes that in this book there are dollars for them, though probably only pennies for myself."

The first call was to Charles Scribner's Sons, who had published his most recent books, *Trails of the Pathfinders*, *Beyond the Old Frontier*, and *Blackfeet Indian Stories*, not to mention *The Wolf Hunters*, a memoir of plainsman Robert M. Peck, which Scribner's had accepted on the condition that Grinnell be credited as author. Almost sheepishly Grinnell sent the manuscript of *The Fighting Cheyennes* to Scribner's editor Edward Burlingame. "I have drawn marks in the margin opposite some paragraphs or pages that on a pinch can be taken out," he hedged. "I suppose that by chopping out all except the most exciting incidents it might be made a popular book."

To his surprise and enormous relief, Burlingame wrote back two weeks later, expressing "our disposition to undertake the publication." He agreed with Grinnell that the manuscript was long and followed the history "with much minuteness," but, all in all, he had only "one or two trifling suggestions" for revision.

Grinnell hurried to share the good news. More than twenty years of dedication and toil had at last paid off. *The Fighting Cheyennes* meant more to him than anything he had published before. "I feel as if there was a whole lot of good stuff in the book," he wrote to Lute North with unmuffled pride after hearing from Scribner's, "and while, no doubt, I have made a lot of mistakes, I really feel as if it was a contribution to the history of the development of the western country. You see how modest I am!"

He celebrated further at his forty-fifth Yale reunion in June. And after he and Elizabeth attended the crew races, baseball game, and other festivities at New Haven, she agreed to accompany him to Glacier, once classmate Gaff Reeve and his wife said they would join them. This would not be a reprise of the last western trip Grinnell and Reeve had taken together, with Professor Marsh in 1870. They promised their wives that they would not have to suffer any hardship. The goal, Grinnell declared, was "to sit on a hotel piazza and jeer at the other tourists."

The first galley proofs of *The Fighting Cheyennes* arrived on July 21, a week before the Grinnells were to depart for Montana. He read all that he could before leaving and forwarded the pages to George Hyde. The remainder he took with him, going over them on the train and during the two weeks at Glacier Park Lodge and Many Glacier Hotel.

After an enjoyable time with the Reeves in Glacier, the Grinnells went west to Seattle, where they looked up Billy Hofer. They contemplated swinging south to San Francisco, to take in the Panama-Pacific Exposition, celebrating the completion of the Panama Canal, but then reconsidered. Instead they chose to come home by way of Salt Lake City. "It was many years since I had been over the Union Pacific Railroad," Grinnell wrote to his sister Laura, "and I was much interested in seeing again places that I had known more than forty years ago."

The rest of the proofs arrived in bunches throughout September and were then passed under Hyde's magnifying glass. When all was out of Grinnell's hands—text, index, and eleven maps—he was stricken with the fear that he had not done enough. "The book is promised for October," he wrote Hyde. "I have read it over so many times that it seems to me now about the most rotten stuff that anybody ever turned out. . . . This same thing happened to me many times before. One gets absolutely sick and disgusted with his stuff before it gets between covers."

Hyde responded with consoling words: "I came to the galleys with a fresh mind and believe the book is very good indeed. . . . I can't remember a single bad mistake. The little faults are so small you cannot get hold of them."

Grinnell received his first copy on October 18. "'The Fighting Cheyennes' crept out of its hole the other day," he wrote Billy Hofer. In a letter to Harriet Audubon, who lived in Louisville, Kentucky, he described the book's arrival more as fatherhood. "You see, the average book is compounded of . . . ideas brought together and cemented by the blood and sweat of the man who got it together," he explained. "He has a feeling toward it that no one else can altogether comprehend."

The preface to *The Fighting Cheyennes* is dated August 10, 1915, likely written on the "piazza" of Many Glacier Hotel, as Grinnell studied the tourists and gazed across Swiftcurrent Lake toward Mount Grinnell and Grinnell Glacier. In his acknowledgments he thanks Lute North, a half dozen military men, and "many Cheyenne friends," though the only Indian he credits by name is George Bent. As for George Hyde's contribution, he states that he "has verified most of the references and given me the benefit of his careful study of the history of early travel on the plains." No mention of the numerous sections rewritten by Hyde.

"This book deals with the wars of the Cheyennes," he begins. "A fighting and a fearless people, the tribe was almost constantly at war with its neighbors, but until 1856 was friendly to the whites."

"Since the Indians could not write," he continues, "the history of their wars has been set down by their enemies, and the story has been told always from the hostile point of view." Make no mistake, he alerts his audience, the book they were reading was unlike any other previous rendering of the subject. "Evidently there is another side to this history," he declares, "and this other side is one which should be recorded."

The Fighting Cheyennes is a tour de force—comprehensive and confident, rich in background and drenched in blood. It begins with the Cheyennes' clashes with other tribes—Crows, Kiowas, Comanches, Pawnees. "The fighting spirit was encouraged," Grinnell observes. "They fought not only to gain the approval of their fellow tribesmen but for pure enjoyment of the struggle—real *gaudium certaminis*" (joy of contest).

Enter next a more lethal enemy: "If the tribes were not generally hostile to the white men, it was not because they lacked cause of complaint against them. Lawless white men roved over the plains, killing the game, often treating the Indians with the utmost arrogance, and bringing liquor and disease among them."

Once the U.S. Army rode onto the field, to open and protect the path of emigrants, gold miners, and railroads, the collisions grew more fierce and more devastating, a chain reaction of defiance and death, a downward spiral of cruelty and defeat—from Sand Creek to Fort Phil Kearny, to the Washita, to the Little Bighorn, to the attack on Dull Knife's camp; and to the Cheyenne breakouts, first from Oklahoma and then from Fort Robinson, interrupted by the occasional untrustworthy truce and disingenuous treaty.

The stories are enlivened and grounded by the testimony of eyewitnesses. George Bent's account of Sand Creek appears virtually verbatim. As a rule, Grinnell trusted the memory of Cheyennes over that of whites. "The old-time Indian was a far better observer than most white men. He saw more clearly what was happening and usually reported facts more accurately," Grinnell asserts.

Whites, meanwhile, were blinkered by prejudice, incompetence, and vainglory. "[Capt. H. E.] Palmer's account of this affair [an attack on an Indian village] is quite graphic," Grinnell remarks, "though written from the point of view of a man who knew nothing of Indians and Indian fighting but wished to impress an audience. . . ."

Or: "General Carrington was a man of great ability and of varied pursuits, but he knew nothing of Indians. . . ."

Or, more bluntly still: "Custer's own account is distorted and exaggerated. . . ."

In Grinnell's opinion, the Cheyennes were a people of upright character and good intentions. "In Black Kettle, White Antelope, and Yellow Wolf, all old men, who were all killed by the whites, we have three examples of high patriotism," Grinnell eulogizes. "These men were constant workers among the Indians in behalf of peace with the white people. They did this not because they loved the white people, from whom they had received nothing good, but because they loved their own tribe and wished to guide it in paths that would be for the tribe's greatest advantage."

If, by the end of four hundred pages of text, there is any question where Grinnell stands, it is answered in his final paragraph. His tone might have been more temperate had the current commissioner of Indian affairs shown him more consideration. But, once aggrieved, Grinnell sets upon his opponents, much as the Cheyennes had done upon theirs:

"If the Indian Bureau should adopt a broad and definitely settled policy—one sufficiently elastic to be adaptable to the needs of each of the different Indian reservations—the progress of the race toward civilization would be hastened; but such a policy cannot be thought out and set on foot without preparation. Before it could be outlined, the Bureau would require a vast amount of information on the conditions on most reservations, which it now absolutely lacks. . . . Even if such a policy were adopted, it seems quite likely that at the end of four years it would be changed again, and the new officials—as their predecessors have so often done—would begin to tear down what the previous administration had built up, and a new Indian commissioner would try out his theories on the helpless people. There is little hope of any rapid advance of the Indians under present conditions."

"Yet, unconsciously," Grinnell concludes, shedding a ray of optimism, "[Indians] are changing, and will continue to change, and the time is coming, perhaps sooner than we think, when the Indians will be a component and useful part of the population of this country."

George Hyde received his copy of *The Fighting Cheyennes* on November 5 and thanked Grinnell for the handwritten note on the flyleaf. "Your share in the volume is more than you have credit for," Grinnell wrote Hyde in a follow-up letter, "and I, of course, am continuingly grateful for the help you gave." Ever obsequious, Hyde assured Grinnell, "I shall always keep the book in remembrance of the pleasant months I have put in on the work."

At the same time that Grinnell's book was reaching bookstores and libraries, Hyde at long last was finishing his own collaboration with George Bent. As he had predicted, no publisher expressed interest. The manuscript would molder in the archives of the Denver Public Library, unseen and unappreciated, for another fifty years.

Grinnell was impatient for reviews; when they appeared, they were mostly flattering, though not all effusive. "The book has not been out long enough to have many opinions passed on it," he wrote Hyde in mid-November, "but on the other hand . . . last Sunday's *Sun* gave it a very nice notice of about two and one-third columns."

The most generous review came from the *Times*: "There is something of the Homeric quality in this story," the newspaper pronounced. "It is an American epic, a romantic chapter of our history seen from a new and wider viewpoint, and told with an understanding of Indian character such as few writers have yet attained."

Grinnell sent a copy to Theodore Roosevelt, explaining to Charles Sheldon that Roosevelt "has not much use for Indians but may possibly be interested in the historical side of the volume." When Roosevelt wrote Grinnell that he was "delighted" with the book, Grinnell responded: "I am glad you like it. I feel myself that it contains some wild meat."

The book's harshest critic turned out to be its author. Grinnell berated himself for misspelling a general's name and for calling the Eighteenth Kansas Regiment the Nineteenth. The blunder that would eventually gall the most, though, was the orientation of the map of the Dull Knife fight. "The lettering on the map must be changed and brought around . . . so that now north shall be east, east shall be south, and so on," he pleaded to Edward Burlingame at Scribner's. The embarrassment was almost more than he could bear, and he was anxious to have the change made on the printing plates—presumably for any future editions. "I have rather a feeling that I am partner in a fraud so long as any of these maps . . . go out wrong, and I should like to have the errors corrected now, even at some cost to myself."

He really had little to complain about, however. Although his Yale classmates were failing, one by one, and his brother-in-law Newell Martin had quit work after a nervous breakdown, Grinnell himself was going strong. "I find that at my time of life it does not at all do either to be ill or to imagine that I am ill, and I think one's imagination has much to do with the way he feels," he explained to Harriet Audubon. "If I am always well, it is, I think, because I have spent most of my time out of doors and have tried to live an active life."

The week after *The Fighting Cheyennes* was published, Grinnell and Elizabeth went up to Woodstock for a week of partridge and woodcock shooting with the Sheldons. Grinnell took along his dog, Partner, who, he told Sheldon, "continues to be one of the joys of my life." As they strode the Vermont uplands, the two men, eighteen years apart, discussed many things—mountain sheep, game preservation, William T. Hornaday's latest antics. And they agreed that after the New Year they would make an effort to introduce themselves to a fellow whom they had heard good things about: Stephen Mather, assistant to the secretary of the interior, with specific responsibility for the national parks.

A railroad was being built in Alaska from the mouth of Cook Inlet north along the eastern side of the Alaska Range, Sheldon's old stomping grounds. Sheldon wanted badly to spare this pristine wilderness, including the tallest peak in North America, Mount McKinley, from harm. Stephen Mather, as Sheldon and Grinnell were soon to discover, was an ambitious and resourceful man. He had already set his sights on something even grander than a national park for McKinley. He envisioned bringing *all* national parks together into a whole, under his supervision.

CHAPTER 31

THE NATIONAL PARK SERVICE

C harles Sheldon had been talking up the Mount McKinley idea for years. In November 1915, with construction of the railroad from Seward to Fairbanks under way, he convened the Game Preservation Committee of the Boone and Crockett Club, including Grinnell and Edward Nelson of the Bureau of Biological Survey, and together they drafted a proposal promoting the park. Next Sheldon approached James Wickersham, Alaska's delegate to Congress, to convince him of the urgency of protecting the region's wildlife; each year market hunters killed thousands of sheep, moose, and caribou in the foothills of the Alaska Range; these numbers were sure to multiply as the railroad made the interior more accessible. Once Sheldon drew the boundaries to exclude the choicest mineral ground and explained that a national park would actually boost the Alaska economy through increased tourism, Wickersham agreed to introduce the Boone and Crockett Club bill. The next man to see was Stephen Mather at the Department of the Interior.

Stephen Tyng Mather was descended from the Puritan Mathers. His father left Connecticut for New York and then moved to San Francisco, where Stephen was born in 1867. As a young man, he summited Mount Rainier, hiked Yosemite, and joined the Sierra Club. After college he went east and worked for the *New York Sun,* where his wizardry with words caught the attention of Francis "Borax" Smith, owner of the Pacific Coast Borax Company. Borax was mined almost exclusively in California and used mostly for water softening and eyewash; Mather soon made Pacific Coast's borax a household essential, trampling the competition through advertisement of its "20 Mule Team" brand. Before long Mather and a partner unseated Borax Smith and made the mule team their own.

Wealthy by his early forties, Mather turned to his first love, America's wild places. He took John Muir's side in the Hetch Hetchy fight, and in 1914 he wrote a letter to Franklin Lane, Woodrow Wilson's secretary of the interior and a fellow Cal alumnus, complaining about the government's shabby treatment of the country's national parks and national monuments. Lane responded by offering Mather the position of assistant secretary, apologizing for the paltry salary. Mather didn't need the money, but Robert Sterling Yard, a friend from the *Sun* whom he hired as *his* assistant, did. Officially the government paid Yard only thirty dollars a month; Mather made up the difference from his own pocket. He also persuaded a bright young law graduate from California named Horace Albright to stay on.

One of Mather's first initiatives was to lead a group of politicians, railroad men, and other swells on a grand tour of western parks. To fan publicity, he invited Emerson Hough, who now wrote for the *Saturday Evening Post,* and Gilbert Grosvenor, editor of *National Geographic.* Stops included Sequoia, Yosemite, Crater Lake, Mount Rainier, Mount Olympus (today's Olympic National Park), Rocky Mountain, Yellowstone, and Glacier.

In Yellowstone Mather completed the first automobile trip of the Grand Loop. In Glacier he rode horseback from Lake McDonald, over Gunsight Pass, to St. Mary, a trip Grinnell had never made. Before leaving Glacier, Mather arranged to purchase, again with his own money, land for the park's much-needed headquarters. By the time he returned to Washington in the fall, the consummate propagandist had broadcast a clear and appealing message, perfectly tailored to the times: Europe and the world were in turmoil, but America's crown jewels remained intact, and they needed protecting and appreciating. Their net value, as Mather so graphically demonstrated during his ballyhooed summer circuit, was far greater than the sum of the many unique and splendid parts.

In December 1915 Grinnell suggested to Charles Sheldon that he approach Mather about Mount McKinley. Sheldon and Mather were only three months apart in age; both had made a great deal of money early in life; and both were indefatigable advocates of preservation. Sheldon began by writing a letter, demonstrating his familiarity with the region and stressing the need to protect its "vast reservoir of game." He also declared that, for sheer grandeur, the only scenery in North America to compare with Mount McKinley was the Grand Canyon.

Mather was sold. The two met in person, and a few days later Sheldon put Mather (who was not a big-game hunter) up for associate membership in the Boone and Crockett Club. Mather was now inside the tent.

At the annual meeting of the Boone and Crockett Club on January 7, 1916, the handsome, hyperactive Mather assured his newly acquired brethren that he would do everything he could to make Mount McKinley National Park a reality. They, in turn, embraced his notion of a unified administration of the country's thirteen national parks and eighteen national monuments.

On April 16 the Mount McKinley bill was introduced in the House and Senate simultaneously. "I wish with all my heart that it might be called Denali Park," Grinnell wrote Robert Sterling Yard, seconding Sheldon's desire to use the native name for the mountain—meaning "the High One." What the park would be called was of minor concern, however. Getting it past Congress came first.

Others went to bat for McKinley—notably Belmore Browne, who knew the mountain as intimately as any man alive; in 1912 he had come within a few windblown steps of its 20,310-foot summit. Representing the large and influential membership of the Camp-Fire Club, Browne had arrived in Washington in early January to lobby for national park designation, only to be informed by Robert Sterling Yard that Sheldon and the Boone and Crockett Club were in the field ahead of him. The two clubs agreed to join forces and lend their assistance to Wickersham and the chief engineer of the Alaska Railroad (and future Alaska governor), Thomas Riggs, in drawing up a park bill.

At a meeting at Sheldon's house in New York, attended by Camp-Fire and Boone and Crockett men, Sheldon proposed that the responsibility of lobbying Congress be entrusted to the man who had been so effective in passing the Weeks-McLean migratory bird act of 1913: John Bird Burnham of the American Game Protective Association (which had dropped *and Propagation* from its name).

Meanwhile, Stephen Mather moved ahead with his scheme to gather all the national parks and monuments under one umbrella. In April two California congressmen, John Raker and William Kent, introduced a national parks bill they had crafted with the guidance of, among others, Mather, Gilbert Grosvenor, landscaper architect and conservationist Frederick Law Olmsted, Jr., and J. Horace McFarland of the American Civic Association, famous for having defended Niagara Falls from commercial encroachment.

Mather figured that the national parks bill, like the Mount McKinley legislation, would swirl in an eddy of red tape before working its way downstream, and so he headed west for another summer of inspections. He was in Yosemite when he received the surprising news that the parks bill had passed the House. Still, the Senate could not be expected to react so nimbly. He was on a pack trip in Sequoia National Park when, by more good fortune, the bill found the requisite votes in the upper house.

As Mather rode out of the mountains on August 26, he was handed a telegram sent from Washington by his able, if underpaid, assistant, Horace Albright. The previous evening Albright had slipped the bill into a packet with another one on army appropriations that the president had been expecting. A call to Wilson from Interior Secretary Lane ensured that the president would not overlook the park document, and before retiring for the night, Wilson signed it. When Mather swung from the saddle in Visalia, California, on the twenty-sixth, he learned that his job title had changed; forthwith he would be director of a brand new federal agency: the National Park Service.

The bill to create Mount McKinley National Park took another year to come to a vote. John Burnham ran another efficient campaign, coaxing the various preservation groups to work in unison. Grinnell went to Washington to testify before the House Committee on Public Lands and nudged the current editor of *Forest and Stream* to run several pro-McKinley items. The Boone and Crockett Club hosted a banquet for key congressmen. Newspapers and magazines, egged on by Mather and Yard, ran stories on the wonders of Mount McKinley.

Congress finally passed the bill on February 20, 1917, and Charles Sheldon was given the honor of delivering it to the White House, where it was signed into law a week later. It was the first addition to the roster of the National Park Service. (Mount McKinley would not be renamed Denali until 1980; Mount McKinley National Park finally became Denali National Park in 2015.)

Afterward—and inevitably—there was bickering over which group had done most for the cause. Grinnell would have none of it. "As I have told you many times," he wrote Madison Grant, "I think that one reason why . . . preservation matters have gone so slowly in this country is because a lot of us have been continually squabbling over who should get the credit of having done something or started something. My view for a good many years has been to try to get results . . . and I know you feel in that way yourself, differing from your excellent subordinate, Hornaday"—a Camp-Fire Club man—"who prefers to have the light held always on himself."

Grinnell was out west when the National Park Service drew its first breath. He and Elizabeth had stored their silver in a vault at Tiffany's for safe-keeping and left New York on June 16. They stopped in Omaha to see the Norths, and Grinnell had a pleasant visit with George Hyde. From Omaha they went to Wyoming, where Elizabeth spent the next two weeks enjoying the comforts of Eatons' Ranch. Grinnell continued to Rosebud, Montana, on the Yellowstone River. There he rendezvoused with three men who shared his interest in the events of 1876.

In firsthand experience, General Edward Godfrey held rank. He had served under Custer at the Washita in 1868. He had been with Custer in the Black Hills in 1874, which is when Grinnell first made his acquaintance. And of course he had been at the Little Bighorn in 1876. After campaigns in Cuba and the Philippines, he retired to New Jersey. Grinnell went there to see him several times while working on *The Fighting Cheyennes.*

Walter M. Camp was from Chicago. He earned his living as editor of the *Railway and Engineering Review*, though his true passion was the Indian wars. He was as fanatical on the subject as Grinnell or George Hyde, and over the years he had interviewed scores of participants in the major battles.

The third member of the party was L. A. Huffman, a photographer from Miles City, Montana, who had come west in 1879 to serve as photographer at nearby Fort Keogh and sustained a respectable career documenting the people and ranch life of the lower Yellowstone.

On the morning of June 21 Grinnell found Godfrey, Camp, and Huffman waiting for him at Rosebud with a three-seat Dougherty wagon. For the next four days they drove upstream along Rosebud Creek, following—by Godfrey's memory—the route the Seventh Cavalry had taken forty years before. The creek was high, bridges were washed out, and they had difficulty finding places to cross. As they made their way, they swapped their considerable knowledge and debated historical details, each night bunking at a roadside ranch.

On the twenty-third they reached the Northern Cheyenne reservation, where they met up with August Stohr, the agency trader, and Willis Rowland, Grinnell's favorite interpreter. From Lame Deer the wagon headed west toward Crow Agency, and at dawn on the twenty-fifth, they reached the south fork of Reno Creek—named for Custer's second in command, Major Marcus Reno—and continued onward to the Little Bighorn River.

"Passed waterhole where Custer's outfit watered," Grinnell wrote in his diary, "and then to [the] hill held by [Captain Frederick] Benteen"—whose three companies had brought up the rear—"and on to the scene of the Reno fight. Saw Benteen's trenches and some fragments of weathered horse bones. Then on to [the] Custer battlefield, which we reached at 12:30." They could not have planned their arrival more perfectly. "[W]e reached the battlefield on the same day of the month and week, and at the same hour of the day that Custer had reached it forty years before," Grinnell reported.

He estimated that five thousand people attended the memorial ceremony that afternoon. Special trains ran from Sheridan and Billings. One local newspaper, the *Hardin Tribune*, reported that as many as one thousand automobiles made the trip—"the greatest number of automobiles ever gathered in one place in the state of Montana." Godfrey led the parade, followed by several other military men and "a lot of Indians in war togs," Grinnell observed. George Herendeen, a scout who had attacked with Reno and lived to tell about it, rode in the procession with Grinnell. A band from the Crow reservation played "Garry Owen," the signature song of the Seventh Cavalry.

Near the monument marking where Custer had fallen, Godfrey stood in a car above the crowd and reflected less on the heroism of June 25, 1876, and instead dwelt, with macabre detail, on the aftermath of the slaughter.

"The day after the arrival of General Terry's relief column and three days after the battle which we now commemorate, the Seventh cavalry under Major Reno broke camp to march to the field to bury the dead," Godfrey told his audience, which stood among the headstones of those very same soldiers. "On reaching yonder hill, the highest point of this field, the command was dismounted to receive instructions. With the glint of the early morning sun the inequalities of the ground were brought out in striking relief. We saw in bewildered astonishment what appeared to be white boulders scattered all over the field. 'What are they?' 'Are those rocks?' There were almost universal exclamations as the troops successively arrived at the top of the hill. An officer raised his field glasses; in a moment his arms dropped limp by his sides, and he said with suppressed feelings: 'My God! They are the bodies of the dead!'" All had been stripped, scalped, and mutilated, Godfrey attested—"except one, General Custer."

Finally Two Moon was given the chance to speak for the Cheyennes and Sioux. "Yes, I was here forty years ago and I helped in the battle," he stated through an interpreter, perhaps Willis Rowland. "I was the foe of the white man then; now I am his ally. We belong to the same country, adore the same flag and serve the same god."

This, anyway, was how the *Billings Gazette* chose to report Two Moon's remarks. The *Hardin Tribune* quoted him somewhat more tersely: "[We] wiped Custer and his followers off the face of the earth, but now the Indians and the whites are friends."

Grinnell, though, absorbed none of this oratory. "I was not near enough to hear them," he wrote to Wyoming historian Grace Raymond Hebard. "No doubt they were good." Afterward he and Walter Camp placed a marker on the spot where they believed Charley Reynolds had met his end in the river bottom of the Little Bighorn.

Two days later Grinnell went south with Willis Rowland, his wife, Nahka, and four other Cheyennes: Two Moon, Dog, Harry Hand, and Braided Locks, all of whom, including Nahka, had been with Dull Knife in November 1876. They traveled past Sheridan, past Buffalo, to Kaycee, Wyoming, where they turned west up the North Fork of the Powder River.

Although *The Fighting Cheyennes* was a fait accompli, Grinnell remained obsessed with the blow-by-blow account of Colonel Ranald Mackenzie's attack that effectively ended the army's war with the Cheyennes. In the course of his research Grinnell had exchanged letters with Leonidas Condit, whose ranch was near the battlefield, and Condit had invited Grinnell to see the site for himself. After a long ride over a twisty road, he and his companions arrived at the Condit ranch on June 29 and were "most kindly received."

Early the next morning they drove to where Dull Knife and more than nine hundred of his people had camped on the frigid night of November 24, 1876. "We climbed the high red butte . . . and from that point got a wide, birds-eye view of [the] valley," Grinnell wrote. Only then did he realize his mapmaking error. He had shown Mackenzie's troops (and the Norths' Pawnee scouts) approaching from the north, when, as was now obvious, they had come from the east. "Who is responsible for this blunder?" he fumed in his diary.

The group spent the day walking over the scene of the fighting. The Cheyennes' memories came flooding back. "We saw where Lt. McKinney fell, where Bull Hump fought, where Long Jaw was cornered and was helped out by the 20 men in war bonnets, and where 6 young men were killed close under the mt," Grinnell recorded.

The next day they went back to Sheridan, where Grinnell paid the Indians for their time and sent them on their way. Later he was driven the twenty-five miles to Eatons' Ranch. "Found all well and E[lizabeth] glad to see me," he mentioned. They took a morning ride in the foothills of the Big Horn Mountains and paused for an hour to watch a golden eagle feast on the entrails of a dead range cow—a raw version of the Audubon painting *The Eagle and the Lamb*, which hung on the wall in Stuyvesant Square. When it was time to leave, Howard Eaton refused to let Grinnell pay for Elizabeth's stay.

Grinnell and Elizabeth arrived at Mammoth Hot Springs, in Yellowstone National Park, on July 4, their first visit in twelve years. All that Grinnell had foreseen—the increase in tourists and concessions—had been borne out. The hotels were full and the roads choked with the dust of automobiles. They took the Grand Loop through the geyser basins and stayed at the Old Faithful Inn, Yellowstone's counterpart to the timber temple of Glacier Park Lodge. They rode a steam launch along the shore of Yellowstone Lake and in the evening watched bears eat garbage put out by hotel employees. "They did not fear the spectators at all," Grinnell remarked.

Glacier, where they arrived on the thirteenth, was no wilder—which was fine by Elizabeth. For two weeks they soaked up the scenery and socialized with other tourists, never venturing long or far from their hotel. On the first night at Many Glacier, Grinnell wrote in his diary: "E[lizabeth] tickled because a Mr. Adams to whom she spoke asked if she was Mr. Grinnell's daughter or his granddaughter!"

On sunny days they rode out from the hotel on hired horses, once as far as Swiftcurrent Pass, but they always returned in time to dress for dinner. One day he and Elizabeth took a picnic to Grinnell Lake, until the bugs became unbearable. The talk among the other guests was of a plan to build a proper horse trail all the way to Grinnell Glacier. On the way out of the park, they stopped at St. Mary, where they missed seeing Jack Monroe but found his two eldest sons, Jesse and Joe, and learned that both were in trouble for horse stealing.

Although Grinnell had been to the Northern Cheyenne reservation earlier in the summer, he could not resist returning. This time Elizabeth agreed to accompany him. Grinnell's diary reveals no particular focus to the trip. There was no medicine lodge or massaum dance to observe. Mostly he seemed content to mingle with old friends and gather up whatever stories they cared to tell.

And still they did not go home. On September 1 they met Lute North and his wife in Sterling, Colorado, and were driven eighteen miles to Summit Springs, where forty-seven years earlier, on July 11, 1869, Frank and Lute North, thirty Pawnee scouts, and six companies of the Fifth Cavalry under the command of Major Eugene Carr had attacked a camp of four hundred Cheyennes and Sioux. Grinnell had learned about the fight directly from Lute and also from Frank North's unpublished memoirs; he had devoted an entire chapter to it in *The Fighting Cheyennes*.

North was pleased that he still recognized the terrain, and he had little difficulty finding where the Indian lodges had stood and where the worst killing had occurred. But, in the end, there was not much to see. "We looked in vain for bones or cartridge shells," Grinnell wrote after the visit. The springs of Summit Springs were now muddy and trampled by the hooves of livestock, the usurpers of plains that had once belonged to the buffalo—buffalo the Cheyennes and Sioux had been hunting when they were suddenly assaulted.

The trip stirred another memory. After saying goodbye in Sterling, the Grinnells headed east to New York, and the Norths continued west to visit other parts of Colorado. Once both couples had arrived home, North wrote Grinnell and evidently made reference to an incident never discussed in previous letters. Grinnell, plainly aroused, replied suggestively: "You say nothing in your account of your trip to Colorado as to whether you visited the Big Thompson"—the Big Thompson River flows from the Rocky Mountains northeastward into the South Platte—"and saw some of the spots where so many events occurred in the years gone by."

Grinnell did not specify precisely *which* events, except to say: "Is that great cottonwood tree standing just below the mouth of that little canyon, where you and I—."

Here he caught himself. "[Y]ou and I dare not put it on paper for fear this letter might fall into other hands than yours. What a mercy it is that those who have known us so well in these later days are ignorant of the frightful events that happened to you and to me during the months that we spent in the heyday of our youth on that historic stream. I need not remind you of those happenings. They are branded on your memory as deeply as on mine."

Neither Grinnell's memoirs nor any of his diaries mentions a trip to the Big Thompson. Grinnell did make a hunting trip to North Park in Colorado in 1878, as recounted in *Forest and Stream* (under the byline "Yo") and later fictionalized in *Jack the Young Trapper*. But Lute North was not along on that outing. The best guess is that he and Grinnell made it as far as the Big Thompson on one of North's subsequent visits to the Shirley Basin ranch. If they did, a record of the outing and its "frightful events" was never kept.

Yet North's response to Grinnell's letter of October 1916 *was* kept. "No, I didn't go over to the Big Thompson," he answered. "You know my wife was with me and there is no telling what might have happened if we had met one of the Oldtimers there. That part of our life would be no longer a secret."

To which Grinnell wrote back: "I am glad you handled the region of the Big Thompson as discreetly as you did. God forbid that anyone dear to us should ever hear of the events of those early days."

What could warrant such secrecy? It was widely known that Lute North had a violent past—had killed his share of Indians. Grinnell, too, was proud of his brief skirmish with the Sioux in 1872. He liked being thought of as a man of arms. If he had ever killed or injured an Indian or anyone he deemed miscreant, he would not have kept the deed to himself. And if he and North had committed some form of unsportsmanlike excess, they would not have been quite so haunted by it. At any rate, the episode on the Big Thompson was not something they wished to advertise. Nor would they ever forget it.

The Indian wars were bygone, but another war was close at hand. Woodrow Wilson was reelected in November, to Grinnell's disappointment. "Wilson is the champion wobbler," he complained to Jay White, who was still in England, "and in his efforts to 'keep us out of the war,' he may dump us into it at any moment."

Like most Americans, Grinnell had hoped that the United States would not be drawn into the clash of nations that was laying waste to Europe, but he was also a proponent of preparedness. His convictions were bolstered by Julius W. Muller's alarmist novel, *The Invasion of America*, which played out a German invasion of Rhode Island, followed by the capture of Boston and New York, and, ultimately, led to "a brave Nation, a greatly capable Nation, made to grovel for her life because, in a world of men, she had failed to prepare for what men might do." Grinnell sent copies to friends, and in correspondence with Muller he commiserated: "I suppose it is hopeless to try to get the American people to think. They do not know how to do it, and it may be questioned if they will ever learn."

In the early months of 1917, as America's participation in the war became likely, Grinnell grew more sanguine and fatalistic. "It is readily conceivable," he wrote Ned Dana in February, "that war, no matter what it cost in blood and suffering, might be a good thing for this country. Certainly the American people need discipline." To George Hyde he added a nativist edge to his frustration: "It is a very humiliating thing that there should be in this country a considerable body of people who seem to consider their own ease and comfort more than honor, not to say decency. I suppose that a good many of them have not been here long enough to have absorbed the American idea."

Already several members of his greater family had stepped forward. An English cousin, George Grinnell-Milne, had two sons in the Royal Flying Corps. And his niece Sylvia Page had married an Italian, Renzo Brusati, who served in the Italian artillery.

Once the United States declared war on Germany on April 3, Grinnell made the customary noises about doing his part. "I have had a senile ambition to go to war, forgetting my years and my infirmities," he told Ned Dana, with whom he shared most infirmities. One was lumbago—a chronic pain in his left hip—that he attributed to the fall he had taken while packing out a sheep in Montana thirty years earlier; another was that he had grown so deaf that he could not even hear the telephone ring.

"You and I are scarcely in condition to totter to the front, though both of us would make excellent food for powder," he wrote Jim Russell. "Since, however, we cannot expect to be shot at, let us try to contribute something to the central good."

One proposal was to recruit Indians—Cheyennes specifically—to form fighting units, a notion he had favored during the Spanish-American War. Grinnell envisioned a Cheyenne battalion, like the Pawnees, possibly under the command of Theodore Roosevelt. And if it were not practical to send the Indians to Europe, he suggested that they be deployed to patrol the volatile Mexican border. He shared his idea with his old friend General Hugh L. Scott, the army chief of staff, who politely explained that Indians were welcome to enlist but must do so as individuals.

In the end the best Grinnell could do was purchase $2,000 in Liberty Bonds and increase the productivity on his Milford farm. "I am hopeful about the war," he wrote his sister Helen in May. "I recognize that the United States Government will make plenty of mistakes. . . . There should, however, be no trouble about our raising what money we require and the men we need." On the other hand, he continued, less brightly, "I am old enough to remember very well the draft riots of the Civil War."

That spring, Elizabeth went upstate to check on her mother and brother. Four years earlier, in 1913, Frank Curtis's mental instability had obliged Elizabeth and Delle to commit him to the state hospital in Middletown, New York. Grinnell paid the hospital bills and felt entitled to offer advice on how Frank might regain his equilibrium. "One of the things you greatly need," he counseled, "is to be freed from the care and control of your mother, and to learn—though so late in life—to stand on your two legs."

Frank spent twenty months at Middletown, seeing his mother and sister only occasionally. When he was finally released in the spring of 1915, John Burnham, as a kindness to the Grinnells, found a job for Frank on a farm in Essex, New York, a few miles from Burnham's game preserve at Willsboro. Grinnell arranged to pay Frank's wages through the farm owner, a man named Mason, with the understanding that Frank would not be told its origin.

Frank did well enough that, after a year, Grinnell reluctantly agreed to let him try farming on another small place in Essex. "It is possible that he may succeed at it, but the chances are against it," Grinnell predicted. To his dismay, Delle Curtis moved to Essex to be with her son. Grinnell was now paying the rent on the farm, a small wage to Frank, a continuing allowance to his mother-in-law, and a little something to neighbor Mason to keep an eye on things. "Frank Curtis has never earned a dollar in his life," Grinnell alerted Mason, and, "Mrs. Curtis is absolutely irresponsible and, if allowed to do so, she will buy anything that she thinks she wants, without any regard to her ability to pay for it."

Grinnell could be testy toward his wife as well. "Elizabeth deserted me last night and has gone away for a month," he wrote George Huntress after she went to Essex in mid-April—desertion being a serious crime during wartime. A week later he wrote her—in one of the few letters to her that has not disappeared—dispensing a measure of stern advice. "I understand how close to your heart is the success of this Essex experiment," he offered, stretching his finite fund of empathy. "I am inclined to think that when you are dealing with a lot of people who have no idea whatever of self-control, this smoothing down and exhibition of good feeling may not last very long."

Elizabeth had a generous spirit. She volunteered at Bellevue Hospital and did other charity work through the Catholic Church, which she attended both in New York and Milford. Her mother had been widowed and left nearly penniless, and the same had happened to Elizabeth after the death of her first husband. She would not let her family down.

Grinnell recognized that it would not be fair to insist Elizabeth stay away from her brother and mother; nonetheless he took steps to ensure that they did not envelop her entirely. In March, before Elizabeth left for Essex, he drafted a codicil to his will. "I do not wish my wife's mother and brother at any time to occupy the house I own, nor to live with my wife, wherever she may be, or at her expense," he stated, "and, in case Mrs. Curtis and her son shall strive to make their home with Mrs. Grinnell, or to make long visits to her, I request that the income provided for them in the codicil above referred be no longer paid to them."

In closing he clarified unequivocally: "My purpose is to protect my wife, if possible, from what would be a serious affliction, of which on her account I should strongly disapprove. I earnestly request my wife to observe and carry out my wishes in this respect, and I hope my executors will be able to assist her to do so."

The strain on the marriage might easily have been greater. Small as it was, however, it was not insignificant. "[M]arriage is a frightful lottery," Grinnell advised Sylvia Page (now Brusati) with avuncular frankness, "and I advise all my friends against it, but when people get their noses set in a certain direction, it is impossible to turn them."

A few days earlier he had joked to A. K. Fisher, the renowned ornithologist and a dear friend in Washington: "You know without me telling you that a man is a very poor authority on the hotels in his own town. I sleep at home, or, if I am driven out of that by any eccentricity of my wife, I go to a club."

Still, it was evident that he admired Elizabeth, for her appearance as well as her virtue. Grinnell kept close watch on his own weight and was quite vain about his slimness. For his wife, though, he preferred the opposite. "Elizabeth is very well and is becoming more roly-poly than ever," he wrote George Huntress, who himself was growing rotund with age. "This perhaps increases her good nature, though she never was a quarrelsome soul."

As spring wore on, though, Grinnell became less patient. "I am altogether disposed to think that the wisest thing is simply to turn these people loose on the farm, giving them allowance and nothing else, and then let them work out their own salvation," he lectured Elizabeth. If he had thought about it, this was precisely what he prescribed for Indians under the General Allotment Act. He all but ordered his wife to come home. "[Y]ou are making a mistake by shilly-shallying . . . and I shall be very glad if you stop this backing and filling," he intoned in early May. "Oblige me by attending to this injunction."

Shortly after Elizabeth complied with his wishes, Grinnell tried another solution to the Curtis problem. Ownership of the family farm near Glenville, in Schenectady County, where Delle Curtis and her children first moved after the death of her husband, was divided among her siblings. Grinnell arranged to buy the parcel owned by Delle's brother Edward Smith, for $2,500; next he leased the adjacent parcel belonging to the other brother, Jacob. At the end of the year, Delle and Frank Curtis would move back to Fair View, as the family place was known. There they promised to live by their own devices (with a stipend from New York) and, if Grinnell had any say, never again make undue demands on him and Elizabeth.

Neither family complications nor the war kept Grinnell and Elizabeth from going west in the summer of 1917. They enjoyed two weeks at Eatons' Ranch and several days with the Condits, who the previous summer had been so hospitable in showing Grinnell around the Dull Knife site. Then, predictably, they spent a week on the Northern Cheyenne reservation, before going on to Glacier.

Grinnell clearly enjoyed being the éminence grise of Glacier—*the* Grinnell of Grinnell Lake, Grinnell Glacier, and Mount Grinnell—but, at the same time, he recognized that popularity had its price. As he had observed in Yellowstone the year before, the wildlife in Glacier had become so accustomed to the presence of tourists that "I might as well be looking at animals in a cage," he complained.

Grinnell and Elizabeth stopped at Jack Monroe's, and this time they found the whole family at home. The two horse-stealing boys were to be sentenced soon (one got seventy-five days, the other ninety), and Grinnell Monroe was refusing to return to Haskell Institute, the Indian boarding school in Lawrence, Kansas, where he had been enrolled for several years. The boy was now sixteen, big and husky, and prone to trouble. From time to time George Bird Grinnell had sent Grinnell Monroe checks and letters of encouragement; now he persuaded him to return to school, knowing that if he did not, he would likely follow in the footsteps of his brothers. "This is one of the things a boy has to bear," Grinnell counseled his namesake, "and [doing] what you ought to do is what makes a man." As with Frank Curtis, he dearly wanted Grinnell Monroe to buckle down and not be a worry to his family. His influence, however, went only so far.

Two weeks after returning east, Grinnell got a new dog, Flossie, another setter, which he kenneled at Milford. His previous setter, Partner—named for the other Partner in his life—had died a year earlier, and Grinnell mourned mightily. "I never expect to see a partridge dog like him again," he wrote to Partner's trainer. "Such dogs occur only once in a generation," he told his sister Helen. "I had but two seasons' use of Partner, but in those two seasons I had much contentment."

Grinnell had been reluctant to fill the void, but Flossie proved to be a welcome successor. He preferred males but this time was willing to try a female. "She is very small and has not the dash and go of old Partner," he remarked, "but is very businesslike, has a good nose, and is very cautious and very staunch." Moreover, "She is a very affectionate dog and has won her way into all our hearts."

Fall was Grinnell's favorite time to be at Milford. "I spend my Sundays about in the fields and woods, and in this church I take great comfort," he told Jim Russell, adding, "I must confess to you secretly that it would give my wife great satisfaction if I should join the Church of Rome." He never even accompanied her to mass.

As winter approached and the upland bird-shooting season ended, Grinnell turned to the task that had been pending for far too long. "I am fiddling away on the big Cheyenne book," he informed George Bent in October. In January he sent the "Early History" chapters to George Hyde for inspection. Grinnell also hired Hyde to edit "When Beaver Skins Were Money," which had last been published in *Beyond the Old Frontier*. With Hyde's sharpening, he hoped to place it in an academic journal. It finally found a home in the *Kansas State Historical Society Collections*, under the more sober title "Bent's Old Fort and Its Builders."

Once the Bent's Fort chore was out of the way, Hyde set to work on the Cheyenne chapters with his customary obsessiveness, checking sources, rooting out errors, and adding details. Grinnell paid the usual rate of $2.50 a day. The work continued throughout the winter and spring—Grinnell sending manuscript pages, Hyde returning them with copious notes. Then, in the midst of their exchanges, they received word that George Bent had died on May 19, at the age of seventy-five.

"He and I, besides being fond of each other, had a common interest in the history of the Cheyenne tribe," Grinnell wrote to Bent's widow. "[H]is keen powers of observation, his extraordinary memory, and his great patience in finding out things that had nearly been forgotten were wonderful and admirable. . . . I loved your husband dearly and am deeply sorry that I shall not shake hands with him again."

As the "big book" began to take shape, Grinnell again contemplated what to do with the coming-of-age story of the Cheyenne boy Wikis, which originally he had thought might provide an engaging introduction to the more staid ethnography to follow. He now sent Wikis to Frederick A. Stokes, publisher of the Jack books. "There is nothing in it that is especially exciting," he confessed, "but it gives, as I conceive, a faithful picture of the way in which Indians thought and talked in the days before they had been greatly changed by the approach of civilization."

But not even Stokes was interested in Wikis. And so he thrust his ambition into the big book.

In 1918 the war was no small distraction. January was bitterly cold, and coal was in short supply. One of the furnaces at the Fifteenth Street house went down and several radiators burst, obliging Grinnell and Elizabeth to retreat to the second-floor library and two or three rooms at the back, warmed by a fireplace. "Americans . . . need some frightful jar to make them think of other things than themselves and their own comfort," he declared. "I believe it is a good thing for the human race to suffer, for it is only by suffering that we learn." He took austere pleasure in discovering ice in the washbasin when he rose in the morning.

Then came honor rationing. "Of course, I eat corn bread and cut out meat pretty regularly," Grinnell wrote Jim Russell. "I think we have had no bacon in this house for two or three months." He was never short of tobacco, for Russell regularly sent Grinnell a supply of a burley blend from his Kentucky farm.

Many made far greater sacrifices. On Good Friday, April 2, Grinnell's cousin Lassie Landon and her two daughters were killed in Paris by a German artillery shell. Duncan and Douglas Grinnell-Milne were both captured by the Germans. Duncan escaped; Douglas never came home. In July another cousin, Galloway Cheston, would be shot down, his body never recovered. Renzo Brusati would survive two wounds and receive the Croix de Guerre, only to die of pneumonia.

"[W]e must fight until Germany makes unconditional surrender," Grinnell wrote in May. "I do not see how it is possible for us to stop until we have spent our last dollar and lost our last man."

The war was hard on conservation, as well. As America mustered to the flag, there were those who saw a chance to unlock the country's treasury of natural resources. In the name of patriotism they urged loosening restrictions on grazing and logging on public lands, including the national parks. The Biological Survey stepped up its campaign to trap and shoot predators of livestock: wolves, coyotes, bears, and mountain lions. Laws regulating hunting seasons, bag limits, and the commercial sale of game were suddenly threatened.

In August 1917 President Wilson signed an executive order creating the United States Food Administration and appointed as its head Herbert Hoover, erstwhile mining engineer and more recently director of the international commission for relief of Belgium. Hoover's new job was to feed American citizens, soldiers, and allies by maximizing productivity—of crops and livestock, but also of fisheries and possibly migratory birds and big game. Conservationists were put in a delicate position: how to support the war effort while defending wildlife. If game was to be killed for the cause, it must be done rationally, in moderation, and, above all, not by market hunters or sportsmen looking for an excuse to abrogate years of hard work by groups such as the Boone and Crockett Club and the American Game Protective Association.

"Increased killing would no doubt give us more food today but vastly less food for next year, when we may require it much more than we do now," Grinnell wrote to Charles Sheldon in November 1917.

At the annual meeting of the Boone and Crockett Club in January, this sentiment was formalized in a resolution—drafted by Sheldon, who still chaired the Game Preservation committee—decrying "the pressure, apparently initiated by hotel and market men, commercial fishermen and other selfish interests" to liberalize or suspend the game and fish laws. The club urged the Food Administration to leave the laws alone "so that an adequate supply [of breeding stock] may be preserved for the essential needs of the country."

It did not hurt that Hoover's right-hand man on the Food Administration was Frederic C. Walcott, who had graduated from Yale a class behind Sheldon and since 1913 had been an associate member of the Boone and Crockett Club. He had also helped John Burnham found the American Game Protective Association. At a meeting the following month at the Cosmos Club in Washington, Walcott and Sheldon were joined by the Biological Survey's Edward Nelson, Horace Albright of the National Park Service, and George Shiras, father of the migratory bird law. Their discussion produced a memorandum, again drafted by Sheldon, that Walcott carried back to Hoover. It read: "Since an attempted relaxation of laws would tend toward a rapid destruction of game, no emergency has as yet arisen sufficiently acute to warrant the Food Administration advocating the destruction of game, which forms a valuable national asset." Hoover signed the memo, and soon it received a bully endorsement from former president Theodore Roosevelt. He called those who would profit from relaxed game laws during wartime "pseudo-patriots."

After a trying winter, Grinnell was eager to get away. In mid-May he and Elizabeth left Stuyvesant Square on the same day—she to see her family in Glenville, he to spend a month examining sites of early Cheyenne villages in North Dakota, followed by a couple of weeks on the Northern Cheyenne reservation. In July, upon their return, they joined the Ardsley Club, overlooking the Hudson between Dobbs Ferry and Irvington, an hour's train ride from New York. Its original membership included J. P. Morgan and Cornelius Vanderbilt. "Mrs. Grinnell's physician has ordered her to play golf," Grinnell wrote to a New York acquaintance, asking the fellow to put him up for membership. "I shall probably never be a golfer myself, but it will be a good thing for Mrs. Grinnell."

The doctor's concern must have been legitimate, for Grinnell soon wrote to Eatons' Ranch, explaining, "Mrs. Grinnell is not very well, and I am inclined to think that a couple of weeks or a month out to your ranch would be good and pleasant for her and certainly would be quite agreeable to me."

They arrived at the ranch on August 19. "As soon as she reached the mountains, she braced up," Grinnell informed Lute North. They spent three weeks doing the things dudes do: riding, admiring wildlife, enjoying cool evenings and cordial company. They caught a glimpse of a wolf—"something I have not seen for a number of years," Grinnell wrote Jay White—and rode up on a family of black bears. "If I had on my saddle a rope, or even some strings, I think that even at my time of life I should have climbed the tree and tied up the little bears to bring into the ranch."

Back in New York in mid-September, Elizabeth pursued golf in earnest. Grinnell occasionally went along to Ardsley-on-Hudson and walked the course with her, but he was still not tempted to play.

He and Elizabeth spent the weekend of November 8–10 hunting woodcock in Milford. As they arrived back in the city on Monday, November 11, they were greeted by the happy news that the armistice ending the First World War had been signed.

"Here in New York . . . they raised something whose name rhymes with 'quell' for about twenty-four hours," Grinnell wrote Billy Hofer, "and a man's life was hardly safe on the street. It was worse than traveling through an Indian country. You had to keep your eye in four directions at once. . . . However," he added, "the Lord takes care of fools, drunken people, and Americans."

Reflecting on the recent war and on war in general, he made another comparison to Indians. "The varnish of civilization which overlies most civilized people is very thin and is easily scratched off," he wrote to L. O. Vaught, a lawyer from Illinois who spent summers on the west side of Glacier

National Park. "I am willing to acknowledge that the Americans were as bad as the Indians but not that they are as bad as the Huns. The Americans and Indians vent their spite on their enemies by cutting them up and possibly even by torturing them, but the Huns started in with a policy of terrorizing their enemies, to frighten them by inhumanity to a point where they would not fight any longer. This only shows that the Hun is a poor psychologist."

On another Monday, eight weeks later, Theodore Roosevelt died of a blood clot at the age of sixty. Grinnell attended the funeral at Oyster Bay, joining former president William Howard Taft, various statesmen, judges, military men, policemen, society men, Rough Riders, and hunting companions. Before being taken from the house to the cemetery, Roosevelt's coffin was placed for viewing in the north room of Sagamore Hill, draped in the Stars and Stripes and resting on the skin of a lion.

"I had known Roosevelt for many years and am deeply saddened at his passing," Grinnell wrote Jim Russell a few days later, "but he said to me in a letter not very long ago: 'You and I and the rest of our generation are now getting within range of the rifle pits. We, all of us, have to face the same fate a few years earlier or a few years later, and I think what really matters is that, according to our lights, we shall have borne ourselves well and rendered what service we were able as long as we could do so.'"

The annual Boone and Crockett Club dinner was already scheduled for Friday, January 10, two days after Roosevelt's funeral. The program was to include speeches memorializing Austin Wadsworth, the club president who had died in May. Wadsworth was only the third president in the Boone and Crockett's thirty-one years. The first, of course, was Theodore Roosevelt. To succeed Wadsworth, the membership chose another of the founders: George Bird Grinnell.

"I am to preside," Grinnell wrote Charles Sheldon the day of Roosevelt's funeral, "and must do the best I can under the painful circumstances."

Thirty-seven men attended the dinner in New York. The main speaker for the night was Stephen Mather, who talked of the proposed enlargement of Sequoia National Park and a similar (and perennial) measure to stretch the boundaries of Yellowstone in order to increase feeding grounds for the park's elk. As Mather finished, a club member suggested that Sequoia

National Park ought to be renamed Roosevelt National Park. Mather thought this a grand idea and promised to look into it.

Grinnell still loathed public speaking. "I am not an orator, not a speech-maker, not even a talker on my feet," he confessed. "[I]f I am ever by any chance called upon for a word in public, my ideas and my command of language take prompt flight, not to return until some time after I have resumed my seat." This time, though, there was no dodging his duty. Once the last plates were cleared and the glasses recharged, he stood and offered brief encomiums to Wadsworth and Roosevelt. If he wrote out his eulogy to Roosevelt in advance, the script does not survive. But the gist of his tribute endures in a letter to Billy Hofer, who had guided both Roosevelt and Grinnell on trips through Yellowstone many years earlier:

"Yes, he was a good fellow, and good man, and a great man, and we who have known him and [have] known him well, were lucky in those respects. I remember him, as you perhaps knew [him]—a slim, fair-haired youngster, not long out of college, and quite crazy about hunting. Of course, I was one of the first people he talked to about the Boone and Crockett Club, and I was present at the dinner when it was formed."

And then more expansively, Grinnell offered: "It is a pity that we haven't more Theodore Roosevelts. We could have them if men would just exercise their wills and plug hard all the time, instead of plugging hard for an hour or two and then taking a month's rest. As I said the other night, there are thousands and thousands of young men in this country, each of whom might make a Theodore Roosevelt of himself, if he would only do so and had brains enough to keep at his job and try to prepare himself for doing the best work that was in him. But men with such a will do not occur more than once in a generation, if so often."

PART SEVEN

GRAY GUARDIAN

(1919–1938)

ALL THIS BETTER WORK

G rinnell grieved, but he did not grieve for long. "As I saw [Roosevelt] carried to his grave, I wondered if it was not well that he died when and as he did," he reflected to an old *Forest and Stream* contributor. "We all miss him, but we can all say he did his work."

Grinnell had lost relations in the war and had observed the worn faces of men fortunate enough to return in one piece. Yet for the United States the fighting had been comparatively short—from April 1917 to November 1918—and the hardship on Grinnell had been indirect and fleeting. In fact, the war had been good to him in at least one respect. He and his siblings still owned a hefty percentage of Campbell Bosworth, the company that manufactured and leased leather-stitching machines. Automobiles were banishing horse-drawn vehicles from American roads, but, for the time being at least, the military still needed horses—and harnesses—in the field. The demand had been robust for the past few years, and the dividends paid to Grinnell stockholders were handsome.

Meanwhile, Grinnell's other investments also paid reliably. He had never taken risks with his money, having learned a hard lesson during his father's reversal in 1873. His portfolio was blue-chip and conservative, including banks, railroads, manufacturing, and throughout the years steady dividends—*not* his writing—covered the bills and then some.

What weighed on Grinnell more was age. "Our horns . . . are getting full of wrinkles, and we are losing our teeth," he commiserated with Jack Monroe in May 1919. "We can no longer [chew] dried meat and are pushed off to the cold side of the lodge."

To George Gould he was no less graphic: "I resemble one of the old wax figures in the Eden Musée"—referring to the entertainment emporium on Twenty-Third Street—"put behind a screen and left there for fifteen or twenty years. Dragged out and exposed to the light, it looks dusty, moth-eaten, and generally in need of renovation." Gould evidently had seen an old photograph of Grinnell in some publication and asked his friend to send one that was more recent. Grinnell had not had a formal photo taken in years, and he was not inclined to sit for another—or, for that matter, to have Gould glimpse him as an older man. In a few months he would turn seventy.

Unlike Roosevelt, Grinnell had not yet completed his life's work. From time to time he sent more chapters of the "fat Cheyenne book" to George Hyde. "[S]omeday [it may] see the light, though I do not feel very sure about this," he told L. O. Vaught. His uncertainty was increased—and his ego nicked—when the only publisher to express any interest in the story of the Cheyenne boy Wikis said that he would be delighted to take the book, provided Grinnell paid for the production. "I have been making copy for the printers now in the neighborhood of fifty years," he replied indignantly, "and in all that time, I have never paid anything to have my copy put in type. I am afraid it is rather late in life for me to begin this practice."

As summer approached, Grinnell and Elizabeth had different ideas on how to spend it. He, as usual, had his eye turned westward. She wanted to take a house on the Massachusetts coast, so she could play golf. This time she could not use nerves or digestion as a pretense. "Mrs. Grinnell is—shall I say it?—as husky as a bear and has had a very good winter," Grinnell informed a friend they had made in Glacier several years before.

On June 18 Elizabeth departed for Manchester, north of Boston, bearing five trunks. Earlier in the year Grinnell had joked to a family friend, "Elizabeth and I are as well as could be expected, considering the fact that we are obliged to live together." For the next two months they would not.

Four days after Elizabeth left, Grinnell departed for New Mexico, where he had arranged to meet up with George Fraser, an attorney in the firm once run by brother-in-law Newell Martin. The idea for the trip had been mostly Fraser's, although Grinnell had been wanting for some time to see more of the pueblo culture of the Southwest. He found Fraser waiting at the station in Laguna, along with a hired driver named Canfield.

Fraser was clearly thrilled to share the excursion with the venerable Dr. Grinnell, writing somewhat fancifully in his journal: "The Doctor's luggage was a suit case and a large leather accordion bag (he said cowhide, but I think it was made of the hide of a buffalo shot by him alongside the Yellowstone in 1873), the bed roll he used when he and Prof. Marsh found the eohippus in 1870, and a copy of the *Saturday Evening Post*." Canfield had brought along a chuck box full of provisions, and, with all the luggage, Fraser could barely squeeze into the back seat of the Dodge. "The Doctor, in light of a lifetime's experience in packing horses, solved the problem," Fraser remarked admiringly, "using the buffalo hide container and the suit case as a foundation, lashing them firmly to the arm supporting the top of the machine, and tying the rest of the things much as a Christmas tree is dressed."

From Laguna they went to Acoma, "the oldest continuously inhabited spot in U.S.," Grinnell noted in his own diary. El Moro, Hubbell's Trading Post, Canyon de Chelly, Ship Rock, Mesa Verde—they examined ruins in four states, hiring different drivers and cars, sleeping outdoors, in the occasional barn, and even at a hotel or two. They spent a day with Grinnell's friend Frederick Hodge, who was leading an excavation of the ruins of the Zuni pueblo Hawikku, where it was believed Spanish conquistador Francisco Vázquez de Coronado had first made contact with Pueblo people. In 1918 Hodge had been hired away from the Smithsonian's Bureau of Ethnology to head the Museum of the American Indian—which in 1922 would open its new building next to the Hispanic Society, in the neighborhood still known as Audubon Park, the ruins of which, like Hawikku's, had been buried by a latter layer of civilization.

It rained a good deal, unusual for the desert, and more than once their car sank to the axles while crossing what normally ought to have been dry washes. "At 4 o'clock it began to rain and in a few minutes we were in a cloud burst," Fraser recorded on July 16. "It was rather like the play of a fire hose than rain. . . . In spite of our raincoats we were thoroughly wet and all our belongings in the car pretty well soaked. . . . I could see this experience was making the Doctor feel thoroughly at home because, for the first time, I succeeded in getting him to tell some tales of his . . . contact with the Indians of the Northwest."

Grinnell's own entry for that day was more matter-of-fact: "I suppose it rained for an hour and a half as hard as seemed possible. . . . Later it stopped, a few stars appeared, and about 11 o'c[lock] we went to bed. Slept well." It hadn't occurred to him to bring a tent.

Arriving back in New York on July 30, he did not relish the thought of joining Elizabeth in Massachusetts. He griped to niece Sylvia Brusati, "The amusements of Manchester are not many—golf, which I do not play, fishing, which I do not indulge in, and walking, of which only a certain amount can be done." He went anyway, and he and Elizabeth stayed until the end of September. His correspondence does not mention how they spent September 20, his seventieth birthday.

He devoted the fall to the Cheyenne manuscript, which, as he told Charles Sheldon, was "slowly pulling itself through the mud," and worked up a reminiscence of his early days at Audubon Park for the journal *Natural History*. Years had passed since Grinnell had paid a visit to his old neighborhood, or what little of it remained. A grand Beaux-Arts apartment building had replaced the Hemlocks, receiving its first tenants in 1911. With a nod to the not-so-distant past, its developers had christened it: The Grinnell.

In December George Bird Grinnell made his annual trip to the Narrows Island Club in North Carolina, though he confessed to Billy Hofer that his agility was not what it once had been. "I still manage to creep around pretty actively on my feet, but . . . I would fall down every time I got into a boat or out of a boat, and often fell over in the blind."

Elizabeth, too, was unsteady. She felt poorly at Christmas, and whatever it was that ailed her continued into the spring. On good days she was able to walk a few blocks. Many others she spent in bed. In April Grinnell had to cancel a trip to Washington on account of her condition. "I have a sick wife who has been laid up pretty much all winter," he explained, "and she likes to have me within call."

A number of conservation matters had commanded his attention in recent months. Alaskans were pressing to loosen the laws against hunting bears and the export of bearskins. (At long last, bears—Alaskan bears, anyway— were deemed worthy of protection.) For years the Boone and Crockett Club had pushed to establish game refuges within national forests; the latest bill toward this end had received a welcome push from a young Forest Service visionary from New Mexico by the name of Aldo Leopold. Yet the issue that aroused Grinnell the most was an imminent threat to Yellowstone.

In early 1920 Senator John Nugent and Representative Addison Smith, both of Idaho, introduced bills to authorize construction of dams on the Falls River and its tributary, the Bechler River, in the southwestern corner of the park, in order to improve irrigation along the Snake River, which these streams supplied. The farmers whose interests Nugent and Smith represented had also concocted an astonishing, and even more invasive, project: a dam at the outlet of Yellowstone Lake, where it flowed into the Yellowstone River, that reportedly would raise the lake level as much as twenty-five feet. By their calculations, the impounded water could then be routed, via a tunnel, or possibly two, beneath the Continental Divide—that is, beneath Two Ocean Plateau—to the Snake River and the thirstier country on the western slope. (Never mind that the tunnel would have to be dug through the still-flexing floor of a volcanic crater.)

Not to be outdone, a group in Livingston, Montana, favored a similar dam at the mouth of the lake to aid irrigation and mitigate flooding on their side of the divide, in the lower Yellowstone River valley.

The Senate bill on the Falls River dams passed without opposition on April 6, and the House bill was placed on the unanimous-consent calendar—which is where it was poised when Grinnell and his cohort of conservationists came awake and took to the ramparts. Grinnell was quick to label this new threat "a second Hetch Hetchy."

More than that, he saw the dam legislation as only the first, ominous step down a far more perilous path. On April 21 he wrote to Connecticut congressman Schuyler Merritt, a friend and fellow Yale man (class of 1873). "The point I make against this [House] bill," Grinnell told Merritt, "is not so much that it destroys the most important range and feeding ground of the moose in Yellowstone Park, but that it is an obvious effort . . . to get a foothold in the Park and to establish a precedent for taking away from the public, which owns these parks, a little bit for the use of some private local people. If they can take water from this corner of the Park, the greater irrigation project which contemplates damming the Yellowstone Lake and flooding a great area of the country will be justified. If they can use these waters for local purposes, why cannot they use the timber or anything else the Park contains for such local purposes? If a beginning is made to nibble away something from a single national park for private purposes, the whole system of national parks will presently come crashing to the ground."

Grinnell also heard credible rumors that, should the Idahoans not get their dams (and even if they did), they contemplated further legislation to have the Yellowstone boundary modified so as to excise the Falls River basin from the park entirely.

The campaign to prevent the damming of Yellowstone was a test of the combined forces of American conservation. Hetch Hetchy had been a bitter defeat; this time would be different. The National Association of Audubon Societies, the Appalachian Mountain Club, the Sierra Club, the National Geographic Society, the American Civic Association, and the American Society of Landscape Architects all passed resolutions against the dams. Robert Sterling Yard used the newly organized auxiliary, the National Parks Association, as a megaphone for the defense of Yellowstone, eventually rallying hundreds of outdoor clubs, automobile associations, teachers' organizations, and scientific groups to take a stand against the dams. Thousands of citizens wrote letters protesting the assault on one of the nation's crown jewels.

Yellowstone Lake was indeed a diadem: 130 square miles of blue purity, fringed nearly to its shoreline by lodgepole pines and accented here and there by geothermal gems. To picture the harm that would befall the lake once a dam was built, critics needed look no farther than Jackson Lake, to the south of the park, where a recently improved dam on the Snake River had left a bathtub ring of mudflats and a stubble of drowned trees in the shallows.

As for the dams in the Falls River basin, few tourists had visited this corner of the park, but its very wildness was reason enough to demand its preservation. Where Idaho farmers and politicians saw a worthless marsh, Yellowstone proponents saw nature untrammeled. "[T]he preservation of remote, unfrequented areas is one of the most attractive and valuable features of . . . the Yellowstone [Park], where the primitive wilderness can remain untouched and undisturbed," Edward Nelson wrote to Wyoming congressman Frank Mondell. "[T]o permit the exploitation of areas within its borders, such as the flooding of large tracts for reservoir sites, would be to vitiate the purpose for which the park has been established."

No voice was more vehement than that of George Bird Grinnell. Here was a battle that hit close to home. "The Yellowstone Park has always been a sort of baby [of mine]," he told the Boone and Crockett Club's vice president, Charles Davison, "and I feel that we ought to take strong ground." (He had said the same thing about Glacier.)

Four months earlier he had bemoaned his physical frailty to Billy Hofer. Now, as he climbed on his steed one more time, he declared to his old guide, who knew the contested country better than almost any man alive, "It seems to me like more or less renewing my youth to be fighting about the Yellowstone Park again." When the *Anaconda* (Montana) *Standard*, a booster of the dams, accused him of being an "eastern faddist" who sought to deny "ample water to 3,000 settlers in the Snake River country of Idaho," Grinnell more than welcomed the rough-and-tumble. "The story tickles me," he wrote a lawyer friend in Helena. So, too, did the *Livingston Enterprise*'s attempt to dismiss him as a "nature faker."

At first the momentum in favor of the dams seemed unstoppable. The worst drought in more than thirty years had parched the northern Rockies in 1918–1919, and the world war had made food production a matter of national urgency—the same urgency that prompted the Water Power Act to maximize the hydroelectric and irrigation potential of federal lands, *including* national parks. (It would become law on June 20, 1920.) The backers of the dam framed the debate as one between yeoman westerners and eastern elites. "It is just a question," Representative Smith said on the House floor, "of whether the Congress is willing to allow the farmers living in eastern Idaho to build reservoirs . . . to save for irrigation purposes the snow and rains which God almighty sends for all of us, or whether a few splendid but overly esthetic people . . . who are living in luxury in Boston, New York, Philadelphia, and other eastern cities, and apparently have little interest or sympathy for those of limited means who are trying to build homes for themselves and families on the arid lands, are to be permitted to [defeat] this legislation."

Secretary of the Interior Franklin Lane supported the Yellowstone dams and the Water Power Act and pressured his national park director, Stephen Mather, to fall in line. Mather equivocated initially, and Grinnell wasted no time in calling him out. "I shall not believe, without seeing a statement from you, that you are in favor of this bill. If you are in favor of it, you cannot, I feel sure, know how far-reaching it is and how it threatens the whole national park system," he wrote with calculated incredulity.

A month later he held Mather's feet closer to the coals: "I am sorry to say that I think you have, to some extent, lost standing with the conservationists by the quasi assent that you [at first] gave to the bill. You have done so much and you are so highly regarded by most of those interested in the national park that I should be very deeply grieved if, for any reason, they felt that you were not measuring up to their ideals."

Mather's heart was in the right place, and although he took longer than Grinnell would have liked, he finally spoke out against the dams— once Secretary Lane stepped down in February and was replaced by the more conservation-minded John Barton Payne of Chicago. "[T]he whole National Park System is facing a grave crisis, where a single false step would be irremediable," Mather wrote in his annual report for 1920. In assessing the various dams under consideration, he described the "pollution," "injury," "havoc," and "ruin" they would inflict in the Falls River basin. The loss of scenic beauty, he stressed, would be "awful to contemplate."

Grinnell worried that Elizabeth's health might prevent him from going to Washington to appear before the House Rules Committee on May 25, but in the end he was able to make the overnight trip. "There were fifty or sixty people present, I should think," he reported to Billy Hofer, "and more than one half of them were opposed to the bill." Among those who spoke against the dams that day were Robert Sterling Yard, landscape architect Frederick Law Olmsted, J. Horace McFarland of the American Civic Association, zoologist Wilfred H. Osgood of Chicago's Field Museum, and John Burnham of the American Game Protective Association. Grinnell carried not only the banner of the Boone and Crockett Club, but also those of the National Association of Audubon Societies, the New York Zoological Society, and the American Museum of National History.

Their testimony dominated the two-hour hearing and apparently was persuasive, for the Smith bill was not brought to a vote and died on the calendar—for the time being at least. "Yellowstone Plan Defeated by Highbrows," sniffed one Idaho paper. "[T]hat this bill would have permitted the creation of a lake where a swamp now exists did not appeal to these easterners at all, for they maintain that nothing but nature shall be allowed to sway in the sacred precincts of the Yellowstone."

Grinnell had a different perspective. "It will be a good many years, I suspect, before the men who come from the further West will absorb the real conservation idea," he wrote to Henry Graves, who had succeeded Gifford Pinchot as chief of the National Forest Service (and, recently, had resigned himself). "The western men want to seize and turn into money everything in sight and are willing to trust to Providence to take care of the next generation."

Grinnell knew the dammers would be back. "The ease and swiftness with which bills to commercialize national parks, national monuments, and national forests slip through Congress seems alarming," he wrote Mather in early June, "and I feel that something should be done to protect the public against these attacks, which usually originate out in a country adjacent to the territory desired by the looters." He asked Mather if he might spare a

Park Service man to keep an eye on Congress. "[I]t might be practicable for the information about any bill . . . to be reported privately to someone here in New York, and we here might have a committee of three or four dependable men who could try to take steps for the protection of the public."

They called themselves the National Parks Committee. Their first meeting took place on June 29 in New York, attended by Grinnell, Burnham, Madison Grant, Charles Davison, and William C. Gregg, a New Jersey industrialist with a deep affection for Yellowstone. The initial idea was to act as a New York counterpart to Washington's National Parks Association, although Grinnell, who was the committee's chairman, enlisted several leaders of the Washington group into his. Jointly and severally, their goal was to prevent plundering of the parks for commercial purposes.

While they girded for the next assault on Yellowstone, they took two more proactive steps toward park protection. Through letter writing, lobbying, and arm-twisting, they tried to amend the Water Power Act so as to exempt the national parks and monuments. "How [this] got into the bill and why [it was] not discovered in the bill by Mr. Mather, Mr. Yard, and the other people in Washington who are supposed to be looking after those things is one of the conundrums I am unable to answer," Grinnell vented to William Gregg.

The second step was to make national park protection an issue in the upcoming presidential election. Grinnell was fed up with Woodrow Wilson and his administration; on the other hand, he could not work up much enthusiasm for the Republicans and their ticket, Ohio senator Warren G. Harding and Massachusetts governor Calvin Coolidge. When the Republican platform endorsed the Water Power Act, Grinnell saw an opportunity to play the Democratic opposition to his advantage. "[I]t seems natural," he wrote to Robert Sterling Yard, "that the Democratic politicians should be glad to do anything that they could to show [that] the Republican politicians are in the wrong."

With this in mind, he pressed Charles Sheldon to call on Franklin D. Roosevelt, the thirty-eight-year old assistant secretary of the navy who was about to be chosen as running mate to James M. Cox, governor of Ohio, on the Democratic ticket. "Would it be possible or practicable for you to write or telegraph him to get put into the Democratic platform a plank advocating the continued protection of our national parks?" Grinnell asked Sheldon and then suggested some talking points that might sway Roosevelt.

"I believe that the parks are actual producers of wealth," he explained, "because they enable the people who visit them to work through the rest of the year harder, longer, and better than they would work if they had not had the change of thought and received the mental stimulus that they got from these novel surroundings, and this contact with nature. I believe that the sum of all this better work done by the people who visit the parks is worth more than all the water, all the power, and all the timber that they contain. I want you to say something of this to Roosevelt, who, I believe, is an active politician, a good fellow, and who might feel an interest."

When it came to loyalty, Grinnell's was to parks over party.

At the end of June, while Grinnell was immersed in forming the National Parks Committee and endeavoring to shape the national political debate, he took time to attend his fiftieth Yale reunion, which he drolly described as "a sort of siesta in New Haven." For three days he mingled and reminisced with thirty "tattering old graybeards" of the class of 1870—a good many of whom, he suspected, he was seeing for the last time. To Jim Russell, who had not made the trip from Kentucky, he reported, "There was no drink"—Prohibition had gone into effect earlier in the year—"so everybody was absolutely decorous."

After New Haven he spent the weekend at Milford. On Saturday, June 26, his brother Willie died in New York, of blood poisoning, at the age of sixty-two.

William Milne Grinnell was buried in the family plot in Woodlawn Cemetery, alongside his parents and brothers Frank and Morton. Whether George or any other kin was in attendance is not known. On July 1 Grinnell wrote to nephew Frank Page, congratulating him on the birth of a daughter, but he was silent on Uncle Willie. On July 6 he wrote a long letter to sister Helen, who was living near Paris, discussing family business and sharing bits of gossip. Not a word about Willie. Finally, on July 28, in response to Donald Page, another nephew, he wrote tersely, "I had not thought it necessary to write you about the death of my brother."

By way of contrast, a few months later he would write to Sylvia Brusati: "I have to announce to you a great misfortune that has happened to the Grinnell family. Our precious Flossie died last week. . . . She was a very affectionate and lovable dog and a good dog in the field. I grieve over her loss."

An obituary published in Yale alumni records states that, after his retirement from architecture, William Grinnell traveled extensively in South America, Egypt, Spain, India, China, and Japan and that he was a member of the Society of Mayflower Descendants and a communicant of the Episcopal Church. The *New York Times* reported that he had willed "all of his Persian antiques, miniatures, faience and other Persian articles now in a cabinet in his home at 850 Seventh Avenue" to the Metropolitan Museum of Art. He gave $10,000 to Yale and $50,000 and a marble bust to Marguerite Cunliffe-Owen, a French countess-turned-author who published, under flamboyant pseudonyms, titles such as *The Martyrdom of an Empress* and *The Tribulations of a Princess*. He also gave $70,000 to James Scott, the former New York City policeman whom Willie had met while playing handball. Scott's two sons each received $5,000 to help with college. To brother George and sisters Helen and Laura he gave nothing, the *Times* noted, "because they are well provided for." He did, however, leave "small bequests" to his sisters' children "as personal remembrances."

Grinnell and Elizabeth had made tentative plans to go west in July, at least as far as Eatons' Ranch, but even as Elizabeth began to regain her strength in June, her doctor advised against an extended trip and forbade her to ride a horse. As an alternative, Grinnell proposed joining Charles and Louisa Sheldon, who, with their four children, were spending their second summer at Kedgemakooge Lodge, located on a serene lake in the interior of Nova Scotia (today's Kejimkujik National Park).

Grinnell inquired about renting one of the lodge's cottages but then had to cancel, again on doctor's orders. Instead he sent Elizabeth with a nurse to a hotel in Briarcliff, New York, and then to a country inn in Sharon, Connecticut. He did not accompany her to either place, though he made at least one visit to Briarcliff in early August. "She looks better—I saw her last night—is gaining weight, and is very cheerful," he informed sister

Helen. His wife was apparently doing well enough that he felt he could get away himself.

He arrived in Columbus, Nebraska, on August 20. Prohibition had ended Lute North's job at the Omaha distillery, and for the next three days one of North's nephews chauffeured him and Grinnell up the Loup River to examine several early Pawnee village sites—a couple of old-timers poking around in the past.

From here on, his itinerary was, if not aimless, then without premeditated purpose. Arriving in Sheridan, Wyoming, he telephoned Leonidas Condit, who drove in from his ranch for a few hours. By chance, while refilling his pen in the office of his Sheridan hotel, Grinnell ran into Walter Camp, the Indian buff with whom he had ridden to the Little Bighorn battlefield in 1916. Camp was there to meet up with a man named John Hoover, a former army sergeant who had participated in the so-called Wagon Box Fight, nine months after the Fetterman Massacre. Grinnell jumped at the invitation to accompany them to the site of the battle, three miles from where Fort Phil Kearny once had stood.

On August 2, 1867, a thousand or more Sioux, led by Crazy Horse and High Backbone, and a small group of perhaps sixty Cheyennes, led by Little Wolf, attacked a party of woodcutters guarded by fifty-three soldiers. But unlike the Fetterman debacle, the day belonged to the army, who forted up in a corral built from fourteen wagon boxes, their running gear removed. The soldiers were armed with new breech-loading Springfield rifles capable of firing as many as twenty rounds per minute.

When the smoke and dust settled, only six whites had been killed; the number of Indians who lost their lives while charging the well-defended barricade can only be conjectured, but some estimates range well into the hundreds. "Hoover believes that they killed 3200 Indians and says that they ought to have killed 7000, as they shot away all of their ammunition," Grinnell recorded skeptically in his diary. "I believe that there were only two or three hundred Indians in the fight and that the Indian loss was 15–25."

The rest of the trip seemed almost rote. He spent three days on the Northern Cheyenne reservation and then went on to Glacier. He motored from Glacier Park Lodge to Many Glacier Hotel. During his six-day stay he did not mount a horse or venture into the mountains; nor did he spend any time among the Piegans. "I used to be very familiar with the condition of the Blackfeet," Grinnell told the *New York Herald* later in the fall, "but have seen little of them in late years."

He arrived back in New York on September 14, having been away less than a month. "I did no work whatever while I was in the West," he remarked almost guiltily, and he confessed to a cousin, "I did not sleep once out of doors."

Elizabeth had arrived at Stuyvesant Square only a half hour before Grinnell. She appeared "quite her old self again," Grinnell remarked. "Her siege was a long one and, to me, very discouraging. However, she possesses a cheerful disposition and did not allow herself to become depressed." She dispensed with her nurse and resumed playing golf at Ardsley, and on weekends at Milford she was eager and able to pursue woodcock, shotgun on her shoulder.

As winter approached, Grinnell and the defenders of Yellowstone readied themselves for the assault they knew was coming. Over the summer William Gregg, the New Jersey industrialist and Yellowstone enthusiast, had made a trip to the seldom-visited Falls River Basin of the park and produced a report puncturing the myth spread by Idahoans that the area they wished to dam was "a dismal swamp which produced nothing but malaria and mosquitoes." On the contrary, Gregg discovered a "region of delight, abounding in . . . forests and meadows, fine trout streams, lakes, waterfalls, cascades and hot springs—an ideal paradise for the camper." He referred to it as "the Cascade Corner."

Interior Secretary Payne also toured Yellowstone over the summer and stated in no uncertain terms that commercial interests—including agricultural—should keep their hands off the national parks. Articles appeared in newspapers and magazines under headlines such as "Pawning the Heirlooms" and, inevitably, "Another Hetch Hetchy." The former, in the *Saturday Evening Post*, was written by Emerson Hough. He and Grinnell may have had a falling-out once upon a time, but they remained on the same page with respect to conservation and the public trust.

None of this posturing deterred the dam proponents, however. A bill to dam the Falls River Basin was reintroduced at the next session of Congress. The proposition to dam Yellowstone Lake and tunnel under the Continental Divide was supplanted by the better-organized campaign of a group of Montanans calling itself the Yellowstone Irrigation Association. In November the association, comprising mostly chamber-of-commerce men of Livingston, published a pamphlet that declared that flooding or its opposite, low water, had cost Montanans $200 million in damage and productivity over the past four years. The problem could be easily solved, the association announced, by "an artistic concrete structure." The pamphlet scoffed at critical reports "circulated by our eastern friends, who are inadvertently permitting their imaginations to run riot." Warnings that "great areas of forest will be submerged; [that] ugly stretches of mud bank [will be] left by the draining of the lake; [that] game [will be] run out of the park; [that] the paint pots, geysers, and other scenic wonders [will be] destroyed" were patently false.

Besides, contested another dam enthusiast, even if the scenery were marred somewhat, "Beauty is only skin deep."

On December 7 a bill was introduced authorizing a dam near the lake's outlet. Its sponsor was Montana senator Thomas J. Walsh, a Democrat.

Earlier in the year Grinnell had figured the Democrats as the better hope for the national parks. But in October, when it became evident that the party of Woodrow Wilson had no chance, he had sought the ear of Warren G. Harding. His emissary to the Republican candidate was Madison Grant, representing Grinnell's new group, the National Parks Committee—with the obvious backing of a much larger network of influential organizations and men. By the end of the month, Grinnell was able to report to Charles Sargent, eminent botanist and protector of forests, "I had a letter of mine shown last week to Senator Harding, who wrote me quite an encouraging note." A few days later he wrote again to Sargent: "If Mr. Harding should be elected . . . the fight [to protect Yellowstone] will be made much easier for us all."

Harding was indeed elected, by a landslide, and as secretary of the interior he chose Senator Albert Fall of New Mexico. At first Grinnell was as optimistic about Fall as he was about Harding. "As a western man acquainted with western conditions . . . you can perform great public service," he flattered the new secretary in March, shortly after Fall's appointment. "On the subject of national parks, I have had lately some intercourse with your predecessor, Judge Payne, whose views on these subjects were [quite] liberal. With a wider territorial experience . . . your viewpoint might be even broader than this."

Soon enough, however, Fall would shatter Grinnell's (and the nation's) rosy expectations for the Harding regime. Fall was exposed not as a protector but as a plunderer of the public trust; and he would wind up in jail for accepting bribes to lease federal lands (Elk Hills in California and Teapot Dome in Wyoming) to private interests (oil). As it happened, the senator who would lead the investigation against Fall was Thomas Walsh—the same Thomas Walsh who, for all the sanctimony he was to exude in his pursuit of a venal colleague, had, in the early months of the Harding administration, been all too willing to side with private interests (the Yellowstone Irrigation Association) against the sanctity of federal land (Yellowstone National Park).

This time the conservationists were ready, and the efforts of Grinnell, Robert Sterling Yard, William Gregg, and fellow members of the National Parks Association and National Parks Committee had the desired effect. Public awareness of the Cascade Corner kept the House's version of the bill to dam the Falls River from coming to a vote before the winter session of Congress ended. Then, in February 1921, two weeks before Harding's inauguration, when Senator Walsh tried to hold surprise hearings on the Yellowstone Lake dam bill, they again presented a stout and orderly front.

Their argument, marshaled over the previous year, was twofold. First, the dam, even if it raised the lake only six feet, would do great harm to the lakefront and would also choke the river's flow over the magnificent upper and lower falls of the river. This disfigurement would do enormous economic harm, Grinnell warned in one of the many letters he wrote to business groups throughout Montana. "Every year [Yellowstone] brings to Montana many thousands of people who leave in Montana a great deal of money," he explained to the Commercial Club of Billings, "which of course helps to develop the country and to make the wheels of business revolve."

Second, they insisted that the dam would, in fact, *not* have much effect on the river's flow beyond the park—that is, in the rest of Montana. Most of the water in the lower Yellowstone comes from streams below the proposed dam site. The lake actually serves as its own flood control, checking, holding, and gradually releasing the water that flows into it each spring from the mountains at the southern (upper) end of the lake. Or as Grinnell put it succinctly to Senator Key Pittman of Nevada: "The proponents of the Walsh bill seem to be ignorant that the Yellowstone Lake is not a source of floods but a preventer of floods."

Grinnell's letters do not mention whether he attended the committee hearing on February 28, when the Yellowstone defenders had their say. But the united resistance held up. The Walsh bill did not make it out of committee. Its fate now rested in the hands of a future Congress and the next administration.

More good news came in March, when Congress passed an amendment to the Water Power Act, exempting *existing* national parks and monuments from hydroelectric exploitation. President Wilson signed the bill on the evening of March 3, one day before he left the White House.

"This result has been attained by the admirable team work of many associations and individuals, all of whom united to inform the public at large of the danger that threatened their playgrounds," Grinnell wrote to L. O. Vaught. "The return of these reservations to the direct control of Congress"—as opposed to a commission appointed under the Water Power Act—"strengthens the hands of those who are striving for the protection of the parks and erects a new barrier against the [future] consideration by Congress of the Walsh Bill."

Even so, he hastened to add, recognizing that the Yellowstone bills were not yet dead and that future national parks and monuments could be vulnerable to water grabbers, "We have still a fight on our hands."

Grinnell's tenacity paid off in another way as well. At the end of 1919 he sent the manuscript of the Wikis story to Yale University Press. If he were not going to make money on a book—the Jack books being exceptions to this rule—then at least he would not spend any. Yale accepted the story on the condition that he forego a royalty on the first five hundred copies. The title they agreed on was *When Buffalo Ran*. It was published in October 1920, accompanied by eight of Elizabeth's photographs.

At 114 pages, with wide margins, it has the leaven of a volume of verse or a child's storybook. "Seventy years ago," it begins, "when some of the events here recounted took place, Indians were Indians, and the plains were the plains indeed." This sets the date at 1850, or earlier, since Grinnell had completed the manuscript several years before it appeared in print.

Wikis, the protagonist, is not identified as Cheyenne, but his tribe can be deduced, if only by the names of the other tribes that surround it.

When Buffalo Ran is an exercise in nostalgia, a mood that infused Grinnell's writing more and more as he aged. After publishing "A Chapter of History and Natural History in Old New York" earlier in the year, he would write a companion piece, "Recollections of Audubon Park," which appeared in the *Auk*, the journal of the American Ornithologists' Union. Soon he would write "An Old Time Bone Hunt," a look back at the Yale expedition of 1870.

Beyond nostalgia, though, *When Buffalo Ran* is also a guide to good conduct for a younger generation. Grinnell had spent his entire life, since college anyway, trying to be a better person, and his guiding principle was one he shared with Theodore Roosevelt: "Do the best you can and do it all the time." He had his nieces and nephews in mind, of course, but others as well, including Grinnell Monroe, who each year was stumbling deeper into trouble. Grinnell Monroe's big brothers stole horses; he would eventually serve time for stealing an automobile.

Like Jack Danvers of the Jack books, Wikis has no father present in his life. In Jack's case his father remains in New York; in Wikis's case his father has died in battle. In both cases the boys are mentored by other elders, who instruct on the proper Way to Live. "[A]ct a man's part," Wikis's uncle tells him. "[A]ct bravely and well, so that people will speak well of you and your relations will be proud." One's standing and status are critical. "It is a good thing to be a member of our tribe, and it is a good thing to belong to a good family in that tribe. You must always remember that you come of good people. . . . You must love your relations and must do everything that you can for them. If the enemy should attack the village, do not run away; think always first of defending your own people."

And there is one final virtue essential to manhood: "If you should chance to perform any brave act, do not speak of it; let your comrades do this; it is not for you to tell of the things that you have done."

Twenty years pass, and Wikis marries Standing Alone, presenting her father ten horses. "It was a few years after I took Standing Alone for my wife, when my oldest boy was four years old," Wikis relates, "that the wars were begun between the white people and my tribe. This was a hard time. It is true we killed many white people and captured much property, but though most of the tribe did not seem to see that it was so, my uncle and I felt that the Indians were being crowded out, pushed further and further away from where we had always been—where we belonged. After each expedition through the country by white troops and after each fight that we had with the white men, we felt as if some great hand that was all around my tribe and all the other tribes, was closing a little tighter about us all, and that at last it would grasp us and squeeze us to death."

At least one reviewer of *When Buffalo Ran* interpreted Grinnell's sensitivity as opportunism. "[W]e are now in the era of apotheosis of the Indian," J. P. Dunn wrote in the *Mississippi Valley Historical Review.* "Our ancestors underestimated, and, as a rule, vilified him; but in the recoil, present-day writers usually go to the other extreme. Possibly this is due to the utilitarian character of the American mind. Having acquired nearly all the material valuables of the Indian, we are now exploiting the romance of his former existence to enhance the value of the place names and other relics that are left to us."

Elizabeth Grinnell took no credit for the eight photographs that appear in *When Buffalo Ran.* While once she had taken pictures enthusiastically, over time she grew frustrated with her inability to master the technical challenges of the medium and eventually lost interest. When Yale University Press sent the early proofs of the book, she was so ashamed of how her work looked on the page that she requested her name be removed.

Yet if Elizabeth was disappointed with her part in *When Buffalo Ran,* Grinnell was quite pleased. He had not expected to make a dime from the book, but in March 1921 he received a royalty payment of $127.88. "In view of the fact that it had practically no advertising and that few reviews or notices had come out," he wrote the press, "I think we may feel that the little book did fairly well," adding, "I hear good words about it myself, but that counts for little or nothing."

———

A month later the news from Yale was more heartening still. Anson Phelps Stokes, the university's secretary, informed Grinnell that he was to be conferred the honorary degree of doctor of letters at the June commencement. Twice now he had turned down invitations to accept master's degrees, but this was a far loftier distinction.

Grinnell had done nothing to promote his candidacy. This was undertaken by classmate George Huntress, a past president of the Yale Alumni Association. "I have never needed assurance of [your] affection, but its visible expression warms my heart," Grinnell wrote Huntress after getting the news. "You may well enough understand that I never thought of receiving such a degree, and I see no reason why it should have been given."

He and Elizabeth went to New Haven on June 21—the same commencement at which James Rowland Angell was inaugurated as Yale president. "Yale University, through some . . . temporary aberration of the mind, decided to give me an honorary degree," Grinnell told Jay White, who had remained in England after the war. "I was of course obliged to go to New Haven and accept it and to march in procession, sit on the platform, [and] listen to orations. . . . However, I lived through it."

Two days after the ceremony, the Grinnells left for Montana. Once again he was struck by how much the national parks had changed since his first visit in 1875. In Yellowstone he and Elizabeth were able to motor all the way to the ten-thousand-foot summit of Mount Washburn. On another day they were "held up" by a black bear begging for food. "We stopped and talked to him," Grinnell wrote in his diary, "and he came up close to [the] car and stretched out his head and, getting nothing, went around to [the] other side. E[lizabeth] stretched out her hand to it and then drew it back, and the bear put his feet on the running board and stuck his head in the car, scaring E[lizabeth] so that she almost tried to get out of [the] car on [the] other side. We flapped our hats at the bear and he withdrew."

On the train to Glacier, Grinnell was stirred by memories of the old buffalo range that he had passed through forty-six years earlier. "Now it is a country of cattle and of farms," he mourned. "Oats, wheat, potatoes, and even corn [are] grown by dry farming. Many of the towns have brick buildings. Automobiles are everywhere, and one sees women and girls dressed like those of Boston, Phila[delphia] & N. Y."

Returning east less than refreshed, Grinnell gave no indication of slowing down. In October he went to Washington and introduced himself to Harding's commissioner of Indian affairs, Charles H. Burke, a former congressman from South Dakota. Grinnell had been granted little, if any, entrée to Woodrow Wilson's commissioner, Cato Sells. "I have been *persona non grata* in the Indian Office and have not . . . shown my face there," he acknowledged to an ally at the Indian Rights Association. But now with the Republicans back in charge, he hoped his access and influence might be restored—in the Indian Bureau at least.

Grinnell found the commissioner most hospitable and, better yet, "very sensible" on the subject of Indians. They talked mostly about the Piegans, and Grinnell made his pitch for having them hired as laborers on the new road that the National Park Service was just beginning to build over the mountains, from St. Mary to Lake McDonald—an engineering wonder that, upon its completion in 1932, would be christened the Going-to-the-Sun Road.

In 1921 Grinnell also lent his support to the Migratory Fish Committee of the American Game Protective Association, chaired by George Shiras. Fish had never been a primary focus of Grinnell's, but the water they swam in was something that weighed on his mind more and more of late.

The Migratory Fish Committee's aim was to draft and enact legislation similar to Shiras's Migratory Bird Act. One early supporter of the cause was Secretary of Commerce Herbert Hoover, who happened to be an avid fisherman. In June Hoover organized a national conference of scientists, public officials, and informed citizens to evaluate the condition of the country's inland fisheries. One of the main topics up for discussion was pollution.

Unable to make it to Iowa for the conference, Grinnell wrote a lengthy letter to Robert Coker, chief of the Division of Scientific Inquiry of the

Bureau of Fisheries, presenting his thoughts about water. "The purity of the waters has always been a difficult subject," he began his rumination. "We have acted on what had apparently been the common belief that streams were laid out by Providence to serve as sewers for those who live along their banks. The waste of cities, towns and villages is emptied into them to save trouble and expense; and to this is added the waste from thousands of factories which, along many streams east and west, has so polluted the water that life is impossible."

The threat, once identified, must be met, he declared: "An effort is now being made to educate public opinion to the point of inducing Congress to enact a migratory fish law which shall hand over to . . . the federal authorities [control of] all those fish which, at certain seasons, run from one place to another.

"The passage of such a law," he continued, finding his stride, "would . . . result in a general purification of our streams and would [direct] communities . . . to devise some other form of disposing of their waste. . . . Our lakes and our streams are the sources of our water supply, and from them the water we drink and that drunk by our domestic animals is drawn. Nothing, it would seem, can be more important than to have this water supply kept pure; and yet, to all appearances, this is the last thing that Americans consider."

(This, twenty-seven years before passage of the federal Water Pollution Act and more than fifty years before passage of the federal Clean Water Act.)

From here he reached to make a larger point: "What seems far more important and more threatening than anything else is that the whole western country—that is to say, the whole Mississippi Valley—is slowly but surely being robbed of its soil because it is being so universally stripped of its timber and shrubbery and so generally ditched and drained that the run-off of the rainstorms continually carries away with it more and more of the soil in which our farmers depend. If our farmers are robbed of their soil and can no longer raise crops, the whole country must feel it. What I was hoping for from your conference is a broadened view which shall enable you to set before the public at large the fact that no conservation activity can be undertaken without its reaction on some other conservation activity—and on the whole conservation movement, and the welfare of the country."

As he entered his seventies, George Bird Grinnell could be forgiven for not having immersed himself more fully in the issues of water and water pollution. If he had been a fisherman, he might have focused on it sooner. Yet it is a measure of his growth as a conservationist that he at last turned his earnest attention to the country's emerging natural crisis. Moreover, although he never used the term *ecology*, meaning the interdisciplinary connectivity between living things and their environment, he had come to understand it, to embrace it, and to preach it.

"I am gratified to think that a certain portion of the public is now awakening to the way in which each measure for the conservation of some particular thing influences the conservation of a multitude of other things," he wrote to Joseph Howe, a fellow New Yorker and member of an organization called the American Game Conference. "It has been in the past too much the practice of conservationists to think only of preserving the forests if they were foresters, the fish if they were anglers, the songbirds if they were farmers, and so on to the end of the chapter. But, a little patient thought will make us all realize that these different interests are interlocking."

In the spring, Grinnell took advantage of his warming relations with Yale and Yale University Press and wrote to the press's founder and president, George Parmly Day, inquiring whether he might like to read the manuscript of the big Cheyenne book. When Day expressed interest, Grinnell took the precaution of first sending the pages to Frederick Hodge, who, in addition to his new position as director of the Museum of the American Indian, had also been editor of the highly respected *Handbook of American Indians North of Mexico* (to which Grinnell had contributed several entries). After Hodge gave the manuscript his blessing, Grinnell sent it on to Day, who kept it through the summer. Finally, in November, a letter arrived from Day's assistant, informing Grinnell that the press would be happy to publish the book.

After thirty years, George Bird Grinnell's Cheyennes had found a respectable home. Under certain conditions, that is.

A COMPLEX LIFE

Yale had such high regard for the Cheyenne manuscript that it decided to publish it in two volumes. However, the press warned Grinnell that it probably would not become a bestseller or, for that matter, even pay for itself. *When Buffalo Ran* had been a pleasant surprise, but it read like a novel. *The Fighting Cheyennes* pulsed with blood and thunder. *The Cheyenne Indians: Their History and Ways of Life*, as it was to be titled, had, for all its firsthand insight, both feet firmly planted in the rich but dry soil of anthropology.

In November 1922 Grinnell agreed to pay Yale University Press $7,000 — $2,500 in advance, $2,000 when the presswork was completed, and another $2,500 when the volumes were formally published. He would then be repaid in royalties: 25 percent on the first three thousand sold, 10 percent thereafter. "I suppose I am willing to safeguard the Press," he conceded to George Parmly Day, who promptly responded, "You can be sure it will be a pleasure for us to cooperate with you in every way possible . . . in order to make you realize how very deeply we appreciate your willingness to cooperate so wholeheartedly with us."

Yale also agreed to include fifty photographs taken by Elizabeth Grinnell and another woman photographer who had spent time among the

Cheyennes, Julia E. Tuell. This time Elizabeth was proud enough to take credit on the books' title pages.

There is no way to know how much the manuscript had changed since an early draft was rejected three times twenty years earlier. But Grinnell was wise enough to recognize that he might never have another chance to have his magnum opus see the light of day. Besides, he could afford it.

At the same time, Yale also agreed to take on publication of the next Boone and Crockett book. Since leaving *Forest and Stream*, Grinnell had scrambled to find a house willing to handle the club's projects, which were essentially vanity endeavors, underwritten entirely by the membership. Ten years had passed since Harper & Brothers had published *Hunting at High Altitudes*, and Grinnell was relieved to have Yale put its imprint on the sixth volume in the series.

The title of the new anthology described in the most succinct terms what the Boone and Crockett Club had come to stand for: *Hunting and Conservation*. Grinnell enlisted Charles Sheldon as coeditor, and their preface to the new book presented a credo that was pragmatic, high-minded, and unapologetic: "We have on the one hand descriptions of hunting—of the killing of animals—on the other hand the advocacy of measures by which these animals may be preserved from being killed," the editors state. "There is no conflict between these two views. Animals are for man's use, and one of those uses is recreation, of which hunting is a wholesome form. So long as it does not interfere with the maintenance of a permanent breeding stock of any species, this recreation is legitimate and praiseworthy."

If *Hunting and Conservation* was the distillation of more than thirty years of sportsman's philosophy, *The Cheyenne Indians* was the sum of a lifetime of observation, reflection, and perspective on Native Americans. Grinnell followed a long line of Indian advocates and admirers, and while it cannot be said that his book was a plea on behalf of the Cheyennes in the twentieth century, as Helen Hunt Jackson's *A Century of Dishonor* was for Indians in the nineteenth, it nonetheless makes a persuasive case for the Cheyennes as exemplary and deserving members of the American family, past and future.

Before Grinnell, no one had ever undertaken such a thorough study of an America Indian tribe. "Certain it is that Dr. Grinnell's work will stand as a monument," declared the *Yale Review*, "not alone to its author but to the people whose life and character he has saved from oblivion."

Ruth Bunzel, a protégée of Franz Boas and an authority on Indians in her own right, would proclaim after Grinnell's death, "Of all the books written about Indians, none comes closer to their everyday life than Grinnell's classic monograph on the Cheyenne. Reading it, one can smell the buffalo grass and the wood fires, feel the heavy morning dew on the prairie."

Grinnell explores and explains every aspect of the Cheyennes. They called themselves *Tsit-sis-tas*—"the people." The name *Cheyenne* was given to them by the Sioux: *Sha hi e la*—"people of alien speech." Grinnell traces their Algonquian origin; their westward movement across the Mississippi and Missouri rivers; their merger with the Suhtai tribe; their acquisition of the horse in the early 1700s; their habitation of the Black Hills; and, at last, their arrival in the buffalo plains of the Powder and Platte rivers. He dates the split between the Northern and Southern Cheyennes to the early 1800s, when some bands were drawn southward by the trading opportunities along the Santa Fe and other trails; Bent's Fort, for instance, was built in 1832.

Yet as confident as Grinnell is at stitching history, his even greater strength is revealed in the other half of the book's subtitle: the Cheyenne ways of life. His narrative is suffused with warmth as he discusses tribal governance, morals, religion, superstitions, manners, marriage, medicine, diet, music, dance, games, clothing, weapons, hunting, warfare, and the sacred ceremonies of the massaum and medicine lodge. His aim is to dispel myths and misperceptions, to set the record straight. He applies neither glaring light nor somber shadow to his subject.

Grinnell's research was exhaustive, to be sure—hundreds of hours spent in lodges, squatting in sun and shade, sitting cross-legged by firelight, enduring dust, mud, and rutted roads, transcribing multiple versions of the same story, seeking out eyewitnesses to key events and keepers of the oldest memories, returning year after year to dig for details missed, absorbing the cadence of the Cheyenne language, building a vocabulary, waiting for interpreters to convert one tongue into another so that he in turn could scribble the translation into the next leather diary to be placed on a shelf with so many others, always feeling that there was more to be done. He cites government reports, archaeology (his own and that of others), and the accounts of early plainsmen, traders, missionaries, and military men. He is not afraid to disagree with outside sources. Yet he writes with an implicit humility, occasionally acknowledging his own unsure footing. And while he continues to use the terms *civilized* and *civilization* to describe white culture, and *savage* and *primitive* still hold a place in his vocabulary, it is plain to him that the gulf between the two is not nearly so wide as most whites presumed.

His greatest advantage was timing. His first encounter with the Cheyennes was at Fort Keogh, Montana, in 1890, well after the Cheyennes had been relegated to reservations, but early enough that many were still alive who were born in the early nineteenth century—men and women who could recall stories told to them by elders who had lived in the mid- or even in the early eighteenth century, at a time when the Cheyennes were just beginning to move onto the plains; when they were first becoming horse people; and before their way of life was entwined with whites.

Grinnell was, of course, the beneficiary of significant work done by George Hyde and George Bent. Hyde continued to live in Omaha, looked after by his mother and later his sister, and in early 1923, when the first page proofs came from Yale, Grinnell paid him to prepare the book's index (at their usual rate of $2.50 per day). In the acknowledgments to *The Cheyenne Indians*, Grinnell thanks Bent, dead now five years, for his "cordial and helpful" friendship. As for Hyde's role in the endeavor, Grinnell mentions only his assistance with the index.

For an anthropological treatise, the book is refreshingly personal, without being overly subjective. "Big Woman told me . . ." begins one anecdote. "My friend Shell . . ." begins another. And so on: "Red Bird's shield, now in my possession. . . ." "The last ceremony of the Medicine Lodge that I witnessed. . . ."

As a hunter himself, Grinnell devotes his longest chapter to Cheyenne subsistence. "The hardships of the Indian war-path have been spoken of, but little seems to have been written of the labor of his hunting," he remarks. "Most civilized writers seem to have assumed that hunting was all pleasure. This view is taken because to the white man hunting is a pastime, a recreation, and we assume that it is to all people. To the Indian, hunting was work, and often work of the hardest kind." In a footnote, he clarifies that, for Indians, the notion of the afterlife as a "happy hunting ground" is oxymoronic.

Grinnell's polite perseverance provides an intimate view of the roles of men and women in Cheyenne society—the former "energetic, brave, and hardy," the latter "virtuous, devoted, and masterful." Husband and wife are "partners, sharing equally in the work of the family, and often in a deep and lasting affection which each bore toward the other. . . . Men tell me that they used to lie awake all night, talking to their newly married wives."

He is at his most cautious when he discusses Cheyenne spirituality. "No subject is more difficult of treatment than one which deals with the beliefs of any people concerning abstract matters," he writes. He follows, day by day, step by step, the proceedings of the medicine lodge and massaum, drawing principally from his observations of August 1911. Yet, he concedes, "[T]he full significance of these ceremonies cannot be comprehended."

In doing his best to get a grip on Cheyenne religion—the creator, the six spirits, seers and ghosts, the sacred arrows and buffalo hat, rituals of the pipe, potency of plants and objects, reverence for animals, expressions of gratitude, purification, and sacrifice—Grinnell does not emphasize the exoticism of their beliefs, but instead finds common ground with all who search for the meaning of life and man's place in it. "[I]n the Cheyenne community," he comments, "there was great individual diversity of faith and feeling. Some men believed firmly in spirits, birds, and animals; others were almost skeptics."

But even the less-than-zealous believer "prayed constantly and offered many sacrifices to propitiate the unseen powers and to enlist their help," Grinnell observes. "He practiced charity, for from earliest youth he had been taught to be kind to his fellow man, to feel sympathy for the unfortunate and to make efforts to assist them. It often costs civilized man to carry out the precept to love his neighbor, but the Cheyenne did kindly, friendly, or charitable acts of his own free will and took no credit for them."

For all the universality of the Cheyennes, Grinnell delineates tastes and taboos that set them apart from other tribes and, more generally, set Indians apart from whites. Cheyennes kill turtles by putting their heads in the fire. Buffalo lungs taste best if dried and roasted on coals. Young dogs are delicious, as are badgers and skunks. Not so otters or magpies. A husband is forbidden to talk to his mother-in-law. Women who touch a gray eagle feather will turn gray; women who burn owl feathers become deaf. Water that stands in a vessel overnight is considered dead and ought not to be drunk. A warrior preserves the protective power of his shield by following a strict diet, for instance not eating entrails.

Grinnell describes scalping in dispassionate detail (choosing not to mention how he once came to possess the scalp of Dull Knife's son). In and of itself, to scalp an enemy was not a "notable feat," he submits. The scalp was "merely taken as a trophy, something to show, something to dance over—a good thing, but of no great importance."

He introduces "a little group of men called *Hee man eh*, 'halfmen-halfwomen.'" They were men, he explains, "but had taken up the ways of women; even their voices sounded between the voice of a man and that of a woman. They were very popular and especial favorites of young people, whether married or not, for they were noted matchmakers."

In the end, *The Cheyenne Indians* is a book shaped by Grinnell's disposition toward his own tribe. The Grinnells lived closely at Audubon Park and in Milford. They were led by a chief, with Grinnell assuming authority after the death of his father. They claimed a proud history, but they were not without their shortcomings: Grinnell's brothers and sisters were spendthrift; none of the men, other than George Bird, had pursued a career for long. Sisters Helen and Laura were more supported than supportive. What the family lacked was self-discipline, Grinnell remarked repeatedly.

By contrast, the Cheyennes had maintained their integrity through thick and thin—or at least that is how Grinnell idealized them. Frustrated by his own family and perhaps unsure of his own domestic niche—he had yet to contemplate either marriage or parenthood when he was first getting acquainted with the Cheyennes—he had sought an alternative environment to inhabit. If a man wanted to separate himself from his immediate surroundings, the Indian life provided an inviting haven. Grinnell was not expressly drawn to the Cheyennes or any other Indians because he thought them "wild" or because he wanted to become in some fashion wild himself.

If anything, it was the Cheyennes' orthodoxy, their sheltering normality, that enamored him. "These primitive people in certain ways live more in accordance with custom and form than we do," he writes in the preface to *The Cheyenne Indians*.

That said, otherness had its appeal. Grinnell enjoyed bridging two worlds, using one to buffer the other. When he was in the East, he was known as a man to be reckoned with in the West. When he was in the West, he was a man of big medicine in the East. He was esteemed in either setting; at the same time, he was also hard to pin down.

Some years earlier, in 1916, Grinnell had written to Montana folklorist Frank Bird Linderman—that middle name again—who had dedicated his first book, *Indian Why Stories*, to him. "I have reached the shell with two or three tribes and perhaps have gotten a little way into the white," he told Linderman, "but way down deeper there is the yolk of the egg—the heart of the whole matter—which I do not penetrate." The same could be said for George Bird Grinnell, who kept his eggs in separate baskets, as a form of self-protection and privacy. Wherever he happened to be, a part of him was elsewhere, shielded by distance and disparity.

Grinnell finished reading the last page proofs of *The Cheyenne Indians* on August 1, 1923, and the next day he and Elizabeth departed for Nova Scotia, to spend the month of August with the Sheldons. As their train crossed into Canada at Vanceboro, Maine, they received word that President Harding had died in San Francisco, most likely of a heart attack, though early reports blamed food poisoning. When Harding succumbed at the Palace Hotel, he was concluding a long cross-country trip that had taken him as far as Alaska—the first president to set foot in the territory—and included stops in Yellowstone and Yosemite.

At the time of Harding's sudden death, Grinnell had not lost faith in the president, as he (and the rest of the public) had long since done with the secretary of the interior. Tarred by Teapot Dome, Albert Fall had been forced to retire in March. "Mr. Fall is not a conservationist and is not interested in our natural things," Grinnell concluded. "He appears to share the common American notion that such things should at once be turned into money and so consumed, rather than preserved as capital which will forever produce an income and so be of permanent value to the country." Harding's demise, on the other hand, "was a tremendous loss to the country," Grinnell lamented. "He had definitely aligned himself on the side of conservation with special reference to the national parks, game, and forests."

As for Harding's successor, "Silent Cal" Coolidge, "[S]ome of us feel very hopeful about him," Grinnell remarked. "He knows enough, at least, to keep quiet."

Grinnell and Elizabeth were back from Canada barely a week when they repacked their trunks and left for Montana. After his previous visit to Glacier, two years earlier, Grinnell was ambivalent about returning. "I have had a part in the establishing of the national parks," he wrote to Aldo Leopold in New Mexico, "and while I have never regretted what I did in this matter because of the pleasure those parks give to a vast multitude of people, still the territory that I used to love and travel through is now ruined for my purposes."

Leopold, the future author of *A Sand Country Almanac*, nowadays revered as a core text in the canon of environmentalist doctrine, got his start in forest and game management. In 1921 he had published a head-turning article in the *Journal of Forestry* entitled, "The Wilderness and Its Place in Forest Recreation Policy," which challenged Gifford Pinchot's notion of "highest use" for national forests and suggested that some forests ought to be left alone entirely—preserved as "wild country" for future generations. Leopold then drew up a plan to designate the Gila National Forest as the nation's first wilderness area. In recent months Leopold and Grinnell had struck up a correspondence over their mutual interest in a related idea: establishment of game refuges within national forests—a perennial ambition of the Boone and Crockett Club and others. Grinnell had long contended that game in federal forests was best managed by the National Forest Service, but he was impressed by the approach Leopold was taking in New Mexico, where, instead of struggling to turn an entire forest into a game refuge—thus far unsuccessfully—he had persuaded the state game commission to set aside and manage smaller refuges within the forests. Neither man acknowledged as much, but the torch of conservation was being passed to a new generation.

Grinnell was still simmering over the rude treatment he had received during his previous visit to Glacier, two years earlier, when a stable manager insisted that he must ride on the park's trails accompanied by a guide. He wrote to Arno Cammerer, the number-two man at the National Park Service, requesting special privileges: "I cannot spend [the] time chasing after officers in order to demonstrate that I am competent to ride a horse, to follow a trail, or to find my way about." Sarcastically he asked Cammerer to provide him with "weapons to use against [any] wooden-headed ranger" who stood in his way.

Arriving at Glacier Park Lodge, he noticed a group of Indians standing around in headdresses, their presence encouraged and likely underwritten by the Great Northern. "I went over to them and found 25 or more I[ndians] with their women & children," he wrote in his diary. "They all called me by name as they shook hands and all seemed glad to see me." Among the men were Bird Rattler, Many Tail Feathers, Curly Bear, and John Two Guns White Calf, son of Chief White Calf.

Later, with Jack Monroe, he inspected a number of Piegan farms and admired the grain fields. Thirty years before, Grinnell had doubted that the Piegans would ever be able to grow crops; he believed that they should stick to raising cattle collectively. But with allotment and land patents now pervasive, and with the advent of strains of wheat that could be planted in the fall and harvested in the spring, many Indians had in fact become farmers.

Grinnell and Elizabeth could not leave the park without paying their respects to Grinnell Glacier. They rode with a group of other tourists to the head of Lake Josephine on horseback (with no apparent guff from the rangers). They climbed the rest of the way on foot. "I had to stop rather often to get my wind," Grinnell confessed. They walked gingerly onto the ice, reaching its highest point, beneath the balcony of today's Salamander Glacier, where they could see down into a deep hollow where the icefield had sunk. "Here were several seemingly unfathomable potholes into which the water from the melting ice was pouring," he observed. "The amount of water daily lost from this ice is stupendous."

The next stop was Lame Deer. The Cheyenne book was finished, on its way to the printer, and Grinnell had no larger purpose than to spend time among the people to whom he had devoted so much of his life.

One night he and Elizabeth attended a council of elders. "We went up to the camp about 7 p.m. and found the big tent up, a dozen or fifteen old men in it and eight or ten women boiling beef over a big fire," he wrote. "It was interesting and reminiscent of old times to see the women working about the fire on which a dozen or fifteen kettles were boiling. Later more people gathered, lights were put up, and the older men, about a dozen, began to sing . . . [M]en stood up, one at a time, and counted coups, relating adventures of the old war days."

At 9:30 Grinnell and Elizabeth bid good night to their friends, and in the morning they left for Eatons' Ranch, with its own customs and hospitality, but none any more welcoming than the council tent of the Northern Cheyennes.

That fall and winter Grinnell made his customary bird-shooting trips—with Elizabeth to the Adirondacks and by himself to North Carolina. "Time has dealt kindly with me," he wrote a Canadian friend, "and at the age of 74 I am still reasonably active."

Elizabeth had been wanting him to take her to Europe again, and in April he relented. They docked at Barcelona and proceeded to Madrid in time for Holy Week, an ambition of Elizabeth's, whose Catholicism had not been dimmed by her husband's indifference. After Spain they went to Paris and spent several days with Grinnell's sister Helen. In France Grinnell tried to locate records of Grinnell ancestors—"Grenelles"—whom he believed (erroneously, it would turn out) had French roots. He had only slightly better luck in Holland, digging up records of his mother's Lansing forebears. Grinnell had always taken a keen interest in genealogy. As he grew older, heritage mattered to him even more.

He spent the summer putting the finishing touches on the Boone and

Crockett book, *Hunting and Conservation*. The preface, signed by "The Editors"—Grinnell and Sheldon—is dated September 5, 1924. One day later Grinnell boarded the Lake Shore Limited, this time without Elizabeth, and arrived in Columbus, Nebraska, two days later.

Early on in the friendship Grinnell had tried in vain to get Lute North to write his memoirs. By 1924, however, Lute, now seventy-seven, was willing to make another stab. Two years earlier he had given a lecture on the Pawnee Battalion at the annual meeting of the Nebraska State Historical Society, and now, with some goading from Grinnell, he filled several pads of paper with further reminiscences of his adventures on the plains. Grinnell took these pages with him when he left Columbus, en route to Colorado and Wyoming. Here perhaps were the makings of a book after all.

In Casper, Wyoming, Grinnell was the guest of Robert Ellison, attorney for the Midwest Refining Company and an avid collector of western books and artifacts. Ellison was only too pleased to drive the acclaimed Indian expert to several nearby spots of interest. First was the site of a bridge over the North Platte where in July 1865 Sioux and Cheyenne, including George Bent's Dog Soldiers, had attacked and severely punished the army protecting this critical crossing on the Bozeman Trail. The surrounding hills were now dotted with oil tanks, but "one could [still] visualize the scene," Grinnell wrote, having already described it in *The Fighting Cheyennes*.

The following day Ellison showed Grinnell a more recent chapter of history: Teapot Dome and the adjacent oil fields of Salt Creek, north of Casper. The rugged terrain, once the bed of an ocean, once the stomping ground of dinosaurs, once the stronghold of the Cheyennes, was "covered with derricks in all directions," Grinnell observed. A town of several thousand people—today's Midwest, Wyoming—had sprung up, with "schools, hospital, churches, club, boarding house, theatre, everything up to date and on grand scale." On the outskirts he noticed a booming tenderloin proffering "girls, liquor & other undesirable things."

From Casper he went to the Northern Cheyennes and made the rounds. He spent September 20, his seventy-fifth birthday, with Young Little Wolf, Porcupine, Dog, and several other old friends.

Then on to Eatons' Ranch. "On the whole, a most delightful visit," he wrote of these few days as a dude. "Everyone asked about E[lizabeth] & I was warned not to come again without her." He was back with her in New York on October 1.

One of the first things he did upon his return was write to Walter Camp, reminding him of the pledge they had made several years earlier to place markers on the graves of Dull Knife and Little Wolf. "We [must] tackle the thing at once," he urged Camp, "because I am reaching a time of life now when my visits to the West cannot be very many more. I should like to have these markers put up before I need a marker myself."

The next thing he did was get to work on Lute North's manuscript. On his way east, he had stopped again at Columbus and found that North had spent the past month writing more recollections. "The stuff seems to me good, but one can't tell how it will strike a reader," Grinnell cautioned. He thought he might try the material on a few publishers: Scribner's, Yale University Press, Doubleday, and Frederick A. Stokes.

Over the coming weeks he cobbled a hybrid of Lute North's stories and the ragged, unpublished biography of Frank North, fleshed out by his own revisions and additions. In February he wrote to Charles Scribner's Sons—a sensible first choice, since they had published Grinnell's *Trails of the Path-finders, Beyond the Old Frontier, The Fighting Cheyennes*, and, even earlier, his Pawnee and Blackfoot books. "I have worked over [the manuscript] to get it in reasonable shape for reading," he explained to Scribner's. "I take it that it is the sort of stuff that you would be glad to have."

Try as he might, however, he could not find a taker. Scribner's took a pass, then Macmillan, Houghton Mifflin, and Doubleday. "Probably if [the] story were told in blood and thunder fashion, with a lot of adjectives, they would look at it differently," he complained to Addison Sheldon of the Nebraska State Historical Society. "But it is told in simple, straightforward style, with no posing and exaggeration." Even Sheldon, an admirer of the North brothers and the Pawnee scouts, declined.

Grinnell's final try was with Yale, which had recently accepted two (now classic) memoirs by plainsmen: one by James H. Cook (*Fifty Years on the Old Frontier*), the other by Grinnell's old friend Luther "Yellowstone" Kelly. He might have had better luck if he had put his own name on the title page, as he had done with one of James Willard Schultz's early manuscripts, but he was determined to give Lute North full credit as author. Yale passed.

Hunting and Conservation, the Boone and Crockett book published by Yale, fared better. Of the three articles by Grinnell, the most noteworthy was a brief history of American game protection. "The natural things we are trying to preserve are useful in two aspects," Grinnell writes. "They have a value measurable in money, and a recreation value not measurable, but expressing itself in renewed vitality in working people, and so indirectly adding to our national well-being. If we treat these natural things solely as commercial assets and turn them into dollars and cents, we expend and destroy them. Their use is ended. They leave nothing behind them. If we preserve them, they reproduce themselves, retain their value for recreation and will yield to us and to our children a never-ending income in health, strength and pleasure. Preserved, they are everlasting; consumed and destroyed, their value is gone for all time."

For all the achievements cited by Grinnell in his history of protection, there were exceptions to this progress. One such disappointment was the Federal Public Shooting Ground and Bird Refuge bill, which had been navigating the crosscurrents of Congress since 1921.

Its predecessor, the Migratory Bird Treaty Act, was generally regarded as a great success; but as restrictions on bag limits and shooting seasons took effect, conservationists and progressive sportsmen recognized that something more must be done to protect the shores, waterways, and wetlands essential to the migration, breeding, nesting, and wintering of wildfowl. Bird shooting was becoming more popular as a recreational pastime; meanwhile, urban and agricultural development was spewing pollutants and draining marshes in these fragile areas. The Boone and Crockett Club and the American Game Protective Association were among the groups to call attention to the necessity for more refuges *and* more shooting grounds for the average citizen, who had no access to exclusive clubs (such as Grinnell's Narrows Island Club).

It was John Bird Burnham's idea that the creation of more game refuges could be underwritten by allowing hunting, carefully controlled, on these refuges; the only cost to the public would be a small fee for a federal hunting license (the germ of today's federal duck stamp). A bill to this effect was introduced by Senator Harry New of Indiana and Representative Dan Anthony of Kansas. The legislation was endorsed by state game commissions and numerous sportsman's groups—the National Association of Audubon Societies, the Camp-Fire Club, Izaak Walton League, National Federation of Women's Clubs, Council on National Parks, Forests and Wildlife (as Grinnell's National Parks Committee was renamed), Aldo Leopold's New Mexico Game Protective Association, and of course the Boone and Crockett Club and American Game Protective Association. Still, the bill was stymied, largely due to the troublemaking of one man, William T. Hornaday, director of the New York Zoological Society and pamphleteer of the Permanent Wild Life Protection Fund.

Over the years, Hornaday had grown ever more adamant and outspoken in his view that hunting ought to be outlawed everywhere. He bore a personal animus toward Burnham and maligned the AGPA for advocating hunting as sport. In the newsletter of his Permanent Wild Life Protection Fund, Hornaday disparaged the proposed new game refuges as potential "slaughter pens" propagated by "game hogs."

Sticking up for Burnham, Grinnell pronounced Hornaday "anything but an outdoor man." He continued to avoid Hornaday and, as he had done in the past, used Madison Grant as intermediary when communication was absolutely necessary. "Bad experience has taught me that it is a pretty difficult matter to restrain Hornaday, who lacks judgment and lacks tact," he confided.

But even Grinnell could not keep from lashing out directly at Hornaday for his hardline antics. "I have been working for game protection longer than most men," he wrote Hornaday in 1920, "and I believe that I appreciate more fully than most people the vast amount of effective work for protection which your great energy has enabled you to accomplish. Yet I have made no secret of the fact that I have not approved of your methods of recent years, because I think that your combative attitude—and as I see them—exaggerated methods injure the cause of game protection by alienating the sympathies of people who, by different handling, might become its friends and partisans, and because I feel it is a waste of energy for the friends of game protection to quarrel among themselves."

Hornaday was not one to hold his tongue. "Your letter was a hostile and dangerous production," he fired back at Grinnell. "On my part, in all the thirty-three years of our acquaintance, I never have laid a straw in your way, and so far as I can recall, I never once have pointedly criticized you or your methods. I have thought, however, that your methods are at times too mild for these times. I have dealt severely with the brutal enemies of wild life, because in these harsh times I think strong methods with such people are necessary in the securing of real results."

Grinnell characterized Hornaday's followers as mostly women and children seduced by sanctimony. Perhaps this was so, but Hornaday made sufficient noise among this constituency that Congress, in a succession of votes, rejected the bill.

"There is one class of people . . . that, lacking apparent balance, readily [becomes] enthusiastic for protection, but do not seem to use their wits about it and are guided solely by their emotions," Grinnell wrote to Secretary of Agriculture Henry Wallace as the game-refuge campaign was stalling. "Often, therefore, those in our own camp give us more trouble than our real opponents."

Conservationists now occupied a big tent; Grinnell was not yet used to it being so crowded.

Another concern nagging Grinnell was the unintended consequence of wildlife preservation: the overprotection and overabundance of wildlife in certain habitats.

Yellowstone, the first national park and the standard for all future national parks, was, in one respect, a flawed design. During Grinnell's trip to Yellowstone with the Ludlow reconnaissance in 1875, he had been alarmed by the slaughter of elk in the Yellowstone River valley, north of the park, and he warned that, if the killing continued, elk might soon become extinct in the region. He, the Boone and Crockett Club, and a familiar coalition of conservationists failed to pass legislation to expand the park's boundaries, but they did persuade Congress to prohibit hunting within the park—and subsequently in all national parks. With protection, the Yellowstone herd recovered rapidly, only to face a fresh existential crisis. Historically the elk had migrated freely in winter—southward into lower country around Jackson Hole and northward into the more temperate valleys of the Lamar and Yellowstone rivers. But by the end of the nineteenth century the animals found their passage impeded by ranches, livestock, fences, and a firing line of hunters. The herd was bottled up, multiplying fast, running short of food, and collaterally threatening the subsistence of the deer, buffalo, and bighorn sheep.

The National Park Service and the Bureau of Biological Survey tried a number of different measures to rectify the situation: feeding hay to the elk through the winter months, as was already done to sustain buffalo in the Lamar Valley; capturing elk and shipping them to other ranges; and purchasing and dedicating land on the park's perimeter as a national elk refuge. Even so, by the mid-1920s there were far too many elk in the greater Yellowstone region—more than forty thousand—and the range had been grazed to a nub. Whereas once Grinnell had been appalled by the wholesale killing of elk, now he sang a different, deadlier tune. "If the elk increase to forty-five thousand next year and to fifty thousand the year afterward, you have always the same problem," Grinnell wrote to Charles Sheldon. With regard to the feeding program and establishment of refuges, he stated, "It is just my personal view that these experiments will come to nothing." In a follow-up letter to Edward Nelson, he offered a solution befitting a conservationist who was also a hunter: "[T]he elk must be kept down to a certain number by killing off the increase each year."

But by 1925 no management program or combination of programs had been put in place to alter the calculus of containing wildlife on an island of finite resources. It was a conundrum that would persist into the twenty-first century—affecting not only elk but also buffalo, grizzly bears, and wolves.

Such setbacks and frustrations scarcely tarnished Grinnell's public reputation. In April 1925 he received a letter from the Roosevelt Memorial Association, informing him that he was to be awarded a medal for his lifetime of good works.

The Memorial Association had formed shortly after Roosevelt's death to honor his exemplary character and deeds. Its members campaigned for a Roosevelt Memorial in Washington (only to be preempted by the Jefferson Memorial). They would soon encourage sculptor Gutzon Borglum to include Roosevelt on the colossal "Shrine of Democracy" being contemplated in the Black Hills—Mount Rushmore.

The Roosevelt Medal for Distinguished Service, first awarded in 1923, was the work of another sculptor, James Earl Fraser, who had designed *The End of the Trail*, of an Indian warrior slumped in the saddle, and the buffalo nickel, which on its "tail" bore the profile of an Indian, said at various times to be modeled on Two Moon, the Cheyenne, and John Two Guns White Calf. The solid gold Roosevelt Medal had the head of the president on one side; on the other a flaming sword and the words, "If I must choose between righteousness and peace, I choose righteousness."

At a ceremony at the White House on May 15, President Coolidge presented three such medals. Martha Berry, the founder of schools for the underprivileged in rural Georgia, was celebrated for her work in promoting the welfare of women and children. Interestingly, Grinnell was not cited for his contribution to conservation explicitly. That honor was bestowed on Gifford Pinchot, "the man to whom the nation owes most for what has been accomplished as regards the preservation of the natural resources of the country." Grinnell, meanwhile, was celebrated for his "promotion of outdoor life."

He was not one to quibble over which man had contributed more to conservation, but he was doubtless pleased by how Coolidge set him apart. "Mr. Grinnell," the president said, "I am struck by the fact that this year I have the pleasure of presenting these Roosevelt medals to three pioneers. You and Miss Berry and Gov. Pinchot [elected governor of Pennsylvania in 1923] have all been trail blazers. In the case of Miss Berry and Mr. Pinchot, however, it is true only in a figurative sense. But you were with Gen. Custer in the Black Hills and with Col. Ludlow in the Yellowstone. You lived among the Indians; you became a member of the Blackfoot tribe. Your studies of the language and customs are authoritative. Few have done so much as you, none have done more, to preserve vast areas of picturesque wilderness for the eyes of posterity in the simple majesty in which you and your fellow pioneers first beheld them. In the Yellowstone Park you prevented the exploitation and, therefore, the destruction of the natural beauty. The Glacier National Park is peculiarly your monument. As editor for 35 years of a journal devoted to outdoor life, you have done a noteworthy service in bringing to the men and women of a hurried and harried age the relaxation and revitalization which comes from contact with nature."

The newspapers did not record Grinnell's reply, but afterward he wrote Luther North, who had sent a letter of congratulation. "I went to Washington and with the other two people stood up, listened to a speech by the President, and received the medal," he explained sparingly. "It was more or less a function at which 75 or 100 people were present. The medal is big enough to knock a man down with and, I suppose, is actually something to be gratified about."

Robert Ellison, the Wyoming oilman, was another who sent an admiring note. "Very many thanks for the kind words," Grinnell replied. "It seems to me there are a good many other people who ought to have received [the medal] before me, for . . . all I have done is to do each day's work as it came along."

At the close of his remarks at the White House, President Coolidge had told Grinnell: "I am glad to have a part in the public recognition which your self-effacing and effective life has won." By nature a reserved man himself, Coolidge had invoked George Bird Grinnell's essence precisely.

MELTING RAPIDLY

For the third summer in a row Grinnell and Elizabeth joined the Sheldons in Nova Scotia. Elizabeth's enthusiasm for golf had waned, and she had let her membership in the Ardsley Club lapse, but she was otherwise quite active and contented. "About 22 or 25 years ago I got married," Grinnell wrote to an old New York friend early in the summer of 1925, "and my wife and I have not done an undue amount of quarreling since; we manage to get along pretty comfortably together."

Elizabeth's well-being and the harmony of their marriage were directly related to the stability of her mother and brother. Grinnell's decision to purchase the Curtis farm in Glenville had proven to be a good one. He continued to pay the bills, as Frank Curtis settled down, with the help of a hired man and his mother, raising a small herd of dairy cows, a few sheep, and sufficient feed to sustain the animals through winters. Although Grinnell remained doubtful that the farm would ever earn money, much less that Frank would prove capable of running it on his own, he and Elizabeth made headway in coaxing Delle Curtis to live more frugally.

After Nova Scotia in July, Grinnell and Elizabeth left New York again on August 4. Elizabeth went only as far as Glenville. Grinnell continued west, making yet another of what were becoming almost compulsive trips. His first stop was Chicago, where he meant to discuss with Walter Camp plans for the memorials of Dull Knife and Little Wolf. Upon arrival, Grinnell learned that Camp had died only two days before. Later he wrote to Camp's widow, urging her to preserve her husband's Indian artifacts—thinking also of his own collection, which he had begun donating to the Peabody Museum at Yale and to the American Museum of Natural History. "Matter such as this," Grinnell wrote to Mrs. Camp, "has, of course, no money value, but it has a very great historical value and ought to be saved."

Grinnell spent two nights with Lute North in Columbus, sharing his frustration over not being able to find a publisher for North's memoir. Next, strictly for nostalgia's sake, he went to Laramie, Wyoming, and was driven to Shirley Basin, which he had not set eyes on since he sold out in 1899. "My place is still known as the Grinnell ranch & [the] lake is G[rinnell] Lake," he remarked in his diary. The road to the basin was barely passable after a recent rain, but Grinnell was delighted to see antelope and sage hens still in abundance.

From Laramie he continued west on the Union Pacific, following the route he had taken with Professor Marsh in 1870. He stopped in Ogden, Utah, and spent two days as a guest of A. P. Bigelow, a local banker and sportsman, who showed him around the marshy delta of the Bear River, where it flows into the northeast arm of the Great Salt Lake. Grinnell, the seasoned naturalist, filled his notebook with the names of birds: avocets, sickle-billed curlews, glossy ibises, godwits, egrets, herons, pelicans, swans, green-winged teals, cormorants, geese, and "numberless ducks." Three years later the wetland would be federally protected as the Bear River Migratory Bird Refuge.

His next destination was Oakland, where he passed two days with nephew Frank Page, wife Flora, and their two daughters, who had been living in California for the past couple of years. Grinnell had always felt a special attachment to Frank Page, named for the older brother who had died so young. Yet to go such a long way to spend only two days was a rather extreme demonstration of affection. The sheer act of traveling, of maintaining motion, was apparently a goal in and of itself.

The last time Grinnell had journeyed all the way to the West Coast, in

1912, he and Elizabeth had continued south to Santa Barbara, where he had made a tentative, and unsuccessful, effort to see George Gould. This time after leaving the Bay Area, he turned north to Crater Lake National Park in Oregon and then carried on to Seattle and Whidbey Island, where Billy Hofer, his beloved Yellowstone guide, was living out his old age.

Hofer was nearly crippled by arthritis and needed two canes to get around, but his recent letters to Grinnell were full of chipper reminiscences. "You know we are now 'old timers' . . . but we did see a little of the tail end of the 'old times'—just the last wiggle of the tail," Hofer wrote after receiving an autographed copy of *The Fighting Cheyennes.* In another letter he declared: "I'm getting so I don't mourn, but sit by my fire, smoke my pipe, and think of the good times I've had, and congratulate myself I had them, saw the country, the game, the Indians and all, and to know that I saw it, and younger folks can never do so. I've got something they can't take away from me."

Hofer, a bachelor, lived with his sister in a cottage on the island's southwest shore, a subdivision called Sunlight Beach (although Grinnell noted on the day he visited, "It was raining—no sunshine"). The understanding that they would never again be together remained unspoken; Grinnell noted, "I enjoyed seeing [Billy] very much and was sorry to part."

Grinnell arrived at Glacier National Park on August 27. At St. Mary he saw Jack Monroe, James Willard Schultz, and several familiar Piegans. Of the Indians' many complaints, the one that troubled Grinnell the most harkened to the treaty he had helped to negotiate thirty summers before. In agreeing to sell the Ceded Strip to the government, the Piegans had reserved the right to hunt and cut timber on the relinquished land, so long as it remained "public." But with the creation of Glacier National Park, which absorbed all of the Ceded Strip, the government had taken the arcane legal position that a national park was no longer *public.*

"It seems a shame," Grinnell commented in his diary, "that the P[iegans] have never been paid anything for the game and timber rights guaranteed them by the treaty of 1895 and taken from them."

He had not fought on behalf of the Blackfeet since Roosevelt was president, and he was too old and too out of touch to start again.

Grinnell did not venture into the mountains, either above the St. Mary Lakes or in the direction of Grinnell Glacier, at the head of Swiftcurrent. Instead he rode the train over Marias Pass to Belton and Lake McDonald, on the west side of the park, where he was met by Charles Kraebel, the park superintendent.

Kraebel received him as a visiting dignitary, driving him along the lake and delivering him to the summer cottage of Charles M. Russell, the famous cowboy artist. Grinnell and Russell had met once or twice in New York, when Russell was exhibiting his energetic western paintings and bronzes on Fifth Avenue. They shared a profound nostalgia for an era when Indians roamed free, buffalo were plenty, and, as Russell reverently put it, "the land belonged to God." Russell was fourteen years younger than Grinnell, but, at the age of sixty-one, he was weakened by a goiter and a bad heart. The paintings Grinnell saw at Lake McDonald were some of the last great pieces of Russell's colorful career. In a year he would be dead, another of Montana's adopted sons gone to the Sand Hills.

On his way east Grinnell spent a week on the Northern Cheyenne reservation, and once back in New York he deliberated on the memorials for Dull Knife and Little Wolf. With Walter Camp's death, the task was his alone. He had Tiffany draw designs for two bronze tablets and at first balked at the price—eighty dollars each. He finally relented and asked Tiffany to ship the pieces in care of August Stohr, the agency trader at Lame Deer. At this point it was too late for Tiffany to cast them in time for him take on his next trip to the Cheyenne reservation.

In several respects the western trip Grinnell and Elizabeth took in the summer of 1926 was like all the others. What set it apart was the fiftieth anniversary of the battle of the Little Bighorn, although, to read Grinnell's account of the ceremony, the day was somewhat anticlimactic: "The show was not very good, for there were so many people that few had a chance to see what went on. The multitude so overwhelmed the soldiers & Indians. We saw no one we knew until after the show." Finally he spotted Lute North; Robert Ellison, the oilman from Casper, was another familiar face. Then he ran into his two companions from the Rosebud trip ten years earlier, General Godfrey and photographer L. A. Huffman. "The celebration was not very impressive," he repeated to an acquaintance in Kansas, "but the [gathering] of the old fellows . . . was very gratifying."

Grinnell had relived the battle over and over in his head and in the company of men who had fought on June 25, 1876. He had read every published account and had written his own version more than once. It was one of the benchmarks of his life—and, of course, it had nearly been the last. If he had accepted William Ludlow's invitation to join the Seventh Cavalry in the summer of 1876, his name might have been on the memorial at the top of the hill, his bones decomposing in one of the coulees leading up from the river, near where his friend Charley Reynolds had fallen.

Grinnell had been twenty-six then; he was now seventy-six. During the interceding years he had made and lost a great many friends and observed what had come after the Indians won the battle, only to lose the war. Airplanes now swooped overhead. Automobiles churned up dust on the white man's road. Trains made it possible for him to shuttle between two worlds with ease. In the end, he had come to the Little Bighorn because, for better or worse, it was a vantage point from which he could size up the past while retracing his own progress through a long, productive, and fortunate life.

After a couple of days at Eatons' Ranch and five days at Lame Deer, Grinnell and Elizabeth spent two weeks at Glacier, including a side trip to the Blackfeet agency to observe the medicine lodge.

On July 14, leaving Elizabeth at Many Glacier Hotel, Grinnell set out for his glacier, accompanied by Morton Elrod, a young science professor from the University of Montana who that summer had established the beginnings of what he hoped would become a park museum. Also in the party were several young hotel guests, a Mr. and Mrs. Noble, a Mrs. Binder, and a Miss Kemey, whom Elrod had agreed to guide. Forty years earlier Grinnell had surmised that he was the first white man to make this trip. In the summer of 1926 nearly a thousand tourists would hike or ride to his glacier.

The first four miles of the six-mile route passed alongside the lower lakes, Swiftcurrent, Josephine, and Grinnell. Then the trail steepened, and the way became more demanding. From Many Glacier Hotel to Grinnell Lake the path ascends only two hundred feet in elevation; the climb from Grinnell Lake to the foot of the glacier is 1,400 vertical feet, every one strewn with boulders. Grinnell drew stamina from his past trips and, with frequent pauses to catch his breath, he and his fellow hikers in due course reached the rubble moraine that marked the terminus of the glacier. Immense, sculpted freight cars of ice, discarded violently by the retreating train of the mother glacier, parked themselves across the basin.

Grinnell's party picked its way cautiously across the moraine and onto the ice, but they were reluctant to proceed farther upon the slushy, uncertain surface. Luckily they were joined by a strapping Swiss guide—Hans, by name—who cheerfully agreed to rope them together and lead the way up the sloping glacier to where it met the exposed face of a towering ridge, its sharp crest limned a thousand feet above them.

Grinnell sensed that this likely would be his last ascent to Grinnell Glacier, and the poignancy of such finality was made more redolent by memories of his earlier visits to this alpine sanctum—with Jack Monroe and especially with George Gould, who had died in Santa Barbara earlier in the year.

Grinnell and Gould had last seen each other in 1890. If Gould came east during that interim, there is no evidence, certainly none in Grinnell's papers, of any such visits. Grinnell was the peripatetic pilgrim, Gould was an emigrant—each to his own nature—but both were motivated by a similar desire for separation from eastern convention and constraint. Given the length of their time apart, it is remarkable that they maintained a correspondence for as long as they did. Eventually, though, their letters became more infrequent. By 1926 Grinnell had not heard from his "Partner" since 1919.

The obituary in the Santa Barbara newspaper provided only the sparest details of Gould's full and active life. "Mr. Gould, believed to be the second oldest barrister in Santa Barbara, was an authority on litigation over water rights and was president of the Montecito county water district," the notice stated. It made no mention, for instance, of Gould's ongoing interest in the history of pre-Anglo settlement of the Pacific Coast; nor of the gardens and olive groves he cultivated on his Montecito estate; nor of any friends, beyond members of the bar. The lone personal anecdote provided was the rather random observation that "Mr. Gould during the war joined with other residents of the county in a protest against high cost of clothing, and donned overalls"—jeans.

The only person reported to have been present at Gould's deathbed was the wife of a nephew. Grinnell was duck-hunting in North Carolina at the time and must have received word through Gould's brother Charles. Again Grinnell's letter books register no acknowledgment.

At the end of the climb to Grinnell Glacier, Grinnell fell twice while descending the trail. He arrived back at the hotel at sundown on weary legs. That night he wrote in his diary, "The glacier is melting very fast, and the amount of water coming from it is very great." (According to Morton Elrod, the ice had receded sixty-five feet in the past year alone.)

Then Grinnell added: "All these glaciers are melting rapidly and after a time will disappear."

Yet even as Grinnell Glacier shrunk, its great gouged basin, at the top of a staircase of lakes, would continue to be flanked by two handsome summits, separated eternally by the cornice of the Continental Divide, complementing each other like carved newel posts: Mount Grinnell and Mount Gould.

Despite his great fatigue, or because of it, Grinnell slept poorly that night. For the rest of his time at the park, he did not attempt anything nearly so strenuous. He and Elizabeth arrived home in New York on July 22. They had been away barely a month.

In the fall of 1926 Grinnell redoubled his effort to see Lute North's manuscript into print. Time was running out. North had recently turned eighty, and in December he had fallen and injured himself badly. "It is a very shocking thing, and I offer you my sympathy," Grinnell wrote his friend. "I hope that . . . before long your various broken bones will knit and become usable again." On the other hand, he added, "We do not recuperate from such accidents now as we did many years ago."

In November Grinnell pitched the project to the Arthur H. Clark Company of Cleveland, distinguished for publishing earnest books of western history—for example, a memoir by Montana pioneer Granville Stuart, and *The Dawn of the World*, C. Hart Merriam's collection of folk tales from the Mewan (today called Miwok) Indians of California.

In his submission letter, Grinnell laid out the strengths as well as the shortcomings. "[North] is one of the most modest and truthful men that I have ever known," he advised. "[He] might have written a story that would show that he was a great hero, but he does not happen to be built on the lines of Bill Cody, Buffalo Bill." Grinnell explained that he intended to merge the original manuscript of Frank North's life with Lute North's story. And he also made clear that he wished the synthesized volume to be published "over the name of its author and that I should merely write an explanatory foreword."

The publisher had other ideas. Clark wanted more than Grinnell's editorial assistance; he wanted Grinnell's name on the title page. Grinnell relayed this proposition to North, knowing in advance what the outcome would be: "As I have probably told you in previous letters, I wanted this story to go out under your name as author, in the hope that you would get glory out of it, and perhaps some money." But, he elaborated, "[I]f I should take hold of the manuscript and make of it a book combining your recollections and Frank's, I should probably have to appear as author and should, of course, hope for some return for the time and work that I put into it."

North conceded that the task of grafting the two manuscripts was beyond his abilities. Besides, Grinnell cared more about the book than he ever had. And so he graciously and gratefully capitulated. By June 1927 Grinnell had woven the material into a single, 70,000-word narrative. He pressed Arthur H. Clark for prompt acceptance. "Captain L. H. North, a dear friend of more than fifty years standing, is an old man and subject to the dangers of age," he explained to the publisher.

After sending off the North manuscript, Grinnell took a train to Columbus, without Elizabeth, and spent two days. Then on July 19 he and North rode west together to Casper, Wyoming, where they were met by Robert Ellison. Grinnell remained fascinated, indeed nearly obsessed, with the attack on the Dull Knife camp, in which the North brothers and Pawnee scouts had led the charge. He still could not forgive himself for the mistake he had made on the map included in *The Fighting Cheyennes*. "[I]t is a frightful, mortifying thing to have such a colossal blunder take place," Grinnell told Ellison, "but it did take place, and there is no excuse for it."

Ellison was as hospitable as ever, driving Grinnell and North one hundred miles to the Dull Knife site, North's first visit since that frigid and ferocious day in November 1876. Everything came back to him: the bugle signaling the charge, the shooting of Dull Knife's son, the Cheyennes' tenacious defense, the capture of the Indian horses, the burning of lodges, and the snowstorm that buried the camp the night after the attack. As they walked the battle-ground, they came upon two other groups of visitors. "[E]ach one had a copy of the Fighting Cheyennes," Grinnell noted in his diary. "They were all studying my map." Whether he alerted them to its error, he did not say.

Ellison took them back to Casper, and the next day North returned to Nebraska. "Sorry to lose him," Grinnell wrote, little knowing that it was the last time the two would see each other.

His own destination was Yellowstone National Park, which, for the first time, he entered from the east, by way of Cody, Wyoming. He spent only three days in the park, driven by a student from Montana State College. They stopped at the popular attractions—Old Faithful, Yellowstone Lake, Mammoth Hot Springs—and one that Grinnell had never seen close-up before: Artist's Point on the Grand Canyon of the Yellowstone, immortalized in the paintings of Albert Bierstadt, Thomas Moran, and many others. Grinnell, who, forty years earlier, had been put off by the increase in visitors to the park, was nonplussed by the traffic in 1927. "Travel last year was over 187,000," he noted. "This year will be larger. Astonishing number of people come and go on buses, and there is a vast auto travel." (Today more than three million visit the park annually.)

His stopover on the Northern Cheyenne reservation was brief—only three nights. He stayed with August Stohr and reunited with familiar faces. One Cheyenne friend said in sign language that the sight of Grinnell was "like the sun shining on him."

With each successive year, train service in Montana got better; this time, it took Grinnell only a day to get from the Cheyenne reservation to Glacier, where his stay was another whistle stop. He saw almost nothing of the park but tracked down Jack Monroe at his home in St. Mary. Some things never changed. "Jack Monroe has told me much about his mine without conveying to me much idea of what he has accomplished," Grinnell joked wryly in his diary.

Grinnell was back in New York on August 6. This latest western trip was one of the shortest: less than two weeks.

As hastily as he had traveled, he came to accept that he was slowing down. At the annual Boone and Crockett meeting in January 1928, he asked not to be reelected president. The members acceded to his wish, but in appreciation of his forty years of dedication, they voted him the title of honorary president. Grinnell expressed his gratitude in a letter to club secretary Kermit Roosevelt, second son of Theodore Roosevelt. "I have always felt that my election as presiding officer of the Boone and Crockett Club was the greatest honor that had ever come to me," he wrote. "Not many of the original members of the Club are still living, but we can all look back with satisfaction on its history. . . . More important than its actual accomplishments has been the force of the Club's example," he continued. "The objects it advocated and what it has done to forward these objects have brought before the public new ideas that outdoor people gradually absorbed. It thus set on foot a system of education, and people began to learn that our natural things should be protected and cherished, and [they] came to understand why this should be done."

Other resignations followed. He gave up the chairmanship of the Council of National Parks, Forests and Wildlife. Increasing deafness—caused by a lifetime of shotguns thundering upon his eardrums—obliged him to quit the board of trustees of the American Game Protective Association. "I paid close attention to the proceedings at yesterday's meeting and missed so much of what went on to convince me that I cannot usefully serve longer," he sheepishly informed John Bird Burnham.

He also made plans for the dispersal of his material possessions. In his will drafted before his 1927 trip, he specified that Indian artifacts previously loaned to the American Museum of Natural History should become outright gifts. These included moccasins, headdresses, leggings, tepee liners, blankets, backrests, baskets, parfleches, pipes, jewelry, charms, games, drums, whistles, flutes, saddles, saddlebags, quirts, shields, lances, clubs, bows, arrows, quivers, a buffalo skull used in a Cheyenne medicine lodge— and an unidentified human scalp. He had already conveyed a trove of several hundred items to the Peabody Museum at Yale, and in his will he bequeathed any "curiosities and other objects relating to American Indians" left in his houses in New York and Milford to the Peabody as well.

He gave the Audubon painting *The Eagle and the Lamb*, plus a smaller Audubon of a warbler, to Elizabeth on the condition that, upon her death, they would be presented to the National Association of Audubon Societies, "in memory of the establishment by me of the first Audubon Society in February 1886." He also wanted Elizabeth to have his father's gold watches.

Grinnell had always been practical, and even the inevitable warranted a plan. "I may disappear at pretty much any time," he wrote to Boone and Crockett treasurer Redmond Cross in the spring of 1928, "and I feel preparation for such an event ought to be made."

Yet there was still time for at least one more trip. Elizabeth persuaded Grinnell to book passage for Europe, departing in July, though he confided to Madison Grant, "I am not very enthusiastic." By June he had talked her out of it. As he explained to his sister Laura, "Elizabeth very generously and nobly gave up her ambition to go to France because she saw that I did not care to go."

Instead they went to Santa Barbara.

Grinnell inferred, somewhat disingenuously, that the choice was more Elizabeth's than his own. "I have no particular reason to go except that I believe Mrs. Grinnell wants to," he wrote Billy Hofer in July. They left New York on July 23, stopped for twenty-four hours in Nebraska, and from there rode straight through to Santa Barbara. No Indians, no Yellowstone, no Glacier this time.

They arrived in the middle of Fiesta, the annual celebration of the city's Spanish colonial heritage—a swirl of parades, barbecues, dances, and polo matches. They stayed at, of all places, the Miramar Hotel, which was not in the center of Santa Barbara, but along the coast on the beachfront of Montecito, only a mile from where George Gould had lived on Olive Mill Road.

Grinnell said nothing about trying to visit Gould's former house or his grave in the Santa Barbara Cemetery, overlooking the Pacific. Nor did he seem to take any interest in the doings of Fiesta. The newspaper society page listed the prominent guests registered at hotels but never mentioned the Grinnells.

By mid-August, they had had enough, and Grinnell and Elizabeth went back to New York, this time without making a single stop. "California is a pleasant place to loaf," he told Jack Monroe, "but loafing very soon becomes mere boredom."

Shortly after his return, he was shocked by the death of Charles Sheldon, who suffered a stroke while in Nova Scotia, just shy of his sixty-first birthday and one day after Grinnell's seventy-eighth. Grinnell had endured the death of many friends, but Sheldon's sudden exit was harder to absorb than most, perhaps because Sheldon was so much younger, so vigorous till the very day he collapsed. "Those of us who were his close friends will not know how to get along very well without Sheldon," Grinnell told Charles Townsend, the director of the New York Aquarium.

In many respects Grinnell had come to see Sheldon as a better version of himself: strenuous sportsman, canny conservationist, and the consummate Yale man. "He entered Yale in the class of 1890, was well liked and popular," Grinnell wrote in an obituary circulated among Boone and Crockett members and other friends. Reckless as an underclassman, Sheldon bore down after his father suffered a series of financial reversals and "retained a remarkable standing in scholarship . . . and graduated in high repute."

Grinnell was concerned that Sheldon would be too quickly forgotten—likely anticipating a similarly faint posterity for himself. "I do not suppose that anybody is interested in the story of my life," he told Robert Sterling Yard two weeks after Sheldon's funeral. A few days later he wrote to Gilbert Pearson of the Audubon Societies: "[Sheldon] was a very fine man . . . constantly working for good things. On the other hand, he was so modest and kept himself so carefully out of the limelight that a great many people knew little of his efforts for good things. I hope that some time his good work may be better known."

Then, too, Grinnell was sensitive to the suggestion that Sheldon's death had been hastened by his smoking, a habit they shared. "If you credit Sheldon's death to the excessive use of tobacco, you are making a mistake," he replied to A. K. Fisher of the Biological Survey. "I have probably used tobacco more in excess than Sheldon, and, while I may perish from that excess this afternoon, I am still feeling pretty well, thank you."

Well enough, but shaken nevertheless. "As the years go by," he wrote to Yale classmate Lewis Hicks, "we must expect to drop off, and it does not make much difference when the dropping comes." On Christmas Eve he wrote to Lute North, informing him of the recent death of Indian scout Yellowstone Kelly. "He was just my age," Grinnell remarked, "and the newspaper account says that his death was attributed to senile debility, so keep your eye on the newspapers for my death."

If Grinnell was at all concerned that his own story would be forgotten—and if he regretted that he had never finished writing it—he made sure that the same fate did not befall the North brothers. Their memoir, as retooled by Grinnell, was published in December 1928. The title was long-winded and not a little hagiographic: *Two Great Scouts and Their Pawnee Battalion: The Experiences of Frank J. North and Luther H. North, Pioneers in the Great West, 1856–1882, and Their Defence of the Building of the Union Pacific Railroad.* As anticipated, the author of record was George Bird Grinnell.

The last time Grinnell had seen Lute North, he appeared "a short, sloped-shouldered man and . . . rather wrinkled." In the pages of *Two Great Scouts* Lute is vital and ageless (as is brother Frank). In Grinnell's telling, Lute's courage and stamina neither wane nor waver. Bullets and arrows can't kill him.

All the fights between the Pawnee scouts and their enemies, the Cheyennes and Sioux, are recounted—Summit Springs, Plum Creek, and, of course, the attack on Dull Knife's camp on the Powder River. Grinnell describes his and Lute's participation in the Black Hills expedition of 1874 and uses the occasion to appraise Custer's prowess as a plainsman—pale in comparison to North's.

In Grinnell's eyes, Luther and Frank North were American archetypes befitting James Fenimore Cooper, Mayne Reid, or the pulp and cinematic westerns that currently captured the national imagination. *Two Great Scouts and Their Pawnee Battalion* was Grinnell's final book, published forty years after his first. Through firsthand experiences with the North brothers, and by absorbing their adventures vicariously, he celebrated everything a western man ought to be. Not Custer, not Buffalo Bill, but the Norths were the heroes Grinnell had conjured as a child in Audubon Park. In its essence, theirs was the story he had been looking to tell all his life.

"The North brothers had been residents of the frontier from boyhood, and experience had taught them the ways of the wild inhabitants and methods of self-dependence in unknown regions," Grinnell writes in the introduction. "More than that, they had long been in close contact with the Pawnee Indians, who then, and for years thereafter, preserved and practiced many of their old time ways of life. . . . With this training and this association, the North brothers became great scouts, singularly fitted to take part in Indian warfare. The service they rendered during their fighting days cannot be too highly praised. Its value to this country was enormous."

Grinnell was eager, somewhat anxious even, for North's response. "Of course, there may be a lot of mistakes in [it], but that is inevitable," he hedged. "It will be gratifying to me if you are interested enough in the book to read it, either in the way of finding fault with what is said or approving the story. A copy of the book goes to you today."

Lute North nearly did not see the book at all. Before Christmas he came down with the flu, and on January 11 he scrawled a short note to Grinnell: "Am still very weak and have a lot of pain. Can't write. My brain won't work." But two weeks later he had regained enough strength to write again. "I have read the book and I think it is all right," he told Grinnell, "but I am [still] so sick that I can't get up much enthusiasm for anything. Sometimes I think I will never be any better. Thank you for the book and when I have read it over again and my head gets right so I can think, I will write again."

North did get better, but he never revisited the subject of *Two Pawnee Scouts*. That was how he was: reserved, short on adjectives, parsimonious when it came to praise, uncomfortable when he received it himself. Grinnell never again pestered him for a review of their book.

Grinnell was feeling none too robust himself in the early months of 1929. To Lute North he confessed: "I have had lately two or three warnings that I am not as young as I used to be. However, these things need not bother us. We will keep plugging until we give out."

He and Elizabeth continued to go to Milford on weekends. They had acquired a new dog, a Chesapeake, and after Charles Sheldon died, Louisa Sheldon asked if Grinnell would take her husband's young setter. "They are both about six months old, just the right age for their education to begin, and if they are able to get that education, it will make them very fond of us, and they will be a comfort to us as long as they live," Grinnell wrote sister Laura Martin in February.

Three months later, though, he informed Billy Hofer that walks with the dogs were "much shorter than those I used to take a few years ago." To Jack Monroe he revealed gamely, "I am getting a little shaky on my pins but hope to last through another hunting season."

As summer approached, Elizabeth once more tried to talk him into going to Europe. He could not summon the enthusiasm to go anywhere, least of all abroad. Even the West seemed too far. "There is really nothing for me to do there," he conceded to sister Helen Page, "and if I go, it will be only to keep up my old habits." In the end he announced that he would prefer to stay in New York and Connecticut.

He did, however, buy Elizabeth an automobile, granting one of her long-standing wishes. Grinnell had never expressed interest in learning to drive, but, with misgivings, he had become accustomed to being driven. Several years earlier he had acquired a small truck for the farm, in which the hired man picked him and Elizabeth up at the station each weekend. His correspondence does not mention the model of the new vehicle, but in June he wrote to a niece: "Last night Elizabeth, who is more or less crazy about her automobile, took me for a drive in Central Park. The day had been a very hot one, and the excursion in the cool of the evening was pleasant."

Grinnell had a lot to be grateful for, especially compared to his peers. Jim Russell, classmate and erstwhile buffalo-hunting companion, had taken his failing lungs to Tucson, Arizona. Madison Grant's health had obliged him to seek the care of a sanatorium in Battle Creek, Michigan. Meanwhile, Grinnell was pleased to learn that the memorial tablets to Dull Knife and Little Wolf had finally been placed in the cemetery at Lame Deer. Perhaps not coincidentally he wrote Helen Page in May, suggesting that they put the family plot in Woodlawn Cemetery "in good order." He encouraged her to plant some new dogwoods.

He took on no more writing assignments that spring, although several articles he had finished during the winter appeared in print: a story for *Boy's Life* entitled "Billy Jackson's Tobacco Trade"; a piece on pronghorn antelope for the *Journal of Mammalogy*; and a review of *The Hunting of the Buffalo*, a book by E. Douglas Branch, which appeared in the *Saturday Review of Literature* under the headline, "An Extinct Beast."

A new Boone and Crockett anthology was in the works. Grinnell declared that it should not be "devoted to the killing of animals, nor even to successful hunting. It should be in my view, devoted to outdoor life—the study of natural things." Yet he begged off from the chore of editing, advising Madison Grant, "I shall probably be in another and better world before we get out another volume."

On Friday, July 12, he wrote to Jim Russell, commiserating on their respective frailties: "Of course, at our time of life we must look at all sorts of breakdowns in our machinery, but with reasonable care we may last for some time yet. As I have already suggested, I am always in pretty good physical shape, and I look forward to continuance of this, though recognizing that there may be a break at any time."

After finishing this letter, Grinnell and Elizabeth took their customary train to Milford. Sometime during the weekend, he suffered a heart attack. A doctor was summoned, and for a while his condition was considered grave. A few days later, after he was judged well enough to return to New York, a specialist discovered a blood clot. Grinnell's latest secretary, George Sheetz, reported: "[T]here was danger that it might cut off the flow of blood to the heart at any moment. However, much to the astonishment of his physician, and the delight of his relatives and friends, he has rallied from the attack, and we are now hopeful that he will be up and about again."

A bed was set up in the dining room of the Fifteenth Street townhouse, so that he would not have to climb stairs. By the first week of September he felt well enough to resume limited correspondence. One of the first to whom he wrote was Lute North. "I have not been out of the house for some weeks. However, I am improving, as I believe, and hope that before very long I shall be in shape to go up to the country and resume my usual pursuits." A few days later he tried to climb the stairs. "My legs immediately gave out, and it may be some time before I can move about as I used to," he wrote Ned Dana, whom he had looked after with such care during their western outings.

In another month he was able to take rides in the car with Elizabeth and short walks in Stuyvesant Square. Soon he was able to return to Milford. Even so, he did not recover his full strength, and, by and large, his public and professional life was finished. His motto, shared with Theodore Roosevelt, to do the best you can for as long as you can, had been fulfilled.

"I have outlived most of my contemporaries," Grinnell wrote to a friend who recently had sent get-well wishes. "I do not feel sure I possess the ambition to complete the hundred years which you hope for in my behalf. I shall accept with contentment such added years as may come to me, but it may be doubted whether, at my time of life, these years will be productive of much usefulness to any of my fellow men."

He had just turned eighty. He had another eight years of life left to live.

A STRONG STRAND

F or five or six years after the heart attack, Grinnell was able to continue his duck-hunting trips to North Carolina. He also managed to write the preface for the seventh Boone and Crockett book, *Hunting Trails on Three Continents*, which appeared in 1933. His letter writing thinned drastically, however, partly because he had ceased to be active in the many causes that had kept the ink flowing for the past half century, and partly because many of his peers were no longer alive. Three months after Grinnell's 1929 collapse, Jim Russell died in Kentucky. Their classmate Charles Gould, brother to George Gould, died in 1931. Billy Hofer in 1933; Lute North and Ned Dana in 1935. Grinnell's sister Helen had also passed away, leaving Laura as his only living sibling. Gone, too, were Emerson Hough, Samuel Mather, William T. Hornaday, and Madison Grant. Even *Forest and Stream* had disappeared—absorbed by *Field and Stream* in 1930. Jack Monroe, James Willard Schultz, C. Hart Merriam, Gifford Pinchot, and Edward Curtis were among the few still active. So, too, was Elizabeth Grinnell, who was fifty-two at the time of her husband's collapse.

As dutiful as Elizabeth had been in accompanying Grinnell on his western trips, and as much as she enjoyed them (up to a point), she also loved the seashore. In the summer of 1932 she talked Grinnell into taking rooms at the Seven Ponds Inn, in Water Mill, Long Island, near Southampton. As he became more sedentary, he became more acquiescent.

Around 1935 his strength and perhaps his mind began to fail. Some years earlier, a newspaper reporter had described him as "this spare gray figure of a man with the scholar's stoop and kindly quizzical eyes." Finally, in early spring of his eighty-ninth year, those eyes, which had seen more than most, shut for the last time. George Bird Grinnell died on Monday, April 11, 1938, at home on Fifteenth Street.

Appreciations of his character and accomplishments began well before his departure. In 1919 Madison Grant had written of his fellow Boone and Crockett Club member: "Mr. Grinnell, perhaps more than any other living man, represents the now disappearing class of educated Easterners who went to the frontier in the buffalo and Indian days and devoted their lives to the welfare of the great West. Many men on the plains and in the mountains did the same, but for the most part they were not unmindful of their own material interests, and the credit they deserve for developing the country is perhaps to be qualified somewhat by the fact that they themselves often profited substantially in doing so. Mr. Grinnell, on the other hand, from the year 1870 has freely given his time, his money, his scientific and literary attainments, and his talents to the cause of the preservation of the forests, the wild life of the country and, above all, the welfare of the Indians of the West."

The *New York Times* quoted Grant in its obituary nineteen years later. Its headline identified Grinnell as "Naturalist . . . Founder of the First Audubon Society . . . Helped Set Up Zoos Here . . . A Sponsor of Yellowstone and Glacier Parks—Authority on Indian Tribes of West." The *Times* also acknowledged him as "the father of American conservation."

The *New York Herald Tribune*'s obituary cited President Coolidge's remarks from the Roosevelt Memorial ceremony and, in a separate column on its editorial page, the *Herald Tribune* added further luster to Grinnell's legacy. "The passing of Dr. Grinnell cuts a strong strand in the remnants of the thinning cable that still links America with the age of its frontier," the paean began. "No doubt his background in the East that was already being ravaged by industrial development, coupled with his happy and penetrating gifts as a naturalist, gave George Bird Grinnell his peculiar foresight with reference to the fate of natural resources in the United States."

The *Herald Tribune* salute bore no byline, but clearly it was written by someone who had known Grinnell in his prime and remembered him well: "[H]is outstanding personal characteristic was that of never-failing dignity. . . . To meet his eye, feel his iron handclasp or hear his calm and thrifty words—even when he was a man in his ninth decade—was to conclude that there was the noblest Roman of them all."

Grinnell's will ensured that Elizabeth would live comfortably. Even after the stock market crash of October 29, 1929, which coincided with Grinnell's convalescence from his heart attack, his portfolio of investments was sound enough to sustain her in the manner to which she had become accustomed—not luxuriously, but worry-free. She lived for a while longer on Fifteenth Street, but she lost interest in Milford, preferring Long Island in the summer.

Besides donating his Indian artifacts to Yale and the American Museum of Natural History and his Audubons to the National Association of Audubon Societies, Grinnell dictated his intentions on the distribution of the rest of his assets, including his papers and books. He left money to his nieces and nephews, and to the latter his guns. More to relieve Elizabeth's anxiety than to express magnanimity, he left $15,000 to her mother. To his namesake, Grinnell Monroe, he gave $1,000—for what good it would do. He left $5,000 to the Boone and Crockett Club.

Elizabeth Grinnell never remarried. She abandoned photography altogether and took up painting, the calling of her first husband, Emery Williams. In 1954 she had an exhibition of landscapes and birds at the Schoneman Galleries on Madison Avenue. "Within their own modest aspiration, these works have a unique charm," complimented *Arts Digest*. "It is rare to see such innocence and joy expressed with a simplicity that is both naïve and knowledgeable."

A year or so before her exhibition, Elizabeth moved to a residential hotel in Manhattan. This reduction in living quarters prompted her to auction off more than four hundred lots of her husband's books. His correspondence—including thirty-eight letter books—she gave to the Connecticut Audubon Society, along with the bird specimens he had collected during the 1874 Black Hills expedition. His leather-bound diaries went to the Southwest Museum in Los Angeles, founded by Charles Lummis in 1907. (The letter books and bird specimens now belong to Yale, and the Southwest Museum library is now part of the Autry Museum of the American West.)

On June 15, 1956, two officials from the National Park Service, a Dr. Pitkin and a Mr. Neubauer, called on Elizabeth Grinnell at her hotel as she was preparing to leave the city for the summer. Their particular objective was to learn more about George Bird Grinnell's involvement with Glacier National Park. A summary of their talk was subsequently written up by Newell Foster, superintendent of Statue of Liberty National Monument.

"They found her a charming person, completely without affectation though obviously intensely and affectionately proud of her late husband and his work," Foster reported. "She had evidently been looking forward to the interview with some interest, and had piled a cocktail table full with books, photographs and other material relating to the Glacier area and her husband's work there."

Elizabeth reminisced about the many trips she and Grinnell had taken. She stressed "the essential modesty of her husband," Newell's memo mentioned, "but she does recall that sometimes, when they were visiting Grinnell glacier, he would, in his delight at seeing it again, refer to it as 'my glacier.'" She also suggested that "her husband deserves a full-length biography," to which Foster added, "Anyone who has made even the most superficial examination of the basic facts of his life must agree whole-heartedly."

Elizabeth Kirby Curtis Williams Grinnell died on February 23, 1960, at the age of eighty-three. With no children of her own and no family to speak of—her mother died in 1942, her brother in 1956—there was no obvious repository for the personal letters and mementos she may have accumulated during thirty-six years of marriage. Without the benefit of these, the depth and details of her relationship to Grinnell are difficult to discern—perhaps as it should be.

Yet without Elizabeth's devotion to his legacy, history never would have been allowed to know George Bird Grinnell so intimately.

DO MORE GOOD

I n the years researching and writing this book, the question most frequently asked this belated biographer has been: Is George Bird Grinnell related to Grinnell College? Answer: *Very* distantly. Grinnell
College, originally Iowa College, was relocated to Grinnell, Iowa, in 1859
by its benefactor, Josiah Bushnell Grinnell, a Vermont-born Congrega-
tionalist minister and outspoken abolitionist. (It was to this Grinnell that
New-York Tribune editor Horace Greeley supposedly said, "Go West, young
man.") Josiah Bushnell Grinnell and George Bird Grinnell doubtless have
common ancestors in the Puritan Grinnells who arrived in New England
in the 1600s.

The second-most-asked question has been: Does George Bird Grinnell
have any connection to Grinnell Glacier? This mainly from Montanans
and those who have hiked the trails of Glacier National Park.

If George Bird Grinnell's name is hard to place nowadays, the reasons
owe more to his effectiveness than to his evanescence. The conservation
movement he inspired and nurtured continues to grow. Grinnell is the pro-
totype of the city-dwelling environmentalist whose conscience and money
today fuel organizations such as the Sierra Club, Environmental Defense
Fund, National Resource Defense Council, Earth Justice, World Wildlife

Fund, Wilderness Society, and, of course, the National Audubon Society. Nearly every national park has an auxiliary organization to support and protect it. Groups like Ducks Unlimited, Trout Unlimited, and Rocky Mountain Elk Foundation ascribe to the Boone and Crockett credo that sportsmen make exemplary stewards of game and wildlife habitat. (In 1993, the Boone and Crockett Club headquarters was fittingly relocated to Montana.) Success, it has been said, has many fathers. To Grinnell's credit, he became a face in an expanding crowd of nature-loving parents.

The field of ethnology has likewise matured. In the introduction to a new edition of *The Cheyenne Indians*, published in 1962, western writer Mari Sandoz declared, "One could wish that other tribes might have had their George Bird Grinnell." In the years that followed publication of Grinnell's tour de force, many other tribes did get their version of Grinnell, although few are so fortunate to have someone of his dedication and sensitivity tell their stories in full. And even as the discipline of studying other "cultures" improves, few of its practitioners write with the ease and accessibility of Grinnell. In reviewing one of his collections of Indian folk tales, Mary Austin, another distinguished western writer, pronounced: "To all who are interested in cultures other than their own . . . a new book by George Bird Grinnell is always welcome. . . . Mr. Grinnell writes pleasantly, with no . . . veil of literary affectation between him and his subject."

What has marginalized Grinnell in the annals of anthropology is his relegation of Native Americans to lower rungs on the ladder of civilization. To describe Indians as "children" is today paternalistic and outright racist. Yet Grinnell's attitude toward Indians, as a race, as tribes, as individuals, was forever evolving. The tendency is to lump men of his generation and class in one foul ball of bigotry. The temptation is to smear Grinnell with the same brush that damns a Madison Grant, who was a devout conservationist but also a white supremacist. But unlike Grant, Grinnell advanced from the romantic, to the Darwinian, to the progressive—that is to say, to the practical.

In 1920 Grinnell picked a bone with Charles Gould, who, like their mutual friend Grant, regarded himself as an amateur social engineer, with an unabashed bias against anyone whose breeding did not resemble his. "I have a feeling that while the immigrant from southern and southeastern

Europe may never adapt himself to American conditions," Grinnell wrote Gould, "his children will make excellent citizens and good Americans. In this, you and the excellent Madison will never agree with me. Races of men have been mixing up ever since bipeds without feathers began to travel on the earth. I, as many of us have, thought and am disposed to think that we shall do more good by trying to polish up and make better the material we have at hand than by keeping more such material out of the country."

Not the most enlightened philosophy, perhaps, but hardly sufficient evidence to quarantine his research or banish its author from posterity.

The better Grinnell got to know the Blackfeet and the Cheyennes, the more he sympathized with their struggle to survive, to assimilate, while endeavoring to maintain self-identity, and the more frustrated he became with whites who would not see things through their eyes. He, more than most of his contemporaries, advocated the preservation of Native American beliefs and customs. He never opposed the medicine lodge, for instance; he wished only that it did not consume so much of the summer. And in the final analysis, it is fair to say that Grinnell spent almost as much time trying to fit into the Indians' world as he did encouraging them to join his own.

And thus he carries on. There is nothing off-key or anachronistic about the example set by Grinnell. Like the thorough-going pathfinder he became, he studied the back trail in order to plot the most prudent way forward. His dedication and compassion—toward nature, toward Native Americans, toward public lands, toward the public interest—are motivational. The pleasure and refreshment he derived from wild places and their wild inhabitants are inspirational. The warnings he sounded against greed, wastefulness, and self-interest are as resonant today as they were a century ago. Regrettably, Grinnell Glacier will melt away in the all-too-near future, but in a world of watchful, resolute, and considerate citizens, the name of George Bird Grinnell deserves to endure as a beacon for all time.

ACKNOWLEDGMENTS

Let the chain of gratitude begin with Elizabeth Grinnell for bequeathing her husband's papers to the Southwest Museum and the Connecticut Audubon Society. Then a link of thanks to then-director of the Connecticut Audubon Society John F. Reiger for seeing that Grinnell's letter books, memoirs, *Forest and Stream* records, and other meaty materials wound up at Yale.

Beyond that, let us praise the timely evolution of technology. Without the typewriter and the letterpress process that created and collected Grinnell's correspondence, he might be a forgotten man today, or a faint silhouette of one. Next came the medium of microfilm, which saved the yellowing letter books and made their pages more accessible to anyone inclined to dig around in the ore of Grinnell's life. I first came upon Grinnell's papers spooled onto forty-seven reels in the Mansfield Library at the University of Montana—duplicates of film made from the original letters acquired by Yale in 1984. Each reel contains roughly one thousand pages—rich veins indeed but still demanding a lot of pick-and-shovel work to extract the high-grade nuggets. I was grinning and grimacing at a couple of years hunched over a finicky film reader in the windowless basement of a building not close enough to home. The best of times, the worst of times.

But then: digital scanning to the rescue—deus ex machina delivered by Glenn Kneebone, manager of the Paw Print, the copy center at the Mansfield. (Go, Grizzlies!) He mentioned, somewhat casually, that the library had recently acquired a magic contraption (I never actually saw it) that could scan an entire reel of microfilm in something like half an hour. He agreed to put me—or, rather, the Grinnell reels—on the night shift and fit me in among other jobs as time allowed. Two months later he placed in my own paw a flash drive containing the entirety of Grinnell's papers. One of the reasons, perhaps *the* reason, no one has been able to tackle a thorough biography of George Bird Grinnell before now is that they could not stretch their arms all the way around him. Having these 40K pages funneled into my laptop allowed me, laboring in my own salt mine, to give the material of Grinnell's life the scale and scrutiny it deserves.

Similarly accommodating was Liza Posas, archivist of the Braun Research Library at the Autry Museum of the American West in Los Angeles. She generously allowed me to hover over Grinnell's diaries with my digital camera and thus to transfer more than fifty years of handwritten notes onto my now-bulging hard drive. The winding trail of George Bird Grinnell became a freeway—still long, to be sure, but well lit, with loads of terrific scenery.

Yet when I reflect on my bountiful fortune in researching this biography, I think of one person above all others. Many years ago, when Matthew Spady arrived in New York, his good sense and taste led him to buy an apartment in The Grinnell, the Beaux-Arts building that stands on the Grinnell (and before that, Audubon) homestead on Riverside Drive in Washington Heights. Raised in a small town in Virginia, Matthew set out to make a small town of his new neighborhood. His immersion in his surroundings and his patient persuasions ensured official recognition of the Audubon Park Historic District in 2009. Along the way, Matthew has learned *everything* about its residents, especially the Grinnells. Without Matthew's help I would never have been able to tell the Audubon and Grinnell family histories with any degree of specificity. He shared his own research without reservation; more than that, his insight and encouragement in all matters Grinnellian gave me confidence to press further in my own deductions. I look forward to Matthew's book on the history of Audubon Park. Its author is a historian and gentleman of the first rank.

Here's to not just the bones but also the brains and heart of Daniel Brinkman of the Division of Vertebrate Paleontology at Yale's Peabody Museum of Natural History. Dan assists in curating not just the museum's fossils, but over the years he has also amassed a file of documents germane to Othniel C. Marsh, George Bird Grinnell, and the Yale Expedition of 1870. He kindly passed along these items and turned me on to goodies I didn't know I was looking for but gobbled up gladly. He also introduced me to Erin Gredell, the Peabody's repatriation coordinator of native artifacts, and Kristof Zyskowski, collections manager of the Peabody's Division of Ornithology and Mammalogy. The former shared with me the inventory of Indian pieces that Grinnell donated to the museum; the latter showed me the collection of bird specimens (astonishingly well preserved) that Grinnell brought back from the Black Hills in 1875.

Time also to applaud Hugh Grinnell, distant kin to the great conservationist, known to perform a lively rendering, period garb and all, of forebear "Bird." Hugh made me feel welcome at a Grinnell family reunion in New Bedford, Massachusetts. The Grinnell tribe continues, robust and proud; Hugh is one of its most gracious ambassadors.

The same goes for Grinnell in-laws. Alison Meyer, wife of Laura Grinnell Martin's great-grandson Scott Meyer, unearthed old family photo albums and other mementos and was nice enough to make them available to Matthew Spady and me. The letter from George Bird Grinnell's grandfather, urging him to "go out beyond his hived home," is one of the unexpected treats from this bundle.

Dear librarians, archivists, clerks, and research rats: You know who you are. Or maybe you don't, since you're so busy guiding the next hunter-gatherer that you don't have time to notice this inadequate genuflection. But let me declare my appreciation anyway to the able and indulgent staffs of the George C. Ruhle Library at Glacier National Park, Glacier National Park Archives, Huntington Library at the University of California at Berkeley,

Archives of Traditional Music and Lilly Library at Indiana University, Milford (Connecticut) Clerk's Office, Montana Historical Society, Maureen and Mike Mansfield Library at the University of Montana (Missoula), Montana State University Library (Bozeman), Montecito Association History Committee, History Nebraska, New York Public Library, Santa Barbara Historical Museum, Saratoga Springs Public Library, Saratoga County Historical Society, Saratoga County Clerk's Office, Seward House Museum, Harry Ransom Center and Perry-Castañeda Library at the University of Texas at Austin, Special Collections of the University of Washington Library, Wildlife Conservation Society Archives at the Bronx Zoo, Sterling Memorial and Beinecke Rare Books & Manuscript libraries at Yale, and Yellowstone Research Library.

The reason this book exists at all is because my agent, Esther Newberg, appreciated that it was what I most wanted to write next, and so she went out and, with *her* restless drive, found just the right people to publish it. That would be Liveright. A young man named Will Menaker opened the door to me initially; then, after Will went his way, I was taken in hand by Gina Iaquinta. Never before has an editor worked so conscientiously to make my work better, and I hope I've done my best to meet her high standards.

And finally a puff of the medicine pipe for George Bird Grinnell himself, who lived such an engaged and engaging life. Not too late to pay my regards. Here's hoping my good readers do the same and are heartened by his admirable example.

NOTES

ABBREVIATIONS

F&S   *Forest and Stream*
GBG   George Bird Grinnell
GBGD   George Bird Grinnell Diary, Braun Research Library, Autry Museum of the American West
GBGM   George Bird Grinnell "Memoirs," 1915, GBG Papers, Yale University
GBGP   George Bird Grinnell Papers, Sterling Memorial Library, Yale University

INTRODUCTION: EVOLUTION AND EXTINCTION

2   *"She is so entirely"*: GBG to Luther North, October 17, 1912, GBGP
4   *"[Thomas] says Arabs"*: GBGD June 22, 1926
5   *"a horrible crowd"*: GBG to E. W. Sawyer, September 7, 1926, GBGP
5   *"a number of my contemporary"*: GBG to Helen Page, July [date illegible], 1926, GBGP
6   *"Here as nowhere"*: J. W. Schultz, "Life Among the Blackfeet," F&S, November 30, 1883
7   *"From this point"*: GBGD, September 15, 1885
9   *"Somewhat annoyed"*: GBGD July 11, 1926
9   *"Rode up under"*: GBGD, July 13, 1926
11   *"The white race"*: GBG to J. W. Schultz, December 15, 1911, GBGP
13   *"Those of us who"*: GBG to Madison Grant, January 4, 1918, GBGP
13   *"natural impulse"*: GBG to E. A. Quarles, July 17, 1918, GBGP

CHAPTER 1: AUDUBON PARK

18 *"turned around at the top"*: GBG to Helen Page, August 26, 1924, GBGP

19 *"The country was wild"*: GBGM, 2

20 *"I have a distinct"*: GBGM, 6–7; GBG to Findlay Sackett, July 10, 1918, GBGP

20 *"[A]s soon as 23rd"*: GBGM, 6

21 *"that he became a mere"*: GBGM, 9

23 *"It was a wild"*: [Lucy Bakewell Audubon], ed., *The Life of John James Audubon*, 441

24 *"simple and unpretending"*: Herrick, *Audubon the Naturalist*, 237

24 *cartloads of caged rodents*: Ford, *John James Audubon*, 382

24 *"In one corner stood"*: Herrick, *Audubon the Naturalist*, 237

24 *"Several graceful fawns"*: Herrick, *Audubon the Naturalist*, 237

25 *"[H]ow I wonder"*: Herrick, *Audubon the Naturalist*, 238

25 *On January 1, 1857*: GBGM, 11

26 *"the notes of the thrushes"*: GBG, "A Chapter of History and Natural History," 24

26 *"It was while we lived"*: GBGM, 13

27 *"a most kindly"*: GBG, "Recollections of Audubon Park," 373

27 *"My father and I"*: GBG, "A Visit to Santa Barbara," typescript, August 13, 1928, GBGP

27 *"I am very proud"*: Helen Lansing Grinnell, diary for Frank Grinnell, August 22, 1860, New York Public Library

28 *"My chief anxiety"*: Helen Lansing Grinnell, diary for Helen Jesup Grinnell, April 26, 1865

28 *"[M]ost of the boys"*: GBGM, 19–20

28 *"to make an Indian"*: GBGM, 19

29 *"I soon became more"*: GBGM, 26

29 *"Georgie is delighted"*: Helen Lansing Grinnell, diary for Frank Grinnell, December 27, 1861

29 *"[A] woodcock one autumn"*: GBGM, 29

29 *"Then after a little"*: GBG, "Recollections of Audubon Park," 375–376

29 *"There were many trophies"*: GBGM, 19

31 *"Where the Prince"*: Helen Lansing Grinnell, diary for Helen Jesup Grinnell, October 15, 1860

31 *"I was overtaken"*: GBGM, 26

31 *"Our country is in"*: Helen Lansing Grinnell, diary for Frank Grinnell, May 18, 1861

34 *"He needs the physical"*: Helen Lansing Grinnell, diary for Frank Grinnell, September 3, 1863

34 *"He is very happy"*: Helen Lansing Grinnell, diary for Frank Grinnell, November 25, 1863

34 *"Hastiness and improper"*: Helen Lansing Grinnell, diary for Frank Grinnell, January 22, 1865

35 *"Today we have the splendid"*: Helen Lansing Grinnell, diary for Frank Grinnell, April 10, 1865

35 *"Alas! Alas!"*: Helen Lansing Grinnell, diary for Frank Grinnell, April 24, 1865

35 *"to see the dead face"*: Helen Lansing Grinnell, diary for Frank Grinnell, April 24, 1865

35 *"I . . . still remember the air"*: GBGM, 33

36 *"I did not in the least"*: GBGM, 33

36 *"practice private prayer"*: George Grinnell to GBG, October 11, 1863, letter from Schuyler M. Meyer family, private collection

CHAPTER 2: MEMBER OF THE CLASS

39 *"The cutting off of hair"*: Baggs, *Four Years at Yale*, 253
39 *"Little of interest"*: GBGM, 34
40 *"detected in hazing"*: GBGM, 34
40 *"Dr. Hurlburt was"*: GBGM, 35
41 *"social element"*: Baggs, *Four Years at Yale*, 179
41 *"a very pleasant one"*: GBGM, 36
41 *"My career in college"*: Yale Class of 1870, *Report of the Thirty-fifth Anniversary*, 54
42 *"You will be saddened"*: GBG to James Russell, May 7, 1929, GBGP

CHAPTER 3: THE YALE EXPEDITION

43 *"Cooper is the American"*: F&S, February 26, 1889
44 *"told of lands"*: Reid, *The Boy Hunters*, 12
44 *"[I]n all the range"*: F&S, February 3, 1900
45 *"naïve love of fine"*: Schuchert and LeVene, *O. C. Marsh*, 342
45 *"the deepest life"*: Timothy Dwight, *Memories of Yale Life and Men* (1903), 409, 412
45 *"Marsh was a peculiar"*: GBG to Ernest Howe, in response to request by Howe to edit papers of O. C. Marsh, February 19, 1929, typescript, O. C. Marsh Papers, courtesy Daniel Brinkman, Peabody Museum of Natural History, Yale
46 *"None of them except"*: GBG, "An Old-Time Bone Hunt," 330
46 *"It was my first visit"*: Schuchert and LeVene, *O. C. Marsh*, 9
47 *"I soon found many"*: Schuchert and LeVene, *O.C. Marsh*, 98
48 *"strode on the platform"*: Henry B. Sargent, "Marsh Expedition in 1870"
48 *"I believed that now"*: GBGM, 37–38
48 *"the most celebrated prairie"*: GBGD, July 14, 1870
48 *"a tall, well-built"*: GBG, "An Old-Time Bone Hunt," 332
48 *Tucky-tee-lous and La-Hoor-a-sac:* Also spelled Tuck-it-te-louks ("Alonc to War") and La-hoo-re-sock ("Head Warrior"); Van de Logt, *War Party in Blue*, 165
49 *"modest almost to diffidence"*: "Frank North," F&S, March 19, 1885
50 *"They wore their hair"*: GBG to "My dear Mother and Father," August 3, 1870, GBGP
50 *"[T]he longest summer"*: Wilson, *Frank J. North*, 177
50 *"I wish it had"*: GBGD July 24, 1870
50 *"can believe the descriptions"*: GBG to "My dear Father and Mother," August 3, 1870, GBGP
51 *"I took some beads"*: GBGD, July 20, 1870
51 *"We created quite"*: GBGD, July 28, 1870
51 *"The friends thou hast"*: GBGD, July 30, 1870
52 *"one of them a little fellow"*: GBG, "An Old-Time Bone Hunt," 334
52 *"[W]hen the flames"*: GBG to "My dear Mother and Father," August 26, 1870. GBGP
53 *"I am happy to say"*: GBG to "My dear Mother and Father," August 26, 1870, GBGP
53 *"We stood upon the brink"*: Betts, "The Yale College Expedition of 1870," 669–670
53 *"I was eager to explore"*: GBG, unpublished introduction to proposed Marsh biography, 1929, O. C. Marsh Papers, Yale
54 *"John Baker and Phil Mass"*: Yo, "The Old West," F&S, April 27, 1901
54 *"The life in the camp"*: GBG, "A Memory of Fort Bridger," typescript, n.d., GBGP

55 *"[W]e sat around the fire"*: Ornis, "A Day with the Sage Grouse," F&S, November 6, 1873

55 *similar creatures inhabit*: Goetzmann, *Exploration and Empire*, 427

55 *"[W]e flirted with twenty-two"*: Betts, "The Yale College Expedition of 1870," 671

56 *"persons of importance"*: GBGM, 43; Fox, *The American Conservation Movement*, 17–18

56 *Before leaving*: Photograph of GBG, GBGP

57 *"peculiar joint"*: Schuchert and LeVene, O. C. *Marsh*, 119–120

58 *"In 1870, I think"*: GBG to Edward W. Nelson, May 11, 1916, GBGP

58 *"I found that he was anxious"*: GBGM, 44

58 *"I desired enormously"*: GBGM, 42

CHAPTER 4: A WILD GALLOP

59 *formed a brokerage firm*: Spady, *The Grinnell at 100*, 31

59 *"His speculations have been"*: *New York Times*, June 21, 1873

59 *"large and profitable"*: GBGM, 44

60 *The Reiches had begun*: Richard W. Flint, "American Showmen and European Dealers," in Hoage and Deiss, *New Worlds, New Animals*, 101–103; Hanson, *Animal Attractions*, 79

60 *"I stopped in at a menagerie"*: GBG to O. C. Marsh, February 20, 1871, O. C. Marsh Papers, Yale

61 *Over the next year*: GBG to O. C. Marsh, January 21, April 4, 1871; March 5, January 4, April 23, January 29, 1872, O. C. Marsh Papers, Yale

61 *"I have now to speak"*: GBG to O. C. Marsh, March 9, 1872, O. C. Marsh Papers, Yale

62 *"Many thanks for the honor"*: GBG to O. C. Marsh, May 24, 1871, O. C. Marsh Papers, Yale

62 *"prowess on the prairie"*: GBG to O. C. Marsh, May 25, 1872, O. C. Marsh Papers, Yale

62 *"in most luxurious fashion"*: GBGM, 50

62 *"Lute North is a splendid"*: GBG to O. C. Marsh, August 22, 1872, O. C. Marsh Papers, Yale

63 *"true Ishmaelites"*: GBG, *Pawnee Hero Stories and Folk-Tales*, 307

63 *"Now, for a little while"*: GBG, *Pawnee Hero Stories and Folk-Tales*, 274

63 *"Many a time during"*: GBG, "Buffalo Hunt with the Pawnees," F&S, December 25, 1873

64 *"the culinary glory"*: Cooper, *The Prairie*, 96, 369, 378

64 *"[E]ach horse sprang"*: Parkman, *The Oregon Trail*, 280, 104

64 *"Bear with me"*: Ornis, "Buffalo Hunt with the Pawnees," F&S, December 25, 1873

64 *"The scene was one"*: Ornis, "Buffalo Hunt with the Pawnees," F&S, December 25, 1873

65 *"spectacle of four thousand"*: Ornis, "Buffalo Hunt with the Pawnees," F&S, December 25, 1873

65 *"The scene we now beheld"*: GBG, *Pawnee Hero Stories and Folk-Tales*, 295–299

66 *"I put spurs"*: Ornis, "Buffalo Hunt with the Pawnees," F&S, December 25, 1873

66 *"Altogether we had"*: GBG to O. C. Marsh, August 22, 1872, O. C. Marsh Papers, Yale

66 *"I have this day"*: GBG to O. C. Marsh, September 2, 1872, O. C. Marsh Papers, Yale

67 *"[W]e were attacked"*: GBGM, 47–49

68 *"I regret now"*: GBG to James Russell, April 13, 1917, GBGP
68 *"a dreadful misfortune"*: GBGM, 50
69 *"Lute—my guide"*: Ornis, "Elk Hunting in Nebraska," F&S, October 2, 1873
69 *"This was for me"*: Ornis, "Elk Hunting in Nebraska, F&S, October 2, 1873
70 *"The panic of 1873"*: GBGM, 51
70 *"The Vanderbilt stocks"*: New York Times, September 20, 1873
71 *"Commodore Vanderbilt"*: GBGM, 51
71 *"farmer and horse-dealer"*: New York Times, October 12, 1873
71 *"an indelible form of disgrace"*: New York World, October 3, 1873
72 *"The conduct of George Bird"*: New York Times, October 12, 1873
72 *"alleged bankruptcy"*: New York World, October 6, 1873
72 *"The trade in stocks"*: New York World, December 15, 1873
72 *"[O]ur customers took"*: GBGM, 52
73 *"The winter was one"*: GBGM, 51
73 *"The Publishers . . . aim"*: F&S, August 14, 1873

CHAPTER 5: THE BLACK HILLS

76 *As a favor:* T. J. Stiles, *Custer's Trials*, 404
77 *"all the gold we could"*: Donald Jackson, *Custer's Gold*, 3
77 *"Custer was a friendly"*: GBG to W. H. Power, November 2, 1927, GBGP
78 *"I have Custer's book"*: GBG to George Hyde, May 14, 1908, GBGP
78 *"Secured several birds"*: GBGD, July 5, 1874
79 *"As we proceed"*: Ludlow, *Report of a Reconnaissance of the Black Hills*, 79
79 *"[Even] if we were"*: GBGD, July 16, 1874
79 *"On the plains General"*: GBG, *Two Great Scouts*, 241
79 *"I will knock the heads"*: GBG, *Two Great Scouts*, 241–242
80 *"I have reached the highest"*: Utley, *Cavalier in Buckskin*, 137
80 *"It was a very old"*: Ludlow, *Report of a Reconnaissance of the Black Hills*, 76
81 *"There is much talk"*: Ludlow, *Report of a Reconnaissance of the Black Hills*, 19
81 *"through a country infested"*: Ludlow, *Report of a Reconnaissance of the Black Hills*, 19
81 *"gold has been found"*: Jackson, *Custer's Gold*, 87–88
81 *"Rich Mines of Gold"*: Jackson, *Custer's Gold*, 89; Krause and Olson, *Prelude to Glory*, 126
82 *"When I heard that"*: GBG, "Charley Reynolds," F&S, December 26, 1896
82 *"Thus ends the expedition"*: GBGD, August 23, 1874
82 *"I shall work as hard"*: GBG to O. C. Marsh, February 20, 1871, GBGP

CHAPTER 6: A NATION'S PARK

85 *"[W]hat a splendid"*: Catlin, *Letters and Notes*, I:261–262
85 *"if there could be secured"*: Nathaniel P. Langford, *Diary of the Washburn Expedition*, 117–118, quoted in Haines, *The Yellowstone Story*, I:129–130
86 *"This is probably the most"*: Chittenden, *The Yellowstone National Park*, 81
87 *"Dana had never been"*: GBGM, 66
89 *"there were buffalo"*: GBGM, 66
89 *"the sort of man"*: Krause and Olson, *Prelude to Glory*, 124–125
90 *"In those days"*: GBG to J. E. Ramsburg, July 9, 1915, GBGP
90 *"Charley and I were"*: GBG, "Stories of an Heroic Age," F&S, January 30, 1897

92 *"The country is beautifully"*: GBGD, August 15, 1875

92 *"Little open prairies"*: GBGD, August 16, 1875

92 *"We had the most magnificent"*: GBGD, August 17, 1875

92 *"a beautiful sheet"*: GBGD, August 19, 1875

92 *"We laid two days"*: GBGD, August 21–22, 1875

93 *"the rude hand of man"*: Ludlow, *Report of a Reconnaissance from Carroll, Montana*, 26

93 *"It may be out"*: GBG, "Letter of Transmittal," June 1, 1876, in Ludlow, *Report of a Reconnaissance from Carroll, Montana*, 61

93 *"The general feeling"*: GBG, "Letter of Transmittal," June 1, 1876, in Ludlow, *Report of a Reconnaissance from Carroll, Montana*, 61

94 *"You have done nothing"*: Helen Lansing Grinnell, diary for Frank Grinnell, March 30, 1959

94 *"You dance beautifully"*: Helen Lansing Grinnell, diary for Frank Grinnell, January 15, 1861

94 *"Georgie has grown"*: Helen Lansing Grinnell, diary for Helen Jesup Grinnell, January 4, 1866

94 *"Frankie got on"*: Helen Lansing Grinnell, Diary for Helen Jesup Grinnell, December 25, 1863

94 *"closet of obedience"*: Helen Lansing Grinnell diary for Helen Jesup Grinnell, June 25, 1859

94 *"Frankie, I must say"*: Helen Lansing Grinnell diary for Frank Grinnell, January 15, 1861

95 *He was not a regular*: *Hartford Daily Courant*, September 9, 1875; *New York Times*, September 13, 1875; *New-York Tribune*, September 13, 1875

95 *"sanatorium city"*: Tompkins, *The Yankee Barbareños*, 273

95 *"the pleasantest of all"*: Nordhoff, *California for Health, Pleasure, and Residence*, 111, 113–114

96 *"father seemed rather"*: GBGM, 74

96 *"a very good time"*: GBGM, 74

96 *"the February strawberries"*: GBG, "A Visit to Santa Barbara," typescript, n.d., GBGP

96 *"I congratulate you"*: William Ludlow to GBG, March 29, 1876, GBGP

97 *"Every little ravine"*: GBG, *The Fighting Cheyenne*, 341

97 *"Reno ordered the retreat"*: GBG, "Charley Reynolds," F&S, December 26, 1896

98 *"One of the bravest"*: GBG, "On the War Path," F&S, May 10, 1877

98 *"Buffalo Bill, who takes"*: "The Little Big Horn Fight," F&S, January 6, 1897

CHAPTER 7: AGE OF SURPRISES

103 *He was another Yale*: Coues, "Charles Hallock," 117–118

104 *"We live in an age"*: GBG, "Birds with Teeth," F&S, February 21, 1878

104 *"Sometime—soon"*: Charles Hallock to GBG, November 18, 1876, GBGP

104 *"George Bird Grinnell, Esq."*: "Our New Dress," F&S, November 16, 1876

104 *collaborate on a short*: Grinnell and Dana, "On a New Tertiary Lake Basin," 126–128

105 *"They were miserably"*: Danker, *Man of the Plains*, 197–198

105 *"fairly climbed over"*: Danker, *Man of the Plains*. 196

105 *"I will tell you"*: "On the War Path," F&S, May 10, 1877

106 *"I tell you they are"*: "On the War Path," F&S, May 10, 1877

106 *"Your good letter came"*: Luther North to GBGH, February 14, 1877, Luther H. North Papers, History Nebraska

106 *"We generally try"*: Luther North to GBG, March 23, 1877, Luther H. North Papers, History Nebraska

107 *fifteen hundred longhorns*: Mcintosh, *The Nebraska Sand Hills*, 135

107 *touring the East*: Russell, *The Lives and Legends of Buffalo Bill*, 259

107 *"worked for two or three"*: GBG to A. [?] McCandless, October 16, 1913, GBGP

108 *"In the old days"*: GBG to Dr. H. N. Moeller, November 29, 1916, GBGP

108 *"what some of those eastern"*: GBG, *Jack the Young Cowboy*, 49

109 *"I was out of my"*: GBGM, 83

109 *"What I have, I hold"*: Schuchert, *Biographical Memoir of Othniel Marsh*, 1; also see Conniff, *House of Lost Worlds*, 108–109

109 *"That Americans, as"*: Yo, "A Trip to North Park," F&S, September 4, 1879

110 *"As I look back"*: Yo, "A Trip to North Park," F&S, October 30, 1879

110 *"[He] had become more"*: GBGM, 86

111 *"With new and better"*: "Note the Change," F&S, April 20, 1880, GBG

111 *"The ground cuckoos"*: GBG, "On the Osteology of *Geococcyx californius*," draft of PhD dissertation, Yale College, 1880, GBGP

111 *"with keen regret"*: GBGM, 87

CHAPTER 8: THOROUGH SPORTSMAN

112 *"narrow in the chest"*: Charles Hallock, "In the Beginning," F&S, June 29, 1893

112 *"A keen lover"*: "Sports and Sportsmen," F&S, April 6, 1877

113 *"Five song bird killers"*: "Aliens and Guns," F&S, October 28, 1905

113 *"[W]hat can be said"*: "At Home and Abroad," F&S, November 6, 1897

113 *"unsportsmanlike and brutal"*: "Adirondack Deer Hounding," F&S, January 15, 1885

114 *"I have no sympathy"*: Yo, "A Band of Bears," F&S, December 27, 1883

114 *"Every right-minded"*: "Pot-Hunters," F&S, April 20, 1882

115 *"It is high time"*: "Loose Moose Morals," F&S, August 10, 1882

115 *"This is another age"*: "Save the Adirondacks," F&S, December 13, 1883

116 *"I regretted exceedingly"*: P.H. Sheridan et al., *Report of an Exploration of Parts of Wyoming, Idaho and Montana, in August and September 1882*, quoted in Haines, *The Yellowstone Story*, I:263

117 *recruited local hunters*: Hutton, *Phil Sheridan and His Army*, 355; Haines, *The Yellowstone Story*, I:267–269

117 *"For many years we"*: "Their Last Refuge," F&S, December 14, 1882

118 *"[T]his project is neither"*: "Leasing the National Park," F&S, December 21, 1882

118 *"The people are a little"*: "The Park Monopolists Checked," F&S, January 11, 1883

118 *"It is the duty"*: "The People's Park," F&S, January 18, 1883

118 *Rallying to the guidon*: Bartlett, "The Senator Who Saved Yellowstone Park," 49–52, 66

118 *"exclusive privileges"*: Haines, *The Yellowstone Story*, I:269

119 *"The Park is at present"*: "Mr. Vest's Victory," F&S, March 8, 1883

119 *"It is only a matter"*: newspapers quoted in "The Drift of Press Opinion," F&S, January 11, 1883

120 *"one of the most attractive"*: GBGM, 96

121 *"It is satisfaction"*: "It Failed to Pass," F&S, March 12, 1885

122 *"The scene in the valley"*: [GBG], "Through Two-Ocean Pass," F&S, January 29, 1885

CHAPTER 9: NO TENDERFOOT HE

123 *"The love of wild life"*: Schultz, *My Life as an Indian*, 3–4
124 *"Bands of the ancient"*: Schultz, "Life Among the Blackfeet," F&S, November 30, 1883
125 *"Never in my life"*: Schultz, "To Chief Mountain," F&S, December 3, 1885.
125 *"He arrived on the mail"*: Schultz, *Blackfeet and Buffalo*, 83
126 *"an old buffalo horse"*: Yo, "To the Walled-In Lakes," December 10, 1885
126 *"which the Indians call"*: GBGD September 3, 1885
126 *"Dimly through changing"*: Yo, "To the Walled-In Lakes," December 17, 1882
127 *"The life of a sheep"*: Yo, "To the Walled-In Lakes," December 24, 1885
127 *"Soon it began"*: GBGD, September 10, 1885
127 *"There is something rather"*: Yo, "To the Walled-In Lakes," F&S, January 14, 1886
128 *"probably the best"*: GBGD, September 10, 1885
128 *"I am a little man"*: Yo, "To the Walled-In Lakes," F&S, January 14, 1886
129 *"pale greenish"*: GBGD, September 15, 1885
129 *"I estimate this glacier"*: GBGD, September 14, 1885
129 *"[A]t length [we] found"*: GBGD, September 15, 1885
129 *"In character it is"*: GBGD, September 15, 1885
129 *"It is quite possible"*: Yo, "To the Walled-In Lakes," F&S, February 18, 1886
130 *"The mountains today"*: GBGD, September 15, 1885
130 *"The children read"*: GBGD, August 31, 1885
130 *performed by Red Eagle*: Hungry-Wolf, *Blackfoot Papers*, 4:1261
131 *"who were nearly as numerous"*: Yo, "To the Walled-In Lakes," F&S, March 11, 1886
131 *"a medicine man of great"*: GBGD, September 22, 1885
132 *made a cooing*: GBGD September 22, 1885
132 *"Four bears stepped up"*: GBGD, September 23, 1885
133 *"the famine winter"*: Yo, "The Famine Winter," F&S, October 15, 1885
134 *"It is quite certain"*: "Indian Education," F&S, October 22, 1885
134 *size of Newfoundlands*: George Gould to GBG, June 14, 1914, GBGP
134 *"Grizzly bears are healthy"*: "Our Grizzly Bears," F&S, December 17, 1885
135 *less than three years*: "The Demise of the Grizzly," F&S, June 21, 1888
135 *"She was, as bears"*: "We Have Lost a Bear," F&S, August 26, 1893
135 *"Each year it is harder"*: Yo, "To the Walled-In Lakes," March 18, 1886

CHAPTER 10: DEAR PARTNER

138 *The book was printed*: Morris, *The Rise of Theodore Roosevelt*, 291
138 *"Luxurious books"*: "New Publications," F&S, July 2, 1885
138 *"I knew enough"*: GBG, "Introduction," in *The Works of Theodore Roosevelt, Memorial Edition*, xv
138 *"[His] experience of the Western"*: "New Publications," F&S, July 2, 1885
139 *"He at once saw"*: GBG, "Introduction," in *The Works of Theodore Roosevelt, Memorial Edition*, xv-xvi
139 *"a sickly boy"*: Roosevelt, *An Autobiography*, 29
139 *"Theodore, you have the mind"*: Robinson, *My Brother, Theodore Roosevelt*, 50
139 *"Four Eyes" . . . "Oscar Wilde"*: Morris, *The Rise of Theodore Roosevelt*; 144; McCullough, *Mornings on Horseback*, 256; Bederman, *Manliness & Civilization*, 170

140 *"The light has gone"*: Morris, *The Rise of Theodore Roosevelt,* 230

140 *"a veritable tragedy"*: Roosevelt, *Hunting Trips of a Ranchman,* 236, 243

140 *"doomed to extinction"*: Roosevelt, *Hunting Trips of a Ranchman,* 286–287

141 *"[I]ndeed, it was over"*: Roosevelt, *Hunting Trips of a Ranchman,* 304–305, 307

141 **For the photograph**: McCullough, *Mornings on Horseback,* 320, 333; Morris, *The Rise of Theodore Roosevelt,* 291

142 *"exceedingly vigorous"*: Harvard College Class of 1872, *Tenth Report of the Secretary,* 1912–1917 (1917)

143 *"now prospecting"*: Fourth Report of the Secretary of the Class of 1872 of Harvard College, *June 1878–June 1881* (1881)

143 *"fruitful farms"*: H. G. Dulog, "Santa Barbara in Spring," F&S, May 21, 1885

143 *"Careful he stands"*: H. G. Dulog, "The Bull Fight," F&S, October 29, 1885

144 *"some lines written"*: Yo, "To the Walled-In Lakes," F&S, January 21, 1886

145 *"Passed a wretched"*: GBGD, September 4, 1886

145 *"Since I saw you"*: GBG to Luther North, January 29, 1887

146 *"He is a very good"*: GBG to H. H. Garr, February 5, 1891

146 *"Gould killed 4"*: GBGD, October 2, 1886

CHAPTER 11: THE AUDUBON SOCIETY

149 *"We must realize how"*: "The Destruction of Small Birds," F&S, August 7, 1884

149 *"we must reflect"*: "Birds, Bonnets and Butchers," F&S, September 25, 1884

149 *"the industry of slaughtering"*: "The Audubon Society," F&S, February 11, 1886

150 *"Very slowly the public"*: "The Audubon Society," F&S, February 11, 1886

152 *"slaughter of the innocents"*: Henry Ward Beecher, letter, F&S, February 25, 1886

152 *"It is barbarous taste"*: John Burroughs, letter, F&S, February 25, 1886

152 *"The streets of New York"*: Chapman, *Autobiography of a Bird-Lover,* 38

152 **tabulated in Forest and Stream**: "Birds and Bonnets," F&S, February 25, 1886

153 *"The movement is confined"*: "The Progress of the Work," F&S, March 25, 1886

154 *"There is nothing inconsistent"*: "Concerning Consistency," F&S, July 8, 1886

154 *"enjoying the support"*: "A Word in Confidence," F&S, December 9, 1886

154 *"a great deal more"*: "Discontinuance of the 'Audubon Magazine,' *Audubon Magazine* 2 (January 1889), 262

155 *"to discourage buying"*: "A New Audubon Society," F&S, April 18, 1896

CHAPTER 12: THE ROCK CLIMBERS

156 *"You ask me to tell"*: GBG to John Fannin, August 25, 1886, GBGP

156 *"Really it begins to look"*: GBG to Luther North, May 19, 1887, GBGP

157 *"was not at home"*: GBG to George Gould, February 22, 1897, GBGP

157 *"[T]he arrival of your"*: GBG to Luther North, January 29, 1887, GBGP

157 *"You said that something"*: GBG to Luther North, February 17, 1887, GBGP

157 *"Four or five men"*: GBG to George Gould, June 3, 1887, GBGP

157 *"He has his law"*: Harvard College Class of 1872, *Tenth Report of the Secretary,* 1912–1917 (1917)

158 *"How I should like"*: GBG to George Gould, June 3, 1887, GBGP

158 *"Well, we have had"*: Theodore Roosevelt to Henry Cabot Lodge, April 20, 1887, in Henry Cabot Lodge, ed., *Selections from the Correspondence of Theodore Roosevelt and Henry Cabot Lodge, 1884–1918* (1925), I:54

158 *"The losses are crippling"*: Roosevelt, *Ranch Life and the Hunting Trail,* 79

158 *"The bills are too heavy"*: GBG to William Reed, April 14, 1887, GBGP

158 *"digestive difficulties"*: GBG to George Gould, March 18, 1887, and GBG to George Gould, June 3, 1887, GBGP

158 *"[F]or a couple of weeks"*: GBG to Luther North, August 22, 1887, GBGP

158 *"My ranch project"*: GBGM, 97

159 *"You must do it"*: GBG to Luther North, August 22, 1887, GBGP

160 *"When I started out"*: GBG to Luther North, February 17, 1888, GBGP

160 *"Hark! The report"*: H. G. Dulog, "The Rock Climbers," F&S, February 2, 1888

160 *"I was sorry to see"*: GBGD, October 26, 1887

160 *"Gould left me"*: GBG to Luther North, January 23, 1888, GBGP

161 *"Then a sadness fell"*: Yo, "The Rock Climbers, F&S, March 22, 1888

161 *"Altogether it was"*: GBGD, November 1, 1887

162 *"Up before light"*: GBGD, October 31 and November 1, 1887

162 *"the solid wall"*: GBGD, November 2, 1887

162 *"white waving line"*: Yo, "The Rock Climbers," F&S, March 29, 1888

163 *"two principal masses"*: Yo, "The Rock Climbers," March 29, 1888

164 *"1500 or 2000 feet"*: GBGD, November 2, 1887

164 *"Blood on the snow"*: Yo, "The Rock Climbers," F&S, April 5, 1888

165 *"Gould Mountain and Grinnell"*: GBG to George Gould, December 23, 1887, GBGP

166 *"It is well for you"*: GBG to George Gould, February 11, 1888, GBGP

CHAPTER 13: FAIR CHASE

167 *"We regretted the unnecessary"*: GBG, "Introduction," *The Works of Theodore Roosevelt*, Memorial Edition, vol. 1, xviii

168 *"the preservation of the large"*: "The Boone and Crockett Club," F&S, March 8, 1888

168 *"The members of the club"*: "Snap Shots," F&S, February 16, 1888

168 *first proper meeting*: Trefethen, *Crusade for Wilderness*, 19

168 *"killed with the rifle"*: GBG and Roosevelt, eds., *American Big-Game Hunting*, 338

169 *"Among the members"*: "The Boone and Crockett Club," F&S, January 17, 1889

170 *"Your delightful letter"*: GBG to George Gould, May 31, 1888, GBGP

170 *"What [if] we do"*: GBG to George Gould, August 9, 1888, GBGP

171 *"The glacier was vocal"*: Yo, "Slide Rock from Many Mountains," October 2, 1890

171 *"This was the most"*: GBGD, October 7, 1888

171 *"Yet this particular mode"*: Yo, "Slide Rock from Many Mountains," F&S, October 2, 1890

172 *"I thought when I plunged"*: Yo, "The Misfortunes of Pani Puk Koats," F&S, December 6, 1888

172 *"This is our home"*: Yo, "The Misfortunes of Pani Puk Koats," F&S December 6, 1888

173 *"Gould kindly did"*: GBGD, October 22, 1889

173 *"the very pink"*: GBG to William T. Hornaday, November 20, 1888, GBGP

174 *twelve acres of potatoes*: Ewers, *The Blackfeet*, 303

174 *"so much of their land"*: Ewers, *The Blackfeet*, 304

174 *"civilization, comfort"*: "An Act to Ratify and Confirm and Agreement with the Gros Ventre, Piegan Blood, Blackfeet, and River Crow Indians in Montana," May 1, 1888, in Charles J. Kappler, comp., *Indian Affairs: Laws and Treaties*, Vol. 1: Laws (1904)

175 *overestimated the amount:* Foley, An Historical Analysis of the Administration of the Blackfeet Reservation, 100

175 *Agent Tomorrow:* Foley, An Historical Analysis of the Administration of the Blackfeet Reservation, 104

175 *"On my way back":* GBG to Luther North, December 13, 1888, GBGP

176 *"I am not in a position":* GBG to George Hyde, May 10, 1915, GBGP

176 *"I will tell you a true":* GBGD, November 7, 1888

176 *"The road made for us":* GBGD, November 7, 1888

176 *"They feel that they":* quoted in Foley, An Historical Analysis of the Administration of the Blackfeet Indian Reservation, 110

177 *"personal investigation":* GBG to John Oberly, November 20, 1888, GBGD

177 *"The cattlemen push":* New York Evening Post, February 6, 1889

178 *"We are too apt":* GBG, The Story of the Indian, x

178 *"do for the Indian":* Quoted in Mardock, The Reformers and the American Indian, 206

CHAPTER 14: GHOST DANCE

180 *"I ought to live":* GBG to Luther North, February 4, 1889, GBGP

181 *"The entire ignorance":* GBG, Pawnee Hero Stories and Folk-Tales, 5–12

181 *"The Indian is neither":* GBG, Pawnee Hero Stories and Folk-Tales, 14

181 *"As a rule [Indians]":* GBG, Pawnee Hero Stories and Folk-Tales, 14–15

182 *Morgan formulated:* Morgan, Ancient Society, 15–18; also see Dippie, The Vanishing American, 102–106

182 *"collection of decided value":* New-York Daily Tribune, January 12, 1890

182 *"my baby—a squally":* GBG to John Nicholson, December 7, 1889, GBGP

182 *"This book is from":* John Elliott Curran, "'Pawnee Hero Stories and Folk-Tales,'" F&S, November 21, 1889

183 *"Here one has woven":* H. G. Dulog, "'Pawnee Hero Stories and Folk-Tales,'" F&S, January 16, 1890

183 *"He bawled just":* GBGD, August 25, 1889; Yo, "Slide Rock from Many Mountains," F&S, January 23, 1890

184 *"I am not married":* GBG to Douglas Miller, April 19, 1890, GBGP

185 *"When I first heard":* GBGD, August 27, 1890

186 *"A most superb prospect":* GBGD, September 20, 1890

186 *"I saw something":* GBG to James R. Murie, December 13, 1890, GBGP

187 *"went to heaven":* Mooney, The Ghost-Dance Religion and the Sioux Outbreak of 1890, 764

187 *All of their ancestors:* Utley, The Last Days of the Sioux Nation, 64–69

187 *"False Christ":* GBGD, October 5, 1890

187 *"This is only what":* GBG to Ralph J. Weeks, December 13, 1890, GBGP

187 *"The dancing usually lasts":* This interview and an article GBG submitted to the New York Times were combined and revised in the Journal of American Folk-Lore; also see GBG, "Account of the Northern Cheyennes Concerning the Messiah Superstition," Journal of American Folklore 4:12 (Jan.-March 1891), 61–69

188 *"the world would be turned":* GBGD, October 5, 1890

188 *"it is quite possible":* GBG to Luther North, December 3, 1890, GBGP

188 *"Some crazy-headed":* GBG to Ralph J. Weeks, December 13, 1890, GBGP

188 *"It is rather pitiful":* GBG to H. H. Garr, December 31, 1890, GBGP

189 *"Both [Casey and Wallace]":* "Snap Shots," F&S, January 15, 1891

CHAPTER 15: SACRED RANGE

190 *"When I came in"*: GBG to Orin Belknap, January 3, 1891, GBGP
191 *"Every sportsman desires"*: "In Behalf of the Park," F&S, March 8, 1888
191 At the Metropolitan: "Boone and Crockett Club Meeting," F&S, January 22, 1891
192 *"We showed [Speaker Reed]"*: GBG to Archibald Rogers, January 17, 1891, GBGP
193 *"I feel that the whole"*: GBG to Arnold Hague, April 6, 1891, GBGP
193 *"printed notices stuck"*: GBG to W. Hallett Phillips, April 10, 1891, GBGP
193 *"nothing on the whole"*: GBG to George Gould, November 12, 1891, GBGP
194 *"Our investigations"*: GBG to George Gould, November 12, 1891, GBGP
195 *"How would it do"*: GBGD, September 17, 1891
195 *"I have the welfare"*: GBG to George Steell, December 24, 1891, GBGP

CHAPTER 16: STANDING MENACE

196 *"lived quietly"*: *New York Times*, December 20, 1891
198 *"[M]y mother's health"*: GBG to H. W. Henshaw, March 24, 1892, GBGP
198 *"I do not say much"*: GBG to George Gould, February 6, 1892, GBGP
198 *"[I] look back"*: GBG to George Gould, March 9, 1892, GBGP
198 *"On the floor"*: GBG, "The Last of the Buffalo," 267
199 *"one robe"*: GBG, "The Last of the Buffalo," 286
199 *"These are the Indians"*: GBG to William Brownell, May 9, 1892, GBGP
199 *"Have been a member"*: GBG to Franz Boas, January 5, 1892, GBGP
200 *"I feel as if you"*: GBG to White Calf, February 8, 1892, GBGP
200 *"During my annual"*: GBG, *Blackfoot Lodge Tales*, 294
200 *"The most shameful"*: GBG, *Blackfoot Lodge Tales*, xi
201 *"I don't go so far"*: Hermann Hagedorn, *Roosevelt in the Bad Lands* (1921), 355
201 *"toward civilization"*: GBG, *Blackfoot Lodge Tales*, 299–300
201 *"The author has that rare"*: James Mooney, review of *Blackfoot Lodge Tales*, *American Anthropologist* (April 1894), 209
202 *"those of us who are"*: "The Senate and the Park," F&S, May 19, 1892; also see Punke, *The Last Stand*, 186–187
202 *"I am sick of fighting"*: GBG to F. A. Boutelle, February 23, 1892, GBGP
202 *"The Park is threatened"*: "Danger to the Park," F&S, May 19, 1892
202 *"[This] is one"*: GBG to W. Hallett Phillips, December 15, 1892, GBGP
203 *"The National Park is"*: "A Standing Menace," F&S, December 8, 1882
203 *"[A]ll public-spirited"*: "A Standing Menace," F&S, December 15, 1882
204 *"This will be a very"*: George Anderson to secretary of the interior, July 24, 1893, Yellowstone National Park Library
204 *"As winter approaches"*: George Anderson to secretary of the interior, September 16, 1893, Yellowstone National Park Library
205 *"I expect probably"*: E. Hough, "'Forest and Stream's' Yellowstone Park Game Exploration," F&S, May 5, 1894
205 *"miserable scoundrels"*: "A Premium on Crime," F&S, March 24, 1894
206 *"which belongs to those"*: "Save the Park Buffalo," F&S, April 14, 1894
207 robbed by masked men: Haines, *The Yellowstone Story*, 2:12
207 *"I have seen half"*: Theodore Roosevelt to George Anderson, March 30, 1894, Yellowstone National Park Archives
207 *"the most important arrest"*: George Anderson to Secretary of the Interior Hoke Smith, March 17, 1894, Yellowstone National Park Archives

207 *"all hunting or killing"*: "National Park Protective Act," in Roosevelt and GBG, eds., *Hunting in Many Lands*, 433–435

208 *"I believe the days"*: *Report of the Superintendent of Yellowstone National Park, 1894,* 10

208 **would be adopted**: Hampton, *How the U.S. Cavalry Saved Our National Parks,* 129

208 *"It is not too much"*: "Protection of the Park," F&S, May 12, 1894

208 *"My mother is no"*: GBG to William M. Collins, April 25, 1894, GBGP

209 *"He is a man"*: GBG to T. E. Hofer, August 8, 1892, GBGP

209 *"If ever I get out"*: GBG to George Gould, November 9, 1892, GBGP

209 *"It is believed"*: n.a., *The Triumph of Reform: A History of the Great Political Revolution, November Sixth, Eighteen Hundred and Ninety-four* (1895), 8

210 *"good Democrat"*: GBG to George Gould, November 30, 1892, GBGP

CHAPTER 17: THE CEDED STRIP

212 *"I had hoped"*: GBG to George Steell, July 2, 1894, GBGP

213 *"We wish you would"*: Foley, "An Historical Analysis of the Administration of the Blackfeet Indian Reservation," 130

213 *"I desire to see"*: GBG to George Steell, July 2, 1894, GBGP

213 *"If I were to accept"*: GBG to George Steell, July 2, 1894, GBGP

213 *"I am anxious to converse"*: GBG to F. J. Whitney, October 17, 1894, GBGP

214 *"very rich"*: GBGD, November 3, 1894

214 *"A long and tiresome"*: GBGD, November 7, 1894

214 *"The shirt and headdress"*: GBGD, November 10, 1894

214 *"While considerable dissatisfaction"*: GBG to Hoke Smith, December 12, 1894, GBGP

215 *"The appointment which"*: GBG to Hoke Smith, July 11, 1895, GBGP

216 *"I don't know anything"*: GBG to Luther North, October 2, 1894, GBGP

216 *"They brought many guns"*: GBGD August 12, 1895

217 *"The bad spirits"*: GBGD, August 13, 1895

217 *"Physically and mentally"*: GBG to Hoke Smith, February 11, 1896, GBGP

218 *"[S]ome old man harangued"*: GBGD, August 18, 1895

219 *"The Blackfeet disdained"*: Schultz, *My Life as an Indian,* 119

219 *"[G]hosts live in these"*: Schultz, *My Life as an Indian,* 416–417

219 *"In the year 1891"*: GBG to Robert Sterling Yard, October 27, 1927, GBGP

221 *"Saw many of the people"*: GBGD, August 31, 1895

221 *"Mort shot her"*: GBGD, September 6, 1895

221 *"I do not like the job"*: GBG to Billy Jackson, July 17, 1895, GBGP

222 *"I do not have it"*: "Proceedings of the Meetings of Commissioners for Reduction of Indian Reservations," 1895, typescript, Ruhle Library, Glacier National Park

225 *"In the afternoon [the offer]"*: GBGD September 25, 1895

225 *"Not a dissenting"*: GBGD, September 28, 1895

227 *"This land which some"*: "Proceedings of the Meetings of Commissioners for Reduction of Indian Reservations"

227 *"I myself think the treaty"*: GBG to Billy Jackson, November 6, 1895, GBGP

CHAPTER 18: A PLANK

228 *"No narrative about"*: GBG, *The Story of the Indian,* ix

228 *"We know in advance"*: F. W. Hodge, "Book Notices," *American Anthropologist* 9 (February 1896), 58. Although the review carries Hodge's byline, correspondence

suggests that James Mooney was the actual author; see GBG to Mooney, January 14, 1896, GBGP

228 *"Mr. Grinnell has drawn"*: [Charles F. Lummis], "That Which Is Written," 143

229 *"Your book is a good one"*: George Gould to GBG, December 15, 1895, GBGP

229 *"Dear Partner . . . A number"*: GBG to George Gould, December 24, 1895, GBGP

229 *"His nose showed none"*: Madison Grant, "A Canadian Moose Hunt," in GBG and Theodore Roosevelt, eds., *Hunting in Many Lands*, 97

230 *"dreaded and accursed"*: Henry T. Allen, "Wolf-Hunting in Russia," in *Hunting in Many Lands*, 156

230 *"About a year ago"*: George H. Gould, "To the Gulf of Cortez," in *Hunting in Many Lands*, 55

230 *"Its sex was female"*: George H. Gould, "To the Gulf of Cortez, in *Hunting in Many Lands*, 58

231 *"Have the sportsmen"*: "A Higher Standard," F&S, August 10, 1895

231 *"We have just been celebrating"*: "A Plank," F&S February 3, 1894

231 *"[I]f anyone shall assume"*: "The Markets and the Game," F&S, February 18, 1895

233 *"We learned the lay"*: Pinchot, *Breaking New Ground*, 98

233 *"In his late fifties"*: Pinchot, *Breaking New Ground*, 100

235 *"It is very important"*: GBG to Billy Jackson, [date unreadable—c. February] 1896, GBGP

235 *"It will be an abiding"*: "Snap Shots," F&S, April 4, 1896

235 *"the iron that floats"*: GBG to Vernon H. Brown, March 20, 1896, GBGP

235 *"Very little wine"*: GBG to The Arena, March 20, 1896, GBGP

235 *"If we could write down"*: "Snap Shots," F&S, April 4, 1896

235 *"[T]he charms of this"*: GBG to Ronald Hilton, September 22, 1896, GBGP

236 *"[O]n the gentler acclivities"*: GBG to Arnold Hague, December 14, 1896, GBGP

237 *"I do not care"*: GBG to J. B. Monroe, June 26, 1896, GBGP

237 *good for $500*: GBG to J. B. Monroe, July 29, 1896, GBGP

237 *"I certainly should have"*: GBG to J. B. Monroe, November 21, 1896, GBGP

237 *"About 200 enthusiasts"*: J. B. Monroe to GBG, quoted in GBG to Luther North, June 16, 1898, GBGP

238 *"probably the highest peak"*: GBG to George Gould, July 8, 1897, GBGP

238 *"soused about"*: GBG, "Climbing Blackfoot," F&S, October 8, 1898

238 *"For the rest of"*: GBG to George Gould, July 8, 1897, GBGP

239 *"camped in the circle"*: GBGD, June 15, 1897

239 *"Slits are cut"*: GBG, *Blackfoot Lodge Tales*, 267

240 *"is almost the only one"*: GBGD, June 15, 1897

240 *"[I]t rained in torrents"*: GBG to J. W. Schultz, July 17, 1897, GBGP

240 *"I was highly honored"*: GBG to George Gould, July 8, 1897, GBGP

240 *"I was greatly touched"*: GBG to J. W. Schultz, July 17, 1897, GBGP

240 *"This last trip"*: GBG to J. B. Monroe, July 16, 1897, GBGP

240 *"I sometimes wish"*: GBG to J. B. Monroe, April 12, 1897, GBGP

241 *"You and I have missed"*: GBG to George Gould, July 15, 1897, GBGP

CHAPTER 19: DIVERSE VOICES

243 *"I have not the gift"*: GBG to W. Hallett Phillips, December 23, 1892, GBGP

243 *"I was induced to make"*: GBG to George Gould December [date unreadable], 1897, GBGP

244 *"The Boone and Crocketters"*: GBG to George Gould, July 29, 1897, GBGP

244 *"My nature is such a gentle"*: GBG to George Gould, April 5, 1901, GBGP

244 *"I know you have had"*: GBG to Washington Matthews, August 10, 1897. GBGP

245 *"Explained graphophone"*: GBGD, September 22, 1897

245 *"I cannot get at"*: GBGD, September 21, 1897

245 *"The great spirit"*: GBGD September 21, 1897

246 *"I married him"*: GBGD, October 15, 1897

246 *"Some day they may"*: GBG to George Gould, November 1, 1897, GBGP

247 *"Recent developments"*: GBG to Indian Rights Association, November 20, 1897, GBGP

248 *"I have not forgotten you"*: GBG to Little Whirlwind, February 4, 1901, GBGP

249 *"A simple murder"*: Hamlin Garland, "A Typical Indian Scare: The Cheyenne Trouble," in Underhill and Littlefield, eds., *Hamlin Garland's Observations of the American Indians, 1895–1905* (1976), 156–157

250 *"The older I grow"*: Garland, *The Captain of the Gray-Horse Troop* (1901), 80–81

250 *"I am exceedingly glad"*: GBG to Hamlin Garland, September 1, 1897, GBGP

250 *"[W]hen he asked me"*: Garland, *Companions on the Trail*, 105

250 *"His house is a joy"*: Garland, *Companions of the Trail*, 191

CHAPTER 20: ECLIPSE OF MEMORY

256 *"The trade of writing"*: GBG to Morton Grinnell, April 3, 1898, GBGP

256 *"As for trying to earn"*: GBG to Morton Grinnell, June 15, 1898, GBGP

257 *"atmosphere of refinement"*: Grinnell, *An Eclipse of Memory*, 10–11

257 *"You know Billie"*: Grinnell, *An Eclipse of Memory*, 72, 86

257 *"harmless" girl*: Grinnell, *An Eclipse of Memory*, 73

257 *"James A. Scott"*: *New York Times*, August 3, 1922

258 of *"a capital book"*: GBG to J. E. North, March 3, 1898, GBGP

258 *"If it were not"*: GBG to Luther North, March 28, 1898, GBGP

259 *"a splendid thing"*: GBG to George Gould, April 20, 1898, GBGP

259 *"If I were a gentleman"*: GBG to George Gould, April 20, 1898, GBGP

259 *"licking it into shape"*: GBG to George Gould, June 6, 1898, GBGP

259 *"vast amount of useless"*: George Gould to GBG, July 27, 1898, GBGP

259 *"The dry & disjointed"*: George Gould to GBG, July 12, 1898, GBGP

260 *"Don't let . . . my small"*: George Gould to GBG, July 27, 1898, GBGP

260 *"It will make a pamphlet"*: GBG to George Gould, August 5, 1898, GBGP

260 *outshot Buffalo Bill*: O'Donnell, *Luther North: Frontier Scout*, 165–166

260 *"My dear Lute"*: GBG to Luther North, August 6, 1898, GBGP

260 *"It was a great shock"*: GBG to George Gould, August 20, 1898, GBGP

261 *"I am somewhat uneasy"*: GBG to Morton Grinnell, March 12, 1898, GBGP

261 *"My dear Roosevelt"*: GBG to Theodore Roosevelt, April 23, 1898, GBGP

262 *"I have watched"*: GBG to Theodore Roosevelt, September 5, 1898, GBGP

263 *"cowboy cavalry"*: GBG to Luther North, June 13, 1898, GBGP

263 *"at almost any sacrifice"*: GBG to N. E. Corthell, May 25, 1898, GBGP

263 *"[I]n summer, when"*: GBG to Rides at the Door, January 5, 1899, GBGP

263 *"[U]ntil somebody goes"*: GBG to J. B . Monroe, December 15, 1897, GBGP

264 *"If one had slipped"*: GBG, "Climbing Blackfoot," F&S, October 8, 1898

264 *"Jack, who was in advance"*: GBG, "Climbing Blackfoot," F&S, October 8, 1898

265 *"It is the purpose"*: James Mooney, "The Indian Congress at Omaha," 128

265 *Piegan friend Mountain*: GBG, "The North American Indian of To-day," 545

265 *"Up and down the field"*: (Omaha) *Evening Bee*, September 21, 1898
265 *photographer Frank Rinehart*: "Frank Rinehart (1862–1928)," Museum of Nebraska Art (http://monet.unk.edu/early/rinehart.shtml)
266 *"When I walked through"*: GBG, *The Indians of To-day* (1900), 5–6
267 *"We cannot deal"*: GBG, "The Wild Indian," 20–29
267 *"The Tame Indian"*: GBG to Walter H. Page, December 19, 1898, GBGP
267 *"which should at once"*: GBG, "The Indian on the Reservation," 255–267

CHAPTER 21: THE ALASKA EXPEDITION

270 *"When I raised"*: Kennan, *E. H. Harriman*, I:186–187
270 *"2 uncleaned human"*: Sterling, *Last of the Naturalists*, 31
272 *"A couple of times"*: Edward S. Curtis to Harriet Leitch, April 10, 1951, Seattle Public Library
272 *One of the men:* A number of sources mistakenly assert that Grinnell first met Curtis while mountain climbing in Washington State, either in 1897 or 1898 (for example, see Goetzmann and Sloan, *Looking North*, 12; Egan, *Short Nights of the Shadow Catcher*, 29–30; Andrews, *Curtis' Western Indians*, 21). But, as Grinnell's diary and correspondence attest, he was not anywhere near the Cascades or Seattle during those summers. Curtis's letter to Harriet Leitch, former librarian at the Seattle Public Library, of April 10, 1951, states, "You are quite right in thinking that I met George Bird Grinnell *on the Expedition* [italics added]," by which he clearly meant the Harriman Alaska Expedition. (Edward S. Curtis to Harriet Leitch, April 10, 1951, Seattle Public Library)
272 *The best Merriam:* Gidley, *Edward S. Curtis and the North American Indian, Incorporated*, 57
272 *"[B]ut so many good men"*: GBG to George Gould, May 5, 1899, GBGP
273 *"a farmer's barnyard"*: John Burroughs, "Narrative of the Expedition," *Alaska* I:17–18
273 *"The ship had no business"*: C. Hart Merriam, "Introduction," *Alaska* I:xxviii
273 *"Steamer stopped"*: GBGD, June 2, 1899
273 *"Dr. Dall was our"*: Burroughs, "Narrative of the Expedition," 18
274 *"The houses of the people"*: GBGD, June 4, 1899
274 *"It would be hard"*: GBG, "The Natives of the Alaska Coast Region," 153, 155
275 *"great range of snowclad peaks"*: GBGD, June 4, 1899
275 *"the pathos of the trail"*: GBGD, June 7, 1899
275 *"like huge monsters"*: Burroughs, "Narrative of the Expedition," I:37
276 *"Slept fairly well"*: GBGD, June 8, 1899
276 *"Mr. Muir talked"*: GBGD, June 9, 1899
276 *"I told her to shoot"*: GBGD, June 15, 1899
277 *"At the house of Chief"*: GBGD, June 17, 1899
277 *dressed in their best:* Goetzmann and Sloan, 92–94
277 *"absolutely reverses"*: GBG, "The Natives of the Alaska Coast Region," *Alaska* I:158–165
278 *"The Indian women frowned"*: Burroughs, "Narrative of the Expedition," *Alaska* I:60–61
279 *"[G]laciers to right"*: Burroughs, "Narrative of the Expedition," *Alaska* I:69
279 *They named this passage:* "Ninth Meeting of the Executive Committee," July 28, 1899, C. Hart Merriam Papers, Huntington Library, University of California at Berkeley
279 *"Some of these are like"*: GBGD, June 26, 1899
279 *"The purity"*: GBGD, July 26, 1899

280 *"They saw the bear"*: GBGD, July 6, 1899

280 **When John Muir saw**: Goetzmann and Sloan, 126

281 *"bump, then a rattling"*: GBGD, July 9, 1899

281 *"The affair was now"*: GBGD, July 9, 1899

281 *"The women are very"*: GBGD, July 11, 1899

281 *"with bad morals"*: Burroughs, "Narrative of the Expedition," *Alaska* I:101

281 *"grotesque dolls"*: Burroughs, "Narrative of the Expedition," *Alaska* I:100

282 *"[They] were a fine"*: GBGD, July 12, 1899

282 *"These people were well"*: GBGD, July 12, 1899

282 *"All the officers"*: GBGD, July 17, 1899

283 *"A grave to [the southwest]"*: GBGD, July 26, 1899

283 *"It is purposed"*: GBGD, July 26, 1899

283 *five totem poles*: Goetzmann and Sloan, 168

283 *"It is pleasant to recall"*: E. H. Harriman, "Preface," *Alaska* I:xxiii

284 *"A great deal was said"*: GBGD, July 27, 1899

284 *"Hitherto they have been"*: GBG, "The Eskimo We Saw," *Alaska* I:183

285 *"I walked about"*: GBG to Luther North, "August 14, 1899, GBGP

285 *"It was the most delightful"*: GBG to George Gould, October 25, 1899, GBGP

285 *"I suppose the fact"*: GBG to George Gould, November 11, 1899, GBGP

CHAPTER 22: INDIANS OF TO-DAY

286 *"very little hard work"*: GBG to J. B. Monroe, August 14, 1899, GBG

286 *"a hack book"*: GBG to George Gould, October 25, 1899, GBGP

286 *"a large, rich and dignified"*: Lummis, "That Which Is Written," 384

287 *"Jack was not a very"*: GBG, "Jack, the Young Ranchman," 4

287 *"walled in by mountains"*: GBG, *Jack, The Young Ranchman*, Preface

287 *Lute North in all but*: "I have been writing a book, and if you read it, you will find yourself appearing in it from time to time." GBG to Luther North, November 11, 1899, GBGP

287 *"once the bottom"* . . . *"it ain't no more"*: GBG, *Jack, the Young Ranchman*, 27, 121

287 *"I have seen quite"*: GBG, *Jack, the Young Ranchman*, 64

287 *"Then he was white"*: GBG, *Jack, the Young Ranchman*, 303

289 *"It is wild"*: Andrews, *Curtis' Western Indians*, 114

289 *"I am by no means"*: GBG to J. W. Schultz, June 14, 1901

290 *"The results which Curtis"*: GBG, "Portraits of Indian Types," 273

290 *"The pictures speak"*: GBG, "Portraits of Indian Types," 273

291 *"My dear Nephews"*: "My dear Nephews and Nieces," GBG, *Jack Among the Indians*, [no page number]

291 *"the smartest"*: GBG, *Jack Among the Indians*, 33

291 *"anybody's country"*: GBG, *Jack Among the Indians*, 50

291 *"kind o' like Christmas"*: GBG, *Jack Among the Indians*, 187

292 *"Pooh! These Indians"*: GBG, *Jack Among the Indians*, 157

292 *"[H]e had never expected"*: GBG, *Jack Among the Indians*, 181

292 *"I wish these occasions"*: GBG to Edward S. Dana, November 10, 1900, GBGP

292 *"It was highly exciting"*: GBG to George Gould, November 30, 1900, GBGP

292 *"I was not particularly cheered"*: GBG to Theodore Roosevelt, August 29, 1900, GBGP

293 *"I do not particularly object"*: GBG to Luther Kelly, January 29, 1901, GBGP

293 *"our time of life"*: GBG to George Gould, November 30, 1901, GBGP

293 *"rather too short"*: GBG to J. W. Schultz, December 5, 1900, GBGP

293 *"I am usually at work"*: GBG to Ripley Hitchcock, February 16, 1901, GBGP

293 *"my families"*: GBG to Edward S. Dana, April 5, 1901, GBGP

293 *"noble namesake"*: GBG to J. B. Monroe, December 18, 1900, GBGP

293 *"I have not forgotten"*: GBG to George Gould, May 2, 1901, GBGP

294 *"I have not been engaging"*: GBG to George Gould, May 21, 1901, GBGP

294 *"To go back to your earlier"*: GBG to George Gould, August 19, 1901, GBGP

CHAPTER 23: WINNING OF THE WEST

295 *"If you thought you could"*: GBG to George Gould, October 2, 1901, GBGP

295 *pleasure trip*: GBG to George Gould, December 6, 1901, GBGP

295 *"the Crown of the Continent"*: GBG, "The Crown of the Continent," 660

296 *"Country defaced"*: GBGD, October 22, 1901

296 *"[A] good bit"*: GBG to Gifford Pinchot, December 4, 1901, GBGP

296 *"My ice as beautiful"*: GBGD, October 23, 1901

296 *"Climbed Gould with infinite"*: GBGD, October 23, 1901

297 *"I wish that you might"*: GBG to George Gould, December 6, 1901, GBGP

298 *"Don't be afraid"*: Halass and Masich, *Halfbreed*, 141

298 *George Bent's memory*: For Bent's firsthand account of Sand Creek, see GBG, *The Fighting Cheyennes*, 170–173 and Hyde, *Life of George Bent*, 151–153

299 *Indians totaling only 10 percent*: Berthrong, *The Cheyenne and Arapaho Ordeal*, 182

299 *"I have squeezed"*: GBG to G. W. H. Stouch, April 30, 1901, GBGP

299 *"It is a great pleasure"*: GBG to George Bent, December 13, 1901, GBGP

300 *"When you come out"*: George Bent to GBG, December 8, 1901, George Bent Papers, Beinecke Rare Books & Manuscript Library, Yale

300 *"We are all troubled"*: GBG to [Eagle] Plume, September 16, 1901, GBGP

300 *"President Roosevelt is a hunter"*: "Sportsmen in the White House," F&S, May 10, 1902

300 *"Within the boundaries"*: "Make Forest Reserves Game Preserves," F&S, February 16, 1901

301 *"race expansion"*: Roosevelt, *The Winning of the West*, vol. 1, *From the Alleghanies to the Mississippi, 1769–1776*, 1–2

301 *"The continent had to be"*: (Boston) *Evening Transcript*, November 19, 1898, quoted in Hagan, *Theodore Roosevelt and Six Friends of the Indian*, 48

301 *"Roosevelt is a man"*: GBG to Hamlin Garland, October 7, 1901, GBGP

302 *"Mr. and Mrs. Roe"*: GBGD, November 12, 1901

303 *"remedying—and keeping"*: Bingham, *Charles F. Lummis*, 115

303 *"We are really launching"*: Charles F. Lummis to GBG, December 12, 1901, GBGP

304 *"to have one real Indian" . . . "a missionary"*: GBG to Charles F. Lummis, December 24, 1901, GBGP

304 *"She is a woman"*: GBG to Charles F. Lummis, January 25, 1902, GBGP

304 *"finding a market"*: GBG to Charles F. Lummis, March 18, 1902, GBGP

305 *"Everybody seemed"*: GBG to Charles F. Lummis, March 21, 1902, GBGP

CHAPTER 24: THE CAPTURED WOMAN

309 *"Nothing special"*: GBG to J. B. Monroe, March 13, 1902, GBGP

309 *"take a lot of photographs"*: GBG to Hamlin Garland, April 2, 1902, GBGP

309 *"If you see her"*: GBG to George Bent, April 5, 1902, GBGP

310 *"Among the shrubbery"* . . . *"a moment's delay"*: "A Charlton Farmer," *Saratogian* (Saratoga Springs, New York), December 31, 1868

312 **Williams's brief story:** *New York Herald*, September 30, 1900

313 *"The Navajo Indians"*: Williams, *An Alphabet of Indians*, [no page number]

313 **Elizabeth would recall:** Newell H. Foster, interview with Mrs. George B. Grinnell, typescript, June 19, 1956, Glacier National Park Archives

313 **At least one source:** "End of Romance," *Bismarck Daily Tribune*, August 28, 1902

314 *"Can you go?"*: Theodore Roosevelt, to GBG, April 28, 1902, Theodore Roosevelt Papers

314 *"I have been in absolute"*: GBG to C. Hart Merriam, April 30, 1902, GBGP

315 *"The Indian Bureau pot"*: GBG to Emerson Hough, May 7, 1902, GBGP

315 *"I want you to be"*: GBG to George Bent, May 1, 1902, GBGP

315 *"The whole trouble"*: GBG to Honorable Secretary of the Interior, May 20, 1902, GBGP

316 *"I think him an absolutely"*: Theodore Roosevelt to GBG, June 13, 1902, Theodore Roosevelt Papers

317 *"I believe absolutely"*: GBG to Theodore Roosevelt, July 18, 1902, GBGP

317 *"The officials who"*: Theodore Roosevelt, Second Annual Message to Congress, December 2, 1902

318 *"Went to Mr. Williams' "*: GBGD, May 14, 1902

318 *"No wagon"*: GBGD, May 31, 1902

318 *"Mrs. Williams has"*: GBGD, June 1, 1902

318 *"Pleasant day with"*: GBGD, June 2, 1902

318 *"Ret'd to El Reno"*: GBGD, July 8, 1902

318 *"Pleasant day sitting"*: GBGD, July 9, 1902

318 *"by dispensation"*: New York *Sun*, August 22, 1902

318 *"long wedding tour"*: *New York Times*, August 22, 1902

319 *"Give my love"*: GBG to J. B. Monroe, November 22, 1902, GBGP

319 *"I am glad to hear"*: GBG to Luther North, November 25, 1902, GBGP

319 *"I am back here now"*: GBG to George Gould, July 30, 1902, GBGP

319 *"There is little"*: GBG to George Gould, January 8, 1903, GBGP

320 *"If I had the time"*: GBG to John Pitcher, February 20, 1903, GBGP

320 *"The Indians . . . did not"*: GBG to Charles Aubrey, February 2, 1903, GBGP

320 *"Many of the diners"*: "Boone and Crockett Club Meeting," F&S, January 31, 1903

321 *"White Calf while here"*: *New York Times*, January 31, 1903

321 *"He was a man"*: "An Indian Chief," F&S, February 7, 1903

321 *"He truly loved"*: Margaret Kipp to GBG, February 9, 1903, Selected Papers of GBG from Southwest Museum, microfilm, Mansfield Library, University of Montana

322 *"I feel as if present"*: GBG to Hamlin Garland, November 22, 1902, GBGP

322 *"I have shown your"*: GBG to Mrs. W. G. Kohlenberg, February 24, 1903, GBGP

323 *"I am the criminal"*: GBG to George Gould, June 4, 1903, GBGP

323 *"I should be greatly"*: GBG to W. C. Brownell, June 3, 1903, GBGP

323 *"All seemed glad"*: GBGD, June 9, 1903

323 *"There was great excitement"*: GBG to H. C. Goodale, July 24, 1903, GBGP

324 *"All day in the saddle"*: GBGD, June 16, 1903

324 *"The women climbed"*: GBGD, July 10, 1903

324 *"Climbed to pass"*: GBGD, July 13, 1903

325 *"This is a bird"*: GBG to Luther North, July 27, 1903, GBGP

325 *"For many centuries"*: "Women in the Field," F&S, October 19, 1903

325 *"My little trip"*: GBG to George Gould, August 21, 1903, GBGP
326 *"I am sorry that you"*: GBG to W. C. Brownell, August 5, 1903, GBGP

CHAPTER 25: TEMPORARY SOJOURNERS

327 *"I came back"*: GBG to Edward S. Dana, August 17, 1903, GBGP
328 *"We had a great time"*: GBG to Edward S. Dana, September 21, 1903, GBGP
328 *"Mrs. Grinnell is up"*: GBG to John Nicholson, December 8, 1903, GBGP
328 *"Mrs. Grinnell has not"*: GBG to Edward S. Dana, February 20, 1904, GBGP
328 *"about again"*: GBG to John Nicholson, February [date unreadable—c. February 29], 1904, GBGP
328 *"practically at our door"*: GBG to John Pitcher, December 27, 1904, GBGP
328 *cutting off the house*: GBG to Mr. Crosby, May 20, 1904, GBGP
328 *"We have our ups"*: GBG to Helen Page, July 12, 1904, GBGP
328 *"I am awakened"*: GBG to Edward S. Dana, July 28, 1904, GBGP
328 *"When properly used"*: "The 'Devil-Wagon,'" F&S, July 23, 1904
328 *"I have done so little"*: GBG to John Pitcher, February 20, 1903, GBGP
329 *"I have recently purchased"*: GBG to Edward S. Dana, September 21, 1903, GBGP
329 *"blasts going off"*: GBG to Edward S. Dana, December 9, 1904, GBGP
329 *"As you know"*: GBG to Madison Grant, May 26, 1904, GBGP
330 *"bring together a number"*: "The Boone and Crockett Club," F&S, January 30, 1904
330 *"to set aside portions"*: "Big-Game Refuges," in GBG, ed., *American Big Game in Its Haunts*, 446
331 *Burroughs's piece*: Lutts, *The Nature Fakers*, 38–41
331 *a snide rebuke*: Hermit, "The Intelligence of the Wild Things," F&S, April 18, 1903
332 *"a paper of the standing"*: Theodore Roosevelt to GBG, April 24, 1903, Theodore Roosevelt Papers
332 *"I am very glad"*: GBG to Theodore Roosevelt, May 1, 1903, GBGP
332 *"The creation and preservation"*: Theodore Roosevelt, "Speech of President Roosevelt at laying of cornerstone of gateway to Yellowstone National Park, Gardiner, Montana, April 24, 1903," typescript, www.theodorerooseveltcenter.org/Research/Digital-Library
333 *"The articles which are"*: GBG, "Trail of the Pathfinders," F&S, February 27, 1904
334 *"Often when he was"*: GBG, *Jack in the Rockies*, 10
334 *" . . . stick the knife"*: GBG, *Jack in the Rockies*, 229
334 *"I don't want you"*: GBG, *Jack in the Rockies*, 30
334 *"And if I should have"*: GBG, *Jack in the Rockies*, 169–170
335 *"all the wonders"*: GBG to Edward S. Dana, November 5, 1904, GBGP
335 *"Mrs. Grinnell had never"*: GBG to Edward S. Dana, November 5, 1904, GBGP
335 *"Mrs. Grinnell alternately"*: GBG to George Gould, November 16, 1904, GBGP
335 *"I had it impressed"*: GBG to Edward S. Dana, November 5, 1904, GBGP
336 *"[F]or many years"*: GBG to Harriet Audubon, November 10, 1916, GBGP
336 *"I want him as"*: GBG to H. L. Allen, March 11, 1903, GBGP
336 *"snapped at members"*: GBG to H. L. Allen, August 19, 1903, GBGP
337 *"The time is coming"*: GBG, *American Duck Shooting*, 608
337 *"Nine men out"*: "Mr. Lacey's Bird Bill," F&S, January 18, 1900
339 *"breed in districts beyond"*: "Federal Protection of Wildfowl," F&S, December 10, 1904
340 *"Hunting without a gun"*: "Hunting with a Camera," F&S, May 5, 1892

340 *"In the migratory game"*: "The Shiras Bill," F&S, February 18, 1905

341 *"[T]he fundamental idea"* ... *"Forestry is Tree Farming"*: Pinchot, *Breaking New Ground*, 29, 31

341 *"delightful innocence"*: quoted in Worster, *A Passion for Nature*, 364

341 *"blood-loving savagery"*: quoted in Worster, *A Passion for Nature*, 369

342 *"Besides the parks"*: "The President's Message," F&S, December 17, 1904

343 *"I managed to suggest"*: GBG to R. N. Wilson, July 18, 1905, GBGP

343 *"a labor of love"*: Leupp, *The Man Roosevelt*, 334

343 *"You sized up Major"*: GBG to Francis E. Leupp, November 15, 1904, GBGP

343 *"I think Mr. Leupp"*: GBG to R. N. Wilson, July 18, 1905, GGP

344 *"If, a few centuries"*: Francis E. Leupp, "Outlines of an Indian Policy," 946

344 *"I don't know exactly how"*: GBG to George Bent, March 27, 1905, GBGP

344 *"These old war"*: GBG to George Bent, May 9, 1905, GBGP

345 *"I read your letter"*: GBG to John J. White, Jr., July 24, 1905, GBGP

345 *"I feel badly"*: GBG to Luther North, August 2, 1905, GBGP

345 *"We had a delightful"*: GBG to John C. Clifford, October 9, 1905, GBGP

345 *"We all of us feel"*: GBG to Hamlin Garland, June 19, 1905, GBGP

346 *"Frank seems to be"*: GBG to Mrs. F. D. Curtis, June 2, 1905, GBGP

346 *"The outdoor life"*: GBG to Mrs. F. D. Curtis, July 28, 1905, GBGP

346 *"[I]t appears to me"*: GBG to Mrs. F. D. Curtis, November 22, 1905, GBGP

347 *"That day he went"*: GBG to Clinton Catherwood, December 21, 1905, GBGP

347 *"It was a sad errand"*: GBG to J. B. Monroe, December 28, 1905, GBGP

347 *"I am feeling his loss"*: GBG to George Gould, January 5, 1906, GBGP

347 *"One of the things"*: GBG to George Gould, February 6, 1906 GBGP

CHAPTER 26: PULVERIZING ENGINE

349 *"It is something"*: GBG to Emerson Hough, September 9, 1900, GBGP

349 *"You do not, of course"*: GBG to George Gould, February 15 and May 12, 1904, GBGP

350 *"I have not got far"*: GBG to J. W. Schultz, March 28, 1905, GBGP

350 *"You make good stuff"*: GBG to J. W. Schultz, June 1, 1905, GBGP

350 *"I would not allow"*: GBG to George Gould, January 5, 1906, GBGP

350 *"I have a certain pity"*: GBG to J. B. Monroe, January 31, 1906, GBGP

350 *"Of course, you are"*: GBG to J. W. Schultz, December 16, 1906, GBGP

350 *"I got tired of being"*: GBG to J. B. Alexander, June 15, 1906, GBGP

351 *"It is a study"*: GBG, "Editorial Note," in J. W. Schultz, *My Life as an Indian* (1907)

351 *"Good books about"*: J. Donald Adams, "Speaking of Books," *New York Times*, December 23, 1945

352 *"I have known Mr. White"*: GBG to Francis E. Leupp, September 4, 1906, GBGP

352 *"He is a very nice"*: GBG to J. B. Monroe, February 3, 1905, GBGP

352 **White was at home**: *New York Times*, September 21, 1907; *New-York Tribune*, September 21, 1907

353 *"a sharp attack"*: GBG to Edward S. Dana, June 13, 1906, GBGP

354 *"She is now not"*: GBG to Edward S. Dana, July 25, 1906, GBGP

354 *"This is less a business"*: GBG to A. V. Boak, February 26, 1906, GBGP

354 *"I have been sick"*: GBG to George Bent, May 16, 1906, GBGP

354 *"As I grow older"*: GBG to J. B. Monroe, December 16, 1904

354 *"I regard allotment"*: GBG to Mrs. F. N. Doubleday, June 10, 1905, GBGP

355 *"The Blackfeet Reservation"*: GBG to Joseph M. Dixon, February 19, 1906, GBGP

355 *"Since the situation"*: "Proceedings of Councils of the Commissioners Appointed to Negotiate with Blackfeet Indians," September 28, 1895, typescript, Ruhle Library, Glacier National Park

355 *"plenary authority"*: Hagan, *Theodore Roosevelt and Six Friends of the Indian*, 103–104; also see Blue Clark, *Lone Wolf v. Hitchcock*

356 *"I think that the people"*: GBG to Jack Monroe, March 20, 1906, GBGP

356 *"mighty pulverizing engine"*: Theodore Roosevelt, Annual Address to Congress, December 3, 1901

356 *"I am inclined to think"*: GBG to F. E. Matthes, June 1, 1906, GBGP

356 *"I have written more"*: GBG to Roswell B. Lawrence, June 4, 1906, GBGP

357 *"The Park proposed"*: François Matthes to GBG, May 20, 1906, GBGP

357 *"I preached to them"*: GBG to J. W. Schultz, November 2, 1906, GBGP

357 *"It was pathetic"*: GBGD, October 3, 1906

357 *"I regarded it as quite"*: GBG to Francis E. Leupp, November 7, 1906, GBGP

358 *"To his newspaper"*: "The Retirement of Mr. Reynolds," F&S, December 1, 1906

358 *"a great misfortune"*: GBG to Edward S. Dana, January 22, 1907, GBGP

358 *"I am unable to supply"*: GBG to Mrs. F. D. Curtis, December 27, 1906, GBGP

359 *"In Paris my purpose"*: GBG to John J. White, Jr., March 28, 1907, GBGP

359 *"There was no one"*: GBG to George Gould, May 28, 1907, GBGP

359 *"Mrs. Grinnell is very"*: GBG to J. B. Monroe, May 31, 1907, GBGP

359 *"Pita ke" . . . "was sick"*: GBG to Little Plume, June 19, 1907, GBGP

360 *"too d[amne]d lazy"*: John J. White, Jr. to GBG, November 9 and 11, 1905, GBGP

360 *"It would be impossible"*: GBG to George Hyde, January 29, 1907, GBGP

361 *"I am sure the story"*: GBG to George Bent, March 25, 1907, GBGP

361 *"I do not clearly see"*: GBG to George Hyde, July 31, 1907, GBGP

362 *"I certainly would not"*: GBG to George Hyde, November 13, 1907, GBGP

362 *"My idea, after looking"*: GBG to John J. White, Jr., April 2, 1908, GBGP

362 *"[I] want to tell"*: GBG to George Bent, April 29, 1908, GBGP

362 *"There is no reason"*: GBG to George Hyde, April 17, 1908, GBGP

363 *"Mrs. Grinnell and I can"*: GBG to George Bent, March 10, 1908. GBGP

363 *"He mounted his horse"*: GBGD, September 19, 1908

364 *"It was not long before"*: GBGD, September 27, 1908; also see GBG, *The Fighting Cheyennes*, 341

366 *"It is, in my opinion"*: GBG to Luther North, October 15, 1908, GBGP

366 no extant correspondence: Young with McCormack, *The Dutiful Son*, 110

366 *"Important men in control"*: Buccholtz, *Man in Glacier*, 46

367 *"Indians of the plains"*: GBG, *Jack the Young Explorer*, v

367 *"crowded out"*: GGB, *Jack the Young Explorer*, 55

367 *"these Indians are so kindly"*: GBG, *Jack the Young Explorer*, 42

367 *"He looked so handsome"*: GBG, *Jack the Young Explorer*, 97

367 *"was perhaps the grandest"*: GBG, *Jack the Young Explorer*, 220

367 *"I expect if no more"*: GBG, *Jack the Young Explorer*, 225

367 *"There is a wonderful"*: GBG, *Jack the Young Explorer*, 306

368 *"If the measure shall"*: GBG, *Jack the Young Explorer*, 307–308

368 *The New York Real*: *Real Estate Record and Builders Guide* 82 (November 28, 1908), 1034

368 *"You will be sorry"*: GBG to Luther North, December 23, 1908, GBGP

369 *"Since writing you last"*: GBG to George Gould, December 31, 1908, GBGP

CHAPTER 27: STUYVESANT SQUARE

370 *"I was turned out"*: GBG to Lewis W. Hicks, January 20, 1910, GBGP
370 *"I . . . have been in great"*: GBG to George Bent, February [date illegible], 1909
371 *"I now think that"*: GBG to Edward S. Dana, March 9, 1909, GBGP
372 *"so that there will be"*: GBG to Sylvia Page, May 27, 1909, GBGP
372 **Double Elephant Folio**: GBG to John Schwab, December 7, 1912, GBGP
372 *"I have not been back"*: GBG to Edward S. Dana, June 16, 1909, GBGP
372 *"We are becoming more"*: GBG to John Nicholson, July 31, 1909, GBGP
373 *"I wish that there were"*: GBG to George Gould, August 17, 1909, GBGP
373 *"The first [was] quite"*: GBGD, September 22, 1909
374 *"still sick and anxious"*: GBGD, September 16, 1909
374 *"This is the third"*: GBGD, September 18, 1909
374 *"E[lizabeth] happened"*: GBGD, September 20, 1909
374 to *"sit with closed"*: GBG to "My dear Aunt Ella [Mrs. Thomas A. Ripley]," November 2, 1909, GBGP
374 *"There can be no"*: "The Glacier National Park," F&S, March 5, 1910
375 *"a frank, downright"*: GBG to Madison Grant, April 1, 1910, GBGP
375 *"this bill, which if it becomes"*: GBG to A. C. Harvey, April 23, 1910, GBGP
375 *"This has been a 'baby'"*: GBG to Hermon C. Bumpus, May 4, 1910, GBGP
376 *"aesthetic conservationism"*: Miller, *Gifford Pinchot and the Making of Modern Environmentalism*, 4
376 *"temple destroyers"*: John Muir, "The Hetch-Hetchy Valley," *Sierra Club Bulletin* 6 (January 1908), 219–220, quoted in Worster, *A Passion for Nature: The Life of John Muir*, 425
376 *"the good of man"*: Pinchot, *Breaking New Ground*, 322; Worster, *A Passion for Nature*, 427
376 *"through economic spectacles"*: GBG to Allen Chamberlain, May 19, 1910, GBGP
376 *"the birth of conservation"*: Pinchot, *Breaking New Ground*, 319
376 *"Injury to Hetch Hetchy"*: Pinchot to Frederick Perry Noble, September 18, 1913, quoted in Miller, *Gifford Pinchot and the Making of Modern Environmentalism*, 140
376 *"Pinchot, of course"*: GBG to William Brewster, June 12, 1911, GBGP
377 *"highest possible use"*: Gifford Pinchot to Theodore Roosevelt, October 11, 1907, quoted in Miller, *Gifford Pinchot and the Making of Modern Environmentalism*, 140
377 *"It is an unfortunate"*: "The Hetch-Hetchy Project," F&S, February 6, 1909
377 **"Forest and Stream"**: "The Glacier National Park," F&S, May 21, 1910
378 *"My dear Belf"*: GBG to C. S. Belford, February 2, 1910, GBGP
379 *"How can I bring"*: GBG to E. A. Lewis, March 2, 1910, GBGP
379 *"The Lord only"*: GBG to James Russell, February 2, 1910, GBGP
379 *"I think you can"*: GBG to James Russell, March 17, 1910, GBGP
379 *"dangerous thing"*: GBG to George Huntress, December 1, 1909, GBGP
380 *"knocked the man"*: GBG to Helen Page, October 13, 1920, GBGP
380 *"our meeting at New Haven"*: GBG to Edward S. Dana, June 23, 1910, GBGP
380 *"Thank the Lord"*: GBG to James Russell, July 18, 1910, GBGP
381 *"[S]ince its establishment"*: GBG, *Brief History of the Boone and Crockett Club*, 58
382 *"One might suppose"*: GBG, "Roosevelt in Africa," 461
382 *"Personally I am"*: GBG to Madison Grant, December 14, 1910, GBGP

CHAPTER 28: BREAK THE OLD HABIT

385 *"If some kind person"*: GBG to George Gould, March 24, 1910, GBGP
386 *"Otis has made"*: GBG to George Huntress, May 10, 1911, GBGP
386 *"getting to look"*: GBG to John J. White, Jr., April 21, 1911, GBGP
386 *"I am inclined to think"*: GBG to J. B. Monroe, May 16, 1911, GBGP
387 *"Your company is directly"*: GBG to George W. Jenkins, May 12, 1912, GBGP
387 *"It is this sort of gun"*: *New York Times*, June 3, 1911
388 *"[T]he association reserves"*: *New York Times*, June 4, 1911
388 *"It is no doubt partly"*: GBG to Madison Grant, February 7, 1912, GBGP
389 *"They continue to degenerate"*: GBG to J. W. Schultz, September 13, 1911, GBGP
389 *"pleasant seeming people"*: GBGD, July 15, 1911
390 *allotment bill in 1907*: Ewers, *The Blackfeet*, 318
390 *"The basest of all"*: J. B. Monroe to GBG, July 28, 1911, Selected Papers of GBG
     from Southwest Museum, University of Montana
390 *"Their memories"*: GBG to J. B. Monroe, January 22, 1912, GBGP
391 *"The instructors knelt"*: GBG, "The Cheyenne Medicine Lodge," AA (April–June
     1914) 253–254
392 *"Now the officers"*: GBGD, August 10, 1911
392 *"The bullets were flying"*: GBGD, August 10, 1911
393 *"I was very much surprised"*: Luther North to GBG, November 5, 1911, Luther H.
     North Papers, History Nebraska
393 *"Take a good rest"*: J. B. Monroe to GBG, October 30, 1911, GBGP
393 *"I have been trying"*: GBG to J. B. Monroe, November 8, 1911, GBGP
394 *"Then would you be"*: GBG to J. B. Monroe, September 13, 1911, GBGP
394 *"Mrs. Grinnell made"*: GBG to John J. White, Jr., October 26, 1911, GBGP
394 *"a keen sportsman"*: GBG, ed., *Hunting at High Altitudes*, 7
395 *"Many of the birds"*: GBG, "Marsh Island," typescript, March 1912, GBGP
396 *"A nephew of mine"*: GBG to John J. White, Jr., January 6, 1912, GBGP
396 *"Long Island sportsman"*: *New York Times*, September 28, 1911
396 *The couple was found*: *New York Times*, February 5, 1912
396 *"As you know, our hearts"*: GBG to John J. White, Jr., March 26, 1912, GBGP
396 *"I have worked more"*: GBG to Luther North, February 5, 1912, GBGP
396 *"I was in four"*: Luther North to GBG, February 8, 1912, Luther H. North Papers,
     History Nebraska
397 *"his heart-strings"*: GBG, *Jack the Young Cowboy*, 278
397 *"I look back"*: GBG to Luther North, May 31, 1912, GBGP
397 *"This we did not"*: GBGD, May 31, 1912
397 *"I was sitting"*: GBGD, June 6, 1912
398 *"All prairie Indians"*: GBGD, June 6, 1912
398 *"There is nothing certain"*: GBG to Charles Reed, February 20, 1912, GBGP
399 *"The leader spoke"*: GBGD, August 9, 1912
399 *"that dangerous animal"*: GBG to John J. White, Jr., May 24, 1912, GBGP
400 *"We had a fine"*: GBG to C. Hart Merriam, October 9, 1912
400 *"[They] are perhaps"*: GBGD, September 10, 1912
400 *"Tried . . . to find Geo. Gould"*: GBGD, September 13 and 14, 1912
401 *"Dear Partner"*: GBG to George Gould, October 10, 1912, GBGP

CHAPTER 29: UNDUE DESTRUCTION

402 *"I believe that many"*: GBG to Maria Audubon, March 3, 1914, GBGP

402 *"You should make"*: GBG to John J. White, Jr., March 12, 1914, GBGP

402 *"probably have to go"*: GBG to John J. White, Jr., November 3,1913, GBGP

403 *"I am a warm friend"*: GBG to H. S. Leonard, February 2, 1914, GBGP

403 *"The Boone and Crockett"*: GBG to John Bird Burnham, December 21, 1911, GBGP

404 *Pancho Villa:* [GBG], sketch of Charles Sheldon, February 8, 1929, GBGP

405 *"We go back"*: Sheldon, *The Wilderness of the Upper Yukon*, 47

405 *"wilderness wanderer"*: Theodore Roosevelt, "The American Hunter-Naturalist," *Outlook* (December 9, 1911), 854–856, quoted in Brinkley, *The Quiet World*, 128

406 *"Sheldon is one"*: GBG to John Nicholson, May 13, 1909, GBGP

406 *"Glancing at Mrs. Sheldon"*: Sheldon, *The Wilderness of the North Pacific Coast Islands*, 176–177

406 *"This is . . . the most"*: Pearson, *Adventures in Bird Protection*, 277

407 *"I am really ashamed"*: Hornaday, "The Passing of the Buffalo," 85

408 *"It possesses the essentials"*: GBG to W. T. Hornaday, May 7, 1896, GBGP

408 *"the enjoyment of the general"*: Bridges, *Gathering of Animals*, 32

409 *"a lamentable failure"*: Dehler, *The Most Defiant Devil*, 121

409 *"A new engine"*: "The Automatic Shot-Gun," *Zoological Society Bulletin* 12 (January 1904), 132

410 *"I am not . . . disposed"*: GBG to Madison Grant, February 7, 1912, GBGP

410 *"He delights in a row"*: GBG to Madison Grant, February 7, 1912, GBGP

411 *"I am positively"*: William T. Hornaday to Rosalie Edge, November 11, 1931, quoted in Dehler, *The Most Defiant Devil*, 1

411 *"the dickey-bird"*: Hornaday, *Thirty Years War for Wild Life*, 163

412 *"our 'song bird' issue"*: Hornaday, *Thirty Years War for Wild Life*, 165

412 *"To my mind"*: GBG to Madison Grant, March 13, 1913, GBGP

412 *"The general conservation"*: GBG to Allen Chamberlain, November 28, 1911, GBGP

CHAPTER 30: FIGHTING CHEYENNES

413 *"I fritter away"*: GBG to Ella D. Barberie, April 2, 1913, GBGP

414 *"Perhaps I am too"*: GBG to Luther North, March 3, 1913, GBGP

414 *"I wish to get"*: GBG to "Box 324," January 20, 1913, GBGP

414 *"The West has become"*: GBG to George Huntress, July 14, 1913, GBGP

414 *"turned into a pleasure"*: GBG to Charles Reed, May 16, 1913, GBGP

414 *"The force of habit"*: GBG to Charles Reed, May 16, 1913, GBGP

415 *"Good room with bath"*: GBGD, July 30, 31, 1913

415 *"A number of these"*: GBG to J. W. Schultz, October 15, 1913, GBGP

415 *"Trip made in about"*: GBGD, July 31, 1913

415 *"There is still quite"*: GBG to T. E. Hofer, August 14, 1914, GBGP

415 *"Mrs. Grinnell gave"*: GBG to John J. White, Jr., September 17, 1913, GBGP

416 *"Mrs. Grinnell worked"*: GBG to T. E. Hofer, December 1, 1913, GBGP

416 *"in Indian fashion"*: GBG to Ripley Hitchcock, January 30, 1914, GBGP

416 *"You know that I"*: GBG to Ripley Hitchcock, February 3, 1914, GBGP

417 *"strenuous Theodore"*: GBG to Edward S. Dana, June 12, 1914, GBGP

417 *"I left word for"*: GBG to J. R. Eddy, January 22, 1914, GBGP

417 *"less about Indians"*: GBG to Editor, *New York Times*, January 4, 1915

418 *"These people are fifty"*: GBG to A. Phimster Proctor, March 26, 1914, GBGP
418 *"the attraction of Woodstock"*: GBG to Mrs. Theodore Porter, April 28, 1914, GBGP
418 *"[M]an is everywhere"*: Marsh, *Man and Nature*, 36
418 *"a man of splendid"*: GBG to Committee of Admissions, Century Association, October 8, 1914, GBGP
419 *"I went over the Ft."*: GBG to T. E. Hofer, August 26, 1914, GBGP
420 *"The European war"*: GBG to Mrs. W. van Straubenzee, September 8, 1914, GBGP
420 *"I carry Elizabeth's"*: GBG to Laura Martin, August 21, 1914, GBGP
420 *"so robust that when"*: GBG to John J. White, Jr., October 27, 1914, GBGP
421 *"My deafness and bad"*: George Hyde to GBG, September 14, 1914, George Bent Papers, Beinecke Rare Books & Manuscripts Library, Yale
421 *"No one, I suppose"*: GBG to General W. S. Schuyler, March 15, 1915, GBGP
421 *"The Cheyennes who"*: GBG to General E. S. Godfrey, September 8, 1914, GBGP
421 *"He has the best"*: GBG to W. J. Dixon, March 27, 1914, GBGP
421 *"I am getting tired"*: Halaas and Masich, *Half Breed*, 345
422 *"I should like"*: GBG to George Hyde, December 9, 1914, GBGP
422 *"most of them are bad"*: George Hyde to GBG, December 23, 1914, George Bent Papers, Beinecke Rare Books & Manuscripts Library, Yale
422 *"I would rewrite"*: GBG to George Hyde, December 28, 1914, GBGP
422 *"I suppose the idea"*: George Hyde to GBG, May 8, 1915, George Bent Papers, Beinecke Rare Books & Manuscript Library, Yale
422 *"He is a very young"*: GBG to Luther North, January [c. 6–7], 1915, GBGP
423 *"for the first time"*: GBG to George Hyde, February 23, 1915, GBGP
423 *"I shall take my bundle"*: GBG to Luther North, January [c. 6–7], 1915, GBGP
423 *"I have drawn marks"*: GBG to Edward L. Burlingame, May 5, 1915, GBGP
423 *"our disposition to undertake"*: Edward L. Burlingame to GBG, May 19, 1915, GBGP
423 *"I feel as if"*: GBG to Luther North, June 2, 1915, GBGP
424 *"to sit on a hotel"*: GBG to John J. White, Jr., June 15, 1915, GBGP
424 *"It was many years"*: GBG to Mrs. Newell Martin, September 13, 1915, GBGP
424 *"The book is promised"*: GBG to George Hyde, October 4, 1915, GBGP
424 *"I came to the galleys"*: George Hyde to GBG, October 7, 1915, George Bent Papers, Beinecke Rare Books & Manuscripts Library, Yale
424 *" 'The Fighting Cheyennes' crept"*: GBG to T. E. Hofer, November 1, 1915, GBGP
424 *"You see, the average"*: GBG to Harriet Audubon, October 30, 1915, GBGP
425 *"many Cheyenne friends"*: GBG, *The Fighting Cheyennes*, vi
425 *"They fought not only"*: GBG, *the Fighting Cheyennes*, 9
425 *"If the tribes were"*: GBG, *The Fighting Cheyennes*, 93–94
426 *"The old-time Indian"*: GBG, *The Fighting Cheyennes*, 270
426 *"[Capt H. E.]"* . . . *"distorted and exaggerated"*: GBG, *The Fighting Cheyennes*, 202, 222, 250
426 *"In Black Kettle"*: GBG, *The Fighting Cheyennes*, 298
427 *"If the Indian Bureau"*: GBG, *The Fighting Cheyennes*, 417–418
427 *"Your share in the volume"*: GBG to George Hyde, November 16, 1915, GBGP
427 *"I shall always keep"*: George Hyde to GBG, November 10, 1915, George Bent Papers, Beinecke Rare Books & Manuscripts Library, Yale
427 *"The book has not"*: GBG to George Hyde, November 16, 1915, GBGP
427 *"There is something"*: *New York Times*, June 30, 1916
428 *"has not much use"*: GBG to Charles Sheldon, November 18, 1915, GBGP

428 *"delighted"* . . . *"I am glad you"*: Theodore Roosevelt to GBG, November 16, 1915, Theodore Roosevelt Papers; GBG to Roosevelt, November 24, 1915, GBGP

428 *"The lettering"*: GBG to Edward L. Burlingame, October 11, 1916, GBGP

428 *"I find that at my"*: GBG to Harriet Audubon, January 13, 1916, GBGP

428 *"continues to be one"*: GBG to Charles Sheldon, November 18, 1915, GBGP

CHAPTER 31: THE NATIONAL PARK SERVICE

432 *"vast reservoir of game"*: Charles Sheldon to Stephen T. Mather, December 15, 1915, National Archives, Record Group 79, Entry 6, Correspondence Mount McKinley, Box 383, cited in National Park Service, "Denali: Historical Resource Study," https://www.nps.gov/parkhistory/online_books/dena/hrs5.htm

432 *"I wish with all"*: GBG to Robert Sterling Yard, May 11, 1916, GBGP

434 *"As I have told you"*: GBG to Madison Grant, June 5, 1916, GBGP

435 *"Passed waterhole"*: GBGD, June 25, 1916

435 *"[We] reached the battlefield"*: GBG to Frank Linabury, September 13, 1916, GBGP

436 *estimated that five thousand*: GBG to Grace Raymond Hebard, September 15, 1916, GBGP

436 *"the greatest number"*: Hardin Tribune, June 30, 1916

436 *"a lot of Indians"*: GBGD June 25, 1916

436 *"The day after the arrival"*: Hardin Tribune, June 30, 1916

436 *"Yes, I was here"*: Billings Gazette, June 26, 1916

437 *"wiped Custer and his followers"*: Hardin Tribune, June 30, 1916

437 *"I was not near"*: GBG to Grace Raymond Hebard, September 15, 1916, GBGP

437 *"most kindly received"*: GBGD, June 29, 1916

437 *"We climbed the high"*: GBGD, June 30, 1916

437 *"We saw where"*: GBGD, June 30, 1916

438 *"Found all well"*: GBGD, July 1, 1916

438 *"They did not fear"*: GBGD, July 8, 1916

438 *"E[lizabeth] tickled"*: GBGD, July 26, 1916

439 *"We looked in vain"*: GBGD, September 2, 1916

439 *"You say nothing"*: GBG to Luther North, October 24, 1916, GBGP

440 *"No, I didn't go"*: Luther North to GBG, November 3, 1916, Luther H. North Papers, History Nebraska

440 *"I am glad you handled"*: GBG to Luther North, November 13, 1916, GBGP

441 *"Wilson is the champion"*: GBG to John J. White, Jr., December 27, 1916, GBGP

441 *"a brave Nation"*: Muller, The Invasion of America, 351–352

441 *"I suppose it is hopeless"*: GBG to Julius W. Muller, January 12, 1916, GBGP

441 *"It is readily conceivable"*: GBG to Edward S. Dana, February 20, 1917, GBGP

441 *"It is a very humiliating"*: GBG to George Hyde, February 20, 1917, GBGP

441 *"I have had a senile"*: GBG to Edward S. Dana, May 8, 1917, GBGP

442 *"You and I are scarcely"*: GBG to James Russell, April 13, 1917, GBGP

442 *"I am hopeful"*: GBG to Helen Page, May 31, 1917, GBGP

442 *"One of the things"*: GBG to Frank Curtis, July 2, 1913, GBGP

443 *"It is possible"*: GBG to E. L. Mason, March 24, 1916, GBGP

443 *"Frank Curtis has never"*: GBG to E. L. Mason, May 16, 1916, GBGP

443 *"Elizabeth deserted me"*: GBG to George Huntress, April 17, 1917, GBGP

443 *"I understand how"*: GBG to Elizabeth Grinnell, April 24, 1917, GBGP

443 *"I do not wish"*: GBG to Louis Dean Speir, March 14, 1917, GBGP

444 *"[M]arriage is a frightful"*: GBG to Sylvia Brusati, February 5, 1917, GBGP

444 *"You know without"*: GBG to A. K. Fisher, January 31, 1917, GBGP

444 *"Elizabeth is very well"*: GBG to George Huntress, February 20, 1917, GBGP

444 *"I am altogether"*: GBG to Elizabeth Grinnell, April 25, 1917, GBGP

444 *"[Y]ou are making"*: GBG to Elizabeth Grinnell, May 7, 1917, GBGP

444 *"I might as well"*: GBG to James Russell, December 6, 1917, GBGP

446 *"I never expect"*: GBG to Paul Stetson, October 18, 1916, GBGP

446 *"Such dogs occur"*: GBG to Helen Page, October 30, 1916, GBGP

446 *"She is very small"*: GBG to Paul Stetson, November 8, 1917, GBGP

446 *"She is a very affectionate dog"*: GBG to Vernon Rice, November 28, 1917, GBGP

446 *"I must confess"*: GBG to James Russell, March 27, 1918, GBGP

446 *"I am fiddling away"*: GBG to George Bent, October 16, 1917, GBGP

447 *"He and I, besides"*: GBG to Mrs. George Bent, June 21, 1918, GBGP

447 *"There is nothing"*: GBG to Frederick A. Stokes, February 4, 1918, GBGP

447 *"Americans . . . need some"*: GBG to Mary C. Collins, September 5, 1917, GBGP

447 *"Of course, I eat"*: GBG to James Russell, January 17, 1918, GBGP

448 *"[W]e must fight until"*: GBG to L. R. A. Condit, May 13, 1918, GBGP

448 *"Increased killing"*: GBG to Charles Sheldon, November 23, 1917, GBGP

449 *"the pressure, apparently"*: Resolution, Annual Meeting of the Boone and Crockett Club, January 10, 1918, GBGP

449 *"Since an attempted"*: Trefethen, *Crusade for Wildlife*, 207

449 *"Pseudo-patriots"*: Trefethen, *Crusade for Wildlife*, 208

449 *"Mrs. Grinnell's physician"*: GBG to W. S. Haskell, July 16, 1918, GBGP

450 *"I shall probably never be"*: GBG to Herman Leroy Edgar, July 8, 1918, GBGP

450 *"Mrs. Grinnell is not"*: GBG to Eaton Brothers, July 26, 1918, GBGP

450 *"As soon as she reached"*: GBG to Luther North, September 30, 1918, GBGP

450 *"something I have not"*: GBG to John J. White, Jr., September 13, 1918, GBGP

450 *"Here in New York"*: GBG to T. E. Hofer, November 12, 1918, GBGP

450 *"The varnish of civilization"*: GBG to L. O. Vaught, February 7, 1919, GBGP

451 *"I had known Roosevelt"*: GBG to James Russell, January 14, 1919, GBGP

451 *"I am to preside"*: GBG to Charles Sheldon, January 8, 1919, GBGP

452 *"I am not an orator"*: GBG to G. Douglas Wardrop, November 16, 1914, GBGP

452 *"Yes, he was a good"*: GBG to T. E. Hofer, January 15, 1919, GBGP

CHAPTER 32: ALL THIS BETTER WORK

455 *"As I saw [Roosevelt]"*: GBG to A. J. Woodcock, March 17, 1919, GBGP

456 *"Our horns"*: GBG to J. B. Monroe, May 12, 1919, GBGP

456 *"I resemble one"*: GBG to George Gould, March 28, 1919, GBGP

456 *"[S]omeday [it may]"*: GBG to L. O. Vaught, January 3, 1919, GBGP

456 *"I have been making"*: GBG to Henry T. Schnittkind, May 13, 1919, GBGP

456 *"Mrs. Grinnell is—shall"*: GBG to Charles B. Reed, March 28, 1919, GBGP

457 *"Elizabeth and I"*: GBG to Nonnie Lyon, February 28, 1919, GBGP

457 *"The Doctor's luggage"*: George C. Fraser, "Notes, A Journey Taken, Dr. George Bird Grinnell and George C. Fraser, June 24 to August 1, 1919 through Portions of Western New Mexico, Eastern Arizona and Southwestern Colorado, including The Navaho Country and Mesa Verde National Park," typescript, GBGP

457 *"The Doctor, in light"*: George C. Fraser, "Notes," 12

457 *"the oldest continuously"*: GBGD, June 28, 1919

458 *"At 4 o'clock"*: George C. Fraser, "Notes," 107

458 *"I suppose it rained"*: GBGD, July 16, 1919

458 *"The amusements"*: GBG to Sylvia Brusati, June 19, 1919, GBGP

458 *"I still manage"*: GBG to T. E. Hofer, December 24, 1919, GBGP

459 *"I have a sick"*: GBG to W. B. Mershon, April 30, 1920, GBGP

460 *"a second Hetch Hetchy"*: GBG to Allen Chamberlain, April 21, 1920, GBGP

460 *"The point I make"*: GBG to Schuyler Merritt, April 21, 1920, GBGP

461 *"[T]he preservation of remote"*: Edward W. Nelson to Frank W. Mondell, April 3, 1920, GBGP

461 *"The Yellowstone Park"*: GBG to Charles S. Davison, April 22, 1920, GBGP

461 *"It seems to me"*: GBG to T. E. Hofer, May 10, 1920, GBGP

461 *"eastern faddist"*: *Anaconda Standard*, May 9, 1920

461 *"The story tickles"*: GBG to J. U. Sanders, May 21, 1920, GBGP

461 a *"nature faker"*: *Livingston Enterprise*, May 11, 1920

462 *"It is just a question"*: *Congressional Record*, April 19, 1920, 6322, clipping in GBGP

462 *"I shall not believe"*: GBG to Stephen Mather, April 22, 1920, GBGP

462 *"I am sorry to say"*: GBG to Stephen Mather, May 26, 1920, GBGP

462 *"[T]he whole National"*: *Report of the Director of the National Park Service to the Secretary of the Interior for the Fiscal Year Ended June 30, 1920 and the Travel Season 1920* (1920), 21

462 *"pollution," "injury"*: *Report of the Director*, 22–23

463 *"There were fifty"*: GBG to T. E. Hofer, June 2, 1920, GBGP

463 *"Yellowstone Plan Defeated"*: Newspaper clipping, Yellowstone Park scrapbook, "Irrigation, 1919–1921," quoted in Bartlett, *Yellowstone: A Wilderness Betrayed*, 353

463 *"It will be a good"*: GBG to Harry S. Graves, June 9, 1920, GBGP

463 *"The ease and swiftness"*: GBG to Stephen Mather, June 9, 1920, GBGP

464 *"How [this] got into"*: GBG to W. C. Gregg, June 24, 1920, GBGP

464 *"[I]t seems natural"*: GBG to Robert Sterling Yard, June 24, 1920, GBGP

464 *"Would it be possible"*: GBG to Charles Sheldon, June 18, 1920, GBGP

465 *"a sort of siesta"*: GBG to Howard Eaton, June 11, 1920, GBGP

465 *"There was no drink"*: GBG to James Russell, June 25, 1920, GBGP

465 *"I had not thought"*: GBG to Frank Page, July 28, 1920, GBGP

466 *"I have to announce"*: GBG to Sylvia Brusati, October 27, 1920, GBGP

466 **An obituary published**: *Obituary Record of Graduates of Yale College: Deceased During the Academic Year Ending July 1, 1920* (1921); *New York Times*, July 1, 1920; *New York Times*, August 3, 1922

466 *"She looks better"*: GBG to Helen Page, August 6, 1920, GBGP

467 *"Hoover believes"*: GBGD, August 29, 1920

468 *"I used to be very familiar"*: GBG to Editor, *New York Herald*, December 29, 1920

468 *"I did no work"*: GBG to A. K. Fisher, September 15, 1920; GBG to George Grinnell-Milne, November 13, 1920, GBGP

468 *"quite her old self"*: GBG to Edward Sawyer, September 30, 1920, GBGP

468 *"a dismal swamp"*: GBG to John Agar, September 16, 1920, GBGP

468 *"region of delight"*: Robert Sterling Yard, "The War on the Yellowstone," *National Parks Association Bulletin* 11 (September 24, 1920), 4–5

468 *"Pawning the Heirlooms"* . . . *"Another Hetch Hetchy"*: Hough, "Pawning the Heirlooms," *Outlook*, July 7, 1920, 448

469 *"artistic concrete structure"*: *The Lake Yellowstone Project: What Is It? Why Is It?* (November 1920)

469 *"great areas of forest"*: Michael J. Yochim, "Conservationists and the Battles to Keep Dams Out of Yellowstone," in Roger J. Anderson and David Harmon, eds., *Yellowstone Lake: Hotbed of Chaos or Reservoir of Resilience?* (2002), 291

469 *"I had a letter"*: GBG to Charles S. Sargent, October 25, 1920, GBGP

469 *"If Mr. Harding"*: GBG to Charles S. Sargent, October 27, 1920, GBGP

469 *"As a western"*: GBG to Albert B. Fall, March 22, 1921, GBGP

470 *"Every year [Yellowstone]"*: GBG to Commercial Club, Billings, Montana, October 27, 1920, GBGP

471 *"The proponents"*: GBG to Key Pittman, May 2, 1921, GBGP

471 *"This result"*: GBG to L. O. Vaught, March 8, 1921, GBGP

472 *"Seventy years ago"*: GBG, *When Buffalo Ran*, 9

472 *"[A]ct a man's part"*: GBG, *When Buffalo Ran*, 36

472 *"It is a good thing"*: GBG, *When Buffalo Ran*, 35

472 *"If you should chance"*: GBG, *When Buffalo Ran*, 27

473 *"It was a few"*: GBG, *When Buffalo Ran*, 113–114

473 *"[W]e are now"*: J. P. Dunn, review of GBG, *When Buffalo Ran*, *Mississippi Valley Historical Review* 7 (March 1921), 409

473 *"In view of the fact"*: GBG to Yale University Press, March 9, 1921, GBGP

474 *"I have never needed"*: GBG to George Huntress, May 26, 1921, GBGP

474 *"Yale University, through"*: GBG to John J. White, Jr., October 145, 1921, GBGP

474 *"We stopped and talked"*: GBGD, July 3, 1921\

474 *"Now it is a country"*: GBGD, August 21, 1921

475 *"I have been persona"*: GBG to M. K. Sniffen, January 18, 1921, GBGP

475 *"very sensible"*: GBG to Thomas Magee, October 7, 1921, GBGP

476 *"The purity of the waters"*: GBG to R. E. Coker, April 28, 1921, GBGP

477 *"I am gratified to think"*: GBG to Joseph P. Howe, April 13, 1921, GBGP

CHAPTER 33: A COMPLEX LIFE

478 *"I suppose I am"* . . . *"You can be sure"*: GBG to George Parmly Day, November 16, 1922; George Parmly Day to GBG, November 25, 1922, GBGP

479 *"We have on the one"*: GBG and Sheldon, eds., *Hunting and Conservation*, xi

480 *"Certain it is"*: *Yale Review* 14 (January 1925), 406

480 *"Of all the books"*: Mead and Bunzel, eds., *The Golden Age of American Anthropology*, 114

481 *"cordial and helpful"*: GBG, *The Cheyenne Indians*, I:vi

481 *"The hardships of the Indian"*: GBG, *The Cheyenne Indians*, I:257

482 *"energetic, brave"*: GBG, *The Cheyenne Indians*, I:128, 145

482 *"No subject is more"*: GBG, *The Cheyenne Indians*, II:192

482 *"[I]n the Cheyenne"*: GBG, *The Cheyenne Indians*, II:87

482 *"prayed constantly"*: GBG, *The Cheyenne Indians*, II:193

483 *"notable feat"*: GBG, *The Cheyenne Indians*, I:29–30

483 *"a little group of men"*: GBG, *The Cheyenne Indians*, II:39

484 *"These primitive people"*: GBG, *The Cheyenne Indians* I:vi

484 *"I have reached the shell"*: GBG to Frank B. Linderman, November 8, 1916, GBGP

484 *"Mr. Fall is not"*: GBG to Nicholas Roosevelt, January 4, 1923, GBGP

485 *"was a tremendous loss"*: GBG to Mrs. Gustave Lewis, October 18, 1923, GBGP

485 *"[S]ome of us feel"*: GBG to George Milne-Grinnell, January 9, 1924, GBGP

485 *"I have had a part"*: GBG to Aldo Leopold, April 4, 1923, GBGP

485 *"highest use"*: Leopold, "The Wilderness and Its Place in Forest Recreation Policy," 720

486 *"I cannot spend"*: GBG to Arno B. Cammerer, July 24, 1923, GBGP

486 *"I went over to them"*: GBGD, September 9, 1923
486 *"I had to stop rather"*: GBGD, September 13, 1923
486 *"Here were several"*: GBGD, September 13, 1923
487 *"We went up"*: GBGD, September 22, 1923
487 *"Time has dealt"*: GBG to H. J. Moberley, October 23, 1923, GBGP
488 *"one could [still] visualize"*: GBGD, September 14, 1924
488 *"covered with derricks"*: GBGD, September 15, 1924
488 *"On the whole"*: GBGD, September 23, 1924
489 *"We [must] tackle"*: GBG to W. M. Camp, October 2, 1924, GBGP
489 *"The stuff seems to me good"*: GBGD, September 27, 1924
489 *"I have worked over"*: GBG to Charles Scribner's Sons, February 3, 1925, GBGP
489 *"Probably if [the] story"*: GBG to A. E. Sheldon, November 2, 1925, GBGP
490 *"The natural things"*: GBG, "American Game Protection," in GBG and Sheldon, eds., *Hunting and Conservation*, 252
491 *"slaughter pens"*: Trefethen, *Crusade for Wildlife*, 257
491 *"anything but an outdoor"*: GBG to T. Gilbert Pearson, July 29, 1924, GBGP
491 *"Bad experience"*: GBG to Redmond Cross, July 1, 1920, GBGP
491 *"I have been working"*: GBG to William T. Hornaday, August 6, 1920, GBGP
492 *"Your letter was a hostile"*: William T. Hornaday to GBG, August 9, 1920, William T. Hornaday and W. Reid Blair, incoming correspondence and subject files, 1895–1940, Collection 1001, Wildlife Conservation Society Archives
492 *mostly women and children*: GBG to Thomas Riggs, Jr., March 9, 1920, GBGP
492 *"There is one class"*: GBG to Henry C. Wallace, July 16, 1924, GBGP
493 *found their passage impeded*: Trefethen, *Crusade for Wildlife*, 231
493 *"If the elk increase"*: GBG to Charles Sheldon, January 27, 1920, GBGP
493 *"[T]he elk must be kept"*: GBG to Edward W. Nelson, February 3, 1920, GBGP
494 *"the man to whom"*: *New York Times*, n.d., news clipping, GBGP
494 *"Mr. Grinnell"*: *Washington Star*, May 16, 1925, news clipping, GBGP
495 *"I went to Washington"*: GBG to Luther North, June 2, 1925, GBGP
495 *"It seems to me"*: GBG to R. S. Ellison, June 3, 1925, GBGP
495 *"I am glad to have"*: *Washington Star*, May 16, 1925, news clipping, GBGP

CHAPTER 34: MELTING RAPIDLY

496 *"About 22 or 25"*: GBG to Edward Judson, May 26, 1925, GBGP
497 *"Matter such as this"*: GBG to Mrs. Walter M. Camp, September 15, 1925, GBGP
497 *"My place is still"*: GBGD, August 11, 1925
497 *"numberless ducks"*: GBGD, August 13–14, 1925
498 *"You know we are now"*: T. E. Hofer to GBG, December 6, 1915, GBGP
498 *"I'm getting so I don't"*: T. E. Hofer to GBG, February 27 1914
498 *"It was raining"*: GBGD, August 24, 1925
498 *"It seems a shame"*: GBGD, August 29, 1925
500 *"The show was not"*: GBGD, June 25, 1926
500 *"The celebration was not"*: GBG to Frank M. Lockard, July 27, 1926, GBGP
501 *"Mr. Gould, believed"*: (Santa Barbara) *Morning Press*, January 26, 1926
502 *According to Morton Elrod*: Morton J. Elrod, "Report of the Park Naturalist, Glacier National Park, 1926," GBGP
502 *"All these glaciers"*: GBGD, July 14, 1926
502 *"It is a very shocking"*: GBG to Luther North, December 27, 1926, GBGP

503 *"We do not recuperate"*: GBG to Luther North, January 3, 1927, GBGP

503 *"[North] is one"*: GBG to Arthur H. Clark, November 24, 1926, GBGP

503 *"As I have probably"*: GBG to Luther North, December 27, 1926, GBGP

503 *"Captain L. H. North"*: GBG to Arthur H. Clark, June 17, 1926, GBGP

504 *"[E]ach one had a copy"*: GBG to R. S. Ellison, March 17, 1926, GBGP

504 *"They were all studying"*: GBGD, July 21, 1927

504 *"Sorry to lose him"*: GBGD, July 22, 1927

504 *"Travel last year"*: GBGD, July 27, 1927

505 *"Jack Monroe has told"*: GBGD, August 2, 1927

505 *"I have always felt"*: GBG to Kermit Roosevelt, January 6, 1928, GBGP

505 *"I paid close attention"*: GBG to John B. Burnham, March 15, 1929, GBGP

506 *"in memory of"*: GBG, Will, June 3, 1927, photocopy in Glacier National Park Archives

506 *"I may disappear"*: GBG to W. Redmond Cross, May 7, 1928, GBGP

506 *"I am not very enthusiastic"*: GBG to Madison Grant, April 30, 1928, GBGP

506 *"Elizabeth very generously"*: GBG to Mrs. Newell (Laura) Martin, July 3, 1928, GBGP

506 *"I have no particular"*: GBG to T. E. Hofer, July 11, 1928, GBGP

507 *"California is a pleasant"*: GBG to J. B. Monroe, September 19, 1928, GBGP

507 *"Those of us who were"*: GBG to C. H. Townsend, October 4, 1928, GBGP

507 *"He entered Yale"*: [GBG], obituary of Charles Sheldon, February 8, 1929, typescript, GBGP

507 *"I do not suppose"*: GBG to Robert Sterling Yard, October 5, 1928, GBGP

507 *"[Sheldon] was a very"*: GBG to Gilbert Pearson, November 16, 1928, GBGP

508 *"If you credit Sheldon's"*: GBG to A. K. Fisher, November 7, 1928, GBGP

508 *"As the years go by"*: GBG to Lewis Hicks, October 26, 1928, GBGP

508 *"He was just my"*: GBG to Luther North, December 24, 1928, GBGP

508 *"a short, sloped-shouldered"*: GBG to Robert Bruce, January 2, 1929, GBGP

509 *"The North Brothers"*: GBG, *Two Great Scouts*, 18

509 *"Of course, there may"*: GBG to Luther North, January 22, 1929

509 *"Am still very weak"*: Luther North to GBG, January 11, 1929, Luther H. North Papers, History Nebraska

509 *"I have read the book"*: Luther North to GBG, January 27, 1929, Luther H. North Papers, History Nebraska

510 *"I have had lately"*: GBG to Luther North, February 13, 1929, GBGP

510 *"They are both"*: GBG to Mrs. Newell Martin, February 19, 1929, GBGP

510 *"much shorter than those"*: GBG to T. E. Hofer, May 7, 1929, GBGP

510 *"I am getting a little"*: GBG to J. B. Monroe, June 20, 1929, GBGP

510 *"There is really nothing"*: GBG to Helen Page, June 12, 1929, GBGP

510 *"Last night Elizabeth"*: GBG to Laura Page, June 12, 1929, GBGP

511 *"in good order"*: GBG to Helen Page, May 23, 1929, GBGP

511 *"devoted to the killing"*: GBG to Henry Bannon, February 13, 1929, GBGP

511 *"I shall probably be"*: GBG to Madison Grant, March 15, 1928, GBGP

511 *"Of course, at our"*: GBG to James Russell, July 12, 1929, GBGP

511 *"[T]here was danger"*: [George Sheetz] to Robert Sterling Yard, August 14 1929, GBGP

512 *"I have not been out"*: GBG to Luther North, September 6, 1929, GBGP

512 *"My legs immediately"*: GBG to Edward S. Dana, September 9, 1929, GBGP

512 *"I have outlived most"*: GBG to R. N. Wilson, September 30, 1929, GBGP

CHAPTER 35: A STRONG STRAND

514 *"this spare gray figure"*: Columbus [Nebraska] *Daily Telegram*, September 27, 1920; news clipping, Luther H. North Papers, History Nebraska

514 *"Mr. Grinnell, perhaps"*: Grant, *Early History of Glacier National Park*, 5–6

514 *"Naturalist . . . Founder"*: *New York Times*, April 12, 1938

514 *"The passing of Dr. Grinnell"*: *New York Herald Tribune*, April 17, 1938

515 *"It is rare to see"*: "Elizabeth Grinnell," *Arts Digest*, 25

516 *"They found her"*: Newell H. Foster, Memorandum, June 19, 1956, Glacier National Park Archives

EPILOGUE: DO MORE GOOD

518 *"One could wish"*: Mari Sandoz, "Introduction" to GBG, *The Cheyenne Indians: Their History and Ways of Life*, xiii

518 *"To all who are interested"*: Mary Austin, review of *By Cheyenne Campfires*, in *Saturday Review of Literature*, November 1, 1920, copy in Selected Papers of GBG from Southwest Museum, University of Montana

518 *"I have a feeling that"*: GBG to Charles Gould, November 1, 1920, GBGP

BIBLIOGRAPHY

ABBREVIATIONS

AA   *American Anthropologist*
F&S   *Forest and Stream*
GBG   George Bird Grinnell
MMWH   *Montana: The Magazine of Western History*

CHRONOLOGY OF WRITINGS BY GEORGE BIRD GRINNELL

(Unsigned articles published in F&S not included)

Ornis, "Elk Hunting in Nebraska," F&S (October 2, 1873)
Ornis, "A Day with the Sage Grouse," F&S (November 6, 1873)
Ornis, "The Green River Country," F&S (November 13, 1873)
Ornis, "Buffalo Hunt with the Pawnees," F&S (December 25, 1873)
GBG and Edward S. Dana, "On a New Tertiary Lake Basin," *American Journal of Science and Arts* (February 1876), 126–128
"On a New Crinoid from the Cretaceous Formation of the West," *American Journal of Science and Arts* (July 1876), 81–83
"Notice of a New Genus of Annelids from the Lower Silurian," *American Journal of Science and Arts* (September 1877), 229–230
"The Ground Dove (*Chaamoepeleia passerina*) in New York," *Bulletin of the Nuttall Ornithological Club* (July 1878), 147
"Sketch of Professor Marsh," *Popular Science Monthly* (September 1878), 612–617
Yo, "A Trip to North Park," F&S (9 installments, beginning September 4, 1879)
"Review of Professor Marsh's Monograph on the *Odontornithes*, or Toothed Birds of North America," *American Journal of Science and Arts* (April 1881), 255–276

Yo, "Bye-Ways of the Northwest," F&S (10 installments, beginning June 14, 1881)

"Snipe-Shooting," *Century* (October 1883), 921–925

Yo, "A Band of Bears," F&S (December 27, 1883)

"Through Two-Ocean Pass," F&S (15 installments, beginning January 29, 1885)

Yo, "Indians at Work," F&S (October 22, 1885)

Yo, "To the Walled-In Lakes," F&S (15 installments, beginning December 10, 1885)

Yo, "The Diamond Hitch," F&S (June 23, 1887)

"The Character of John James Audubon," *Audubon Magazine* (October 1887), 195–197

Yo, "The Rock Climbers," F&S (18 installments, beginning December 29, 1887)

Yo, "The Misfortunes of Pani Puk' Koats," F&S (December 6, 1888)

Yo, "After Stolen Horses," F&S (January 10, 1889)

"The Fur Fisheries of the Northwest Seas," F&S (6 installments, beginning June 13, 1889)

Pawnee Hero Stories and Folk-Tales (1889)

"The Dun Horse," F&S (November 28, 1889)

Yo and H. G. Dulog, "Slide Rock from Many Mountains," F&S (20 installments, beginning January 2, 1890)

"Two Pawnian Tribal Names," AA (April 1891), 197–199

"Marriage Among the Pawnees," AA (July 1891), 275–281

"The Young Dog's Dance," *Journal of American Folk-Lore* (October-December 1891), 307–313

"Early Blackfoot History," AA (April 1892), 153–164

"Chief Mountain Lakes: Disagreement as to Location," *Science* (August 12, 1892), 85

"The Last of the Buffalo," *Scribner's* (September 1892), 267–286; excerpt, "The Indians' Buffalo Piskun," F&S (September 29, 1892)

Blackfoot Lodge Tales: The Story of a Prairie People (1892)

Theodore Roosevelt and GBG, eds., *American Big-Game Hunting* (1893)

"In Buffalo Days," in Theodore Roosevelt and GBG, eds., *American Big-Game Hunting* (1893), 155–211

"Climbing for White Goats," *Scribner's* (May 1894), 643–648

"Western Big Game Preserves," *Harper's Weekly* (February 23, 1895), 190

Theodore Roosevelt and GBG, eds., *Hunting in Many Lands: The Book of the Boone and Crockett Club* (1895)

The Story of the Indian (1895)

"Charley Reynolds," F&S (December 26, 1896)

"The Return of the War Party; A Reminiscence of Charley Reynolds," F&S (January 30, 1897)

Review of *The Ghost-Dance Religion*, AA (July 1897), 230–233

"Alpine Climbing in America," *Harper's Weekly* (October 2, 1897), 979–980

"The Native American Hunter," F&S (7 installments, beginning October 9, 1897)

Theodore Roosevelt and GBG, eds., *Trail and Camp-Fire* (1897)

"Wolves and Wolf Nature," in *Trail and Camp-Fire* (1897), 152–203

"A Berry Picker," in *Trail and Camp-Fire* (1897), 223–225

"Climbing Blackfoot," F&S (October 8, 1898)

"The Wild Indian," *Atlantic Monthly* (January 1899), 20–29

"The Butterfly and the Spider Among the Blackfeet," AA (January 1899), 194–196

"The Indian on the Reservation," *Atlantic Monthly* (February 1899), 255–267

"The North American Indian of To-day," *Cosmopolitan* (March 1899), 537–548

"Some Indian Natural History Comments," F&S (May 6, 1899)

Jack the Young Ranchman (1899)

Yo, "Glimpses of Canvasbacks," F&S (January 20, 1900)

"The Harriman Alaska Expedition," F&S (14 installments, beginning February 24, 1900)
"Eskimo," F&S (June 2, 1900)
The Indians of To-day (1900)
Jack Among the Indians (1900)
"Punishment of the Stingy," *Harper's Monthly* (August 1900), 323–328
"Present Distribution of Big Game in America," *Outing* (December 1900), 250–259
Yo, "The Old West," F&S (April 27, 1901)
The Punishment of the Stingy and Other Indian Stories (1901)
American Duck Shooting (1901)
"Girl Who Was the Ring," *Harper's Magazine* (February 1901), 425–430
"The Crown of the Continent," *Century* (September 1901), 660–672
"The Lodges of the Blackfeet," AA (October–December 1901), 650–668
"Cheyenne Woman Customs," AA (January–March 1902), 13–16
"The Natives of the Alaska Coast Region," in John Burroughs, John Muir, GBG, eds.,
    Harriman Alaska Series I: *Narrative, Glaciers, Natives* (1902), 137–183
"The Salmon Industry," in William H. Dall, Charles Keeler et al., *Harriman Alaska
    Series* II: *History, Geography, Resources* (1902), 337–355
"Notes on Some Cheyenne Songs," AA (April–June 1903), 312–322
"Cheyenne Songs," AA (July–September 1903), 582–583
"The Indians and the Outing System," *Outlook* (September 19, 1903), 167–173
"Antelope Hunting Thirty Years Ago and To-day," *Outing* (November 1903), 195–204
"The Lodges of the Blackfeet, F&S (November 14, 1903)
"President Roosevelt as a Sportsman," F&S (December 5, 1903)
"Trails of the Pathfinders," F&S (34 installments, beginning February 27, 1904)
"The Cheyenne Medicine Lodge," AA (April–June 1904), 245–256
Jack in the Rockies (1904)
GBG, ed., *American Big Game in Its Haunts* (1904)
"The Mountain Sheep and Its Range," in *American Big Game in Its Haunts* (1904),
    270–348
"Some Cheyenne Plant Medicines," AA (January–March 1905), 37–43
"Portraits of Indian Types," *Scribner's* (March 1905), 259–273
"The Great Fight with the Kiowas and Comanches," F&S (March 18, 1905)
"Social Organization of the Cheyennes," *International Congress of Americanists, Thir-
    teenth Session Held in New York in 1902* (1905), 135–146
"Theodore Roosevelt as a Sportsman," *Country Calendar* (November 1905), 623–626, 666
"Cheyenne Stream Names," AA (January–March 1906), 15–22
Jack the Young Canoeman (1906)
"Tenure of Land among the Indians," AA (January–March 1907), 1–11
"Buffalo Memorials," F&S (February 16, March 2, and March 9, 1907)
"Horses," in Frederick Webb Hodge, ed., *Handbook of American Indians North of Mex-
    ico*, Part 1 (1907), 569–571
Jack the Young Trapper (1907)
"The Horse and the Indian," F&S (June 22, 1907)
"Some Early Cheyenne Tales," *Journal of American Folk-Lore* (July–September 1907),
    169–194
"Primitive Bows and Their Uses," F&S (November 23, 1907)
"A Bloodless Coup, F&S (March 28, 1908)
"Wild Horses and the Indians," F&S (3 installments, beginning August 8,1908)
"Indian Camp-Fire Tales, F&S (3 installments, beginning September 19, 1908)
"A Generous Leader," F&S (October 3, 1908)

"Some Early Cheyenne Tales II," *Journal of American Folk-Lore* (October–December 1908), 269–320

"A Fur Trader of the North," F&S (December 12, 1908)

"The Fleetness of Crow Chief," F&S (December 26, 1908)

Jack the Young Explorer: A Boy's Experiences in the Unknown Northwest (1908)

"An Old Story of Astoria," F&S (January 23, 1909)

Ornis, "With Goats and Sheep in British Columbia," F&S (4 installments, beginning April 10, 1909)

Yo, "Was I Lost or Not?" F&S (November 13, 1909)

"When Beaver Skins Were Money," F&S (4 installments, beginning January 1, 1910)

Oldster, "With the Ducks on Currituck Sound," F&S (February 19, 1910)

"Winter War Stories," F&S (February 26 and March 5, 1910)

American Game-Bird Shooting (1910)

"Coup and Scalp Among the Plains Indians," AA (April–June 1910), 296–310

"Othniel Charles Marsh," in David Starr Jordan, ed., *Leading American Men of Science* (1910), 283–312

"Great Mysteries of the Cheyenne," AA (October–December 1910), 542–575

"Roosevelt in Africa," *Review of Reviews* (October 1910), 457–461

Brief History of the Boone and Crockett Club, 1910

"A Peculiar People," F&S (June 18, 1910)

"Unusual Antelope Horns," F&S (August 13, 1910)

"A Boy in Indian Camps," F&S (December 3, 1910)

"Lands of the Antarctic," F&S (June 17, 1911)

"When Antelope Were Plenty," F&S (October 14, 1911)

Trails of the Pathfinders (1911)

"Ruffed Grouse," *Bird-Lore* 15 (January 1913), 63–66

"Some Indian Stream Names," AA (April–June 1913), 327–331

Beyond the Old Frontier (1913)

Blackfeet Indian Stories (1913)

Jack the Young Cowboy (1913)

GBG, ed., *Hunting at High Altitudes* (1913)

"Notes on Memories of a Bear Hunter," in *Hunting at High Altitudes* (1913), 242–294

"Brief History of the Boone and Crockett Club," in *Hunting at High Altitudes* (1913), 435–491

The Wolf Hunters: A Story of the Buffalo Plains; Edited and Arranged from the Manuscript Account of Robert M. Peck (1914)

"The Cheyenne Medicine Lodge," AA (April–June 1914), 245–256

"Death of General Anderson," F&S (April 1915)

The Fighting Cheyennes (1915)

"Memoirs," typescript, 1915, GBG Papers, Special Collections, Sterling Memorial Library, Yale

"Some Adventures of Sweet Root," *The Teepee Book*, January 1916, 3–17

"What We May Learn from the Indians," F&S (March 1916)

"Some Audubon Letters," *Auk* 33 (April 1916), 119–120

"Communication," *American Historical Review* (July 1916), 866–867

Audubon Park: The History of the Site of the Hispanic Society of America and Neighbouring Institutions (1927)

"Indian Trap Pits on the Missouri," AA (January–March 1917), 148

"The Mt. McKinley National Park," F&S (April 1917)

"Recollections of the Old West: Appreciation of the Historical Canvas of Indian and Pioneer American Life Painted by William de la Montagne Cary," *American Museum Journal* (May 1917), 332–340

"What About the Yellowstone Elk?" F&S (June 1918)

"Early Cheyenne Villages," AA (October–December 1918), 359–380

"A Buffalo Sweatlodge," AA (October–December 1919), 361–375

"A Chapter of History and Natural History in Old New York," *Natural History* (January–February 1920), 23–27

When Buffalo Ran (1920)

"Recollections of Audubon Park," *Auk* (July 1920), 372–380

"Who Were the Padouca?" AA (July–September 1920), 248–260

"As to the Wolverine," *Journal of Mammalogy* (August 1920), 182–184

"Falling Star," *Journal of American Folk-Lore* (July–September 1921), 308–315

"The Medicine Wheel," AA (July–September 1922), 299–310

"An Old-Time Bone Hunt," *Natural History* (1923), 330

"Bent's Old Fort and Its Builders," *Kansas State Historical Society Collections* 15 (1923)

The Cheyenne Indians: Their History and Ways of Life, 2 vols. (1923)

"Introduction" to *The Works of Theodore Roosevelt*, Memorial Edition, Vol. 1 (Scribner, 1923), xiii–xxviii

"Starving Deer of the Kaibab Forest," *Outlook* (January 30, 1924), 186–187

"Old-Time Range of Virginia Deer, Moose and Elk," *Natural History* (1925), 136–143

GBG and Charles Sheldon, eds., *Hunting and Conservation: The Book of the Boone and Crockett Club* (1925)

"American Game Protection," in *Hunting and Conservation* (1925), 201–257

"The American Bison in 1924," in *Hunting and Conservation* (1925), 356–411

"The National Recreation Conference," in *Hunting and Conservation* (1925), 471–491

By Cheyenne Campfires (1926)

"Some Habits of the Wolverine," *Journal of Mammalogy* (February 1926), 30–34

Audubon Park: The History of the Site of the Hispanic Society of America and Neighboring Institutions (1927)

"Mountain Sheep," *Journal of Mammalogy* (February 1928), 1–9

Two Great Scouts and Their Pawnee Battalion (1928)

"Billy Jackson's Tobacco Trade," *Boy's Life* (January 1929), 11, 32

"Pronghorn Antelope," *Journal of Mammalogy* (May 1929), 135–141

"An Extinct Beast," review of E. Douglas Branch, *The Hunting of the Buffalo, Saturday Review of Literature* (July 20, 1929), 1193

"The King of the Mountains and How It Beckoned Explorers to the Country That Is Now Glacier National Park," *American Forests and Forest Life* (August 1929), 487–493

"Preface," in GBG et al., eds., *Hunting Trails on Three Continents* (1933), vii–xi

"A Letter from Mr. Grinnell," *Bird-Lore* (January–February 1934), 84–85

"A White Blackfoot," *Masterkey for Indian Lore and History* (October–December 1972), 143–151; (January–March 1973), 12–22

GENERAL SOURCES

Dan Aadland, *Women and Warriors of the Plains: The Pioneer Photography of Julia E. Tuell* (1996)

Horace M. Albright, *The Birth of the National Park Service: The Founding Years, 1913–33* (1985)

J. A. Allen, "The North American Bison and Its Extermination," *Penn Monthly*, March 1876, 214–224

J. A. Allen, "The Present Wholesale Destruction of Bird-Life in the United States," *Science* (Supplement, February 26, 1886), 191–195

Robert P. Allen, "The Wild-Life Sanctuary Movement in the United States; Part I: Historical Aspects," *Bird-Lore* (January–February 1934), 80–84

Roger J. Anderson and David Harmon, eds., *Yellowstone Lake: Hotbed of Chaos or Reservoir of Resilience?* Proceedings of the 6th Biennial Scientific Conference on the Greater Yellowstone Ecosystem (2002)

Walter B. Anderson [James Willard Schultz], "In the Lodges of the Blackfeet," F&S (34 installments, beginning November 25, 1905)

Ralph A. Andrews, *Curtis' Western Indians* (1962)

Archives of Traditional Music, Indiana University, "Montana, Northern Cheyenne Indians, George Bird Grinnell, 1897–1898," digital audio file of wax-cylinder recordings by GBG, Accession No. 54–104-F

Archives of Traditional Music, Indiana University, "Montana, Piegan Agency, Blackfoot Indians, George Bird Grinnell, 1897," digital audio files of wax-cylinder recordings by GBG, Accession No. 54–095-F

Stanley Clisby Arthur, *Audubon: An Intimate Life of the American Woodsman* (1937)

[Lucy Bakewell Audubon], *The Life of John James Audubon, the Naturalist, Edited by His Widow* (1869)

Maria R. Audubon, ed., *Audubon and His Journals*, vol. 2 (1897, reprint 1960)

Christopher S. Ashby, "The Blackfeet Agreement of 1895 and Glacier National Park: A Case History," master's thesis, University of Montana, 1985

Lyman Hotchkiss Bagg, *Four Years at Yale by a Graduate of '69* (1871)

Shawn Patrick Bailey, "Colonization of the Crown: Hunting, Class, and the Creation of Glacier National Park, 1885–1915," master's thesis, University of Montana, 2009

Stuart Banner, *How the Indians Lost Their Land: Law and Power on the Frontier* (2005)

Eric Baratay and Elisabeth Hardouin-Fugier, *Zoo: A History of Zoological Gardens in the West* (2002)

Jeff Barnes, *Forts of the Northern Plains* (2008)

Mark V. Barrow, Jr., *A Passion for Birds: American Ornithology after Audubon* (1998)

Glen Barrett, "Stock Raising in the Shirley Basin," *Journal of the West* (July 1973)

Richard A. Bartlett, "The Senator Who Saved Yellowstone Park," (Denver) *Westerners Brand Book* (1969), 49–52, 66

Richard A. Bartlett, *Yellowstone: A Wilderness Besieged* (1985)

Larry Barsness, *Head, Hide & Horns: The Compleat Buffalo Book* (1985)

Seward Beacom, *The Colonel from Yellow Creek* (1999)

Ralph L. Beals, *History of Glacier National Park with Particular Emphasis on the Northern Developments* (1935)

Gail Bederman, *Manliness and Civilization: A Cultural History of Gender and Race in the United States, 1880–1917* (1995)

Stefan Bechtel, *Mr. Hornaday's War: How a Peculiar Victorian Zookeeper Waged a Lonely Crusade for Wildlife That Changed the World* (2012)

Charles Beecher, "Othniel Charles Marsh," *Journal of American Science* (June 1899), 402–428

Jacquelin Beidl, "The Blackfeet and the Badger-Two Medicine: An Evaluation of Potential Traditional Cultural Significance Drawn from Archival Sources," January 1992, typescript, Ruhle Library, Glacier National Park

William Benemann, *Men in Eden: William Drummond Stewart and Same-Sex Desire in the Rocky Mountain Fur Trade* (2012)

George Bent, "Forty Years with the Cheyennes," *Frontier* (October, November, December 1905; January, February, March 1906)

Robert F. Berkhofer, Jr., *The White Man's Indian: Images of the American Indian from Columbus to the Present* (1978)

Iver Bernstein, *The New York City Draft Riots: Their Significance for American Society and Politics in the Age of the Civil War* (1990)

Donald J. Berthrong, *The Cheyenne and Arapaho Ordeal: Reservation and Agency Life in the Indian Territory, 1875–1907* (1976)

Donald J. Berthrong, *The Southern Cheyennes* (1963)

Charles Wyllys Betts, "The Yale College Expedition of 1870," *Harper's New Monthly Magazine* (June–November 1871), 663–671

J. R. Betts, "Sporting Journalism in Nineteenth-Century America," *American Quarterly* (Spring 1953), 39–56

Robert E. Bieder, *Science Encounters the Indian, 1820–1880: The Early Years of American Ethnology* (1986)

Edwin R. Bingham, *Charles F. Lummis: Editor of the Southwest* (1955)

Theodore Binnema, *Common and Contested Ground: A Human and Environmental History of the Northwestern Plains* (2001)

Franz Boas, *The Shaping of American Anthropology, 1883–1911: A Franz Boas Reader* (1974)

Christine Bold, *The Frontier Club: Popular Westerns and Cultural Power, 1880–1924* (2013)

John G. Bourke, "Mackenzie's Last Fight with the Cheyennes," *Journal of the Military Institution* (November-December 1913), 343–385

Phillips Verner Bradford and Harvey Blume: *Ota Benga: The Pygmy in the Zoo* (1992)

Brent H. Breithaupt, "Biography of William Harlow Reed: The Story of a Frontier Fossil Collector," *Earth Science Quarterly* (1990), 6–13

William Bridges, *Gathering of Animals: An Unconventional History of the New York Zoological Society* (1974)

Douglas Brinkley, *The Quiet World: Saving Alaska's Wilderness Kingdom, 1879–1960* (2011)

Douglas Brinkley, *The Wilderness Warrior: Theodore Roosevelt and the Crusade for America* (2009)

George Bristol, *Glacier National Park: A Culmination of Giants* (2017)

Sarah E. Broadbent, "Sportsmen and the Evolution of the Conservation Idea in Yellowstone: 1882–1894," master's thesis, Montana State University, 1997

Robert Bruce, *The Fighting Norths and Pawnee Scouts: Narratives and Reminiscences of Military Service on the Old Frontier* (1932)

William L. Bryan, Jr., *Montana's Indians: Yesterday and Today* (2nd edition, 1996)

Curtis W. Buchholtz, *Man in Glacier* (1976)

C. W. Buchholtz, "The National Park as Playground," *Journal of Sport History* (Winter 1978), 21–36

Philip Burnham, *Indian Country, God's Country: Native Americans and the National Parks* (2000)

John Burroughs, *Camping and Tramping with Roosevelt* (1905)

John Burroughs, "Imagination in Natural History: A Letter from John Burroughs on the Roosevelt-Long Controversy; and a Reply," *Outlook* (June 29, 1907), 457–460

John Burroughs, "Narrative of the Expedition," in Burroughs, John Muir, and GBG, eds., *Harriman Alaska Series* I: *Narrative Glaciers, Natives* (1902), 1–118

John Burroughs, "On Humanizing the Animals," *Century* (March 1904), 773–780

John Burroughs, "Real and Sham Natural History," *Atlantic Monthly* (March 1903), 298–309

Polly Burroughs, "George Bird Grinnell, Pioneer Conservationist," in *George Bird Grinnell, Alaska 1899: Essays from the Harriman Expedition* (1995), xii–xxxv

Edwin G. Burrows and Mike Wallace, *Gotham: A History of New York City to 1898* (1999)

Jenks Cameron, *The Bureau of Biological Survey: Its History, Activities, and Organizations* (1929), 21–27

Stephen R. Capps, "A Game Country Like No Other: The Proposed Mount McKinley National Park," *National Geographic* (January 1917), 69–84

Theodore W. Cart, "The Lacey Act: America's First Nationwide Wildlife Statute," *Forest History* (October 1973), 4–13

George Catlin, *Lectures and Notes on the Manners, Customs and Conditions of the North American Indians*, 2 vols. (1844, reprint 1973)

L. W. Chaney, Jr., "A Glacier in the Montana Rockies," *Science* (December 13, 1895), 792–796

Frank M. Chapman, *Autobiography of a Bird-Lover* (1933)

Frank M. Chapman, "Birds and Bonnets," F&S (February 25, 1886), 84

C. Walter Chessman, *Governor Theodore Roosevelt: The Albany Apprenticeship, 1898–1900* (1965)

Hiram Chittenden, *The Yellowstone National Park* (1895, reprint 1964)

Blue Clark, *Lone Wolf v. Hitchcock: Treaty Rights and Indian Law at the End of the Nineteenth Century* (1999)

Edward B. Clark, "Real Naturalists on Nature Faking," *Everybody's* (September–October 1907), 423–427

Edward B. Clark, "Roosevelt on the Nature Fakirs," *Everybody's* (June 1907), 770–774

J. S. Clark, "A Pawnee Buffalo Hunt," *Chronicles of Oklahoma* (December 1942), 387–395

Douglas Coffman, *Reflecting the Sublime: The Rebirth of an American Icon* (2013)

Douglas Coffman, "William Hornaday's Bitter Mission: The Mysterious Journey of the Last Buffalo," *Montana Magazine* (February 1991), 58–71

Michael Cohen, *The Pathless Way: John Muir and American Wilderness* (1984)

Michael L. Collins, *That Damned Cowboy: Theodore Roosevelt and the American West, 1883–1898* (1989)

Steven Conn, *History's Shadow: Native Americans and Historical Consciousness in the Nineteenth Century* (2004)

Evan S. Connell, *Son of the Morning Star* (1984)

William E. Connelly, review of *Two Great Scouts and the Pawnee Battalion*, *Mississippi Valley Historical Review* (December 1929), 426–428

Richard Conniff, *House of Lost Worlds: Dinosaurs, Dynasties & the Story of Life on Earth* (2016)

Rebecca Conrad, "John F. Lacey: Conservation's Public Servant," in David Harman et al., eds., *The Antiquities Act: A Century of American Archaeology, Historic Preservation, and Nature Conservation* (2006), 48–63

James Fenimore Cooper, *The Prairie* (1827, reprint 1987)

Herbert V. Coryell, "James Willard Schultz: He Made the Indians' Ways and Tales His Own," *St. Nicholas* (August 1929), 815, 850

Elliott Coues, "Charles Hallock," *Osprey* 3 (April 1899), 117–118

Margaret Curry, *The History of Platte County, Nebraska* (1950)

Edward S. Curtis, "As It Was," manuscript, Special Collections, University of Washington

Edward S. Curtis, letters to Harriet Leitch, Edward S. Curtis Digital Collection, Seattle Public Library

Edward S. Curtis, *The North American Indians: The Complete Portfolios* (1997)

Edward S. Curtis, "The Rush to the Klondike over the Mountain Pass," *Century* (March 1898), 692–697

Edward S. Curtis, *A Souvenir of the Harriman Alaska Expedition: May–August, 1899*, portfolio, 2 vols., Harry Ransom Center, University of Texas at Austin

Elizabeth B. Custer, *Boots and Saddles; Or, Life in Dakota with General Custer* (1885, reprint 1961)

Paul Russell Cutright, *Theodore Roosevelt: The Making of a Conservationist* (1985)

Paul Russell Cutright, *Theodore Roosevelt: The Naturalist* (1956)

Donald F. Danker, ed., "The Journal of an Indian Fighter: The 1869 Diary of Frank J. North," *Nebraska History* (June 1958), 87–177

Donald F. Danker, ed., *Man of the Plains: Recollections of Luther North, 1856–1882* (1961)

Kathleen Dalton, *Theodore Roosevelt: A Strenuous Life* (2002)

Jane Pierce Davidson, *The Bone Sharp: The Life of Edward Drinker Cope* (1997)

Gregory J. Dehler, *The Most Defiant Devil: William Temple Hornaday & His Controversial Crusade to Save American Wildlife* (2013)

Carolyn E. Delatte, *Lucy Audubon: A Biography* (1982)

Hugh A. Dempsey, *The Amazing Death of Calf Shirt and Other Blackfoot Stories: Three Hundred Years of Blackfoot History* (1994, reprint 1996)

Hugh A. Dempsey, *The Great Blackfoot Treaties* (2015)

George M. Dennison, *Montana's Pioneer Naturalist: Morton J. Elrod* (2016)

Jerome DeSanto, "Drilling in Kintla Lake: Montana's First Oil Well," MMWH (Winter 1985), 24–37

Maitland C. De Sormo, *John Bird Burnham: Klondiker, Adirondacker and Eminent Conservationist* (1978)

Brian W. Dippie, *The Vanishing American: White Attitudes and U.S. Indian Policy* (1982)

Christine Diehl-Taylor, "Passengers, Profits, and Prestige: The Glacier Park Hotel Company, 1914–1929," MMWH (Summer 1997), 26–43

G. M. Dillard, "A Rocky Mountain Goat-Hunt," *Outing* (October 1894), 41–43

Robert W. Doughty, *Feather Fashions and Bird Preservation: A Study in Nature Protection* (1975)

Ray Djuff and Chris Morrison, *View with a Room: Glacier's Historic Hotels and Chalets* (2001)

H. G. Dulog, "The Angel of the Guard," F&S (September 11 and 18, 1897)

H. G. Dulog, "The Bull Fight," F&S (October 29, 1885)

H. G. Dulog, "Friendly Screech Owls," letter to editor, F&S (October 10, 1908)

H. G. Dulog, "The Island of Marquez," F&S (April 23 and 30, 1898)

H. G. Dulog, "Jim McLane's Bay Pony," F&S (December 31, 1891)

H. G. Dulog, "Santa Barbara in Spring," F&S (May 21, 1885)

H. G. Dulog, "Some Old Indian Songs" F&S (July 7, 1887)

H. G. Dulog, "The Story of a Stump," F&S (December 5, 1903)

H. G. Dulog, "A Trip to Wyoming," F&S (November 10, 1892)

John B. Dunbar, "The Pawnee Lands" and "The Pawnee Indians; Their Habits and Customs," *Magazine of American History* (November 1880) 343–345

Thomas W. Dunlay, *Wolves for the Blue Soldiers: Indian Scouts and Auxiliaries with the United States Army, 1860–1890* (1982)

J. P. Dunn, review of *When Buffalo Ran*, *Mississippi Valley Historical Review* (March 1921), 409

Verne Dusenberry, "An Appreciation of James Willard Schultz," MMWH (October 1960), 22–23

William Dutcher, "History of the Audubon Movement," *Bird-Lore* (January–February 1905), 43–53

Paul Dyck, "Lone Wolf Returns to the Soil of His Indian Forebears," MMWH (Winter 1972), 18–41

Charles Eastman, *Indian Boyhood* (1902)

Zelda Edelson, "The Ordeal of the Peabody Museum; The Struggle for a Building, 1882–1925," *Discovery* (1979), 30–39

Timothy Egan, *Short Nights of the Shadow Catcher: The Epic Life and Immortal Photographs of Edward Curtis* (2012)

Loren Eiseley, *Darwin's Century: Evolution and the Men Who Discovered It* (1958)

"Elizabeth Grinnell," *Arts Digest* (December 15, 1954), 25

"End of Romance," *Bismarck Daily Tribune*, August 28, 1902

John C. Ewers, *The Blackfeet: Raiders of the Northwestern Plains* (1958)

John C. Ewers, *The Horse in Blackfoot Indian Culture* (1955)

John C. Ewers, *Indian Life on the Upper Missouri* (1968)

Lincoln B. Faller and George Bent, "Making Medicine against 'White Man's Side of Story': George Bent's Letters to George Hyde," *American Indian Quarterly* (Winter 2000), 64–90

William E. Farr, *Blackfoot Redemption: A Blood Indian's Story of Murder, Confinement, and Imperfect Justice* (2012)

William E. Farr, "A Point of Entry: The Blackfeet Adoption of Walter McClintock," in Steven L. Grafe, ed., *Lanterns on the Prairie: The Blackfeet Photographs of Walter McClintock* (2009), 43–81

William E. Farr, *The Reservation Blackfeet, 1882–1945: A Photographic History of Cultural Survival* (1984)

"Fete Columbus Plainsman on 88th Birthday," Columbus (Nebraska) *Daily Telegram*, March 7, 1939

Final Report on Custer's 1874 Black Hills Expedition (1875)

"The First National Parks," *American Forestry* (February 1910), 118–119

Albert Kenrick Fisher, "In Memoriam: George Bird Grinnell, *Auk* (January 1939), 1–12

Turbesé Lummis Fiske and Keith Lummis, *Charles F. Lummis: The Man and His West* (1975)

Dan Flores, *American Serengeti: The Last Big Animals of the Great Plains* (2016)

Michael F. Foley, "An Historical Analysis of the Administration of the Blackfeet Reservation by the United States, 1855–1950's," typescript, Ruhle Library, Glacier National Park (1974)

Alice Ford, *John James Audubon: A Biography* (1988)

William E. Ford, "Memorial of Edward Salisbury Dana," *American Mineralogist* (March 1936), 173–177

Stephen Fox, *The American Conservation Movement: John Muir and His Legacy* (1985)

"A Friend of the Indian," *Outlook* 103 (April 5, 1913), 789–980

Henry E. Fritz, *The Movement for Indian Assimilation, 1860–1890* (1963)

Michael Frome, *The Forest Service* (1971)

Michael Frome, "George Bird Grinnell: Grandfather of Conservation," *Field and Stream* (June 1970), 52, 170–172

Hamlin Garland, *The Book of the American Indian* (1923)

Hamlin Garland, *The Captain of the Gray-Horse Troop* (1902)

Hamlin Garland, *Cavanagh: Forest Ranger* (1910)

Hamlin Garland, *Companions on the Trail: A Literary Chronicle* (1931)

Hamlin Garland, "The Red Man's Present Needs," *North American Review* (April 1902), 476–488

Hamlin Garland, *Roadside Meetings* (1930)

Martin S. Garretson, *The American Bison: The Story of Its Extermination as a Wild Species and Its Restoration under Federal Protection* (1938)

Andrew Giarelli, "An Indian Understanding of the Nature of Things: One Man's Education in the Field," *Yale Alumni Magazine* (March 1982), 18–22

Mick Gidley, *Edward S. Curtis and the North American Indian, Incorporated* (1998)

Mick Gidley, ed., *Edward S. Curtis and the North American Indian Project in the Field* (2003)

Mick Gidley, "Edward S. Curtis Goes to the Mountain," *Pacific Northwest Quarterly* (October 1984), 164–170

E. S. Godrey, "Custer's Last Battle," *Century* (January 1892), 358–384

William H. Goetzmann, *Exploration and Empire: The Explorer and the Scientist in the Winning of the American West* (1966)

William H. Goetzmann and Kay Sloan, *Looking Far North: The Harriman Expedition to Alaska, 1899* (1982)

G. B. Gordon, review of *The North American Indian*, AA, New Series (July–September 1908), 435–441

Charles W. Gould, *America: A Family Matter* (1922)

George H. Gould, "To the Gulf of Cortez," in Theodore Roosevelt and GBG, eds., *Hunting in Many Lands* (1895), 55–83

Ernest Grafe and Paul Horsted, *Exploring with Custer: The 1874 Black Hills Expedition* (2002)

Frank Graham, Jr., *The Audubon Ark: A History of the National Audubon Society* (1990)

Frank Graham, Jr., *Man's Dominion: The Story of Conservation in America* (1971)

Otis L. Graham, *Presidents and the American Environment* (2015)

Madison Grant, "America for the Americans," *Forum* (1925), 346–355

Madison Grant, "Discussion of Article on Democracy and Heredity," *Journal of Heredity* (April 1919), 164–165

Madison Grant, *Early History of Glacier National Park* (1919)

Madison Grant, "Ethics in Hunting Game," *Forum* (January 1917), 103–112

Madison Grant, "George Bird Grinnell," *American Review of Reviews* (June 1925), 600–602

Madison Grant, "History of the Zoological Society," *Zoological Society Bulletin* (January 1910), 589–601

Madison Grant, *The Passing of the Great Race; or, The Racial Basis of European History* (1916)

Madison Grant, "The Racial Transformation of America," *North American Review* (March 1924), 345–352

Madison Grant, "The Vanishing Moose and Their Extermination in the Adirondacks," *Century Illustrated* (January 1894), 345–356

Madison Grant and Charles Stewart Davison, *The Founders of the Republic on Immigration, Naturalization and Aliens* (1928)

Henry S. Graves, "A Crisis in National Recreation," *American Forestry* (July 1920), 391–400

Andrew R. Graybill, *The Red and the White: A Family Saga of the American West* (2013)

Alfred W. Greeley, "Our Unknown Scenic Wonders: The Crown of the Continent," *World's Work* (May 1908), 10248–10253

Joel Greenberg, *A Feathered Ribbon Across the Sky: The Passenger Pigeon's Flight to Extinction* (2014)

Jerome A. Greene, *American Carnage: Wounded Knee, 1890* (2014)

Jerome A. Greene, *Lakota and Cheyenne: Indian Views of the Great Sioux War, 1876–1877* (1994)

Jerome A. Greene and Douglas D. Scott, *Finding Sand Creek: History, Archeology, and the 1864 Massacre Site* (2004)

Helen Lansing Grinnell, diary for Frank Grinnell, manuscript, Manuscripts and Archives Division, New York Public Library, Astor, Lenox, and Tilden Foundations

Helen Lansing Grinnell, diary for Helen Jesup Grinnell, manuscript, Lilly Library, Indiana University

Morton Grinnell, *An Eclipse of Memory* (1899)

Morton Grinnell, *Neighbors of Field, Wood and Stream: Through the Years with Nature's Children* (1901)

Theodore Grivas, "The Arthur H. Clark Company: Publisher of the West; A Review of 60 Years of Service, 1902–1962," *Arizona and the West* (Spring 1963), 63–78

Erna Gunther, review of *When Buffalo Ran*, AA (April–June 1921), 222–223

C. W. Guthrie, *All Aboard for Glacier: The Great Northern Railway and Glacier National Park* (2004)

William T. Hagan, *The Indian Rights Association: The Herbert Welsh Years, 1882–1904* (1985)

William T. Hagan, *Theodore Roosevelt and Six Friends of the Indian* (1997)

Arnold Hague, "The Yellowstone Park as a Forest Reservation," *Nation* (January 5, 1988), 9–10

Aubrey L. Haines, *The Yellowstone Story: A History of Our First National Park*, 2 vols. (1997, revised 1996)

David Fridtjof Halaas and Andrew E. Masich, *Halfbreed: The Remarkable True Story of George Bent—Caught Between the Worlds of the Indian and the White Man* (2004)

Ansel F. Hall, "With the Ranger Naturalists," *American Forests* (August 1926), 451–454

Charles Hallock, *An Angler's Reminiscences: A Record of Sport, Travel and Adventure, with an Autobiography of the Author* (1913)

Charles Hallock, *The Sportsman's Gazetteer and General Guide* (1877)

Kenneth Hammer, ed., *Custer in '76: Walter Camp's Notes on the Custer Fight* (1976)

W. T. Hamilton, *My Sixty Years on the Plains: Trapping, Trading, and Indian Fighting* (1905)

H. Duane Hampton, *How the U.S. Cavalry Saved Our National Parks* (1971)

H. Duane Hampton, "U.S. Army and the National Parks," *Forest History* (October 1966), 14

Warren L. Hanna, *The Life of James Willard Schultz (Apikuni)* (1986)

Warren L. Hanna, *Montana's Many-Splendored Glacierland* (1976)

Warren L. Hanna, *Stars over Montana: Men Who Made Glacier National Park History* (Glacier Natural History Association, 1988)

Elizabeth Hanson, *Animal Attractions: Nature on Display in American Zoos* (2002)

Richard G. Hardoff, ed., *Cheyenne Memories of the Custer Fight* (1995)

David Harmon et al., eds., *The Antiquities Act: A Century of American Archaeology, Historic Preservation, and Nature Conservation* (2006)

Andrew C. Harper, "Conceiving Nature: The Creation of Montana's Glacier National Park," MMWH (Summer 2010), 3–24

Andrew C. Harper, "The Crown and the Jewel: George Bird Grinnell, Louis Warren Hill, and Glacier National Park," PhD dissertation, Northern Arizona University, 1999

Richard H. Harper, "The Missionary Work of the Reformed (Dutch) Church in America in Oklahoma," *Chronicles of Oklahoma* (September 1940), 252–265

Edward Day Harris, "Preserving a Vision of the American West: The Life of George Bird Grinnell," PhD dissertation, University of Texas at Austin (1995)

William E. Haskell, *The American Game Protective and Propagation Association* (1937)

F. V. Hayden, "The Wonders of the West. II. More About Yellowstone," *Scribner's Monthly* (February 1872), 388–396

James B. Haynes, *History of the Trans-Mississippi and International Exposition of 1898* (1910)

Samuel P. Hays, *Conservation and the Gospel of Efficiency: The Progressive Conservation Movement, 1890–1920* (1959)

James B. Hedges, review of *Two Great Scouts and Their Pawnee Battalion*, *American Historical Review* (July 1929), 890–891

H. W. Henshaw, review of *Pawnee Hero Stories and Folk-Tales*, AA (January 1890), 94–96

Francis Hobart Herrick, *Audubon the Naturalist: A History of His Life and Times* (1917, second edition 1938)

R. J. Hoage and William A. Deiss, eds., *New Worlds, New Animals: From Menagerie to Zoological Park in the Nineteenth Century* (1996)

Frederick Webb Hodge, ed., *Handbook of American Indians North of Mexico*, 2 vols. (1907–1910)

F. W. Hodge, review of *The Story of the Indian*, AA (February 1896), 58–59

Jean Holloway, *Hamlin Garland: A Biography* (1960)

Jack Holterman, *Place Names of Glacier/Waterton National Parks* (1985)

Jack Holterman, *Who Was Who in Glacier Land* (2001)

William T. Hornaday, *The American Natural History: A Foundation of Useful Knowledge of the Higher Animals of North America* (1904)

William T. Hornaday, *Camp-Fires in the Canadian Rockies* (1906)

William T. Hornaday, "Ethics Hunting Game," *Forum* (January 1917), 103–112

William T. Hornaday, *Extermination of the American Bison* (1889)

William T. Hornaday, *Our Vanishing Wild Life* (1913)

William T. Hornaday, "The Passing of the Buffalo," *Cosmopolitan* (October 1887), 85–98

William T. Hornaday, "The Seamy Side of the Protection of Wild Game," *New York Times Magazine*, March 8, 1914

William T. Hornaday, *Thirty Years War for Wild Life* (1931)

William T. Hornaday, *Two Years in the Jungle: The Experience of a Hunter and Naturalist in India, Ceylon, the Malay Peninsula and Borneo* (1885)

Reginald Horsman, "Scientific Racism and the American Indian in the Mid-Nineteenth Century," *American Quarterly* (May 1975), 152–168

Emerson Hough, *The Covered Wagon* (1922)

Emerson Hough, *The Girl at the Halfway House: A Story of the Plains* (1900)

Emerson Hough, "Made in America," *Saturday Evening Post* (June 5, 1915), 12–14, 57–58, 61–62

Emerson Hough, "Pawning the Heirlooms," *Saturday Evening Post* (September 25, 1920), 12–13, 90, 95–96, 98, 102

Emerson Hough, "The President's Forest," *Saturday Evening Post* (January 14, 1922), 6–7, 65, 69, 72, 75; (January 21, 1922), 23, 57–58, 60, 63

Emerson Hough, *The Story of the Cowboy* (1897)

Emerson Hough, "There Is No Dead Line at Forty," *American Magazine* (June 1918), 37, 106–109

Robert West Howard, *The Dawnseekers: The First History of American Paleontology* (1975)

Ernest Howe, partial biography of O. C. Marsh, including four chapters written by Howe and one by GBG, manuscript, O. C. Marsh Papers, Yale

Frederick Hoxie, *A Final Promise: The Campaign to Assimilate the Indians, 1880–1920* (1984)

Adolf Hungry Wolf, *The Blackfoot Papers*, Vol. 1: *Pikunni History and Culture* (2006); Vol. 4: *Pikunni Biographies* (2006)

Elizabeth Hutchinson, *The Indian Craze: Primitivism, Modernism, and Transculturation in American Art, 1890–1915* (2009)

Paul A. Hutton, *Phil Sheridan and His Army* (1985)

Paul Hutton, "Phil Sheridan's Crusade for Yellowstone," *American History Illustrated* (February 1985), 10–15, 7

George E. Hyde, *Life of George Bent: Written from His Letters* (1968)

George E. Hyde, *The Pawnee Indians* (1951, reprint 1974)

Joseph P. Iddings, "Biographical Memoir of Arnold Hague, 1840–1917," in *Biographical Memoirs of National Academy of Sciences* (May 1919)

Iowa Park and Forestry Association, *Major John F. Lacey: Memorial Volume* (1915)

John Ise, *Our National Park Policy: A Critical History* (1961, reprint 1979)

John Ise, *The United States Forest Policy* (1920)

Andrew C. Isenberg, *The Destruction of the Bison* (2000)

Donald Jackson, *Custer's Gold: The United States Cavalry Expedition of 1874* (1966)

Helen Hunt Jackson, *A Century of Dishonor: A Sketch of the United States Government's Dealings with Some of the Indian Tribes* (1885, reprint 1995)

Harry C. James, "Apikuni's Ageless Audience," MMWH (October 1960), 24–26

"John F. Lacey: Champion of Birds and Wildlife," Iowa National History Foundation, Des Moines

W. A. Jones, "The Standing Rock Case; Commissioner Jones's Statement," *Outlook* (April 19, 1902), 951–955

Neil M. Judd, *The Bureau of American Ethnology: A Partial History* (1967)

Jerry Keenan, *The Life of Yellowstone Kelly* (2006)

Jerry Keenan, *The Wagon Box Fight: An Episode of Red Cloud's War* (2000)

Robert H. Keller and Michael F. Turek, *American Indians and National Parks* (1998)

Luther S. Kelly, "Memoirs of Experiences in Alaska and the Philippines," typescript, Beinecke Rare Books & Manuscripts Library, Yale

George Kennan, E. H. *Harriman: A Biography*, 2 vols. (1922)

George Kennan, "Have Reservation Indians Any Vested Rights?" *Outlook* (March 29, 1902), 759–765

George Kennan, "Have the Standing Rock Indians Been Fairly Treated?" *Outlook* (May 3, 1902), 90–96

George Kennan, "A New Statement from Mr. Kennan," *Outlook* (April 19, 1902), 956–958

George Kennan, "Settlement of the Standing Rock Indian Case," *Outlook* (December 13, 1902)

David and Jim Kimball, *The Market Hunter* (1969)

Charles Kingsley, *Glaucus; or, The Wonders of the Shore* (1855)

Jim Kipp, "Blackfeet Oral Tradition of the 1895 Agreement," master's thesis, University of Montana, 2002

Adolph Knopf, "Biographical Memoir of Edward Salisbury Dana," *Biographical Memoirs*, Vol. 18, National Academy of Sciences, 1937

Michael F. Kohl and John S. McIntosh, eds., *Discovering Dinosaurs in the Old West: The Field Journals of Arthur Lakes* (1997)

Sidney Kramer, *A History of Stone & Kimball and Herbert S. Stone & Co.* (1940)

Herbert Krause and Gary D. Olson, *Prelude to Glory: A Newspaper Account of Custer's 1874 Expedition to the Black Hills* (1974)

Theodora Kroeber, *Ishi in Two Worlds: A Biography of the Last Wild Indian in North America* (1961)

Robert M. Kvasnicka and Herman J. Viola, eds., *The Commissioners of Indian Affairs, 1824–1977* (1979)

John F. Lacey, "Let Us Save the Birds," *Recreation* (July 1900), 33–35

Richard Lancaster, *Piegan: A Look from Within at the Life, Times, and Legacy of the American Indian Tribe* (1966)

Earl Lanham, *The Bone Hunters* (1973)

D. C. Lansing, *Sermons on Important Subjects of Doctrine and Duty* (1825)

Aldo Leopold, "Forestry and Game Conservation," *Journal of Forestry* (April 1918), 404–411

Aldo Leopold, *Game Management* (1948)

Aldo Leopold, *A Sand Country Almanac* (1968)

Aldo Leopold, "The Wilderness and Its Place in Forest Recreation Policy," *Journal of Forestry* (November 1921), 718–721

Aldo Leopold, "Wilderness as a Form of Land Use," *Journal of Land & Public Utility Economics* (October 1925), 398–404

John G. and Sue Lepley, eds., *The Vanishing West: Hornaday's Buffalo* (n.d.)

Francis E. Leupp, *The Indian and His Problem* (1910)

Francis E. Leupp, *The Man Roosevelt* (1904)

Francis E. Leupp, "Outlines of an Indian Policy," *Outlook* (April 15, 1905), 946–950

Francis E. Leupp, *In Red Man's Land: A Study of the American Indian* (1914)

Francis Leupp, "Roosevelt the Politician," *Atlantic Monthly* (June 1912), 843–852

Bruce R. Liddick and Paul Harbaugh, eds., *Custer and Company: Walter Camp's Notes on the Custer Fight* (1995)

Ralph Linton, review of *The Fighting Cheyennes*, *Mississippi Valley Historical Review* (December 1916), 417–418

Daniel F. Littlefield, Jr., and Lonnie E. Underhill, "Renaming the American Indian, 1890–1913," *American Studies* (Fall 1971), 33–45

Thomas S. Litwin, ed., *The Harriman Alaska Expedition Retraced: A Century of Change, 1899–2001* (2005)

William J. Long, "The Modern School of Nature-Study and Its Critics," *North American Review* (May 1903), 688–698

Dale F. Lott, *American Bison: A Natural History* (2002)

"Low Flying and Speed Event Proves Fatal," *Aero* (January 27, 1912), 333

David Lowenthal, *George Perkins Marsh: Prophet of Conservation* (2000)

William Ludlow, *Report of a Reconnaissance from Carroll, Montana Territory, on the Upper Missouri, to the Yellowstone National Park, and Return, Made in the Summer of 1875* (1876)

William Ludlow, *Report of a Reconnaissance of the Black Hills of Dakota, Made in the Summer of 1874* (1875)

Richard Swann Lull, "Early Fossil Hunting in the Rocky Mountains," *Natural History* (September–October 1926), 455–461

Richard S. Lull, "The Yale Collection of Fossil Horses," *Yale Alumni Weekly* (supplement, 1913)

Charles F. Lummis, "In Western Letters," *Land of Sunshine* (May 1900), 350–351

Charles F. Lummis, "A New Indian Policy," *Land of Sunshine* (December 1901), 457–464

[Charles F. Lummis], "To Make Better Indians," *Out West* (February 1902) 177–179

[Charles F. Lummis], "That Which Is Written," *Land of Sunshine* (May 1900), 384

Darrin Lunde, *The Naturalist: Theodore Roosevelt, A Lifetime of Exploration, and the Triumph of American Natural History* (2016)

"Luther North's Recollections as Told to George Bird Grinnell," manuscript, History Nebraska

Ralph H. Lutts, *The Nature Fakers: Wildlife, Science & Sentiment* (1990)

Mark J. McCarren, *The Scientific Contributions of Othniel Charles Marsh: Birds, Bones, and Brontotheres* (1993)

Laton McCartney, *The Teapot Dome Scandal* (2008)

Douglas C. McChristian, "Burying the Hatchet: The Semi-Centennial of the Battle of the Little Bighorn," MMWH (Summer 1996), 50–65

Walter McClintock, "The Blackfoot Beaver Bundle," *Southwest Museum Leaflets* (1935)

Walter McClintock, "The Blackfoot Tipi," *Southwest Museum Leaflets* (1936)

Walter McClintock, "Blackfoot Warrior Societies," *Southwest Museum Leaflets* (1937)

Walter McClintock, "Dances of the Blackfoot Indians," *Southwest Museum Leaflets* (1937)

Walter McClintock, "Four Days in a Medicine Lodge," *Harper's Monthly*, (September 1900), 519–532

Walter McClintock, *The Old North Trail: Life, Legends and Religion of the Blackfeet Indians* (1910, reprint 1999)

Walter McClintock, *Old Indian Trails* (1923, reprint 1992)

Walter McClintock, "Painted Tipis and Picture-Writing of the Blackfoot Indians," *Southwest Museum Leaflets* (1936)

Walter McClintock, "The Tragedy of the Blackfoot," *Southwest Museum Leaflets* (1930)

David McCullough, *Mornings on Horseback* (1981)

M. Nelson McGeary, *Gifford Pinchot: Forester-Politician* (1960)

Chris J. Magoc, *Yellowstone: The Creation and Selling of an American Landscape, 1870–1903* (1909)

Edward A. McIlhenny, *The Autobiography of an Egret* (1939)

Charles Barron McIntosh, *The Nebraska Sand Hills: The Human Landscape* (1996)

C. Barron McIntosh, "The Route of a Sand Hills Bone Hunt: The Yale College Expedition of 1870," *Nebraska History* (Summer 1988), 84–94

James McLaughlin, *My Friend the Indian* (1910, reprint 1926 with introduction by GBG)

Michael P. Malone, *James J. Hill: Empire Builder of the Northwest* (1996)

Robert Winston Mardock, *The Reformers and the American Indian* (1971)

Thomas B. Marquis, *The Cheyennes of Montana* (1978)

Thomas B. Marquis, *A Warrior Who Fought Custer* (1931)

George Perkins Marsh, *Man and Nature* (1864, reprint 1965)

O. C. Marsh, "Discovery of a Remarkable Fossil Bird," *American Journal of Science and Arts* (January 1872), 56–57

O. C. Marsh, "Fossil Horses in America," *American Naturalist* (May 1874), 288–294

O. C. Marsh, "Notice of a New and Diminutive Species of Fossil Horse (*Equus parvulus*), from the Tertiary of Nebraska," *American Journal of Science and Arts* (November 1868), 374–375

O. C. Marsh, "Notice of New Equine Mammals from the Tertiary Formation," *American Journal of Science and Arts* (March 1874), 247–258

Othniel Marsh, *Odontornithes: A Monograph on the Extinct Toothed Birds of North America* (1880)

O. C. Marsh, "On the Geology of the Eastern Uintah Mountains," *American Journal of Science and Arts* (March 1871), 191–198

O. C. Marsh, "Scientific Expedition to the Rocky Mountains," *American Journal of Science and Arts* (February 1871), 142–143

Albro Martin, *James J. Hill and the Opening of the Northwest* (1976)

Francois E. Matthes, "The Alps of Montana," *Appalachia* (April 1904), 255–276

Peter Matthiessen, *Wildlife in America* (1959)

Margaret Mead and Ruth Bunzel, eds., *The Golden Age of American Anthropology* (1960)

Curt Meine, *Aldo Leopold: His Life and Work* (1988)

Carolyn Merchant, *Spare the Birds!: George Bird Grinnell and the First Audubon Society* (2016)

C. Hart Merriam, *The Dawn of the World: Myths and Weird Tales by the Mewan Indians of California* (1910)

C. Hart Merriam, ed., *Harriman Alaska Series*, 14 vols. (1902–1914)

C. Hart Merriam, "Introduction," in *Harriman Alaska Series* I: *Narratives, Glaciers, Natives* (1910), xxv–xxxi

C. Hart Merriam, "Theodore Roosevelt, the Naturalist," *Science* (February 12, 1932), 181–183

William B. Mershon, *Recollections of My Fifty Years Hunting and Fishing* (1923)

David W. Messer, *Henry Roe Cloud: A Biography* (2010)

Harvey Meyerson, *Nature's Army: When Soldiers Fought for Yosemite* (2001)

Gregory F. Michno, *Encyclopedia of Indian Wars: Western Battles and Skirmishes, 1850–1890* (2003)

John C. Miles, *Guardians of the Parks: A History of the National Parks and Conservation Association* (1995)

Char Miller, ed. *American Forests: Nature, Culture, and Politics* (1997)

Char Miller, *Gifford Pinchot and the Making of Modern Environmentalism* (2001)

Char Miller, "Landmark Decision: The Antiquities Act, Big Stick Conservation, and the Modern State," in David Harmon et al., *The Antiquities Act* (2006), 64–78

Richard Milner, *The Encyclopedia of Evolution: Humanity's Search for Its Origins* (1990)

Guy Elliott Mitchell, "A New Playground for the Nation," *American Review of Reviews* (June 1910), 710–717

John Mitchell, "A Man Called Bird," *Audubon* (March 1987), 81–104

Frederick Monsen, "The Destruction of Our Indians: What Civilization is Doing to Extinguish an Ancient and Highly Intelligent Race by Taking Away Its Arts, Crafts, Industries and Religion," *Craftsman* (March 1901), 683–691

John H. Moore, *The Cheyenne* (1966)

James Mooney, *The Cheyenne Indians*, American Anthropological Association Memoirs, vol. 1, part 6 (1907), 360–442

James Mooney, *The Ghost-Dance Religion and the Sioux Outbreak of 1890* (1896, reprint 1991)

James Mooney, "The Indian Congress at Omaha," AA (January 1899), 126–149

James Mooney, review of *Blackfoot Lodge Tales*, AA (April 1894), 209–211

James Mooney, review of *The Fighting Cheyennes*, *American Historical Review* (April 1916), 612–614

Lewis H. Morgan, *Ancient Society* (1877, reprint 1964)

Elting Morison, ed., *The Letters of Theodore Roosevelt*, 8 vols. (1951–1954)

Edmund Morris, *The Rise of Theodore Roosevelt* (1979)

Travis Morris, *Untold Stories of Old Currituck Duck Clubs* (2010)

Terry Mort, *Thieves' Road: The Black Hills Betrayal and Custer's Path to Little Bighorn* (2015)

L. G. Moses, *The Indian Man: A Biography of James Mooney* (1984)

Frank Luther Mott, *A History of American Magazines: 1850–1865* (1938)

Frank Luther Mott, *A History of American Magazines: 1865–1885* (1938)

Bridget Moylan, *Glacier's Grandest: A Pictorial History of the Hotels and Chalets of Glacier National Park* (1995)

John Muir, "The American Forests," *Atlantic Monthly* (August 1897), 145–159

John Muir, "Features of the Proposed Yosemite National Park," *Century* (September 1890)

John Muir, *The Mountains of California* (1894, reprint 1988)

John Muir, *Nature Writings* (1997)

John Muir, *Our National Parks* (1901, reprint 1991)

John Muir, "The Treasures of Yosemite," *Century* (August 1890)

John Muir, "The Wild Parks and Forest Reservations of the West," *Atlantic Monthly* (January 1898), 15–28

John Muir, *The Yosemite* (1914, reprint 1988)

Julius W. Muller, *The Invasion of America: A Fact Story Based on the Inexorable Mathematics of War* (1916)

Robert Winston Murdock, *The Reformers and the American Indian* (1971)

James E. Murphy, *Half Interest in a Silver Dollar: The Saga of Charles E. Conrad* (1983)

David F. Myrick, *Montecito and Santa Barbara*; Vol. 2: *The Days of the Great Estates* (1991)

The Narrows Island Club: Charter, Constitution and By-Laws (1923)

Roderick Nash, "Gifford Pinchot," in Nash, *In These Beginnings: A Biographical Approach to American History* (1984)

Roderick Nash, *The Rights of Nature: A History of Environmental Ethics* (1989)

Roderick Nash, *Wilderness and the American Mind* (1967)

E. W. Nelson, "Charles Sheldon," *American Forests and Forest Life* (November 1928), 659–660

Pamela Newkirk, *Spectacle: The Astonishing Life of Ota Benga* (2015)

Keith Newlin, *Hamlin Garland: A Life* (2008)

"New Publications: The Wilderness Hunter," *F&S* (July 29, 1893)

Charles Nordhoff, *California for Travellers and Settlers* (1872)

L. H. North, "The Fighting Norths and the Pawnee Scouts: Stirring Scenes in the Old Northwest, Recalled for Motor Tourists," *Motor Travel* (10 installments, beginning March 1931)

Ronald Numbers, *Darwinism Comes to America* (1998)

Eric Nye and Sheri Hoem, eds., "Big Game on the Editor's Desk: Roosevelt and Bierstadt's Tale of a Hunt," *New England Quarterly* (September 1987), 454–465

Jeff O'Donnell, *Luther North: Frontier Scout* (1995)

Cleophas C. O'Harra, "Custer's Black Hills Expedition of 1874," *Black Hills Engineer* (November 1929), 286–299

"The Omaha Exposition and the Indian Congress," *Scientific American* (October 15, 1898), 248–249

Oliver H. Orr, Jr., *Saving American Birds: T. Gilbert Pearson and the Founding of the Audubon Movement* (1992)

Simon J. Ortiz, ed., *Beyond the Reach of Time and Change: Native American Reflections on the Frank A. Rinehart Photograph Collection* (2004)

Henry Fairfield Osborn, *The American Museum of Natural History, Its Origins and History* (1911)

Wilfred H. Osgood, "Clinton Hart Merriam—1855–1942," *Journal of Mammalogy* (November 17, 1943), 421–457

John H. Ostrom and John S. McIntosh, *Marsh's Dinosaurs: The Collections from Como Bluff* (1966)

"Our Game Protectors at War," *Literary Digest* (September 5, 1925), 16

Elizabeth M. Page, *In Camp and Tepee: An Indian Mission Story* (1915)

T. S. Palmer, "In Memoriam: William Dutcher," *Auk* (October 1921), 501–513

Mary Faith Pankin, ed., "The Yale Scientific Expedition of 1871: A Student's-Eye View, *Oregon Historical Quarterly* (Winter 1998–99), 374–435

Franklin Parker, *George Peabody: A Biography* (1971)

Francis Parkman, Jr., *The Oregon Trail* (1859, reprint 1982)

Frederick E. Partington, *The Story of Mohonk* (1911)

Eli Paul, ed., *The Nebraska Indian Wars Reader, 1865–1877* (1998)

Thomas Gilbert Pearson, *Adventures in Bird Protection* (1937)

[T. Gilbert Pearson], "The Feather Proviso" and accompanying articles, *Bird-Lore* (September–October 1913), 331–333

Thomas Gilbert Pearson, "The Passing of the Feather Trade," *Craftsman* (June 1913), 303–308

T. Gilbert Pearson, "Regulations for the Protection of Migratory Birds," *Bird-Lore* (July–August 1913), 231–235

Dan. W. Peery, "The Indians Friend John H. Seger," *Chronicles of Oklahoma* (September 1932), 348–368; (December 1932), 570–591

James Penick, "Professor Cope vs. Professor Marsh," *American Heritage* (August 1971), 5–13

John M. Peterson, ed., "Buffalo Hunting in Montana in 1886: The Diary of W. Harvey Brown," MMWH (August 1981), 2–13

Louis L. Pfaller, *James McLaughlin: The Man with the Indian Heart* (1978)

John C. Phillips, *A Bibliography of American Sporting Books* (1930)

John C. Phillips, "Naturalists, Nature Lovers, and Sportsmen," *Auk* (January 1931), 40–46

Nathaniel P. Phister, "The Indian Messiah," AA (April 1891), 105–108

Ralph Pierson, The Czar of Wonderland," (Denver) *Westerners Brand Book* 11 (1955), 375–386

Gifford Pinchot, *Breaking New Ground* (1947, reprint 1998)

Gifford Pinchot, *The Fight for Conservation* (1910)

Gifford Pinchot, *To the South Seas* (1930)

Kenneth Pitt, "The Ceded Strip: Blackfeet Treaty Rights in the 1890s," manuscript, Ruhle Library, Glacier National Park

Miles A. Powell, *Vanishing America: Species Extinction, Racial Peril, and the Origins of Conservation* (2016)

Peter J. Powell, *Sweet Medicine: The Continuing Role of the Sacred Arrows, the Sun Dance, and the Sacred Buffalo Hat in Northern Cheyenne History*, 2 vols. (1969, reprint 1979)

Charles N. Pray, *Recollections Concerning the Establishment of Glacier National Park* (1954)

Charlie Presti, "Then and Now: Blackfeet Subsistence and Glacier National Park," master's thesis, University of Montana, 2005

Douglas J. Preston, *Dinosaurs in the Attic: An Excursion into the American Museum of Natural History* (1986)

Loring Benson Priest, *Uncle Sam's Stepchildren: The Reformation of United States Indian Policy, 1865–1887* (1942, reprint 1975)

"Proceedings of the Meetings of Commissioners for Reduction of Indian Reservations: Blackfeet Reservation," typescript, Ruhle Library, Glacier National Park

Francis Paul Prucha, *American Indian Policy in Crisis: Christian Reformers and the Indian, 1865–1900* (1976)

Francis Paul Prucha, *The Churches and the Indian Schools, 1888–1912* (1980)

Francis Paul Prucha, ed., *Americanizing the American Indian: Writings by "Friends of the Indian," 1880–1900* (1973)

Francis Paul Prucha, *The Great Father: The United States Government and the American Indians* (1984)

Raphael Pumpelly, *My Reminiscences*, vol. 2 (1918)

Michael Punke, *Last Stand: George Bird Grinnell, the Battle to Save the Buffalo, and the Birth of the New West* (2007)

M. M. Quaife, ed. *"Yellowstone Kelly": The Memoirs of Luther S. Kelly* (1926)

Ronald Rainger, *An Agenda for Antiquity: Henry Fairfield Osborn & Vertebrate Paleontology at the American Museum of Natural History* (1949)

W. S. Rainsford, *The Land of the Lion* (1909)

Richard C. Rattenbury, *Hunting the American West: Pursuit of Game for Life, Profit, and Sport, 1800–1900* (2008)

Charles Burt Reed, *Masters of the Wilderness* (1914)

Brian Reeves and Sandra Peacock, *"Our Mountains Are Our Pillows": An Ethnographic Overview of Glacier National Park* (2001)

Mayne Reid, *The Boy Hunters, or, Adventures in Search of a White Buffalo* (1856)

John F. Reiger, *American Sportsmen and the Origin of Conservation* (1975)

John F. Reiger, *Escaping into Nature: The Making of a Sportsman-Conservationist and Environmental Historian* (2013)

John F. Reiger, ed., *The Passing of the Great West: Selected Papers of George Bird Grinnell* (1972)

Edward J. Renehan, Jr., *John Burroughs: An American Naturalist* (1992)

Elmo R. Richardson, *The Politics of Conservation: Crusade and Controversies, 1897–1913* (1962)

Robert W. Righter, "National Monuments to National Parks: The Use of the Antiquities Act of 1906," *Western Historical Quarterly* (August 1989), 281–301

Richard Rhodes, *John James Audubon: The Making of an American* (2006)

Walter C. Roe, "The Mohonk Lodge: An Experiment in Indian Work," *Outlook* (May 18, 1901), 176–179

Alfred S. Romer, "Cope Versus Marsh," *Systematic Zoology* (December 30, 1964), 201–207

Corrine Roosevelt Robinson, *My Brother, Theodore Roosevelt* (1921)

Theodore Roosevelt, *African Game Trails* (1910)

Theodore Roosevelt, *An Autobiography* (1913)

Theodore Roosevelt, *A Book-Lover's Holidays in the Open* (1916)

Theodore Roosevelt, *The Deer Family* (1902)

Theodore Roosevelt, *Hunting Trips of a Ranchman* (1885)

Theodore Roosevelt, "John Muir: An Appreciation," *Outlook* (January 6, 1915), 27–28

Theodore Roosevelt, "My Life as a Naturalist," *American Museum Journal* (May 1918), 320–350

Theodore Roosevelt, "Nature Fakers," *Everybody's* (September–October 1907), 427–430

Theodore Roosevelt, *Outdoor Pastimes of an American Hunter* (1905)

Theodore Roosevelt, *Ranch Life and the Hunting-Trail* (1888)

Theodore Roosevelt, "Ranch Life and Game-Shooting in the West," *Outing* (March 1886), 611–616

Theodore Roosevelt, *The Strenuous Life: Essays and Addresses* (1902)

Theodore Roosevelt, *The Wilderness Hunter* (1893)

Theodore Roosevelt, *The Winning of the West; Vol. 1: From the Alleghanies to the Mississippi, 1769–1776* (1894, reprint 1995)

"The Roosevelt-Long Controversy," *Outlook* (June 8, 1907), 263

Paul C. Rosier, *Rebirth of the Blackfeet Nation, 1912–1954* (2001)

Nigel Rothfels, *Savages and Beasts: The Birth of the Modern Zoo* (2002)

Martin J. S. Rudwick, *The Meaning of Fossils: Episodes in the History of Palaeontology* (revised edition, 1976)

Cynthia Eagle Russett, *Darwin in America: The Intellectual Response 1865–1912* (1976)

Don Russell, *The Lives and Legends of Buffalo Bill* (1960)

John P. Russo, *The Kaibab North Deer Herd: Its History, Problems and Management* (1964)

Douglas Cazaux Sackman, *Wild Men: Ishi and Kroeber in the Wilderness of Modern America* (2011)

Mari Sandoz, *Cheyenne Autumn* (1953, reprint 1992)

Mari Sandoz, "Introduction" to George Bird Grinnell, *The Cheyenne Indians: Their History and Ways of Life* (reprint, 1962)

Harry B. Sargent, "Marsh Expedition in 1870," prepared for the Colby Club, typescript, Sterling Memorial Library; courtesy of Daniel Brinkman, Peabody Museum of Natural History, Yale

Barnet Schecter, *The Devil's Own Work: The Civil War Draft Riots and the Fight to Reconstruct America* (2005)

Michael G. Schene, "The Crown of the Continent: Private Enterprise and Public Interest in the Early Development of Glacier National Park, 1910–1917," *Forest and Conservation History* (April 1990), 69–75

Charles Schuchert, *Biographical Memoir of Othniel Charles Marsh, 1831–1899* (1938)

Charles Schuchert, "The Rise of Natural History Museums in the United States," in Addresses Delivered on the Occasion of the Dedication of the New Museum Building, 29 December 1925, *Bulletin of the Peabody Museum of Natural History* 1 (1926)

Charles Schuchert and Clara Mae LeVene, *O. C. Marsh: Pioneer in Paleontology* (1940)

Paul Schullery, *The Bear Hunter's Century: Profiles from the Golden Age of Bear Hunting* (1988)

Paul Schullery, "Buffalo Jones and the Bison Herd in Yellowstone," MMWH (July 1986), 40–51

James Willard Schultz, *Blackfeet and Buffalo: Memories of Life among the Indians* (1962)

James Willard Schultz, *Blackfeet Tales from Apikuni's World* (2002)

James Willard Schultz, *Blackfeet Tales of Glacier National Park* (1916, reprint 2002)

James Willard Schultz, *Floating on the Missouri* (1979)

James Willard Schultz, *Friends of My Life as an Indian* (1923)

James Willard Schultz, "The Glaciers of Montana," *Alpine Journal* (February 1897), 354

James Willard Schultz, "Indian Names in Glacier National Park," *Outlook* (July 28, 1926), 442–444

James Willard Schultz, *My Life as an Indian: The Story of a Red Woman and a White Man in the Lodges of the Blackfeet* (1907)

James Willard Schultz, *Recently Discovered Tales of Life Among the Indians* (1988)

James Willard Schultz, *Rising Wolf, the White Blackfoot; Hugh Monroe's Story of His First Year on the Plains* (1919)

James Willard Schultz, "Sale of Glacier National Park Had Inception in Ouija Board Job," *Great Falls Tribune*, November 15, 1936

James Willard Schultz, *Signposts of Adventure: Glacier National Park as the Indians Know It* (1926)

James Willard Schultz, *Why Gone Those Times?* (1974)

James Willard Schultz, *William Jackson, Indian Scout; His True Story Told by His Friend* (1926, reprint 1976)

James Willard Schultz, "Winter Hunting of Goat and Sheep in the Rockies," *Outing* (January 1901), 413–418

Jesse Donaldson Schultz, "Adventuresome, Amazing Apikuni," MMWH (October 1960), 2–18

"Scientific Expedition to the Rocky Mountains," *American Journal of Science and Arts*, (February 1871), 142–143

Hugh Lenox Scott, *Some Memories of a Soldier* (1928)

John Seger, "Tradition of the Cheyenne Indians," *Chronicles of Oklahoma* (September 1928), 260–270

Richard West Sellars, *Preserving Nature in the National Parks: A History* (1997)

Marguerite S. Shaffer, *See America First: Tourism and National Identity, 1880–1940* (2001)

Robert Shankland, *Steve Mather of the National Parks* (1951)

Charles Sheldon, *The Wilderness of Denali* (1930, reprint 1960)

Charles Sheldon, *The Wilderness of the North Pacific Coast Islands* (1912)

Charles Sheldon, *The Wilderness of the Upper Yukon* (1911)

Margaret E. Thompson Sheldon, "The Trumpeter's Last Call: The Epic of a Season in the Life of the Swan," *Nature Magazine* (July 1929), 11–13

Morgan Sherwood, *Big Game in Alaska: A History of Wildlife and People* (1981)

George Shiras 3rd, *Hunting Wild Life with Camera and Flashlight*, 2 vols., (1906)

George Shiras 3rd, "Photographing Wild Game with Flashlight and Camera," *National Geographic* (July 1906), 367-423

Elizabeth Noble Shor, *The Fossil Feud Between E. D. Cope and O. C. Marsh* (1974)

Frank E. Smith, *The Politics of Conservation* (1966)

Katherine L. Smith, "For a National Park," *Technical World* (August 1909), 642–644

Katherine Louise Smith, "An Ice Playground for Tourists," *Harper's Weekly* (December 26, 1908), 26

Sherry L. Smith, "George Bird Grinnell and the 'Vanishing' Plains Indians," (Autumn 2000), 18–31

Sherry L. Smith, *Reimagining Indians; Native Americans through Anglo Eyes, 1880–1940* (2000)

Alfred Sorenson, "A Quarter of a Century on the Frontier; or, The Adventures of Frank North, the 'White Chief of the Pawnees,'" typescript, History Nebraska

William Souder, *Under a Wild Sky: Audubon and the Making of* The Birds of America (2014)

Matthew Spady, *The Grinnell at 100: Celebrating Community, History, and an Architectural Gem* (2010)

Matthew Spady, *How Audubon Park Disrupted Manhattan's Grid: Images to Accompany a Guided Walk Through the Audubon Park Historic District to Northern Manhattan* (2016)

Mark David Spence, "Crown of the Continent, Backbone of the World: The American Wilderness Ideal and Blackfeet Exclusion from Glacier National Park," *Environmental History* (July 1996), 29–49

Mark David Spence, *Dispossessing the Wilderness: Indian Removal and the Making of the National Parks* (1999)

Lyman B. Sperry, "Avalanche Basin, Montana Rockies," *Appalachia* (January 1896), 57–69

Jonathan Peter Spiro, *Defending the Master Race: Conservation, Eugenics, and the Legacy of Madison Grant* (2009)

Harold K. Steen, *The U.S. Forest Service: A History* (1976)

Wallace Stegner, *Beyond the Hundredth Meridian: John Wesley Powell and the Second Opening of the West* (1954)

Keir B. Sterling, *Last of the Naturalists: The Career of C. Hart Merriam* (1977)

Keir B. Sterling, ed., *Selected Works of Clinton Hart Merriam* (1974)

Charles H. Sternberg, *The Life of a Fossil Hunter* (1931)

T. J. Stiles, *Custer's Trials: A Life on the Frontier of a New America* (2015)

T. J. Stiles, *The First Tycoon: The Epic Life of Cornelius Vanderbilt* (2009)

Henry L. Stimson, *My Vacations* (1949)

George W. Stocking, ed., *Race, Culture, and Evolution* (1982)

David H. Stratton, *Tempest over Teapot Dome: The Story of Albert B. Fall* (1998)

Douglas H. Strong, *The Conservationists* (1971)

General W. E. Strong, *A Trip to the Yellowstone National Park in July, August and September, 1875* (1968)

"Telling History by Photographs: Records of Our North American Indians Being Preserved by Pictures," *Craftsman* (March 1906), 846–849

Lowell Thomas, *With Lawrence in Arabia* (1924)

Mark Thompson, *American Character: The Curious Life of Charles Fletcher Lummis and the Rediscovery of the Southwest* (2001)

Sally Thompson, *People Before the Park: The Kootenai and Blackfeet Before Glacier National Park* (2015)

James A. Tober, *Who Owns the Wildlife? The Political Economy of Conservation in Nineteenth Century America* (1981)

Walter A. Tompkins, *The Yankee Barbareños: The Americanization of Santa Barbara County, California, 1796–1925* (2003)

Alan Trachtenberg, *Shades of Hiawatha: Staging Indians, Making Americans, 1880–1930* (2004)

James B. Trefethen, *Crusade for Wildlife: Highlights in Conservation Progress* (1961)

James B. Trefethen, *An American Crusade for Wildlife* (1975)

Frederick Turner, *Rediscovering America: John Muir in His Time and Ours* (1985)

Lonnie E. Underhill and Daniel F. Littlefield, Jr., "Cheyenne 'Outbreak' of 1897" MMWH (Autumn 1974), 30–41

Lonnie E. Underhill and Daniel F. Littlefield, Jr., *Hamlin Garland's Observations on the American Indians, 1895–1905* (1976)

Richard Upton, ed., *The Battle of the Little Big Horn and Custer's Last Fight Remembered by Participants at the Tenth Anniversary, June 25, 1886, and the Fiftieth Anniversary, June 25, 1926* (2007)

Robert M. Utley, *Cavalier in Buckskin: George Armstrong Custer and the Western Military Frontier* (1988)

Robert M. Utley, *The Last Days of the Sioux Nation* (1963)

Robert M. Utley, "The Ordeal of Plenty Horses," *American Heritage* (December 1974), 15–19, 82–86

Mark Van de Logt, *War Party in Blue: Pawnee Scouts in the U.S. Army* (2010)

J. Hansford C. Vest, "Traditional Blackfeet Religion and the Sacred Badger Two-Medicine Wildlands," *Journal of Law and Religion* (1988), 455–489

David Rains Wallace, *The Bonehunters' Revenge: Dinosaurs, Greed, and the Greatest Scientific Feud of the Gilded Age* (1999)

Dave Walter, "The Ceded Strip: The Blackfeet, GNP, and Badger Two Medicine," MMWH (September/October 1998), 55–61

George B. Ward and Richard E. McCabe, "Trail Blazers in Conservation: The Boone and Crockett Club's First Century," in *Records of North American Big Game* (4th ed., 1980)

George B. Ward and Richard E. McCabe, *Records of North American Big Game* (1952), 62–63

Louis S. Warren, *God's Red Son: The Ghost Dance Religion and the Making of Modern America* (2017)

Louis Warren, *The Hunter's Game: Poachers and Conservationists in Twentieth-Century America* (1997)

Francis E. Watkins, "Charles F. Lummis and the Sequoya League," *The Quarterly: Historical Society of Southern California* (June-September 1944), 99–114

T. H. Watkins, "Father of the Forests," *American Heritage* (February-March 1991), 86–98

Robert Henry Welker, *Birds and Men: American Birds in Science, Art, and Literature, 1800–1900* (1955)

Thomas R. Wessel, "George Bird Grinnell," in *Historians of the American Frontier* (1988)

Thomas R. Wessel, "Historical Report on the Blackfeet Reservation in Northern Montana," Indian Claims Commission Docket 279-D (1975)

Helen B. West, "Starvation Winter of the Blackfeet," MMWH (January 1959), 2–19

Christopher White, *The Melting World: A Journey Across America's Vanishing Glaciers* (2013)

John J. White, Jr., "Hunting Ahead of Roosevelt in Africa," *Harper's Weekly* (March 13, 1909), 10–11; (March 20, 1909), 16–17; (March 27, 1909), 16–17; (April 3, 1909), 24–25

Henry Whittemore, *The Signers of the Mayflower Compact and Their Descendants* (1899)

Caspar Whitney, GBG, and Owen Wister, *Musk-Ox, Bison, Sheep and Goat* (1904)

John Noble Wilford, *The Riddle of the Dinosaur* (1985)

Emery Leverett Williams, *An Alphabet of Indians* (1900)

John Perrin Williams, *John Burroughs and the Place of Nature* (2006)

Ruby E. Wilson, *Frank J. North, Pawnee Scout Commander and Pioneer* (1984)

Clark Wissler, *The American Indian: An Introduction to the Anthropology of the New World* (1917)

Donald Worster, *A Passion for Nature: The Life of John Muir* (2008)

Jacob L. Wortman, "Othniel Charles Marsh," *Science*, New Series (1899), 562, 565

Paul R. Wylie, *Blood on the Marias: The Baker Massacre* (2016)

Robert Sterling Yard, *The Book of the National Parks* (1919)

Robert Sterling Yard, *Our Federal Lands: A Romance of American Development* (1928)

Robert Sterling Yard, *The Top of the Continent: The Story of a Cheerful Journey Through Our National Parks* (1917)

Biloine W. Young with Eileen R. McCormack, *The Dutiful Son: Louis W. Hill: Life in the Shadow of the Empire Builder, James J. Hill* (2010)

Harry Ziegler, "The Rocky Mountains," *New York Herald*, December 24, 1870

ILLUSTRATION CREDITS

FRONTISPIECE

George Bird Grinnell Papers, Manuscripts and Archives, Sterling Memorial Library, Yale University.

MAPS

John Wilson.

INSERTS

Victor Audubon, *View of the Hudson River*: Courtesy of the Museum of the City of New York.

John James Audubon: [Lucy Bakewell Audubon], *The Life of John James Audubon, the Naturalist* (1869).

Lucy Bakewell Audubon with granddaughters: Courtesy of the John James Audubon Museum, Henderson, Kentucky.

George Bird Grinnell as a Yale undergraduate: Manuscripts and Archives, Sterling Memorial Library, Yale University.

The Hemlocks: Private collection, Schuyler M. Meyer family.

Grinnell's study: Private collection, Schuyler M. Meyer family.

Frank North: History Nebraska.

Luther "Lute" North: History Nebraska.

William F. "Buffalo Bill" Cody: Buffalo Bill Center of the West.

Charley Reynolds: National Park Service, Little Bighorn Battlefield National Monument, LIBI 00019 00171.

Yale College scientific expedition: Peabody Museum of Natural History, Yale University.

Custer with grizzly bear: South Dakota State Historical Society.

Theodore Roosevelt: Theodore Roosevelt Collection, Houghton Library, Harvard University.

George H. Gould: Santa Barbara Historical Museum.

Grinnell Glacier, 1885: Morton J. Elrod Papers, University of Montana Archives and Special Collections, Mansfield Library, University of Montana.

Edward S. Dana: Manuscripts and Archives, Sterling Memorial Library, Yale University.

James Willard "Appekunny" Schultz: George Bird Grinnell Papers, Manuscripts and Archives, Sterling Memorial Library, Yale University.

Forest and Stream, December 25, 1873: New-York Historical Society.

Grinnell with Piegans and notebook: Seward House Museum, Auburn, New York.

Grinnell and Billy Jackson: Seward House Museum, Auburn, New York.

Edward Howell: Photograph by Frank Jay Haynes, courtesy of the Montana Historical Society Research Center Photograph Archives, Helena, MT.

Buffalo heads: Photograph by Frank Jay Haynes, courtesy of the National Park Service, Yellowstone National Park.

George W. Elder: Photograph by Edward S. Curtis, courtesy of the Harry Ransom Center, University of Texas.

The Two Johnnies: Photograph by Edward S. Curtis, courtesy of the Harry Ransom Center, University of Texas.

Harriman Alaska Expedition: Photograph by Edward S. Curtis, Harry Ransom Center, University of Texas.

Clinton Hart Merriam: Library of Congress.

Chief American Horse, Sioux: Photograph by Frank Rinehart, courtesy of the Boston Public Library.

Edward S. Curtis: Christopher Cardozo Fine Art.

White Calf—Piegan: Christopher Cardozo Fine Art.

The Three Chiefs: Christopher Cardozo Fine Art.

George and Elizabeth Grinnell, shooting in the Adirondacks: Glacier National Park Museum and Archives.

George and Elizabeth Grinnell on Grinnell Glacier, 1925: Glacier National Park Museum and Archives.

Honeymoon camp, Chief Mountain, 1902: Photograph by Elizabeth Grinnell, Glacier National Park Museum and Archives.

Grinnell with Northern Cheyennes: Glacier National Park Museum and Archives.

Grinnell with Two Moon: Glacier National Park Museum and Archives.

Little Wolf and Dull Knife: L. Tom Perry Special Collections, Harold B. Lee Library, Brigham Young University.

Northern Cheyenne woman: Photograph by Elizabeth Grinnell, courtesy of the Buffalo Bill Center of the West.

George Bent: Oklahoma Historical Society.

Charles F. Lummis: Library of Congress.

Hamlin Garland: University of Southern California, on behalf of the USC Libraries Special Collections.

George Shiras III: National Geographic Society.

Charles Sheldon: Unidentified maker, Sheldon and jays near cabin, November 20, 1907. Gelatin silver print, 4 × 5 in. Collection of Shelburne Museum Archives, given by the Sheldon family in memory of their father, Charles Sheldon. MS430_D6.33A.

John Bird Burnham: Collection of the Adirondack History Museum.

William T. Hornaday: Library of Congress.

Stephen Mather: Library of Congress.

Gifford Pinchot: TRC-PH-2 507.P65-002 (olvwork563259), Houghton Library, Harvard University.

George Vest: State Historical Society of Missouri.

John F. Lacey: Library of Congress.

Grinnell on Grinnell Glacier, 1926: Morton J. Elrod Papers, Archives & Special Collections, Mansfield Library, University of Montana.

Grinnell and Lute North: Private collection, Samuel N. Smith.

Thomas Elwood "Billy" Hofer: Morton J. Elrod Papers, Archives & Special Collections, Mansfield Library, University of Montana.

Grinnell at Narrows Island Club: Private collection, John F. Reiger.

INDEX